Lecture Notes in Com

Founding Editors

Gerhard Goos
Juris Hartmanis

Editorial Board Members

Elisa Bertino, *Purdue University, West Lafayette, IN, USA*
Wen Gao, *Peking University, Beijing, China*
Bernhard Steffen , *TU Dortmund University, Dortmund, Germany*
Moti Yung , *Columbia University, New York, NY, USA*

The series Lecture Notes in Computer Science (LNCS), including its subseries Lecture Notes in Artificial Intelligence (LNAI) and Lecture Notes in Bioinformatics (LNBI), has established itself as a medium for the publication of new developments in computer science and information technology research, teaching, and education.

LNCS enjoys close cooperation with the computer science R & D community, the series counts many renowned academics among its volume editors and paper authors, and collaborates with prestigious societies. Its mission is to serve this international community by providing an invaluable service, mainly focused on the publication of conference and workshop proceedings and postproceedings. LNCS commenced publication in 1973.

Michael Wand · Kristína Malinovská ·
Jürgen Schmidhuber · Igor V. Tetko
Editors

Artificial Neural Networks and Machine Learning – ICANN 2024

33rd International Conference on Artificial Neural Networks
Lugano, Switzerland, September 17–20, 2024
Proceedings, Part II

Springer

Editors
Michael Wand
IDSIA USI-SUPSI
Lugano, Switzerland

MeDiTech, SUPSI
Lugano, Switzerland

Jürgen Schmidhuber
KAUST Center of Generative AI
Thuwal, Saudi Arabia

IDSIA USI-SUPSI
Lugano, Switzerland

Kristína Malinovská
Comenius University
Bratislava, Slovakia

Igor V. Tetko
Helmholtz Zentrum München
Neuherberg, Germany

BigChem GmbH
Unterschleißheim, Germany

ISSN 0302-9743 ISSN 1611-3349 (electronic)
Lecture Notes in Computer Science
ISBN 978-3-031-72334-6 ISBN 978-3-031-72335-3 (eBook)
https://doi.org/10.1007/978-3-031-72335-3

© The Editor(s) (if applicable) and The Author(s), under exclusive license
to Springer Nature Switzerland AG 2024

This work is subject to copyright. All rights are solely and exclusively licensed by the Publisher, whether the whole or part of the material is concerned, specifically the rights of translation, reprinting, reuse of illustrations, recitation, broadcasting, reproduction on microfilms or in any other physical way, and transmission or information storage and retrieval, electronic adaptation, computer software, or by similar or dissimilar methodology now known or hereafter developed.
The use of general descriptive names, registered names, trademarks, service marks, etc. in this publication does not imply, even in the absence of a specific statement, that such names are exempt from the relevant protective laws and regulations and therefore free for general use.
The publisher, the authors and the editors are safe to assume that the advice and information in this book are believed to be true and accurate at the date of publication. Neither the publisher nor the authors or the editors give a warranty, expressed or implied, with respect to the material contained herein or for any errors or omissions that may have been made. The publisher remains neutral with regard to jurisdictional claims in published maps and institutional affiliations.

This Springer imprint is published by the registered company Springer Nature Switzerland AG
The registered company address is: Gewerbestrasse 11, 6330 Cham, Switzerland

If disposing of this product, please recycle the paper.

Preface

In recent years, Machine Learning has become more important than ever before. Large Language Models have revolutionized language-based tasks, with an impact far beyond the research community and IT-related industries: Artificial Intelligence for solving day-to-day tasks has become available for a wide range of end users across the world.

Machine Learning not only influences our daily lives, but also many fields of science and technology. As a specific example, we present Artificial Intelligence in organic chemistry and pharmaceutical research: a variety of tasks in this field are tackled with state-of-the-art Neural Network methods, leading to improved design and higher security of medical drugs, and to better solutions for chemical tasks in general, improving the quality of life of a large number of persons across the globe.

It is in this context that we proudly present the Proceedings of the 33th International Conference on Artificial Neural Networks (ICANN 2024). ICANN is the annual flagship conference of the European Neural Network Society (ENNS). This edition was co-organized by Istituto Dalle Molle di studi sull'intelligenza artificiale (IDSIA USI-SUPSI https://www.idsia.usi-supsi.ch) and by the Marie Skłodowska-Curie (MSC) Innovative Training Network European Industrial Doctorate "Advanced machine learning for Innovative Drug Discovery" (AIDD https://ai-dd.eu), supported by the MSC Doctoral Network "Explainable AI for Molecules" (AiChemist https://aichemist.eu). After two years of on-line and two years of hybrid conferences, ICANN 2024 was again organized as an in-person event, held on the premises of Università della Svizzera italiana (USI) and Scuola Universitaria Professionale della Svizzera italiana (SUPSI) in Lugano from September 17 to September 20, 2024.

ICANN 2024 featured three main conference tracks, namely Artificial Intelligence and Machine Learning, Bio-inspired Computing, and an Application Track. Dedicated members of the ICANN community also organized three workshops:

- AI in Drug Discovery
- Explainable AI in Human-Robot Interaction
- Reservoir Computing

  as well as three special sessions:

- Spiking Neural Networks and Neuromorphic Computing
- Accuracy, Stability, and Robustness in Deep Neural Networks
- Neurorobotics.

  Two tutorial sessions

- FEDn – A scalable federated machine learning framework for cross-device and cross-silo environments
- TSFEL - A Hands-on Introduction to Time Series Feature Extraction

were likewise proposed and organized by the community, as well as the

- Tox24 Challenge (prediction of toxicity of chemical compounds).

The proceedings of the conference are published as Springer volumes belonging to the Lecture Notes in Computer Science series. The conference had a total of 764 articles submitted to it. The papers went through a double-blind peer-review process supervised by experienced Area Chairs who suggested decisions to Program Chairs. In total, 564 Area Chairs, Program Committee (PC) members, and reviewers participated in the review process. The reviewers were on average assigned 3–4 articles each and submissions received on average 2.03 reviews each. A list of reviewers/PC Members who agreed to publish their names is included in the proceedings.

Based on the Area Chairs' and reviewers' comments, 310 articles (40.5% of initial submissions) were accepted, including 180 manuscripts selected for oral presentations. Out of the total number of accepted articles the majority (285 papers) were full articles with an average length of 15 pages, 20 manuscripts were short articles with an average length of 10 pages, and 5 were abstracts with an average length of 3 pages.

The accepted papers of the 33rd ICANN conference are published as 11 volumes, including one open-access volume with papers supported by the AIDD project.

The authors of accepted articles came from 29 different countries. As indicated by first author affiliation the largest number of articles came from China, followed by Germany, Japan, and Italy. While the majority of the articles were from academic researchers, the conference also attracted contributions from many industries including large pharmaceutical companies (Pfizer, Bayer, AstraZeneca, Johnson & Johnson), information and communication technology companies (Fujitsu and Baidu inc.), as well as multiple startups. This speaks to the increasing use of artificial neural networks in industry. Four keynote speakers were invited to give lectures on the timely aspects of advances in understanding the brain (Michael Reimann); new insights into cortical attention mechanisms and context-dependent gating and how they might inspire future developments in AI (Walter Senn); the current state of cognitive systems and how the full range of bio-signals can be utilized to further enhance human-robot interactions (Tanja Schultz); and a general overview of the past, present and future of machine learning (Jürgen Schmidhuber).

These proceedings provide comprehensive and up-to-date coverage of the dynamically developing field of Artificial Neural Networks. They are of major interest both for theoreticians as well as for applied scientists who are looking for new innovative approaches to solve their practical problems. We sincerely thank the Program and Steering Committee, Area Chairs, and the reviewers for their invaluable work.

September 2024

Michael Wand
Kristína Malinovská
Jürgen Schmidhuber
Igor V. Tetko

Organization

General Chairs

Jürgen Schmidhuber   KAUST Center of Generative AI, Saudi Arabia, and IDSIA USI-SUPSI, Switzerland
Igor V. Tetko   Helmholtz Munich, Germany and BigChem GmbH, Germany

Program Chairs

Michael Wand   IDSIA USI-SUPSI, Switzerland and MeDiTech, SUPSI, Switzerland
Kristina Malinovska   Comenius University Bratislava, Slovakia

Honorary Chair

Stefan Wermter   University of Hamburg, Germany

Organizing Committee Chairs

Katya Ahmad   Helmholtz Munich, Germany
Alessandra Lintas   University of Lausanne, Switzerland

Local Organizing Committee

Stefano van Gogh   IDSIA USI-SUPSI, Switzerland
Qinhan Hou   IDSIA USI-SUPSI, Switzerland
Nicolò La Porta   SUPSI, Switzerland
Alessandro Giusti   IDSIA USI-SUPSI, Switzerland
Vittorio Limongelli   USI, Switzerland
Cesare Alippi   IDSIA USI-SUPSI, Switzerland
Elena Invernizzi   IDSIA USI-SUPSI, Switzerland
Alessia Gianinazzi   IDSIA USI-SUPSI, Switzerland

Communication Chairs

Sebastian Otte University of Lübeck, Germany
R. Omar Chavez-Garcia IDSIA USI-SUPSI, Switzerland

Steering Committee

Stefan Wermter University of Hamburg, Germany
Angelo Cangelosi University of Manchester, UK
Igor Farkaš Comenius University Bratislava, Slovakia
Chrisina Jayne Teesside University, UK
Matthias Kerzel University of Hamburg, Germany
Alessandra Lintas University of Lausanne, Switzerland
Kristína Malinovská Comenius University Bratislava, Slovakia
Alessio Micheli University of Pisa, Italy
Jaakko Peltonen Tampere University, Finland
Brigitte Quenet ESPCI Paris, France
Ausra Saudargiene Lithuanian University of Health Sciences, and Vytautas Magnus University, Lithuania
Roseli Wedemann Rio de Janeiro State University, Brazil
Sebastian Otte University of Lübeck, Germany

Area Chairs

Alessandro Antonucci IDSIA USI-SUPSI, Switzerland
Alessandro Facchini IDSIA USI-SUPSI, Switzerland
Alessio Micheli University of Pisa, Italy
Anthony Cioppa University of Liège, Belgium
Ausra Saudargiene Lithuanian University of Health Sciences, and Vytautas Magnus University, Lithuania
Brigitte Quenet ESPCI Paris PSL, France
Chen Zhao King Abdullah University of Science and Technology, Saudi Arabia
Daniele Palossi IDSIA USI-SUPSI, Switzerland
Davide Bacciu University of Pisa, Italy
Fabio Rinaldi IDSIA USI-SUPSI, Switzerland
Felix Putze University of Bremen, Germany
Francesca Faraci MeDiTech/BSP SUPSI-DTI, Switzerland
Gabriela Andrejková P. J. Šafárik University in Košice, Slovakia
Hui Liu University of Bremen, Germany

Igor Farkaš	Comenius University Bratislava, Slovakia
Kevin Jablonka	Friedrich Schiller University Jena, Germany
Marcello Restelli	Politecnico di Milano, Italy
Marco Forgione	IDSIA USI-SUPSI, Switzerland
Matthias Karlbauer	University of Tübingen, Germany
Michela Papandrea	ISIN, DTI, SUPSI, Switzerland
Mihai Andries	IMT Atlantique, France
Oleg Szehr	IDSIA USI-SUPSI, Switzerland
Rafael Cabañas de Paz	University of Almería, Spain
Silvio Giancola	King Abdullah University of Science and Technology, Saudi Arabia
Thang Vu	University of Stuttgart, Germany
Yibo Yang	King Abdullah University of Science and Technology, Saudi Arabia
Zuzana Černeková	Comenius University Bratislava, Slovakia

Workshop and Special Session Chairs

Workshop: AI in Drug Discovery

Djork-Arné Clevert	Pfizer GmbH, Germany
Igor Tetko	Helmholtz Munich, Germany

Workshop: Explainable AI in Human-Robot Interaction

Stefan Wermter	University of Hamburg, Germany
Angelo Cangelosi	University of Manchester, UK
Igor Farkaš	Comenius University Bratislava, Slovakia
Theresa Pekarek-Rosin	University of Hamburg, Germany

Workshop: Reservoir Computing

Alessio Micheli	University of Pisa, Italy
Gouhei Tanaka	Nagoya Institute of Technology, Japan
Claudio Gallicchio	University of Pisa, Italy
Benjamin Paassen	University of Bielefeld, Germany
Domenico Tortorella	University of Pisa, Italy

Special Session: Spiking Neural Networks and Neuromorphic Computing

Sander Bohté	CWI Amsterdam, Netherlands
Sebastian Otte	University of Lübeck, Germany

Special Session: Accuracy, Stability, and Robustness in Deep Neural Networks

Vera Kurkova	Institute of Computer Science of the Czech Academy of Sciences, Prague Czech Republic
Ivan Tyukin	King's College, London, UK

Special Session: Neurorobotics

Igor Farkaš	Comenius University Bratislava, Slovakia
Kristína Malinovská	Comenius University Bratislava, Slovakia
Andrej Lúčny	Comenius University Bratislava, Slovakia
Pavel Petrovič	Comenius University Bratislava, Slovakia
Michal Vavrečka	Czech Technical University in Prague, Czechia
Matthias Kerzel	University of Hamburg, Germany
Hassan Ali	University of Hamburg, Germany
Carlo Mazzola	Italian Institute for Technology, Italy

Program Committee

Abraham Yosipof	CLB, Israel
Adam Arany	KU Leuven, Belgium
Adrian Mirza	Helmholtz Institute for Polymers in Energy Applications, Germany
Adrian Ulges	RheinMain University of Applied Sciences, Germany
Alan Anis Lahoud	Örebro University, Sweden
Albert Weichselbraun	University of Applied Sciences of the Grisons (FHGR), Switzerland
Alessandra Roncaglioni	Istituto di Ricerche Farmacologiche Mario Negri, Italy
Alessandro Giusti	IDSIA USI-SUPSI, Switzerland
Alessandro Manenti	USI, Switzerland

Alessandro Trenta	University of Pisa, Italy
Alessio Gravina	University of Pisa, Italy
Alex Doboli	Stony Brook University, USA
Alex Shenfield	Sheffield Hallam University, UK
Alexander Schulz	Bielefeld University, Germany
Alexandra Reichenbach	Heilbronn University of Applied Sciences, Germany
Ali Rodan	University of Jordan, Jordan
Alireza Raisiardali	Pragmatic Semiconductor Limited, UK
Aliza Subedi	Tribhuvan University, Nepal
Amir Mohammad Elahi	EPFL, Switzerland
Ana Claudia Sima	SIB Swiss Institute of Bioinformatics, Switzerland
Ana Sanchez-Fernandez	Johnson & Johnson Innovative Medicine, Belgium/JKU Linz, Austria
Andrea Licciardi	ICAR-CNR, Italy
Andreas Mayr	Johannes Kepler University Linz, Austria
Andreas Plesner	ETH Zurich, Switzerland
Andrej Lucny	Comenius University Bratislava, Slovakia
Aneri Muni	University of Montreal and Mila AI Institute, Canada
Angeliki Pantazi	IBM Research - Zurich, Switzerland
Angelo Moroncelli	IDSIA USI-SUPSI, Switzerland
Anne-Gwenn Bosser	Lab-STICC, ENIB, France
Anthony Strock	Stanford University, USA
Antonio Liotta	Free University of Bozen-Bolzano, Italy
Aparna Raj	BITS Pilani, Dubai Campus, United Arab Emirates
Ardian Selmonaj	IDSIA USI-SUPSI, Switzerland
Arnaud Gucciardi	University of Ljubljana, Slovenia
Artur Xarles	Universitat de Barcelona, Spain
Asma Sattar	University of Pisa, Italy
Aurelio Raffa Ugolini	Politecnico di Milano, Italy
Baohua Zhang	Beijing Institute of Technology, China
Baojin Huang	Wuhan University, China
Barbara Hammer	Bielefeld University, Germany
Bikram Kumar De	Texas State University, USA
Blerina Spahiu	University of Milan-Bicocca, Italy
Bo Li	Baidu Inc., China
Bogdan Kwolek	AGH University of Krakow, Poland
Bojian Yin	Innatera B.V., Netherlands
Brian Moser	German Research Center for Artificial Intelligence, Germany

Bulcsú Sándor	Babeş-Bolyai University, Romania
Cesare Donati	Politecnico di Torino, Italy
Chengeng Liu	Wuhan University, China
Chenxing Wang	Beijing University of Posts and Telecommunications, China
Chi Xie	Tongji University, China
Chong Zhang	Xi'an Jiaotong-Liverpool University, China
Chrisina Jayne	Teesside University, UK
Christoph Reinders	Leibniz University Hannover, Germany
Chrysoula Kosma	École Normale Supérieure Paris-Saclay, France
Cleber Zanchettin	Universidade Federal de Pernambuco, Brazil
Congcong Zhou	Sir Run Run Shaw Hospital, Zhejiang University, China
Coşku Can Horuz	University of Lübeck, Germany
Cunjian Chen	Monash University, Australia
Cyril Zakka	Stanford University, USA
Dania Humaidan	University Hospital Tübingen and Hertie Institute for Clinical Brain Research, Germany
Daniel Frank	University of Stuttgart, Germany
Daniel Nissani (Nissensohn)	Independent Research, Israel
Daniel Ortega	University of Stuttgart, Germany
Daniel Rose	University of Vienna, Austria
Daniele Angioletti	Università della Svizzera italiana, Switzerland
Daniele Castellana	Università degli Studi di Firenze, Italy
Daniele Malpetti	IDSIA USI-SUPSI, Switzerland
Daniele Zambon	IDSIA USI-SUPSI, Switzerland
Darío Ramos López	University of Almería, Spain
Davide Borra	University of Bologna, Italy
Dehui Kong	Sanechips; ZTE, China
Denis Kleyko	Örebro University, Sweden
Diana Borza	Babeş-Bolyai University, Romania
Dinesh Kumar	Bennett University, India
Dirk Väth	University of Stuttgart, Germany
Dongmian Zou	Duke Kunshan University, China
Doreen Jirak	Istituto Italiano di Tecnologia, Italy
Douglas McLelland	BrainChip, France
Duarte Folgado	Fraunhofer Portugal AICOS, Portugal
Dulani Meedeniya	University of Moratuwa, Sri Lanka
Dumitru-Clementin Cercel	Politehnica University of Bucharest, Romania
Dylan Muir	SynSense, Switzerland
Dylan R. Ashley	IDSIA USI-SUPSI, Switzerland

E. J. Solteiro Pires	Universidade de Trás-os-Montes e Alto Douro, Portugal
Elena Šikudová	Charles University, Czech Republic
Elia Cereda	IDSIA USI-SUPSI, Switzerland
Elia Piccoli	University of Pisa, Italy
Emmanuel Okafor	King Fahd University of Petroleum and Minerals, Saudi Arabia
Evaldo Mendonça Fleury Curado	Centro Brasileiro de Pesquisas Físicas and National Institute of Science and Technology for Complex Systems, Brazil
Evgeny Mirkes	University of Leicester, UK
Farhad Nooralahzadeh	Zurich University of Applied Sciences, University of Zurich, Switzerland
Fatemeh Hadaeghi	University Medical Center Hamburg-Eppendorf (UKE), Germany
Fatima Ezzeddine	Università della Svizzera italiana, Switzerland
Federico Errica	NEC Laboratories Europe, Germany
Fedor Scholz	University of Tübingen, Germany
Filipe Miguel Cardoso Micu Menezes	Helmholtz Munich, Germany
Flávio Arthur Oliveira Santos	Universidade Federal de Pernambuco, Brazil
Florian Lux	University of Stuttgart, Germany
Francesco Faccio	IDSIA USI-SUPSI, Switzerland/KAUST AI Initiative, Saudi Arabia
Francesco Landolfi	Università di Pisa, Italy
Francis Colas	Inria, France
Frédéric Alexandre	Inria, France
Gabriel Haddon-Hill	Keio University, Japan
Gabriela Sejnova	Czech Technical University in Prague, Czech Republic
Gabriele Lagani	ISTI-CNR, Italy
Gerrit A. Ecke	Mercedes-Benz AG, Germany
Gianvito Losapio	Politecnico di Milano, Italy
Giorgia Adorni	IDSIA USI-SUPSI, Switzerland
Giovanni Dispoto	Politecnico di Milano, Italy
Giovanni Donghi	University of Padua, Italy
Giuliana Monachino	University of Applied Sciences and Arts of Southern Switzerland (SUPSI), Switzerland
Gugulothu Narendhar	TCS Research, India
Guillaume Godin	BigChem, Switzerland
Habib Irani	Texas State University, USA
Hanno Gottschalk	TU Berlin, Germany
Haoran Yang	Sichuan University, China

Hasby Fahrudin	AIBrain, South Korea
Hicham Boudlal	Mohammed First University of Oujda, Morocco
Hitesh Laxmichand Patel	Oracle/New York University, USA
Houssem Ouertatani	IRT SystemX & Univ. Lille, CNRS, Inria, France
Huang Yifan	Northeast Electric Power University, China
Hubert Cecotti	California State University, Fresno, USA
Hugo Cesar de Castro Carneiro	Universität Hamburg, Germany
Huifang Ma	Northwest Normal University, China
Igor Tetko	Helmholtz Munich, Germany
Ivor Uhliarik	Comenius University Bratislava, Slovakia
Jan Kalina	Czech Academy of Sciences, Institute of Computer Science, Czech Republic
Jan Niehues	KIT, Germany
Jan Prosi	University of Tübingen/International Max Planck Research School for Intelligent Systems, Germany
Jan Wollschläger	Bayer Pharmaceuticals, Germany
Jannis Vamvas	University of Zurich, Switzerland
Jérémie Cabessa	University of Versailles Saint-Quentin, France
Jia Cai	Guangdong University of Finance and Economics, China
Jiahui Chen	Xiamen University, China
Jialiang Xu	Soochow University, China
Jian Zhang	Zhejiang University, China
Jing Han	University of Cambridge, UK
Jingzehua Xu	Tsinghua University, China
Jinlai Ning	King's College London, UK
Jiong Wang	Beijing Normal University, China
Jiwen Yu	Peking University, China
Jizhe Yu	Dalian University of Technology, China
João Ricardo Sato	Universidade Federal do ABC, Brazil
Johannes Kriebel	University of Münster, Germany
Johannes Zierenberg	Max Planck Institute for Dynamics and Self-Organization, Germany
Jorge Lo Presti	University of Pavia, Italy
Julian Cremer	Pfizer, Germany
Julie Keisler	EDF R&D, Inria, France
Julien Marteen Akay	Bielefeld University of Applied Sciences and Arts, Germany
Jun Zhou	Wuhan University, China
Junjie Zhou	Nanjing University of Aeronautics and Astronautics, China
Junzhou Chen	College of William and Mary, USA

Kai Mao	Xi'an Jiaotong University, China
Kevin Scheck	University of Bremen, Germany
Keyan Jin	Macao Polytechnic University, Macao SAR, China
Khoa Phung	University of the West of England, UK
Kiran Lekkala	University of Southern California, USA
Kohei Nakajima	University of Tokyo, Japan
Konstantinos Chatzilygeroudis	University of Patras, Greece
Krechel Dirk	RheinMain University of Applied Science, Germany
Kristína Malinovská	Comenius University Bratislava, Slovakia
Lapo Frascati	ODYS, Italy
Laura Azzimonti	IDSIA USI-SUPSI, Switzerland
Laurent Larger	FEMTO-ST Institute, Université Bourgogne-Franche-Comté, France
Laurent Mertens	KU Leuven, Belgium
Laurent Udo Perrinet	Institut des Neurosciences de la Timone, Aix Marseille Univ - CNRS, France
Lazaros Iliadis	Democritus University of Thrace, Greece
Lea Multerer	IDSIA USI-SUPSI, Switzerland
Lei Li	University of Copenhagen, Denmark
Lenka Tetkova	Technical University of Denmark, Denmark
Leon Scharwächter	University of Tübingen, Germany
Leonardo Olivetti	Uppsala University, Sweden
Lewis Mervin	AstraZeneca, UK
Lina Humbeck	Boehringer Ingelheim Pharma GmbH & Co. KG, Germany
Lindsey Vanderlyn	University of Stuttgart, Germany
Logofatu Doina	Frankfurt University of Applied Sciences, Germany
Lu Yang	Wuhan University, China
Lubomir Antoni	Pavol Jozef Šafárik University in Košice, Slovakia
Luca Butera	IDSIA USI-SUPSI, Switzerland
Luca Sabbioni	ML cube, Italy
Luís Gonçalves	Universidade Federal de Pernambuco, Brazil
Lyra Puspa	Vanaya NeuroLab, Indonesia and Canterbury Christ Church University, UK
Maëlic Neau	ENIB, France/Flinders University, Australia
Mahsa Abazari Kia	Northeastern University London, UK
Maksim Makarenko	Saudi Aramco, Saudi Arabia
Manas Mejari	IDSIA USI-SUPSI, Switzerland
Manon Dampfhoffer	Univ. Grenoble Alpes, CEA, List, France
Manuel Traub	University of Tübingen, Germany

Marco Paul E. Apolinario	Purdue University, USA
Marco Podda	University of Pisa, Italy
Marco Tarabini	Politecnico di Milano, Italy
Marcondes Ricarte da Silva Júnior	Federal University of Pernambuco, Brazil
Marek Suppa	Comenius University Bratislava, Slovakia
Marina Garcia de Lomana	Bayer AG, Germany
Markus Heinonen	Aalto University, Finland
Marta Lenatti	Consiglio Nazionale delle Ricerche, Italy
Martin Lefebvre	Université catholique de Louvain, Belgium
Martin Ritzert	Georg-August Universität Göttingen, Germany
Masanobu Inubushi	Tokyo University of Science, Japan
Matej Fandl	Comenius University Bratislava, Slovakia
Matej Pecháč	Tachyum s.r.o., Slovakia
Matteo Rufolo	IDSIA USI-SUPSI, Switzerland
Matthias Kerzel	Universität Hamburg, Germany
Matthias Rupp	Luxembourg Institute of Science and Technology, Luxembourg
Matus Tuna	Comenius University Bratislava, Slovakia
Maximilian Kimmich	University of Stuttgart, Germany
Maynara Donato de Souza	Federal University of Pernambuco, Brazil
Mengdi Li	University of Hamburg, Germany
Mengjia Zhu	IMT School for Advanced Studies Lucca, Italy
Michal Bechny	UNIBE/SUPSI, Switzerland
Michal Burgunder	Università della Svizzera italiana, Switzerland
Michal Vavrecka	CIIRC CTU, Czech Republic
Michela Sperti	Politecnico di Torino, Italy
Michele Fontanesi	University of Pisa, Italy
Mikhail Andronov	Università della Svizzera Italiana, Switzerland
Mingyang Li	Stanford University, USA
Mingyong Li	Chongqing Normal University, China
Miroslav Strupl	IDSIA USI-SUPSI, Switzerland
Moritz Wolter	Rheinische Friedrich-Wilhelms-Universität Bonn, Germany
Muhammad Arslan Masood	Aalto University, Finland
Muhammad Burhan Hafez	University of Southampton, UK
Mykhailo Sakevych	Texas State University, USA
Nabeel Khalid	German Research Center for Artificial Intelligence, Germany
Navdeep Singh Bedi	IDSIA USI-SUPSI, Switzerland
Nicolò La Porta	Università della Svizzera Italiana, Switzerland
Niklas Beuter	Technische Hochschule Lübeck, Germany
Niko Dalla Noce	University of Pisa, Italy

Oh-hyeon Choung	dsm-firmenich, Switzerland
Olivier J. M. Béquignon	Leiden University, The Netherlands
Omran Ayoub	University of Applied Sciences and Arts of Southern Switzerland, Switzerland
Oscar Mendez Lucio	Recursion, Spain
Osvaldo Simeone	King's College London, UK
Otto Brinkhaus	Spleenlab GmbH, Germany
Pascal Tilli	University of Stuttgart, Germany
Paul Czodrowski	JGU Mainz, Germany
Paul Kainen	Georgetown University, USA
Paula Štancelová	Comenius University Bratislava, Slovakia
Paula Torren-Peraire	Johnson & Johnson Innovative Medicine, Belgium
Pavel Denisov	University of Stuttgart, Germany
Pavel Kordík	Czech Technical University in Prague, Czech Republic
Pavel Petrovič	Comenius University Bratislava, Slovakia
Peiyu Liang	Temple University, USA
Peng Qiao	NUDT, China
Pengjie Liu	Southern University of Science and Technology, China
Pengyu Li	Yanshan University, China
Petia Koprinkova-Hristova	Institute of Information and Communication Technologies, Bulgarian Academy of Sciences, Bulgaria
Petra Vidnerová	Institute of Computer Science, Czech Academy of Sciences, Czech Republic
Philipp Allgeuer	University of Hamburg, Germany
Plinio Moreno	Instituto Superior Técnico/University of Lisbon, Portugal
Qinhan Hou	IDSIA USI-SUPSI, Switzerland
Quentin Jodelet	Tokyo Institute of Technology, Japan
Raphael Yokoingawa de Camargo	Universidade Federal do ABC, Brazil
Răzvan-Alexandru Smădu	National University of Science and Technology POLITEHNICA Bucharest, Romania
Reyan Ahmed	University of Arizona, USA
Ricardo O. Chávez García	IDSIA USI-SUPSI, Switzerland
Riccardo Massidda	Università di Pisa, Italy
Riccardo Renzulli	University of Turin, Italy
Robert Legenstein	Graz University of Technology, Austria
Robertas Damaševičius	Kaunas University of Technology, Lithuania
Robin Winter	Pfizer, Germany

Rodolphe Vuilleumier	École normale supérieure-PSL, Sorbonne Université, CNRS, France
Rodrigo Braga	NOVA School of Science and Technology, Portugal
Rodrigo Clemente Thom de Souza	Federal University of Paraná, Brazil
Roseli S. Wedemann	Universidade do Estado do Rio de Janeiro, Brazil
Roxane Jacob	University of Vienna, Austria
Ru Zhou	RuiJin Hospital LuWan Branch, Shanghai Jiaotong University School of Medicine, China
Ruinan Wang	University of Bristol, UK
Ruixi Zhou	Beijing University of Posts and Telecommunications, China
Rupesh Raj Karn	New York University Abu Dhabi, United Arab Emirates
Samuel Genheden	AstraZeneca R&D, Sweden
Sandra Mitrovic	IDSIA USI-SUPSI, Switzerland
Sankalp Jain	NCATS-NIH, USA
Sara Joubbi	University of Pisa, Italy
Seema Dilipkumar Aswani	BITS Pilani, Dubai Campus, UAE
Seiya Satoh	Tokyo Denki University, Japan
Semih Beycimen	Cranfield University, UK
Senhui Qiu	Ulster University, UK
Sergei Katkov	Free University of Bozen-Bolzano, Italy
Sergio Mauricio Vanegas Arias	LUT University, Finland
Shangchao Su	Fudan University, China
Sheng Xu	Chinese University of Hong Kong, Shenzhen, China
Shenyang Liu	University of Central Florida, USA
Sherjeel Shabih	Humboldt University, Germany
Shi Haoran	China Water Northeastern Investigation, Design & Research Co., Ltd., China
Shingo Murata	Keio University, Japan
Shinnosuke Matsuo	Kyushu University, Japan
Shiyao Zhang	University of Bremen, Germany
Sho Shirasaka	Osaka University, Japan
Simiao Zhuang	TUM Beijing, China
Simon Heilig	Ruhr University Bochum, Germany
Šimon Horvát	Slovakia
Simone Bonechi	University of Siena, Italy
Simone Lionetti	Hochschule Luzern, Switzerland
Siyu Wu	Central South University of Forests and Technology, China
Stefano Damato	IDSIA USI-SUPSI, Switzerland

Stéphane Meystre	MeDiTech/SUPSI, Switzerland
Steve Azzolin	University of Trento, Italy
Sudip Roy	Indian Institute of Technology Roorkee, India
Sujala D. Shetty	BITS Pilani, Dubai Campus, United Arab Emirates
Taoran Fu	Hunan University & Hunan Institute of Engineering, China
Teste Olivier	Université Toulouse 2, IRIT (UMR5505), France
Thierry Viéville	Inria, France
Tianyi Wang	Nanyang Technological University, Singapore
Tim Schlippe	IU International University of Applied Sciences, Germany
Tingyu Lin	TU Wien, Austria
Tuan Le	Pfizer, Germany
Valerie Vaquet	Bielefeld University, Germany
Vangelis Metsis	Texas State University, USA
Vani Kanjirangat	IDSIA USI-SUPSI, Switzerland
Varun Ojha	Newcastle University, UK
Veronica Lachi	Fondazione Bruno Kessler, Italy
Viktor Kocur	Comenius University Bratislava, Slovakia
Vincenzo Palmacci	University of Vienna, Austria
Wei Dai	Robo Space, China
Weiqi Li	Peking University, China
Weiran Chen	Soochow University, China
Wenjie Zhang	Shandong University, China
Wenwei Gu	Chinese University of Hong Kong, China
Wolfram Schenck	Bielefeld University of Applied Sciences and Arts, Germany
Xavier Hinaut	Inria, France
Xi Wang	National University of Defense Technology, China
Xiangxian Li	Shandong University, China
Xiangyuan Peng	Technical University of Munich, Germany
Xiaochen Yuan	Macao Polytechnic University, Macao SAR, China
Xiaomeng Fu	University of Chinese Academy of Sciences, China
Xiaowen Sun	University of Hamburg, Germany
Xiaoxiao Miao	Singapore Institute of Technology, Singapore
Xingda Yao	Zhejiang University of Technology, China
Xinxin Luo	Southeast University, China
XinZhi Lin	Beihang University, China
Xun Lin	Beihang University, China

Yan Jiang	Nanjing University of Information Science and Technology, China
Yang Cao	Shanghai University of Finance and Economics, China
Yangfan Zhou	Southwest University of Science and Technology, China
Yangxun Ou	East China Normal University, China
Yao Du	Beihang University, China
Yaxin Hu	University of Lübeck, Germany
Ye Hu	Pfizer, Germany
Yi Li	Lancaster University, UK
Yichi Zhang	Fudan University, China
Yiming Tang	Shanghai Lixin University of Accounting and Finance, China
Ying Tan	Key Laboratory for Computer Systems of State Ethnic Affairs Commission, Southwest Minzu University, China
Yiqing Shen	Johns Hopkins University, USA
Yixuan Xiao	University of Stuttgart, Germany
Yong Luo	Wuhan University, China
Yongtao Tang	National University of Defense Technology, China
Yuankun Chen	University of Science and Technology, China
Yuansheng Ma	Soochow University, China
Yuchen Guo	Institute of Information Engineering, Chinese Academy of Sciences, China
Yuichi Katori	Future University Hakodate, Japan
Yuji Kawai	Osaka University, Japan
Yusen Wu	Sichuan University, China
Yutaka Nakamura	Riken, Japan
Yuya Okadome	Tokyo University of Science, Japan
Zdravko Marinov	Karlsruhe Institute of Technology, Germany
Zeyao Liu	Key Institute of Information Engineering, Chinese Academy of Sciences, China
Zhang Ke	China University of Petroleum (Beijing), China
Zhenjie Yao	Institute of Microelectronics of the Chinese Academy of Sciences, China
Zheyan Gao	Tianjin University, China
Zhiheng Qiu	City University of Macau, China
Zhihuan Xing	Beihang University, China
Zuzana Berger Haladova	Comenius University Bratislava, Slovakia

Plenary Talks

Past, Present, Future, and Far Future of Machine Learning

Jürgen Schmidhuber

IDSIA USI-SUPSI, Switzerland, and KAUST AI Initiative, Saudi Arabia

I'll discuss modern Artificial Intelligence and how the principles of the G, P and T in Chat GPT emerged in 1991. I'll also discuss what's next in AI, and its expected impact on the future of the universe.

Dendritic Computations and Deep Learning in the Brain

Walter Senn

University of Bern, Institut für Physiologie, Computational Neuroscience Lab,
Switzerland

Artificial Intelligence, through its working horse of neural networks, is inspired by the biological example of the brain. The unprecedented success of AI in modeling cognitive processes, in turn, inspires functional models of the brain. Yet, when looking into the brain, additional biological structures become apparent, such as dendritic morphologies, interneuron circuits, recurrent connectivity, error representations, top-down signaling and various gating hierarchies. I will give a review on these biological elements and show how they may integrate in an energy-based theory of cortical computation. Dendrites and cortical microcircuits turn out to implement a real-time version of error-backpropagation based on prospective errors. The theory is inspired by the least-action principle in physics from which all dynamical equations of motions are derived. We likewise derive the neuronal dynamics, including the synaptic dynamics with gradient-descent learning, from our Neuronal Least-Action (NLA) principle. The principle tells that the cortical activities and the real-time learning follows a path that minimizes prospective errors across all neurons of the network. Prospective errors in output neurons relate to behavioral errors, while prospective errors in deep network neurons relate to errors in the neuron-specific dendritic prediction of somatic firing. I will explain how these ideas relate to cortical attention mechanisms and context-dependent gating that link to, and potentially inspires, recent developments in AI.

Biosignal-Adaptive Cognitive Systems

Tanja Schultz

University of Bremen, Fachbereich 3 - Mathematik und Informatik, Cognitive Systems Lab, Germany

I will describe technical cognitive systems that automatically adapt to users' needs by interpreting their biosignals: Human behavior includes physical, mental, and social actions that emit a range of biosignals which can be captured by a variety of sensors. The processing and interpretation of such biosignals provides an inside perspective on human physical and mental activities, complementing the traditional approach of merely observing human behavior. As great strides have been made in recent years in integrating sensor technologies into ubiquitous devices and in machine learning methods for processing and learning from data, I argue that the time has come to harness the full spectrum of biosignals to understand user needs. I will present illustrative cases ranging from silent and imagined speech interfaces that convert myographic and neural signals directly into audible speech, to interpretation of human attention and decision making in human-robot interaction from multimodal biosignals.

A Model of Neocortical Micro- and Mesocircuitry and Its Applications

Michael Reimann

Blue Brain, Swiss Federal Institute of Technology Lausanne, Switzerland

We present a large-scale, biophysically detailed model of rat non-barrel somatosensory regions. Building upon an earlier version of such a model, we increased the spatial scale of the model and enhanced its biological realism. The most salient improvements are: First, construction of realistic synaptic connectivity as the union of two algorithms, one for local connections, and another for long-range connections. Second, introduction of methods to build a model inside a standardized voxel atlas. This, combined with the connectivity algorithms allows models of brain regions to be developed separately and then easily integrated. Third, improvements in the methods to compensate for missing extrinsic inputs and to validate an in-vivo-like activity regime.

We demonstrate several applications of the model that make use of its specific advantages over more simplified models: First, studying the rules of synaptic plasticity at the population level. Second, studying the effect of heterogeneous and non-random connectivity on circuit function and reliability. Third, studying the accuracy and biases inherent in spike sorting algorithms.

Contents – Part II

Computer Vision: Classification

A Weakly Supervised Part Detection Method for Robust Fine-Grained Classification 3
   Yang Liu, Le Jiang, Guoming Li, Xiaozhou Ye, and Ye Ouyang

An Energy Sampling Replay-Based Continual Learning Framework 17
   Xingzhong Zhang, Joon Huang Chuah, Chu Kiong Loo, and Stefan Wermter

Coarse-to-Fine Granularity in MultiScale FeatureFusion Network for SAR Ship Classification 31
   Wei Lin, Hao Zheng, Zhigang Hu, Meiguang Zheng, and Liu Yang

Multi-scale Convolutional Attention Fuzzy Broad Network for Few-Shot Hyperspectral Image Classification 46
   Xiaopei Hu, Guixin Zhao, Lu Yuan, Xiangjun Dong, and Aimei Dong

Self Adaptive Threshold Pseudo-labeling and Unreliable Sample Contrastive Loss for Semi-supervised Image Classification 61
   Xuerong Zhang, Li Huang, Jing Lv, and Ming Yang

Computer Vision: Object Detection

CIA-Net: Cross-Modal Interaction and Depth Quality-Aware Network for RGB-D Salient Object Detection 79
   Xiaomei Kuang, Aiqing Zhu, Junbin Yuan, and Qingzhen Xu

CPH DETR: Comprehensive Regression Loss for End-to-End Object Detection 93
   Jihao Wu, Shufang Li, Guxia Kang, and Yuqing Yang

DecoratingFusion: A LiDAR-Camera Fusion Network with the Combination of Point-Level and Feature-Level Fusion 108
   Zixuan Yin, Han Sun, Ningzhong Liu, Huiyu Zhou, and Jiaquan Shen

EMDFNet: Efficient Multi-scale and Diverse Feature Network for Traffic Sign Detection 120
   Pengyu Li, Chenhe Liu, Tengfei Li, Xinyu Wang, Shihui Zhang, and Dongyang Yu

Global-Guided Weighted Enhancement for Salient Object Detection 137
Jizhe Yu, Yu Liu, Hongkui Wei, Kaiping Xu, Yifei Cao, and Jiangquan Li

KDNet: Leveraging Vision-Language Knowledge Distillation
for Few-Shot Object Detection 153
Mengyuan Ma, Lin Qian, and Hujun Yin

MUFASA: Multi-view Fusion and Adaptation Network with Spatial
Awareness for Radar Object Detection 168
Xiangyuan Peng, Miao Tang, Huawei Sun, Kay Bierzynski, Lorenzo Servadei, and Robert Wille

One-Shot Object Detection with 4D-Correlation and 4D-Attention 185
Qiwei Lin, Xinzhi Lin, Junjie Zhou, and Qinghua Long

Small Object Detection Based on Bidirectional Feature Fusion
and Multi-scale Distillation 200
Lingyu Wang, Zijie Zhou, Guanqun Shi, Junkang Guo, and Zhigang Liu

SRA-YOLO: Spatial Resolution Adaptive YOLO for Semi-supervised
Cross-Domain Aerial Object Detection 215
Junhao Huang, Jian Xue, Yuqiu Li, Hao Wu, and Ke Lu

Computer Vision: Security and Adversarial Attacks

BiFAT: Bilateral Filtering and Attention Mechanisms in a Two-Stream
Model for Deepfake Detection 231
Lei Zhang, Ceyuan Yi, and Liang Liu

EL-FDL: Improving Image Forgery Detection and Localization
via Ensemble Learning 248
Bin Wang, Feifan Wang, Jingge Wang, Haonan Yan, Shaopeng Zhou, and Chaohao Li

Enhanced Image Manipulation Detection with TPB-Net: Integrating
Triple-Path Backbone and Dual-Path Compressed Sensing Attention 263
Huaqing Song

Generalizable Deepfake Detection with Unbiased Feature Extraction
and Low-Level Forgery Enhancement 275
Zhihan Yu, JiaXin Li, Guangshuo Wang, Yuesheng Zhu, and Guibo Luo

Generative Universal Nullifying Perturbation for Countering Deepfakes
Through Combined Unsupervised Feature Aggregation 289
   Yuchen Guo, Xi Wang, Xiaomeng Fu, Jin Liu, Zhaoxing Li,
   and Jizhong Han

HFDA-Net: Utilizing High-Frequency Feature and Dual-Attention
to Enhance Image Manipulation Detection and Localization 304
   Chengeng Liu, Xu Chen, Tian Xu, and Xiangyang Jia

Noise-NeRF: Hide Information in Neural Radiance Field Using Trainable
Noise 320
   Qinglong Huang, Haoran Li, Yong Liao, Yanbin Hao, and Pengyuan Zhou

Unconventional Face Adversarial Attack 335
   Ruoxi Wang, Baojin Huang, Zhen Han, and Dengshi Li

Computer Vision: Image Enhancement

A Study in Dataset Pruning for Image Super-Resolution 351
   Brian B. Moser, Federico Raue, and Andreas Dengel

EDAFormer: Enhancing Low-Light Images with a Dual-Attention
Transformer 364
   Jin Zhang, Haiyan Jin, Haonan Su, Yuanlin Zhang, Zhaolin Xiao,
   and Bin Wang

Image Matting Based on Deep Equilibrium Models 379
   Xinshuang Liu and Yue Zhao

Computer Vision: 3D Methods

ControlNeRF: Text-Driven 3D Scene Stylization via Diffusion Model 395
   Jiahui Chen, Chuanfeng Yang, Kaiheng Li, Qingqiang Wu,
   and Qingqi Hong

Interactive Color Manipulation in NeRF: A Point Cloud and Palette-Driven
Approach 407
   Haolei Qiu, Chenqu Ren, and Yeheng Shao

Multimodal Monocular Dense Depth Estimation with Event-Frame Fusion
Using Transformer 419
   Baihui Xiao, Jingzehua Xu, Zekai Zhang, Tianyu Xing, Jingjing Wang,
   and Yong Ren

SAM-NeRF: NeRF-Based 3D Instance Segmentation with Segment
Anything Model 434
   *Xi Wang, Linglin Xie, Peng Qiao, Yong Dou, Sidun Liu, Wenyu Li,
   and Kaijun Yang*

Towards High-Accuracy Point Cloud Registration with Channel
Self-attention and Angle Invariance 449
   Jinhong Hong, Songwei Pei, and Shuhuai Wang

Author Index 463

Computer Vision: Classification

A Weakly Supervised Part Detection Method for Robust Fine-Grained Classification

Yang Liu[1], Le Jiang[1(✉)], Guoming Li[1], Xiaozhou Ye[1], and Ye Ouyang[1,2]

[1] AsiaInfo Technologies (China) Inc., Beijing, China
{liuyang46,jiangle,ligm,yexz,ye.ouyang}@asiainfo.com
[2] AsiaInfo Technologies, Guangzhou, China

Abstract. Fine-grained classification is a challenging task due to the subtle differences between subclasses, therefore, locating discriminative part features has become a key capability of fine-grained algorithms. In this paper, we design a sophisticated module to obtain the most discriminative part features by weakly supervised learning, which can be combined with multiple backbone networks, such as CNN-based or Transformer-based networks. Besides, we propose a self-knowledge distillation method that combines random homography transformation with a consistency loss in the training stage, which motivates the model to become more robust to pose variation and learns richer knowledge. The experimental results demonstrate that our model outperforms current fine-grained algorithms based on weakly supervised learning. Meanwhile, it follows a single stage design and does not require iterative optimization, thus having good training and inference efficiency.

Keywords: Fine-grained Classification · Weakly Supervised Learning · Self-Knowledge Distillation

1 Introduction

The purpose of fine-grained image recognition (FGVC) tasks is to identify different subcategory under the same category. Compared with traditional image recognition tasks, the differences and difficulties of fine-grained image recognition are as follows: Firstly, the differences between different subclass are very subtle, which usually reflected in local details; Secondly, for fine-grained categories, intra-class differences are relatively large, that is, different objects of the same subcategory also have huge differences in shape, posture, color, background and so on. Fine-grained image recognition usually requires a lot of professional knowledge to distinguish from subtle details, making it a huge challenge for both humans and computers.

In the past few years, many algorithms [1–7] have processed fine-grained recognition by locating the local regions with strong discrimination, then extract

---

Yang Liu, Le Jiang : IEEE Fellow.

those local region features to assist models in classification. However, these methods either require a large amount of part annotations [1–3], or have very complex model structures [4–7], which hinder the deployment and application of algorithms. In this paper, inspired by object detection area [8–10], we propose a weakly superwised part detection method (WSPD) to extract the most discriminative part features, which can be combined with multiple backbone networks (such as CNN-based or Transformer-based networks) and without bringing a significant burden on training and inference efficiency. Specifically, our contributions include:

- We design a sophisticated module to extract the most discriminative part features by weakly supervised learning, thus assisting the model in classification;
- We introduce a self-knowledge distillation method by combining a random homography transformation with a consistency loss at training stage to motivate model to become more robust and learn richer knowledge;
- We achieve surprising experimental results at three publicly fine-grained classification datasets: CUB-200-2011, Stanford Cars and FGVC aircraft, which demonstrating the effectiveness of our algorithm.

2 Related Work

According to whether use extra annotations except category-level annotations or not, fine-grained image recognition (FGVC) algorithms can be divided into two categories: fine-grained image recognition algorithm based on strong supervised learning and fine-grained image recognition algorithm based on weak supervised learning.

FGVC Based on Strong Supervised Learning: Because the differences between different sub-categories is only reflected in local details, it is often difficult to accurately identify object by using category labels alone. Therefore, in addition to use category labels, some research works [1–3,11] also uses extra manual annotation information, such as object bounding box [1,2], part annotation points [3], and text description [11]. For instance, MetaFormer [11] is a unified multi-modality framework which effectively improve the accuracy of FGVC task with the assistance of meta-information. It encodes geographic information and image together at a bird dataset [12], because species distribution presents a trend of clustering geographically, and the living habits of different species are different so that spatio-temporal information can assist the fine-grained task of species classification. Although these fine-grained image recognition algorithms based on strong supervised learning have achieved high recognition rates, their disadvantage is that they require a large amount of additional annotations in addition to category level annotations, which greatly increases training costs. Therefore, it is difficult for these algorithms to be put into practical applications.

FGVC Based on Weakly Supervised Learning: In recent years, a growing number of researchers [4–7,13,14] have focused on fine-grained image recognition algorithms based on weakly supervised learning. CCFR [13] proposed a retrieval based coarse-to-fine framework, which re-rank the Top-N classification results by using the local region enhanced embedding features to improve the Top-1 accuracy. TransFG [14] is a novel transformer-based framework which integrates all raw attention weights of the transformer into an attention map for guiding the network to effectively and accurately select discriminative image patches and compute their relations. NTS-Net [5] attempts to detect informative regions without any part annotations. It utilizes a Region Proposal Network (RPN) to predict a score which represents the informativeness of each corresponding region. Its main idea is that regions assigned with high probability on ground-truth class should contain more object-characteristic semantics. However, it needs to resize the localized regions to a fixed resolution and extract the feature again, which consumes too much computation and inference time, making it ineffective for practical applications. PIM [7] is a plug-in module which builds a feature pyramid on the backbone network and applies an auxiliary classifier at each scale of the feature pyramid. Its main idea is that the max predicted class score after softmax can represent the informativeness of the corresponding region. However, it may not be reasonable to directly use the maximum predicted class score after softmax. Due to the minor difference between each sub-classes, a part feature may be a common feature shared by several sub-classes, instead of a specific character which only belongs to ground-truth class. In this paper, we propose a part feature discriminator module (PFDM) to locate the discriminative part features with only class-level annotations. Different from the above works, it uses a weakly supervised approach to learn and rate the features of the region, which also follows a single stage design, making it more efficient and flexible.

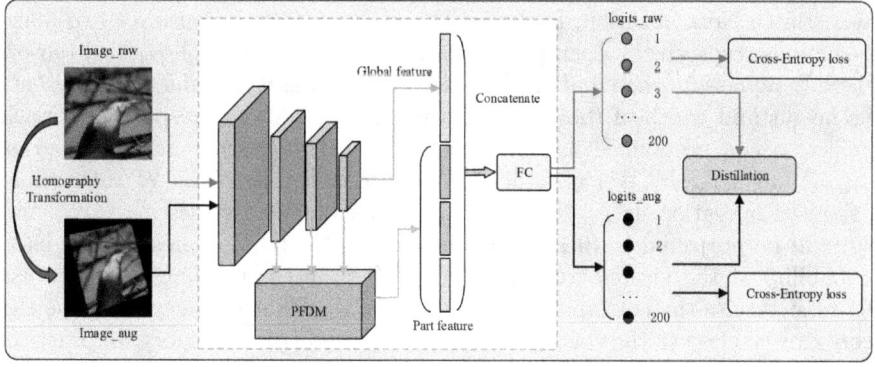

Fig. 1. The overall architecture of WSPD. We employ a shared architecture and parameters between the training graph of the raw images and its augment counterparts which generated by homography transformation.

3 Method

Figure 1 shows the main architecture of our proposed method WSPD. During the training stage, we first construct image pairs by applying random homography transformations on each input image. Then, we input the image pairs into the feature extractor to obtain the global features of each image. A part feature discriminator module (PFDM) is constructed at multiple layers of the backbone network, which helps the model to locate the most discriminative part regions and extract the corresponding part features. Next, we concatenate the global features and part features together and input them into a fully connected layer to generate the final classification logits. At the training stage, in addition to the cross entropy loss applied to the classification tasks, a consistency loss is also applied on two classification logits corresponding to the image pair, which motivates the model to be more robust to pose variation and to excavate richer information.

3.1 Part Feature Discriminator Module

In this section, we mainly introduce how the PFDM module is implemented. Firstly, we should clarify that the purpose of designing PFDM is to identify the most discriminative regions and extract corresponding features. Secondly, we can only rely on category labels during the training process, it means that PFDM can only be trained in a weakly supervised manner. Based on the above premises, we design the PFDM to predict a score map that reflects the informativeness of each part region. Meanwhile, we use feature classification probability at the ground-truth position as the supervisory signal for the score map.

Figure 2 shows the architecture of our proposed Part Feature Discriminator Module (PFDM). Take ResNet-50 [15] as an example, we first construct a feature pyramid on the last three stages (C3, C4, C5), and then input (P3, P4, P5) into a feature classification head (Implemented by a sequence of 3×3 convolution layer, Batch Normalization, LeakyReLU and 1×1 convolution layer.) to make predictions respectively. Each prediction is encoded as a $(C+1, H_i, W_i)$ tensor, where C represents the number of classes in the dataset, H_i and W_i represents the height and width of the output feature map for stage i respectively. Each prediction can be divided into two parts: a $(1, H_i, W_i)$ score map denoted as F_{score}, and a (C, H_i, W_i) classification map denoted as F_{cls}. We then apply a sigmoid operation at F_{score} and F_{cls}, so the range of values on F_{score} and F_{cls} will be projected to (0,1). Assuming $F_{gt} \in \mathbb{R}^{1 \times H_i \times W_i}$ represents the class probability at the ground-truth position of F_{cls}. In the training stage, we use F_{gt} to supervise the corresponding score at F_{score}. That is to say, we hope the score can be close to the class probability of ground truth category. In practice, we employ a squared l2-norm for mutual alignment between F_{score} and F_{gt}:

$$L_{MSE} = \frac{1}{HWC} ||F_{score} - F_{gt}||^2 \tag{1}$$

where H, W, C represent the height, width, and channel number of the F_{score}, respectively.

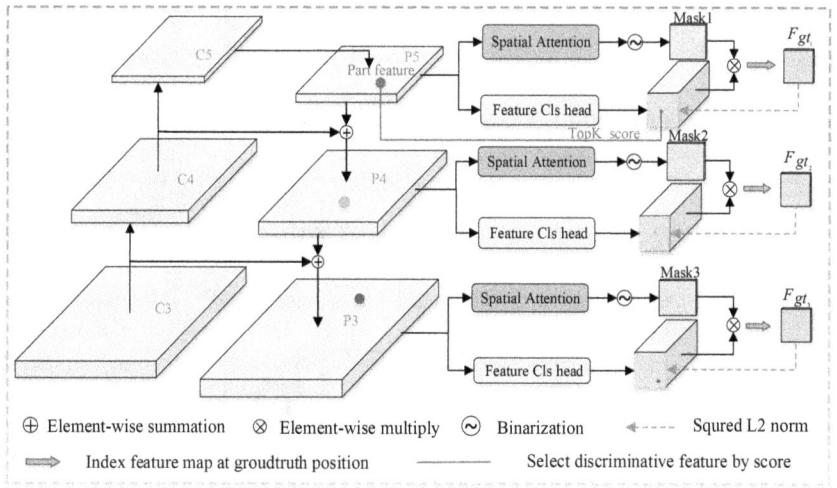

Fig. 2. The architecture of the part feature discriminator module (PFDM). C3, C4 and C5 respectively represent the output of the last 3 stages of backbone network. P3, P4 and P5 represent the the output feature maps of the feature pyramid for each stage.

However, directly apply the loss function (1) is unreasonable, because there exists a large part of background area that can not be seen as a part of the object. Thus, those areas should not be supervised. To solve this problem, during the trainning stage, we input (P3, P4, P5) into a designed spatial attention module to generate an attention map $F_{att} \in \mathbb{R}^{H_i \times W_i}$ respectively. We implement spatial attention module as following: Firstly, we perform average operation and max operation through channel dimension at the input feature map F respectively, which are formulated as: $F_{max} = MAP(F), F_{avg} = AAP(F)$. Then, we concatenate F_{max} and F_{avg} together, followed by a sequence of $K \times K$ convolution, Batch Normalization, RELU, $K \times K$ convolution and a sigmoid operation, where K represents the kernel size. Assuming the mean value of the attention map F_{att} is denoted as F_{mean}, we then generate a binary mask $F_{mask} \in \mathbb{R}^{H_i \times W_i}$ by performing a binary operation on F_{att} as following equation:

$$F_{mask_{j,k}} = \begin{cases} 1, & if F_{mask_{j,k}} \geq F_{mean} \\ 0, & otherwise \end{cases} \quad (2)$$

Here, $j \in 0, 1, .., H_{i-1}$, $k \in 0, 1, .., W_{i-1}$. Thus, the value of each location at the F_{mask} is either 0 or 1. We then use F_{mask} to guide the supervision between F_{score} and F_{gt}, so that only positions with a value of 1 at the corresponding binary mask will receive supervision. Specifically, before applying the equation (1), we multiply the F_{cls} with the corresponding binary mask:

$$F_{cls} = F_{cls} \times F_{mask} \quad (3)$$

After applying the function (3), the values at the drop position of F_{cls} change to 0. Consequently, the score at drop position of F_{score} will be encouraged to get close to 0.

Finally, we should apply a feature classification loss to F_{cls}. In the experiments, we use the following focal loss [16]:

$$L_{focal} = -\alpha_t(1-p_t)^\gamma log(p_t), p_t = \begin{cases} p, & if \quad y=1 \\ 1-p, & if \quad y=0 \end{cases} \quad (4)$$

where $y \in \{0,1\}$ specifies the groud-truth class and $p \in [0,1]$ denotes the estimated probability for the class with label y=1. α_t and γ are hyper-parameters, we set $\alpha_t = 0.25$, $\gamma = 2$. Because F_{cls} has multiplied with the binary mask, the gradient at the drop position will be cut off. Thus, F_{cls} only gets supervision at the non-drop area.

During the inference stage, we will remove the spatial attention module at each stage of feature pyramid. Finally, we choose the top-k max score at F_{score} and find the features at the corresponding location of (P3, P4, P5), thus get the most discriminative part features at each scale.

3.2 Self-knowledge Distillation

In this section, we mainly introduce the proposed self-knowledge distillation method, it mainly includes two parts: homography transformation and a consistency loss.

Homography Transformation. Homography transformation relationship can be described by a 3 × 3 matrix, which requires at least four pairs of matching points to calculate. Therefore, to sample a good homography that represents reasonable camera transformations, we first initialize two pairs of points: pt_1 : $[[0,0],[0,1],[1,1],[1,0]]$, pt_2 : $[[0,0],[0,1],[1,1],[1,0]]$. Next, we use truncated normal distribution to sample within predefined ranges of translation, scaling, in-plane rotation, and symmetric perspective distortion, and then apply these operations on pt_2 to obtain the transformed points pt_2 : $[[x_1,y_1],[x_2,y_2],[x_3,y_3],[x_4,y_4]]$. Assuming the homography matrix to be solved is H, we can obtain the following equation:

$$pt_2' = H \times pt_1 \quad (5)$$

We can use the polynomial solving function in NumPy to solve this function, thus get the result of H. Assuming I represents the raw input image, thus the augmented image by homography transformation can be formulated as:

$$I' = H \times I \quad (6)$$

Consistency Loss. In this work, we propose incorporating the homography transformation and Self-KD [17–19] into a unified framework. We hope to encourage the model to behave consistently in logits-based class posterior distributions between original images and their augmented images generated by homography transformation. To this end, we maximize the consistency of logit-based class probability distribution via KL-divergence:

$$L_{consistent}(x_{raw}, x_{aug}; \theta, T) = L_{KL}(\sigma(\frac{f(x_{raw}; \theta)}{T}), \sigma(f(x_{aug}; \theta)/T)) \quad (7)$$

where L_{KL} denotes Kullback-Leibler (KL) divergence, T is a temperature following the original KD [20]. σ represents a softmax function to normalize the logits to model posterior probability distributions. $f(x; \theta)$ represents the output logits of the fully connected layer of the backbone network which is parameterized by θ.

3.3 Overall Loss

Finally, we apply a cross-entropy loss at the final prediction logits, which formulated as:

$$L_{CLS} = L_{CE}(f(x; \theta), y) \quad (8)$$

here L_{CE} is a common cross-entropy loss, y is the class-level label of the input image x. Thus, the overall loss function of the network can be formulated as:

$$L_{total} = \alpha L_{consistent} + \beta L_{MSE} + \mu L_{focal} + \delta L_{CLS} \quad (9)$$

We set $\alpha = \beta = \mu = \delta = 1$ in our experiments.

4 Experiments

We conduct experiments on three published fine-grained image datasets: CUB-200-2011 [12], Stanford Cars [21] and FGVC Aircraft [22]. The number of categories of these three datasets and the division of training sets and test sets are shown in Table 1.

Table 1. Category data of data set and division of training set and test set.

Dataset	Category-num	Training-set	Test-set
CUB-200-2011	200	5994	5794
Stanford Cars	196	8144	8041
FGVC Aircraft	100	6667	3333

4.1 Implementation Details

We apply our algorithm to two backbones, ResNet-50 [15] and Swin-T [23], where ResNet-50 are pretrained on Image-Net-1K or ImageNet-21K, respectively, Swin-T is pretrained on Image-Net-22K. While using ResNet-50 as the backbone, the size of the input image is first sampled to 600 × 600, then randomly crop to 448 × 448. While using Swin-T as the backbone, the size of the input image is first sampled to 510 × 510, then randomly crop to 384 × 384. Gaussian blur and random adjust sharpness are applied during training phase. We use SGD and momentum optimizer with initial learning rate, momentum, and weight decay set to 0.001, 0.9, and 0.0001, respectively. The number of features selected for each layer (top-k) is set to 2. It is worth mentioning that the spatial attention module can be removed during the inference stage, so it does not incur any computational overhead.

Table 2. Comparison of TOP-1 accuracy with different methods on three public datasets.

Method	Backbone	CUB-200-2011	Stanford Cars	FGVC-Aircraft
NTS-Net [5]	ResNet-50	87.5%	93.9%	91.4%
DCL [24]	ResNet-50	87.8%	94.5%	93.0%
PIM [7]	ResNet-50(21k)	89.5%	-	-
StackedLSTM [6]	GoogleNet	90.4%	-	-
CCFR [13]	ResNet-50	91.1%	95.49%	94.1%
MetaFormer [11]	MetaFormer-1 (21K)	91.3%	95.0%	94.2%
TransFG [14]	ViT-B16	91.7%	94.8%	-
SIM-Trans [25]	ViT-B16	91.8%	-	-
CMAL-Net [26]	ResNet-50	-	94.9%	94.7%
CAP [27]	Xception [28]	91.8%	95.7%	94.9%
ViT-SAC [29]	Xception	91.8%	-	93.1%
DCAL [30]	R50-ViT-Base	92.0%	95.3%	93.3%
WSPD (ours)	ResNet-50(1K)	88.3%	94.8%	93.0%
WSPD (ours)	ResNet-50(21K)	89.9%	95.1%	93.8%
WSPD (ours)	Swin-T (22K)	**92.6%**	**95.8%**	**95.0%**

4.2 Main Results

Table 2 compares our WSPD with other existing methods at three main datasets. Remarkblely, our model outperforms current fine-grained algorithms based on weakly supervised learning. While using ResNet-50 (1K) as the backbone, our WSPD achieves 88.3%, 94.8%, and 93.0% Top-1 accuracy on CUB-200-2011, Stanford Cars, and FGVC Aircraft, respectively. While using ResNet-50 (21K)

Table 3. The influence of each component in WSPD.

Method	TOP-1 accuracy
ResNet-50	86.0%
+ Homography transformation	86.4% (+0.4%)
+ Consistency loss	86.9% (+0.5%)
+ PFDM	**88.3%** (+1.4%)

as the backbone, we achieve 89.9%, 95.1%, and 93.8%, respectively. While using Swin-T as the backbone, we achieve 92.6%, 95.8%, and 95.0%, respectively. Compared to NTS-Net [5] which has similar ideas to our WSPD, we have surpassed 0.8%, 0.9%, and 1.6% under the same backbone ResNet-50 (1K), respectively. In addition, compared with PIM [7], for the sake of fairness, we use ResNet-50 pretrained on Image-Net-21K as the backbone. As a result, we have an 0.4% advantage over PIM on CUB-200-2011. It is worth mentioning that unlike some multi-stage methods such as NTS-Net [5] and StackedLSTM [6], our approach follows a single stage design, making its training and deployment more efficient.

4.3 Ablation Study

Module Analysis. In this section, we analyze the influence of each component in WSPD on CUB-200-2011 dataset, and all models are based on ResNet-50. As shown in Table 3, after applying random homography transformation to the training data, we improved by 0.4% compared to ResNet-50. We analyze this because it augments more samples from various views, making the model more robust to some hard samples caused by pose variations. Then, we combine the consistency loss with homography transformation, which further improved the accuracy by 0.5%. This result to some extent proves that the consistency loss can encourage the model to excavate richer information while combining with homography transformation. The most important component is PFDM, which further improves the accuracy by 1.4%. This result proves that the PFDM module can effectively learn discriminative features, thereby helping the model better distinguish fine-grained categories.

Table 4. The influence of selection number k.

Selector number k	TOP-1 accuracy
1	88.1%
2	**88.3%**
3	88.1%
4	87.9%

Different Selection Number k. In this section, we investigated the effect of the number of choices k on each layer. For ResNet-50, we select top k part features at P3 and P4. Table 4 shows that we achieved the best performance while k=2, which reflects that selecting too few or too many part features does not necessarily lead to improved results. When k is too small, the model can not obtain sufficient auxiliary information well; when k is too large, the model will obtain a large amount of redundant information.

Fig. 3. Visualization results of the spatial attention map at each layer. (top is the input image, middle is the $F_{att_{P3}}$, bottom is the $F_{att_{P4}}$)

4.4 Visual Analysis

Visualization of Attention Map. As shown in Fig. 3, we perform visualization of the spatial attention maps $F_{att_{P3}}$, and $F_{att_{P4}}$ related to P3 and P4, respectively. The images are selected from CUB200-2011. It can be observed that both $F_{att_{P3}}$ and $F_{att_{P4}}$ activate a certain range of areas. Specifically, $F_{att_{P3}}$ tends to activate the entire target area. There are also some regions activated in the background, indicating that the shallow layers of convolutional neural networks focus more on low-level features, typically the detailed information such as colors, edges, angles, gradients, and so on. On the other hand, $F_{att_{P4}}$ tends to focus on some special part of the object, like head,wings,torso, because $F_{att_{P4}}$ is generated from deeper feature maps, which contain more semantic information, so it focuses more on some important regions.

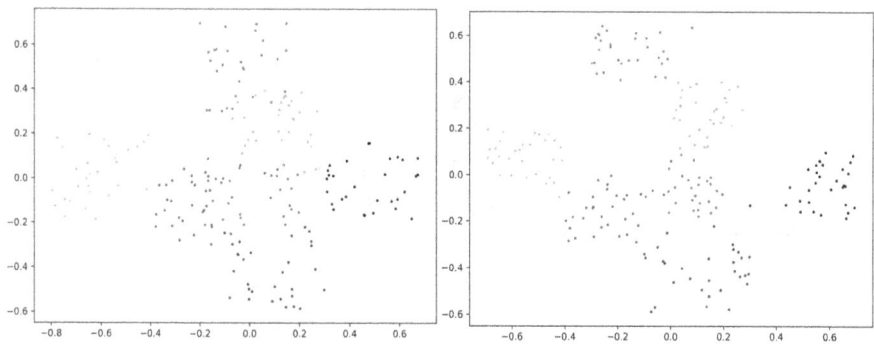

Fig. 4. Feature learned without self-knowledge distillation (left) vs with self-knowledge distillation (right). In which different color represent different categories of Gulls.

Robustness Analysis. To further analyse the effectiveness of our proposed self-knowledge distillation, we visualize the feature distribution of eight Gull categories selected from CUB-200-2011 dataset. The reason is that there are significant posture changes in the samples of these Gull categories. Specifically, we extract the final logits output from the fully connected layer. Then, we use principal component analysis (PCA) to reduce the dimension of the raw data into a two-dimensional coordinate system. Thus, we generate a clustering scatter graph of multidimensional data, as shown in Fig. 4. We can observe that after applying self-knowledge distillation, features from the same subcategories

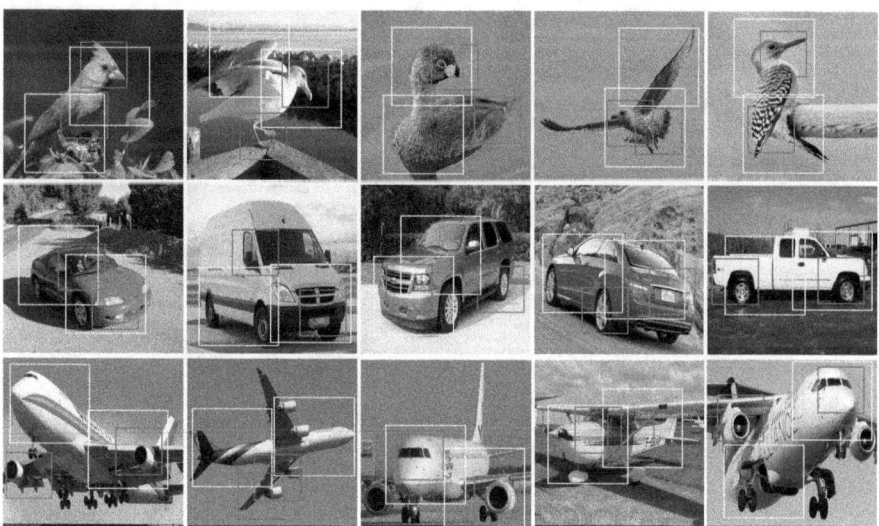

Fig. 5. Part detection visualization results, boxes with different colors are detected by different layers.

become more clustered, indicating that the algorithm does indeed become more robust to variations (like shape variations) exist in these fine-grained categories.

Part Detection Visualization. Fig. 5 shows the visualization results of discriminative part regions detected by PFDM. In bird recognition tasks, it can be found that PFDM is mainly focuses on the head, torso, wings, and other parts. In vehicle type recognition, it is more concerned with locating areas such as the tires, lights, and body. In aircraft recognition tasks, the areas such as the wings, nose, and tail are located. It can be concluded that PFDM can effectively locate multiple different information parts of identified targets.

5 Conclusion

In this paper, we propose a weakly supervised part feature detection method, which can help the model find the most discriminative features without any part annotations. Besides, we introduce a self-knowledge distillation method to motivate the model to be more robust to pose variation and learn richer knowledge. Our model has good flexibility and efficiency, and experiments on three public datasets demonstrated the effectiveness of our method. In the future, we will focus on combining multimodality information to better solve the problem of manual annotation costs.

References

1. Zhang, N., Donahue, J., Girshick, R., Darrell, T.: Part-based R-CNNs for fine-grained category detection. In: Computer Vision–ECCV 2014: 13th European Conference, Zurich, Switzerland, September 6–12, 2014, Proceedings, Part I, vol. 13, pp. 834–849 (2014)
2. Wei, X.S., Xie, C.W., Wu, J.: Mask-CNN: localizing parts and selecting descriptors for fine-grained image recognition. arXiv preprint arXiv:1605.06878 (2016)
3. Branson, S., Van Horn, G., Belongie, S., et al: Bird species categorization using pose normalized deep convolutional nets. arXiv preprint arXiv:1406.2952 (2014)
4. Sun, M., Yuan, Y., Zhou, F., Ding, E.: Multi-attention multi-class constraint for fine-grained image recognition. In: Proceedings of the European Conference on Computer Vision (ECCV), pp. 805–821 (2018)
5. Yang, Z., Luo, T., Wang, D., Hu, Z., Gao, J., Wang, L.: Learning to navigate for fine-grained classification. In: Proceedings of the European Conference on Computer Vision (ECCV), pp. 420–435 (2018)
6. Ge, W., Lin, X., Yu, Y.: Weakly supervised complementary parts models for fine-grained image classification from the bottom up. In: IEEE Conference on Computer Vision and Pattern Recognition, pp. 3034–3043 (2019)
7. Chou, P.Y., Lin, C.H., Kao, W.C.: A novel plug-in module for fine-grained visual classification. arXiv preprint arXiv:2202.03822 (2022)
8. Lin, T.Y., Dollár, P., Girshick, R., He, K., Hariharan, B., Belongie, S.: Feature pyramid networks for object detection. In: Proceedings of the IEEE Conference on Computer Vision and Pattern Recognition, pp. 2117–2125 (2017)

9. Redmon, J., Divvala, S., Girshick, R., Farhadi, A.: You only look once: unified, real-time object detection. In: Proceedings of the IEEE Conference on Computer Vision and Pattern Recognition, pp. 779–788 (2016)
10. Zong, Z., Song, G., Liu, Y.: DETRs with collaborative hybrid assignments training. In: Proceedings of the IEEE/CVF International Conference on Computer Vision, pp. 6748–6758 (2023)
11. Diao, Q., Jiang, Y., Wen, B., Sun, J., Yuan, Z.: MetaFormer: a unified meta framework for fine-grained recognition. arXiv preprint arXiv:2203.02751 (2022)
12. Wah, C., Branson, S., Welinder, P., Perona, P., Belongie, S.: The Caltech-UCSD Birds-200-2011 Dataset. California Institute of Technology (2011)
13. Yang, S., Liu, S., Yang, C., Wang, C.: Re-rank coarse classification with local region enhanced features for fine-grained image recognition. arXiv preprint arXiv:2102.09875 (2021)
14. He, J., et al.: Transfg: a transformer architecture for fine-grained recognition. In: Proceedings of the AAAI Conference on Artificial Intelligence, pp. 852–860 (2022)
15. He, K., Zhang, X., Ren, S., Sun, J.: Deep residual learning for image recognition. In: Proceedings of the IEEE Conference on Computer Vision and Pattern Recognition, pp. 770–778 (2016)
16. Lin, T.Y., Goyal, P., Girshick, R., He, K., Dollár, P.: Focal loss for dense object detection. In: Proceedings of the IEEE International Conference on Computer Vision, pp. 2980–2988 (2017)
17. Zhang, L., Bao, C., Ma, K.: Self-distillation: towards efficient and compact neural networks. IEEE Trans. Pattern Anal. Mach. Intell. **44**, 4388–4403 (2021)
18. Yang, C. et al.: MixSKD: self-knowledge distillation from Mixup for image recognition. In: European Conference on Computer Vision, pp. 534–551 (2022)
19. Oquab, M., Darcet, T., Moutakanni, T., et al.: Dinov2: learning robust visual features without supervision. arXiv preprint arXiv:2304.07193 (2023)
20. Hinton, G., Vinyals, O., Dean, J.: Distilling the knowledge in a neural network. arXiv preprint arXiv:1503.02531 (2015)
21. Krause, J., Stark, M., Deng, J. and Fei-Fei, L.: 3D object representations for fine-grained categorization. In: Proceedings of the IEEE International Conference on Computer Vision Workshops, pp. 554–561 (2013)
22. Maji, S., Kannala, J., Rahtu, E., Blaschko, M., Vedaldi, A.: Fine-grained visual classification of aircraft. Technical report (2013)
23. Liu, Z.,, et al.: Swin transformer: hierarchical vision transformer using shifted windows. In: Proceedings of the IEEE/CVF International Conference on Computer Vision, pp. 10012–10022 (2021)
24. Chen, Y., Bai, Y., Zhang, W., Mei, T.: Destruction and construction learning for fine-grained image recognition. In: Proceedings of the IEEE/CVF Conference on Computer Vision and Pattern Recognition, pp. 5157–5166 (2019)
25. Sun, H., He, X., Peng, Y.: Sim-trans: structure information modeling transformer for fine-grained visual categorization. In: Proceedings of the 30th ACM International Conference on Multimedia, pp. 5853–5861 (2022)
26. Liu, D., Zhao, L., Wang, Y., Kato, J.: Learn from each other to Classify better: cross-layer mutual attention learning for fine-grained visual classification. Pattern Recogn. **140**, 109550 (2023)
27. Behera, A., Wharton, Z., Hewage, P.R., Bera, A.: Context-aware attentional pooling (CAP) for fine-grained visual classification. In: Proceedings of the AAAI Conference on Artificial Intelligence, pp. 929–937 (2021)

28. Chollet, F.: Xception: deep learning with depthwise separable convolutions. Proceedings of the IEEE Conference on Computer Vision and Pattern Recognition, pp. 1251–1258 (2017)
29. Do, T., Tran, H., Tjiputra, E., Tran, Q.D., Nguyen, A.: Fine-grained visual classification using self assessment classifier. arXiv preprint arXiv:2205.10529 (2022)
30. Zhu, H., Ke, W., Li, D., Liu, J., Tian, L., Shan, Y.: Dual cross-attention learning for fine-grained visual categorization and object re-identification. In: Proceedings of the IEEE/CVF Conference on Computer Vision and Pattern Recognition, pp. 4692–4702 (2022)

An Energy Sampling Replay-Based Continual Learning Framework

Xingzhong Zhang[1], Joon Huang Chuah[1,2](✉), Chu Kiong Loo[3], and Stefan Wermter[4]

[1] Faculty of Engineering, University of Malaya, Kuala Lumpur, Malaysia
`22063370@siswa.um.edu.my, jhchuah@suc.edu.my`
[2] Faculty of Engineering and Information Technology, Southern University College, Skudai, Johor, Malaysia
[3] Faculty of Computer Science and Information Technology, University of Malaya, Kuala Lumpur, Malaysia
`ckloo.um@um.edu.my`
[4] Knowledge Technology, Department of Informatics, Universität Hamburg, Hamburg, Germany
`stefan.wermter@informatik.uni-hamburg.de`

Abstract. Continual Learning represents a significant challenge within the field of computer vision, primarily due to the issue of catastrophic forgetting that arises with sequential learning tasks. Among the array of strategies explored in current continual learning research, replay-based methods have shown notable effectiveness. In this paper, we introduce a novel Energy Sampling Replay-based (ESR) structure for image classification. This framework enhances the selection process of samples for replay by leveraging the energy distribution of the samples, thereby improving the effectiveness of memory samples during the replay phase and increasing accuracy. We have conducted extensive experiments across various continual learning methodologies and datasets. The results demonstrate that our approach effectively mitigates forgetting on CIFAR-10, CIFAR-100 and CIFAR-110 datasets by optimizing the replay strategy.

Keywords: Image classification · Continual learning · Catastrophic forgetting · Energy-based sampling

1 Introduction

In the rapidly evolving field of machine learning, the concept of Continual Learning (CL) emerges as a crucial paradigm to address the challenge of learning new tasks sequentially without forgetting previously acquired knowledge. This paper focuses on developing an Energy Sampling Replay-based Continual Learning Framework for image classification aimed at enhancing the efficiency and effectiveness of CL models.

CL methodologies can be broadly categorized into three groups of approaches: regularization-based approaches, replay-based approaches, and optimization-based approaches. Regularization-based approaches [11,14,20] aim to mitigate catastrophic forgetting by limiting the variation of learned knowledge, employing techniques like Elastic Weight Consolidation (EWC) [8] and Memory Aware Synapses (MAS) [2] to preserve knowledge of previous tasks while learning new knowledge. Replay-based approaches [5,19,24], such as experience replay and generative replay, counteract forgetting by emulating and restoring data distributions of previous tasks, ensuring the model's adaptability and memory retention. Optimization-based approaches [4,16,23], including gradient projection and meta-learning strategies, focus on modifying the optimization process to balance the preservation of old knowledge with the incorporation of new insights, thereby fostering a dynamic learning environment.

Energy-based models (EBMs) have become a method that has received increasing attention in recent years. Some studies have already applied it in domains such as domain adaptation and active learning. Among methods in [7,25,26], EBMs offer a promising alternative by leveraging the concept of energy functions to model the probability distribution of data. EBMs have the distinct advantage of addressing both probabilistic and non-probabilistic unsupervised learning tasks, making them particularly suitable for CL scenarios. By replacing the conventional softmax layer with an energy-based model classifier, [12,13,15] utilize energy scores as a novel output metric, theoretically aligned with the input's probability density and less prone to overconfidence issues. This approach does not only address the limitations of softmax in continual learning tasks but also provides a more flexible framework for managing sequential task learning.

In this paper, we present a novel Energy Sampling Replay-based (ESR) framework for Continual Learning in the context of computer vision, specifically tackling the challenge of catastrophic forgetting that arises when models are trained on sequential learning tasks. Leveraging the principles of energy models, our framework enhances the selection process of memory samples during the replay phase by utilizing the energy distribution of the samples. This approach improves the effectiveness of replay and contributes to increasing the overall accuracy of the model across various tasks. Through extensive experiments conducted across multiple datasets and CL methodologies, our framework demonstrates significant improvements in mitigating forgetting, particularly on CIFAR-10, CIFAR-100, and CIFAR-110 datasets [9]. The key contributions of this paper are as follows:

- We propose an energy-based sampling strategy that significantly improves the selection of memory samples for replay by analyzing their energy distribution, leading to more effective learning processes.
- We introduces a novel approach that combines random sampling with a Minimum versus Second-Minimum strategy. This hybrid sampling technique enables the selection of samples from the memory buffer that exhibit greater

uncertainty and representativeness, enhancing the model's ability to handle diverse and dynamic data distributions effectively.
- The framework's effectiveness and efficiency are validated across a variety of datasets, demonstrating adaptability to different visual tasks and environments. By optimizing with energy-based sampling, our method improves model accuracy, offering substantial advantages for continual learning.

2 Related Work

Continual Learning methods are crucial for addressing catastrophic forgetting in computer vision, primarily employing regularization, replay, and optimization strategies. Regularization methods, such as Elastic Weight Consolidation (EWC) [8] and Memory Aware Synapses (MAS) [2], aim to maintain the integrity of previously learned information by imposing constraints on the model's parameters, assessing the significance of each through mechanisms like the Fisher Information Matrix or unsupervised online assessments. These methods, while effective in preserving old knowledge, demand meticulous balancing to avoid overfitting on new tasks or eroding prior learning outcomes. Replay strategies [5,19,24], including experience, generative, and feature replay, focus on reconstructing past data distributions to bolster memory retention. The GEM [16] tackles catastrophic forgetting by leveraging episodic memory to reduce impacts on prior tasks and facilitate beneficial knowledge transfer, yet it requires further development in task descriptor utilization, memory management, and computational efficiency. The A-GEM [4] method refines GEM by averaging episodic memory losses, significantly boosting computational and memory efficiency, at the cost of some task-specific performance to gain broader applicability and simplicity. CLEAR [21] effectively mitigates catastrophic forgetting by combining on-policy learning with off-policy replay and behavioral cloning, thus enhancing stability and plasticity without needing detailed task knowledge; however, its extensive memory needs for storing past experiences pose limitations. Techniques such as the AQM [3] for experience replay or generative models for feature replay address issues like data imbalance or representation shifts, aiming for resource-efficient learning across tasks. Optimization-based methods [4,16,23] complement these by adjusting the optimization process to balance new and old information, ensuring dynamic adaptation and learning efficiency.

Researchers have significantly advanced the field of energy-based models, moving from the foundational Boltzmann machines [1,22] to more sophisticated frameworks that suitable for deep learning architectures [10,17,18]. This progression highlights their efforts to provide a versatile approach to addressing unsupervised learning challenges, including clustering and feature extraction. EBMs, by defining an energy function that represents an unnormalized probability distribution, allow for a nuanced handling of data occurrence probabilities. Notably, in the context of CL [7,25], EBMs have been explored for their potential to minimize interference between new and existing knowledge, providing an alternative to the softmax classifier's limitations. For instance, approaches like

Energy-Aware Domain Adaptation (EADA) [26] leverage energy distributions to address domain adaptation, while novel methods [6] interpret classifier logits as energy functions, facilitating a seamless integration of data and label distributions. This advancement in EBMs showcases their effectiveness in mitigating overconfidence issues prevalent in softmax-based classifiers and enhancing model adaptability and generalization across continuous learning tasks.

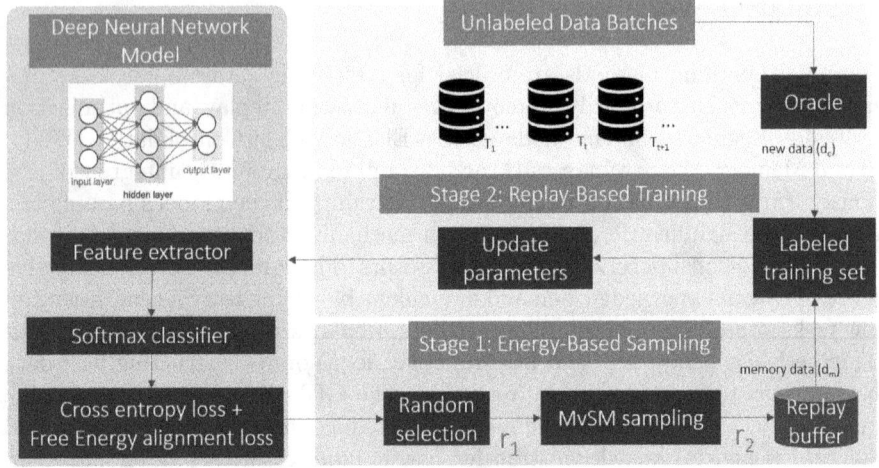

Fig. 1. Proposed framework of ESR.

3 Methodology

The CL framework proposed in this article is illustrated in Fig. 1. A dataset that is divided into several tasks, is fed into the network model for training in consecutive batches. T_1 represents the data for the first task, T_t represents the data for the t_{th} task, and $T_t + 1$ for the data of the $(t + 1)_{th}$ task. Each round of learning corresponding to a task is called an experience (E), and in the context of image classification tasks, each experience typically includes training samples from several classes. After an Oracle annotates the data at time T_t, it becomes new current data (d_c) for training E_t. Subsequently, a portion of samples from the previous round of training is randomly selected, and then, through a Minimum versus second-minimum method, samples are chosen to be stored in the replay buffer. This part of the data, referred to as memory data (d_m), and the previous current data (d_c) together form the labeled training set for the current experience. In stage two, the neural network model is trained using a replay-based approach, and the parameters are updated.

3.1 Replay-Based Method

The replay-based method helps consolidate knowledge learned from previous tasks and improve the stability and performance of learning by retaining a subset of training samples from earlier tasks in a memory buffer and retraining these samples in subsequent training processes. Therefore, when selecting samples to store in the memory buffer, it's essential to consider the balance between memory data and current data, allowing the model to learn new tasks while losing as little knowledge as possible from old tasks.

Random sampling for selecting training samples in replay-based CL methods encompasses numerous pitfalls, such as producing a biased and unrepresentative selection, especially from imbalanced datasets, leading to a model bias towards over-represented classes. This randomness may exclude diverse and informative samples crucial for a comprehensive understanding of previously learned tasks, undermining the memory buffer's role in effectively supporting new task learning or old task recall. Additionally, this approach may inefficiently allocate buffer space to less informative samples, increasing computational demands and diminishing learning efficiency. Performance-wise, indiscriminate sampling fosters learning imbalances, causing the model to disproportionately forget under-represented tasks and negatively impacting performance across a variety of tasks, a situation exacerbated in dynamic environments where data distributions evolve, and randomly selected samples swiftly become outdated. Therefore, we utilize an energy-based sampling method to improve upon this aspect.

3.2 Energy-Based Sampling

Within energy-based methods, the energy function outlines an unnormalized probability distribution, where lower energy levels indicate higher probabilities of data occurrence. Leveraging this property, we introduce an Energy Alignment Loss to address the issue of the model's inability to distinguish between old classes and new classes. Suppose the three shapes in Fig. 2 represent two old classes (rectangle and triangle) and one new class (circle), and their samples have biases as well as overlapping sections in the feature space. By setting a regularization term, samples on the feature domain boundaries of each class can be filtered out, similar to identifying samples that reflect domain divergence in domain adaptation tasks.

In the energy-based loss used for memory data sampling, the concept of free energy is pivotal for understanding the distribution and likelihood of input data. The free energy, denoted as $F(x)$, quantifies the "energy" or likelihood of an input instance x, with lower values indicating higher probabilities or more favorable states according to the model. Here, x represents an input instance, a feature vector derived from the dataset. The formula for calculating free energy is given by:

$$\mathcal{F}(x) = -\log \sum_{y \in \mathcal{Y}} \exp(-E(x,y)) \qquad (1)$$

Within this formula, Y stands for the set of all possible labels in the classification task, and $E(x, y)$ is the energy function that assigns a scalar value representing the energy associated with the input x having a label y. This energy function is designed to yield lower energies for configurations of x and y that are more probable or correct, based on the model's training. The summation aggregates the exponentiated negative energies over all possible labels y, which is then transformed by the negative logarithm into the free energy $F(x)$. This transformation ensures that the free energy reflects a probabilistic measure, indicating the likelihood of the input x within the model's learned energy landscape. Utilizing free energy in this way allows ESR to effectively assess and select informative unlabeled data from the old data, crucial for memory data sampling strategies.

The Free Energy Alignment (FEA) loss is employed to address the challenge of feature confusion by aligning the free energy distributions of memory data and current data. The calculation of FEA loss begins with the evaluation of the model's output on a batch of previous data to obtain the previous energy output. Meanwhile, the current data energy, which represents the free energy of samples from the current data, is used to calculate the current data batch's mean free energy. This mean acts as a reference (global mean) for aligning the free energy of the memory data.

The FEA loss itself is computed using a custom loss criterion, the Free Energy Alignment Loss, applied to the current energy output of the current data with respect to the global mean free energy. Mathematically, it is defined as:

$$\mathcal{L}_{fea}(x;\theta) = \max\left(0, \mathcal{F}(x;\theta) - \delta\right) \tag{2}$$

where $\mathcal{F}(x;\theta)$ is the energy output of the current data batch, and δ is the dynamically updated global mean free energy of memory samples. This approach effectively reduces the free energy bias between classes. It selects samples near the overlap of class features, which promotes more effective knowledge transfer from memory data to current data.

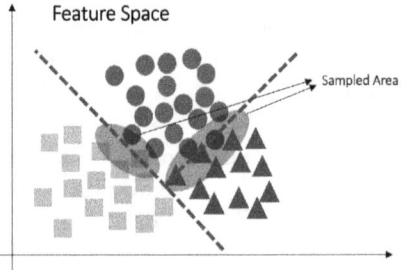

Fig. 2. Feature space representation of three classes.

3.3 Minimum Versus Second-Minimum Strategy

The selection process of stage one in Fig. 1 is divided into two steps: First, a certain number of samples, denoted as r_1 are randomly selected from the trained data. Then, from this subset, r_2 samples are selected using a Minimum versus Second-Minimum (MvSM) sampling strategy designed based on the energy distribution. During this process, the ratio between the two rounds of selection is defined as the parameter α, which determines the relationship between α and the number of selected samples as follows:

$$\alpha = \frac{r_2}{r_1} \tag{3}$$

The selection strategy integrates a two-step approach beginning with the MvSM method to gauge the certainty of the model's predictions by calculating the difference between the two lowest energy scores for each sample. The equation is:

$$U(x) = E(x, y^*; \theta) - E(x, y'; \theta) \tag{4}$$

where y^* and y' are the lowest and the second-lowest energy output from the model. Samples with larger differences are seen as having clearer classification boundaries, making them prime candidates for initial selection. This approach first filters samples based on their free energy, prioritizing those with lower energy as more critical or representative, and selects a subset based on a predetermined ratio. The process then refines this selection by arranging the chosen samples according to their MvSM uncertainty values, with a preference for higher values to ensure training focuses on samples where the model is most confident. This strategy optimizes the learning process by carefully balancing exposure to both informative and challenging samples, enhancing the effectiveness of training within a CL setup.

4 Experiments and Analysis

4.1 Experimental Settings

In this section, we will detail the experimental setup and results analysis of our study. The ESR method proposed in this paper was implemented as a plugin within the Avalanche Continual Learning Library framework, and added to the training strategy. Since our method builds upon the basic Replay Plugin, the experimental results of the Replay Plugin were used as the baseline for comparison with our method in Sects. 4.2 and 4.4. The datasets were divided into several experiences for sequential training. The model was evaluated after each experience.

Dataset. We evaluate the ESR Continual Learning Framework using CIFAR-10, CIFAR-100, and CIFAR-110 datasets. CIFAR-10 and CIFAR-100 are popular datasets for machine learning, featuring images across 10 and 100 classes, respectively. CIFAR-110 combines both to create a unique Continual Learning benchmark, starting with CIFAR-10 and incrementally introducing the diverse classes of CIFAR-100.

Network. We adopt the ResNet50 backbone for feature extraction, modifying its initial convolutional layer to accommodate different input channels. A bottleneck linear layer reduces feature dimensionality, enhanced by batch normalization. Class predictions were made through a linear classifier mapping the compressed features to their respective classes.

Our training employs a composite loss function that combines the FEA loss, as detailed in Sect. 3.2, with CrossEntropyLoss, essential for classification tasks. The total loss function $\mathcal{L}$ for our model, incorporating these components, is formally defined as:

$$\mathcal{L}(\theta; \mathcal{D}) = \sum_{i \in \mathcal{D}} \mathcal{L}_{fea}(x_i; \theta) + \sum_{i \in \mathcal{D}} -\log\left(\frac{\exp(o_{y_i})}{\sum_j \exp(o_j)}\right) \quad (5)$$

In this equation, θ denotes the parameters of our model, and $\mathcal{D}$ represents the dataset used for training. Each instance i in $\mathcal{D}$ contributes to the loss through the Free Energy Alignment loss $\mathcal{L}_{fea}(x_i; \theta)$ and the CrossEntropyLoss. The latter is calculated by taking the negative logarithm of the predicted probability for the true class y_i, normalized by the sum of exponential scores of all class logits o_j. This mechanism pushes the model to fine-tune its parameters to increase the probability of the actual class label while decreasing that of the incorrect labels.

After experimenting with various configurations, we ultimately selected specific parameters for the Stochastic Gradient Descent (SGD) optimizer that yielded the best experimental results. The final configuration for SGD that we employed uses a learning rate of 0.001 and a momentum of 0.9. These parameters were found to be optimal in achieving efficient convergence and robust training outcomes in our continual learning tasks.

Evaluation Metrics. In our project, we utilize specific metrics from the Avalanche library to evaluate our CL model, including the Forgetting metric which is particularly crucial for assessing how well the model retains previously learned knowledge while acquiring new tasks. The formula for the Forgetting metric for a particular task k is simplified as follows:

$$\text{Forgetting}(k) = \left(\frac{C_{\text{init}}(k)}{N(k)}\right) - \left(\frac{C_{\text{sub}}(k)}{N(k)}\right) \quad (6)$$

Here, $C_{\text{init}}(k)$ represents the number of correct predictions immediately after the model is first trained on task k, capturing the initial mastery of the task. $C_{\text{sub}}(k)$ denotes the number of correct predictions after the model has been trained on subsequent tasks, indicating the retention of task k abilities amidst new learning experiences. $N(k)$ is the total number of predictions made for task k during assessments, ensuring that accuracy measurements are comparable.

This metric quantifies the decline in task performance, aiming for minimal forgetting to ensure effective knowledge retention across different learning tasks. By maintaining low values of Forgetting(k), the model demonstrates its capability to handle new information without significant loss of performance on previously learned tasks, an essential feature for continual learning models.

Additionally, the Average Mean Class Accuracy (AMCA) is utilized to evaluate the model's confidence and accuracy in predictions. The AMCA is computed as follows:

$$AMCA = \frac{1}{C} \sum_{i=1}^{C} \text{Accuracy}_i \qquad (7)$$

where C is the number of classes in the task, and Accuracy_i is the accuracy for the ith class. This metric provides insights into the model's predictive confidence, with a higher AMCA value indicating better performance and higher prediction certainty.

Ideally, we aim for the model to retain as much knowledge of previous tasks as possible while learning new information, hence a lower forgetting metric is preferred. We desire a model not only to make accurate predictions but also to have high confidence in its predictions, making a higher AMCA value more desirable.

4.2 Comparison with State-of-the-Art Methods

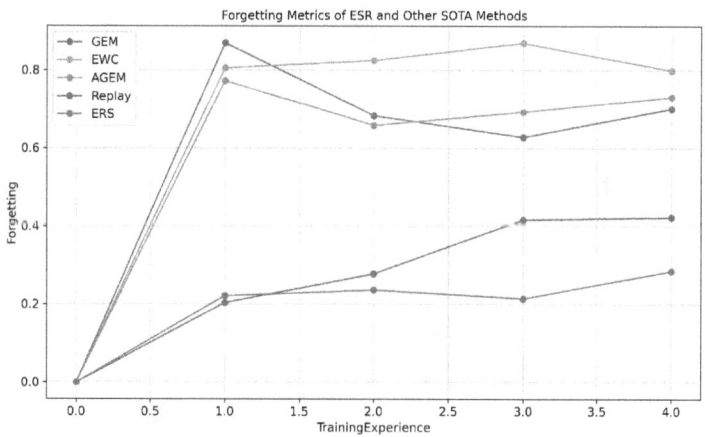

Fig. 3. Forgetting metrics of ESR and other state-of-the-art methods.

In this section, we compare the ESR method with four other state-of-the-art methods (EWC [8], GEM [16], AGEM [4], and Replay [21]) implemented as plugins within the Avalanche Continual Learning Library framework, using the SplitCIFAR10 dataset for our experiments. We set the number of experiences to 5, with CIFAR-10 comprising a total of 10 classes, meaning each experience involves learning two new classes. Figure 3 displays the forgetting metrics for these five methods. It is noticeable that the Forgetting values for the ESR (purple) and Replay (red) methods are lower compared to the other three methods, with our ESR method achieving a Forgetting value of 0.285. Thus, in this round of experiments, ESR demonstrates good performance in mitigating the model's forgetting of old knowledge. As seen in Fig. 4, the purple line representing the ESR method scores higher on the AMCA metric compared to the other four methods. This indicates that ESR can improve the quality of selected memory data based on the Replay method, thereby achieving greater confidence of the model in its classification of a sample.

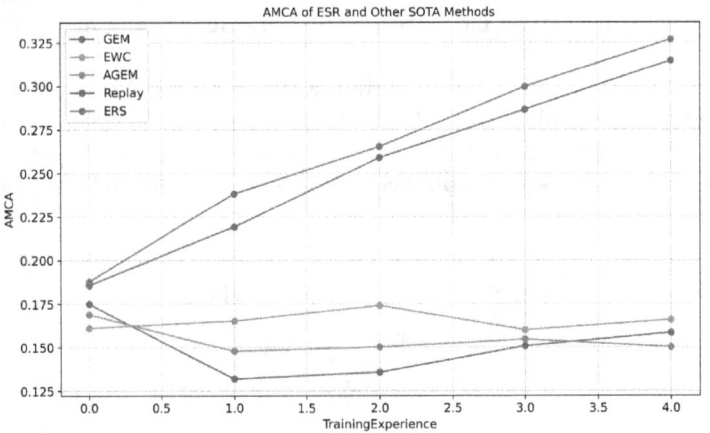

Fig. 4. AMCA of ESR and other state-of-the-art methods.

4.3 Effect of α in Sampling Memory Data

In this section, we analyze the impact of the ratio of energy-based sampling to random sampling, denoted as α, on the experimental results. The selection of specific α values was based on two primary considerations:

1. **Sampling Density and Efficiency:** It was essential to ensure that the number of samples in the random sampling step was sufficient to maintain a dispersed representation across the feature space. This dispersion is critical for capturing the diversity of the dataset while enhancing the efficiency of the sample selection process by reducing the number of samples to a manageable size.

2. **Effectiveness of MvSM Sampling:** The chosen α values needed to allow the effectiveness of the MvSM to be clearly demonstrated. Values of α higher than 1/2 (0.5) yield samples that are not diverse enough to showcase the uncertainty of classes within the feature space. Conversely, values below 1/6 (0.1667) result in too few samples, diminishing their representativeness and the ability to generalize the sampling method's effectiveness.

Based on these considerations, the following α values were selected: 1/2 (0.5), 1/3 (0.3333), 1/4 (0.25), 1/5 (0.2), and 1/6 (0.1667). These values provide a balanced range from a lower to a higher preference for energy-based sampling over random sampling, allowing us to explore the influence of varying degrees of bias towards energy-efficient samples on learning dynamics.

Table 1. The results of ESR with different α.

Strategy Name	r_1	r_2	α	Accuracy	AMCA	Forgetting
ESR-0.1667	4800	800	0.1667	0.4265	0.3084	0.295
ESR-0.2	4000	800	0.2	0.4304	0.3069	0.3264
ESR-0.25	3200	800	0.25	0.4635	0.3193	0.31
ESR-0.3333	**2400**	**800**	**0.3333**	**0.4967**	**0.3329**	**0.2695**
ESR-0.5	1600	800	0.5	0.4447	0.3283	0.343

From Table 1, it can be seen that when α equals 0.3333, the values of the Forgetting metrics are lower compared to the other four experiments after the last experience was trained. In the assessment of classification accuracy and confidence, the accuracy and AMCA at α equal to 0.3333 surpassed the other four experiments. This indicates that at this point in the training process, the energy-based sampling strategy can better balance the learning efficiency of new tasks and the consolidation of knowledge from old tasks.

4.4 Ablation Studies

In order to investigate the impact of the ESR method on the replay-based approach, we systematically compared the approach incorporating the energy-based sampling strategy with the baseline replay-based method, which solely uses random sampling, across three datasets: CIFAR-10, CIFAR-100, and CIFAR-110. As shown in Sect. 4.2, the ESR employing energy-based sampling method outperforms the Replay Plugin on the CIFAR-10 dataset.

Table 2. The results of ESR and Replay on the CIFAR-100 and CIFAR-110 datasets.

Strategy Name	Evaluation Metrics	Exp-3	Exp-7	Exp-11	Exp-15	Exp-19
ESR-CIFAR100	accuracy	**0.0969**	**0.1149**	**0.1368**	**0.1511**	**0.1897**
	forgetting	**0.3413**	**0.4226**	**0.4367**	**0.4703**	**0.4582**
Replay-CIFAR100	accuracy	0.0799	0.1053	0.1162	0.1167	0.1295
	forgetting	0.3733	0.58	0.6358	0.6856	0.6957
		Exp-2	Exp-4	Exp-6	Exp-8	Exp-10
ESR-CIFAR110	accuracy	0.2408	0.1663	0.1474	**0.1696**	**0.1598**
	forgetting	**0.3124**	**0.3892**	**0.4163**	**0.4403**	**0.4702**
Replay-CIFAR110	accuracy	**0.2591**	**0.2026**	**0.1661**	0.1227	0.1187
	forgetting	0.3848	0.51	0.5797	0.6535	0.7064

Table 2 presents the accuracy and forgetting metrics for experiments conducted on the CIFAR-100 and CIFAR-110 datasets. In this experiment, we utilized an α value of 0.25. It's notable that although the proposed sampling strategy may slightly reduce the classification accuracy in the early stages of training, the advantages of employing energy-based sampling gradually become apparent as tasks accumulate, and the gap between this method and the baseline widens.

4.5 Discussion

The introduction of our ESR method marks a significant advancement in enhancing the information content of the samples selected for replay by utilizing their energy distribution. However, this strategy incurs increased computational overhead during the data loading phase. This involves computing the energy for each candidate sample and sorting these samples based on their energy levels. Although this meticulous selection process ensures the quality and representativeness of the samples, it also leads to a substantial increase in time consumption. Specifically, when training on the CIFAR-10 dataset using the ESR method, preparing for each round of experience requires approximately three times more time to select the replay data compared to a basic replay approach that utilizes random sampling.

To effectively balance sampling speed with the quality of samples, we conducted extensive experiments with different settings of the parameter α, as outlined in Sect. 4.3. These experiments are critical for understanding how variations in α affect the efficiency and effectiveness of the learning process. While these studies demonstrate that adjusting α enables fine-tuning the trade-off between operational efficiency and sample quality, optimizing the CL process to meet various constraints and learning goals, it is important to acknowledge the limitations in the choice of α values. The range of α tested was limited, and there is a lack of deeper exploration into the optimal balancing points for sampling efficiency. This limitation points to a promising direction for future research. Further investigations could refine the balance between exploring new knowledge and exploiting learned experiences, potentially through adaptive mechanisms that dynamically adjust energy thresholds based on evolving data distributions. Such advancements could enhance the model's applicability and performance across diverse CL scenarios.

5 Conclusion

In this work, we propose an energy-based sampling strategy applied to the replay-based approach, which can effectively filter samples from old tasks that have a similar energy distribution to current data as memory data. The trained model is better at distinguishing classes between old and new tasks. The Energy Sampling Replay-based method outperforms several state-of-the-art methods in mitigating forgetting on the CIFAR-10 dataset. This approach also exceeds the performance of replay-based methods that do not utilize this strategy on the CIFAR-100 and CIFAR-110 datasets, demonstrating a strong ability to learn new tasks without forgetting the knowledge of old tasks. In our future work, we will attempt to apply the energy-based sampling method to more tasks, such as active learning.

Acknowledgement. We express our profound gratitude to Universiti Malaya for awarding the Universiti Malaya Scholarship Scheme as a Graduate Research Assistant under the government grant, MOHE - Kementerian Pendidikan Tinggi (KPT). This support has been crucial for the research (PPRN001A-2023) conducted at the Department of Artificial Intelligence, Faculty of Computer Science and Information Technology, under the guidance of Professor Dr. Loo Chu Kiong.

References

1. Ackley, D.H., Hinton, G.E., Sejnowski, T.J.: A learning algorithm for Boltzmann machines. Cogn. Sci. **9**(1), 147–169 (1985)
2. Aljundi, R., Babiloni, F., Elhoseiny, M., Rohrbach, M., Tuytelaars, T.: Memory aware synapses: learning what (not) to forget. In: Proceedings of the European Conference on Computer Vision (ECCV), pp. 139–154 (2018)
3. Caccia, L., Belilovsky, E., Caccia, M., Pineau, J.: Online learned continual compression with adaptive quantization modules. In: International Conference on Machine Learning, pp. 1240–1250. PMLR (2020)
4. Chaudhry, A., Ranzato, M., Rohrbach, M., Elhoseiny, M.: Efficient lifelong learning with a-gem. arXiv preprint arXiv:1812.00420 (2018)
5. Chaudhry, A., et al.: On tiny episodic memories in continual learning. arXiv preprint arXiv:1902.10486 (2019)
6. Grathwohl, W., Wang, K.C., Jacobsen, J.H., Duvenaud, D., Norouzi, M., Swersky, K.: Your classifier is secretly an energy based model and you should treat it like one. arXiv preprint arXiv:1912.03263 (2019)
7. Joseph, K., Khan, S., Khan, F.S., Balasubramanian, V.N.: Towards open world object detection. In: Proceedings of the IEEE/CVF Conference on Computer Vision and Pattern Recognition, pp. 5830–5840 (2021)

8. Kirkpatrick, J., et al.: Overcoming catastrophic forgetting in neural networks. Proc. Natl. Acad. Sci. **114**(13), 3521–3526 (2017)
9. Krizhevsky, A., Hinton, G., et al.: Learning multiple layers of features from tiny images (2009)
10. LeCun, Y., Chopra, S., Hadsell, R., Ranzato, M., Huang, F.: A tutorial on energy-based learning. In: Predicting Structured Data (2006)
11. Lee, S.W., Kim, J.H., Jun, J., Ha, J.W., Zhang, B.T.: Overcoming catastrophic forgetting by incremental moment matching. Adv. Neural Inf. Process. Syst. **30** (2017)
12. Li, J., Chen, P., He, Z., Yu, S., Liu, S., Jia, J.: Rethinking out-of-distribution (OOD) detection: masked image modeling is all you need. In: Proceedings of the IEEE/CVF Conference on Computer Vision and Pattern Recognition, pp. 11578–11589 (2023)
13. Li, S., Du, Y., van de Ven, G., Mordatch, I.: Energy-based models for continual learning. In: Conference on Lifelong Learning Agents, pp. 1–22. PMLR (2022)
14. Li, Z., Hoiem, D.: Learning without forgetting. IEEE Trans. Pattern Anal. Mach. Intell. **40**(12), 2935–2947 (2017)
15. Liu, W., Wang, X., Owens, J., Li, Y.: Energy-based out-of-distribution detection. Adv. Neural. Inf. Process. Syst. **33**, 21464–21475 (2020)
16. Lopez-Paz, D., Ranzato, M.: Gradient episodic memory for continual learning. Adv. Neural Inf. Process. Syst. **30** (2017)
17. Ranzato, M., Poultney, C., Chopra, S., Cun, Y.: Efficient learning of sparse representations with an energy-based model. Adv. Neural Inf. Process. Syst. **19** (2006)
18. Ranzato, M., Boureau, Y.L., Chopra, S., LeCun, Y.: A unified energy-based framework for unsupervised learning. In: Artificial Intelligence and Statistics, p. 379. PMLR (2007)
19. Razdaibiedina, A., Mao, Y., Hou, R., Khabsa, M., Lewis, M., Almahairi, A.: Progressive prompts: continual learning for language models. arXiv preprint arXiv:2301.12314 (2023)
20. Rebuffi, S.A., Kolesnikov, A., Sperl, G., Lampert, C.H.: icarl: incremental classifier and representation learning. In: Proceedings of the IEEE Conference on Computer Vision and Pattern Recognition, pp. 2001–2010 (2017)
21. Rolnick, D., Ahuja, A., Schwarz, J., Lillicrap, T., Wayne, G.: Experience replay for continual learning. Adv. Neural Inf. Process. Syst. **32** (2019)
22. Salakhutdinov, R., Larochelle, H.: Efficient learning of deep Boltzmann machines. In: Proceedings of the Thirteenth International Conference on Artificial Intelligence and Statistics, pp. 693–700. JMLR Workshop and Conference Proceedings (2010)
23. Tang, S., Chen, D., Zhu, J., Yu, S., Ouyang, W.: Layerwise optimization by gradient decomposition for continual learning. In: Proceedings of the IEEE/CVF Conference on Computer Vision and Pattern Recognition, pp. 9634–9643 (2021)
24. Vitter, J.S.: Random sampling with a reservoir. ACM Trans. Math. Softw. **11**(1), 37–57 (1985)
25. Wang, Y., Li, B., Che, T., Zhou, K., Liu, Z., Li, D.: Energy-based open-world uncertainty modeling for confidence calibration. In: Proceedings of the IEEE/CVF International Conference on Computer Vision, pp. 9302–9311 (2021)
26. Xie, B., Yuan, L., Li, S., Liu, C.H., Cheng, X., Wang, G.: Active learning for domain adaptation: An energy-based approach. In: Proceedings of the AAAI Conference on Artificial Intelligence, vol. 36, pp. 8708–8716 (2022)

Coarse-to-Fine Granularity in MultiScale FeatureFusion Network for SAR Ship Classification

Wei Lin, Hao Zheng, Zhigang Hu[✉], Meiguang Zheng, and Liu Yang

School of Computer Science and Engineering, Central South University,
Chang Sha, China
{linwei,zghu}@csu.edu.cn

Abstract. The classification of Synthetic Aperture Radar (SAR) ships is a challenging task due to the small inter-class differences and large intra-class variance. Previous methods have used multiscale feature fusion to solve this problem, but most of them are too rough to extract fine-grained features. In this paper, we propose a new coarse-to-fine granularity multiscale feature fusion network (C2F-MFF) to address this issue. C2F-MFF consists of two stages, i.e., coarse-grained multiscale feature extraction and adaptive fine-grained multiscale feature refining. The first stage is used to capture and augment the discriminative scale-rich fusion features, while the second stage is able to adaptively assign varying importance to individual scale features. Notably, the first stage contains two novel blocks, feature focus (FF) block and feature enhance (FE) block are interactively introduced to capture significant and abundant information. Extensive ablation studies can confirm the effectiveness of each contribution. Results on the three-category and six-category Open-SARShip datasets demonstrate that our network surpasses the modern CNN-based methods and other feature fusion methods.

Keywords: Multiscale Feature Fusion · Synthetic Aperture Radar (SAR) · SAR Ship Classification · Fine-Grained Feature Refining

1 Introduction

In recent years, SAR ship surveillance, encompassing both ship monitoring [1] and ship recognition [2], has increasingly captured the interest of classification. Notably, SAR ship recognition, which identifies different types of ships, plays a crucial role in providing essential information for maritime decision-making and is a key component of maritime ship detection.

Initially, researchers innovatively developed manual feature extraction methods for recognizing SAR ships, which included analyzing color, texture and shape features. These methods exhibited commendable performance in certain specific

---

W. Lin and H. Zheng— Equal contribution.

contexts. However, they are labor-intensive and their applicability in complex situations cannot be reliably guaranteed.

With the advancement of artificial intelligence, researchers have begun utilizing convolutional neural networks (CNN) for SAR ship classification. CNNs offer an advantage over manual feature extraction methods as they can automatically extract features from various ship types using given labels and corresponding ship images. However, while CNN-based methods have shown notable performance, they often overlook a critical aspect of SAR ship images: the significant variation in target size. This variation manifests as considerable shape differences within the same ship type and minimal shape differences among different types [3]. For instance, general cargo ships vary in size from 90 to 200 m long and 15 to 33 m wide, whereas bulk carriers range from 150 to 275 m long and 23 to 38 m wide. This size diversity poses a challenge and limits the classification performance of existing CNN-based methods.

Numerous studies have proposed solutions to this challenge, with one effective approach being the utilization of ships' multiscale features [4]. However, these methods do not fully exploit multiscale features. This limitation is evident in their reliance on only the terminal features of the network for recognition and the insufficient extraction of multiscale features during the feature extraction stage.

Therefore, to address these challenges, this paper introduces a novel coarse-to-fine granularity multiscale feature fusion network (C2F-MFF). In C2F-MFF, aiming to fully extract fine-grained multiscale features, we propose a coarse-grained multiscale feature extraction (CMFE) module. This module enhances the extraction of multiscale features and establishes remote channel relationships, directing the network's focus toward important features. Additionally, we introduce an adaptive fine-grained multiscale feature refining (AFMF) module, which assigns varying importance to multiscale features and adaptively fuses them to obtain the most discerning features. We conducted a comprehensive evaluation on the three-category and six-category subsets of the public dataset OpenSARship, validating the performance of each module through ablation experiments. The experimental results demonstrate that C2F-MFF achieves superior SAR ship classification accuracy compared to modern CNN-based methods and other feature fusion methods. In summary, the main contributions of this paper can be summarized as follows:

- We propose a C2F-MFF network to accurately extract multiscale features for SAR ship classification.
- We introduce a CMFE module to enhance the extraction of multiscale features and guide the network to focus on crucial features. This module also establishes remote channel relationships between features.
- We propose an AFMF module that refines multiscale features by assigning varying importance based on their distinct information and adaptively fuses them to achieve optimal classification results.

2 Related Work

2.1 SAR Ship Classification Method

In earlier times, researchers introduced various manual feature extraction methods. Snapir et al. [5] proposed a Random Forest (RF) based method for distinguishing fishing vessels from non-fishing vessels, applying it to a region in the North Sea. Xu et al. [6] presented the Geometric Transfer Metric Learning (GTML) method, which enhances SAR ship classification performance by integrating pairwise constraints (PC), joint distribution adaptation (JDA) and manifold regularization (MR) into a unified optimization function. While these methods have demonstrated good performance in specific cases, they often rely on the knowledge and expertise of domain experts for design.

Convolutional Neural Networks (CNNs) have become increasingly popular in the field of SAR ship classification in recent years. Researchers like Huang et al. [7] have developed an adapted-domain multi-source data delivery method to bridge the gap between source data and SAR target. Similarly, He et al. [8] proposed a multi-task learning framework to improve ship classification efficiency in MR SAR images. While these CNN-based methods have shown impressive results, they primarily focus on modifying the model and do not fully account for the significant variation in target size within SAR ship images.

2.2 Multiscale Feature Fusion

The fusion of features at different scales is advantageous for combining the benefits and complementarities of each image, enhancing feature diversity and improving the model's ability to generalize SAR images in complex scenes.

In recent years, researchers have been working on improving the performance of SAR (Synthetic Aperture Radar) ship classification by incorporating multiscale features [9–11]. Some studies have focused on fusing features at different scales to enhance SAR ship recognition. For instance, Zhang et al. [9] introduced a new Deep Learning (DL) network called HOG-ShipCLSNet, which uses a histogram of oriented gradients (HOG) feature fusion network to classify features obtained at different scales. They fused these features using an average weighted method. Similarly, Bai [10] proposed a multiscale feature fusion covariance network (MF2CNet) with octave convolution (Oct Conv) to extract multifrequency and multiscale features from Remote Sensing Images (RSIs). In contrast, Wang et al. [11] developed an adaptive channel dimensionality reduction method that enhances channel attention by incorporating semantic information and adaptive channel features.

Studies have investigated fusion methods for multiscale features, but there are still challenges in extracting fine multiscale features. These difficulties are especially apparent when classifying SAR ship targets with large size variation.

3 Method

3.1 Proposed Coarse-to-Fine Granularity Multiscale Feature Fusion Network

Many existing methods for extracting multiscale features lack precision, so we created a C2F-MFF. It consists of two stages. In the first stage, we obtain abundant multiscale features and process them. In the second stage, we assign different importance to these features before fusing them. We also incorporate downsampling after each stage of the CMFE module to minimize overfitting caused by deeper convolutional layers. You can see the framework graph of C2F-MFF in Fig. 1.

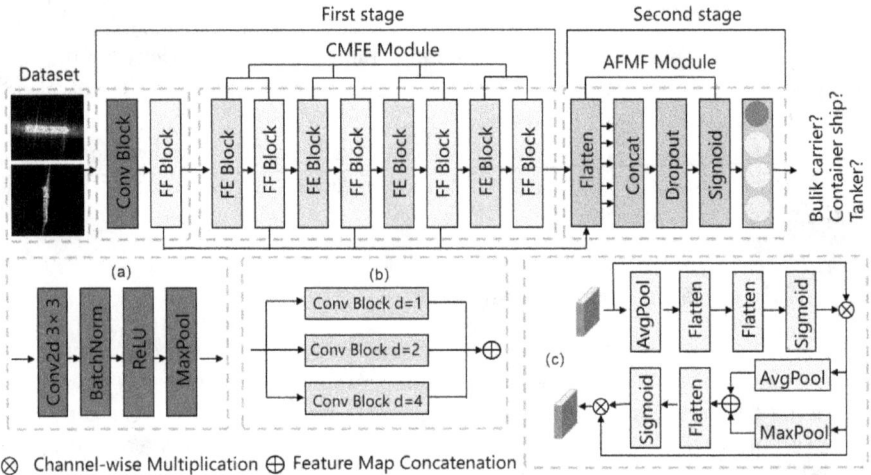

Fig. 1. The framework structure of C2F-MFF which mainly consists of two stages with two modules: CMFE module and AFMF module. The CMFE module consists of a FE block and a FF block. (a) Conv Block. (b) FE Block. d is the expansion rate of conv block. (c) FF Block.

3.2 Coarse-Grained Multiscale Feature Extraction Module

It is critical to obtain the most discriminative features, but existing multiscale feature fusion methods may not provide the required precision for feature extraction. To address this issue, we have introduced a CMFE module. Firstly, we use the FE block to obtain features at each scale. The FE block comprises of three dilated convolutions in parallel with different expansion rates.

Each convolution is followed by a BatchNorm (BN) layer and a MaxPooling layer to extract multiscale features effectively. The features of different scales are then connected in the channel direction. Let the obtained feature map be F, then F can be denoted as

$$F = Cat([F_0, F_1, \ldots F_n]) \tag{1}$$

where F_n represents features at different scales. When aggregating features at different scales, it is possible that important regions may be weakened due to interference from unimportant regions. Our approach addresses this issue by introducing the FF Block, which refines multiscale features by paying more attention to visually important regions. The FF block is capable of establishing remote channel dependencies, unlike spatial attention and channel attention. You can refer to its structure in Fig. 1.

Specifically, Let $F \in R^{C \times H \times W}$ denote the input feature map, where the quantity H, W, C represent its height, width, number of input channels respectively. Firstly, global average pooling is used to embed global spatial information into the channel descriptors. The global average pooling can be calculated as follows

$$g_c = \frac{1}{H \times W} \sum_{i=1}^{H} \sum_{j=1}^{W} x_c(i, j) \tag{2}$$

the information flow between different channels is combined using two fully connected layers in order to effectively enhance the interaction between high and low channel dimension information. After this, a Sigmoid function is applied to assign weights to the channels based on their interactions in order to extract information more efficiently. The resulting attentional weight of F can be expressed as

$$W(F) = \sigma(W_1 \delta(W_0(g_F))) \tag{3}$$

the symbol δ denotes the Rectified Linear Unit (ReLU) operation, $W_0 \in R^{\frac{C}{r} \times C}$ and $W_1 \in R^{\frac{C}{r} \times C}$ denote the Fully Connected (FC) layer.

After obtaining a multiscale feature map that establishes remote channel dependencies, we generate two 2D graphs by employing two pooling operations to aggregate the channel information from the feature maps: $F_{avg}^s \in R^{1 \times H \times W}$ and $F_{max}^s \in R^{1 \times H \times W}$. Each represents the average pooled features across channels and the maximum pooled features. These are then concatenated and convolved by a standard convolutional layer to produce our 2D spatial attention map. Briefly, the spatial attention map is computed as follows

$$M_s(F) = \sigma(f^{7 \times 7}([AvgPool(F); MaxPool(F)])) \tag{4}$$

where σ denotes a sigmoid function and $f^{7\times 7}$ denotes a convolution operation with a filter size of 7×7. Finally, we obtain the feature map F_{end} as follows

$$F_{end} = F \otimes M_s(F) \otimes W(F) \tag{5}$$

3.3 Adaptive Fine-Grained Multiscale Feature Refining Module

To further refine the multiscale features, we have designed an AFMF module. The AFMF module is capable of assigning varying importance to individual scale features. Recognizing that the gap between different scale features results in distinct spatial features and semantic information, we note that the addition operation may overwrite information, potentially leading to the loss of critical details. Conversely, the concatenation operation retains more dimensional and positional information but fails to account for the varying importance of features at different scales. Therefore, building upon the concatenation operation, the AFMF module transforms the diverse information carried by features at each stage into weights through the ReLU function and concatenation operation. This is followed by the sigmoid function to constrain the feature matrix within the range [0,1].

Let F_1 and F_2, F_3, F_4, F_5 denote the features of each scale after the fully connected layer, respectively. The weights are computed using the following formula

$$\alpha = \delta[\theta(F_1 \oplus F_2 \oplus F_3 \oplus F_4 \oplus F_5)] \tag{6}$$

where θ denotes the ReLU function, δ denotes the sigmoid function, and $\oplus$ denotes the linking operation. Each element in θ denotes the importance of the corresponding channel and then the last feature I is calculated using the following equation

$$I = \alpha \cdot \sum_{i=1}^{i} F_i \tag{7}$$

Finally, we multiply the obtained weights with the fused features to obtain the final features used for classification and i$\in (1 \cdots 5)$.

The AFMF module can assign varying importance to multiscale features at different stages based on the distinct information they carry. This adaptability characterizes the fusion approach of the AFMF module. Consequently, the features obtained from fusion are biased towards those that are more instrumental for classification.

4 Experiments

4.1 Dataset

OpenSARShip [14] was compiled from 41 Sentinel-1 images captured under diverse environmental conditions, offering 11346 SAR ship chips with integrated Automatic Identification System (AIS) messages. It boasts five key attributes: specificity, large scale, diversity, reliability and public availability. These attributes position OpenSARShip as a benchmark dataset, empowering researchers to develop purpose-built and adaptive ship interpretation algorithms, thereby elevating the performance standard for data analysis. Sentinel-1 is a C-band SAR satellite system in operation.

Table 1. Training-Test Division of the Dataset

Dataset	Category	Training	Test	All
Three-Category	Bulk	169	164	333
	Container	169	404	573
	Tanker	169	73	242
Six-Category	Bulk	100	233	333
	Cargo	100	571	671
	Container	100	473	573
	Fishing	100	25	125
	General cargo	100	42	142
	Tanker	100	142	242

Many researchers utilize SAR ship images from this dataset [15–17]. As described in the paper [4], two data subsets were employed for the experiments: a three-categorized subset and a six-categorized subset. Table 1 provides detailed data descriptions.

1) Three-Category: In OpenSARShip, the number of samples in the three classes is imbalanced. To achieve a class-balanced dataset, similar to HOG-ShipCLSNet [9], the number of training samples for each class is set to be equal. The training-test ratio was determined to be 7:3 based on the minimum number of samples in the three-Category dataset. Table 1 displays the number of samples for the three ship classes in OpenSARShip.
2) Six-Category: Following Zhang et al. [4], another challenging six-category dataset was constructed to further validate our work. The six-ship categories were selected based on the number of Bulk carriers, Container ships, Tanker, Cargo, Fishing, and General cargo, all exceeding 100. Similarly, to obtain a category-balanced training set, 80% of the number of samples from all categories of vessels were set as the training set ($125 \times 80\% = 100$), with the remaining samples allocated to the test set. Figure 2. illustrates the six types of ships.

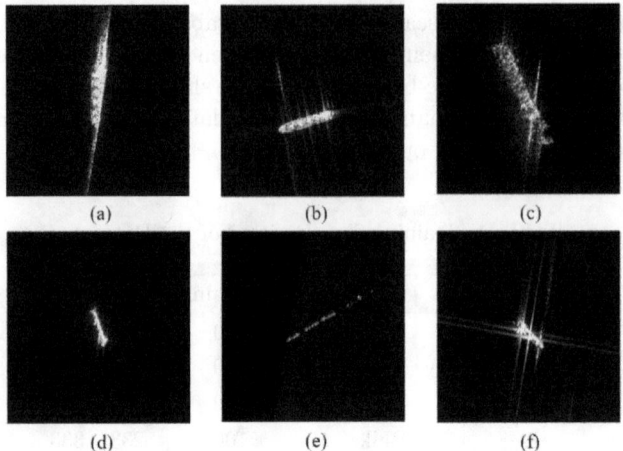

Fig. 2. Six-category of SAR ship images in the OpenSARShip-1.0 dataset. (a) Bulk. (b) Container. (c) Tanker. (d) Cargo. (e) Fishing. (f) Genral cargo.

4.2 Training Details

We resized the SAR image to 64 × 64. We use Adaptive Moment Estimation (Adam) as the optimization method in training C2F-MFF for 100 epochs, with beta-1 set to 0.9 and beta-2 set to 0.999. We empirically set the batch size of training to 16. To offset the possible negative effect of the gradient vanishing, we set the learning rate at 0.0004, which is a relatively small value.

4.3 Loss Function

We use the CE loss as the loss function for C2F-MFF, defined as?

$$L_s = -\frac{1}{N_x} \sum_{i=1}^{N_x} log(p_i) \qquad (8)$$

where p_i denotes the ith sample classification result and N_x denotes the number of all training samples.

4.4 Evaluation Criteria

We adopted Accuracy (Acc) to evaluate the ability of C2F-MFF to ship classification, Acc was used as the core evaluation criterion to measure the classification performance, defined as

$$Accuracy = \frac{TP + TN}{TP + TN + FN + FP} \qquad (9)$$

TP for True Positive, TN for True Negative, FP for False Positive and FN for False Negative. Furthermore, four other performance metrics are employed for more result verifications in the experiments, including 1) precision; 2) recall; 3) F1; and 4) confusion matrix.

5 Results and Discussion

5.1 Results and Comparisons

Table 2 and Table 3 presents the SAR ship classification results of C2F-MFF on the three-category and six-category datasets. Each combination was executed five times and the reported accuracy is in the form of "mean ± std." The table indicates that C2F-MFF achieves the highest classification accuracy. In the three-category dataset, its accuracy is 78.22%, surpassing the sub-optimal method by Zhang et al. [9] by 0.07%. For the six-category dataset, its classification accuracy is 57.11%, outperforming the sub-optimal method by Zeng et al. [18] by 1.85%.

Furthermore, C2F-MFF outperforms other methods in all metrics on both datasets, except for the Precision-Recall metric, where it ranks second in the three-category dataset and the Recall metric, where it ranks second in the six-category dataset.

Table 4 and Table 5 show the top-1 accuracy of C2F-MFF for both datasets, presenting the classification performance for each ship category through confusion matrices. Notably, both tables reveal instances of misclassifications, primarily attributed to significant interference from background noise in the images of both datasets. However, Table 4 exhibits superior performance compared to Table 5, attributed to the six-category dataset having fewer training images. It achieves an accuracy of 57.54%, which is notably lower than the three-category dataset's accuracy of 78.94%. The category prediction confusion in the six-category dataset mainly arises in the Tanker and General Cargo categories due to their similar geometries. Cargo, Fishing, and Tanker ships exhibit better classification performance.

Considering Fig. 3, C2F-MFF exhibits significantly lower standard deviation compared to both deep feature methods and feature fusion methods, registering values of 0.18 and 0.25 on the two datasets, respectively. These results underscore the effectiveness of the AFMF module and the CMFE module in achieving fine-grained fusion of multiscale features, contributing to a more robust generalization ability of the network.

6 Ablation Experiments

6.1 Ablation Study on Coarse-Grained Multiscale Feature Extraction Module

We conducted ablation experiments to compare the performance of the CMFE module with that of ordinary convolution.

Table 2. Comparison of C2F-MFF with Deep Feature and State-of-the-Art Feature Fusion Methods on the Three-Category Dataset. Each Combination was Executed Five Times and the Reported Accuracy is in the Form of "MEAN ± STD." Bolded Fonts in the Table Represent the Best Results

Feature	Method	Three-Category			
		Acc (%)	Recall (%)	Precision (%)	F1 (%)
Deep Feature	VGG-11 [22]	73.42 ± 0.75	73.21 ± 0.96	68.64 ± 1.49	70.85 ± 1.07
	VGG-13 [22]	73.03 ± 0.86	72.59 ± 1.29	67.24 ± 1.75	69.79 ± 0.92
	Resnet-18 [23]	74.64 ± 0.68	73.76 ± 1.61	69.40 ± 1.92	71.49 ± 1.0
	Resnet-34 [23]	73.40 ± 1.09	71.43 ± 2.72	68.11 ± 1.73	69.69 ± 1.47
	DenseNet-121 [24]	74.65 ± 0.68	72.55 ± 3.88	69.56 ± 2.17	70.93 ± 1.60
	DenseNet-169 [24]	74.31 ± 0.76	71.40 ± 1.80	68.83 ± 1.50	70.07 ± 1.00
	SqueezeNet-v1.0 [25]	72.15 ± 1.25	71.47 ± 1.31	66.73 ± 1.70	69.01 ± 1.28
	SqueezeNet-v1.1 [25]	70.89 ± 1.11	67.42 ± 4.67	65.67 ± 1.87	66.45 ± 2.61
	Xception [26]	73.74 ± 0.86	71.56 ± 3.00	68.60 ± 1.67	70.00 ± 1.29
	Wang et al. [20]	69.27 ± 0.27	57.72 ± 1.37	58.72 ± 4.76	58.12 ± 2.67
	Hou et al. [21]	67.41 ± 1.13	69.33 ± 2.00	69.44 ± 2.42	66.76 ± 1.64
	Huang et al. [16]	74.98 ± 1.46	74.74 ± 1.60	69.56 ± 2.38	72.04 ± 1.60
	Zeng et al. [18]	77.41 ± 1.74	74.99 ± 1.55	**74.05 ± 1.75**	74.52 ± 1.02
Feature fusion	Xiong et al. [19]	75.44 ± 2.68	73.87 ± 1.16	71.50 ± 3.00	72.67 ± 2.04
	CLSNet [9]	78.15 ± 0.57	77.87 ± 1.14	72.42 ± 1.06	75.05 ± 1.10
	C2F-MFF (ours)	**78.22 ± 0.18**	**79.24 ± 0.61**	73.04 ± 0.47	**75.47 ± 0.18**

Table 3. Comparison of C2F-MFF with Deep Feature and State-of-the-Art Feature Fusion Methods on the Six-Category Dataset

Feature	Method	Six-Category			
		Acc (%)	Recall (%)	Precision (%)	F1 (%)
Deep Feature	VGG-11 [22]	49.41 ± 0.99	51.38 ± 0.82	43.27 ± 1.63	47.21 ± 1.25
	VGG-13 [22]	49.70 ± 1.36	51.32 ± 0.38	43.06 ± 1.68	46.83 ± 0.90
	Resnet-18 [23]	45.91 ± 0.43	50.19 ± 0.47	42.85 ± 1.20	46.23 ± 0.35
	Resnet-34 [23]	48.27 ± 2.75	48.12 ± 0.57	42.18 ± 0.57	44.95 ± 0.83
	DenseNet-121 [24]	53.49 ± 1.47	55.51 ± 1.30	46.52 ± 1.48	50.62 ± 0.74
	DenseNet-169 [24]	54.26 ± 2.97	55.55 ± 0.81	47.21 ± 1.67	**51.07 ± 1.49**
	SqueezeNet-v1.0 [25]	53.12 ± 1.12	53.24 ± 0.75	45.55 ± 0.79	49.10 ± 0.85
	SqueezeNet-v1.1 [25]	50.83 ± 1.74	52.72 ± 1.13	43.73 ± 0.94	47.81 ± 1.33
	Xception [26]	49.56 ± 1.47	52.21 ± 0.94	44.03 ± 1.15	47.77 ± 1.11
	Wang et al. [20]	48.43 ± 3.71	50.53 ± 1.85	41.77 ± 1.34	45.73 ± 1.28
	Hou et al. [21]	47.44 ± 2.01	48.76 ± 0.79	41.22 ± 0.74	44.67 ± 1.21
	Huang et al. [16]	54.78 ± 2.08	54.09 ± 0.81	47.58 ± 1.66	50.63 ± 1.79
	Zeng et al. [18]	55.26 ± 2.36	55.66 ± 1.23	47.16 ± 0.70	50.96 ± 1.18
Feature fusion	Xiong et al. [19]	54.93 ± 2.61	53.57 ± 0.33	45.74 ± 0.82	49.35 ± 0.69
	CLSNet [9]	53.77 ± 3.63	54.20 ± 1.09	46.66 ± 1.07	50.15 ± 1.24
	C2F-MFF (ours)	**57.11 ± 0.25**	**56.54 ± 0.52**	**49.06 ± 0.13**	50.80 ± 0.25

Table 4. Confusion Matrix of C2F-MFF Classification Results on the Three-Category Dataset

Predicted				
True	Bulk	Container	Tanker	**Recall (%)**
Bulk	120	37	6	73.62
Container	53	327	24	80.94
Tanker	7	7	59	80.82
Precison (%)	66.67	88.14	66.29	**Accuracy**
F1(%)	69.97	84.39	72.84	**78.94%**

Table 5. Confusion Matrix of C2F-MFF Classification Results on the Six-Category Dataset

Predicted							
True	Bulk	Container	Tanker	Cargo	Fishing	Genral cargo	**Recall (%)**
Bulk	144	24	6	43	1	15	61.80
Container	98	252	12	105	0	6	53.28
Tanker	13	4	40	44	7	34	28.17
Cargo	58	74	37	378	6	4	67.86
Fishing	1	0	0	0	15	9	60.00
Genral cargo	3	1	6	1	5	26	61.90
Precison(%)	45.43	70.99	39.60	66.20	44.12	27.66	**Accuracy**
F1(%)	52.37	60.87	32.92	67.02	50.85	38.23	**57.54%**

Table 6 indicates that the CMFE module enhances recognition accuracy by 5.83% for the three-category dataset and by 1.76% for the six-category dataset. The experimental results affirm that the CMFE module effectively enhances the abundance of multiscale features at each stage through the rational fusion of features at different scales. This provides clear evidence of the effectiveness of the CMFE module.

Table 6. Effectiveness of the CMFE Module

CMFE	Three-Category Acc (%)	Six-Category Acc (%)
✓	78.22 ± 0.20	57.11 ± 0.25
✗	72.39 ± 11.87	55.35 ± 2.10

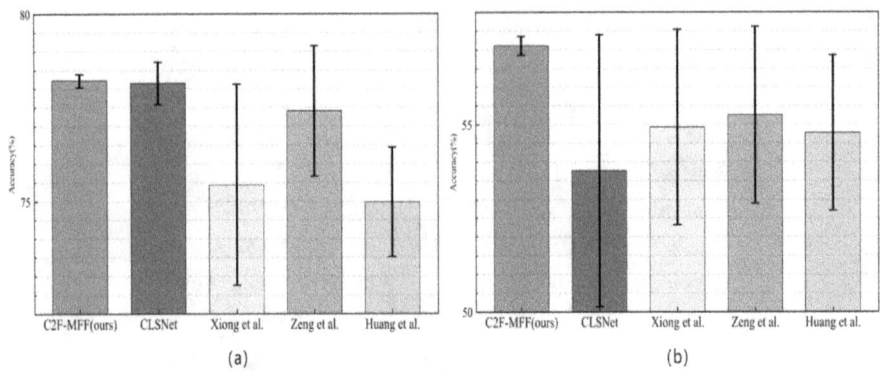

Fig. 3. Comparison results of "mean ± std" accuracy between the proposed C2F-MFF and the state-of-the-art. (a) Three-category. (b) Six-category.

Table 7. Effectiveness of the AFMF Module

Method	Three-Category Acc (%)	Six-Category Acc (%)
Element-by-element Addition	72.76 ± 1.04	54.60 ± 1.20
Use of the Terminal Features	73.17 ± 5.68	54.68 ± 2.33
Concatenation	76.19 ± 3.52	56.30 ± 1.55
Average Weighting	75.98 ± 1.45	56.51 ± 0.12
AFMF(ours)	**78.22 ± 0.20**	**57.11 ± 0.25**

6.2 Ablation Study on Adaptive Fine-Grained Multiscale Feature Refining Module

We set up two groups of ablation experiments to demonstrate the effectiveness of the AFMF module.

1) Experiment 1: effectiveness of module. To verify the effectiveness of the AFMF module, we compared it with a method utilizing terminal features, involving concatenation, element-by-element addition and average weighting.

The experimental results for terminal features, element-by-element addition, concatenation, average weighting method and adaptive refinement method are presented in Table 7. The Element-by-Element Addition method yields the least favorable results, potentially attributed to the obscuring of semantic information contained in features at each stage, leading to final features that deviate from crucial aspects for recognition. The method using Terminal Features neglects the importance of earlier features for ship recognition, resulting in lower accuracy. The Average Weighting method partly ensures the importance of key features, while the Concatenation method preserves both spatial and semantic information in each phase, outperforming the method using Terminal Features. Our proposed method achieves classification accuracy 2.03% and 0.60% higher than the second-ranked method on the three-category and six-category datasets, respectively. These experiments underscore the importance of considering the significance of earlier features and recognizing the distinct importance of multiscale features at each stage.

2) Experiment 2: effectiveness of every stage feature. From Table 8, we can see that on the three-category dataset, the multiscale features at each stage contribute to the accuracy of ship classification and we conjecture that it is because dropping the terminal features causes the network to become worse at recognizing small ships. Meanwhile, there are recognizable results on the six-category dataset. Thus, our ablation experiments demonstrate that dropping the terminal features of the network without consideration is not justified.

Table 8. Effectiveness of Every Stage Feature

Dataset	F_1	F_2	F3	F4	F_5	Acc (%)
Three-Category	✗	✗	✗	✗	✓	72.76 ± 1.04
	✗	✗	✗	✓	✓	75.35 ± 6.07
	✗	✗	✓	✓	✓	76.13 ± 1.23
	✗	✓	✓	✓	✓	75.78 ± 2.57
	✓	✓	✓	✓	✓	**78.22 ± 0.20**
Six-Category	✗	✗	✗	✗	✓	54.68 ± 2.33
	✗	✗	✗	✓	✓	55.90 ± 0.83
	✗	✗	✓	✓	✓	55.93 ± 1.10
	✗	✗	✓	✓	✓	56.76 ± 0.97
	✓	✓	✓	✓	✓	**57.11 ± 0.25**

7 Conclusion

This paper proposes C2F-MFF to fully leverage multiscale features. Initially, the CMFE module is employed to enrich multiscale features at each stage. Subsequently, the AFMF module is utilized to assign varying importance to multiscale features at different stages, ensuring the comprehensive utilization of these features to enhance the performance and generalization ability of the model. Our experimental results on the three-category and six-category OpenSARShip datasets demonstrate that C2F-MFF achieves the state-of-the-art results among modern CNN-based methods and other feature fusion methods.

References

1. Zhang, T., Zhang, X., Shi, J., et al.: HyperLi-Net: A hyper-light deep learning network for high-accurate and high-speed ship detection from synthetic aperture radar imagery. ISPRS J. Photogramm. Remote. Sens. **167**, 123–153 (2020)
2. Cui, Z., Wang, X., Liu, N., et al.: Ship detection in large-scale SAR images via spatial shuffle-group enhance attention. IEEE Trans. Geosci. Remote Sens. **59**(1), 379–391 (2020)

3. Ai, J., Mao, Y., Luo, Q., et al.: SAR target classification using the multikernel-size feature fusion-based convolutional neural network. IEEE Trans. Geosci. Remote Sens. **60**, 1–13 (2021)
4. Zhang, T., Zhang, X.: Squeeze-and-excitation Laplacian pyramid network with dual-polarization feature fusion for ship classification in SAR images. IEEE Geosci. Remote Sens. Lett. **19**, 1–5 (2021)
5. Snapir, B., Waine, T.W., Biermann, L.: Maritime vessel classification to monitor fisheries with SAR: demonstration in the North Sea. Remote Sens. **11**(3), 353 (2019)
6. Xu, Y., Lang, H., Niu, L., et al.: Discriminative adaptation regularization framework-based transfer learning for ship classification in SAR images. IEEE Geosci. Remote Sens. Lett. **16**(11), 1786–1790 (2019)
7. Huang, Z., Pan, Z., Lei, B.: What, where, and how to transfer in SAR target recognition based on deep CNNs. IEEE Trans. Geosci. Remote Sens. **58**(4), 2324–2336 (2019)
8. He, J., Wang, Y., Liu, H.: Ship classification in medium-resolution SAR images via densely connected triplet CNNs integrating Fisher discrimination regularized metric learning. IEEE Trans. Geosci. Remote Sens. **59**(4), 3022–3039 (2020)
9. Zhang, T., Zhang, X., Ke, X., et al.: HOG-ShipCLSNet: a novel deep learning network with hog feature fusion for SAR ship classification. IEEE Trans. Geosci. Remote Sens. **60**, 1–22 (2021)
10. Bai, L., Liu, Q., Li, C., et al.: A lightweight and multiscale network for remote sensing image scene classification. IEEE Geosci. Remote Sens. Lett. **19**, 1–5 (2021)
11. Wang, G., Zhang, N., Liu, W., et al.: MFST: a multi-level fusion network for remote sensing scene classification. IEEE Geosci. Remote Sens. Lett. **19**, 1–5 (2022)
12. Zhang, H., Zu, K., Lu, J., et al.: Epsanet: an efficient pyramid split attention block on convolutional [12] network. arXiv preprint arXiv:2105.14447 (2021)
13. Woo, S., Park, J., Lee, J.-Y., Kweon, I.S.: CBAM: convolutional block attention module. In: Ferrari, V., Hebert, M., Sminchisescu, C., Weiss, Y. (eds.) ECCV 2018. LNCS, vol. 11211, pp. 3–19. Springer, Cham (2018). https://doi.org/10.1007/978-3-030-01234-2_1
14. Huang, L., Liu, B., Li, B., et al.: OpenSARShip: a dataset dedicated to Sentinel-1 ship interpretation. IEEE J. Select. Topics Applied Earth Observ. Remote Sens. **11**(1), 195–208 (2017)
15. Wang, C., Shi, J., Zhou, Y., et al.: Semisupervised learning-based SAR ATR via self-consistent augmentation. IEEE Trans. Geosci. Remote Sens. **59**(6), 4862–4873 (2020)
16. Huang, G., Liu, X., Hui, J., et al.: A novel group squeeze excitation sparsely connected convolutional networks for SAR target classification. Int. J. Remote Sens. **40**(11), 4346–4360 (2019)
17. He, J., Wang, Y., Liu, H.: Ship classification in medium-resolution SAR images via densely connected triplet CNNs integrating Fisher discrimination regularized metric learning. IEEE Trans. Geosci. Remote Sens. **59**(4), 3022–3039 (2020)
18. Zeng, L., Zhu, Q., Lu, D., et al.: Dual-polarized SAR ship grained classification based on CNN with hybrid channel feature loss. IEEE Geosci. Remote Sens. Lett. **19**, 1–5 (2021)
19. Xiong, G., Xi, Y., Chen, D., et al.: Dual-polarization SAR ship target recognition based on mini hourglass region extraction and dual-channel efficient fusion network. IEEE Access **9**, 29078–29089 (2021)
20. Wang, Y., Wang, C., Zhang, H.: Ship classification in high-resolution SAR images using deep learning of small datasets. Sensors **18**(9), 2929 (2018)

21. Hou, X., Ao, W., Song, Q., et al.: FUSAR-Ship: building a high-resolution SAR-AIS matchup dataset of Gaofen-3 for ship detection and recognition. Sci. China Inf. Sci. **63**, 1–19 (2020)
22. Simonyan, K., Zisserman, A.: Very deep convolutional networks for large-scale image recognition. arXiv preprint arXiv:1409.1556 (2014)
23. He, K., Zhang, X., Ren, S., et al.: Deep residual learning for image recognition. In: Proceedings of the IEEE Conference on Computer Vision and Pattern Recognition, pp. 770–778 (2016)
24. Huang, G., Liu, Z., Van Der Maaten, L., et al.: Densely connected convolutional networks. In: Proceedings of the IEEE Conference on Computer Vision and Pattern Recognition, pp. 4700–4708 (2017)
25. Szegedy, C., Liu, W., Jia, Y., et al.: Going deeper with convolutions. In: Proceedings of the IEEE Conference on Computer Vision and Pattern Recognition, pp. 1–9 (2015)
26. Chollet, F.: Xception: deep learning with depthwise separable convolutions. In: Proceedings of the IEEE Conference on Computer Vision and Pattern Recognition, pp. 1251–1258 (2017)

Multi-scale Convolutional Attention Fuzzy Broad Network for Few-Shot Hyperspectral Image Classification

Xiaopei Hu[1,2,3], Guixin Zhao[1,2,3(✉)], Lu Yuan[1,2,3], Xiangjun Dong[1,2,3], and Aimei Dong[1,2,3]

[1] Key Laboratory of Computing Power Network and Information Security, Ministry of Education, Shandong Computer Science Center (National Supercomputer Center in Jinan), Qilu University of Technology(Shandong Academy of Sciences), Jinan, China
[2] Shandong Provincial Key Laboratory of Computer Networks, Shandong Fundamental Research Center for Computer Science, Jinan, China
[3] Faculty of Computer Science and Technology, Qilu University of Technology (Shandong Academy of Sciences), Jinan 250353, China
zgx@qlu.edu.cn

Abstract. Hyperspectral image (HSI) classification is a challenging research hotspot in the field of hyperspectral remote sensing. Due to the limited number of labeled samples, most existing classification models cannot fully utilize the spatial-spectral features of HSI to improve classification performance under few-shot conditions. In this paper, we propose a multi-scale convolutional attention fuzzy broad network (MCAFBN) for few-shot HSI classification. First, we design a multi-scale feature extraction module with convolution and self-attention to extract deep local and global features, in which an active learning (AL) training strategy is adopted. Then, fuzzy broad learning system (FBLS) can not only use a small number of fuzzy rules to learn the complex mapping relationship between the extracted fusion features and HSI labels but also use the enhancement layer to capture more nonlinear feature intersections to improve the fitting ability of the model. We use the classification results of FBLS to generate initial probability maps. Finally, we use guided filter to further correct misclassified samples in the initial probability map, which can better utilize spatial-spectral features to improve classification accuracy under few-shot conditions. Experimental results on three public HSI datasets show that the proposed model achieves state-of-the-art classification performance compared with eight popular models.

Keywords: Hyperspectral image classification · Active learning · Fuzzy broad learning system · Few-shot · Multi-scale convolution

---

This work was supported in part by the National Natural Science Foundation of China under Grant Nos. 62076143, 62173193 and 11901325, in part by Fundamental research promotion plan of Qilu University of Technology (Shandong Academy of Sciences) No. 2021JC02009 and in part by the Natural Science Foundation of Shandong Province, China, under Grant Nos. ZR2022MF237 and ZR2020MF041.

© The Author(s), under exclusive license to Springer Nature Switzerland AG 2024
M. Wand et al. (Eds.): ICANN 2024, LNCS 15017, pp. 46–60, 2024.
https://doi.org/10.1007/978-3-031-72335-3_4

1 Introduction

HSI classification is an important task in the field of hyperspectral remote sensing. Early HSI classification mainly used machine learning models such as support vector machine (SVM) [1], K-nearest neighbor (KNN) [2], and multinomial logistic regression (MLR) [3]. However, these traditional models only use the spectral features of HSI, so they cannot achieve good classification results.

In recent years, researchers have applied deep learning (DL) models to HSI classification to exploit spatial-spectral features and achieved excellent performance. Li et al. [4] used 3D convolutions based on 2DCNN to extract local spatial-spectral joint features in image patches. Zhong et al. [5] proposed a spatial-spectral residual network (SSRN) model using 3D convolutions and residual connections to obtain robust HSI classification results. Lightweight spatial-spectral Attention Feature Fusion Network (LMAFN) [6] extracts spatial-spectral features by combining multi-scale Ghost with efficient channel attention modules. However, these DL models are difficult to capture nonlinear feature interactions under few-shot conditions, resulting in insufficient learning and fitting capabilities.

As a difficult research, labeling hyperspectral remote sensing images requires a lot of manpower, material resources and time, so currently only a small number of labeled samples are available for HSI classification. To solve the problem of low classification accuracy caused by few training samples, researchers have proposed different models for few-shot HSI classification. For example, Liu et al. [7] utilized semi-supervised learning for few-shot HSI classification, which can simultaneously minimize the sum of supervised and unsupervised cost functions. Bai et al. [8] used 3D convolution, ECA attention module and residual learning to extract spatial-spectral features of few-shot HSI and achieved good classification results. The lightweight convolutional neural network (LWCNN) [9] maintains the discriminative ability of feature extraction in the few-shot case by designing and connecting multiple dual-scale convolution (DSC) modules. HyperLiteNet [10] utilizes a parallel structure to extract and optimize diverse spatial and spectral features. In addition, active learning (AL) [11–13] based models have also been proposed and used for few-shot HSI classification. For example, li [14] proposed a semi-supervised multinomial logistic regression model combined with an active selection strategy based on entropy (EP). Later, an AL framework [15] based on the MRF model was proposed, and a SVM classifier [15] with six different AL sampling strategies was designed for HSI classification.

To more fully extract HSI features when the number of samples is limited, researchers combine AL and DL to apply to few-shot HSI classification [16–18]. Specifically, Li [16] proposed a method that combines the multi-class level uncertainty (MCLU) active criterion with SAE neural networks. Liu [17] proposed a model that combines the weighted incremental dictionary learning criterion with RBM. However, it is difficult for these models to fully extract deep, multi-scale spatial spectral fusion features to achieve good classification performance under few-shot conditions.

Aiming at the problem of insufficient extraction of deep spatial-spectral features and nonlinear features under limited labeled samples, this paper proposes a multi-scale convolutional attention fuzzy broad network (MCAFBN) for few-shot HSI classification. MCAFBN combines multi-scale convolutional attention (MSCA) block with AL strategy, fuzzy broad learning system (FBLS) [19] and guided filter. Specifically, the MSCA block utilizes self-attention and multi-scale convolution of different dimensions to extract local and global spatial spectral features in HSI. Then, we use FBLS with a small number of fuzzy rules to learn the complex mapping relationship between the extracted fusion features and HSI labels, and its enhancement layer can capture more nonlinear feature intersections to improve the fitting ability of the model. The classification results of FBLS are used to generate initial probability maps. Finally, we use a guided filter to correct misclassified samples in the initial probability map guided by the grayscale map generated by principal component analysis (PCA). Therefore, the proposed MCAFBN can better utilize the advantages of spatial-spectral features to improve classification accuracy under few-shot conditions. To evaluate the proposed model, we conduct extensive experiments on three public HSI datasets.

The main contributions of this study can be summarized as: (1) We design a MSCA block using multi-scale convolution and self-attention to extract deep local and global spatial spectral features. We introduced the AL training strategy, which can select informative samples from the validation set to join training under few-shot conditions to improve model performance. (2) We use FBLS to learn the complex mapping relationship between spatial-spectral features and HSI labels, while fuzzy processing can learn rich discriminative features to enhance classification balance. The enhancement layer of FBLS can capture more nonlinear feature interactions, thus making up for the lack of DL's learning and fitting capabilities under few-shot conditions. (3) Experimental results on three public HSI datasets show that the proposed MCAFBN achieves state-of-the-art classification.

2 Methodology

The overall framework of the proposed MCAFBN is shown in Fig. 1. To fully extract spatial-spectral features to improve classification performance under few-shot conditions, The proposed MCAFBN mainly consists of 3 parts, including MSCA block with AL strategy, FBLS and guided filter. (1) The MSCA block simultaneously uses self-attention and multi-scale convolution of different dimensions to extract local and global spatial spectral features of deep layers in HSI. We use the AL strategy for training, which can proactively select the most informative samples from the validation set to add to the next iteration to adjust model weights and improve performance when training samples are limited. (2) The Takagi-Sugeno (TS) fuzzy subsystem in FBLS can learn the complex mapping relationship between the extracted fusion features and HSI labels, thereby transforming the spectral fusion features in the input space into more expressive fuzzy features. In addition, fuzzy features are directly extended on enhancement nodes for nonlinear learning and feature interaction to improve fitting capabilities. Finally, we use the output of defuzzification and enhancement nodes to perform pseudo-inverse calculations to obtain the output weights, thereby completing the preliminary classification of HSI. The classification results of FBLS are used to generate initial probability maps. (3) We use PCA to generate grayscale guidance images. Guided by the grayscale image, we use guided filter to correct misclassified samples in the initial probability map, thereby further improving the classification accuracy under few-shot conditions.

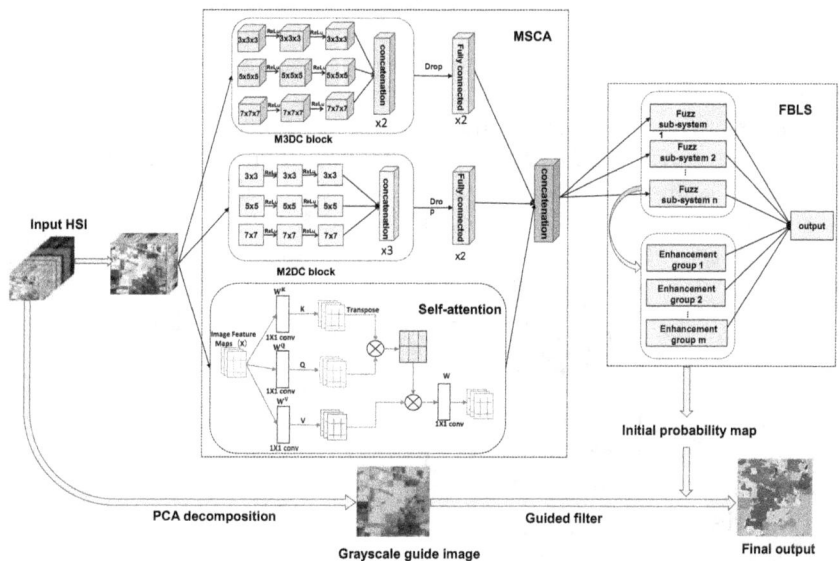

Fig. 1. The detailed architecture of the proposed MCAFBN

2.1 Multi-scale Convolution Attention Block

In this section, we design an MSCA block aimed at capturing long- and short-range temporal features, which combines self-attention with multi-scale convolution in parallel. As shown in Fig. 1, this module mainly contains three parts: a multi-scale 2D convolution block for capturing local features of different dimensions, a multi-scale 3D convolution block and a self-attention block for capturing global features. Let O_{M3DC}, O_{M2DC} and $O_{attention}$ represent the output of the multi-scale 3D convolution (M3DC) block, multi-scale 2D convolution (M2DC) block and self-attention respectively, then the output O of the MSCA block can be expressed as:

$$O = concatenate\left((O_{M3DC} + O_{M2DC}), O_{attention}\right). \tag{1}$$

Multi-scale Convolution In this paper, we simultaneously use 3D convolution and 2D convolution to extract spatial-spectral features from limited HSI labeled samples, which can more comprehensively integrate features in the spatial and spectral dimensions, thereby improving the classification performance of the model. As shown in Fig. 1, the proposed MSCA consists of a multi-scale 3D convolution (M3DC) block and a multi-scale 2D convolution (M2DC) block. We use 2 M3DC blocks and 3 M2DC blocks respectively to improve local spatial-spectral features. In few-shot HSI classification, it is difficult to fully extract spatial-spectral features with a single convolution operation. Therefore, we use multi-scale convolution based on the idea of inception to increase the network width. In the M3DC block and M2DC block, we respectively use three convolution kernels of different scales to capture features while fusing the rich spatial-spectral information in HSI. To extract deep features, we stack 3 convolutional layers at each scale to extract features at different levels, so the network can gradually learn more complex and abstract features. After each convolution layer, we use the ReLU activation function to prevent the gradient from vanishing. We also use fully connected layers to compress weights and add Dropout to avoid the risk of overfitting of the model during training.

In the M2DC block, the 2D convolution operation is calculated as follows:

$$z_{x.y}^{l.r} = f\left(\sum_m \sum_{i=0}^{I_l-1} \sum_{j=0}^{J_l-1} w_{i.j}^{l.r.m} * z_{x+i.y+j}^{l-1.m} + b^{l.r}\right), \quad (2)$$

where l is the layer to be considered, r represents the number of feature maps in layer l. The output $z_{x.y}^{l.r}$ at position (x, y) is the r-th feature map in layer i. $b^{l.r}$ is the bias of the network. $f(\cdot)$ represents the layer activation function. The m index is the feature map of layer $(l-1)$, which is used as the input of layer l. $w_{i.j}^{l.r.m}$ is a value in position (i, j) where the convolution kernel is related to the r-th feature map in the l-th layer, I_l and J_l represent the kernel row and column sizes.

Similar to 2D convolution, the 3D convolution operation formula is:

$$z_{x.y.d}^{l.r} = f\left(\sum_m \sum_{i=0}^{I_l-1} \sum_{j=0}^{J_l-1} \sum_{k=0}^{K_l-1} w_{i.j.k}^{l.r.m} * z_{x+i.y+j.d+k}^{l-1.m} + b^{l.r}\right), \quad (3)$$

where where d is the band of the HSI. The $K_l - 1$ represents the size of the 3-D kernel along the spectral dimension and k is the number of kernel in layer l. The $w_{i.j.k}^{l.r.m}$ is a value in position (i, j, k) whose convolution kernel is related to the r-th feature map in the l-th layer.

Self-attention It is obviously not comprehensive to only focus on local features in HSI classification, so we utilize self-attention blocks to model the global features of HSI. Self-attention maps input X to three feature spaces: the query Q, the key K, and the value V.

$$Q = W^Q X, \quad (4)$$

$$K = W^K X, \tag{5}$$
$$V = W^V X, \tag{6}$$

among them, W^Q, W^K and W^V are the weight matrices of linear mapping. Next, the output of self-attention can be calculated as follows:

$$A = softmax\left(\frac{QK^T}{\sqrt{d_q}}\right) V, \tag{7}$$

where d_q is the parameter to avoid saturation caused by the *softmax* function.

2.2 Active Learning

The AL strategy is widely used in DL training, which can systematically select the most informative and heterogeneous samples for users to label and train classifiers, so that the model can obtain the best possible performance when labeled samples are limited. AL is mainly based on the availability of the initial training set, the availability of the validation set, and the function of selecting and obtaining information samples. The process of AL training strategy is shown in Fig. 2.

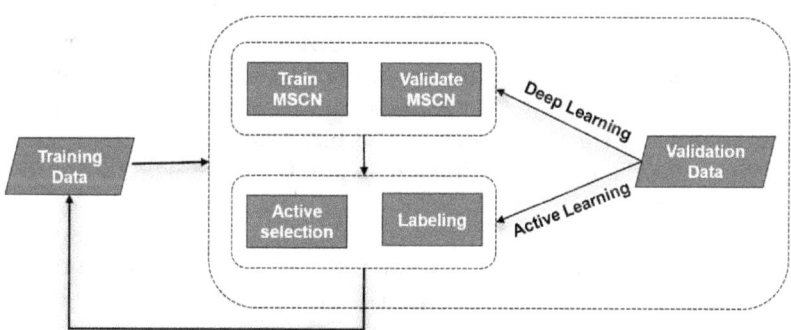

Fig. 2. The detailed architecture of the proposed MCAFBN

In this paper, the HSI cube can be expressed as $X = \{x_i, y_i\} \in R^L$, where each $x_i = \{x_{i,1}, x_{i,2}, x_{i,3}, ..., x_{i,L}\} \in R^L$, and y_i be the class label of each x_i. Let $X_{train} = \{x_i, y_i\}_{i=1}^{l}$ as a training set consisting l samples. Let $X_{val} = \{x_i\}_{i=l+1}^{u}$ as a validation set consisting u samples. In our model, we train MSCA using a small number of training samples. Then, AL iteratively selects informative and heterogeneous samples from the validation set to form a new training sample set to continue to update the training MSCA, which can fine-tune the network weights without retraining. This process provides the maximum information of the HSI training set, thereby improving the model's classification accuracy.

In our research, we rely on the posterior probability-based AL strategy, that is, to rank the candidates in X_{val} based on the ambiguity calculated from the membership function produced by the classifier. The calculation formula for the fuzziness of $n = (l+1 \longrightarrow u)$ samples of Y class is:

$$x_f = \frac{-1}{n \times Y} \sum_{n}^{i=1} \sum_{Y}^{j=1} [\lambda_{i,j} log\,(\lambda_{i,j}) + (1 - \lambda_{i,j})\, log\,(1 - \lambda_{i,j})], \tag{8}$$

where $\lambda_{i,j}$ is the output matrix produced by the trained probabilistic classification model, which represents the membership of sample x_i to class y_j.

2.3 Fuzzy Broad Learning System

Broad learning system (BLS) [20–22] is a flat network designed based on random vector functional-link neural networks(RVFLNN) [23,24]. Compared with the deep network architecture, BLS has the advantages of simple structure, fast calculation speed, and dynamic incremental update. FBLS is a new neuro-fuzzy model that integrates BLS and TS fuzzy systems. In FBLS, we use multiple fuzzy subsystems to process the input data respectively to obtain the output of the TS fuzzy system. Then we send the output of the fuzzy system to the enhancement layer for nonlinear transformation. In this paper, to make full use of the spatial-spectral fusion features of HSI, we first use MSCA to extract multi-scale spatial-spectral features, and then use FBLS to optimize and expand the extracted spatial-spectral fusion features to further enhance the representation ability of the features. Figure 1 shows the detailed framework of FBLS.

Supppose that there are n groups of TS fuzzy subsystems and m groups of enhancement nodes in FBLS. The input data are $X = (x_1, x_2, ..., x_N)^T \in R^{N \times M}$, and the s-th training sample be $x_s = (x_{s1}, x_{s2}, ..., x_{sM}), s = 1, 2, ..., N$, where N and M are the dimensions and number of samples. We map the input features to the TS fuzzy subsystem, and the fuzzy hypothesis rule can be expressed as

if x_{s1} is A^i_{k1} and x_{s2} is A^i_{k2} and x_{sM} is A^i_{kM}
then $z^i_{sk} = f^i_k(x_{s1}, x_{s2}, ...x_{sM}) = \sum_{t=1}^{M} \alpha^i_{kt} x_{st}, k = 1, 2, ..., K_i$.
where A^i_{kM} represents the fuzzy set, f^i_k is the polynomial of the input variable, α^i_{kt} represents the coefficient and K_i represents the number of fuzzy rules in the i-th fuzzy subsystem.

The activation level of the k-th fuzzy rule in the i-th fuzzy subsystem is defined as:

$$\tau^i_{sk} = \prod_{t=1}^{M} \mu^i_{kt}(x_{st}), \tag{9}$$

where μ^i_{kt} is the Gaussian membership function corresponding to the fuzzy set A^i_{kt}, which can be expressed as:

$$\mu^i_{kt}(h) = e^{-(\frac{-c^i_{kt}}{\sigma^i_{kt}})^2}. \tag{10}$$

The weighted activation level for each fuzzy rule is:

$$w_{sk}^i = \frac{\tau_{sk}^i}{\sum_{k=1}^{K_i} \tau_{sk}^i}. \tag{11}$$

The defuzzification output of the i-th fuzzy subsystem can be expressed as:

$$\begin{aligned}F_{si} &= \left(\sum_{k=1}^{K_i} w_{sk}^i \left(\sum_{t=1}^{M} \delta_{K1}^i \alpha_{kt}^i x_{st}\right), \ldots, \sum_{k=1}^{K_i} w_{sk}^i \left(\sum_{t=1}^{M} \delta_{kC}^i \alpha_{kt}^i x_{st}\right)\right) \\ &= \sum_{t=1}^{M} \alpha_{kt}^i x_{st} \left(w_{s1}^i, \ldots, w_{sK_i}^i\right) \begin{pmatrix} \delta_{11}^i & \cdots & \delta_{1C}^i \\ \vdots & & \vdots \\ \delta_{K_i 1}^i & \cdots & \delta_{K_i C}^i \end{pmatrix},\end{aligned} \tag{12}$$

where δ is the parameter calculated by pseudo-inverse. The output matrix of the i-th fuzzy subsystem for all training samples X is $F_i = (F_{1i}, F_{2i}, \ldots, F_{Ni})^T$. The aggregative output of n fuzzy subsystems is $F^n = \sum_{i=1}^{n} F_i$.

We express the output matrix of the i-th fuzzy subsystem of the unaggregated training sample h_s as

$$Z_{si} = (w_{s1}^i z_{s1}^i, w_{s2}^i z_{s2}^i, \ldots, w_{sK_i}^i z_{sK_i}^i). \tag{13}$$

The output matrix of the i-th fuzzy subsystem for all training samples is

$$Z_i = (Z_{1i}, Z_{2i}, \ldots Z_{Ni})^T \in R^{N \times K_i}, i = 1, 2, \ldots, n. \tag{14}$$

To maintain notational consistency, we represent the output of n fuzzy subsystems as

$$Z^n = (Z_1, Z_2, \ldots, Z_n). \tag{15}$$

We send the output Z^n of n fuzzy subsystems to the enhancement layer for further nonlinear transformation. Assuming that the enhancement layer has m groups of enhancement nodes, and L_j is the number of neurons in the j-th enhancement node, then the output of the j-th enhancement node can be expressed as

$$T_j = \xi_j(Z^n W_{xj} + \beta_{xj}), \tag{16}$$

where W_{xj} and β_{xj} are weights and bias terms connecting the output Z^n of fuzzy subsystems to the corresponding enhancement nodes.

The final output of the enhancement layer can be expressed as

$$T^m = (T_1, T_2, \ldots, T_m). \tag{17}$$

We map the defuzzification output and enhancement layer output to the output layer of FBLS, and the final output can be obtained as

$$\hat{Y} = F^n + T^m W_e, \tag{18}$$

where F^n is the defuzzification output of the TS fuzzy system. Finally, we calculate the optimal weight through the pseudo-inverse W_e.

2.4 Guided Filter Correction for Misclassified Samples

In the proposed MCAFBN, the guided filter [25] can correct misclassified samples in the initial probability map constructed from the FBLS classification results based on the grayscale guided map obtained after dimensionality reduction of the original HSI by PCA. Let $p_c(c = 1, 2, ..., C)$ denote the input image and G denote the guided image, where c is the label type. The output image q_c can be obtained by a linear transformation of G in a window ω_k, where pixel k is the center, the radius of k is r, and the size of the local window is $(2r+1)^2$. Let a_k and b_k denote the linear coefficient and bias, respectively. The output $q_{i,c}$ of the guided filter can be calculated as:

$$q_{c,i} = a_k G_i + b_k, \forall i \in \omega_k. \tag{19}$$

It can be observed from the network that $\nabla q_c = a \nabla G$, so the edges of the output q_c and the guide image G are similar. a_k and b_k can be calculated by the minimum cost function in the window ω_k:

$$E(a_k, b_k) = \sum_{i \in \omega_k} \left((a_k G_i + b_k - p_{c,i})^2 + \varepsilon a_k^2 \right), \tag{20}$$

where ε is a regularization parameter that affects how blurry the guided filter is.

Let $|\omega|$ denote the number of pixels in the local window, $\bar{p}_{c,k}$ denote the mean of p_c in the window, and μ_k and σ_k^2 denote the mean and variance of G in the window, respectively. According to the literature [25], the calculation of a_k and b_k can be expressed as follows:

$$a_k = \frac{\frac{1}{|\omega|} \sum_{i \in \omega_k} G_i p_{c,i} - \mu_k \bar{p}_{c,k}}{\sigma_k^2 + \varepsilon}, \tag{21}$$

$$b_k = \bar{p}_{c,k} - a_k \mu_k.$$

3 Experiments

In this section, we evaluate the proposed MCAFBN on three public datasets: Indian Pines (IP), Pavia University (PU), Salinas (SA). The evaluation metrics are Overall Accuracy (OA), Average Accuracy (AA) and kappa coefficient. For fair comparison, the training samples for all experiments are five labeled samples randomly selected from each category, and the testing samples are the remaining samples. To ensure the stability of the experimental results, all experimental results are the average value of ten experiments.

3.1 Ablation Experiment

As can be seen from Table 1, when using 5 training samples, the classification effect of MSCA is better than FBLS. This is because MSCA can extract key information deep between consecutive frequency bands. It can be seen from the table that introducing self-attention to capture global dependencies can improve the classification effect. M2DC+M3DC is better than M3DC and M2DC because single feature extraction will inevitably ignore important information in HSI. The table shows that the AL strategy training of the multi-scale feature extraction module is better than the traditional training method. This is mainly because AL can continue training by labeling informative samples and adding them to the training set, thereby achieving better classification results under the condition of limited labeled samples. Compared with the MSCA block, the classification accuracy OA of introducing FBLS on the three data sets increased by 2.54%, 2.91% and 1.98% respectively. The main reason is that the combination of multi-scale feature extraction module and FBLS can not only better extract local and global spatial spectral information and discernible information in few-shot HSI, but also perform fuzzy feature mapping to improve the learning ability of complex features, while Capture more nonlinear feature interactions to improve the model's learning and fitting capabilities.

As can be seen from the table, compared with MSCA+AL+FBLS, the classification accuracy of MCAFBN has been significantly improved on the three data sets. This is because the proposed MCAFBN can further correct misclassified samples guided by the grayscale image generated from the original image based on the extracted rich diversity features, thereby improving the classification performance.

Table 1. OA of five models on three datasets. Bold indicates best performance

Model	IP	PU	SA
FBLS	41.49	56.98	83.12
M2DC	52.39	64.98	82.10
M3DC	56.70	70.61	84.53
M2DC+M3DC	60.37	72.34	85.10
MSCA	67.30	74.85	86.17
MSCA+AL	70.91	78.96	88.42
MSCA+AL+FBLS	73.45	81.87	90.40
MCAFBN	**78.61**	**91.19**	**93.04**

3.2 Performance Evaluation of the Proposed MCAFBN

In this section, we compare the proposed model with eight popular models on three public HSI datasets. The eight models include: a machine learning model SVM [1], 2 DL models SSRN [5], LWCNN [9], 3 few-shot HSI classification models LMAFN [6], deep cross-domain few-shot learning (DCFSL) [26], and CTFSL [27]. In addition, we compare with a parallel structure model HyperLiteNet [10], and a broad learning model SSBLS [28]. LMAFN is a multi-layer feature fusion model, which extracts the fusion information of spatial-spectral features of each layer by considering the complementary information of different hierarchical structures. DCFSL uses a conditional adversarial domain adaptation strategy for HSI classification. SSBLS use gaussian filter and BLS to realize the extraction of spatial-spectral fusion features. CTFSL uses a convolutional transformer network to extract local-global features in HSI. For fair comparison, the training set of all models uses five randomly selected labeled samples from each class.

To evaluate the classification performance of the proposed network under the few-shot condition, we use OA, AA and kappa coefficient as evaluation criteria. The comparison results of the proposed network and eight popular methods on three datasets are shown in Tables 2, 3, and 4.

Table 2. Comparison of the MCAFBN model and other models on the IP dataset

Model	OA (%)	AA (%)	Kappa
SVM	47.45	61.77	0.41
SSBLS	65.73	65.79	0.62
SSRN	67.10	65.05	0.63
LMAFN	73.41	82.35	0.70
DCFSL	64.96	77.03	0.60
LWCNN	74.78	84.85	0.72
HyperliteNet	75.75	**86.05**	0.72
CTFSL	66.96	79.42	0.62
MCAFBN	**78.61**	81.18	**0.82**

Table 3. Comparison of the MCAFBN model and other models on the PU dataset.

Model	OA (%)	AA (%)	Kappa
SVM	64.10	68.10	0.55
SSBLS	55.18	73.13	0.42
SSRN	82.03	82.62	0.77
LMAFN	80.15	81.87	0.74
DCFSL	80.66	81,13	0.74
LWCNN	82.30	87.27	0.62
HyperliteNet	85.89	88.86	0.82
CTFSL	83.53	83.87	0.78
MCAFBN	**91.19**	**90.89**	**0.88**

These tables show that MCAFBN outperforms the traditional machine learning model SVM in all cases on three public HSI datasets. This is because SVM only utilizes the spectral features of HSI, while the proposed model can effectively extract spatial features.

Compared with four DL models, the OA of the proposed MCAFBN is improved by at least 9.83%, 8.89% and 4.25% on the three datasets respectively. This is because DL-based models require a large number of training samples to better learn the correspondence between deep spatial-spectral features and HSI labels. Therefore, they cannot fully obtain the spatial-spectral fusion features in HSI to improve classification accuracy in the case of a small number of training samples. In addition, the improvement of model accuracy is also attributed to the proposed MCAFBN combines the advantages of DL and FBLS. The MCAFBN model not only enhances the representation ability of spatial-spectral information in few-shot HSI classification, but also better extracts and expands spatial-spectral features to capture more nonlinear feature interactions.

Table 4. Comparison of the MCAFBN model and other models on the SA dataset

Model	OA(%)	AA(%)	Kappa
SVM	80.7	87.5	0.78
SSBLS	90.86	95.40	0.90
SSRN	88.95	93.67	0.87
LMAFN	85.51	92.22	0.83
DCFSL	88.79	93.25	0.87
LWCNN	88.61	93.77	0.84
HyperliteNet	90.70	93.49	0.89
CTFSL	92.07	**95.02**	0.91
MCAFBN	**93.04**	90.94	**0.92**

It can be seen from the table that compared with the three few-shot HSI classification models, the OA of the proposed model achieves better performance on the three datasets. The main reason is that the MSCA block in the proposed MCAFBN can fully extract local and global spatial-spectral features in HSI, thereby better utilizing diversity features to express HSI information. In addition, FBLS can further utilize multi-scale fusion features to learn the relationship between HSI and labels, and nonlinear feature enhancement can improve the fitting ability of the model. Therefore, the proposed model can learn more discriminative features from limited labeled samples to enhance the feature representation ability of the model, thereby further improving the classification performance of the model.

Compared with the model HyperLiteNet with parallel structure, the proposed model achieves better classification performance. The OA of MCAFBN on the three datasets increased by 2.68%, 3.62% and 2.34% respectively. This is because the proposed MCAFBN can fully extract spatial-spectral features using MSCA while using fuzzy rules to learn complex mapping relationships and using enhancement layers to capture more feature relationships. However, the AA of the proposed model is lower than HyperLiteNet on the IP and SA datasets. This is because HyperLiteNet can utilize the diverse features extracted by the parallel structure to distinguish the classification boundaries of rare classes, thereby enhancing the classification accuracy of rare classes.

The table shows that the proposed MCAFBN is consistently better than the broad model SSBLS in terms of OA, AA, and kappa coefficient in the three public datasets. This is because the gaussian filter cannot fully express the complex spatial-spectral information in HSI in the few-shot case. The proposed MCAFBN can utilize multi-scale convolution blocks and self-attention to extract multi-scale deep spatial-spectral information while automatically learning more complex feature representations. In addition, FBLS can fully simulate the complex mapping relationship between spatial-spectral features and HSI labels to improve classification performance.

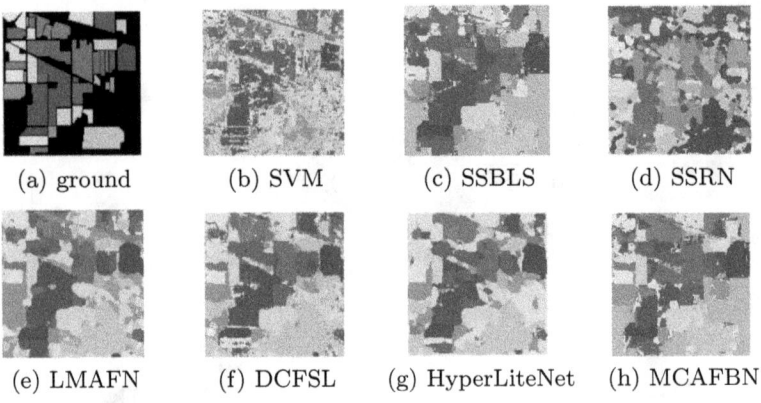

Fig. 3. Classification plots of eight models on the IP dataset

To further compare the classification performance of the above models, we compare the corresponding classification maps of the eight models on different target domains. As shown in Fig. 3, the other models classified more samples into the wrong class than the proposed MCAFBN. It can be seen that the map generated by the proposed network is the most similar to the real map. The proposed MCAFBN can better capture the spatial-spectral information of HSI with a small number of training samples, thereby achieving state-of-the-art classification performance.

4 Conclusion

In this paper, to solve the problem of insufficient spatial-spectral feature extraction in few-shot HSI classification, we propose a classification model MCAFBN that combines MSCA blocks with AL, FBLS and guided filter. We design a MSCA block utilizing M3DC block, M2DC block and self-attention to extract local and global spatial spectral features. We use AL to actively select the most valuable samples for labeling and add them to the training set to train MSCA, which can alleviate to a certain extent the problem of low classification accuracy of HSI when labeled samples are limited. Then, FBLS utilizes a small number of fuzzy rules to fully simulate the complex mapping relationship between spatial-spectral features and labels while capturing more nonlinear feature interactions to improve the expression and fitting capabilities of the model. Finally, the guided filter can further correct misclassified samples based on the guidance map generated by PCA. The proposed model can make full use of the advantages of spatial-spectral features to improve few-shot classification performance. However, the feature extraction of the model under the few-shot condition will lose information and lead to classification imbalance. We will further study the classification imbalance problem in the future.

References

1. Tarabalka, Y., Fauvel, M., Chanussot, J., Benediktsson, J.A.: "SVM-and MRF-based method for accurate classification of hyperspectral images. IEEE Geosci. Remote Sens. Lett. **7**(4), 736–740 (2010)
2. Huang, K., Li, S., Kang, X., Fang, L.: Spectral-spatial hyperspectral image classification based on KNN. Sens. Imaging **17**, 1–13 (2016)
3. Li, J., Bioucas-Dias, J.M., Plaza, A.: Spectral-spatial hyperspectral image segmentation using subspace multinomial logistic regression and Markov random fields. IEEE Trans. Geosci. Remote Sens. **50**(3), 809–823 (2011)
4. Li, Y., Zhang, H., Shen, Q.: Spectral-spatial classification of hyperspectral imagery with 3d convolutional neural network. Remote Sens. **9**(1), 67 (2017)
5. Zhong, Z., Li, J., Luo, Z., Chapman, M.: Spectral-spatial residual network for hyperspectral image classification: a 3-d deep learning framework. IEEE Trans. Geosci. Remote Sens. **56**(2), 847–858 (2017)
6. Wang, J., et al.: Nas-guided lightweight multiscale attention fusion network for hyperspectral image classification. IEEE Trans. Geosci. Remote Sens. **59**(10), 8754–8767 (2021)
7. Liu, B., Yu, X., Zhang, P., Tan, X., Yu, A., Xue, Z.: A semi-supervised convolutional neural network for hyperspectral image classification. Remote Sens. Lett. **8**(9), 839–848 (2017)
8. Bai, J., et al.: Few-shot hyperspectral image classification based on adaptive subspaces and feature transformation. IEEE Trans. Geosci. Remote Sens. **60**, 1–17 (2022)
9. Jia, S., et al.: A lightweight convolutional neural network for hyperspectral image classification. IEEE Trans. Geosci. Remote Sens. **59**(5), 4150–4163 (2020)
10. Wang, J., Huang, R., Guo, S., Li, L., Pei, Z., Liu, B.: Hyperlitenet: extremely lightweight non-deep parallel network for hyperspectral image classification. Remote Sens. **14**(4), 866 (2022)
11. Rajan S., Ghosh, J., Crawford, M.M.: An active learning approach to hyperspectral data classification. IEEE Trans. Geosci. Remote Sens. **46**(4), 1231–1242 (2008)

12. Tuia, D., Ratle, F., Pacifici, F., Kanevski, M.F., Emery, W.J.: Active learning methods for remote sensing image classification. IEEE Trans. Geosci. Remote Sens. **47**(7), 2218–2232 (2009)
13. Crawford, M.M., Tuia, D., Yang, H.L.: Active learning: any value for classification of remotely sensed data? Proc. IEEE **101**(3), 593–608 (2013)
14. Li, J., Bioucas-Dias, J.M., Plaza, A.: Semisupervised hyperspectral image segmentation using multinomial logistic regression with active learning. IEEE Trans. Geosci. Remote Sens. **48**(11), 4085–4098 (2010)
15. Sun, S., Zhong, P., Xiao, H., Wang, R.: An MRF model-based active learning framework for the spectral-spatial classification of hyperspectral imagery. IEEE J. Select. Topics Signal Process. **9**(6), 1074–1088 (2015)
16. Li, J.: Active learning for hyperspectral image classification with a stacked autoencoders based neural network. In: 7th Workshop on Hyperspectral Image and Signal Processing: Evolution in Remote Sensing (WHISPERS), vol. 2015, pp. 1–4 . IEEE (2015)
17. Liu, P., Zhang, H., Eom, K.B.: Active deep learning for classification of hyperspectral images. IEEE J. Select. Topics Appl. Earth Observ. Remote Sens. **10**(2), 712–724 (2016)
18. Haut, J.M., Paoletti, M.E., Plaza, J., Li, J., Plaza, A.: Active learning with convolutional neural networks for hyperspectral image classification using a new Bayesian approach. IEEE Trans. Geosci. Remote Sens. **56**(11), 6440–6461 (2018)
19. Feng, S., Philip Chen, C.L.: Fuzzy broad learning system: a novel neuro-fuzzy model for regression and classification. IEEE Trans. Cybernet. **50**(2), 414–424 (2018)
20. Philip Chen, C.L., Liu, Z.: Broad learning system: an effective and efficient incremental learning system without the need for deep architecture. IEEE Trans. Neural Netw. Learn. Syst. **29**(1), 10–24 (2017)
21. Philip Chen, C.L., Wan, J.Z.: A rapid learning and dynamic stepwise updating algorithm for flat neural networks and the application to time-series prediction. IEEE Trans. Syst. Man Cybernet. Part B Cybernet. **29**(1), 62–72 (1999)
22. Philip Chen, C.L.: A rapid supervised learning neural network for function interpolation and approximation. IEEE Trans. Neural Netw. **7**(5), 1220–1230 (1996)
23. Pao, Y.-H., Park, G.-H., Sobajic, D.J.: Learning and generalization characteristics of the random vector functional-link net. Neurocomputing **6**(2), 163–180 (1994)
24. Kumpati, S.N., Kannan, P., et al.: Identification and control of dynamical systems using neural networks. IEEE Trans. Meural Netw. **1**(1), 4–27 (1990)
25. He, K., Sun, J., Tang, X.: Guided image filtering. IEEE Trans. Pattern Anal. Mach. Intell. **35**(6), 1397–1409 (2012)
26. Zhong, C., Zhang, J., Sifan, W., Zhang, Y.: Cross-scene deep transfer learning with spectral feature adaptation for hyperspectral image classification. IEEE J. Select. Topics Appl. Earth Observ. Remote Sens. **13**, 2861–2873 (2020)
27. Peng, Y., Liu, Y., Bing, T., Zhang, Y.: Convolutional transformer-based few-shot learning for cross-domain hyperspectral image classification. IEEE J. Select. Topics Appl. Earth Observ. Remote Sens. **16**, 1335–1349 (2023)
28. Zhao, G., Wang, X., Kong, Y., Cheng, Y.: Spectral-spatial joint classification of hyperspectral image based on broad learning system. Remote Sens. **13**(4), 583 (2021)

Self Adaptive Threshold Pseudo-labeling and Unreliable Sample Contrastive Loss for Semi-supervised Image Classification

Xuerong Zhang[1], Li Huang[2], Jing Lv[1]([✉]), and Ming Yang[1]

[1] Nanjing Normal University, Nanjing, China
05275@njnu.edu.cn
[2] Jiangsu Open University, Nanjing, China

Abstract. Semi-supervised learning is attracting blooming attention, due to its success in combining unlabeled data. However, pseudo-labeling-based semi-supervised approaches suffer from two problems in image classification: (1) Existing methods might fail to adopt suitable thresholds since they either use a pre-defined/fixed threshold or an ad-hoc threshold adjusting scheme, resulting in inferior performance and slow convergence. (2) Discarding unlabeled data with confidence below the thresholds results in the loss of discriminating information. To solve these issues, we develop an effective method to make sufficient use of unlabeled data. Specifically, we design a self adaptive threshold pseudo-labeling strategy, which thresholds for each class can be dynamically adjusted to increase the number of reliable samples. Meanwhile, in order to effectively utilise unlabeled data with confidence below the thresholds, we propose an unreliable sample contrastive loss to mine the discriminative information in low-confidence samples by learning the similarities and differences between sample features. We evaluate our method on several classification benchmarks under partially labeled settings and demonstrate its superiority over the other approaches.

Keywords: Semi-supervised learning · Pseudo-labeling · Contrastive learning

1 Introduction

In the past several years, our computer vision community has witnessed inspiring progress, thanks to fast developments of deep learning [1]. Such a big success is closely dependent on supervised training with sufficient labeled data. However, a large amount of labeled data are usually laborious and expensive to obtain. To mitigate the demand for labeled data, Semi-supervised learning(SSL) [2,3] has been proposed as a powerful approach to leverage unlabeled data.

Consistency regularization [4–6] and pseudo labeling [7,8] are two powerful techniques in modern SSL, where SSL methods based on pseudo-labeling have achieved good performance. Briefly, the method first train the model based on the labeled data and then use the model's predictions on unlabeled data as pseudo-labels. It is obvious that predictions on unlabeled data are not reliable. If the model is iteratively trained with incorrect pseudo labels, it will suffer the confirmation bias issue [9]. To address this dilemma, Sohn et al. [3] proposed FixMatch, which simply set a fixed confidence threshold to discard potentially unreliable samples. While this strategy can make sure that only high-quality unlabeled data contribute to the model training, it also incurs a low utilization of the whole unlabeled set. Xu et al. proposed Dash [10], which proposes to gradually grow the fixed global threshold as the training progresses. Although the utilization of unlabeled data is improved, their ad-hoc threshold adjusting scheme is arbitrarily controlled by hyper-parameters. Zhang et al. [11] proposed the curriculum pseudo-labeling method to flexibly adjust the thresholds and achieve best result in several SSL benchmark testing datasets.

However, these pseudo-labeling SSL methods alleviate confirmation bias to some extent, but still have many problems and can be summarized in two key aspects: (1) The dynamic thresholding strategies, while taking into account the learning difficulties of different classes, are still mapped from predefined fixed global thresholds and are not sufficient to adjust the thresholds according to the actual learning progress of the models. (2) These methods discards low-confidence pseudo labels and does not fully utilize the unlabeled data and consumes a longer training time.

To solve the above issues, a novel method for semi-supervised image classification is proposed, we call our method as **S**elf Adaptive **T**hreshold Pseudo-labeling and **U**nreliable Sample **C**ontrastive Loss for **S**emi-supervised **I**mage **C**lassification (STUC-SSIC), which consists of self-adaptive threshold pseudo-labeling (SATPL) and unreliable sample contrastive loss (USCL). SATPL proposes that different datasets have different global thresholds, and each class has its own local threshold based on the dynamic global threshold. The number of reliable samples is gradually increased by adjusting the threshold for each class in an adaptive manner. At the same time, we believe that unlabeled data below the thresholds can provide discriminating information to the model. Unlike previous methods [3,10], which discard unlabeled data below the thresholds, we construct an unreliable sample contrastive loss (USCL) to mine discriminating information in the unreliable samples and improve the utilization of the unlabeled dataset. Experimental results show that STUC-SSIC improves the utilization of unlabeled data and improves the classification performance on semi-supervised image classification tasks on three datasets, including CIFAR-10, CIFAR-100 and STL-10.

In summary, the following are the main contributions of our paper:

- We design a self-adaptive threshold pseudo-labeling (SATPL) strategy, considering that the model performance gradually improves with the training process, the threshold of each class is adjusted in an adaptive manner to gradually increase the number of reliable samples.
- An unreliable sample contrastive loss (USCL) is proposed, which can effectively mines the discriminative information in low-confidence samples by learning the similarities and differences between sample features, enabling

the model to utilize all unlabeled samples and speeding up the convergence of the model.
- Experimental results on the CIFAR-10, CIFAR-100 and STL-10 datasets show the superiority of our method.

2 Related Work

2.1 Confidence-Based Pseudo-labeling SSL

Semi-supervised learning has been researched for decades, and the essential idea is to learn from the unlabeled data to enhance the training process. In semi-supervised learning, a confidence-based strategy has been widely used along with pseudo labeling so that the unlabeled data are used only when the predictions are sufficiently confident. Sohn et al. [3] proposed FixMatch, which simply set a fixed confidence threshold to discard potentially unreliable samples. While this strategy can make sure that only high-quality unlabeled data contribute to the model training, it also incurs a low utilization of the whole unlabeled set. Xu et al. [10] proposed Dash, which proposes to gradually grow the fixed global threshold as the training progresses. Although the utilization of unlabeled data is improved, their ad-hoc threshold adjusting scheme is arbitrarily controlled by hyper-parameters. Zhang et al. [11] proposed the curriculum pseudo-labeling method to flexibly adjust the thresholds and achieve best result in several SSL benchmark testing datasets. However, these methods do not use the full unlabeled data for model training.

2.2 Contrastive Learning

Recent contrastive learning studies have presented promising results to directly leverage the unlabeled data. Such methods are to train a representation learning model by automatically constructing similar and dissimilar instances, which essentially encourage similar feature representations between two random crops from the same image and distinct representations among different images. SimCLR [12,13] shows that image augmentation, nonlinear projection head and large batch size plays a critical role in contrastive learning. Since large batch size usually requires a lot of GPU memory, which is not very friendly to most of researchers. MoCo [14] proposed a momentum contrast mechanism that forces the query encoder to learn the representation from a slowly progressing key encoder and maintain a memory buffer to store a large number of negative samples. In Corporate relative valuation(CRV), Yang et al. [15] proposed HM2, which adopted additional triplet loss with embedding of competitors as the constraint to learn more discriminative features. Consequently, HM2 can explore company intrinsic properties to improve CRV. In Class-Incremental Learning (CIL), Yang et al. [16] proposed a semi-supervised style Class Incremental Learning without Forgetting (CILF) method, designs to regularize classiffcation with decoupled prototype based loss, which can improve the intra-class and inter-class structure signiffcantly, and acquires a compact embedding representation for novel class detection in result. In Semi-Supervised Image Captioning, Yang et al. [17] developed a novel relation consistency between augmented images and corresponding generated sentences to retain the important relational knowledge. In Course Recommendation System, Yang et al. [18] applied contrastive learning to learn effective representations of talents and courses. Especially in an open environment, Yang et al. [19] proposed to introduce a sampling mechanism to actively select valuable out-of distribution(OOD) instances, balancing pseudo-ID and pseudo-OOD instances to enhance ID classifiers and OOD detectors. Due to the superior performance of contrastive learning at directly exploiting unlabelled samples, we joint contrastive learning to use unlabeled data below the thresholds to increase the model's performance. Also in this paper, we use the idea of how to select negative samples in contrastive learning.

2.3 Self-Supervision in Semi-supervised Learning

Many recent state-of-the-art semi-supervised learning methods adopt the self-supervised representation learning methods [13,20] to jointly learn good feature representation, which are similar considerations to our method. Specifically, S4L [20] integrated two pretext-based self-supervised approaches in SSL and showed that unsupervised representation learning complements existing SSL methods. CoMatch [21] proposed graph-based contrastive learning to learn better representations. LaSSL [22] enjoys benefits from exploring wider sample relations and more label information, through injecting class-aware contrastive learning and label propagation into the standard self-training. However, methods with instance discrimination [12,14], which treats each image as its own class, can hurt semi-supervised image classification as it partially conflicts with it.

3 Methods

In this section, we will first revisit the preliminary work on semi-supervised learning. Then, we will introduce our proposed STUC-SSIC framework. After that, the algorithm and the implementation details will also be explained.

3.1 Preliminaries on Semi-Supervised Learning

For a semi-supervised image classification problem, where we train a model using M labeled samples and N unlabeled samples, where $N \gg M$. We use mini-batches of labeled instances, $\mathcal{X} = \{(x_i, y_i)\}_{i=1}^{B}$ and unlabeled instances, $\mathcal{U} = \{(u_i)\}_{i=1}^{\mu B}$, where the scalar μ denotes the ratio of unlabeled samples to labeled samples in a batch, and y is is the one-hot vector of the class label $c \in \{1, 2, ..., C\}$. The goal of semi-supervised learning is to use the dataset to train a model with parameter θ, which consists of an encoder network f and a softmax classifier g to produce a distribution over classes $p = f(g(\cdot))$ [22]. Referring to FixMatch [3], We apply weak augmentations $\omega(\cdot)$ on all images and an additional strong augmentation $\Omega(\cdot)$ only on unlabeled samples, which can enhance the model's ability to adapt to changes in the data. The supervised loss for labeled data is:

$$\mathcal{L}_s = \frac{1}{B} \sum_{i=1}^{B} H(y_i, p_\theta(y|\omega(x_i))) \tag{1}$$

where B is the batch size, $H(\cdot,\cdot)$ refers to cross-entropy loss, $p_\theta(\cdot)$ is the output probability from the model.

3.2 STUC-SSIC

In order to solve the problems of inability to fully utilize unlabeled data and low quality of pseudo-labels in deep semi-supervised image classification, we propose STUC-SSIC method, and the overall architecture is shown in Fig. 1. It mainly consists of two parts: self-adaptive threshold pseudo-labeling (SATPL) and unreliable sample contrastive loss (USCL). SATPL can generate reliable pseudo-labels, and USCL can improve the utilization of unlabeled data, and the combination of the two can improve both the classification accuracy and the convergence speed of the model.

Self Adaptive Threshold Pseudo-labeling. The pseudo-labeling-based SSL method has the following drawbacks: due to the high fixed threshold, most of the samples cannot be added to the model training, which prevents the model from identifying classes that are difficult to learn. In addition, some recent approaches [10,11] have proposed different strategies for screening samples with dynamically adjusted thresholds. Although those strategies take into account the degree of learning difficulty of different classes, are still mapped from pre-defined fixed global thresholds, which are not sufficient to adjust the thresholds according to the actual learning progress of the model. Therefore, we introduce SATPL, which global thresholds are varied according to different datasets, and local thresholds are scaled on top of global thresholds.

We propose that at the beginning of training, when the model's learning ability is weak, a lower global threshold is needed to utilize more unlabeled data thus accelerating the model's convergence. As training progresses and the model's learning ability becomes stronger, a higher global threshold is needed to filter out erroneous pseudo-labels and mitigate the confirmation bias in order to improve the quality of pseudo-labels. In addition, since each class has different learning difficulties and different confidence predictions for the samples, the local threshold for each class is dynamically adjusted during the training process to allow the learning-difficulty classes to produce more pseudo-labels, to keep the pseudo-labels' classes balanced, and to alleviate confirmation bias issues.

First define the global thresholds of the model for different datasets. Inspired by FreeMatch [23], we estimate the global confidence as the exponential moving average (EMA) of the confidence at each training time step. We initialize τ_t as $\frac{1}{C}$ where C indicates the number of classes. The global threshold τ_t is defined

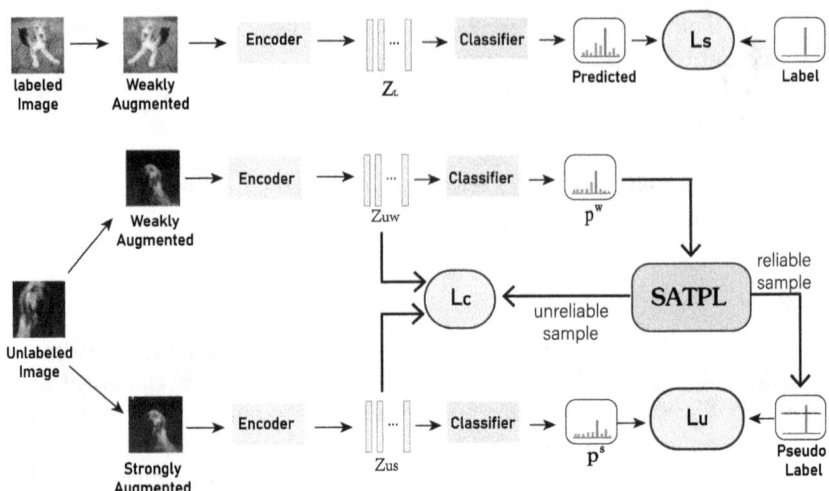

Fig. 1. Illustration of STUC-SSIC. Weak data augmentation labeled data (top) with true labels constitutes a supervised loss. For unlabeled data (bottom), self-adaptive threshold pseudo-labeling (SATPL) generate the current local threshold, pseudo-labels are generated only when the class probability of weak data augmented samples is higher than the local threshold. The prediction of strong data augmented samples with pseudo-labels constitute an unsupervised loss. Unreliable samples (samples below the thresholds) construct a new contrastive loss for training

and adjusted as:

$$\tau_t = \begin{cases} \frac{1}{C}, & t = 0 \\ \lambda \tau_{t-1} + (1-\lambda)\frac{1}{\mu B}\sum_{i=1}^{\mu B} \max(p_{\theta,t}(y|\omega(u_i))), & otherwise \end{cases} \quad (2)$$

where t denotes the t-th iteration of model training, $\lambda \in (0,1)$ is the momentum decay of EMA.

Then local thresholds for each class are obtained by scaling the global threshold using the learning effect of the current class. The learning status of the model for each class during training can be calculated as follows:

$$\phi_t(c) = \sum_{i=1}^{N} \mathbb{I}(\max(p_{\theta,t}(y|\omega(u_i))) > \tau_t)\mathbb{I}(\arg\max(p_{\theta,t}(y|\omega(u_i))) = c) \quad (3)$$

where $\phi_t(c)$ denotes the learning effect of the current class, which can be reflected by the number of samples that are predicted to fall into this class and above the global threshold at round t of training. Larger $\phi_t(c)$ indicates a better estimated learning effect. By applying the following normalization to $\phi_t(c)$ to make its range between 0 to 1, it can then be used to scale the local threshold $\sigma_t(c)$:

$$\Phi_t(c) = \frac{\phi_t(c)}{\max_c(\phi_t)} \quad (4)$$

$$\sigma_t(c) = \Phi_t(c) \cdot \tau_t \tag{5}$$

Thus, the unsupervised loss in STUC-SSIC can be expressed as:

$$\mathcal{L}_u = \frac{1}{\mu B} \sum_{i=1}^{\mu B} I(\max(q_b) \geq \sigma_t(\mathrm{argmax}(q_b))) H(\hat{q}_b, p_\theta(y|\Omega(u_i))) \tag{6}$$

where $q_b = p_\theta(y|\omega(u_i))$, $\hat{q}_b$ is the pseudo-label, and H is the cross-entropy loss function.

Unreliable Sample Contrastive Loss. The key to contrastive learning is to construct positive and negative instance sample pairs. Most existing contrastive learning methods [12,14] focus on instance-level information, which to separate different (negative) data pairs while aggregating similar (positive) data. However, such method will inevitably cause class collision problems, which hurts the quality of the learned representation. Moreover, this contrast loss of treating an instance image as a class introduced into a semi-supervised image classification algorithm would contradict the semi-supervised classification task and affect the performance of the classification.

Therefore, we construct a contrastive loss function suitable for semi-supervised image classification tasks, and the expression is as follows:

$$\mathcal{L}_c = \frac{1}{\mu B} \sum_{i=1}^{\mu B} -\xi(u_i) \log \frac{e^{\mathrm{sim}(Z_i, Z_i^+)/T}}{e^{\mathrm{sim}(Z_i, Z_i^+)} + \sum_{u_i \in N(u_b)} e^{\mathrm{sim}(Z_j, Z_j^-)/T}} \tag{7}$$

where $\xi(u_i) = I(\max(q_b) < \sigma_t(\mathrm{argmax}(q_b)))$ denotes select unreliable samples below the threshold for training. Z_i is the feature representation of sample, Z_i^+ is the feature representation of positive sample, $N(u_b)$ is the set of negative samples, obtained by randomly sampling uniformly from dissimilar negative samples, Z_j^- is the feature representation of negative sample, $\mathrm{sim}(\cdot, \cdot)$ denotes the cosine similarity function, T is the temperature hyper-parameters, these parameters are set from the design of the InfoNCE [14] loss.

Given an unlabeled image u_i in a batch of samples, weak and strong augmented views can be obtained by $\omega(u_i), \Omega(u_i)$ respectively, and calculate the corresponds embedding $Z_{uw}^i = f(\omega(u_i))$, $Z_{us}^i = f(\Omega(u_i))$. Then, we calculate the similarities between the instances of the weakly augmented images and other instance image. A softmax layer can be adopted to process the calculated similarities, which then produces a relationship distribution:

$$\gamma_w^i = \frac{e^{\mathrm{sim}(Z_{uw}^i, Z^j)/T_w}}{\sum_{k=1}^{K} e^{\mathrm{sim}(Z_{uw}^i, Z^k)/T_w}} \tag{8}$$

$$\gamma_s^i = \frac{e^{\mathrm{sim}(Z_{us}^i, Z^j)/T_s}}{\sum_{k=1}^{K} e^{\mathrm{sim}(Z_{us}^i, Z^k)/T_s}} \tag{9}$$

where T_w and T_s is the temperature parameter, which is used to control the clarity of the distribution. The smaller the temperature coefficient, the clearer the distribution, highlighting the most similar features in the distribution. In order to save parametric quantities, T_w and T_s are taken to be 0.1 in the experiments. When a sample is similar to a sample with both strong augmentations as well as weak augmentations, this sample is considered as a positive sample, which added to the set of positive samples, and the rest of the samples are regarded as negative samples. The positive sample was selected as follows:

$$\Lambda = \{Z_i | \gamma_w^i > \varepsilon_1, \gamma_s^i > \varepsilon_2\} \tag{10}$$

which ε_1 and ε_2 are thresholds for filtering similarity. In general, the strong augmentation image is too different from the original image, so the threshold is set smaller than the threshold of weak augmentation image. Then, calculate the mean of all positive samples in the set as the final positive sample:

$$Z_i^+ = \frac{1}{|\Lambda|} \sum_{Z^i \in \Lambda} Z^i \tag{11}$$

3.3 Overall Loss

In summary, the total loss at each mini-batch is:

$$\mathcal{L} = \mathcal{L}_s + \lambda_u \mathcal{L}_u + \lambda_c \mathcal{L}_c \tag{12}$$

where $\mathcal{L}_s$ is the supervised loss on labeled data, λ_u and λ_c are two weight parameter for the unsupervised loss and the unreliable sample contrastive loss respectively. We follow the setting of FixMatch [3], set λ_u to 1.0. We adjust λ_c in an exponentially ramping down manner:

$$\lambda_c = \begin{cases} \lambda_c^0, & t = 0 \\ \lambda_c^0 e^{-\frac{t}{T_t}}, & otherwise \end{cases} \tag{13}$$

which λ_c^0 is set as the maximum value of λ_c, and T_t is the total number of training iterations. The purpose of USCL is to learn a better representation of the features and is not related to the downstream task. Early in training, the contrastive loss can make a relatively large contribution to the model. As the training progresses to the later stages of training, the model should focus more on the downstream classification task, so it will be decreasing and training to the later stages focuses more on the classification task. We present the procedure of STUC-SSIC in Algorithm 1.

Algorithm 1. STUC-SSIC algorithm

Require: Batch of labeled samples $\mathcal{X} = \{(x_b, y_b)\}_{b=1}^{B}$, batch of unlabeled samples $\mathcal{U} = \{(u_b)\}_{b=1}^{\mu B}$, weak augmentation strategy $\omega(\cdot)$, strong augmentation strategy $\Omega(\cdot)$, total number of iterations T_t, the number of class C;
Ensure: Parameters of the image classification model θ.
1: Initialize global thresholds $\tau_0 = \frac{1}{C}$, local thresholds $\sigma_t(c) = \emptyset$;
2: **for** t to T_t **do**
3:     **for** $x_b \in \chi$ **do**
4:         $Z_L = f(\omega(x_b))$; //Extracting features of the labeled samples
5:         $p_\theta(y \mid \omega(x_b)) = g(f(\omega(x_b)))$; //Getting the predicted probabilities
6:     **end for**
7:     Calculate the supervised loss $\mathcal{L}_s$ via Eq. (1);
8:     **for** $c = 1$ to C **do**
9:         Calculate the learning status of each class $\phi_t(c)$ via Eq. (3);
10:         Calculate the normalization of learning status $\Phi_t(c)$ via Eq. (4);
11:         Calculate local thresholds $\sigma_t(c)$ via Eq. (5);
12:     **end for**
13:     **for** $u_b \in u$ **do**
14:         $Z_{uw} = f(\omega(u_b))$, $Z_{us} = f(\Omega(u_b))$; //Extracting features
15:         $p_\theta(y \mid \omega(u_b)) = g(f(\omega(u_b)))$, $p_\theta(y \mid \Omega(u_b)) = g(f(\Omega(u_b)))$;
16:         **if** $\max(p_\theta(y \mid \omega(u_b))) > \sigma_t(c)$ **then**
17:             $\hat{q}_b = \operatorname{argmax}(p_\theta(y \mid \omega(u_b)))$; //Getting Pseudo Labels
18:         **else**
19:             The set of positive samples and negative samples are obtained via Eq. (8), Eq. (9), Eq. (10);
20:         **end if**
21:     **end for**
22:     Update global thresholds τ_t via Eq. (2);
23:     Calculate the unsupervised loss $\mathcal{L}_u$ via Eq. (6);
24:     Positive samples in contrastive loss are obtained via Eq. (11);
25:     Calculate the contrastive loss $\mathcal{L}_c$ via Eq. (7);
26:     Calculate total loss $\mathcal{L}$ via Eq. (12);
27: **end for**

4 Experiments

We evaluated the STUC-SSIC and other semi-supervised algorithms on three public datasets. In addition, we studied STUC-SSIC's performance with varying ratios of labeled data to highlight the benefits of including unlabeled data in training. Finally, we conducted an extensive ablation experiment to validate the efficacy of each component of our method.

4.1 Datasets and Experimental Setup

Small Dataset. CIFAR-10 [24] and CIFAR-100 [24]. The CIFAR-10 dataset consists of 60000 32 ×32 colour images in 10 classes, with 6000 images per class. There are 50000 training images and 10000 test images. CIFAR-100 is just like

Table 1. Comparison of our STUC-SSIC to other relevant works. Top-1 testing accuracy (%) for CIFAR-10, CIFAR-100 and SVHN on 5 different folds. Each result is reported as the average of 5 runs. Bold indicates the best result.

Dataset	CIFAR-10			CIFAR-100			STL-10		
Label Amount	40	250	4000	400	2500	10000	40	250	1000
Mean-Teacher [28]	40.38±3.21	62.30±0.78	83.18±0.12	12.35±1.63	46.40±0.48	54.18±0.11	28.36±2.26	50.34±1.21	53.17±1.08
MixMatch [29]	50.98±4.23	83.80±0.45	86.71±0.09	25.64±1.23	50.80±0.43	61.71±0.19	37.28±3.19	62.50±0.56	64.31±0.09
ReMixMatch [30]	76.84±3.21	88.98±0.08	90.76±0.13	44.82±1.62	62.98±0.18	66.96±0.23	40.89±2.04	66.38±0.09	69.74±0.12
FixMatch [3]	85.90±3.01	89.09±0.62	91.26±0.04	40.21±2.01	61.71±0.11	66.26±0.16	42.45±3.11	68.02±0.13	71.26±0.07
FlexMatch [11]	88.26±0.06	88.95±0.46	91.38±1.01	45.52±1.22	63.11±0.19	67.01±0.12	47.23±2.62	68.82±0.19	72.63±0.22
FullMatch [31]	89.77±3.21	91.76±0.42	92.82±1.12	45.19±0.51	65.37±0.27	68.46±0.18	52.18±0.66	72.11±0.11	73.99±0.21
STUC-SSIC	**91.89±1.06**	**93.09±0.06**	**94.21±0.09**	**46.88±0.21**	65.39±0.19	68.55±0.15	**55.89±0.32**	**73.08±0.09**	**75.00±0.18**

the CIFAR-10, except it has 100 classes containing 600 images each. There are 500 training images and 100 testing images per class.

Medium Dataset. STL-10 [25]. The images in STL-10 are from ImageNet, and there are 113,000 color images of 96×96 resolution, with 5,000 labeled training samples and 8,000 labeled test samples, and 100k unlabeled color images are also provided. There are some samples in these unlabeled color images with different classes than the training set, making this dataset a challenging task.

Implementation Details. Following FixMatch [3], for CIFAR-10 and CIFAR-100, we adopt WideResNet-28-2 and WideResNet-28-8 [26] as the backbone, respectively, while using Wide ResNet-37-2 [27] for STL-10. The batch size of the labeled sample dataset B is set to 64, and the ratio of unlabeled samples to labeled samples μ is set to 7. The unsupervised loss λ_u is set to 1. The temperature coefficient in the contrastive loss term is set to 0.1. For the CIFAR-10 dataset 800k iterations of training were performed, for the CIFAR-100 dataset 300k iterations of training were performed, and for the STL-10 dataset 500k iterations of training were performed. We use an exponential moving average with a decay rate of 0.999 to test our model and repeat the same experiment for five runs with different seeds to report the mean accuracy.

4.2 Comparison Experiment Results

In Table 1, we compare the testing accuracy of our proposed method against recent SSL methods with a varying number of labeled samples. These results demonstrate that STUC-SSIC achieves the best performance on CIFAR-10 and STL10 datasets, and it produces very close results on CIFAR-100 to the best competitor.

On CIFAR-10 task with 40 labels, our method achieves the mean accuracy of 91.89%, which outperforms the FixMatch [3] method by 6%. This is mainly due to the fact that FixMatch uses a fixed threshold to filter the samples, and cannot dynamically change the threshold according to the learning state of the model. On CIFAR-100 task with 40 labels, our method achieves the mean accuracy of 46.88%, which outperforms the FullMatch [31] and FixMatch [3] method by 1% and 6%, respectively. And with a high number of labels, the accuracy of the our proposed method can be slightly higher than the FullMatch [31] method. On a complex dataset like STL-10, our method achieves good classification results, which may be attributed to the fact that the self-supervised loss component gives the model additional information, allowing the model to obtain additional self-supervised information when it lacks supervisory information in the case of very few labels thus allowing the model's performance to be improved. In addition the design of the local dynamic thresholds for each class allows the model to produce more balanced pseudo-labels, resulting in improved classification performance.

In addition, semi-supervised image classification methods all have longer training time on datasets like CIFAR-100, which has more number of classifications. We can see that our proposed method improves the accuracy of the model while reducing the training time of the model from Table 2. This is mainly due to the design of the unreliable sample contrastive loss, this contrastive loss utilizes unreliable samples with confidence below the threshold, mines the discriminative information of unreliable samples, involves all the unlabeled data in the training, and improves the utilization of unlabeled data, which accelerates the convergence speed of the model.

Table 2. Top-1 testing accuracy (%) and runtime (sec./iter.) on CIFAR-100 with 400 labels.

Method	Acc	Runtime
FixMatch [3]	40.31	**0.08**
FlexMatch [11]	45.50	0.14
STUC-SSIC	**46.89**	**0.08**

4.3 Ablation Study

Impact of Different Components. To investigate the impact of two different components in STUC-SSIC (SATPL,USCL), we test STUC-SSIC with different combinations of two components on CIFAR-10 with four labels per class. To better analyze the performance, follow LaSSL [22], we introduce quantity and quality of pseudo-labels. "Quantity" refers to the amount of high confidence pseudo-labels, calculated by the ratio of the number of high-confidence predictions to the total number of unlabeled samples. "Quality" measures how many high-confidence predictions are consistent to ground-truth labels, which can be obtained by using the real labels from CIFAR-10.

It can be seen from Table 3 that each component matters compared to the vanilla version. And that the best classification performance of the model is achieved when the two modules are used jointly. From Table 3, it can be seen that the STUC-SSIC-V2 method using the adaptive threshold pseudo-labeling strategy has a higher number and quality of pseudo-labels and a higher accuracy of the model relative to the STUC-SSIC-V1 method, which is mainly due to the way of dynamically changing thresholds in STUC-SSIC-V2, where the thresholds are low at the beginning of the training period, and more samples will produce pseudo-labels. In the late stage of training, the model's learning

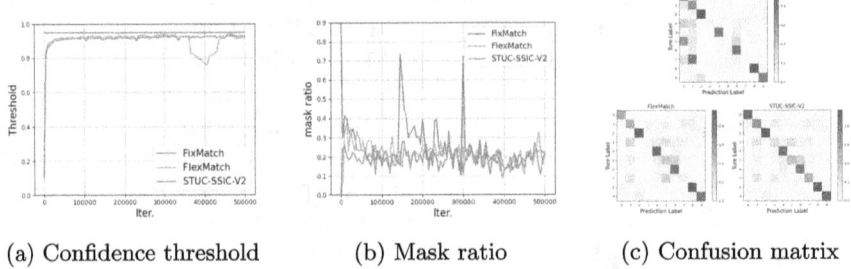

(a) Confidence threshold (b) Mask ratio (c) Confusion matrix

Fig. 2. Ablation Study of SATPL on STL-10 with 40 labels, compared to previous methods. (a) Class-average confidence threshold; (b) Mask ratio; (c) Confusion matrix, where the fading color of diagonal elements refers to the disparity of the accuracy

Table 3. Ablation study (%) of different components on CIFAR-10 with 40 labels.

Method	SATPL	USCL	Quant	Qual	Acc
FixMatch [3]	×	×	82.62	81.57	85.85
STUC-SSIC-V1	×	√	95.72	91.25	90.81
STUC-SSIC-V2	√	×	96.14	92.00	91.18
STUC-SSIC	√	√	**96.77**	**92.42**	**91.71**

ability is stronger, at which time only samples with high confidence will produce pseudo-labels, improving the quality of pseudo-labels.

Impact of the Self-adaptive Threshold Pseudo-labeling. To investigate the validity of SATPL further, we performed an ablation study on the STL-10 with 40 labeles and solely SATPL added to FixMatch. Comparison of the FixMatch method, which uses only a fixed threshold of 0.95, and the FlexMatch method, which uses only dynamic global thresholds. As shown in Fig. 2, where (a) is the class-average confidence threshold, and (b) is the ratio of the number of unlabeled samples screened out to the total number of unlabeled samples, and (c) is the confusion matrix. From Fig. 2a and Fig. 2b, it can be seen that the threshold change of the STUC-SSIC-V2 method is consistent with the previous theoretical analysis, and in the early stage of training, STUC-SSIC-V2 has a lower threshold value relative to the FixMatch and FlexMatch methods, and the rate of unlabeled samples screened out is lower, so that the utilization rate of unlabeled data increases, thus speeding up the convergence of the model. As the learning ability of the model increases, the STUC-SSIC-V2 threshold is gradually increased to a higher value, alleviating the problem of confirmation bias, improving the quality of pseudo-labels, increasing the classification accuracy of the model, and yielding better classification accuracy (as shown in Fig. 2c).

Impact of the Different Thresholding EMA Decay λ. We validate the effect of EMA decay parameter λ on CIFAR-10 with 40 labels in Table 4, it can be observed that the results of the different λ are close, which indicates that STUC-SSIC is robust to λ and it is not recommended to use too large a value as it would prevent the updating of the global and local thresholds. The value was set to 0.999 for all experiments.

Table 4. Ablation Study of different thresholding EMA decay λ on CIFAR-10 with 40 labels.

Thresholding EMA decay	Acc (%)
0.9	91.67
0.99	91.69
0.999	**91.71**
0.9999	91.75

Impact of the Different ε_1 and ε_2. The contrastive loss proposed in our method introduces two threshold parameters for constructing positive and negative samples, in order to study their effects on the classification performance of the model, we conduct ablation experiments on CIFAR-10 datasets with 40 labels, as shown in Fig. 3. In general, the strong augmentation image is too different from the original image, so the threshold ε_2 for screening the strong augmentation similarity is smaller than the ε_1 one. In order to ensure that the screened samples are similar enough, so often set a larger threshold value, in this experiment, the threshold ε_1 value is set to 0.5 as well as 0.8, and let the threshold ε_2 vary in the range of 0.1 to 0.8. As can be seen from the result, the test performance achieve the best when $\varepsilon_1=0.8$, $\varepsilon_2=0.6$.

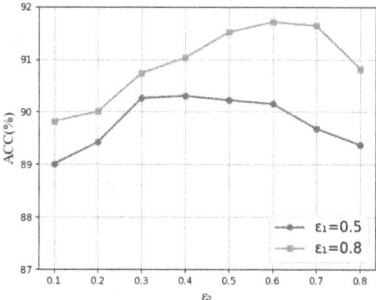

Fig. 3. Ablation study of different ε_1 and ε_2 on CIFAR-10 with 40 labels

5 Conclusion

In this paper, we have proposed a novel semi-supervised learning method STUC-SSIC, which combined with self adaptive threshold pseudo-labeling (SATPL) and unreliable sample contrastive loss (USCL), effectively improves the model's performance. SATPL adjusts in an adaptive manner to generate more reliable pseudo-labels. In addition, unlike previous approaches, we do not discard samples below the threshold, we propose USCL, which can mine the discriminative information in low-confidence samples by learning the similarities and differences between sample features, enabling the model to utilize all unlabeled samples and speeding up the convergence of the model. Experiment results show that STUC-SSIC can effectively improve pseudo-labels generations in terms of quantity and quality, resulting in better performance over other SSL approaches. Besides, in an open environment, how to utilize contrastive learning for image classification is one of our future work.

Acknowledgement. This work is supported by the National Natural Science Foundation of China (Nos. 62276138, 62076135, 61876087).

References

1. Goodfellow, I., Bengio, Y., Courville, A.: Deep Learning. MIT Press (2016)
2. Kervadec, H., Dolz, J., Granger, É., Ben Ayed, I.: Curriculum semi-supervised segmentation. In: International Conference on Medical Image Computing and Computer-Assisted Intervention, pp. 568–576 (2019)
3. Sohn, K., et al.: Fixmatch: simplifying semi-supervised learning with consistency and confidence. Adv. Neural. Inf. Process. Syst. **33**, 596–608 (2020)
4. Bachman, P., Alsharif, O., Precup, D.: Learning with pseudo-ensembles. Adv. Neural Inf. Process. Syst. 3365–3373 (2014)
5. Laine, S., Aila, T.: Temporal ensembling for semi-supervised learning. In: International Conference on Learning Representations (2017)
6. Sajjadi, M., Javanmardi, M., Tasdizen, T.: Regularization with stochastic transformations and perturbations for deep semi-supervised learning. Adv. Neural Inf. Process. Syst. 1171–1179 (2016)
7. Lee, D.H., et al.: Pseudo-label: the simple and efficient semi-supervised learning method for deep neural networks. Int. Conf. Mach. Learn. **3**, 896 (2013)
8. Xie, Q., Luong, M.T., Hovy, E., Le, Q.V.: Self-training with noisy student improves imagenet classification. In: IEEE Conference on Computer Vision and Pattern Recognition, pp. 10687–10698 (2020)
9. Arazo, E., Ortego, D., Albert, P., O'Connor, N.E., McGuinness, K.: Pseudo-labeling and confirmation bias in deep semi-supervised learning. In: International Joint Conference on Neural Networks, pp. 1–8 (2020)
10. Xu, Y., et al.: Dash: semi-supervised learning with dynamic thresholding. In: International Conference on Machine Learning, pp. 11525–11536 (2021)
11. Zhang, B., et al.: Flexmatch: boosting semi-supervised learning with curriculum pseudo labeling. Adv. Neural Inf. Process. Syst. 18408–18419 (2021)
12. Chen, T., Kornblith, S., Norouzi, M., Hinton, G.: A simple framework for contrastive learning of visual representations. In: International Conference on Machine Learning, pp. 1597–1607 (2020)
13. Chen, T., Kornblith, S., Swersky, K., Norouzi, M., Hinton, G.E.: Big self-supervised models are strong semi-supervised learners. Adv. Neural Inf. Process. Syst. 22243–22255 (2020)
14. He, K., Fan, H., Wu, Y., Xie, S., Girshick, R.: Momentum contrast for unsupervised visual representation learning. In: IEEE Conference on Computer Vision and Pattern Recognition, pp. 9729–9738 (2020)
15. Yang, Y., et al.: Corporate relative valuation using heterogeneous multi-modal graph neural network. IEEE Trans. Knowl. Data Eng. **35**(1), 211–224 (2023)
16. Yang, Y., et al.: Learning adaptive embedding considering incremental class. IEEE Trans. Knowl. Data Eng. **35**(3), 2736–2749 (2023)
17. Yang, Y., Wei, H., Zhu, H., Yu, D., Xiong, H., Yang, J.: Exploiting cross-modal prediction and relation consistency for semisupervised image captioning. IEEE Trans. Cybernet. **54**(2), 890–902 (2024)
18. Yang, Y., Zhang, C., Song, X., Dong, Z., Zhu, H., Li, W.: Contextualized knowledge graph embedding for explainable talent training course recommendation. ACM Trans. Inf. Syst. **42**(2), 1–27 (2023)

19. Yang, Y., Zhang, Y., Song, X., Xu, Y.: Not all out-of-distribution data are harmful to open-set active learning. Adv. Neural. Inf. Process. Syst. **36**, 13802–13818 (2023)
20. Zhai, X., Oliver, A., Kolesnikov, A., Beyer, L.: S4l: self-supervised semi-supervised learning. In: IEEE International Conference on Computer Vision, pp. 1476–1485 (2019)
21. Li, J., Xiong, C., Hoi, S.C.: Comatch: semi-supervised learning with contrastive graph regularization. In: IEEE International Conference on Computer Vision, pp. 9475–9484 (2021)
22. Zhao, Z., Zhou, L., Wang, L., Shi, Y., Gao, Y.: Lassl: label-guided self-training for semi-supervised learning. AAAI Conf. Artif. Intell. **36,** 9208–9216 (2022)
23. Wang, Y., et al.: Freematch: self-adaptive thresholding for semi-supervised learning. In: International Conference on Learning Representations (2023)
24. Krizhevsky, A., Hinton, G., et al.: Learning multiple layers of features from tiny images (2009)
25. Coates, A., Ng, A., Lee, H.: An analysis of single-layer networks in unsupervised feature learning. In: International Conference on Artifcial Intelligence and Statistics, pp. 215–223 (2011)
26. Zagoruyko, S., Komodakis, N.: Wide residual networks. In: British Machine Vision Conference (2016)
27. Zhou, T., Wang, S., Bilmes, J.: Time-consistent self-supervision for semi-supervised learning. In: International Conference on Machine Learning, pp. 11523–11533 (2020)
28. Tarvainen, A., Valpola, H.: Mean teachers are better role models: Weight-averaged consistency targets improve semi-supervised deep learning results. Adv. Neural Inf. Process. Syst. 1195–1204 (2017)
29. Berthelot, D., Carlini, N., Goodfellow, I., Papernot, N., Oliver, A., Raffel, C.A.: Mixmatch: a holistic approach to semi-supervised learning. Adv. Neural Inf. Process. Syst. 5050–5060 (2019)
30. Berthelot, D., et al.: Remixmatch: semi-supervised learning with distribution alignment and augmentation anchoring. arXiv preprint arXiv:1911.09785 (2019)
31. Peng, Z., Tian, S., Yu, L., Zhang, D., Wu, W., Zhou, S.: Semi-supervised medical image classification with adaptive threshold pseudo-labeling and unreliable sample contrastive loss. Biomed. Signal Process. Control **79**, 104142 (2023)

Computer Vision: Object Detection

CIA-Net: Cross-Modal Interaction and Depth Quality-Aware Network for RGB-D Salient Object Detection

Xiaomei Kuang, Aiqing Zhu, Junbin Yuan, and Qingzhen Xu[✉]

School of Computer Science, South China Normal University, Guangzhou, China
xqz1997@163.com

Abstract. Depth information has been proven beneficial in RGB-D salient object detection (SOD). However, the depth maps are usually of low quality in existing RGB-D SOD datasets. Most RGB-D SOD models lack cross-modal interaction or fail to consider the quality of depth maps during cross-modal interaction, which could lead to inaccurate encoder features when facing low-quality depth maps. In this paper, we propose a novel network called CIA-Net to measure depth map quality and effectively integrate complementary information across modalities. Through the depth quality-aware module, feature alignment of low-order information generates weights to represent the quality of the depth map. The weighted modality interaction module controls the weight of the depth map to perform interactions, which applies attention mechanisms to interact with the cross-modal features at each scale. Extensive experiments show that our proposed model significantly outperforms ten existing state-of-the-art models on four challenging benchmark datasets. Codes and results will be available after this work is accepted.

Keywords: Salient object detection · RGB-D images · Depth quality

1 Introduction

Salient object detection (SOD) aims to locate image regions that attract human visual attention. It is useful in many computer vision tasks [1] such as object segmentation, tracking, and image/video compression. Despite the significant advancements in RGB SOD methods attributed to the advent of deep learning in recent years, they still encounter problems in challenging scenarios such as similar foregrounds and backgrounds, cluttered or complex backgrounds, or low-contrast environments.

With the popularity of depth sensors/devices, RGB-D SOD has become a prominent research topic, as the additional spatial information provided by depth maps can serve as complementary cues for more robust detection [2]. Meanwhile, depth data has been widely integrated into many mobile devices [3]. Introducing depth information into SOD does address these challenging scenarios to some extent.

Depth maps are sometimes inaccurate and can contaminate the results of SOD [3]. Previous work has often integrated RGB and depth information in an indiscriminate manner, which can produce negative results when encountering inaccurate or ambiguous depth maps. Furthermore, simple strategies such as cascading and multiplication are usually not sufficient to fuse and capture the complementary information of different modalities in RGB images and depth maps, which may lead to less significant results. Therefore, there are two main problems to be solved for RGB-D SOD: (1) how to effectively integrate the complementary nature of cross-modal RGB-D data; and (2) how to prevent low-quality depth maps from adversely affecting model reliability.

To address the above problems, we propose the Cross-modal Interaction and depth quality-Aware Network for RGB-D salient object detection (CIA-Net), which simultaneously evaluates the quality of the depth map and optimises the fusion process of RGB and depth information in the weighted modality interaction (WMI) module. Instead of indiscriminately integrating multimodal information in RGB images and depth maps, we adaptively fuse the two modal data by considering depth potential perception. The Depth Quality-Aware (DQA) module is designed to generate weights that facilitate the integration of cross-modal information, thereby mitigating the potential adverse effects of unreliable depth maps.

For the DQA module, depth quality is difficult to determine based only on the depth map itself [4], because it is hard to discern whether a salient region in the depth map is noise or a target object. Since RGB-D SOD takes two paired images as input, i.e., an RGB image and a depth map, high-quality depth maps usually have some boundaries that are well-aligned with the corresponding RGB image. A similar phenomenon is discussed in [5] for reference-free depth evaluation, and we refer to this assumption as "edge matching" (EM). The alignment of low-level RGB and depth features partially reflects the quality of depth. When the depth quality is poor, avoiding the injection of noisy or misleading depth features can effectively enhance the detection accuracy of the model. Therefore, lower weights are assigned to low-quality depth features, and the depth features are enhanced when judged to be of good quality.

Considering the complementary and inconsistent nature of RGB and depth information, we design a WMI module. Cross-modality features are interacted at each scale, while the interaction information is fed back to the current layer of the respective feature extraction network to improve the respective feature learning. Therefore, we designed the WMI module to control the fusion rate of cross-modal information using the weights of the DQA module to reduce the negative impact of unreliable depth maps. In addition, in the decoding stage, we design a multi-level feature fusion mechanism to better integrate different levels of features. As shown in Fig. 5, the proposed network can handle some challenging scenarios such as background interference (similar appearance), complex scenes, and unreliable depth maps. Finally, we construct a unified end-to-end trainable framework for accurate RGB-D salient object detection. The main contributions of this paper are summarized as follows:

- We propose a new cross-modal interaction and depth quality-aware network for RGB-D salient object detection, which is robust to the unstable quality of depth maps.
- We design a depth quality-aware (DQA) module that adaptively learns weighting terms to represent the quality of the depth map through feature alignment of low-order information. Our quality module is end-to-end trainable and unsupervised.
- We design a weighted modality interaction (WMI) module for efficiently aggregating cross-modal complements of RGB and depth images and controlling the interactive weighting of depth maps through depth weights.
- Extensive experiments on four public datasets under four commonly used evaluation metrics show that the proposed CIA-Net outperforms ten existing state-of-the-art RGB-D salient object detection methods.

2 Related Work

The utilisation of RGB-D data for SOD has been extensively studied in recent years. In this section, we review salient target detection models for RGB and RGB-D images, especially deep learning-based approaches that have made impressive progress in recent years.

2.1 RGB Salient Object Detection

Due to the rapid development of deep learning, substantial progress has been made in deep learning-based salient object detection (SOD) methods for RGB images compared to traditional methods. In this direction, much attention has been paid to designing various effective strategies to fuse multiscale features generated by multilevel CNN layers [6]. A detailed description of the SOD work can be found in recent popularity surveys [1]. Despite the performance gains, RGB SOD is hampered by indistinguishable foreground and background textures, which can be largely mitigated by combining depth information (i.e., RGB-D SOD).

2.2 RGB-D Salient Object Detection

In recent years, RGB-D salient object detection has been developing rapidly. Early methods for RGB-D salient object detection focused on extracting handcrafted features [7] and then fusing RGB images and depth maps. However, due to the limitations of feature representation, most of these methods cannot explore high-level semantic information, resulting in poor performance. With the development of deep learning, various deep learning-based methods [8] have been proposed to explore the correlation between RGB images and depth maps and integrate multimodal information to generate final saliency maps with improved performance. For this task, the central idea is how to effectively fuse the information between the two modalities [9]. From the fusion point of view, existing methods can be classified into three categories: early fusion, middle fusion, and late fusion.

In early fusion, Qu et al. [10] designed a new convolutional neural network (CNN) that fuses different low-level saliency cues into hierarchical features for automatic detection of salient objects in RGB-D images, inputting RGB images and depth maps into two separate networks and combining their original features for predicting the saliency maps and subsequent networks. Some other methods [11] directly connect RGB images and depth maps, and the fused pictures are fed into a unique network branch for RGB-D saliency detection. This type of fusion ignores the differences between the different modalities, resulting in poor performance. In late fusion, some methods [12] input RGB images and depth maps into two network branches separately to learn salient features, and then the obtained saliency predictions are fused. In middle fusion, there are two types. One is to fuse the multilayer features of RGB images and depth maps and then input them into sub-networks (e.g., decoder networks) to generate the final saliency maps [13]. This approach does not take into account the complementary nature of the modal information in the encoder stage. Another is to first learn cross-modal interactions and then inject them into the feature learning network [14]. Our proposed method belongs to the latter of the middle fusion strategies.

Since the quality of depth usually affects model performance, some researchers have considered the issue of depth quality in RGB-D SOD to mitigate the effects of low-quality depth. As an early attempt, some work [15] suggested performing depth quality assessment from a global perspective and obtaining quality-inspired scores. Later, Fan et al. [3] used a triple network sharing the same structure to process the RGB, RGB-D, and depth inputs separately. Chen et al. [16] proposed to locate the most valuable depths by comparing the pseudo ground truth (GT) generated by the sub-networks with RGB-D as input, and comparing the depth region with two salient maps generated by two sub-networks of RGB/depth as input. Unlike the above existing methods with high time complexity, our depth quality assessment is more efficient and more suitable to favor lightweight models. Moreover, compared to methods [16], our quality module is end-to-end trainable and unsupervised.

3 Proposed Method

Figure 1 shows the block diagram of the proposed CIA-Net, which follows a typical encoder-decoder architecture. We divide the encoder into six layers, each with an output stride of 2, except for layer 5, which implies that the feature resolution does not change at layer 5, and thus layer 5 has the same output resolution as layer 4. For brevity, we denote the output features of the RGB branch in the encoder component as f_{Ri} (i = 1...6) and the features of the depth branch in the encoder component as f_{Di} (i = 1...6). The low-level features f_{R1} and f_{D1} are input into the DQA module to undergo feature alignment operations aimed at learning the weighting term α_i (i = 1,2,3,4). Subsequently, the learned weighting term α_i (i = 1,2,3,4) along with the features f_{Ri} (i = 1,2,3,4) and f_{Di}

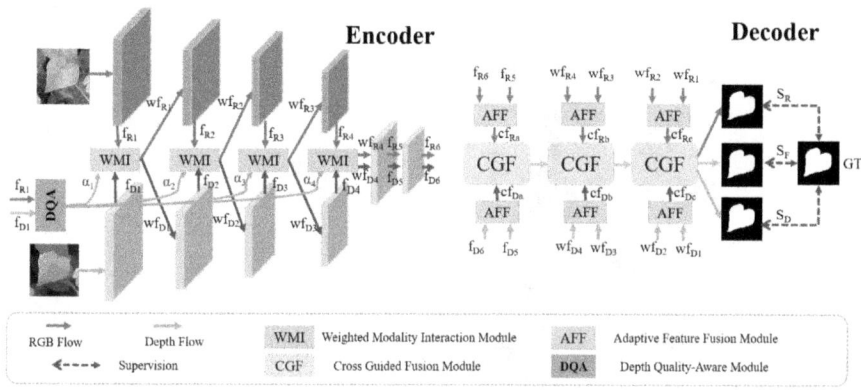

Fig. 1. The overall architecture of our proposed network, which follows the typical encoder-decoder architecture. The encoder is shown on the left, whereas the decoder is shown on the right

(i = 1,2,3,4) are fed into the WMI module to obtain the corresponding enhanced features wf_{Mi} (M ∈ {R,D}, i = 1,2,3,4), respectively. After encoding, wf_{Mi} (M ∈ {R,D}, i = 1,2,3,4) and f_{Mi} (M ∈ {R,D}, i = 5,6) are fed into the refinement decoder. As shown in Fig. 1, the decoder consists of three cross-guided fusion (CGF) modules.

3.1 Depth Quality-Aware Module

Previous studies [17] [18] commonly fuse multi-modal features from RGB and corresponding depth information without discriminating their reliability. However, as mentioned earlier, issues arise when depth maps are unreliable due to contamination. In response to this challenge, Fan et al. [3] introduced a depth depurator unit to mechanically and unsupervisedly switch between the RGB path and RGB-D path. In contrast to this approach [3], our proposed network explicitly captures the confidence response of the depth map, allowing for controlled fusion through a soft mechanism, rather than opting for the outright rejection of low-quality depth maps.

Inspired by the previously mentioned EM in Sect. 1, DQA adaptively learns the weighting term α_i (i = 1,2,3,4) from the low-level features f_{R1} and f_{D1}, since such low-level features characterize the image boundaries. To this end, we first apply 1 × 1 convolution with BatchNorm and ReLU activation to f_{R1} and f_{D1} to obtain transmitted features that are expected to capture more edge-related activation f_{Rv} and f_{Dv}. To evaluate the low-level feature alignment and inspired by the loss layer in [19], given the edge activations f_{Rv} and f_{Dv}, the alignment feature vector EM is computed as:

$$W = \frac{\mathbf{GAP}(\mathbf{BConv}_{1\times1}(f_{R1}) \otimes \mathbf{BConv}_{1\times1}(f_{D1}))}{\mathbf{GAP}(\mathbf{BConv}_{1\times1}(f_{R1}) + \mathbf{BConv}_{1\times1}(f_{D1}))}, \quad (1)$$

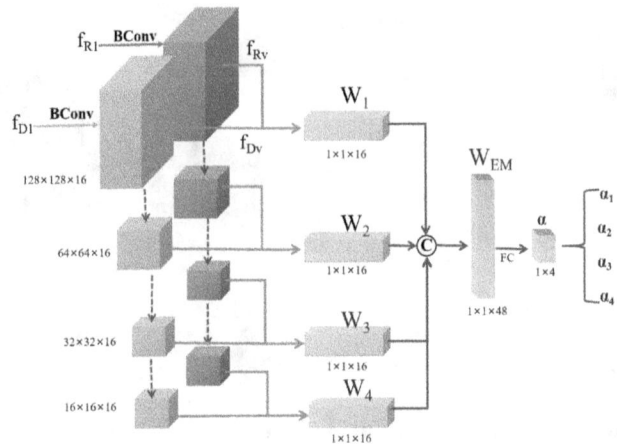

Fig. 2. Architecture of the depth quality-aware (DQA) module

where $BConv_{1\times 1}$ denotes a 1×1 convolution with BatchNorm and ReLU activation. GAP denotes a global average pooling operation that aggregates elemental information, and $\otimes$ denotes element-by-element multiplication.

In order to improve the robustness of W to slight edge offsets, W is computed at multiple scales and the results are concatenated to generate enhancement vectors. As shown in Fig. 2, this multiscale computation is performed by downsampling the initial features edge activations f_{Rv} and f_{Dv} by maximum pooling with a step size of 2, and then calculating the alignment feature vectors. Assuming that W_i (i=1,2,3,4) is an aligned feature vector computed from four scales, as shown in Fig. 2, the enhancement vector computes the W_{EM} as the connection of the four channels of W_i (i=1,2,3,4).

$$W_{EM} = [W_1, W_2, W_3, W_4], \qquad (2)$$

Next, two fully-connected hierarchies are applied to derive α_i from the W_{EM}, and hence the resulting vector α contains $\alpha_i \in (0,1)$ ($i = 1,2,3,4$) as its elements. We use different weights for different hierarchies rather than the same weights.

3.2 Weighted Modality Interaction Module

How to effectively integrate multi-modal information is a challenging problem. For that purpose, we propose a WMI module. As shown in Fig. 3, the detailed structure of the WMI module is based on the spatial attention mechanism. Given features f_{Ri} (i = 1,2,3,4) or f_{Di} (i = 1,2,3,4), which represent the RGB features and depth features of layer i, respectively, we use a 3×3 convolution with a Sigmoid activation function (with the number of output channels as 1) to generate spatial attention maps to enhance the feature representations of f_{Ri} and f_{Di}.

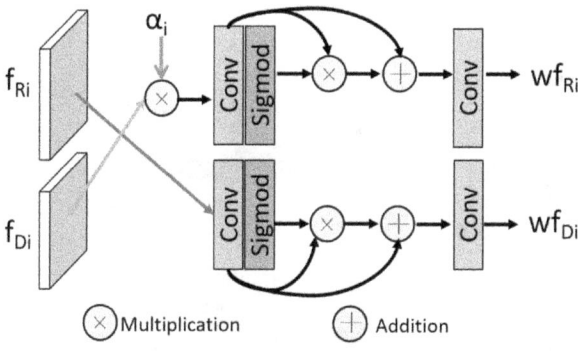

Fig. 3. Architecture of the weighted modality interaction (WMI) module

One modality is guided to focus on important regions of the other modality. The attention map from one modality is used to augment the other modality. Residual connections are then used to combine the enhanced features with their original features.

Given the complementarity and inconsistency of cross-modal RGB-D data, direct integration of cross-modal information may lead to negative results, such as contamination from unreliable depth maps. Furthermore, single-modal features usually have an impact in terms of space or channel, but also include information redundancy. To address these issues, we propose a WMI module. This module uses an attention mechanism to automatically select and enhance important features for significance detection and merges depth map weights into the WMI module to prevent the negative impact of low-quality depth maps. Given the layer i depth features f_{Di} (i=1, 2,3,4), the weights α_i (i=1, 2,3,4) output from the WMI module are used adaptively to control the weighting of depth maps in modal fusion. This can be formulated as:

$$f_{Di} - \alpha_i \times f_{Di}, \tag{3}$$

Given features f_{Ri} (i = 1, 2,3,4) or f_{Di} (i = 1, 2,3,4), which represent the RGB features and depth features of layer i, respectively, we use a 3×3 convolution with a Sigmoid activation function (with the number of output channels as 1) to generate spatial attention maps to enhance the feature representations of f_{Ri} and f_{Di}. One modality is guided to focus on important regions of the other modality. The attention map from one modality is used to augment the other modality. Residual connections are then used to combine the enhanced features with their original features. The process can be described as:

$$wf_{Ri} = f_{Ri} \otimes \sigma\big(\text{Conv}_{3\times 3}(f_{Di})\big) + f_{Ri}, \tag{4}$$

$$wf_{Di} = f_{Di} \otimes \sigma\big(\text{Conv}_{3\times 3}(f_{Ri})\big) + f_{Di}, \tag{5}$$

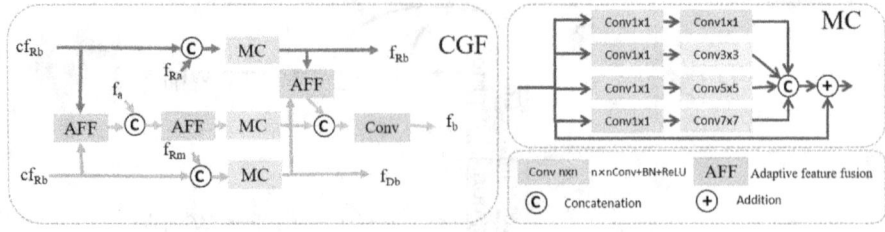

Fig. 4. Architecture of the cross guided fusion (CGF) module

where Conv$_{3\times3}$ denotes the 3 × 3 convolution, σ is the Sigmoid function, and $\otimes$ denotes element-by-element multiplication. The features wf$_{Ri}$ (i = 1, 2,3,4) and wf$_{Di}$ (i = 1,2,3,4) will be fed into the decoder and the next layer of the encoder.

3.3 Decoder

Figure 1 shows the decoder, consisting of adaptive feature fusion (AFF) module and cross guided fusion (CGF) module. We firstly fuse the neighbouring features through the AFF module, and input the fused features cf_{Ma}, cf_{Mb}, cf_{Mc} ($m \in \{R, D\}$) into each of the three CGF modules, respectively. The detailed structure of the CGF module is shown in Fig. 4, which consists of an AFF module and an efficient multi-scale convolution (MC) module. The CGF module has three branches, i.e., RGB branch, depth branch, and fusion branch.

The MC module is shown on the right side of Fig. 4. The MC module contains four parallel branches to expand the receptive domain and residual connections to preserve the original information. For all parallel branches, a CNN block consisting of 1 × 1 convolution, batch normalisation and ReLU is first applied to change the channels. Then, similar CNN blocks with different kernel sizes are used to adjust the sense field and explore the global context information. Finally, the outputs of the four parallel branches are concatenated and residuals are concatenated to produce the final enhanced cross-modal features.

The CGF module consists of two cross-modal feature fusion steps designed to fulfill distinct purposes. The first step integrates the original cross-modal features, refining the coarse features generated by the fusion branch in the preceding stage ("pre-refinement fusion"). Subsequently, the second step merges the refined features from both the RGB branch and the depth branch in the ongoing stage ("post-refinement fusion"). Ultimately, these cross-modal features are effectively fused and refined to produce the final saliency map.

3.4 Loss Function

We use the pixel position aware loss $\mathcal{L}_{ppa}$ [20] to implement three-way supervision to S_R, S_D, and S_F, which is formulated as:

$$\mathcal{L}_{total} = \sum_{m \in \{R,D,F\}} \mathcal{L}_{ppa}(S_m, G) \qquad (6)$$

where $\mathcal{L}_{total}$ is the total loss, $\mathcal{L}_{ppa}$ is the pixel position aware loss, and G denotes the ground truth.

4 Experiments

4.1 Experimental Setup

Implementation Details. We implement our network in PyTorch. If not specified, we use MobileNetV3 [21] as our backbone, and RGB and depth images are both resized to 352×352 for input. For training, in order to generalize the network on limited training samples, we apply various data augmentation techniques, i.e., random translation/cropping, horizontal flipping, color enhancement, and so on. We train CIA-Net for 150 epochs on a single 2080 Ti GPU, taking about 5 h. The initial learning rate is set as $1e-4$ for the Adam optimizer, and the batch size is 10.

Datasets and Metrics. We conduct experiments on four public datasets, including STERE [22] (1,000 samples), NJU2K [23] (1,985 samples), NLPR [24] (1,000 samples), and SIP [3] (929 samples).

We adopt four commonly used metrics in SOD task to quantitatively evaluate the performance. F-measure [22] indicates the weighted harmonic average of precision and recall by comparing the binary saliency map with ground truth. E-measure [25] leverages image-level statistics and local pixel match information to measure the difference. S-measure [26] evaluates the object-aware (S_o) and region-aware structural (S_r) similarity between the predicted saliency map and ground truth. MAE score [2] calculates the difference pixel by pixel.

4.2 Comparisons with SOTA Methods

We compared our proposed models with ten deep learning-based models, including BBSNet [27], S2MA [28], JLDCF [29], DCF [30], HAINet [31], DSA2F [32], C2DFNet [33], DCMF [34], SSL [35], and SPSN [36]. For a fair comparison, we re-tested these models with the open-source codes using their default settings. In addition, for some models without publicly available source codes, we use their reported results directly.

Quantitative Evaluation Table 1 intuitively shows the quantitative results of the proposed CIA-Net on four widely used datasets. Our methods consistently outperforms all the other SOTAs across all the datasets in terms of different metrics. Specifically, the performance gains of the metrics (F_β^{max}, E_ξ^{max}, S_α, MAE) and the state-of-the-art comparison method (SPSN [36]) on all four datasets are ($0.96\% \sim 2.01\%, 0.37\% \sim 1.08\%, 0.44\% \sim 1.15\%, 0.002 \sim 0.004$), and the performance gains of the metrics (F_β^{max}, E_ξ^{max}, S_α, MAE) achieves a gain of ($2.96\% \sim 3.76\%, 1.78\% \sim 2.17\%, 1.85\% \sim 2.90\%, 0.011 \sim 0.024$) over that of S2MA [28]. Overall, our proposed model has shown promising results in detecting RGB-D salient objects with promising performance.

Table 1. Quantitative comparisons on max F-measure, max E-measure, S-measure, and MAE of different RGB-D SOD methods trained with the combined subsets of NJU2K [23] and NLPR [24]. "↑" ("↓") means that higher (lower) is better. The best, second best, and third best results are highlighted in red, blue, and **bold**, respectively.

	Metric	BBSNet ECCV 2020	S2MA CVPR 2020	JLDCF TPAMI 2021	DCF CVPR 2021	HAINet TIP 2021	DSA2F CVPR 2021	C2DFNet TMM 2022	DCMF TIP 2022	SSL AAAI 2022	SPSN ECCV 2022	CIA-NeT Our
STERE	$F_\beta^{max}\uparrow$	.903	.882	.907	.890	.885	.900	.892	.906	**.914**	.902	.912
	$E_\xi^{max}\uparrow$	.942	.932	.949	.931	.925	.942	.927	.946	.939	.945	.952
	$S_a\uparrow$	.908	.890	.911	.907	.907	.898	.902	.910	.904	.906	.912
	MAE↓	.041	.051	.039	.037	.038	.039	.038	.043	.039	**.036**	.034
NJU2K	$F_\beta^{max}\uparrow$	.920	.889	.903	.893	.900	.907	.899	.915	**.923**	.921	.927
	$E_\xi^{max}\uparrow$	.949	.929	.944	.924	.922	.939	.919	.948	.939	.952	.956
	$S_a\uparrow$	.921	.894	.903	.918	.912	.904	.908	.913	.909	.918	.923
	MAE↓	.035	.054	.043	.038	.038	.039	.038	.043	.038	**.033**	.029
NLPR	$F_\beta^{max}\uparrow$	.918	.902	.889	.891	.897	.906	.899	.906	**.923**	.912	.932
	$E_\xi^{max}\uparrow$	.961	.953	.957	.956	.957	.952	.958	.954	.960	.960	.971
	$S_a\uparrow$	.930	.916	.931	.922	.924	.919	.928	.922	.922	**.923**	.935
	MAE↓	.023	.030	.022	.021	.024	.024	.021	.029	.025	**.023**	.019
SIP	$F_\beta^{max}\uparrow$	.883	.877	.900	.051	.875	.875	.867	-	**.909**	.900	.909
	$E_\xi^{max}\uparrow$	.922	.918	.949	.920	.919	.912	.872	-	.927	.936	.940
	$S_a\uparrow$	.879	.872	.892	.880	.880	.862	.872	-	.888	**.892**	.896
	MAE↓	.055	.057	.051	.051	.053	.057	.054	-	.046	**.043**	.040

Visual Comparisons Figure 5 shows a visual comparison of the different methods. As shown, our method achieves better results compared to these SOTA methods, which is consistent with the quantitative comparison. Rows 1–2 demonstrate the superiority of our method for unreliable depth maps. In these scenarios, existing RGB-D methods fail to detect the significant parts and are misled by low-quality depth maps. On the other hand, our network can cope with these scenarios by mining useful information through the proposed module. Additionally, rows 3–4 show challenging scenarios including low contrast (row 3), multiple objects (row 4). These results show that our network is able to accurately capture salient regions in these challenging situations. Furthermore, we chose examples with complex salient object boundaries (rows 5–6) to demonstrate that our model not only locates salient objects but also segments objects with more accurate boundary details.

4.3 Ablation Study

In order to verify the relative contributions of the different components of our model, we perform ablation studies by removing or replacing them from our full model, including the WMI and DQA modules. Model a consists of the backbone network MobileNetV3 and the remaining multiscale refinement modules; model b adds the cross-modal information exchange (CIE) module [37] to Model a; model c adds the WMI module to Model a, with the α weights set at 1, meaning that the fusion weights of RGB and depth information are the same; model d adds the DQA module and WMI module to Model a. Model e is our final model. We evaluate the five models on three benchmark datasets. The results of the quantitative experiments are shown in Table 1.

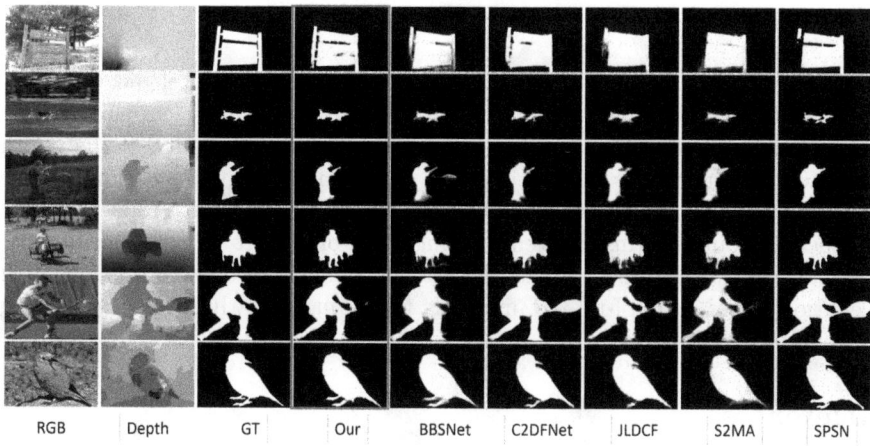

Fig. 5. Visual comparisons between our method and six state-of-the-art methods (including BBSNet [27], C2DFNet [33], JLDCF [29], S2MA [28], DCF [30], and SPSN [36]) are presented. Our results are indicated in the figures with red bounding boxes (Color figure online)

Effectiveness of Weighted Modality Interaction Module. In comparing model a with model b, we observe that model b is inferior to model a in all the evaluation metrics, which means that an inappropriate cross-modality interaction module can have a negative impact on the model, and it is crucial to select an appropriate cross-modality interaction module. Then, by comparing model a with model c, we observe that model c outperforms model a in all evaluation metrics, which implies that our model can perform better by adding the weighted modality interaction (WMI) module. The significant improvement in the evaluation metrics suggests that WMI can improve the accuracy of SOD by automatically selecting and enhancing important features for significance detection using the attention mechanism.

Effectiveness of Depth Quality-Aware Module. To verify the effectiveness of the depth DQA module architecture, we first compare the results of Model c and Model e. The performance of the model decreases after removing the DQA module. Additionally, we compare the results of Model c and Model d, and the model performance is better with the DQA module. Since negative results arise when inaccurate or ambiguous depth maps are present, the DQA module guides the aggregation of cross-modal information by generating weights through feature alignment of low-order information, preventing unreliable depth map contamination, and thus adaptively fusing the two modal data by taking into account the depth latent sensing.

5 Conclusion

In this paper, we propose a novel framework, CIA-Net, to implement RGB-D SOD. Unlike previous networks, our DQA module adaptively learns weighting terms from underlying low-level features to evaluate the quality of the depth map, while dynamically interacting with RGB and depth information via the WMI module. Across four challenging benchmark datasets, our proposed model significantly outperforms the ten existing state-of-the-art models. Specifically, our model enhances salient object detection capability in numerous challenging scenarios where state-of-the-art methods falter, particularly in cases involving low-quality depth maps.

References

1. Keren, F., Jiang, Y., Ji, G.-P., Zhou, T., Zhao, Q., Fan, D.-P.: Light field salient object detection: a review and benchmark. Comput. Visual Media **8**(4), 509–534 (2022)
2. Cong, R., Lei, J., Huazhu, F., Cheng, M.-M., Lin, W., Huang, Q.: Review of visual saliency detection with comprehensive information. IEEE Trans. Circuits Syst. Video Technol. **29**(10), 2941–2959 (2018)
3. Fan, D.-P., Lin, Z., Zhang, Z., Zhu, M., Cheng, M.-M.: Rethinking RGB-D salient object detection: models, data sets, and large-scale benchmarks. IEEE Trans. Neural Netw. Learn. Syst. **32**(5), 2075–2089 (2020)
4. Chen, Z., Cong, R., Qianqian, X., Huang, Q.: Dpanet: depth potentiality-aware gated attention network for RGB-D salient object detection. IEEE Trans. Image Process. **30**, 7012–7024 (2020)
5. Xiang, S., Yu, L., Chen, C.W.: No-reference depth assessment based on edge misalignment errors for t + d images. IEEE Trans. Image Process. **25**(3), 1479–1494 (2016)
6. Wang, X., Liu, Z., Liesaputra, V., Huang, Z.: Feature specific progressive improvement for salient object detection. Pattern Recogn. **147**, 110085 (2024)
7. Yang, K.-F., Li, H., Li, C.-Y., Li, Y.-J.: A unified framework for salient structure detection by contour-guided visual search. IEEE Trans. Image Process. **25**(8), 3475–3488 (2016)
8. Jiang, B., Zhou, Z., Wang, X., Tang, J., Luo, B.: Cmsalgan: RGB-D salient object detection with cross-view generative adversarial networks. IEEE Trans. Multimedia **23**, 1343–1353 (2020)
9. Liang, F., Duan, L., Ma, W., Qiao, Y., Cai, Z., Miao, J., Ye, Q.: Cocnn: RGB-D deep fusion for stereoscopic salient object detection. Pattern Recogn. **104**, 107329 (2020)
10. Liangqiong, Q., He, S., Zhang, J., Tian, J., Tang, Y., Yang, Q.: RGBD salient object detection via deep fusion. IEEE Trans. Image Process. **26**(5), 2274–2285 (2017)
11. Zhu, X., Li, Y., Huazhu, F., Fan, X., Shi, Y., Lei, J.: RGB-D salient object detection via cross-modal joint feature extraction and low-bound fusion loss. Neurocomputing **453**, 623–635 (2021)
12. Liu, Z., Zhang, W., Zhao, P.: A cross-modal adaptive gated fusion generative adversarial network for rgb-d salient object detection. Neurocomputing **387**, 210–220 (2020)

13. Chen, H., Li, Y., Dan, S.: Multi-modal fusion network with multi-scale multi-path and cross-modal interactions for RGB-D salient object detection. Pattern Recogn. **86**, 376–385 (2019)
14. Zongwei, W., Allibert, G., Meriaudeau, F., Ma, C., Demonceaux, C.: Hidanet: RGB-D salient object detection via hierarchical depth awareness. IEEE Trans. Image Process. **32**, 2160–2173 (2023)
15. Cong, R., Lei, J., Zhang, C., Huang, Q., Cao, X., Hou, C.: Saliency detection for stereoscopic images based on depth confidence analysis and multiple cues fusion. IEEE Signal Process. Lett. **23**(6), 819–823 (2016)
16. Chen, C., Wei, J., Peng, C., Qin, H.: Depth-quality-aware salient object detection. IEEE Trans. Image Process. **30**, 2350–2363 (2021)
17. Cong, R., et al.: Cir-net: cross-modality interaction and refinement for RGB-D salient object detection. IEEE Trans. Image Process. **31**, 6800–6815 (2022)
18. Sun, F., Ren, P., Yin, B., Wang, F., Li, H.: Catnet: a cascaded and aggregated transformer network for RGB-D salient object detection. IEEE Trans. Multimedia (2023)
19. Milletari, F., Navab N., Ahmadi, S.-A.: V-net: fully convolutional neural networks for volumetric medical image segmentation. In: 2016 Fourth International Conference on 3D Vision (3DV), pp. 565–571. IEEE (2016)
20. Wei, J., Wang, S., Huang, Q.: F^{3}net: fusion, feedback and focus for salient object detection. Proc. AAAI Conf. Artif. Intell. **34**, 12321–12328 (2020)
21. Howard, A., et al.: Searching for mobilenetv3. In: Proceedings of the IEEE/CVF International Conference on Computer Vision, pp. 1314–1324 (2019)
22. Niu, Y., Geng, Y., Li, X., Liu, F.: Leveraging stereopsis for saliency analysis. In: Proceedings of the IEEE/CVF Conference on Computer Vision and Pattern Recognition, pp. 454–461. IEEE (2012)
23. Ju, R., Ge, L., Geng, W., Ren, T., Wu, G.: Depth saliency based on anisotropic center-surround difference. In: 2014 IEEE International Conference on Image Processing (ICIP) (2014)
24. Peng, H., Li, B., Xiong, W., Hu, W., Ji, R.: RGBD Salient Object Detection: A Benchmark and Algorithms, pp. 92–109 (2014)
25. Fan, D.-P., Ji, G.-P., Qin, X., Cheng, M.-M.: Cognitive vision inspired object segmentation metric and loss function. Scientia Sinica Informationis **6**(6) (2021)
26. Fan, D.-P., Cheng, M.-M., Liu, Y., Li, T., Borji, A.: Structure-measure: a new way to evaluate foreground maps. In: Proceedings of the IEEE International Conference on Computer Vision, pp. 4548–4557 (2017)
27. Fan, D.-P., Zhai, Y., Borji, A., Yang, J., Shao, L.: BBS-Net: RGB-D salient object detection with a bifurcated backbone strategy network. In: Vedaldi, A., Bischof, H., Brox, T., Frahm, J.-M. (eds.) ECCV 2020. LNCS, vol. 12357, pp. 275–292. Springer, Cham (2020). https://doi.org/10.1007/978-3-030-58610-2_17
28. Liu, N., Zhang, N., Han, J.: Learning selective self-mutual attention for RGB-D saliency detection. In: Proceedings of the IEEE/CVF Conference on Computer Vision and Pattern Recognition, pp. 13756–13765 (2020)
29. Fu, K., Fan, D.-P., Ji, G.-P., Zhao, Q.: Jl-dcf: joint learning and densely-cooperative fusion framework for RGB-D salient object detection. In: Proceedings of the IEEE/CVF Conference on Computer Vision and Pattern Recognition, pp. 3052–3062 (2020)
30. Ji, W., et al.: Calibrated rgb-d salient object detection. In: Proceedings of the IEEE/CVF Conference on Computer Vision and Pattern Recognition, pp. 9471–9481 (2021)

31. Li, G., Liu, Z., Chen, M., Bai, Z., Lin, W., Ling, H.: Hierarchical alternate interaction network for RGB-D salient object detection. IEEE Trans. Image Process. **30**, 3528–3542 (2021)
32. Sun, P., Zhang, W., Wang, H., Li, S., Li, X.: Deep RGB-D saliency detection with depth-sensitive attention and automatic multi-modal fusion. In: Proceedings of the IEEE/CVF Conference on Computer Vision and Pattern Recognition, pp. 1407–1417 (2021)
33. Zhang, M., Yao, S., Hu, B., Piao, Y., Ji, W.: C^2 dfnet: criss-cross dynamic filter network for RGB-D salient object detection. IEEE Trans. Multimedia (2022)
34. Wang, F., Pan, J., Shoukun, X., Tang, J.: Learning discriminative cross-modality features for RGB-D saliency detection. IEEE Trans. Image Process. **31**, 1285–1297 (2022)
35. Zhao, X., Pang, Y., Zhang, L., Huchuan, L., Ruan, X.: Self-supervised pretraining for RGB-D salient object detection. Proc. AAAI Conf. Artif. Intell. **36**, 3463–3471 (2022)
36. Lee, M., Park, C., Cho, S., Lee, S.: SPSN: superpixel prototype sampling network for RGB-D salient object detection. In: Avidan, S., Brostow, G., Cissé, M., Farinella, G.M., Hassner, T. (eds.) ECCV 2022, Part XXIX, pp. 630–647. Springer, Cham (2022). https://doi.org/10.1007/978-3-031-19818-2_36
37. Bi, H., Ranwan, W., Liu, Z., Zhu, H., Zhang, C., Xiang, T.-Z.: Cross-modal hierarchical interaction network for RGB-D salient object detection. Pattern Recogn. **136**, 109194 (2023)

CPH DETR: Comprehensive Regression Loss for End-to-End Object Detection

Jihao Wu, Shufang Li, Guxia Kang, and Yuqing Yang[✉]

Beijing University of Posts and Telecommunications, Beijing 100876, China
{wujihao,yangyuqing}@bupt.edu.cn

Abstract. In the DEtection TRansformer (DETR) model, one-to-one matching is employed for categorizing positive and negative samples. However, this approach presents an issue: among multiple predictions highly overlapping with the target, only one is labeled as a positive sample, while the remainder are categorized as negative samples. Consequently, these negative samples cause misalignment of low category confidence and accurate position regression, and interfere with the classification branch judging positive samples. To address this issue, we propose a novel regression loss termed Comprehensive Regression Loss (CPH Regression Loss). It optimizes not only the positive samples but also the suboptimal samples, which are negative samples highly overlapping with the positive ones. Compared with traditional regression loss based on L1 loss and Generalized Intersection over Union loss, our loss incorporates the proximity between suboptimal samples and positive samples as new loss term, so as to devise the one-dimensional spatial constraint ComPreHensive L1 Loss (CPH L1 Loss) and the two-dimensional spatial constraint ComPreHensive Generalized Intersection over Union Loss (CPH GIoU Loss). The approach aligns regression accuracy and confidence scores by moving suboptimal samples away from positive samples, thus facilitating optimization. We refer to the model trained with CPH Regression Loss as ComPreHensive DETR (CPH DETR). Compared to the base model, our optimal model achieves a notable improvement of +3.7% AP.

Keywords: Object detection · Negative samples · Regression loss

1 Introduction

DETR (DEtection TRansformer) [3] stands out as the pioneering model to introduce Transformer [17] architecture into object detection, marking a significant milestone in computer vision. Key to its success is the adoption of the end-to-end detection paradigm, characterized by set prediction and one-to-one matching. This paradigm eliminates the reliance on traditional prior-based components such as anchors, proposals, and Non-Maximum Suppression (NMS) post-processing. Meanwhile, leveraging the efficient feature extraction and interaction capabilities inherent to Transformer, DETR can maintain or even surpass the performance of traditional detectors based on convolutional networks in many scenarios [3].

While DETR has demonstrated excellent performance, it is also associated with several drawbacks, including slow training convergence, large parameters and high computational complexity [22,29]. Subsequent research efforts have aimed to address these issues from various perspectives [4,9,11,19,20,29]. Moreover, in addition to drawbacks inherent in Transformer architecture, the performance of DETR may also be limited by implementation flaws in its paradigm.

As shown in Fig. 1, unlike the traditional detectors based on NMS post-processing, DETR adopts one-to-one matching paradigm, where each target corresponds to only one positive sample (pos). Consequently, a considerable portion of predictions is classified as negative samples (neg), including many special instances that closely approach target positions. Moreover, for these special negative samples, the classification branch must predict with a low confidence level that does not correspond to their accurate regression. Thus several problems arise along with the one-to-one paradigm, such as imbalanced positive and negative samples, sparse supervision, task misalignment and classification dilemmas [2,5,8,23,24], which collectively hinder detection performance.

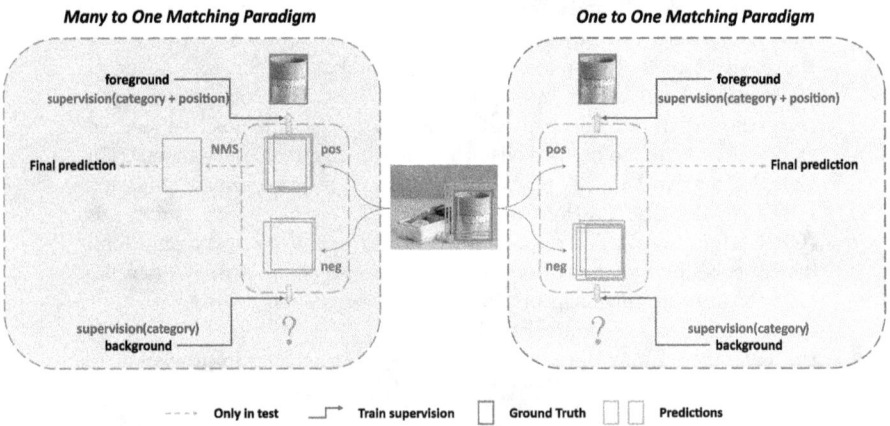

Fig. 1. Comparison of many-to-one matching paradigm and one-to-one matching paradigm

Some subsequent studies have been devoted to increasing the number of positive samples and strengthening supervisory information [2,5,7,8,23,26]. For instance, in H-DETR [7] and CO-DETR [30], auxiliary branches are devised to incorporate traditional two-stage detection structures such as ATSS [25] and Faster-RCNN [12] to assist training. Other efforts, such as DDQ-DETR [26], reintroduce the NMS layer-by-layer to filter model's predictions, aiming to mitigate matching sparsity and instability. Nevertheless, the above approaches deviate from the end-to-end paradigm and directly or indirectly shake the original one-to-one matching by incorporating additional components or branches.

Upon closer examination, the underlying issue with one-to-one matching is not its rigid matching. Rather, the crux of the problem lies in its failure to achieve true one-to-one matching. In practice, positive samples are matched with their corresponding targets not only in terms of category confidences but also in positional coordinates. However, negative samples are only aligned with the background based on category confidence, while their positional coordinates remain unmatched, as illustrated in Fig. 1. This incomplete matching results in sparse regression supervision, and extensive hard negative samples whose positions closely resemble those of positive samples. Additionally, it introduces confusion into the category optimization, as the classification branch struggles to differentiate positive samples from numerous samples with similar locations.

In this paper, our proposed ComPreHensive DETR (CPH DETR) works on the incomplete matching and sparse supervision of one-to-one matching paradigm by involving hard negatives samples in the regression optimization. Specifically, we present ComPreHensive Regression Loss (CPH Regression Loss) to optimize not only positive samples but also negative samples highly overlapping with positive samples. Building upon the study of L1 loss and Generalized Intersection over Union loss, by taking the spatial proximity of negative and positive samples as new loss component, CPH Regression Loss innovates one-dimensional constraint ComPreHensive L1 Loss (CPH L1 Loss) and two-dimensional constraint ComPreHensive Generalized Intersection over Union Loss (CPH GIoU Loss). To the best of our knowledge, this is the first work that explicitly incorporates regression loss of negative samples into DETR-based models.

2 Related Work

2.1 NMS

NMS is a crucial post-processing operation for removing redundant predictions during evaluation of traditional object detectors. Its operation process unfolds as follows: firstly, the prediction boxes are sorted in descending order based on the confidence score, and the box with the highest confidence is retained. Among the remaining boxes, those overlapping with the retained box beyond a predefined Intersection over Union (IoU) threshold are deemed redundant and thus slated for rejection. Should any boxes persist post-rejection, the aforementioned process recurs until all boxes have been either retained or rejected.

NMS enables conventional object detectors to focus on searching targets without the burden of distinguishing between positive and hard negative samples in DETR. However, NMS does have its drawbacks. Its judgment criterion, i.e., IoU threshold needs to be set empirically, and the confidence score ranking does not adequately describe the performance of the predictions [27]. Moreover, for images featuring tightly packed target positions, NMS employing a rigid judgment strategy encounters issues, with high IoU thresholds prone to false positives (FP) and low IoU thresholds susceptible to false negatives (FN) [1].

2.2 Paradigm of DETR

While DETR is not the first end-to-end object detection model, it has significantly advanced this paradigm, building upon previous works [6,14,16]. DETR achieves end-to-end paradigm through one-to-one matching and classification loss [15], setting a successful precedent that has influenced subsequent models. However, a closer examination reveals that DETR still performs traditional many-to-one detection based on anchors or proposals: multiple redundant predictions and the positive sample are simultaneously highly overlapping with the target. The difference is only that DETR relies on the confidence score rather than NMS to filter redundant predictions.

3 Why the Regression Loss of Negative Samples Can Benefit DETR

In the field of traditional detectors, some efforts have been made to address the drawbacks of NMS outlined in Sect. 2.1 by designing auxiliary losses. In [18], Repulsion Loss is designed for a stricter location constraint for positive samples. It requires positive samples to stay away from neighboring irrelevant targets and other irrelevant positive samples. This approach enhances the distinguishability between predictions, aiding NMS in identifying true negative samples without generating FN. While in [10], Pull Loss was proposed to reduce FP. Specifically, this loss pulls FP and corresponding positive samples close to each other, facilitating NMS to eliminate FP.

Motivated by these studies, to address the problem of hard negative samples in DETR as discussed in Sect. 1, we propose a potentially viable solution by directing spatial information differentiation between negative and positive samples through regression loss. Due to the abandonment of NMS in DETR, the above losses related to NMS cannot be directly applied to DETR. Therefore, there is a need to devise new regression losses.

4 Method

4.1 Overview

The previous discussion has shown that redundant hard negative samples in the absence of NMS actually increase the difficulty of distinguishing samples and optimizing the classification branch. To eliminate this situation, hard negative samples and their corresponding positive samples should be far away from each other, which implies reconsidering the positional regression of negative samples. In the following, we augment the missing regression of hard negative samples to refine the training as shown in Fig. 1 and Fig. 2.

Specifically, we define the notion of hard negative samples with a high degree of overlap with targets, called suboptimal samples (sub). And inspired by traditional regression losses of positive samples, we devise new regression losses that consider suboptimal samples.

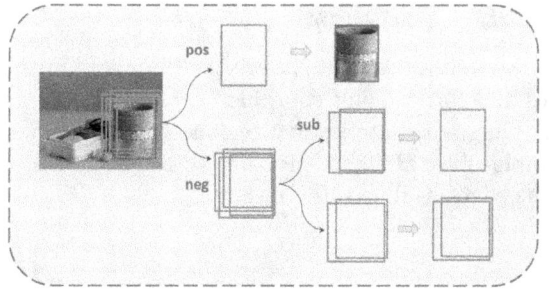

Fig. 2. Regression matching for all predictions. Pos represents positive samples and neg represents negative samples. Sub means our proposed suboptimal samples

4.2 CPH Regression Loss

Suboptimal Samples. We initially establish the concept of suboptimal samples. As implied by the term, such samples possess certain qualities but are inferior to optimal predictions. In the context of real images, we define a suboptimal sample as a negative sample whose overlap with a positive sample of the same category exceeds a specific threshold. In this paper, this level of overlap is quantified by the IoU, and a threshold of 0.8 is considered optimal.

Regression Loss Considering Suboptimal Samples

CPH L1 Loss. The bounding-box (bbox) loss based on one-dimensional Manhattan distance, also known as L1 loss, is a commonly utilized position optimization objective. Generally, the bbox is represented by either center point or corner point coordinates as shown in Fig. 3. For the matched pairs of the positive sample bbox and the ground truth bbox in center point or corner point coordinates, their Manhattan distance is directly calculated as the loss.

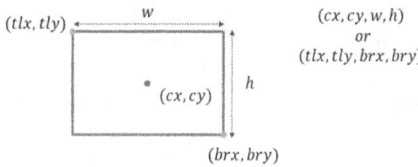

Fig. 3. The center point coordinates and corner point coordinates of a bbox

Assume we have a ground truth bbox A and a positive sample bbox B, where $A = (cx_1, cx_1, w_1, h_1)$, $B = (cx_2, cx_2, w_2, h_2)$, or $A = (tlx_1, tly_1, brx_1, bry_1)$, $B = (tlx_2, tly_2, brx_2, bry_2)$. The loss functions are as follows:

$$L1\ Loss_{center} = |cx_1 - cx_2| + |cy_1 - cy_2| + |w_1 - w_2| + |h_1 - h_2| \quad (1)$$

$$L1\ Loss_{corner} = |tlx_1 - tlx_2| + |tly_1 - tly_2| + |brx_1 - brx_2| + |bly_1 - bly_2| \quad (2)$$

where $L1\ Loss_{center}$ and $L1\ Loss_{corner}$ are the bbox loss in the form of center point coordinates and corner point coordinates, respectively.

For matching pairs with intersecting regions between ground truth bbox A and positive sample bbox B, there are three cases according to the inclusion relationship of the edges as illustrated in Fig. 4.

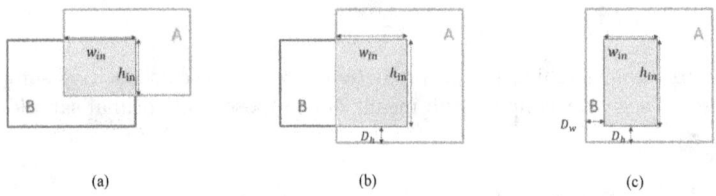

Fig. 4. Three cases of intersections of box boundaries. (a) No inclusion relationship for width or height. (b) There is an inclusion relationship for only one dimension. (c) The inclusion relationship exists for both width and height

The L1 loss of corner point coordinates in the above three cases can be converted as follows:

$$L1\ Loss_{corner} = [w_1 + w_2 - 2w_{in}] + [h_1 + h_2 - 2h_{in}] \quad (3)$$

where w_{in} and h_{in} mean respectively the width and height of the intersecting region. When expressed in terms of center point coordinates, the L1 loss in these three cases can be converted as follows:

$$L1\ Loss_{center} = [\frac{w_1 + w_2}{2} + |w_1 - w_2| - w_{in}] - D_w \\ + [\frac{h_1 + h_2}{2} + |h_1 - h_2| - h_{in}] - D_h \quad (4)$$

where D_w and D_h are factors about the deviation on the two dimensions of the center point in the inclusion case, respectively. For two fixed-size bboxes, in cases where inclusion occurs along a specific dimension, the closer the center points are within this dimension, the greater the corresponding D-value. Conversely, when no inclusion is observed in a dimension, the corresponding D-value is 0.

From the converted expressions, it can be seen that for two bboxes with fixed sizes, the L1 loss describes the proximity between them, primarily based on the width w_{in} and height h_{in} of the intersecting region. As the value of w_{in} or h_{in} increases, the loss decreases, indicating a higher degree of proximity between the two bboxes. Naturally, w_{in} and h_{in} can measure the one-dimensional separation of two intersecting bboxes. It should be noted that there are specific reasons for disregarding D_w and D_h. D_w and D_h mainly describe the distribution difference between the center and the edges, while the importance of the center and edges varies depending on the specific distribution of targets.

Since the definition of suboptimal samples suggests that there must be a high IoU between the suboptimal sample and its corresponding positive sample, it is reasonable to assume that w_{in} and h_{in} apply to represent the separation between suboptimal samples and positive samples.

With the above discussion, we present the CPH L1 Loss, which incorporates suboptimal samples. CPH L1 loss is calculated in two coordinate forms as follows:

$$CPH\ L1\ Loss_{center} = \begin{cases} L1\ Loss_{center}, & if\ bbox \in pos; \\ w_{in} + h_{in}, & if\ bbox \in sub; \\ 0, & otherwise. \end{cases} \quad (5)$$

$$CPH\ L1\ Loss_{corner} = \begin{cases} L1\ Loss_{corner}, & if\ bbox \in pos; \\ 2w_{in} + 2h_{in}, & if\ bbox \in sub; \\ 0, & otherwise. \end{cases} \quad (6)$$

Note that in the equation, when bbox is pos, the loss is calculated between the positive sample and the corresponding ground truth. When bbox is sub, the loss is calculated between the suboptimal sample and the corresponding positive sample. When bbox is neg other than the suboptimal sample, its similarity with positive samples is low, which does not bring about the interference, and thus its loss is not taken into account.

CPH GIoU Loss Another important metric of position optimization is the IoU loss, which describes the proximity between bboxes in a two-dimensional space, and is commonly implemented in the form of IoU or its variant, Generalized IoU (GIoU) [13,21,28]. Details of the IoU and GIoU are present in Algorithm 1 and Fig. 5.

Algorithm 1: Generalized Intersection over Union

Input: Two arbitrary convex shapes: $A,\ B \subseteq S \in R^2$
Output: $GIoU$

1 For A and B, find the smallest enclosing convex object C, where $C \subseteq S \in R^2$
2 $IoU = \frac{|A \cap B|}{|A \cup B|}$
3 $GIoU = IoU - \frac{|C \backslash (A \cap B)|}{|C|}$

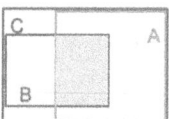

Fig. 5. Illustration of the IoU and GIoU

GIoU extends the IoU concept by allowing spatial relationship to be optimized in the case of non-overlapping bounding boxes (IoU = 0). GIoU spans from -1 to

1. A value of 1 suggests complete overlap between the two bboxes, where the IoU term in the equation equals 1 and the additional term is 0. Conversely, a value of -1 implies no intersecting regions between the bboxes, and they are infinitely far apart, with the IoU term being 0 and the additional term being 1.

When optimizing positive samples, GIoU is transformed into 1-GIoU as loss. The larger the GIoU, the smaller the loss. Similar to the discussion of CPH L1 Loss, the GIoU between the suboptimal sample and its corresponding positive sample can serve as the two-dimensional regression metric for the suboptimal sample. Therefore, CPH GIoU Loss is proposed as in Eq. 7.

$$CPH\ GIoU\ Loss = \begin{cases} 1 - GIoU, & if\ bbox \in pos; \\ 1 + GIoU, & if\ bbox \in sub; \\ 0, & otherwise. \end{cases} \quad (7)$$

4.3 Additional Improvements and Variants for CPH DETR

SideGIoU. During regression optimization, the interplay between the scales of width and height within the loss function impacts each other's optimization trajectory, potentially resulting in suboptimal outcomes. To mitigate this effect, the width-height decoupled SideGIoU is designed in Algorithm 2.

Algorithm 2: Side Generalized Intersection over Union

Input: Two arbitrary bboxes: $A, B \subseteq S \in R^2$
Output: $SideGIoU$
1 For A and B, find the smallest enclosing bbox object C, where $C \subseteq S \in R^2$
2 $SideIoU = \frac{|z_A \cap z_B|}{|z_A \cup z_B|}$, where z stands for w or h of bbox
3 $SideGIoU = SideIoU - \frac{|z_C \setminus (z_A \cap z_B)|}{|z_C|}$

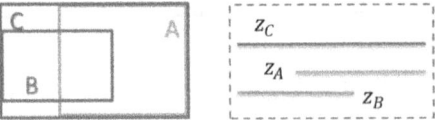

Fig. 6. Illustration of the SideGIoU

Following the same principle for CPH GIoU Loss in Sect. 4.2, the SideGIoU is further transformed into the ComPreHensive SideGIoU Loss (CPH SideGIoU Loss) that takes into account the case of negative sample regression. The formulation of CPH SideGIoU Loss is as follows:

$$CPH\ SideGIoU\ Loss = \begin{cases} 1 - SideGIoU, & if\ bbox \in pos; \\ 1 + SideGIoU, & if\ bbox \in sub; \\ 0, & otherwise. \end{cases} \quad (8)$$

Dynamic Anchor Boxes and Dynamic Label Scores. In DAB Deformable DETR [9], to enhance the content-plus-location query composition, the learnable positional queries are replaced with dynamic positional queries. Motivated by this study, we further devise category query which carries prior knowledge of category. In our method named Dynamic Anchor Boxes and Dynamic Label Scores (DAB&DLS), except for dynamic positional query, dynamic category query obtained by transforming the predicted scores of each layer will be incorporated into the query composition. This approach makes position and category information available for all parts of the query in the decoder (Fig. 6).

We present the frameworks of Deformable DETR, DAB Deformable DETR, and our proposed DAB&DLS Deformable DETR in Fig. 7.

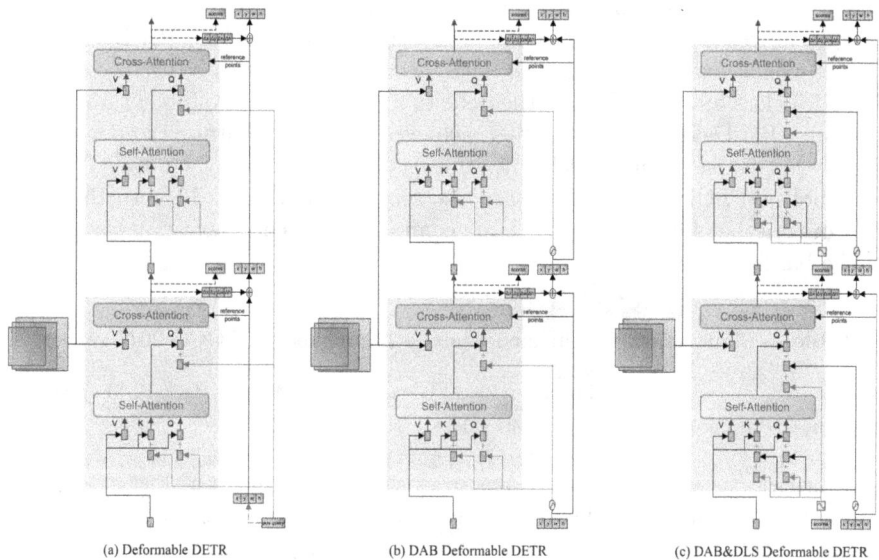

Fig. 7. Frameworks of Deformable DETR, DAB Deformable DETR, and our proposed DAB&DLS Deformable DETR

5 Experiments

5.1 Setup

Dataset. We conduct the experiments on the COCO object detection dataset. All models are trained on the train set, and evaluated on the val set.

Implementation Details We use a layer-by-layer bbox refined Deformable DETR consisting of 6 encoder layers and 6 decoder layers as the baseline model.

Unless otherwise stated, all hyperparameters follow the original configuration of the baseline model. For example, the number of object query is set to 300. We also use Focal Loss with loss weight of 2 for classification, L1 loss with loss weight of 5 and GIoU loss with loss weight of 2 for box regression in Hungarian matching. Our models are trained and evaluated on 2 NVIDIA A6000 GPUs.

We mainly test the effectiveness of the CPH Regression Loss on the baseline model by CPH-Deformable DETR. Moreover, additional improvements are obtained by introducing SideGIoU and DAB&DLS.

5.2 Main Results

As shown in Table 1, we compared our proposed CPH-Deformable DETR with several typical models, including Faster R-CNN [12] and DETR-like models [3, 9,19]. The results show that, compared with other models, CPH-Deformable DETR yields better performance with 12 training epochs. With the help of SideGIoU loss and DAB&DLS, the detection accuracy can be further improved.

Our CPH-Deformable DETR++ achieves 41.9% AP within 12 epochs with the ResNet-50 backbone, which outperforms baseline model by +3.7% AP. Moreover, both GFLOPS and Params are also reported in Table 1. It is worth noting that our methods do not impose large computational complexity or parameters to the baseline model.

Table 1. Main results for our models and other models on COCO 2017 val set

Model	Epochs	AP	AP_{50}	AP_{75}	AP_S	AP_M	AP_L	GFLOPs	Params
Faster R-CNN-FPN-R50	12e	37.9	58.8	41.1	22.4	41.1	49.1	180	40M
DETR-R50	12e	15.5	29.4	14.5	4.3	15.1	26.7	86	41M
DAB-DETR-DC5-R50	12e	38.0	60.3	39.8	19.2	40.9	55.4	216	44M
Anchor-DETR-DC5-R50	12e	38.2	58.6	40.6	20.3	41.9	53.1	-	37M
Deformable DETR-Refine-R50 (Baseline)	12e	38.2	57.3	40.9	22.1	41.5	52.3	195.5	40.61M
CPH-Deformable DETR-R50	12e	39.8	59.5	42.8	22.0	42.8	54.9	195.5	40.61M
+SideGIoU	12e	40.2	59.5	43.1	22.3	43.1	55.2	195.5	40.61M
++DAB&DLS	12e	41.9	60.1	45.0	24.3	45.0	57.3	196.13	40.91M

To provide a more intuitive understanding of our model, we visualize the improvement of CPH Regression Loss in Fig. 8. The left side of each subgraph (with orange background) represents the predictions of the baseline model without CPH Regression Loss, and the right side (with green background) represents the detection results of our model with CPH Regression Loss. We visualize True Positives (TPs) in the upper section of each color block, along with their respective confidence scores. Moreover, suboptimal samples are represented in the lower portion of each color block. For the sake of clarity, we omit the display of confidence scores for suboptimal samples, but it can be inferred that their scores fall below the scores for their corresponding TPs. The figure shows that CPH Regression Loss effectively reduces suboptimal samples and increases confidence scores of TPs and FNs in baseline model.

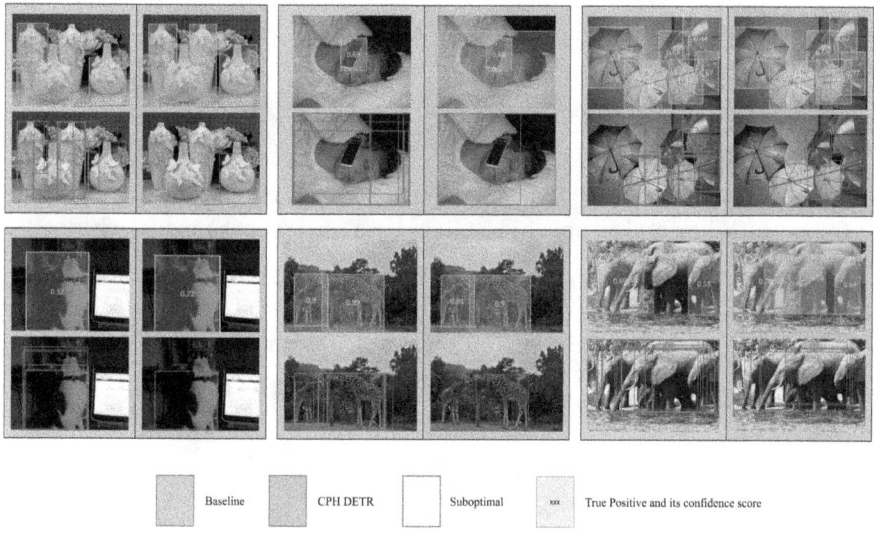

Fig. 8. Visualization of the effect of CPH Regression Loss on suppressing suboptimal samples

5.3 Ablation

In order to assess the contribution of each proposed component, we conduct three ablation studies and the results are reported in Table 2, Table 3 and Table 4.

CPH Loss. We analyze the influence of different IoU thresholds used to filtering suboptimal samples for CPH Regression Loss, as shown in Table 2. Referring to the distinct criterion in [26], we evaluate the accuracy performances of the model trained with IoU thresholds of 0.7, 0.8, and 0.9, respectively. Keeping the main configuration unchanged, the model extend training to 50 epochs, which is more indicative of the method's ability to continuously improve.

In Table 2, the three sets of thresholds lead to slight performance fluctuations. However, the performance of all groups consistently surpasses the baseline performance. The results show that CPH Regression Loss have good robustness with different IoU thresholds.

SideGIoU. To demonstrate the effect of SideGIoU Loss, based on the baseline model, we use SideGIoU and GIoU as regression loss individually and compare

Table 2. Performances of CPH-DETR when CPH Loss adopts different IoU thresholds

Model	Epochs	Thresholds	AP	AP_{50}	AP_{75}	AP_S	AP_M	AP_L
Baseline	50e	-	44.2	63.4	47.4	26.2	47.3	61.0
CPH-Deformable DETR		0.7	44.9	64.4	48.0	27.1	48.0	61.0
		0.8	45.3	64.7	49.0	27.8	48.4	60.9
		0.9	45.0	64.2	48.7	26.9	48.5	60.9

them on 1x and 2x training settings. As presented in Table 3, the results indicate that the width-height decoupled SideGIoU Loss can train the model with better performance.

Table 3. Comparison of different metrics in matching cost and loss function

Epochs	AP	
	GIoU	SideGIoU
1x(12e)	38.2	38.5
2x(24e)	42.6	43.1

DAB&DLS. Table 4 shows the effectiveness of DAB&DLS. Following dynamic anchor boxes proposed by DAB-DETR, DLS is able to further improve the model performance. While DAB&DLS performs weakly on the AP50 metric, it notably improves on the AP75, which is a more stringent measure for IoU criterion. This suggests that DAB&DLS achieves better regression for predictions and aligns predictions' confidence scores more relevant to regression positions.

Table 4. Ablation results for DAB&DLS

Model	Epochs	AP	AP_{50}	AP_{75}	AP_S	AP_M	AP_L
Baseline	12e	38.2	57.3	40.9	22.1	41.5	52.3
DAB-Deformable DETR	12e	40.4	58.8	43.2	22.3	43.4	55.8
DAB&DLS-Deformable DETR	12e	40.9	58.9	43.9	23.3	43.4	57.0

6 Conclusion

In this paper, we thoroughly analyze the current flaws of the DETR-based models and their underlying reasons. Building on these thoughts, we pioneered the CPH Regression Loss to significantly improve the model's performance. Its core is to guide negative samples away from positive samples, thereby easing the difficulty of selecting positive samples for the classification branch, while also promoting alignment between regression accuracy and category confidence. Furthermore, the SideGIoU Loss is introduced to tackle the width-height coupling issue in optimization and the DAB&DLS is proposed to enhance model's prior knowledge. A series of experiment results demonstrate that our methods are effective without incurring excessive costs. Importantly, these methods are generalizable and easily extended to other DETR-based models. We anticipate more experiments to advance our work in the future.

Acknowledgements. This work was supported by the National High Level Hospital Clinical Research Funding (2022-PUMCH-B-066, 2022-PUMCH-C-017) and the National Natural Science Foundation of China (62203060).

References

1. Bodla, N., Singh, B., Chellappa, R., Davis, L.S.: Soft-nms–improving object detection with one line of code. In: Proceedings of the IEEE International Conference on Computer Vision, pp. 5561–5569 (2017)
2. Cai, Z., Liu, S., Wang, G., Ge, Z., Zhang, X., Huang, D.: Align-DETR: Improving DETR with simple iou-aware bce loss. arXiv preprint arXiv:2304.07527 (2023)
3. Carion, N., Massa, F., Synnaeve, G., Usunier, N., Kirillov, A., Zagoruyko, S.: End-to-end object detection with transformers. In: Vedaldi, A., Bischof, H., Brox, T., Frahm, J.-M. (eds.) Computer Vision – ECCV 2020: 16th European Conference, Glasgow, UK, August 23–28, 2020, Proceedings, Part I, pp. 213–229. Springer International Publishing, Cham (2020). https://doi.org/10.1007/978-3-030-58452-8_13
4. Chen, P., et al.: Efficient decoder-free object detection with transformers. In: Avidan, S., Brostow, G., Cissé, M., Farinella, G.M., Hassner, T. (eds.) Computer Vision – ECCV 2022: 17th European Conference, Tel Aviv, Israel, October 23–27, 2022, Proceedings, Part X, pp. 70–86. Springer Nature Switzerland, Cham (2022). https://doi.org/10.1007/978-3-031-20080-9_5
5. Chen, Q., et al.: Group DETR: fast DETR training with group-wise one-to-many assignment. In: Proceedings of the IEEE/CVF International Conference on Computer Vision, pp. 6633–6642 (2023)
6. Hu, H., Gu, J., Zhang, Z., Dai, J., Wei, Y.: Relation networks for object detection. In: Proceedings of the IEEE Conference on Computer Vision and Pattern Recognition, pp. 3588–3597 (2018)
7. Jia, D., et al.: DETRs with hybrid matching. In: Proceedings of the IEEE/CVF Conference on Computer Vision and Pattern Recognition, pp. 19702–19712 (2023)
8. Li, F., Zhang, H., Liu, S., Guo, J., Ni, L.M., Zhang, L.: Dn-DETR: accelerate DETR training by introducing query denoising. In: Proceedings of the IEEE/CVF Conference on Computer Vision and Pattern Recognition, pp. 13619–13627 (2022)
9. Liu, S., et al.: Dab-DETR: dynamic anchor boxes are better queries for DETR. arXiv preprint arXiv:2201.12329 (2022)
10. Luo, Z., Fang, Z., Zheng, S., Wang, Y., Fu, Y.: NMS-loss: learning with non-maximum suppression for crowded pedestrian detection. In: Proceedings of the 2021 International Conference on Multimedia Retrieval, pp. 481–485 (2021)

11. Pu, Y., et al.: Rank-DETR for high quality object detection. In: Advances in Neural Information Processing Systems, vol. 36 (2024)
12. Ren, S., He, K., Girshick, R., Sun, J.: Faster r-cnn: towards real-time object detection with region proposal networks. In: Advances in Neural Information Processing Systems, vol. 28 (2015)
13. o Rezatofighi, H., Tsoi, N., Gwak, J., Sadeghian, A., Reid, I., Savarese, S.: Generalized intersection over union: a metric and a loss for bounding box regression. In: Proceedings of the IEEE/CVF Conference on Computer Vision and Pattern Recognition, pp. 658–666 (2019)
14. Stewart, R., Andriluka, M., Ng, A.Y.: End-to-end people detection in crowded scenes. In: Proceedings of the IEEE Conference on Computer Vision and Pattern Recognition, pp. 2325–2333 (2016)
15. Sun, P., et al.: What makes for end-to-end object detection? In: International Conference on Machine Learning, pp. 9934–9944. PMLR (2021)
16. Sun, P., et al.: Sparse r-cnn: end-to-end object detection with learnable proposals. In: Proceedings of the IEEE/CVF Conference on Computer Vision and Pattern Recognition, pp. 14454–14463 (2021)
17. Vaswani, A., et al.: Attention is all you need. In: Advances in Neural Information Processing Systems, vol. 30 (2017)
18. Wang, X., Xiao, T., Jiang, Y., Shao, S., Sun, J., Shen, C.: Repulsion loss: detecting pedestrians in a crowd. In: Proceedings of the IEEE Conference on Computer Vision and Pattern Recognition, pp. 7774–7783 (2018)
19. Wang, Y., Zhang, X., Yang, T., Sun, J.: Anchor DETR: query design for transformer-based detector. In: Proceedings of the AAAI Conference on Artificial Intelligence, vol. 36, pp. 2567–2575 (2022)
20. Yao, Z., Ai, J., Li, B., Zhang, C.: Efficient DETR: improving end-to-end object detector with dense prior. arXiv preprint arXiv:2104.01318 (2021)
21. Yu, J., Jiang, Y., Wang, Z., Cao, Z., Huang, T.: Unitbox: an advanced object detection network. In: Proceedings of the 24th ACM International Conference on Multimedia, pp. 516–520 (2016)
22. Zhang, G., Luo, Z., Yu, Y., Cui, K., Lu, S.: Accelerating DETR convergence via semantic-aligned matching. In: Proceedings of the IEEE/CVF Conference on Computer Vision and Pattern Recognition, pp. 949–958 (2022)
23. Zhang, H., et al.: Dino: DETR with improved denoising anchor boxes for end-to-end object detection. arXiv preprint arXiv:2203.03605 (2022)
24. Zhang, M., Song, G., Liu, Y., Li, H.: Decoupled DETR: spatially disentangling localization and classification for improved end-to-end object detection. In: Proceedings of the IEEE/CVF International Conference on Computer Vision, pp. 6601–6610 (2023)
25. Zhang, S., Chi, C., Yao, Y., Lei, Z., Li, S.Z.: Bridging the gap between anchor-based and anchor-free detection via adaptive training sample selection. In: Proceedings of the IEEE/CVF Conference on Computer Vision and Pattern Recognition, pp. 9759–9768 (2020a
26. Zhang, S., et al.: Dense distinct query for end-to-end object detection. In: Proceedings of the IEEE/CVF Conference on Computer Vision and Pattern Recognition, pp. 7329–7338 (2023)
27. Zhao, H., Wang, J., Dai, D., Lin, S., Chen, Z.: D-NMS: a dynamic NMS network for general object detection. Neurocomputing **512**, 225–234 (2022)
28. Zheng, Z., Wang, P., Liu, W., Li, J., Ye, R., Ren, D.: Distance-iou loss: faster and better learning for bounding box regression. In: Proceedings of the AAAI Conference on Artificial Intelligence. vol. 34, pp. 12993–13000 (2020)

29. Zhu, X., Su, W., Lu, L., Li, B., Wang, X., Dai, J.: Deformable DETR: Deformable transformers for end-to-end object detection. arXiv preprint arXiv:2010.04159 (2020)
30. Zong, Z., Song, G., Liu, Y.: DETRs with collaborative hybrid assignments training. In: Proceedings of the IEEE/CVF International Conference on Computer Vision, pp. 6748–6758 (2023)

DecoratingFusion: A LiDAR-Camera Fusion Network with the Combination of Point-Level and Feature-Level Fusion

Zixuan Yin[1], Han Sun[1(✉)], Ningzhong Liu[1], Huiyu Zhou[2], and Jiaquan Shen[3]

[1] Nanjing University of Aeronautics and Astronautics, Nanjing, China
sunhan@nuaa.edu.cn
[2] University of Leicester, Leicester, UK
[3] Luoyang Normal University, Luoyang, China

Abstract. Lidars and cameras play essential roles in autonomous driving, offering complementary information for 3D detection. The state-of-the-art fusion methods integrate them at the feature level, but they mostly rely on the learned soft association between point clouds and images, which lacks interpretability and neglects the hard association between them. In this paper, we combine feature-level fusion with point-level fusion, using hard association established by the calibration matrices to guide the generation of object queries. Specifically, in the early fusion stage, we use the 2D CNN features of images to decorate the point cloud data, and employ two independent sparse convolutions to extract the decorated point cloud features. In the mid-level fusion stage, we initialize the queries with a center heatmap and embed the predicted class labels as auxiliary information into the queries, making the initial positions closer to the actual centers of the targets. Extensive experiments conducted on two popular datasets, i.e. KITTI, Waymo, demonstrate the superiority of DecoratingFusion.

Keywords: Lidar-Camera Fusion · 3D Object Detection · Feature Fusion · Autonomous Driving

1 Introduction

In recent years, lidar-camera fusion methods have been increasingly applied in 3D object detection for autonomous driving scenarios [16]. Point cloud data provides spatial geometric information, describing object shape, position, and size, while image data provides color, texture, and visual features. However, due to significant domain gaps between the two modalities, feature alignment has become a key challenge.

After undergoing the development of late-fusion at the result level and early-fusion at the point level, the current state-of-the-art fusion method is mid-level feature fusion [19]. This kind of method maximizes the complementarity between the two types of data but is also the most challenging to implement. Due to the high abstraction level of the features, the key challenge lies in how to match the data from the two modalities in the feature space effectively.

Existing feature fusion methods mostly rely on learning-based approaches to obtain soft correlations between point clouds and images. However, these soft correlations lack interpretability, making it difficult to ensure their reliability. In contrast, the hard correlations commonly used in point-level fusion methods (such as calibration matrices between LiDAR and cameras, which are usually provided by data collectors) are intuitive, ensuring the alignment between point clouds and images. However, hard correlations are rarely applied in feature fusion methods because they become feature-to-feature mappings in the feature space, rendering the use of hard correlations impractical.

To introduce hard correlations into feature fusion methods, we combine early fusion and mid-level fusion and propose an efficient multi-modal fusion strategy called DecoratingFusion. Specifically, we utilize a 2D CNN to extract image features and employ them to decorate the original point cloud data. These convolutional layers, along with other network components, are trained in an end-to-end manner. Considering the domain gaps between the two modalities, two independent sparse convolutions are used to extract the decorated point cloud features, which are then concatenated. These concatenated features are utilized to generate object queries and fuse point cloud and image features through cross-attention mechanisms. Additionally, to optimize the initialization process of object queries, we first predict a center heatmap using the decorated point cloud features and select the initialization position of the query from the heatmap. Finally, the fused features are fed into the prediction head to obtain the final results.

In brief, our contributions can be summarized as follows:

- We combine the early fusion and mid-level fusion approaches, utilizing the hard correlations established through calibration matrices to guide the generation of object queries, and fuse the point cloud and image features using cross-attention mechanisms.
- We use two independent sparse convolutions to extract the decorated point cloud features. Additionally, we initialize the object queries using a center heatmap and embed the predicted class from the center heatmap as auxiliary information into the object queries.
- We validate our method on two prominent autonomous driving datasets, namely KITTI and Waymo. The experimental results demonstrate the effectiveness of our proposed approach.

2 Related Work

According to the fusion stage, existing fusion methods can be divided into three categories: early fusion, mid-level fusion, and late fusion. Below, we will introduce each of them in chronological order of their development.

2.1 Late Fusion

Late fusion methods refer to fusion performed at the later stages of the network, also known as result-level fusion. Early multi-modal fusion methods are mostly late fusion methods, where each modality's data is independently predicted, and the detection results are subsequently fused. This category of methods has the simplest fusion approach and high reliability because they can still operate normally under single-modality conditions. However, their fusion granularity is the lowest among the three categories, often resulting in poor performance. Classic late fusion methods include F-PointNets [7], CLOCs [6]. In recent years, early fusion methods and mid-level fusion methods have gained more attention, while research on late fusion methods has been relatively limited.

2.2 Early Fusion

Early fusion methods refer to fusion performed at the early stages of the network, where different modalities of data are fused to create a new modality, which serves as the input to the feature extraction network. For example, PointPainting [11] utilizes pixel-level semantic segmentation scores to decorate point cloud data as camera features, while PointAugmenting [12] decorates point cloud data with image features. Although PointPainting and PointAugmenting provide novel approaches for multi-modal fusion, researchers quickly discover the bottleneck in them. While these fusion approach allow for the alignment of 3D and 2D coordinates using calibration matrices, existing feature extractors struggle to directly process the fused data. Typical 3D backbone networks are designed specifically to extract sparse point cloud features, and as point cloud and image data have significant differences in characteristics, using existing 3D backbone networks to extract features from the fused data is not suitable.

2.3 Mid-Level Fusion

Mid-level fusion methods refer to fusion performed during the feature extraction stage of the network. Compared to early fusion, which can only fuse data at the raw data level, mid-level fusion methods can operate at the feature level. Therefore, in theory, mid-level fusion methods can maximize the advantages of fusion. However, most existing mid-level fusion methods rely on learned soft correlations between point clouds and images. We consider this approach to be unreliable because it lacks interpretability, and existing feature-level fusion methods often overlook the presence of hard correlations. For example, TransFusion [1] introduces the SMCA (Spatially Modulated Cross Attention) module, which allows the network to adaptively determine which parts of the image features are more important and suitable for fusion. DeepFusion [5] enables a voxel in the point cloud to match multiple pixels in the image and assigns weights to the pixels using cross-attention mechanisms.

3 DecoratingFusion

3.1 Motivations and Pipeline

Before our work, early fusion methods and mid-level fusion methods are completely different approaches. We aimed to leverage the advantages of both by incorporating the hard correlations established through calibration matrices to achieve better detection results. To utilize the hard correlations between point clouds and images to guide the fusion of the two modalities at the feature level, we employ 2D CNN features of correspondingly matched pixels to decorate the original point cloud data. We use the decorated point cloud features to initialize the object queries, aiding the cross-attention module in capturing the correlations between the two types of features more effectively.

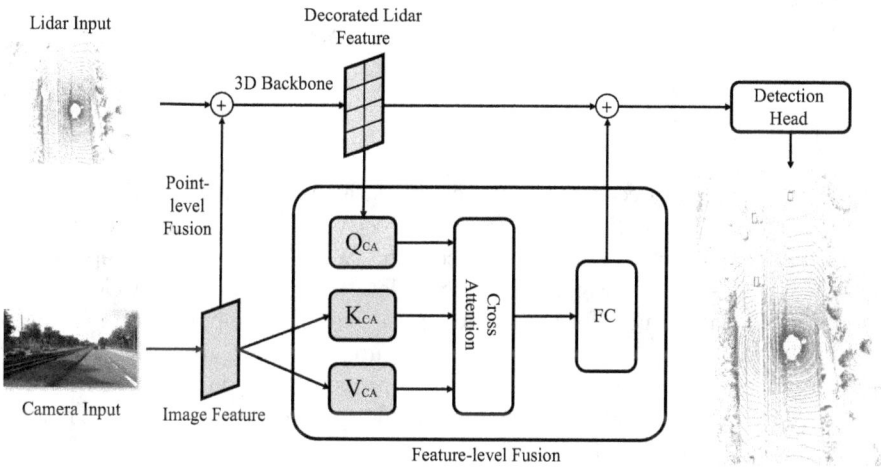

Fig. 1. An overview of DecoratingFusion framework.

DecoratingFusion consists of two parts: the point-level fusion stage and the feature-level fusion stage, as illustrated in Fig. 1. First, in the point-level fusion stage, we use a 2D backbone network to extract features from the input image. Then, using calibration matrices, we project the points of the point cloud onto the image plane, obtaining the corresponding pixel points. We attach the image features of those pixel points to the original point cloud. Next, in the feature fusion stage, the decorated point cloud is passed through a 3D backbone network to obtain the decorated lidar features, which are used to generate object queries. Simultaneously, the image features are used to derive keys and values. Then, through cross-attention, we learn the soft correlations between the two types of features. Finally, the fused features are obtained by connecting the point cloud features with the learned soft correlations. Lastly, the fused features are fed into the existing prediction heads to obtain the final detection results.

3.2 Point-Level Fusion

DecoratingFusion utilizes DLA34 from CenterNet [18] as the 2D backbone network, which produces feature maps with a channel size of 64 and a scale factor of 4. We represent the original point cloud points as (x, y, z, r), where x, y, z represent the coordinates of the point in 3D space, and r represents the reflectance. Each point can be projected onto the image using the calibration matrix $T_{\text{camera} \leftarrow \text{lidar}}$. In this stage, the decorated point cloud, denoted as (x, y, z, r, f), is obtained, where f represents the image features attached to each point.

In addition, the 2D backbone network of DecoratingFusion is trained end-to-end with other network components, unlike PointPainting [11] or PointAugmenting [12], which are independently learned in other tasks such as 2D semantic segmentation or object detection. This approach reduces computational costs, mitigates cross-domain differences, decreases the amount of required data annotation, and avoids suboptimal feature extraction due to heuristic feature selection.

3.3 Feature-Level Fusion

After obtaining the decorated point cloud data, considering the domain gap between the two modalities, we do not directly feed them into the existing 3D backbone network. Instead, we process the two types of features separately. Specifically, as shown in Fig. 2, we first voxelate the decorated point cloud data and extract local features for each voxel. Then, we split the point cloud features and image features, and perform further feature extraction using two independent 3D sparse convolutions. Finally, we compress both modalities' features into a BEV representation and concatenate them along the channel dimension, resulting in the final augmented point cloud features.

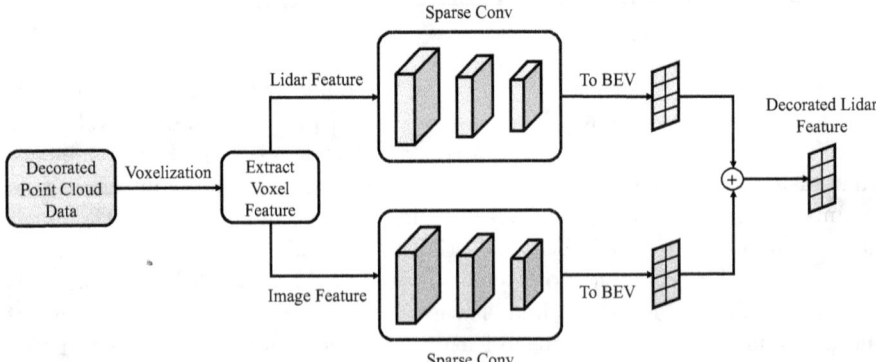

Fig. 2. The two independent sparse convolutions used to extract lidar and image feature.

With the point cloud features F^{Lidar} and image features F^{Camera}, we can transform F^{Lidar} into queries Q_{CA} and F^{Camera} into keys K_{CA} and values V_{CA}. Then, we use cross-attention to learn the correlations between the two types of features. However, unlike DeepFusion [5], which directly uses fully connected layers to transform F^{Lidar} into queries Q_{CA}, we are inspired by CenterPoint [15] and use a center point heatmap for better initialization of object queries. Specifically, we first predict a center point heatmap $\hat{Y} \in \mathbb{R}^{X \times Y \times K}$, where $X \times Y$ represents the size of F^{Lidar} and K represents the number of classes. We treat this heatmap as $X \times Y \times K$ candidate objects and select the top n per class as initial object queries. To prevent queries from being too densely concentrated in a local region, we choose the local maxima as queries, which means their values must be greater than or equal to their eight neighboring points. The query initialization method of DecoratingFusion has the following advantages compared to DeepFusion [5]: (1) The initial positions of the queries are closer to the actual center positions of the objects. (2) The initial positions of the queries are no longer randomly generated, but related to the input data, which can accelerate the convergence speed of the model.

Additionally, inspired by TransFusion [1], we also incorporate class information into each object query. Since the decorated point cloud features are in the BEV space, where object scales are absolute, the scale differences between objects of the same class are minimal. Taking advantage of this characteristic in the BEV space, we encode the class of each query obtained from the center heatmap as a one-hot encoding and concatenate it with the query Q_{CA}. This provides additional class information to assist the cross-attention module, allowing it to focus more on intra-class variations.

Finally, by performing an inner product operation between the query Q_{CA} and the key K_{CA}, we obtain a correlation matrix that captures the relationship between the point cloud features and image features. After applying softmax normalization, this correlation matrix is used to weight and sum the values V_{CA}, resulting in image features that are relevant to the queries. These image features are then processed through a fully connected layer and concatenated with the decorated point cloud features. The concatenated features are fed into the existing 3D detection head to obtain the final detection results.

3.4 Loss Function

The loss function of DecoratingFusion consists of a classification loss $\mathcal{L}_{\text{cls}}$, and a regression loss $\mathcal{L}_{\text{reg}}$. The classification loss is calculated using focal loss, while the regression loss is calculated using Smooth-L1 loss:

$$\mathcal{L} = \mathcal{L}_{\text{cls}} + w\mathcal{L}_{\text{reg}} \tag{1}$$

where w is set to 2, following the empirical settings of SECOND [13].

4 Experiments

To evaluate the effectiveness of DecoratingFusion, we conduct experiments on two commonly used outdoor autonomous driving datasets: the KITTI dataset and the Waymo dataset.

4.1 Datasets

The KITTI dataset is one of the most commonly used datasets in the field of autonomous driving before 2020. It consists of 7481 training samples and 7518 testing samples from 3D scenes in autonomous driving. Following the convention, we divide the training data into a training set with 3712 samples and a validation set with 3769 samples. In accordance with the requirements of the KITTI object detection benchmark, we conduct experiments on three categories: cars, pedestrians, and cyclists, and evaluate the results using the average precision with an IoU threshold of 0.7.

In 2020, Waymo released a training dataset called WOD (Waymo OpenDataset) for autonomous driving. It consists of 798 training sequences, 202 validation sequences, and 150 testing sequences. Each sequence contains approximately 200 frames, which include lidar points, camera images, and labeled 3D bounding boxes. We evaluate the performance of different models using the official metrics, AP and APH. We report the results for the LEVEL1 (L1) and LEVEL2 (L2) difficulty levels. LEVEL1 is used for anchor boxes with more than 5 lidar points, while LEVEL2 is used for anchor boxes with at least one lidar point.

4.2 Implementation Details

We implement DecoratingFusion using the open-source MMDetection3D framework in PyTorch. For the KITTI dataset, we set the voxel sizes to (0.05 m, 0.05 m, 0.1 m). Since the KITTI dataset only provides annotations from the front camera's perspective, the detection ranges on the X, Y, and Z axes are respectively set as [0, 70.4 m], [−40 m, 40 m], and [−3 m, 1 m]. For the Waymo dataset, we set the voxel sizes to (0.1 m, 0.1 m, 0.15 m). The detection range on the X and Y axes is set as [−75.2 m, 75.2 m], and the detection range on the Z axis is set as [−2 m, 4 m]. During the training process, we utilize the AdamW optimizer with a momentum range of 0.85 to 0.95. The learning rate is adjusted using the one-cycle policy. For both the KITTI and Waymo datasets, the initial learning rates are set to $2e-3$ and $3e-3$, respectively, with a weight decay coefficient of 0.01.

We use a pre-trained CenterNet [18] with DLA34 as the 2D backbone network, with the image size set to 448 × 800. For the 3D backbone network, we utilize SECOND [13]. In the Cross Attention Module, we apply a dropout strategy to the correlation matrix to prevent overfitting, with a dropout rate of 0.3. The subsequent fully connected layer has 192 filters. Additionally, we employ the GT-Paste strategy for data augmentation during training. This strategy aids in the convergence of the network but may disrupt the true data distribution. Therefore, following PointAugmenting [12], we use a fading strategy during training. Specifically, we apply the GT-Paste data augmentation strategy throughout the early stages of training but disable it in the final 5 epochs, allowing the network to better adapt to the real data distribution.

4.3 Experimental Results and Analysis

Table 1. Performance comparison on the KITTI *val* set with AP calculated by 40 recall positions.

Method	mAP	Car			Cyclist			Pedestrian		
		Easy	Mod.	Hard	Easy	Mod.	Hard	Easy	Mod.	Hard
SECOND [13]	68.06	88.61	78.62	77.22	80.58	67.15	63.10	56.55	52.98	47.73
PointRCNN [9]	70.67	88.72	78.61	77.82	86.84	71.62	65.59	62.72	53.85	50.25
PV-RCNN [8]	73.27	92.10	84.36	82.48	88.88	71.95	66.78	64.26	56.67	51.91
SE-SSD [17]	-	90.21	**86.25**	79.22	-	-	-	-	-	-
F-PointNet [7]	65.58	83.76	70.92	63.65	77.15	56.49	53.37	70.00	61.32	53.59
CLOCs [6]	70.5	89.49	79.31	77.36	87.57	67.92	63.67	62.88	56.2	50.1
EPNet [4]	70.97	88.76	78.65	78.32	83.88	65.60	62.70	66.74	59.29	54.82
FocalsConv [2]	-	**92.26**	85.32	82.95	-	-	-	-	-	-
CAT-Det [16]	75.42	90.12	81.46	79.15	87.64	72.82	68.20	74.08	66.35	58.92
DecoratingFusion	**77.30**	92.25	85.04	**83.82**	**90.41**	**74.24**	**70.51**	**73.22**	**66.41**	**59.57**

KITTI. To demonstrate the effectiveness of DecoratingFusion, we compare it with nine representative 3D object detection methods on the KITTI dataset. The selected methods include SECOND [13], PointRCNN [9], PVRCNN [8], SE-SSD [17] (four lidar-only methods), as well as F-PointNet [7], CLOCs [6], EPNet [4], FocalsConv [2], and CAT-Det [16] (five multi-modal fusion methods). The experimental results are shown in Table 1, where the top-ranking score is displayed in bold, and the second-ranking score is underlined. From Table 1, it can be observed that DecoratingFusion achieves the highest mAP across all three categories, outperforming all nine representative methods. Although DecoratingFusion does not achieve the best performance in the easy and moderate difficulty levels for car detection, it ranks first in the difficult difficulty level. For small objects (pedestrians and bicycles) detection, DecoratingFusion achieves the top rank across various difficulty levels.

Waymo. On the larger and more diverse Waymo dataset, we also compare DecoratingFusion with several state-of-the-art methods, and the experimental

Table 2. Performance comparison on the Waymo *val* set for 3D vehicle (IoU = 0.7) and pedestrian (IoU = 0.5) detection.

Method	Modality	mAPH L2	Vehicle(AP/APH) L1	Vehicle(AP/APH) L2	Pedestrian(AP/APH) L1	Pedestrian(AP/APH) L2
SECOND [13]	L	57.32	72.27/71.69	63.85/63.33	68.70/58.18	60.72/51.31
3D-MAN [14]	L	63.05	74.50/74.00	67.60/67.10	71.70/67.70	62.60/59.00
Part-A^2 [10]	L	63.30	77.10/76.50	68.50/68.00	75.20/66.90	66.20/58.60
PDV [3]	L	63.55	76.85/76.33	69.30/68.81	74.19/65.96	65.85/58.28
CenterPoint [15]	L	64.40	-	-/66.20	-	-/62.60
Centerformer [19]	L	**74.40**	78.80/78.30	**74.30/73.80**	82.10/79.30	77.80/75.00
PointAugmenting [12]	L+C	63.40	67.40/-	62.70/62.20	75.04/-	70.60/64.60
DeepFusion [5]	L+C	74.20	80.60/80.10	72.90/72.40	85.80/83.00	78.70/76.00
DecoratingFusion	L+C	**74.80**	**81.52/81.08**	73.74/73.11	**86.21/83.65**	**79.15/76.49**

results are presented in Table 2. It can be observed that on Waymo's official primary difficulty metric, L2, DecoratingFusion achieves first place in pedestrian detection and is only 0.69% behind the top-ranking method, CenterFormer, in vehicle detection. Although CenterFormer, a lidar-only method, achieves the top rank in vehicle detection at L2 difficulty, its performance in pedestrian detection is not remarkable. This is due to the inherent limitation of lidar-only methods, as point cloud data itself is sparse in 3D space and has limited coverage of small object instances. In terms of L1 difficulty, DecoratingFusion not only achieves first place in pedestrian detection but also attains the best performance in vehicle detection, surpassing the second-ranking method, DeepFusion, by 0.98%. Overall, considering all categories, DecoratingFusion secures the first rank in L2 difficulty mAPH. Similar to its performance on the KITTI dataset, DecoratingFusion demonstrates advantages in small object recognition on the Waymo dataset as well.

4.4 Ablation Study

To demonstrate the effectiveness of each component in DecoratingFusion, we conduct two sets of experiments on the Waymo dataset, specifically on the L2 difficulty level. These experiments focused on evaluating the point-level fusion module and the feature fusion module separately.

Table 3. Effect of each component in the point-level fusion module.

Decoration	E2E	2SparseConv	Vehicle	Pedestrian
			72.40	76.00
✓			72.84(+0.44)	76.35(+0.35)
✓	✓		72.93(+0.53)	76.4(+0.40)
✓		✓	72.87(+0.47)	76.38(+0.38)
✓	✓	✓	72.97(+0.57)	76.42(+0.42)

The point-level fusion module consists of three components: Decoration, E2E, and 2SparseConv. Decoration indicates whether to use image features to decorate the original point cloud data, E2E represents whether to train the 2D network independently or in an end-to-end manner with other network components, and 2SparseConv indicates whether to use two separate sparse convolutions to extract the decorated point cloud data. In this set of experiments, the baseline method chosen is DeepFusion, and the results are shown in Table 3. From the results, it can be observed that Decoration brings the largest improvement, indicating that the hard correlation between point cloud and image can significantly enhance the feature fusion. Additionally, both the E2E and 2SparseConv modules contribute positively to the model's performance, with E2E providing a relatively larger improvement.

Table 4. Effect of each component in the feature fusion module.

Heatmap Init.	Category Embedding	Vehicle	Pedestrian
		72.84	76.35
✓		72.97(+0.13)	76.41(+0.06)
✓	✓	73.02(+0.18)	76.43(+0.08)

The feature fusion module consists of two components: HeatmapInit. (which initializes the query with a center point heatmap) and Category Embedding (which embeds category information into the query). It is important to note that the Category Embedding component relies on the HeatmapInit. component, as the category information is derived from the predictions of the center heatmap. The baseline method for this set of experiments is DeepFusion + Decoration. From Table 4, it can be seen that both modules contribute positively to the model's performance, with the main improvement coming from the HeatmapInit. component.

5 Conclusion

We combine the early fusion and mid-level fusion in multi-modal fusion methods and propose a new 3D object detection network called DecoratingFusion. The core idea of DecoratingFusion is to establish a hard correlation between point cloud and image using calibration matrices. It utilizes the decorated point cloud features to guide the generation of object queries and finally fuses the point cloud and image features through cross-attention mechanisms. DecoratingFusion consists of two stages: point-level fusion and feature fusion. In the point-level fusion stage, instead of using independently pre-trained networks, image features are learned in an end-to-end manner. Additionally, two separate sparse convolutions are used to extract the decorated point cloud features. In the feature fusion stage, the object query is initialized with a center point heatmap, which brings the initial position of the query closer to the actual center of the object. Moreover, the predicted category from the center point heatmap is embedded as supplementary information into the object query. Experiments conducted on the KITTI and Waymo datasets demonstrate the superiority of DecoratingFusion in 3D object detection.

References

1. Bai, X., Hu, Z., Zhu, X., Huang, Q., Chen, Y.: Transfusion: Robust lidar-camera fusion for 3d object detection with transformers. In: Proceedings of the IEEE/CVF Conference on Computer Vision and Pattern Recognition, pp. 1090–1099 (2022)
2. Chen, Y., Li, Y., Zhang, X., Sun, J., Jia, J.: Focal sparse convolutional networks for 3d object detection. In: Proceedings of the IEEE/CVF Conference on Computer Vision and Pattern Recognition, pp. 5428–5437 (2022)
3. Hu, J.S., Kuai, T., Waslander, S.L.: Point density-aware voxels for lidar 3D object detection. In: Proceedings of the IEEE/CVF Conference on Computer Vision and Pattern Recognition, pp. 8469–8478 (2022)
4. Huang, T., Liu, Z., Chen, X., Bai, X.: EPNet: Enhancing point features with image semantics for 3D object detection. In: Vedaldi, A., Bischof, H., Brox, T., Frahm, J.-M. (eds.) Computer Vision – ECCV 2020: 16th European Conference, Glasgow, UK, August 23–28, 2020, Proceedings, Part XV, pp. 35–52. Springer International Publishing, Cham (2020). https://doi.org/10.1007/978-3-030-58555-6_3
5. Li, Y., Yu, A.W., Meng, T., Caine, B., Ngiam, J.: Deepfusion: lidar-camera deep fusion for multi-modal 3D object detection. In: Proceedings of the IEEE/CVF Conference on Computer Vision and Pattern Recognition, pp. 17182–17191 (2022)
6. Pang, S., Morris, D., Radha, H.: Clocs: camera-lidar object candidates fusion for 3D object detection. In: 2020 IEEE/RSJ International Conference on Intelligent Robots and Systems (IROS), pp. 10386–10393 IEEE (2020)
7. Qi, C.R., Liu, W., Wu, C., Su, H., Guibas, L.J.: Frustum pointnets for 3D object detection from rgb-d data. In: Proceedings of the IEEE Conference on Computer Vision and Pattern Recognition, pp. 918–927 (2018)
8. Shi, S., et al.: PV-rCNN: point-voxel feature set abstraction for 3D object detection. In: Proceedings of the IEEE/CVF Conference on Computer Vision and Pattern Recognition, pp. 10529–10538 (2020)
9. Shi, S., Wang, X., Li, H.: Pointrcnn: 3D object proposal generation and detection from point cloud. In: Proceedings of the IEEE/CVF Conference on Computer Vision and Pattern Recognition, pp. 770–779 (2019)
10. Shi, S., Wang, Z., Shi, J., Wang, X., Li, H.: From points to parts: 3D object detection from point cloud with part-aware and part-aggregation network. IEEE Trans. Pattern Anal. Mach. Intell. **43**(8), 2647–2664 (2020)
11. sbibitemvora2020pointpainting Vora, S., Lang, A.H., Helou, B., Beijbom, O.: Pointpainting: sequential fusion for 3D object detection. In: Proceedings of the IEEE/CVF Conference on Computer Vision and Pattern Recognition, pp. 4604–4612 (2020)
12. Wang, C., Ma, C., Zhu, M., Yang, X.: Pointaugmenting: cross-modal augmentation for 3d object detection. In: Proceedings of the IEEE/CVF Conference on Computer Vision and Pattern Recognition, pp. 11794–11803 (2021)

13. Yan, Y., Mao, Y., Li, B.: Second: sparsely embedded convolutional detection. Sensors **18**(10), 3337 (2018)
14. Yang, Z., Zhou, Y., Chen, Z., Ngiam, J.: 3D-man: 3D multi-frame attention network for object detection. In: Proceedings of the IEEE/CVF Conference on Computer Vision and Pattern Recognition, pp. 1863–1872 (2021)
15. Yin, T., Zhou, X., Krahenbuhl, P.: Center-based 3D object detection and tracking. In: Proceedings of the IEEE/CVF Conference on Computer Vision and Pattern Recognition, pp. 11784–11793 (2021)
16. Zhang, Y., Chen, J., Huang, D.: Cat-det: contrastively augmented transformer for multi-modal 3d object detection. In: Proceedings of the IEEE/CVF Conference on Computer Vision and Pattern Recognition, pp. 908–917 (2022)
17. Zheng, W., Tang, W., Jiang, L., Fu, C.W.: Se-ssd: self-ensembling single-stage object detector from point cloud. In: Proceedings of the IEEE/CVF Conference on Computer Vision and Pattern Recognition, pp. 14494–14503 (2021)
18. Zhou, X., Wang, D., Krähenbühl, P.: Objects as points. arXiv preprint arXiv:1904.07850 (2019)
19. Zhou, Z., Zhao, X., Wang, Yu., Wang, P., Foroosh, H.: CenterFormer: center-based transformer for 3D object detection. In: Avidan, S., Brostow, G., Cissé, M., Farinella, G.M., Hassner, T. (eds.) Computer Vision – ECCV 2022: 17th European Conference, Tel Aviv, Israel, October 23–27, 2022, Proceedings, Part XXXVIII, pp. 496–513. Springer Nature Switzerland, Cham (2022). https://doi.org/10.1007/978-3-031-19839-7_29

EMDFNet: Efficient Multi-scale and Diverse Feature Network for Traffic Sign Detection

Pengyu Li[1], Chenhe Liu[1], Tengfei Li[1], Xinyu Wang[1], Shihui Zhang[1]([✉]), and Dongyang Yu[2]

[1] Yanshan University, Qinhuangdao City 066000, Hebei Province, China
{202111130221,202211200217,funlee,zora030}@stumail.ysu.edu.cn,
sshhzz@ysu.edu.cn
[2] Beijing Rigour Technology Co., Ltd., Beijing, China

Abstract. The detection of small objects, particularly traffic signs, is a critical subtask within object detection and autonomous driving. Despite the notable achievements in previous research, two primary challenges persist. Firstly, the main issue is the singleness of feature extraction. Secondly, the detection process fails to effectively integrate with objects of varying sizes or scales. These issues are also prevalent in generic object detection. Motivated by these challenges, in this paper, we propose a novel object detection network named Efficient Multi-scale and Diverse Feature Network (EMDFNet) for traffic sign detection that integrates an Augmented Shortcut Module and an Efficient Hybrid Encoder to address the aforementioned issues simultaneously. Specifically, the Augmented Shortcut Module utilizes multiple branches to integrate various spatial semantic information and channel semantic information, thereby enhancing feature diversity. The Efficient Hybrid Encoder utilizes global feature fusion and local feature interaction based on various features to generate distinctive classification features by integrating feature information in an adaptable manner. Extensive experiments on the Tsinghua-Tencent 100K (TT100K) benchmark and the German Traffic Sign Detection Benchmark (GTSDB) demonstrate that our EMDFNet outperforms other state-of-the-art detectors in performance while retaining the real-time processing capabilities of single-stage models. This substantiates the effectiveness of EMDFNet in detecting small traffic signs.

Keywords: Small object detection · Traffic signs · Multi-scale fusion · Feature diversity

1 Introduction

Traffic sign detection and recognition (TSD and TSR) are crucial in intelligent transportation and autonomous driving. They aim to detect traffic signs and

---

The work is partially supported by the Hebei Natural Science Foundation No. F2023203012.

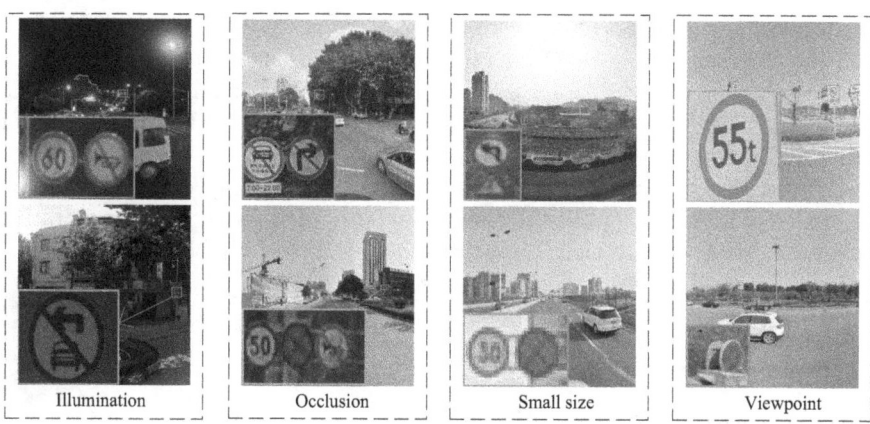

Fig. 1. The difficulties in traffic sign detection. In real traffic scenes, traffic sign detection faces many difficulties including illumination, occlusion, small size, viewpoint and so on.

identify their types for information extraction and safety enhancement. Unlike some studies that separate "detection" (localization) and "recognition" (classification), we consider that TSD includes both in a broader range of object detection.

TSD faces challenges, notably inefficiency due to small sign sizes at long distances, exemplified by signs covering only about 25×25 pixels in 2000×2000 pixel images. The issue of size, combined with the tendency of generic detection models to focus on smaller input resolutions, increases the risk of missing small signs. Additionally, as shown in Fig. 1, detection accuracy is compromised by factors such as complex background, occlusion, deformation, and change in lighting.

Motivated by the above problems, we propose an Efficient Multi-scale and Diverse Feature Network for traffic sign detection in complex background. The contributions of this paper are summarized as four-folds:

- We propose an Efficient Multi-scale and Diverse Feature Network (EMDFNet) for small object detection in complex background. The network possesses a highly powerful capability for feature extraction and multi-scale interaction, thereby enhancing the robustness of small object detection. The network achieves good trade-offs in terms of completeness, real-time processing, and accuracy.

- We propose an Augmented Shortcut Module (ASM) to address the issue of feature singularity. The module combines different spatial semantic information and channel semantic information through multiple branches to enhance feature diversity. Our ASM excels at capturing the fundamental visual patterns and semantic information of small objects, thereby enhancing the effectiveness of small object detection.

• To enhance multi-scale detection capability of the network, we introduce the Efficient Hybrid Encoder (EHE) to improve the neck structure. This encoder combines intra-scale feature interaction and cross-scale feature fusion. To the best of our knowledge, we are the first to apply the idea of EHE to the field of traffic sign detection.

• Extensive experiments are conducted on two widely used datasets TT100K and GTSDB. The experimental results in both qualitative and quantitative dimensions demonstrate that the proposed EMDFNet reliably achieves state-of-the-art performance in traffic sign detection.

2 Related Work

2.1 Object Detection

Deep convolutional neural networks (CNNs) have become the preferred choice for various computer vision tasks in recent years. They have significantly improved the accuracy and speed of object detection, as evidenced in benchmarks such as Pascal VOC [1] and MS COCO [2]. The R-CNN series, including R-CNN [3], Fast R-CNN [4], Faster R-CNN [5], and Mask R-CNN [6], extract region proposals before classifying and regressing them for detection results. However, their two-stage process is computationally intensive, limiting their practical use. Single-stage detectors like SSD [7] and YOLO eliminate the proposal step to enable real-time performance but face challenges with small objects because of the loss of spatial and channel details. This paper aims to preserve spatial and channel feature information to enhance the detection performance of small traffic signs.

2.2 Traffic Sign Detection

Traffic sign detection (TSD) is a specialized area within object detection, where generic methods are less effective due to the small size and complex detection requirements of traffic signs. Traditional techniques focus on handcrafted features such as color, shape, and edges, often combined with machine learning classifiers. However, these methods struggle with environmental variations such as lighting and motion blur.

Recent advancements have seen the rise of CNN-based approaches, utilizing strategies such as fully convolutional networks (FCN) [8] for sign proposals and deep CNNs for classification. Additionally, techniques involving image pyramids and Generative Adversarial Networks (GANs) have been employed to enhance detection performance, particularly for small objects. Despite successes, limitations remain in data availability and sign size, impacting the balance between speed, accuracy, and detection completeness. This paper focuses on the trade-off between accuracy and speed.

3 Proposed Network

3.1 Network Overview

As illustrated in Fig. 2, our EMDFNet, an end-to-end object detection network that incorporates multi-scale feature fusion and diverse features. EMDFNet leverages Res2Net [9] as the backbone to extract three feature maps. The feature map with the largest receptive field is first fed into the Augmented Shortcut Module (ASM). Subsequently, the feature map processed by ASM and the other two feature maps are input into the Efficient Hybrid Encoder (EHE). The ASM enhances feature representation and preserves details, while the EHE achieves better cross-scale fusion. Ultimately, the network integrates three detection heads to obtain detection results after classification and regression tasks.

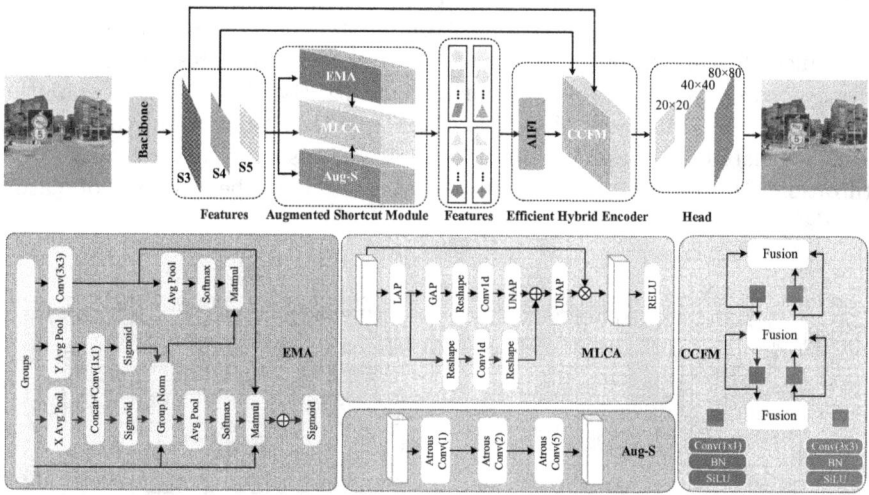

Fig. 2. The EMDFNet can be roughly divided into four parts. The first part consists of a backbone composed of Res2Net. The second part is the Augmented Shortcut Module, which enhances feature diversity. The third part is the Efficient Hybrid Encoder for integrating multi-scale features. Finally, the fourth part comprises three prediction heads for bounding box prediction.

3.2 Augmented Shortcut Module

To address the issue of too single features extracted by the backbone, we propose a powerful Augmented Shortcut Module (ASM) to increase feature diversity in our EMDFNet through refining shortcut connections. ASM includes spatial feature selection, channel feature selection and Aug-S. The module parallelizes three branches and then outputs diversified features. The final structure of the ASM is shown in Fig. 2. The ASM can be formulated as follows:

$$ASM = MLCA(\Gamma(Z_l, \Theta_l), shortcut(Z_l), FS(Z_l)) \tag{1}$$

The augmented shortcut connection, denoted as Γ with parameters Θ, enhances the original shortcut by adding alternative paths that incorporate attention mechanisms. Unlike simple identity projection, Γ transforms input features into a new space using various transformations dictated by Θ. The feature selection (FS) utilizes Efficient Multi-scale Attention (EMA) [10] to select spatial features, and all branches undergo processing by the Mixed Local Channel Attention (MLCA) [11] channel selection module before concatenation.

The original residual connection is updated with two main components: a feature selection layer for spatial and channel features, and an enhanced shortcut connection Aug-S. We utilize spatial feature selection to uniformly distribute spatial semantics and utilize channel feature selection to fuse local and global channel information. In addition, Aug-S consists of a set of dilated convolutions that expand the receptive field while keeping the image size unchanged. Aug-S enhances feature diversity as an alternative route. To preserve details lost during downsampling by the backbone, we utilize Hybrid Dilated Convolution (HDC) with dilation rates of $[1, 2, 5]$. This approach helps avoid the gridding effect associated with uniform dilation rates and ensuring comprehensive pixel utilization. As shown in Fig. 3. This approach improves the retention of feature map details.

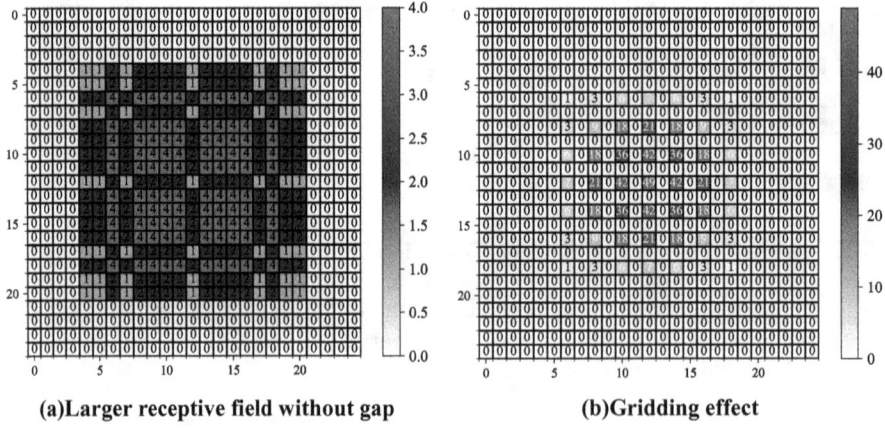

(a)Larger receptive field without gap   (b)Gridding effect

Fig. 3. The dilation rates used in (a) are $[1, 2, 5]$, where all pixel values are effectively utilized, while in (b), the dilation rates are $[2, 2, 2]$, resulting in a gridding effect.

3.3 Efficient Hybrid Encoder

To enhance the multi-scale fusion capability of the proposed EMDFNet, we introduce the Efficient Hybrid Encoder (EHE) for the first time in the field of traffic sign detection, as illustrated in Fig. 2. EHE is an excellent component accepted in CVPR 2024, which can achieve multi-scale fusion through intra-scale interaction and cross-scale interaction [12]. EHE comprises two main units: an Attention-based Intrascale Feature Interaction (AIFI) for reducing computational redundancy by emphasizing high-level intra-scale interactions, and a CNN-based Cross-scale Feature-fusion Module (CCFM), which introduces fusion blocks to combine adjacent feature levels. As shown in formula 2, AIFI prioritizes high-level features for their richer semantic content, avoiding lower-level interactions that could lead to duplication or confusion. As shown in formula 3, CCFM's fusion blocks, combine features through element-wise addition, optimizing feature integration to enhance object detection and recognition performance.

$$F_5 = \text{AIFI}(S_5) \qquad (2)$$

$$\text{Output} = \text{CCFM}(\{S_3, S_4, F_5\}) \qquad (3)$$

where $S3, S4, S5, F5$ are feature maps. AIFI first decomposes the feature map into sequence vectors, and then resynthesizes the feature map through the attention mechanism. CCFM fuses feature maps of different sizes.

3.4 Loss Function

IoU Loss has several limitations, including its inability to optimize when boxes do not intersect (IoU=0), its failure to indicate the distance between boxes, and its inaccuracy in showing the degree of overlap. To overcome IoU Loss limitations, we introduce SIoU Loss [13] for calculating rectangular box loss, enhancing training speed and detection precision.

The SIoU Loss function is defined as follows:

$$L_{box} = 1 - IoU + \frac{L_{dis} + L_{shape}}{2} \qquad (4)$$

$$L = W_{box}L_{box} + W_{cls}L_{cls} \qquad (5)$$

where L_{box} represents shape cost. IoU (Intersection over Union) represents the intersection of the union loss. L_{dis} and L_{shape} represent the distance cost and the shape loss, respectively. W_{box} and W_{cls} represent weights assigned to the bounding box and classification losses, respectively. L_{cls} represents the focal loss. From these we can obtain the final loss function L.

4 Experiment

4.1 Dataset

We use the TT100K and GTSDB datasets to evaluate our EMDFNet.
- **TT100K** [14] provides 1,000,000 images and 30,000 annotated traffic signs that are collected from Tencent Street Views in Chinese Cities. The resolution of the provided images is uniform 2048 × 2048 pixels. We ignore categories

with fewer than 100 instances following, thus leaving 45 categories to detect, as illustrated in Fig. 4. The publicly available benchmark dataset can be found at http://cg.cs.tsinghua.edu.cn/traffic-sign/. To avoid the impact of various augmentation policies, we fine-tune the proposed EMDFNet and other detectors on the original training set, which includes 6105 images, and test them on the original testing set, which comprises 3071 images, for a fair comparison. Three categories labeled as 'ph5', 'w32', and 'wo' are excluded due to their mixed content of several traffic signs.

- **GTSDB** [15] provides 900 images and 1213 annotated traffic signs. All these images are captured from video sequences recorded near Bochum, Germany. The benchmark dataset is publicly available at https://benchmark.ini.rub.de/gtsdb_dataset.html. The final images are clipped to 1360 × 800 pixels. The standard task for GTSDB focuses on traffic signs, and all traffic signs are classified into four major categories: prohibitory, danger, mandatory, and other.

Fig. 4. Illustrations of 45 remaining traffic sign categories from the TT100K dataset.

4.2 Implementation Details

We develop EMDFNet using PyTorch 1.8.0 on an RTX 3090 GPU, utilizing pretrained Res2Net-101 weights to expedite training. Our batch size is 8 for 640 × 640 inputs, dropping to 4 for 1024 × 1024 inputs due to memory constraints. We apply multi-scale inputs, mosaics, and mixup augmentations for better generalization. Training involves 400 epochs on the TT100K dataset and 100 epochs on the GTSDB dataset, starting with a five-epoch warm-up at a zero learning rate. We utilize Stochastic Gradient Descent (SGD) with a weight decay of 0.0005 and momentum of 0.9. The learning rate is adjusted using linear warm-up and cosine annealing techniques, customizing for each stage of training.

4.3 Evaluation Metrics

To assess network performance, we utilize Average Precision (AP), parameters, GFLOPs, and Frames Per Second (FPS) as metrics.

Average Precision (AP) is an evaluation index of detection accuracy, calculated as the average value of the average accuracy across multiple categories. AP is defined as the area under the curve, which depends on recall and accuracy. The function to calculate AP is shown below formula 6. $P(R)$ is the curve based on the recall rate and precision rate. Mean Average Precision (mAP) is a comprehensive criterion that is shown below formula 7. N is the number of categories in the function.

$$AP = \int_0^1 P(R)dR \tag{6}$$

$$\text{mAP@}IoU = \frac{1}{N}\sum_{i=1}^{N} AP@IoU \tag{7}$$

mAP@.5 represents the model's accuracy in object detection with a minimum 50% overlap between predicted and actual bounding boxes. mAP@.75 evaluates precision with a stricter 75% overlap requirement. mAP@.5:.95 averages mAP over IoU thresholds from 0.5 to 0.95. It provides a comprehensive overview of the model's performance across a range of criteria from lenient to strict. In object detection, AP_s, AP_m, and AP_l represent average precision metrics calculated for objects of small, medium, and large sizes detected within images.

Parameters calculate the number of parameter in the model, indicating memory resource usage. GFLOPs measure computational complexity as billions of operations per second. FPS, the rate of image processing, reflects real-time performance and is affected by image resolution. Higher resolutions reduce FPS with the same model and conditions.

4.4 Quantitative Analysis

Comparisons of SOTA on TT100K Dataset. We compare the proposed approach with state-of-the-art traffic sign detection methods. Table 1 presents the mAP@.5, mAP@.75, mAP@.5:.95, AP_s, AP_m, and AP_l values of the proposed method compared to other well-known detectors on the TT100K testing dataset. It can be observed that EMDFNet (640) and EMDFNet (1024) achieve 84.4% mAP@.5 and 93.3% mAP@.5, respectively.

From Table 1, we can know when input sizes are similar, EMDFNet significantly outperforms other models. At an input size of 640, it achieves 84.4%, surpassing SSD (68.7%), ScratchDet (74.0%), CAB Net (78.0%), and OpenTransMind (83.0%). At an input size of 1024, EMDFNet achieves 93.3% accuracy. A 23.8% increase over Sparse R-CNN's 69.5%, surpassing Mask R-CNN (70.8%), Faster R-CNN (74.1%), and Cascade R-CNN (80.1%), setting a new benchmark in object detection.

EMDFNet outperforms models with larger inputs, reaching 84.4% mAP@.5 at an input size of 640. This surpasses RetinaNet (61.9%, 2048 input), Sparse R-CNN (69.5%, 1024 input), Faster R-CNN (74.1%, 1024 input), and Cascade R-CNN (80.1%, 1024 input). Despite using smaller inputs, EMDFNet significantly enhances mAP, demonstrating its exceptional efficiency.

It can be seen from Table 1 that our network focuses on detecting small and medium traffic signs, with a particular emphasis on AP_s. Sparse R-CNN, Faster R-CNN, Cascade R-CNN, and SwinT + Cascade R-CNN achieve AP_s of 35.6%, 27.7%, 36.2%, and 44.5%, respectively. EMDFNet achieves 55.4% and 61.1% AP_s at input sizes of 640 and 1024, respectively, demonstrating its effectiveness in detecting smaller objects.

To further verify the performance of the proposed network, Table 2 shows the detection accuracy of EMDFNet in each category and compares it with other networks. From the Table 2 we can see that EMDFNet achieves SOTA in almost all categories. In particular, the accuracy of p27 reach 100.0%, il60 reach 99.8%, and il80 reach 98.9%.

In summary, it can be concluded that our EMDFNet's efficacy is clear: Res2Net enhances feature extraction, Augmented Shortcut Module diversifies input features, and Efficient Hybrid Encoder enhances multi-scale integration, thereby enhancing small traffic sign detection. Additionally, larger input sizes yield higher AP_s, indicating the potential for further enhancements in small object detection performance.

Table 1. The performance of different models on the TT100K dataset. The best results are shown in bold.

Model	Year	Input Size	mAP@.5	mAP@.75	mAP@.5:.95	AP_s	AP_m	AP_l	FPS	Param.	GFLOPS
Faster R-CNN [5]	2015	1024 × 1024	74.1	69.3	58.9	27.7	73.1	81.8	21	41.6	211.5
SSD512 [7]	2016	512 × 512	68.7	-	-	-	-	-	-	-	-
TT100K [14]	2016	640 × 640	83.3	79.0	65.8	-	-	-	-	35.1	-
RetinaNet [16]	2017	2048 × 2048	61.9	-	-	-	-	-	-	-	-
Mask R-CNN [6]	2017	1000 × 800	70.8	-	-	-	-	-	-	-	-
Cascade-RCNN [17]	2018	1024 × 1024	80.1	74.8	63.5	36.2	74.6	83.0	17.0	69.3	239.2
ScratchDet [18]	2019	512 × 512	74.0	-	-	-	-	-	-	-	-
FCOS [19]	2019	2048 × 2048	83.3	-	-	-	-	-	-	-	-
PCN [20]	2020	2048 × 2048	92.0	86.6	72.1	-	-	-	-	34.3	-
Sparse R-CNN [21]	2021	1024 × 1024	69.5	62.8	53.2	35.6	61.2	70.6	21.0	106.2	153.3
Swint-T+Cascade R-CNN [22]	2021	1024 × 1024	86.3	79.1	68.6	44.5	73.7	85.2	14.0	74.6	245.5
CAB Net [23]	2022	512 × 512	78.0	-	-	-	-	-	-	-	-
TRD-YOLO [24]	2023	640 × 640	37.5	-	30.1	26.8	34.5	40.2	-	-	-
YOLO-SG [25]	2023	640 × 640	75.8	-	-	-	-	60.2	-	-	-
Open-TransMind [26]	2023	512 × 512	83.0	-	-	-	-	-	-	-	-
Transformer Fusion [27]	2024	640 × 640	53.5	-	39.5	43.6	43.7	58.6	-	-	-
EMDFNet(ours)	-	640 × 640	84.4	76.8	64.9	55.4	68.5	81.7	**46.7**	29.7	**98.4**
EMDFNet(ours)	-	1024 × 1024	**93.3**	**87.1**	**73.8**	**61.1**	**78.8**	**85.4**	31.0	**29.6**	187.8

Comparisons of SOTA on GTSDB Dataset. To further verify the performance of our EMDFNet, we conduct experiments based on the GTSDB dataset. We fix the input size of the model to match the original image size of the dataset for comparison under consistent condition. The experimental results are shown in Table 3. From Table 3, we can observe that under the same input condition, the mAP@.5 value of EMDFNet reach 97.0%, significantly surpassing the performance of other models. Among them, the most notable improvement is that EMDFNet is 35.4% higher than SSD Mobilenet (from 61.6% to 97.0%).

When compared with Faster R-CNN Inception ResNet V2, the increase in mAP@.5 value is significant (from 95.7% to 97.0%), and the FPS of EMDFNet is about eight times higher, with a significant reduction in the number of parameters and computational cost. This demonstrates that EMDFNet not only performs well in accuracy but also achieves good results in speed and real-time performance.

Through comparisons of different datasets (TT100K and GTSDB), it is found that EMDFNet consistently achieves state-of-the-art performance levels, indicating that EMDFNet demonstrates excellent generalization capability.

Analyzing Object Detection Errors. We compare EMDFNet and YOLOX using the TIDE toolkit to tabulate error distributions on the TT100K testing set, as presented in Table 4. EMDFNet exhibites a lower classification error than YOLOX (10.02% vs. 11.22%), attributed to the Augmented Shortcut Module enhancing feature diversity and Efficient Hybrid Encoder improving feature spatial distribution for classification. EMDFNet also demonstrates a decreased miss error rate (0.98% vs. 1.87%), attributed to its effective feature extraction, which reduces the omission of essential details, thereby enhancing localization and classification accuracy. Both and Dupe are basically the same, which may be caused by dataset noise. The remaining error rates decrease.

Table 2. Comparisons of AP for each category on the TT100K testing set. Each column represents a traffic sign. The EMDFNet outperforms other detectors, achieving the SOTA performance.

Method	i2	i4	i5	il100	il60	il80	io	ip	p10	p11	p12	p19	p23	p26
Faster R-CNN [5]	44.0	46.0	45.0	41.0	57.0	62.0	41.0	39.0	45.0	38.0	60.0	59.0	65.0	50.0
Faster R-CNN [28]	59.3	73.8	79.7	76.6	76.3	68.5	64.9	66.8	52.2	58.5	45.9	48.2	74.4	66.1
FPN [29]	72.5	79.6	88.3	90.2	88.2	84.9	77.4	75.8	62.7	75.9	60.2	53.7	75.8	76.0
Mask R-CNN [6]	71.4	85.6	89.0	89.4	86.3	82.3	78.0	77.6	59.6	76.9	63.8	52.0	72.9	81.7
SSD512 [7]	70.1	79.3	85.3	77.1	86.4	78.7	72.3	71.6	64.5	57.1	67.7	73.0	80.4	70.7
DSSD512 [30]	65.0	86.2	88.6	62.7	87.7	76.2	60.2	85.5	66.2	55.1	54.4	78.4	79.3	75.5
RFB Net 512 [31]	75.6	79.4	87.9	87.4	89.9	88.4	77.2	79.0	66.1	66.9	71.1	72.8	83.4	74.9
ScratchDet [18]	76.6	86.9	89.2	82.2	88.8	81.3	73.9	77.3	68.8	65.3	70.8	67.2	80.2	74.9
CAB Net [23]	76.0	87.5	89.4	80.6	89.9	85.3	80.5	78.0	69.1	77.6	74.3	87.6	87.1	81.4
CAB-s Net [23]	75.2	86.4	89.4	84.9	89.2	89.1	81.6	77.8	69.7	72.4	72.3	89.0	88.3	81.6
EMDFNet(ours)	**84.0**	**93.5**	**96.1**	**95.1**	**99.8**	**98.9**	**84.6**	**86.9**	**81.8**	**89.9**	**85.8**	81.5	**89.9**	**87.6**

continued

Table 2. continued

Method	i2	i4	i5	il100	il60	il80	io	ip	p10	p11	p12	p19	p23	p26
Method	p3	p5	p6	pg	ph4	ph4.5	pl100	pl120	pl20	pl30	pl40	pl5	pl50	pl60
Faster R-CNN [5]	48.0	57.0	75.0	80.0	68.0	58.0	68.0	67.0	51.0	43.0	52.0	53.0	39.0	53.0
Faster R-CNN [28]	65.4	74.9	39.1	78.2	58.0	36.5	77.6	74.6	40.5	48.5	60.2	65.4	49.0	51.2
FPN [29]	71.6	79.2	39.1	78.2	58.0	36.5	87.5	85.5	55.7	55.6	71.5	77.3	60.8	58.7
Mask R-CNN [6]	78.5	78.9	48.3	88.5	63.9	58.1	86.7	82.4	58.6	53.3	68.2	76.4	63.5	56.6
SSD512 [7]	66.5	74.9	63.9	84.2	62.1	51.2	85.1	84.2	45.4	66.6	65.7	60.5	58.3	64.0
DSSD512 [30]	56.1	79.6	55.4	85.8	60.7	88.6	79.1	69.6	65.3	68.3	68.2	61.5	65.5	64.7
RFB Net 512 [31]	69.0	77.6	68.8	88.9	67.6	63.0	88.8	84.9	66.8	71.8	71.6	75.0	62.9	70.4
ScratchDet [18]	71.2	87.3	65.4	79.1	66.8	55.7	85.8	84.7	63.6	67.1	73.2	65.4	69.9	72.8
CAB Net [23]	74.7	84.5	82.5	87.5	**71.8**	64.4	88.4	87.9	68.6	73.3	74.8	79.3	75.1	**76.3**
CAB-s Net [23]	76.8	85.4	78.0	86.4	71.7	62.3	89.2	88.7	71.5	73.5	75.3	75.9	73.1	75.9
EMDFNet(ours)	**88.0**	**93.6**	**82.9**	**94.9**	63.2	**88.8**	**92.5**	**91.6**	**78.0**	**80.0**	**85.0**	**89.2**	**84.1**	75.3
Method	pl80	pm20	pm30	pm55	pn	pne	po	pr40	w13	w55	w57	w59	p27	pl70
Faster R-CNN [5]	52.0	61.0	67.0	61.0	37.0	47.0	37.0	75.0	33.0	39.0	48.0	39.0	79.0	61.0
Faster R-CNN [28]	59.0	50.5	29.1	68.5	77.8	87.5	47.7	86.9	30.9	62.1	67.0	57.2	64.3	61.2
FPN [29]	70.9	55.5	40.1	75.7	89.0	89.8	60.2	87.6	45.3	65.9	70.3	62.3	84.8	63.5
Mask R-CNN [6]	71.5	58.0	41.5	68.8	88.6	90.5	63.0	87.5	51.3	66.6	71.1	61.8	87.5	66.3
SSD512 [7]	70.5	69.6	51.3	71.2	71.7	86.4	51.8	87.9	46.1	64.6	74.0	58.8	76.2	70.6
DSSD512 [30]	75.6	66.3	50.6	76.5	67.2	88.9	51.7	88.0	60.6	70.1	83.6	75.1	60.9	71.0
RFB Net 512 [31]	71.9	73.7	54.0	**86.5**	78.0	88.2	59.8	84.5	64.8	72.4	81.5	69.3	79.8	64.9
ScratchDet [18]	75.9	73.3	52.2	76.5	76.7	89.4	62.9	85.0	69.1	70.3	84.7	76.5	79.7	70.2
CAB Net [23]	78.8	73.8	**67.3**	80.5	85.4	89.5	63.5	88.9	70.7	66.8	83.5	79.4	81.0	**72.9**
CAB-s Net [23]	78.4	71.2	67.0	83.3	82.2	89.2	64.0	88.2	57.2	75.2	80.1	66.6	87.5	70.7
EMDFNet(ours)	**80.5**	**79.5**	60.3	83.5	**96.3**	**96.6**	**80.7**	**92.7**	**92.7**	**80.9**	**87.8**	**87.9**	**100.0**	72.0

4.5 Qualitative Analysis

To demonstrate the effectiveness of EMDFNet in small object detection, we conduct visualization experiments on the TT100K testing set, as illustrated in Fig. 5.

As shown in the second line of the Fig. 5, there are a total of six ground truth objects in the images. MDNet successfully detects all six objects and correctly classifies them with high confidence scores. This can be attributed to the good performance of MDNet in detecting small objects, demonstrating its robustness and high stability in small traffic sign detection. In contrast, YOLOX only detects two of them and Mask R-CNN only detects four of them. More dramatically, the detected objects 'p19' and 'w55' by YOLOX are completely different from the ground truth objects 'p5' and 'w57'. This discrepancy may be attributed to that the objects are relatively distant and small in the images, resulting in poor classification and detection performance. Results framed in red highlight EMDFNet's ability to accurately detect and classify small, distant, or

Table 3. The performance of different models on the GTSDB dataset.

Model	mAP@.5	FPS	Params	GFLOPS
SSD Mobilenet [7]	61.6	66.0	5.5	2.3
SSD Inception V2 [7]	66.1	42.1	13.4	7.5
Cascade R-CNN [17]	70.4	-	-	-
Faster R-CNN + IFA-FPN [32]	78.0	-	-	-
YOLO V2 [33]	78.8	46.5	50.5	62.7
Cascade R-CNN + IFA-FPN [32]	80.3	-	-	-
Faster R-CNN Inception V2 [5]	90.6	17.0	12.8	120.6
Faster R-CNN ResNet 50 [5]	91.5	9.6	43.3	533.5
Faster R-CNN ResNet 101 [5]	95.0	8.1	62.3	625.7
R-FCN ResNet 101	95.1	11.7	64.5	269.9
Faster R-CNN Inception ResNet V2 [5]	95.7	2.2	59.4	1837.5
EMDFNet(ours)	**97.0**	16.7	29.7	190.4

edge-located signs with high confidence, addressing YOLOX and Mask R-CNN limitations in edge detection and small object classification.

4.6 Ablation Study

To investigate the performance of various components of our EMDFNet, we add the separate component to the baseline to observe the detection performance. All experiments are performed on the TT100K dataset. The ablation results about ASM, EHE, SIoU and Res2net are illustrated in Table 5.

Impact of Augmented Shortcut Module. we first verify ASM's feature diversity capability. As observed in Table 5, mAP@.5 increase by 0.9%, mAP@.75 increase by 1.5%, and mAP@.5:.95 increase by 1.4%. The results show that the mAP value comprehensively improves, proving the ability of ASM feature diversity. ASM enhances input feature diversity beyond standard shortcuts by introducing a transformative multiple branches.

Impact of Efficient Hybrid Encoder. To preserve crucial discriminative information and enhance feature fusion during aggregation and path selection, we integrate EMDFNet's EHE into YOLOX, resulting in significant improvements across various metrics. According to experimental in Table 5, AP_s, AP_m, and AP_l comprehensively enhance. The increase in AP_s, AP_m, and AP_l are 2.0%, 1.5%, and 3.5%, respectively. Therefore, EHE has a very good effect on the fusion of small, medium and large targets.

Impact of SIoU. To verify the impact of different loss functions, we conduct ablation experiments on the original IoU Loss and SIoU Loss. EMDFNet's SIoU Loss considers spatial distances and angles between predicted and actual bounding boxes, improving training efficiency compared to YOLOX's traditional IoU

Loss. Experimental results in Table 5 confirm these improvements, enhancing metrics such as mAP@.5, mAP@.75, and mAP@.5:.95, without adding complexity. Notably, mAP@.5 increases by 1.2% to 81.8%.

Table 4. Detection error distribution of YOLOX and EMDFNet on the TT100K testing set. TIDE categorizes errors into six types: Cls (correct localization but incorrect classification), Loc (correct classification but incorrect localization), Both (incorrect classification and localization), Dupe detection (correct classification and localization with a prior matching detection), Bkg (detected background as foreground), and Miss (undetected ground truths outside of classification or localization errors).

Model	Cls	Loc	Both	Dupe	Bkg	Miss	FalsePos(FP)	FalseNeg(FN)
YOLOX	11.22	0.44	**0.01**	**0.05**	2.71	1.87	7.90	9.67
EMDFNet(ours)	**10.02**	**0.31**	0.03	0.08	**2.63**	**0.98**	**7.47**	**7.62**

Table 5. Ablation Experiment on the TT100K Dataset. We conduct ablation experiments on ASM, EHE, SIoU and Res2Net.

Model	mAP@.5	mAP@.75	mAP@.5:.95	AP_s	AP_m	AP_l
YOLOX [34]	80.6	72.8	61.2	53.1	66.1	72.4
YOLOX+ASM	81.5	74.3	62.6	52.7	67.8	73.0
YOLOX+EHE	82.2	74.6	63.1	55.1	67.6	75.9
YOLOX+SIoU	81.8	73.0	61.7	53.4	66.6	71.2
YOLOX+Res2Net	82.5	74.8	63.2	54.0	68.4	76.0
EMDFNet(ours)	**84.4**	**76.8**	**64.9**	**55.4**	**68.5**	**81.7**

Impact of Res2Net. Finally, we assess EMDFNet's Res2Net backbone, which enhances multi-scale features and expands the receptive field of per layer compared to YOLOX's Darknet53. Theoretically, Res2Net offers superior feature extraction, leading to enhanced detection performance. By partitioning input features into different groups and processing them through varying numbers of convolutional blocks, Res2Net achieves multi-scale effect, which is particularly advantageous for small object detection. Experimental results in Table 5 demonstrate improvements across all metrics, with mAP@.5, mAP@.75, mAP@.5:.95, AP_s, AP_m, and AP_l increasing by 1.9%, 2.0%, 2.0%, 0.9%, 2.3%, and 3.6%, respectively. These enhancements, achieving with minimal increase in parameters and computational complexity, affirm the efficacy of Res2Net in EMDFNet.

Fig. 5. Comparison of detection performance between EMDFNet and other models on the TT100K testing set. Zoom in to see details.

5 Conclusion

This paper proposes a novel detector EMDFNet to address the issues of feature singularity and weak multi-scale fusion capability. EMDFNet consists of two key components: an Augmented Shortcut Module and an Efficient Hybrid Encoder. The Augmented Shortcut Module utilizes extracted features as input for different branches, conducts various feature selection operations, and ultimately combines them to enhance feature diversity. The Efficient Hybrid Encoder performs information interaction based on intra-scale feature interaction and cross-scale feature fusion. Extensive experiments on challenging datasets such as TT100K and GTSDB demonstrate that our EMDFNet achieves state-of-the-art performance. We will continue to explore lightweight network to better apply them in autonomous driving.

References

1. Everingham, M., Van Gool, L., Williams, C.K., Winn, J., Zisserman, A.: The pascal visual object classes (voc) challenge. Int. J. Comput. Vision **88**, 303–338 (2010)
2. Lin, T.-Y., et al.: Microsoft COCO: common objects in context. In: Fleet, D., Pajdla, T., Schiele, B., Tuytelaars, T. (eds.) ECCV 2014. LNCS, vol. 8693, pp. 740–755. Springer, Cham (2014). https://doi.org/10.1007/978-3-319-10602-1_48
3. Girshick, R., Donahue, J., Darrell, T., Malik, J.: Rich feature hierarchies for accurate object detection and semantic segmentation. In: Proceedings of the IEEE Conference on Computer Vision and Pattern Recognition, pp. 580–587 (2014)
4. Girshick, R.: Fast R-CNN. In: Proceedings of the IEEE International Conference on Computer Vision, pp. 1440–1448 (2015)
5. Ren, S., He, K., Girshick, R., Sun, J.: Faster R-CNN: towards real-time object detection with region proposal networks. In: Advances in Neural Information Processing Systems, vol. 28, (2015)
6. He, K., Gkioxari, G., Dollár, P., Girshick, R.: Mask R-CNN. In: Proceedings of the IEEE International Conference on Computer Vision, pp. 2961–2969 (2017)
7. Liu, W., et al.: SSD: single shot multibox detector. In: Leibe, B., Matas, J., Sebe, N., Welling, M. (eds.) ECCV 2016. LNCS, vol. 9905, pp. 21–37. Springer, Cham (2016). https://doi.org/10.1007/978-3-319-46448-0_2
8. Zhu, Y., Zhang, C., Zhou, D., Wang, X., Bai, X., Liu, W.: Traffic sign detection and recognition using fully convolutional network guided proposals. Neurocomputing **214**, 758–766 (2016)
9. Gao, S.-H., Cheng, M.-M., Zhao, K., Zhang, X.-Y., Yang, M.-H., Torr, P.: Res2net: a new multi-scale backbone architecture. IEEE Trans. Pattern Anal. Mach. Intell. **43**(2), 652–662 (2019)
10. Ouyang, D., et al.: Efficient multi-scale attention module with cross-spatial learning. In: ICASSP 2023-2023 IEEE International Conference on Acoustics, Speech and Signal Processing (ICASSP), IEEE, 2023, pp. 1–5 (2023)
11. Wan, D., Lu, R., Shen, S., Xu, T., Lang, X., Ren, Z.: Mixed local channel attention for object detection. Eng. Appl. Artif. Intell. **123**, 106442 (2023)
12. Lv, W., et al.: DETRs beat yolos on real-time object detection. arXiv preprint arXiv:2304.08069 (2023)
13. Gevorgyan, Z.: Siou loss: More powerful learning for bounding box regression. arXiv preprint arXiv:2205.12740 (2022)
14. Zhu, Z., Liang, D., Zhang, S., Huang, X., Li, B., Hu, S.: Traffic-sign detection and classification in the wild. In: Proceedings of the IEEE Conference on Computer Vision and Pattern Recognition, pp. 2110–2118 (2016)

15. Houben, S., Stallkamp, J., Salmen, J., Schlipsing, M., Igel, C.: Detection of traffic signs in real-world images: the German traffic sign detection benchmark. In: International Joint Conference on Neural Networks, no. 1288 (2013)
16. Lin, T.Y., Goyal, P., Girshick, R., He, K., Dollár, P.: Focal loss for dense object detection. In: Proceedings of the IEEE International Conference on Computer Vision, 2017, pp. 2980–2988 (2017)
17. Cai, Z., Vasconcelos, N.: Cascade R-CNN: delving into high quality object detection. In: Proceedings of the IEEE Conference on Computer Vision and Pattern Recognition, 2018, pp. 6154–6162 (2018)
18. Zhu, R.,: Scratchdet: training single-shot object detectors from scratch. In: Proceedings of the IEEE/CVF Conference on Computer Vision and Pattern Recognition, pp. 2268–2277 (2019)
19. Tian, Z., Shen, C., Chen, H., He, T., et al.: Fcos: fully convolutional one-stage object detection. In: Proceedings of the IEEE/CVF International Conference on Computer Vision, pp. 9627–9636 (2019)
20. Liang, Z., Shao, J., Zhang, D., Gao, L.: Traffic sign detection and recognition based on pyramidal convolutional networks. Neural Comput. Appl. **32**, 6533–6543 (2020)
21. Sun, P., et al.: Sparse R-CNN: end-to-end object detection with learnable proposals. In: Proceedings of the IEEE/CVF Conference on Computer Vision and Pattern Recognition, pp. 14 454–14 463 (2021)
22. Liu, Z., et al.: Swin transformer: hierarchical vision transformer using shifted windows. In: Proceedings of the IEEE/CVF International Conference On Computer Vision, pp. 10 012–10 022 (2021)
23. Cui, L., et al.: Context-aware block net for small object detection. IEEE Trans. Cybern. **52**(4), 2300–2313 (2020)
24. Chu, J., Zhang, C., Yan, M., Zhang, H., Ge, T.: Trd-yolo: a real-time, high-performance small traffic sign detection algorithm. Sensors **23**(8), 3871 (2023)
25. Han, Y., Wang, F., Wang, W., Li, X., Zhang, J.: YOLO-SG: small traffic signs detection method in complex scene. J. Supercomput. **80**(2), 2025–2046 (2024). https://doi.org/10.1007/s11227-023-05547-y
26. Shi, Y.: Open-transmind: A new baseline and benchmark for 1st foundation model challenge of intelligent transportation. In: Proceedings of the IEEE/CVF Conference on Computer Vision and Pattern Recognition, pp. 6327–6334 (2023)
27. Zeng, G., Huang, W., Wang, Y., Wang, X., Wenjuan, E.: Transformer fusion and residual learning group classifier loss for long-tailed traffic sign detection. IEEE Sensors J. 1–1 (2024)
28. He, K., Zhang, X., Ren, S., Sun, J.: Deep residual learning for image recognition. In: Proceedings of the IEEE Conference on Computer Vision and Pattern Recognition, pp. 770–778 (2016)
29. Lin, T.-Y., Dollár, P., Girshick, R., He, K., Hariharan, B., Belongie, S.: Feature pyramid networks for object detection. In: Proceedings of the IEEE Conference on Computer Vision and Pattern Recognition, pp. 2117–2125 (2017)
30. Fu, C.Y., Liu, W., Ranga, A., Tyagi, A., Berg, A.C.: Dssd: deconvolutional single shot detector. arXiv preprint arXiv:1701.06659 (2017)
31. Liu, S., Huang, D., et al.: Receptive field block net for accurate and fast object detection. In: Proceedings of the European Conference on Computer Vision (ECCV), pp. 385–400 (2018)
32. Tang, Q., Cao, G., Jo, K.H.: Integrated feature pyramid network with feature aggregation for traffic sign detection. IEEE Access **9**, 117 784–117 794 (2021)

33. Redmon, J., Farhadi, A.: Yolo9000: better, faster, stronger. In: Proceedings of the IEEE Conference on Computer Vision and Pattern Recognition, pp. 7263–7271 (2017)
34. Ge, Z., Liu, S., Wang, F., Li, Z., Sun, J.: Yolox: exceeding yolo series in 2021. arXiv preprint arXiv:2107.08430 (2021)

Global-Guided Weighted Enhancement for Salient Object Detection

Jizhe Yu[1](), Yu Liu[1], Hongkui Wei[2], Kaiping Xu[1], Yifei Cao[1], and Jiangquan Li[1]

[1] DUT School of Software Technology and DUT-RU International School of Information Science and Engineering, Dalian University of Technology, Dalian, China
yujizhe@mail.dlut.edu.cn
[2] State Key Laboratory of Intelligent Manufacturing System Technology, Beijing Institute of Electronic System Engineering, Beijing, China

Abstract. Salient Object Detection (SOD) benefits from the guidance of global context to further enhance performance. However, most works focus on treating the top-layer features through simple compression and nonlinear processing as the global context, which inevitably lacks the integrity of the object. Moreover, directly integrating multi-level features with global context is ineffective for solving semantic dilution. Although the global context is considered to enhance the relationship among salient regions to reduce feature redundancy, equating high-level features with global context often results in suboptimal performance. To address these issues, we redefine the role of global context within the network and propose a new method called Global-Guided Weighted Enhancement Network (GWENet). We first design a Deep Semantic Feature Extractor (DSFE) to enlarge the receptive field of network, laying the foundation for global context extraction. Secondly, we construct a Global Perception Module (GPM) for global context modeling through pixel-level correspondence, which employs a global sliding weighted technique to provide the network with rich semantics and acts on each layer to enhance SOD performance by Global Guidance Flows (GGFs). Lastly, to effectively merge multi-level features with the global context, we introduce a Comprehensive Feature Enhancement Module (CFEM) that integrates all features within the module through 3D convolution, producing more robust feature maps. Extensive experiments on five challenging benchmark datasets demonstrate that GWENet achieves state-of-the-art results.

Keywords: Salient object detection · Global context guidance · Sliding weighted enhancement · Comprehensive feature fusion · 3D convolution

1 Introduction

Salient Object Detection (SOD) mimics the human visual perception system to capture the most attractive parts of an image, and is widely applied in the pre-processing stages of visual tasks such as image editing, AR, VR, and autonomous

Fig. 1. The prediction results are more accurate than the predictions of other state-of-the-art networks in the field, such as GCPANet [9] and EDN [7].

driving. The popularity of SOD owes to the exceptional feature extraction capabilities of Convolutional Neural Networks (CNNs) in computer vision, marking a significant shift from traditional handcrafted feature extraction [1] to advanced feature representation based on encoder-decoder architectures [2]. Many CNN-based models [3,4] have significantly improved SOD performance through the collaborative work of high-level and low-level features. High-level features have a lower resolution but are rich in semantic information, making them ideal for generating coarse saliency maps. In contrast, low-level features offer larger spatial scales and finer details, crucial for reconstructing object structures. Unfortunately, the dilution of high-level features in the top-down transmission process and the large amount of noise in low-level features have prompted many studies to solve this issue by introducing global features. Some studies [5–7] utilize attention mechanisms to focus the global context on critical areas within high-level features. Other studies [8–11] integrate global context into various stages of the decoder, aiming to enhance the coherence of object prediction. Although these two strategies significantly improve, there remains room for enhancing the prediction integrity for irregular-scale objects in complex scenes, as shown in Fig. 1. Therefore, to enhance the semantics and minimize errors, we identify two main issues that need to be addressed: (1) Most previous works generate global context through simple spatial compression and nonlinear activation of deep features in the encoder, overlooking the fundamental differences between high-level features and global context within the network; (2) While global context guides the fusion of multi-level features by scene understanding of the overall image, simply combining semantic information, detail information, and global context is suboptimal. This way fails to consider the interference of complex backgrounds and utilize the potential of global guidance in restoring object integrity.

To redefine the role of global context within networks, we propose a novel network called the Global-guided Weighted Enhancement Network (GWENet), comprising three key components and one enhancement technique. To address the first issue, we design a Global Perception Module (GPM) that focuses on learning the correspondence of each pixel to extract global context, which is then applied in the decoding stage through Global Guidance Flows (GGFs). According to EDN [7], further downsampling of the existing CNN backbone network can extract semantics and locate objects more effectively. For this purpose, we design a Deep Semantic Feature Extractor (DSFE) positioned before GPM, which lays the foundation for capturing global context by mining the correlations among feature channels. To enhance learning object integrity from a global view, we construct a Comprehensive Feature Enhancement Module (CFEM) to gradually aggregate multi-level features from the top-down. CFEM comprises two submodules: an Adaptive Feature Interaction Fusion Module (AFIFM) and a Scale Diversity Integration Module (SDIM), which enable the model to enrich feature diversity while extracting valuable complementary information. To address the second issue, the currently common practice involves element-wise addition, multiplication, or concatenation of global context with multi-level features, which is intuitive but not optimal. Therefore, we propose a more stable and efficient enhancement technique, namely a learnable weighted operator. We utilize the global attention guidance generated by GPM to perform sliding weighting on the appearance details and body region maps, which imparts low-level features with semantics and effectively prevents the dilution of high-level features. Furthermore, at the end of the feature aggregation stage in the CFEM module, we employ 3D convolution to capture more accurate and prosperous inter-feature correspondence, thereby enhancing the comprehensive feature fusion. As the visualization results in Fig. 1 show, our GWENet primarily employs global sliding weighted technique, complemented by comprehensive feature fusion, to maximize shape integrity and minimize background interference, as displayed with objects like tennis rackets and bamboo poles.

To sum up, our contributions are as follows:

- We explore the global context from a new perspective to restore object integrity learning, and propose a global sliding weighted enhancement technique to effectively address issues such as dilution and noise instead of previous improved high-level features acting as the global context to locate salient objects, which is expected to provide a new idea for SOD.
- We propose a novel Global-guided Weighted Enhancement Network for accurate salient object detection, which introduces three key components: the Global Perception Module (GPM), the Deep Semantic Feature Extractor (DSFE), and the Comprehensive Feature Enhancement Module (CFEM), where CFEM comprises the Adaptive Feature Interaction Fusion Module (AFIFM) and the Scale Diversity Integration Module (SDIM).

– Compared with the state-of-the-art methods on five challenging datasets, the proposed GWENet achieves the best performance in quantitative and qualitative evaluations.

2 Related Work

2.1 Methods Based on Global Context Guidance

In recent years, global context learning plays a vital role in enhancing the performance of SOD. Wei et al. [10] introduce the Side-out Aggregation Module to enhance the receptive field of the entire network, enabling it to capture more comprehensive information while avoiding the omission of crucial information. Zhao et al. [6] add a global average pooling layer at the end of the encoder to obtain global context, resulting in complete segmentation outcomes. Wu et al. [7] propose an extreme downsampling block to effectively capture global context, thereby achieving accurate salient object localization. To better address the semantic dilution problem of high-level features, Chen et al. [9] design a global context flow module to generate global context information for different decoding stages. Liu et al. [11] utilize the existing semantic segmentation module PPM [4] to capture global guiding information, compensating for the gradual dilution from the top-down.

2.2 Methods Based on Multi-level Feature Fusion

Most multi-level feature fusion methods adopt the principle of feature complementarity [12], that is, combining global structures with local detail information to aggregate multi-scale information. Wu et al. [8] develop a cascaded feedback decoder to fuse multi-level features through multiple iterations, narrowing the feature differences between different layers. Zhou et al. [3] design a two-stream feature decoder for details and structures to capture complementary information. Pang et al. [13] propose a mutual learning aggregation strategy, fusing only adjacent layer features to enhance the representational capability of different resolution features. To obtain richer scale information, Ma et al. [14] introduce atrous convolution in the feature fusion module, aimed at enhancing valuable information and suppressing noise. Zhuge et al. [15] believe that the rich receptive field of convolution kernels can further help the network capture features of different scales, hence a diversity aggregation module is designed to extract feature diversity.

3 Method

3.1 Overview of GCWNet

As shown in Fig. 2, our proposed GWENet employs a U-shaped network architecture based on the encoder-decoder. The encoder utilizes the VGG16 network as

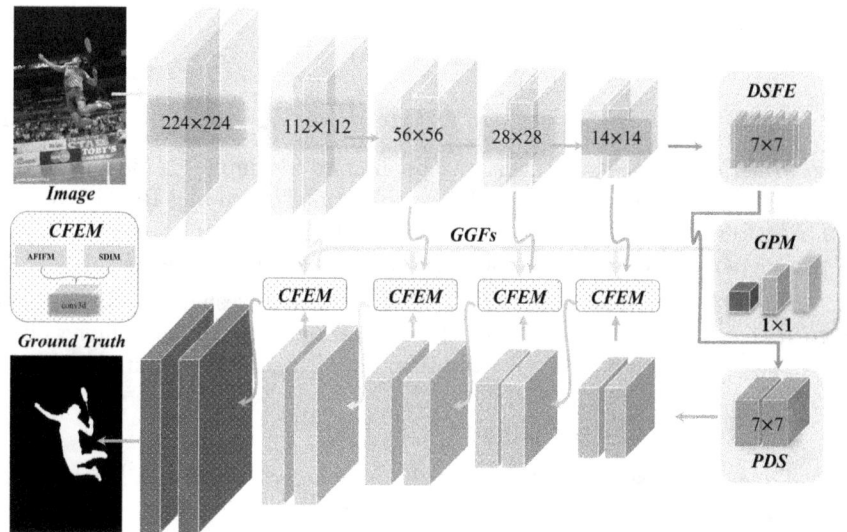

Fig. 2. Illustration of the overall network architecture of GWENet.

its backbone to extract initial features. Following prior studies [4,10], we remove the last pooling and fully connected layers for end-to-end saliency prediction. The network input is images with a resolution of [224 × 224] pixels. Given that VGG comprises four pooling layers, the subsequent output scales are [112 × 112], [56 × 56], [28 × 28], and [14 × 14], respectively. For simplicity, we denote these five stages as a set V = $\{V_{E1}, V_{E2}, V_{E3}, V_{E4}, V_{E5}\}$.

Next, we further downsample the network through the Deep Semantic Feature Extractor (DSFE) to fully extract high-level features rich in semantic and localization information. Thereafter, the high-level features are passed to the Global Perception Module (GPM) to obtain a global view of the image by learning the relationship among pixels and act on the comprehensive feature enhancement module (CFEM) at each decoding stage through the Global Gudance Flow (GFFs). Then, we enhance multi-level feature aggregation with the Adaptive Feature Interaction Fusion Module (AFIFM) and capture multi-scale information using the Scale Diversity Integration Module (SDIM) under the guidance of the global context. Finally, we use 3D convolution to integrate features within the CFEM and output a robust prediction map.

3.2 Deep Semantic Feature Extractor

Wu et al. [7] indicates that further downsampling the network can capture a broader field of view to enhance high-level features, which play a crucial role in scene understanding and object localization [5,10,13]. To this end, we design the Deep Semantic Feature Extractor (DSFE) at the end of the encoder to fully extract high-level semantics. First, we adopt max pooling to downsample the feature maps to 7×7, obtaining feature denoted as $F_{down} \in R^{N \times C \times H \times W}$ (C, H, W are the channel number, height, and width):

$$F_{down} = Conv^{3\times3}\left(MaxPool\left(V_{E5}\right)\right) \tag{1}$$

where $MaxPool(\cdot)$ means 2 times max pooling downsampling. $Conv^{3\times3}(\cdot)$ represents a 3×3 convolution followed by batch normalization and ReLU layers.

Thereafter, inspired by the self-attention [17], three 1×1 convolution layers are deployed to get three feature maps, namely $F_Q \in R^{N \times C \times H \times W}$, $F_K \in R^{N \times C \times H \times W}$, and $F_V \in R^{N \times C \times H \times W}$. After reshaping F_Q, F_V and F_K to $R^{N \times HW \times C}$. Then we reshape the correlation strength map among pixels $F_S \in R^{N \times HW \times C}$ to $R^{N \times C \times H \times W}$, and the above process is computed as:

$$F_S = Softmax\left(F_Q F_K^T\right) F_V + F_{down} \tag{2}$$

where T means transpose, and $Softmax(\cdot)$ represents the softmax layer for feature normalization.

Inspired by the Squeeze-and-Excitation [18], three 3×3 convolution layers are deployed to enhance global dependencies among channels. This process is calculated by

$$F_{D6} = Conv_3^{3\times3}\left(Conv_2^{3\times3}\left(Conv_1^{3\times3}\left(F_S\right)\right)\right) + F_S \tag{3}$$

where $Conv_1^{3\times3}(\cdot) \in R^{C \to C/2}$, $Conv_2^{3\times3}(\cdot) \in R^{C/2 \to C/2}$, and $Conv_3^{3\times3}(\cdot) \in R^{C/2 \to C}$. $F_{D6} \in R^{N \times C \times H \times W}$ represents the deep high-level semantics that are the final output of DSFE.

Finally, we conduct max pooling to highlight salient regions and average pooling to suppress background on the F_{D6}, which captures 'pure' deep semantics F_{PDS} ("PDS" in Fig. 2) applied for top-down.

3.3 Global Perception Module

In the above, we have discussed that existing SOD methods often generate global features via simple compression and nonlinear activation of high-level features but overlook the fundamental differences between the two. Therefore, we design the GPM to capture the global context based on DSFE, enhancing object integrity learning.

We first model F_{D6} in pixel-level corresponding relationship to determine salient region. A location with a high correlation suggests a higher likelihood of being a salient region. Specifically, We pass F_{D6} through two 1×1 convolutional layers followed by matrix multiplication to obtain the affinity matrix map $A_{D6} \in R^{N \times HW \times HW}$:

$$A_{D6} = Conv_1^{1\times1}\left(F_{D6}\right) \otimes Conv_2^{1\times1}\left(F_{D6}\right)^T \tag{4}$$

where $Conv^{1\times1}(\cdot)$ is the 1×1 convolution, $\otimes$ represents matrix multiplication.

Next, To further get the global correlation of each pixel about spatial location, we apply max pooling on the affinity matrix A_{D6} by row to obtain an affinity matrix $A_{D6}^{max} \in R^{N \times HW \times 1}$, then normalize and reshape it into affinity matrix $A'_{D6} \in R^{N \times 1 \times HW}$:

$$A'_{D6} = Softmax\left(Maxpool\left(A_{D6}\right)\right) \tag{5}$$

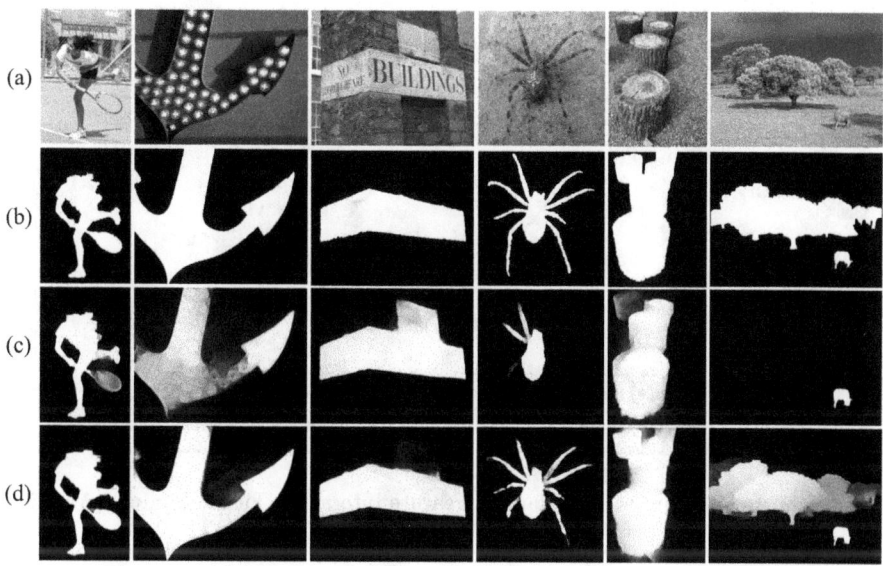

Fig. 3. The effectiveness of GPM. (a) Input images. (b) Ground Truth. (c) Results of our method w/o GPM. (d) Results of our method. We can see that without the GPM, the proposed method will suffer from semantic dilution, interference from non-salient objects, and inaccurate localization of objects.

where $MaxPool(\cdot)$ is the max pooling along the row. Similarly, we repeat Eq. (5) for A'_{D6} to obtain the global affinity vector $A''_{D6} \in R^{N \times 1 \times 1}$.

Thereafter, We transform the affinity vector A''_{D6} into an affinity weight map $A^w_{D6} \in R^{N \times 1 \times 1 \times 1}$ by unsqueeze operation, then we combine the affinity weight map A^w_{D6} and deep high-level semantic F_{D6} in an element-wise multiplication manner, thereby getting the correlation feature map $C^w_{D6} \in R^{N \times C \times H \times W}$ with a high position relationship.

$$C^w_{D6} = A^w_{D6} \odot \rho\left(F_{D6}\right) \tag{6}$$

where $\odot$ is element-wise multiplication, $\rho(\cdot)$ represents L2 normalized function.

Finally, We sum C^w_{D6} along the width and height dimensions to get $R^{N \times C}$, and then convert to $R^{N \times C \times 1 \times 1}$ by two unsqueeze operations. After that, we can get the global context $A^w_G \in R^{N \times C \times 1 \times 1}$ in final feature aggregation.

By applying GPM, we learn a global correspondence for each pixel to learn a global understanding of the entire image. Figure 3 shows some examples. We can see that the proposed model without GPM is easily disturbed by background noise, e.g., the tennis racket and spider legs in Fig. 3(c). In contrast, the proposed GPM effectively prevents semantic dilution and accurately locates salient regions.

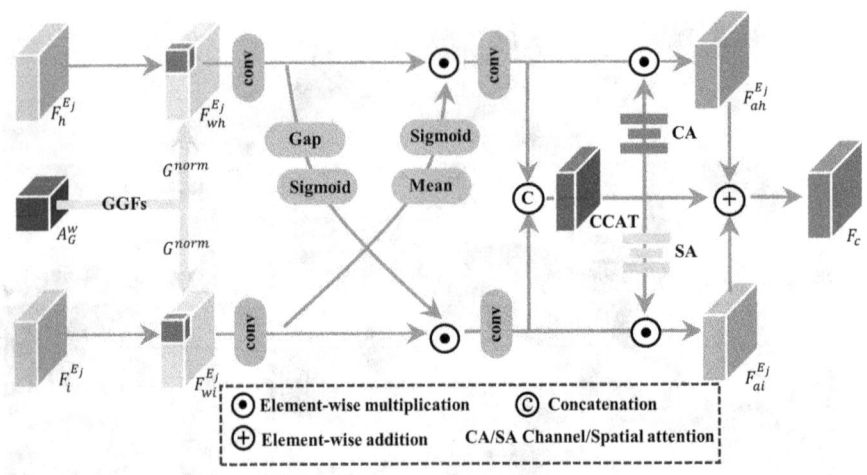

Fig. 4. The architecture of the Adaptive Feature Interactive Fusion Module (AFIFM).

3.4 Comprehensive Feature Enhancement Module

Recent work [8,11] has shown that fusing features from different levels can effectively preserve detail information and capture semantics. For this purpose, we propose the CFEM to better merge multi-level features. We first pass the initial and deep features to the AFIFM, which address the resolution differences between semantics and details under the guidance of global context. Thereafter, features are passed to the SDIM for extracting multi-scale and diverse features. Finally, 3D convolution is used to integrate complementary and multi-scale features.

Adaptive Feature Interactive Fusion Module. As shown in Fig. 4, we construct the AFIFM to address feature misalignment and noise interference in the feature fusion process. Suppose that $F_h^{Ej} \in R^{N \times C \times H \times W}$ represents the deep feature, $F_i^{Ej} \in R^{N \times C \times H \times 1}$ (j=2,3,4,5) represents the initial feature (j denotes the decoding layer). We first apply 1×1 convolutional layer for $A_G^w \in R^{N \times C \times 1 \times 1}$ followed by L2 normalization to obtain global attention guidance map $G^{norm} \in R^{N \times C \times 1 \times 1}$. Then, the proposed global sliding weighted technique is used to enhance F_h^{Ej} and F_i^{Ej}, making them fully considering the corresponding relationship between each pixel and global attention map G^{norm} to enhance the recognition of salient regions and suppress irrelevant background. We can get weight features $F_{wh}^{Ej} \in R^{N \times C \times H \times W}$ and $F_{wi}^{Ej} \in R^{N \times C \times H \times W}$ in a residual connection manner, which can be represented as:

$$\begin{cases} F_{wh}^{Ej} = Conv^{G^{norm}} \left(F_h^{Ej} \right) \odot F_h^{Ej} + F_h^{Ej} \\ F_{wi}^{Ej} = Conv^{G^{norm}} \left(F_i^{Ej} \right) \odot F_i^{Ej} + F_i^{Ej} \end{cases} \qquad (7)$$

where $Conv^{G^{norm}}(\cdot)$ denotes the convolution with G^{norm} as the convolution kernel. It is worth noting that the global sliding weighted technique is not used without the GPM module. With the enhancement of the sliding weighted technique, the model can recognize non-salient objects (billboard in the 3rd column) is illustrated in Fig. 3. Furthermore, unlike [6,7,22], we considered the distinct contributions to different stages, that is, transmitting the global context to each decoding stage through GGFs.

Next, inspired by PFSNet [14], we utilize dynamic weights to fuse semantic and detail features. We first use F_{wh}^{Ej} to generate the channel weights $F_{ch}^{Ej} = \sigma \left(\mathcal{G} \left(Conv_1^{1 \times 1} \left(F_{wh}^{Ej} \right) \right) \right)$ for F_{wi}^{Ej}, and F_{wi}^{Ej} to generate the spatial weights $F_{si}^{Ej} = \sigma \left(\mathcal{M} \left(Conv_1^{1 \times 1} \left(F_{wh}^{Ej} \right) \right) \right)$ for F_{wh}^{Ej}. Both work on opposite branches, which can help us accumulate more salient features at each level. The specific process can be described as follows:

$$CCAT = Concat \left(\left(F_{wi}^{Ej} \odot F_{ch}^{Ej} \right), \left(F_{wh}^{Ej} \odot F_{si}^{Ej} \right) \right) \qquad (8)$$

where $CCAT \in R^{N \times C \times H \times W}$ represents comprehensive feature map, $\sigma(\cdot)$ represents the Sigmoid activation function. $\mathcal{G}(\cdot)$ is global average pooling operation, and $\mathcal{M}(\cdot)$ means that the channel dimensions are averaged. $Concat$ is concatenation operation.

Finally, we use channel and spatial attention [9] to further refine the two branch features, which can be expressed as follows.

$$F_c = CCAT + \left(F_{ai}^{Ej} \odot CA(CCAT) \right) + \left(F_{ah}^{Ej} \odot SA(CCAT) \right) \qquad (9)$$

where CA denotes channel attention, and SA is spatial attention. $F_{ai}^{Ej} = F_{wi}^{Ej} \odot F_{ch}^{Ej}$, $F_{ah}^{Ej} = F_{wh}^{Ej} \odot F_{si}^{Ej}$. The final result $F_c \in R^{N \times C \times H \times W}$ is obtained by fusing all the information through the residual connection.

Scale Diversity Integrated Module. As shown in Fig. 5, we construct SDIM for efficient multi-scale learning. Inspired by the UNet architecture [16], we design SDIM with a U-shaped structure, where the resolution of the deepest feature is

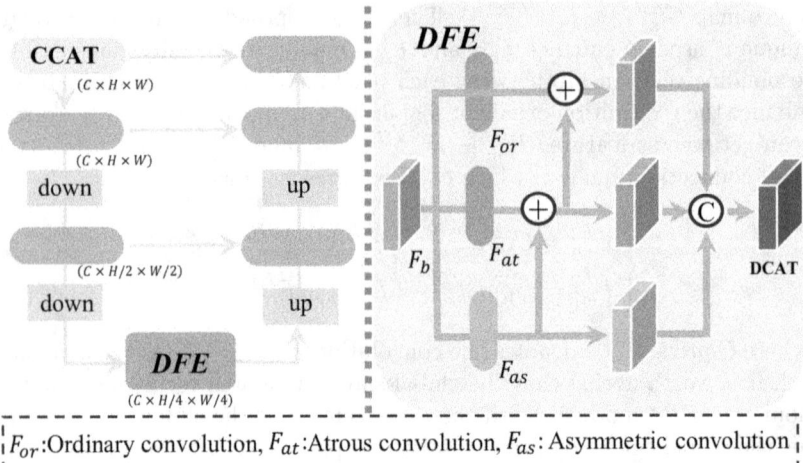

Fig. 5. Illustration of Scale Diversity Integrated Module(SDIM) for enriching feature space.

1/4 of the input size. This is mainly because features of adjacent layers are similar, and integrating features over a wide range can introduce noise [13,14]. Specifically, we first take the $CCAT$ as input of the SDIM to extract and aggregate multi-scale context information $U(CCAT)$. $U(\cdot)$ represents UNet architecture. At the last, we finish with a residual connection:

$$F_u = U(CCAT) + CCAT \tag{10}$$

Due to the challenge of predicting irregular-scale objects in complex scenes, we combine convolutional kernels of different shapes at the bottleneck layer of SDIM to capture features of various object sizes. The DFE is shown in Fig. 5. We employ ordinary convolution (or), atrous convolution [19] (at), and asymmetric convolution [7] (as) to enrich the diversity of the feature space. Furthermore, according to [7,11,21,22], inter-branch interaction helps enhance the multi-scale representation ability. Therefore, we achieve information communication and sharing between the three convolution branches.

$$\begin{cases} F_{\text{orc}} = Conv_{or}^{3\times3}(F_b) \\ F_{\text{asc}} = Conv_{as}^{3\times3}(F_b) + F_{\text{orc}} \\ F_{\text{atc}} = Conv_{at}^{3\times3}(F_b) + F_{\text{asc}} \end{cases} \tag{11}$$

Finally, we concatenate multi-scale features, like

$$DCAT = Conv^{1\times1}\left(Concat\left(F_{\text{orc}}, F_{\text{asc}}, F_{\text{atc}}\right)\right) \tag{12}$$

In this way, SDIM effectively learns irregular-scale features by integrating features of different scales. Notably, SDIM adopts average pooling for downsampling and bilinear interpolation for upsampling, thereby achieving efficient transmission.

Final Aggregation. Due to the high efficiency of 3D convolution in processing video sequences [20], we employ 3D convolution to integrate comprehensive features $CCAT$ with multi-scale features $DCAT$, aiming to enhance model performance and reduce redundancy. This process can be represented as

$$F_A = \delta \left(Conv3D^{2 \times 3 \times 3}(Concat(CCAT, DCAT)) \right) \quad (13)$$

where $Conv3D^{2 \times 3 \times 3}$ represents a 3D convolution with a kernel size of $2 \times 3 \times 3$, δ is RELU activation function. $DCAT$ and $CCAT \in R^{N \times C \times 1 \times H \times W}$. As you know, our network can further enhance the integrity of salient objects.

3.5 Supervision Strategy

Inspired by F3Net [8], we adopt a hybrid loss scheme, utilizing BCE and IoU to train our model, where BCE is used to maintain smooth gradients of the loss function, and IoU is employed to draw more attention to object structures. BCE loss is defined as:

$$\mathcal{L}_{bce} = -\sum_{x=1}^{H}\sum_{y=1}^{W}[G(x,y)\log(P(x,y)) + (1-G(x,y))\log(1-P(x,y))] \quad (14)$$

where $G(x,y)$ and $P(x,y)$ are the ground truth label and the predicted saliency label at the location (x,y), respectively. H and W are the height and width of the images, respectively. Meanwhile, L_{iou} is defined as:

$$\mathcal{L}_{iou} = 1 - \frac{\sum_{x=1}^{H}\sum_{y=1}^{W}P(x,y)G(x,y)}{\sum_{x=1}^{H}\sum_{y=1}^{W}[P(x,y) + G(x,y) - P(x,y)G(x,y)]} \quad (15)$$

4 Experiments

4.1 Experimental Settings

Implementation Details. We use ImageNet to pre-train the backbone network and then use the DUTS-TR to fine-turn the proposed GWENet. Input images are resized to [352 × 352], [320 × 320], [288 × 288], [256 × 256], and [224 × 224] for data augmentation. Adam optimizer [7,16] is used to train our network and its hyper parameters are set to default (initial learning rate lr=1e-4, betas=(0.9, 0.999), eps=1e-8, weight decay=0). The warm-up learning rate strategy is also adopted. The batch size is set to 8 (VGG16) and 32 (ResNet50). We run all experiments on the publicly available Pytorch 1.10.0 platform. The network is trained for 50 epochs. Inference for a testing image takes around 30 fps on a single GPU. The code can be available at https://github.com/Gi-gigi/GWENet.

Testing Datasets and Evaluation Criteria. We evaluate all the models on five popular datasets: ECSSD, PASCAL-S, DUT-OMRON, DUTS, HKU-IS. We adopt the Mean Absolute Error (M), the mean E-measure (E_ξ^m), the weighted F-measure (F_β^ω), and the S-measure (S_m) to assess SOD models [15]. We plot Precision-Recall (PR) curves and F-measure curves to show overall performance.

4.2 Comparison with the State-of-the-Arts

We compare the proposed GWENet with twelve recent state-of-the-art models, including CPD [2], EGNet [12], ITSD [3], GateNet [5], MINet [13], F³Net [8], U²Net [16], GCPANet [9], PFSNet [14], PA-KRN [10], ICON [15], EDN [7], and CTD-L [22]. For a fair comparison, the saliency maps are either provided by the authors or obtained by running their released codes under the default parameters.

Table 1. Comparison of GWENet with state-of-the-art SOD methods. The best performance in each column is highlighted in bold.

Summary		ECSSD				PASCAL-S				DUTS-TE				HKU-IS				OMRON			
Method	Params	S_m	E_ξ^m	F_β^ω	M	S_m	E_ξ^m	F_β^ω	M	S_m	E_ξ^m	F_β^ω	M	S_m	E_ξ^m	F_β^ω	M	S_m	E_ξ^m	F_β^ω	M
VGG16-Based Methods																					
CPD	29.23	.91	.938	.895	.04	.845	.882	.796	.072	.867	.902	.8	.043	.904	.94	.879	.033	.818	.845	.715	.057
EGNet	108.07	.919	.936	.892	.041	.848	.877	.788	.077	.878	.898	.797	.044	.91	.938	.875	.035	.836	.853	.728	.057
ITSD	17.08	.914	.937	.897	.04	.856	.891	.811	.068	.877	.905	.814	.042	.906	.938	.881	.035	.829	.853	.734	.063
GateNet	100.02	.917	.932	.886	.041	.857	.886	.797	.068	.87	.893	.786	.045	.91	.934	.872	.036	.821	.84	.703	.061
MINet	47.56	.919	.943	.905	.036	.854	.893	.808	.064	.875	.907	.813	.039	.912	.944	.889	.031	.822	.846	.718	.057
ICON	19.17	.919	.946	.905	.036	.861	.902	.82	.064	.878	.915	.822	.043	.915	.95	.895	.032	.833	**.865**	.743	.065
EDN	21.83	**.928**	**.951**	**.915**	.034	.86	.896	.815	.066	.883	.912	.822	.041	.921	.95	.9	.029	.838	.863	.746	.057
Ours-V	18.47	**.928**	.950	**.915**	**.031**	**.87**	**.905**	**.833**	**.059**	**.895**	**.926**	**.848**	**.035**	**.922**	**.951**	**.906**	**.027**	.84	**.865**	**.756**	**.056**
ResNet50-Based Methods																					
CPD	47.85	.918	.942	.898	.037	.848	.882	.794	.071	.869	.898	.795	.043	.905	.938	.875	.034	.825	.847	.719	.056
EGNet	111.69	.925	.943	.903	.037	.852	.881	.795	.074	.887	.907	.815	.039	.918	.944	.887	.031	.841	.857	.738	.053
ITSD	26.47	.925	.947	.91	.034	.859	.894	.812	.066	.885	.913	.823	.041	.917	.947	.894	.031	.84	.865	.75	.061
GateNet	128.63	.92	.936	.894	.04	.858	.886	.797	.067	.885	.906	.809	.04	.915	.937	.88	.033	.838	.855	.729	.055
MINet	126.38	.925	.95	.911	.033	.856	.896	.809	.064	.884	.917	.825	.037	.919	.952	.897	.029	.833	.86	.738	.056
F³Net	25.54	.924	.948	.912	.033	.861	.898	.816	.061	.888	.92	.835	.035	.917	.952	.9	.028	.838	.864	.747	.053
U²Net	46.21	.928	.924	.91	.033	.844	.841	.797	.074	.861	.886	.804	.044	.916	.948	.89	.031	.847	.871	.757	.054
GCPANet	67.06	.927	.920	.903	.036	.858	.846	.808	.063	.89	.89	.82	.038	.92	.949	.889	.031	.839	.860	.734	.057
PFSNet	31.18	.929	.927	**.919**	.031	.853	.855	.818	.062	.892	.902	.842	.036	.924	.956	.909	.026	.842	.874	.756	.055
PAKRN	141.06	.927	.924	.918	.032	.851	.857	.816	066	.9	.916	.86	**.033**	.923	.955	.909	.027	**.853**	**.885**	.779	.05
ICON	33.09	.929	**.954**	.918	.032	.861	.899	.818	.064	.888	.924	.836	.037	.92	.953	.902	.029	.844	.876	.761	.057
EDN	42.85	.927	.951	.918	.033	.865	.902	.827	.062	.892	.925	.844	.035	.924	.955	.908	.027	.849	.877	.77	.05
CTD-L	26.48	.921	.925	.913	.032	.868	.870	.825	.059	.891	.914	.849	.034	.922	.954	.905	**.026**	.845	.878	.776	.052
Ours-R	27.73	**.931**	**.954**	**.919**	.03	**.872**	**.907**	**.835**	**.058**	**.901**	**.931**	**.863**	**.033**	**.926**	**.957**	**.91**	**.026**	.851	.882	**.781**	.05

Quantitative Comparison. Table 1 reports the quantitative results on five benchmark datasets using the backbone networks VGG16 and ResNet50 in terms of S-measure, E-measure, weighted F-measure, and MAE. Obviously, the

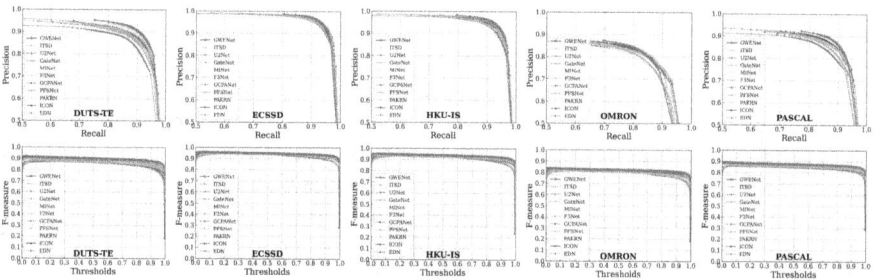

Fig. 6. Illustration of PR curves (1st row), F-measure curves (2nd row) on five datasets.

proposed GWENet outperforms other methods in both performance and efficiency. Although GWENet reach a competitive or comparable level on individual metrics, its overall performance emerged as the leader. In terms of the MAE metric, our GWENet achieves the lowest scores across all datasets, which demonstrates that the GPM assists in enhancing the model to locate salient objects. Compared with EDN [7] and GCPANet [9], the global sliding weighted technique can enhance the capability to prevent semantic dilution and suppress background interference. PR and F-Measure curves are shown in Fig. 6, respectively. GWENet performs best overall on PR and F-Measure curves, which further demonstrates the effectiveness of the proposed method based on the global context guidance.

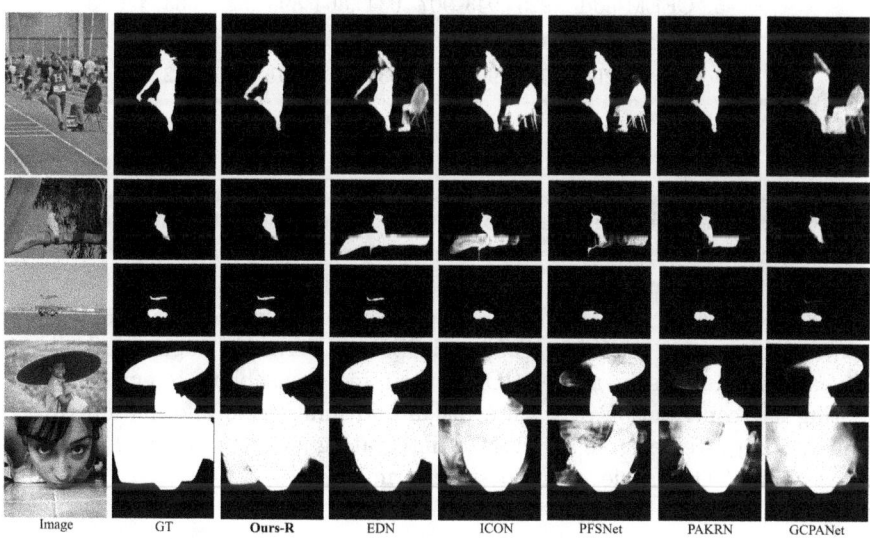

Fig. 7. Qualitative comparison of our method with five SOTA methods: GCPANet [9], PA-KRN [10], PFSNet [14], ICON [15], and EDN [7]. The proposed GWENet produces more accurate localization and complete objects with fewer background noises for various complex scenes.

Qualitative Evaluation. The qualitative comparison is shown in Fig. 7. Our GWENet generates more accurate and complete saliency maps than other methods for diverse challenging cases, e.g., Regular-scale objects in cluttered backgrounds (1st row), Small-scale objects and multi-object scenes (2nd and 3rd row), Large-scale objects (4th and 5th row). Besides, our model can highlight salient regions more clearly and suppress background noise. All visualization results demonstrate the accuracy and robustness of the proposed method.

4.3 Ablation Study

In this part, we conduct the ablation study to verify the effectiveness of the key components and technique proposed in our model. All studies are conducted on the ECSSD and PASCAL-S datasets, and VGG-16 is adopted as the backbone.

Table 2. Ablation study with different components combinations on ECSSD and PASCAL-S dataset.

Summary		ECSSD				PASCAL-S			
ID	Methods	S_m	E_ξ^m	F_β^ω	M	S_m	E_ξ^m	F_β^ω	M
1	Ours	**.928**	**.95**	**.915**	**.031**	**.87**	**.905**	**.833**	**.059**
2	w/o GPM	.921	.943	.903	.036	.865	.899	.819	.065
3	w/o AFIFM	.926	.944	.909	.035	.864	.897	.82	.064
4	w/o SDIM	.924	.948	.912	.034	.862	.902	.822	.063
5	CFEM-add	.925	.943	.907	.034	.864	.896	.82	.063
6	CFEM-multi	.926	.945	.908	.034	.869	.903	.828	.061
7	CFEM-2D	.925	.944	.909	.033	.868	.901	.826	.062

Effectiveness of Different Components. Table 2 shows that removing GPM (ID:2) significantly declines network performance on two datasets, with a 16% and 10% decrease in MAE, respectively. The effectiveness of GPM is exhaustively demonstrated in Fig. 3. We observe further performance degradation after separately removing AFIFM (ID:3) and SDIM (ID:4). Although the decline is not as significant as in model (ID:2), their indispensability is evident, highlighting the contribution of feature fusion and multi-scale information to performance improvement. As anticipated, integrating all components into the proposed model (ID:1) achieves the best performance.

Effectiveness of 3D Convolution from CFEM. In this part, we verify the effectiveness of 3D convolution in the CFEM module. Obviously, the performance of conventional aggregation methods experiences a significant decline. Compared to these models (ID:6 and ID:7), the model performance (ID:5) on the PASCAL-S dataset is particularly notable, with M decreased by 6.8%, F_β^ω by 1.6%, E_ξ^m by

0.9%, and S_m by 0.7%. These findings underscore that 3D convolution is more efficient than 2D convolution in learning relative relationships among features.

5 Conclusion

We propose a novel Global-guided Weighted Enhancement Network, GWENet, to detect irregular-scale objects in complex scenes by utilizing a global sliding weighted enhancement technique. To effectively address issues such as semantic dilution, noise interference, and feature misalignment, we construct the Deep Semantic Feature Extractor (DSFE) to generate pure high-level semantics for top-down, the Global Perception Module (GPM) to extract global context for guidance from pixel-level correspondence, and the CFEM, employing 3D convolution to explore feature correlation. The three complement each other and jointly enhance the object integrity. Comprehensive experiments on five benchmarks demonstrate that GWENet achieves the new state-of-the-art for SOD.

Acknowledgements. This work is Supported by the National Natural Science Foundation of China under Grant 61672128.

References

1. Wang, W., et al.: Salient object detection in the deep learning era: an in-depth survey. IEEE Trans. Pattern Anal. Mach. Intell. **44**, 3239–3259 (2019)
2. Wu, Z., et al.: Cascaded partial decoder for fast and accurate salient object detection. In: 2019 IEEE/CVF Conference on Computer Vision and Pattern Recognition, pp. 3902–3911 (2019)
3. Zhou, H., et al.: Interactive two-stream decoder for accurate and fast saliency detection. In: 2020 IEEE/CVF Conference on Computer Vision and Pattern Recognition, pp. 9138–9147 (2020)
4. Liu, J., et al.: A simple pooling-based design for real-time salient object detection. In: 2019 IEEE/CVF Conference on Computer Vision and Pattern Recognition, pp. 3912–3921 (2019)
5. Zhao, X., et al.: Suppress and Balance: A Simple Gated Network for Salient Object Detection. ArXiv abs/2007.08074 (2020)
6. Zhao, Z., et al.: complementary trilateral decoder for fast and accurate salient object detection. In: Proceedings of the 29th ACM International Conference on Multimedia (2021)
7. Wu, Y.H., et al.: EDN: salient object detection via extremely-downsampled network. IEEE Trans. Image Proc. **31**, 3125-3136 (2020)
8. Wei, J., et al.: F3Net: Fusion, Feedback and Focus for Salient Object Detection. ArXiv abs/1911.11445 (2019)
9. Chen, Z., et al.: Global Context-Aware Progressive Aggregation Network for Salient Object Detection. ArXiv abs/2003.00651 (2020)
10. Xu, B., et al.: Locate globally, segment locally: a progressive architecture with knowledge review network for salient object detection. In: AAAI Conference on Artificial Intelligence (2021)

11. Liu, J., et al.: PoolNet+: exploring the potential of pooling for salient object detection. IEEE Trans. Pattern Anal. Mach. Intell. **45**, 887–904 (2022)
12. Zhao, J., et al.: EGNet: edge guidance network for salient object detection. In: 2019 IEEE/CVF International Conference on Computer Vision, pp. 8778-8787 (2019)
13. Pang, Y., et al.: Multi-scale interactive network for salient object detection. In: 2020 IEEE/CVF Conference on Computer Vision and Pattern Recognition, pp. 9410–9419 (2020)
14. Ma, M., et al.: Pyramidal feature shrinking for salient object detection. In: AAAI Conference on Artificial Intelligence (2021)
15. Zhuge, M., et al.: Salient object detection via integrity learning. IEEE Trans. Pattern Anal. Mach. Intell. **45**, 3738–3752 (2021)
16. Qin, X., et al.: U2-Net: going deeper with nested u-structure for salient object detection. Pattern Recogniton. **106** , 107404 (2020)
17. Vaswani, A., et al.: Attention is all you need. Neural Inf. Proc. Syst. (2017)
18. Hu, J., et al.: Squeeze-and-excitation networks. In: 2018 IEEE/CVF Conference on Computer Vision and Pattern Recognition, pp. 7132–7141 (2017)
19. Chen, L.C., et al.: Encoder-decoder with atrous separable convolution for semantic image segmentation. In: European Conference on Computer Vision (2018)
20. Chen, Q., et al.: 3-D convolutional neural networks for RGB-D salient object detection and beyond. IEEE Trans. Neural Netw. Learn. Syst. **35**, 4309–4323 (2022)
21. Tan, Z., Xiaodong, G.: Feature recalibration network for salient object detection. In: International Conference on Artificial Neural Networks (2022). https://doi.org/10.1007/978-3-031-15937-4_6
22. Li, J., et al.: Rethinking lightweight salient object detection via network depth-width tradeoff. IEEE Trans. Image Proc. **32**, 5664–5677 (2023)

KDNet: Leveraging Vision-Language Knowledge Distillation for Few-Shot Object Detection

Mengyuan Ma, Lin Qian, and Hujun Yin(✉)

University of Manchester, M13 9PL Manchester, UK
{mengyuan.ma,hujun.yin}@manchester.ac.uk,
lin.qian-3@postgrad.manchester.ac.uk

Abstract. Few-shot object detection (FSOD) aims to detect new categories given only few instances for training. Recently emerged vision-language models (VLMs) have shown great performances in zero-shot and open-vocabulary object detection due to their strong ability to align object-level embedding with textual embedding of categories. However, few existing models distill VLMs' object-level knowledge in FSOD, which can help FSOD to learn novel semantic concepts to gain further improvement. Inspired by the recent knowledge distillation approaches with VLMs, we propose an end-to-end few-shot object detector with knowledge distillation from pre-trained VLMs, termed KDNet. A knowledge distillation branch is introduced alongside the object detector to distill knowledge from VLMs' visual encoder to the object detector. Also, we propose a pre-training mechanism with large-scale dataset to inject more semantic concepts to the detector to improve the performance on small datasets. The KDNet achieved state-of-the-art performance on both PASCAL VOC and MS COCO benchmarks over most of the shot settings and evaluation metrics.

Keywords: Object detection · Few-shot learning · Vision-language model · Knowledge distillation

1 Introduction

Owing to the advances in deep learning, object detectors have made impressive progresses recently. Deep learning-based object detectors often require large-scale datasets to achieve desirable performances. In contrast, we humans can recognize novel instances with very limited samples. Therefore there has been increasing attention on few-shot object detection (FSOD) that can learn to detect novel instances from only few annotated training samples.

Current FSOD methods usually adopt the Faster-RCNN [3] as the base detector and can be categorized into two groups: two-stage fine-tuning methods [12,14,25–27,30] and meta-learning based methods [6,7,9,11]. The former learns knowledge from data-abundant base classes to improve the detection of novel categories. Whilst the latter uses support images to generate meta-knowledge to aggregate with query images for final box classification and bounding box regression. Despite tremendous progresses made, it is still challenging to extract sufficient features for novel classes.

Vision-language models (VLMs), such as CLIP [20] and ALIGN [21], are trained on abundant image-text pairs and have shown great potential in improving zero-shot object detection and open-vocabulary object detection. There have been several attempts to introduce VLMs to FSOD tasks but they mainly focus on utilizing CLIP's text embeddings, such as knowledge distillation [32] and data augmentation [33], to gain considerable promotion. As pre-trained VLMs can align visual embeddings with textual embeddings, distilling knowledge from CLIP's visual encoder to base detectors can help capture more semantic concepts, thus improving performance. To this end, we propose KDNet, consisting of a knowledge distillation branch and a detection branch to boost the performance. Specifically speaking, the CLIP's visual encoder works as a teacher model while the detection branch works as a student model, and the detection branch learns the abundant semantic information from the large-scale pre-trained CLIP.

Contributions of the paper are as follows:

- KDNet is proposed for FSOD with a knowledge distillation branch to inject abundant semantic information from large-scale pre-trained VLMs.
- We devise a large-scale dataset pre-training mechanism for KDNet to accommodate small detection datasets.
- The proposed KDNet outperforms SOTA results on the standard FSOD settings on PASCAL VOC and challenging MS COCO dataset.

2 Related Work

2.1 Object Detection

Object Detection is a foundational task in computer vision, and it localizes and recognizes objects in images. A line of prior detectors focuses on the one-stage paradigm [1,2], which directly predicts category class confidence scores and bounding boxes over a dense feature grid. Another line of work such as Faster-RCNN [3] and FPN [4] adopts a two-stage strategy, which generates class-agnostic region proposals and then performs bounding regression and proposal classification. The two-stage approach can filter out background region proposals and often surpasses one-stage methods but suffers from more inference delays. Classic object detectors are usually trained on large-scale datasets and are not adapted well to novel classes in few-shot training regime because of the severe class imbalance.

2.2 Few-Shot Object Detection

FSOD aims to build detectors toward data scarcity scenarios, and existing methods can be grouped into two categories: fine-tune based [12,14,25–27,30] and meta-learning based [6,7,9,11]. Fine-tune based methods train detectors with abundant sufficient base classes samples in the base training phase and fine-tune the models with few-shot novel class samples. TFA [25] only fine-tunes the box regressor and classifier with novel categories while freezing the remaining parameters of the detector and has achieved better performance than the previous meta-learning based approaches. DeFRCN [30] introduces a Gradient Decoupled Layer for multi-stage decoupling and Prototypical Calibration Block for multi-task decoupling. Meta-learning based methods develop a meta-learner to acquire meta-knowledge that can be transferred to novel classes. FSRW [6] leverages fully annotated base classes and quickly adapts to novel classes, using a meta feature learner and a re-weighting module within a one-stage detection architecture. VFA [41] introduces Variational autoencoder to a meta-learner to estimate class distributions. Orthogonal to the existing work, we distill knowledge from VLMs' visual encoder to detectors to acquire sufficient semantics of novel classes.

2.3 Vision-Language Models

The contrastive VLMs such as CLIP [20] and ALIGN [21] are pre-trained on large-scale image-text pairs to learn the semantics alignment between vision and language modalities at different levels. With handcraft prompts, VLMs can extract categories' text embeddings as classifiers for images, thus benefiting zero-shot classification tasks [23]. Unlike image classification methods that can directly extract visual features from CLIP's image encoder, object detectors have to generate region proposals for further vision-language alignment. CLIP has been widely used in open-vocabulary object detection [24] to distill knowledge to detectors. In FSOD, only a few methods distill CLIP's knowledge to generate effective features. In [33] CLIP's semantic embedding was employed to augment training data in the latent space, and method in [32] distilled CLIP's text embeddings to enhance visual features. We are the first to introduce CLIP's image encoder to align the visual features and text semantic features for FSOD.

2.4 Knowledge Distillation for Object Detection

Knowledge distillation (KD) [5] helps train compact student models under the supervision of powerful teacher models. Chen *et al.* [16] proposed feature-based and response-based loss for the Faster-RCNN to distill knowledge to object detectors. GID [17] distills selected regions where the student and teacher perform differently and DeFeat [18] distills the foreground and background regions with different instances factors. FGD [19] introduces focal and global distillation modules to force the student model to focus on the teacher's critical pixels and channels. Compared to the existing KD methods in object detectors, our work is focused on distilling knowledge from VLMs to object detectors to improve few-shot object detection.

3 Proposed Methods

3.1 Preliminaries

Problem Definition. Following the FSOD experiment settings in the existing work [25,30], the training dataset $\mathcal{D}$ with a set of classes $\mathcal{C}$ is split into a base set $\mathcal{D}^B$ with abundant labelled images of base classes $\mathcal{C}^B$, and a novel set $\mathcal{D}^N$ comprising few-shot labeled data of novel classes $\mathcal{C}^N$, where $\mathcal{C}^B \cup \mathcal{C}^N = \mathcal{C}$ and $\mathcal{C}^B \cap \mathcal{C}^N = \varnothing$. Formally, $\mathcal{D}^B = \{(x,y)|y = (c_i, b_i)\}, c_i \in \mathcal{C}^B\}$, $\mathcal{D}^N = \{(x,y)|y = (c_i, b_i)\}, c_i \in \mathcal{C}^N\}$, where $x \in \mathcal{X}$ is an input image and $y \in \mathcal{Y}$ is the corresponding annotation, and c_i and b_i are denoted as class label and bounding box coordinates of each instance i in an image, respectively. We have abundant samples of $\mathcal{C}^B$ and K shots samples of $\mathcal{C}^N (K = 1, 2, 3, 5, 10, ...)$. The goal of FSOD is to train a detector with the base set and novel set to detect both base class and novel class instances.

FSOD models usually adopt a two-stage training procedure: base training and novel training. The former trains the model on $\mathcal{C}^B$ with abundant instances while the latter fine-tunes/re-trains the model with few-shot samples of the whole classes $\mathcal{C}$ or the novel classes $\mathcal{C}^N$.

3.2 Overview of KDNet

The proposed KDNet is the first attempt that distills knowledge from a pre-trained VLM visual encoder to FSOD, and it is built upon the Faster-RCNN [3], shown in Fig. 1. The proposed KDNet consists of two branches: a knowledge distillation (KD) branch and a detection branch. The KD branch injects VLMs' visual knowledge to the detection branch and the idea may also be adapted to other detectors.

Detection Branch. The detection module is built on Faster-RCNN [3] but we replace the fully-connected layers with cosine embedding layers for object classification. Let's first recap its framework. Given an image, $\mathbf{I} \in \mathbb{R}^{H \times W \times 3}$, the backbone extracts multi-level features, and then the Region Proposal Network (RPN) generates a series of region proposals bounding boxes, $\mathcal{B} \subset \mathbb{R}^4$. Same as the RoI Align in Faster-RCNN [3], it extracts proposal features $\mathbf{r} \in \mathbb{R}^{h \times w \times d}$ and projects $\mathbf{r}$ to $\mathcal{E} = \{e_b\}_{b \in \mathcal{B}} \subset \mathbb{R}^d$ with convolutional and pooling layers, on different feature maps, where d denotes the length of e_b, h and w represent the height and width of the region proposals, respectively. Different from Faster-RCNN, we regard $\mathcal{E}$ as visual words and repeat them for s times and feed them as sentences to CLIP's text encoder to generate feature embeddings, $\mathcal{F} = \{f_b\}_{b \in \mathcal{B}} \subset \mathbb{R}^d$.

For each category $c \in \mathcal{C}$, we encode its corresponding text words to generate language prompts, which are fed to the frozen CLIP's text encoder to extract text embeddings, $\mathcal{T} = \{t_c\}_{c \in \mathcal{C}} \subset \mathbb{R}^d$. Additionally, we set the background text embedding t_{bg} as a learnable embedding instead of extracting the embedding of

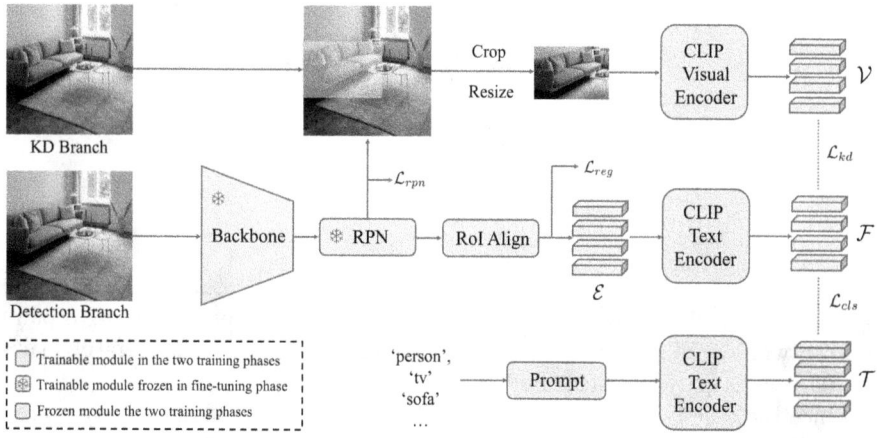

Fig. 1. Illustration of KDNet. Blue blocks denote the frozen modules while the green blocks denote trainable modules in both base training phase and fine-tuning phase. Green blocks with snowflakes are trainable in the base training phase but frozen in the fine-tuning phase. Best viewed in colours. (Color figure online)

the word 'background'. The logits of feature embedding f_b belonging to category c is computed by cosine similarity between f_b and t_c, defined as:

$$l(b,c) = \frac{f_b \cdot t_c}{||f_b|| \cdot ||t_c||} \quad (1)$$

where $\cdot$ denotes dot product, and the probability of a feature embedding f_b belong to a category c is defined as:

$$P(b,c) = \frac{\exp(\tau \cdot l(b,c))}{\sum_{c' \in \mathcal{C}} \exp(\tau \cdot (l(b,c')))} \quad (2)$$

where τ is the temperature to re-scale the value. We calculate cross-entropy loss over $P(b,c)$ as the classification loss L_{cls}.

Knowledge Distillation Branch. Given an input image **I**, this branch crops the image with region proposals $\mathcal{B}$ and resizes the regions to a fixed dimension for further visual encoding. The CLIP's visual encoder extracts region embeddings, $\mathcal{V} = \{v_b\}_{b \in \mathcal{B}} \subset \mathbb{R}^d$. KDNet aligns the region embeddings $\mathcal{V}$ encoded by CLIP's visual encoder and feature embeddings $\mathcal{F}$ from the detection branch. The knowledge distillation branch works as a teacher model and injects visual concepts into the detection branch working as a student model. Given region proposal set $\mathcal{B}$ in image **I**, We adopt the InfoNCE loss [35] as the knowledge distillation loss, defined as follows:

$$\mathcal{L}_{kd} = -\frac{1}{2}(\sum_{b \in \mathcal{B}} \log(p_{f,v}^b) + \log(p_{v,f}^b)) \quad (3)$$

where $p_{f,v}^b$ and $p_{v,f}^b$ are defined as

$$p_{f,v}^b = \frac{\exp(\tau' \cdot \langle f_b, v_b \rangle)}{\sum_{l \in \mathcal{B}} \exp(\tau' \cdot \langle f_b, v_l \rangle)} \quad (4)$$

$$p_{v,f}^b = \frac{\exp(\tau' \cdot \langle v_b, f_b \rangle)}{\sum_{l \in \mathcal{B}} \exp(\tau' \cdot \langle v_b, f_l \rangle)} \quad (5)$$

τ' is the temperature for re-scaling and $\langle \cdot \rangle$ represents cosine similarity. The loss encourages the convergence of embeddings corresponding to positive pairs $\{v_b, f_b\}$, while simultaneously driving embeddings associated with negative pairs $\{v_b, f_l\}(b \neq l)$ apart, as illustrated in Fig. 2.

Since the region embeddings $\mathcal{V}$ and text semantic embeddings $\mathcal{T}$ are aligned by CLIP pre-training, the knowledge distillation loss $\mathcal{L}_{kd}$ can narrow the gap between detection feature embeddings $\mathcal{F}$ and text embeddings $\mathcal{T}$, thus aligning the detection embeddings $\mathcal{F}$ and text embeddings $\mathcal{T}$ also. The overall training objective can be written as:

$$\mathcal{L} = \mathcal{L}_{rpn} + \mathcal{L}_{cls} + \mathcal{L}_{reg} + \mathcal{L}_{kd} \quad (6)$$

where $\mathcal{L}_{reg}$ and $\mathcal{L}_{rpn}$ represent the regression loss and RPN loss employed by Faster-RCNN, respectively.

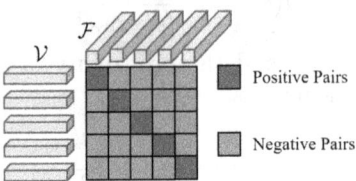

Fig. 2. Illustration of InfoNCE loss. Red patches represent positive pairs and gray patches represent negative pairs, best viewed in colours. (Color figure online)

3.3 External Datasets Knowledge Transferring

Knowledge distillation methods usually require large-scale datasets to obtain satisfying performance [42]. However, when dealing with small datasets with fewer categories, it can be hard for the student model to learn the semantic concepts from the teacher model well. PASCAL VOC dataset is an FSOD benchmark much smaller than MS COCO [37] and LVIS [38]. To fully exploit the capability of the proposed KDNet, we transfer the knowledge KDNet learned from the large-scale detection dataset MS COCO and LVIS and fine-tune KDNet with the novel samples from PASCAL VOC dataset. In detail, we train KDNet on external base classes and then fine-tune the pre-trained model with few-shot PASCAL VOC 20 class samples, and there are no class overlaps between the two sets. As validated in [22], training on base classes can recall enough region proposals of novel categories, the detection branch can learn novel concepts from CLIP's visual encoder. Following previous work [25,41], we freeze the backbones and RPN of the detection branch to prevent over-fitting during the fine-tuning phase.

4 Experiments

4.1 Datasets and Evaluation Metrics

We conducted experiments on PASCAL VOC [39] and MS COCO [37], and used MS COCO and LVIS [38] datasets as external data for PASCAL VOC. For a fair comparison, the same fixed data splits were adopted as previous work [25].

PASCAL VOC is a small object detection dataset containing 20 classes and it is randomly divided into 15 base classes and 5 novel classes for FSOD. It has a total of three such splits and there are $K = 1, 2, 3, 5, 10$ shots available in each novel split. We adopted the VOC2007 trainval set and VOC2012 trainval sets for training and evaluated the models on VOC2007 test set. Mean Average Precision (mAP) on novel set at IoU threshold 0.5 was employed for evaluation.

MS COCO has 80 object classes, where the 20 classes within PASCAL VOC are denoted as novel classes and the rest 60 object classes are set as base classes. We utilized the MS COCO 2014 trainval dataset as training set and 5K images from minival dataset as testing set, and $k = 1, 2, 3, 5, 10, 30$ novel shots were adopted. We evaluated the models on the standard, widely used MS COCO metrics: Average Precision (IoU=0.5: 0.95) and Average Precision (IoU=0.75) on the novel classes, abbreviated as nAP and nAP75, respectively.

LVIS is a large dataset built on images of MS COCO with more detailed annotations. It contains object detection and instance segmentation labels for 1,203 object categories, split into 'frequent', 'common' and 'rare' groups. The 20 classes of PASCAL VOC are in the frequent and common groups (866 classes), and we removed the 20 categories and used the remaining 846 classes as external data in our experiments.

4.2 Implementation Details

In our implementation, we used MMdetection [36] with PyTorch to build the proposed model. We employed the Faster-RCNN with ResNet-50 as our base detector. CLIP model with ViT-B/32 backbone trained on DataComp-1B [40]

Table 1. Few-shot object detection results on MS COCO dataset. The best results are in **bold**.

Method	nAP						nAP75					
	1	2	3	5	10	30	1	2	3	5	10	30
TFA w/fc [25]	2.9	4.3	6.7	8.4	10.0	13.4	2.8	4.1	6.6	8.4	9.2	13.2
TFA w/cos [25]	3.4	4.6	6.6	8.3	10.0	13.7	3.8	4.8	6.5	8.0	9.3	13.2
MPSR [26]	2.3	3.5	5.2	6.7	9.8	14.1	2.3	3.4	5.1	6.4	9.7	14.2
Meta FR-CNN [11]	5.1	7.6	-	-	12.7	16.6	4.3	6.2	-	-	10.8	15.8
FADI [27]	5.7	7.0	8.6	10.1	12.2	16.1	6.0	7.0	8.3	9.7	11.9	15.8
FCT [28]	-	7.9	-	-	17.1	21.4	-	7.9	-	-	17.0	22.1
Pseudo-Labelling [29]	-	-	-	-	17.8	24.5	-	-	-	-	17.8	25.0
DeFRCN [30]	6.6	11.7	13.3	15.6	**18.7**	22.4	7.0	12.2	13.6	15.1	17.6	22.2
FS-DETR [33]	7.0	8.9	10.0	10.9	11.3	-	7.5	9.0	10.0	10.8	11.1	-
D&R [32]	8.3	12.7	14.3	16.0	18.7	21.8	-	-	-	-	-	-
Norm-VAE [33]	9.5	13.7	14.3	15.9	**18.7**	**22.5**	8.8	13.7	14.2	15.3	**17.8**	**22.4**
KDNet (Ours)	**12.8**	**14.1**	**15.0**	**16.0**	17.2	19.0	**12.3**	**13.9**	**14.7**	**15.6**	16.8	18.4

Table 2. Average results over 10 random seeds on MS COCO dataset.

Method	nAP					
	1	2	3	5	10	30
FRCN	1.7	3.1	3.7	4.6	5.5	7.4
TFA	1.9	3.9	5.1	7.0	9.1	12.1
DeFRCN	4.8	8.5	10.7	13.5	**16.7**	**21.0**
D&R	6.1	9.5	11.5	13.9	16.4	20.0
KDNet	**11.9**	**13.5**	**14.6**	**15.4**	16.3	18.7

with 12.8 billion image-text pairs was used as the teacher model in the experiments. During the base training phase, our model was trained by an SGD optimizer with a total batch size of 16, a momentum of 0.9 and a weight decay of 0.0005. For the MS COCO dataset, we trained the base model for 180k iterations with an initial learning rate of 0.01 and decreased it by a factor of 10 after the 140k and 160k iterations. As for the PASCAL VOC dataset, KDNet was trained for 30k iterations with an initial learning rate of 0.01 and it was reduced to 0.001 and 0.0001 at 24k iteration and 28k iteration. We set the temperatures τ and τ' to 50. The repeated times of visual words s was set to 4. All of the experiments were implemented on 8 NVIDIA TITAN V GPUs with 2 image samples per GPU. It took 36 h with 9,733 MB GPU memory consumption per GPU for base training on COCO dataset, while basing training on PASCAL VOC took 5 h with similar GPU consumption.

4.3 Main Results

We compared the performance of the proposed KDNet with state-of-the-art (SOTA) methods on two benchmarks: PASCAL VOC and MS COCO.

Experiments on MS COCO Dataset. Table 1 summarizes the evaluation results for KDNet and competing SOTA methods on MS COCO. When the low shot number $K = 1, 2, 3, 5$, KDNet improved the performance by 3.3%, 0.4%, 0.7%, and 0.1%, respectively, demonstrating its superiority under extreme few-shot settings. When shot number is 10 or higher, its performance fell behind SOTA methods by 1.5%~3.5%.

Furthermore, the average results of 10 repeated runs over different few-shot training samples are reported in Table 2. The proposed KDNet improved the performance by 5.8%, 4.0%, 3.1%, 1.5% on average when shot number $K = 1, 2, 3, 5$, respectively. When the shot number was 10 or 30, the KD branch with pre-trained CLIP would not help, which is in agreement with the results on single runs.

Table 3. Few-shot object detection results on PASCAL VOC dataset. The best results are in **bold** and second best are underlined.

Method	Novel Set 1					Novel Set 2					Novel Set 3				
	1	2	3	5	10	1	2	3	5	10	1	2	3	5	10
FSRW [6]	14.8	15.5	26.7	33.9	47.2	15.7	15.3	22.7	30.1	40.5	21.3	25.6	28.4	42.8	45.9
MetaDet [7]	18.9	20.6	30.2	36.8	49.6	21.8	23.1	27.8	31.7	43.0	20.6	23.9	29.4	43.9	44.1
Meta R-CNN [8]	19.9	25.5	35.0	45.7	51.5	10.4	19.4	29.6	34.8	45.4	14.3	18.2	27.5	41.2	48.1
TFA [25]	39.8	36.1	44.7	55.7	56.0	23.5	26.9	34.1	31.5	39.1	30.8	34.8	42.8	49.5	49.8
CME [9]	41.5	47.5	50.4	58.2	60.9	27.2	30.2	41.4	42.5	46.8	34.3	39.6	45.1	48.3	51.5
MPSR [26]	41.7	42.5	51.4	55.2	61.8	24.4	29.3	39.2	39.9	47.8	35.6	41.8	42.3	48.0	49.7
QA-FewDet [10]	42.4	51.9	55.7	62.6	63.4	25.9	37.8	46.6	48.9	51.1	35.2	42.9	47.8	54.8	53.5
Meta FR-CNN [11]	43.0	54.5	60.6	66.1	65.4	27.7	35.5	46.1	47.8	51.4	40.6	46.4	53.4	50.9	58.6
FSCE [12]	44.2	43.8	51.4	61.9	63.4	27.3	29.5	43.5	44.2	50.2	37.2	41.9	47.5	54.6	58.5
Hallue [13]	47.0	44.9	46.5	54.7	54.7	26.3	31.8	37.4	37.4	41.2	40.4	42.1	43.3	51.4	49.6
SRR-FSD [14]	47.8	50.5	51.3	55.2	56.8	32.5	35.3	39.1	40.8	43.8	40.1	41.5	44.3	46.9	46.4
Meta-DETR [15]	40.6	51.4	58.0	59.2	63.6	37.0	36.6	43.7	49.1	54.6	41.6	45.9	52.7	58.9	60.6
FADI [27]	50.3	54.8	54.2	59.3	63.2	30.6	35.0	40.3	42.8	48.0	45.7	49.7	49.1	55.0	59.6
FCT [28]	49.9	57.1	57.9	63.2	67.1	27.6	34.5	43.7	49.2	51.2	39.5	54.7	52.3	57.0	58.7
DeFRCN [30]	53.6	57.5	61.5	64.1	60.8	30.1	38.1	47.0	53.3	47.9	48.4	50.9	52.3	54.9	57.4
ICPE [34]	54.3	59.5	62.4	65.7	66.2	33.5	40.1	48.7	51.7	52.5	50.9	53.1	55.3	60.6	60.1
D&R [32]	60.4	64.0	65.2	64.7	66.3	37.9	46.8	48.1	52.7	53.1	55.7	57.9	57.6	60.6	61.9
VFA [41]	57.7	64.6	64.7	67.2	67.4	41.4	46.2	51.1	51.8	51.6	48.9	54.8	56.6	59.0	58.9
Norm-VAE [33]	62.1	64.9	67.8	69.2	67.5	39.9	46.8	54.4	54.2	53.6	**58.2**	<u>60.3</u>	61.0	64.0	65.5
KDNet+COCO-60	<u>65.1</u>	<u>67.0</u>	<u>71.2</u>	<u>72.2</u>	<u>73.6</u>	<u>63.9</u>	<u>64.0</u>	<u>67.2</u>	<u>69.0</u>	<u>71.2</u>	55.6	57.5	<u>64.7</u>	<u>65.6</u>	<u>66.8</u>
KDNet+LVIS-846	**67.3**	**68.9**	**72.6**	**73.9**	**74.6**	**65.9**	**66.5**	**67.9**	**70.9**	**72.4**	<u>56.7</u>	<u>58.9</u>	**65.8**	**66.9**	**67.5**

Experiments on PASCAL VOC Dataset. PASCAL VOC is a smaller dataset with respect to the category number and the sample size. In order to fully transfer knowledge from CLIP, KDNet was pre-trained with MS COCO base classes and LVIS base classes and fine-tuned on PASCAL VOC few-shot instances. As shown in Table 3, KDNet with LVIS-846 pre-training significantly outperformed the existing methods. In Novel Set 1, it surpassed the previous best results by 4.0%~7.1%, while there were greater improvements in Novel Set 2, with 16.7%~26.0%. For Novel Set 3, KDNet outperformed the other models when $K = 3, 5, 10$, though it achieved the second best results when $K = 1, 2$.

4.4 Ablation Studies

Table 4. Ablation study of different loss functions on MS COCO. The best results are in **bold**.

Method		nAP						nAP75				
$\mathcal{L}_{cls}$	$\mathcal{L}_{kd}$	1	2	3	5	10	30	1	2	3	5	10	30
✓		1.0	1.2	1.4	2.5	4.5	8.4	1.2	1.5	2.3	2.7	5.1	9.1
	✓	2.1	3.5	4.2	4.9	5.5	9.2	2.2	3.7	4.5	5.1	5.7	9.4
✓	✓	**12.8**	**14.1**	**15.0**	**16.0**	**17.2**	**19.0**	**12.3**	**13.4**	**14.7**	**15.6**	**16.8**	**18.4**

Table 5. Ablation study on CLIP text encoder in the detection branch.

Method	nAP						nAP75					
	1	2	3	5	10	30	1	2	3	5	10	30
w/o visual word encoder	12.3	13.4	14.6	15.6	16.5	18.4	11.9	12.9	14.4	15.2	16.2	17.9
w/ visual word encoder	**12.8**	**14.1**	**15.0**	**16.0**	**17.2**	**19.0**	**12.3**	**13.4**	**14.7**	**15.6**	**16.8**	**18.4**

Table 6. Ablation study on external base samples pre-training. The best results are in **bold**.

Method	Novel Set 1					Novel Set 2				
	1	2	3	5	10	1	2	3	5	10
KDNet	19.7	31.4	34.6	40.9	50.4	12.9	19.9	29.3	31.9	44.2
KDNet + COCO-60	65.1	67.0	71.2	72.2	73.6	63.9	64.0	67.2	69.0	71.2
KDNet + LVIS-846	**67.3**	**68.9**	**72.6**	**73.9**	**74.6**	**65.9**	**66.5**	**67.9**	**70.9**	**72.4**

Effect of Different Loss Functions. If the knowledge distillation loss $\mathcal{L}_{kd}$ is removed, KDNet degrades into a specific version of Faster-RCNN without the knowledge distillation branch. We compared the performances of KDNet, KDNet without $\mathcal{L}_{kd}$ and KDNet without $\mathcal{L}_{cls}$, as shown in Table 4. The knowledge distillation loss improved nAP by 11.6%~13.6% under various few-shot settings, demonstrating the effectiveness of knowledge distillation from the pre-trained CLIP visual encoder to the object detection branch. KDNet trained without $\mathcal{L}_{cls}$ fell behind KDNet by a large margin, validating the importance of classification loss.

Ablation Study on the Effect of CLIP Text Encoder in the Detection Branch. We investigated the effect of the CLIP text encoder used in the detection branch. Table 5 gives the performance comparisons of KDNet with the text encoder and the one without the text encoder. The text encoder can bring consistent improvement to the performance under the whole few-shot settings.

Effect of External Base Samples Pre-Training on PASCAL VOC Dataset. We examined how large-scale dataset pre-training affected the knowledge distillation process. KDNet was trained with abundant MS COCO-60 base

Fig. 3. Detection results based on the 1-shot case of Novel Set 1 of PASCAL VOC dataset. The first row shows the detection results of VFA [41]. The second row is our results.

instances and LVIS-846 base instances and fine-tuned on PASCAL VOC few-shot instances. Table 6 shows that the pre-training process improved the performance of KDNet by a large margin (i.e., 24.2%~53.0%), especially under extreme few-shot settings. The results indicate that the MS COCO and LVIS datasets can provide KDNet with more base semantic concepts for knowledge distillation and KDNet can adapt to PASCAL VOC and achieve impressive performance after fine-tuning.

4.5 Qualitative Visualization

Figure 3 compares the detection results of VFA [41] and KDNet. In Novel Set 1 of PASCAL VOC dataset. 'Cow', 'sofa' and 'bird' belong to the novel categories. We can see that our KDNet can detect the novel instances with more precise boundaries.

5 Conclusion

In this paper, we introduced large-scale vision-language models, particularly CLIP, to few-shot object detection. Unlike existing methods which only utilize CLIP's textual embeddings for further knowledge distillation and data augmentation, the proposed KDNet aligns the object-level embedding from CLIP's visual encoder and object detector, thus distilling knowledge from pre-trained CLIP to base object detector. For small datasets like PASCAL VOC, we proposed a large-scale dataset pre-training mechanism to let KDNet learn sufficient base visual concepts from the MS COCO base instances and LVIS bases instances and then fine-tune it on the PASCAL VOC dataset. Experiments showed that KDNet outperformed the existing methods on the two benchmarks. The proposed KDNet is the first attempt at distilling visual knowledge from pre-trained CLIP for dealing with FSOD tasks. How to distill knowledge with fewer base training samples is still under-explored and it is worth further investigation.

References

1. Liu, W., et al.: SSD: single shot multibox detector. In: Leibe, B., Matas, J., Sebe, N., Welling, M. (eds.) ECCV 2016. LNCS, vol. 9905, pp. 21–37. Springer, Cham (2016). https://doi.org/10.1007/978-3-319-46448-0_2
2. Tian, Z., Shen, C., Chen, H., He, T.: FCOS: a simple and strong anchor-free object detector. IEEE Trans. Pattern Anal. Mach. Intell. **44**(4), 1922–1933 (2020)
3. Ren, S., He, K., Girshick, R., Sun, J.: Faster R-CNN: towards real-time object detection with region proposal networks. Adv. Neural Inf. Process. Syst. **28** (2015)
4. Lin, T.Y., Dollár, P., Girshick, R., He, K., Hariharan, B., Belongie, S.: Feature pyramid networks for object detection. In: Proceedings of the IEEE Conference on Computer Vision and Pattern Recognition, pp. 2117–2125 (2017)
5. Hinton, G., Vinyals, O., Dean, J.: Distilling the knowledge in a neural network. arXiv preprint arXiv:1503.02531 (2015)

6. Kang, B., Liu, Z., Wang, X., Yu, F., Feng, J., Darrell, T.: Few-shot object detection via feature reweighting. In: Proceedings of the IEEE/CVF International Conference on Computer Vision, pp. 8420–8429 (2019)
7. Wang, Y.X., Ramanan, D., Hebert, M.: Meta-learning to detect rare objects. In: Proceedings of the IEEE/CVF International Conference on Computer Vision, pp. 9925–9934 (2019)
8. Yan, X., Chen, Z., Xu, A., Wang, X., Liang, X., Lin, L.: Meta R-CNN: towards general solver for instance-level low-shot learning. In: Proceedings of the IEEE/CVF International Conference on Computer Vision, pp. 9577–9586 (2019)
9. Hu, H., Bai, S., Li, A., Cui, J., Wang, L.: Dense relation distillation with context-aware aggregation for few-shot object detection. In: Proceedings of the IEEE/CVF Conference on Computer Vision and Pattern Recognition, pp. 10185–10194 (2021)
10. Han, G., He, Y., Huang, S., Ma, J., Chang, S.F.: Query adaptive few-shot object detection with heterogeneous graph convolutional networks. In: Proceedings of the IEEE/CVF International Conference on Computer Vision, pp. 3263–3272 (2021)
11. Han, G., Huang, S., Ma, J., He, Y., Chang, S.F.: Meta faster R-CNN: towards accurate few-shot object detection with attentive feature alignment. In: Proceedings of the AAAI Conference on Artificial Intelligence, Vol. 36, pp. 780-789 (2022)
12. Sun, B., Li, B., Cai, S., Yuan, Y., Zhang, C.: FSCE: few-shot object detection via contrastive proposal encoding. In: Proceedings of the IEEE/CVF Conference on Computer Vision and Pattern Recognition, pp. 7352–7362 (2021)
13. Zhang, W., Wang, Y.X.: Hallucination improves few-shot object detection. In: Proceedings of the IEEE/CVF Conference on Computer Vision and Pattern Recognition, pp. 13008–13017 (2021)
14. Zhu, C., Chen, F., Ahmed, U., Shen, Z. and Savvides, M.: Semantic relation reasoning for shot-stable few-shot object detection. In: Proceedings of the IEEE/CVF Conference on Computer Vision and Pattern Recognition, pp. 8782-8791 (2021)
15. Zhang, G., Luo, Z., Cui, K., Lu, S., Xing, E.P.: Meta-DETR: image-level few-shot detection with inter-class correlation exploitation. In: Proceedings of the IEEE Transactions on Pattern Analysis and Machine Intelligence (2022)
16. Chen, G., Choi, W., Yu, X., Han, T., Chandraker, M.: Learning efficient object detection models with knowledge distillation. Adv. Neural Inf. Process. Syst. **30** (2017)
17. Dai, X., Jiang, Z., Wu, Z., Bao, Y., Wang, Z., Liu, S., Zhou, E.: General instance distillation for object detection. In: Proceedings of the IEEE/CVF Conference on Computer Vision and Pattern Recognition, pp. 7842–7851 (2021)
18. Guo, J., et al.: Distilling object detectors via decoupled features. In: Proceedings of the IEEE/CVF Conference on Computer Vision and Pattern Recognition, pp. 2154–2164 (2021)
19. Yang, Z., et al.: Focal and global knowledge distillation for detectors. In: Proceedings of the IEEE/CVF Conference on Computer Vision and Pattern Recognition, pp. 4643–4652 (2022)
20. Radford, A., et al.: Learning transferable visual models from natural language supervision. In: International Conference on Machine Learning, pp. 8748–8763 (2021)
21. Jia, C., et al.: Scaling up visual and vision-language representation learning with noisy text supervision. In: International Conference on Machine Learning, pp. 4904–4916 (2021)
22. Ma, Z., et al.:Open-vocabulary one-stage detection with hierarchical visual-language knowledge distillation. In: Proceedings of the IEEE/CVF Conference on Computer Vision and Pattern Recognition, pp. 14074–14083 (2022)

23. Zhou, K., Yang, J., Loy, C.C., Liu, Z.: Learning to prompt for vision-language models. Int. J. Comput. Vision **130**(9), 2337–2348 (2022)
24. Wu, S., Zhang, W., Jin, S., Liu, W., Loy, C.C.: Aligning bag of regions for open-vocabulary object detection. In: Proceedings of the IEEE/CVF Conference on Computer Vision and Pattern Recognition, pp. 15254–15264 (2023)
25. Wang, X., Huang, T.E., Darrell, T., Gonzalez, J.E., Yu, F.: Frustratingly simple few-shot object detection. arXiv preprint arXiv:2003.06957 (2020)
26. Wu, J., Liu, S., Huang, D., Wang, Y.: Multi-scale positive sample refinement for few-shot object detection. In: Computer Vision-ECCV 2020: 16th European Conference, Glasgow, UK, August 23-28, 2020, Proceedings, Part XVI 16, pp. 456–472 (2020)
27. Cao, Y., et al.: Few-shot object detection via association and discrimination. Adv. Neural Inf. Process. Syst. **34**, 16570–16581 (2021)
28. Han, G., Ma, J., Huang, S., Chen, L., Chang, S.F.: Few-shot object detection with fully cross-transformer. In: Proceedings of the IEEE/CVF Conference on Computer Vision and Pattern Recognition, pp. 5321–5330 (2022)
29. Kaul, P., Xie, W., Zisserman, A.: Label, verify, correct: a simple few shot object detection method. In: Proceedings of the IEEE/CVF Conference on Computer Vision and Pattern Recognition, pp. 14237–14247 (2022)
30. Qiao, L., Zhao, Y., Li, Z., Qiu, X., Wu, J. and Zhang, C.: Defrcn: Decoupled faster r-cnn for few-shot object detection. In: Proceedings of the IEEE/CVF International Conference on Computer Vision, pp. 8681-8690 (2021)
31. Bulat, A., Guerrero, R., Martinez, B., Tzimiropoulos, G.: FS-DETR: few-shot detection transformer with prompting and without re-training. In: Proceedings of the IEEE/CVF International Conference on Computer Vision, pp. 11793–11802 (2023)
32. Li, J., et al.: Disentangle and remerge: interventional knowledge distillation for few-shot object detection from a conditional causal perspective. In: Proceedings of the AAAI Conference on Artificial Intelligence, vol. 37, pp. 1323–1333 (2023)
33. Xu, J., Le, H., Samaras, D.: Generating features with increased crop-related diversity for few-shot object detection. In: Proceedings of the IEEE/CVF Conference on Computer Vision and Pattern Recognition, pp. 19713–19722 (2023)
34. Lu, X., et al.: Breaking immutable: information-coupled prototype elaboration for few-shot object detection. In: Proceedings of the AAAI Conference on Artificial Intelligence, vol. 37, pp. 1844–1852 (2023)
35. Oord, A.V.D., Li, Y., Vinyals, O.: Representation learning with contrastive predictive coding. arXiv preprint arXiv:1807.03748 (2018)
36. Chen, K., et al.: MMDetection: open MMLab detection toolbox and benchmark. arXiv preprint arXiv:1906.07155 (2019)
37. Lin, T.Y., et al.: Microsoft COCO: common objects in context. In: Fleet, D., Pajdla, T., Schiele, B., Tuytelaars, T. (eds.) Computer Vision – ECCV 2014, pp. 740–755. Springer, Cham (2014). https://doi.org/10.1007/978-3-319-10602-1_48
38. Gupta, A., Dollar, P., Girshick, R.: LVIS: a dataset for large vocabulary instance segmentation. In: Proceedings of the IEEE/CVF Conference on Computer Vision and Pattern Recognition, pp. 5356–5364 (2019)
39. Everingham, M., Van Gool, L., Williams, C.K., Winn, J., Zisserman, A.: The pascal visual object classes (VOC) challenge. Int. J. Comput. Vis. **88**, 303–338 (2010)
40. Gadre, S.Y., et al. : DataComp: in search of the next generation of multimodal datasets. Adv. Neural Inf. Process. Syst. **36** (2024)

41. Han, J., Ren, Y., Ding, J., Yan, K., Xia, G.S.: Few-shot object detection via variational feature aggregation. In: Proceedings of the AAAI Conference on Artificial Intelligence, vol. 37, pp. 755–763 (2023)
42. Cui, J., Wang, R., Si, S., Hsieh, C.J.: Scaling up dataset distillation to ImageNet-1K with constant memory. In: International Conference on Machine Learning, pp. 6565–6590. PMLR (2023)

MUFASA: Multi-view Fusion and Adaptation Network with Spatial Awareness for Radar Object Detection

Xiangyuan Peng[1,2]($\boxtimes$), Miao Tang[3], Huawei Sun[1,2], Kay Bierzynski[2], Lorenzo Servadei[1], and Robert Wille[1]

[1] Technical University of Munich, Chair for Design Automation, Munich, Germany
Xiangyuan.Peng@infineon.com
[2] Infineon Technologies AG, Neubiberg, Germany
[3] China University of Geosciences (Wuhan), Wuhan, China

Abstract. In recent years, approaches based on radar object detection have made significant progress in autonomous driving systems due to their robustness under adverse weather compared to LiDAR. However, the sparsity of radar point clouds poses challenges in achieving precise object detection, highlighting the importance of effective and comprehensive feature extraction technologies. To address this challenge, this paper introduces a comprehensive feature extraction method for radar point clouds. This study first enhances the capability of detection networks by using a plug-and-play module, GeoSPA. It leverages the Lalonde features to explore local geometric patterns. Additionally, a distributed multi-view attention mechanism, DEMVA, is designed to integrate the shared information across the entire dataset with the global information of each individual frame. By employing the two modules, we present our method, MUFASA, which enhances object detection performance through improved feature extraction. The approach is evaluated on the VoD and TJ4DRaDSet datasets to demonstrate its effectiveness. In particular, we achieve state-of-the-art results among radar-based methods on the VoD dataset with the mAP of 50.24%.

Keywords: 3D object detection · radar point cloud · distributed multi-view attention · Lalonde feature · autonomous driving

1 Introduction

Object detection plays an important role in autonomous driving systems, providing essential perception capabilities. Initially, object detection relied heavily on camera-based methods, leveraging high-resolution RGB images to accomplish 2D detection [1]. However, cameras lack 3D geometric clues, which is crucial for accurate perception. Hence, Light Detection and Ranging (LiDAR) sensors are integrated into systems to generate 3D point clouds, which are capable of offering geometric details and lead to more accurate object detection [2]. Nevertheless,

LiDAR's performance diminishes under adverse weather conditions, including fog, rain, and snow [3]. The high cost also limits its widespread application [4].

As an alternative, radar has gained sufficient interest due to its robust performance under adverse conditions and capability to provide 3D spatial and velocity information [5]. Yet, radar point clouds pose a unique challenge: sparsity. Numerous methods have been proposed to extract rich features from the sparse points, including sparse theory and advanced signal processing techniques [6,7]. However, these methods are still insufficient to fully explore the information in radar point clouds.

Currently, most feature extraction technologies for sparse radar point clouds primarily focus on extracting local and global features within individual frames [8,9]. While understanding the global semantic information within each frame is essential for scene comprehension, the hidden shared information across the entire dataset is often neglected. For instance, the locations of cars and pedestrians are usually in the center and at the edges of different scenes, respectively. These dataset-wide features can enhance detection confidence by incorporating shared information across different frames. Moreover, local feature extraction often overlooks the significance of geometric spatial patterns. Accurately distinguishing between similar objects, such as pedestrians and signposts, or cars and square trash bins, heavily relies on precise analysis of local geometric patterns. However, during the learning process in feature extraction, the details of these patterns can be missed. These considerations underscore the need for more comprehensive and sophisticated feature extraction strategies.

Therefore, an advanced feature extraction network, MUFASA, is proposed to leverage complex local and global information within each radar point cloud frame, along with shared dataset-wide features.

Contribution. This study focuses on enhancing radar point cloud object detection capabilities through comprehensive feature extractions. The main contributions are as follows:

- A flexible plug-and-play Geometric Spatial Pattern Analysis module, GeoSPA, is designed to explore local geometric features within various detection networks. It enhances the extraction of local features and provides a deep understanding of spatial information in the feature extraction backbone.
- A Distributed External Multi-View Attention module, DEMVA, is designed to integrate dataset-wide features across different frames. It merges the dataset-wide information with the global features of each frame from the cylinder and Bird's Eye View (BEV) projections.
- Extensive experiments on the View-of-Delft (VoD) [10] and TJ4DRadSet [11] datasets demonstrate the superior efficiency and accurate detection performance of the proposed method.

2 Related Work

2.1 Radar-Based 3D Object Detection

Radar point cloud detection methods, often inspired by LiDAR techniques, are classified into voxel-based, pillar-based, point-based, and fusion-based networks [12]. Voxel-based strategies [13,14] convert point clouds into 3D voxel grids, sacrificing some information due to discretization. Pillar-based approaches, such as FastPillars [15], transform point clouds into 2D pseudo-images for BEV analysis, effectively utilizing 2D convolutional neural networks (CNNs) for feature extraction. Point-based methods, highlighted by PointNet [16], directly extract features from raw points, preserving fine-grained details. However, they may suffer higher computational costs. Fusion-based strategies, like PV-RCNN [17], integrate multiple approaches to improve detection performance while considering computational demands.

Despite advancements, extracting precise features from radar point clouds with a single method remains a significant challenge because of the sparsity. Therefore, our network integrates pillar and point-based approaches to ensure comprehensive feature extraction while balancing computational efficiency and detection accuracy.

2.2 Descriptors for Feature Extraction

The inherent sparsity and irregular distribution of radar point clouds necessitate efficient feature extraction in 3D spaces. An effective point cloud descriptor is capable of capturing spatial geometric characteristics while being invariant to translation, scaling, and rotation. Optimizing these descriptors can improve object detection accuracy while reducing the computational cost.

Conventional descriptors combine spatial statistical information of feature points and their neighbors to extract geometric features [18,19]. With the advancement of deep learning, integrating hand-crafted and deep learning-derived features has marked a significant evolution. For instance, [20] employs spherical histograms for spatial mapping around points, with neural networks transforming these representations into Euclidean space. PPFNet [21] and PPF-FoldNet [22] leverage Fisher Vectors in CNNs to navigate the unstructured characteristic of point clouds. The fusion of traditional 3D feature descriptors with deep learning approaches represents a noteworthy advancement in point cloud processing, resulting in more robust and invariant feature representations.

However, a major drawback of most feature extraction methods is the descriptors are tightly coupled with specific network structures, limiting their applicability across different detection systems. To address this limitation, we introduce our GeoSPA, which can integrate into various detection networks, enhancing the generalization of feature extraction.

2.3 Attention Mechanism in 3D Object Detection

The attention mechanism achieves permutation invariance, dynamically focuses on relevant features, and adapts to sparsity and density variations. Also, the ability of attention mechanisms to stably extract information makes them particularly suitable for the complex point cloud analysis [23].

For instance, Box attention [24] introduces a grid-based attention weighting for 3D object detection in outdoor scenes. TANet [25] enhances point cloud discrimination by applying attention at multiple levels to refine the feature representation. CSANet [26] employs self-attention to fuse point cloud features with coordinate information. Additionally, Point-BERT [27] designs a transformer-based pre-training for point clouds.

These advancements, mainly based on the self-attention mechanism, highlight the flexibility and effectiveness of the attention mechanism in 3D object detection. However, external attention, which has a strong learning ability to integrate the information across the entire dataset, is not commonly employed in point cloud detection. Therefore, we designed DEMVA to capture the shared dataset-wide information.

3 Proposed Method

In this section, we outline the overall architecture of MUFASA. Subsequently, the GeoSPA module, designed to extract local geometric patterns within the point clouds, is presented. Later, the DEMVA module is introduced, which utilizes shared information across the entire dataset and the global features in each frame, thereby enhancing the model's overall performance and robustness.

3.1 Overall Structure

The structure of MUFASA is illustrated in Fig. 1. Initially, the radar point clouds undergo transformation into multi-view representations, including BEV and cylindrical projections, inspired by the MVFAN [28]. On the one hand, extracted features through the cylindrical branch maintain the integrity of 3D information. On the other hand, the BEV branch captures a comprehensive scene perspective, effectively mitigating obstruction by obstacles. Subsequently, the features from both representations are fed into the DEMVA. The distributed attention mechanisms enhance feature comprehension by exploring relationships across the entire dataset, addressing and mitigating potential information loss.

In parallel, our network incorporates a point-wised branch with Farthest Point Sampling (FPS) and our GeoSPA module, designed to capture point-wise features. The point-wise features are then fused with the multi-view features derived from the DEMVA branch. Enriched point-wise features are subsequently reprojected back into the BEV. The final features are treated as input for the detection heads to generate proposals.

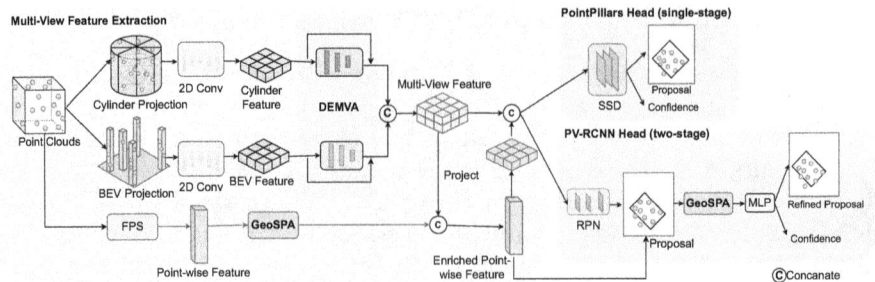

Fig. 1. Overall Structure of MUFASA

The GeoSPA is designed for integration with various detection frameworks, acting as a flexible plug-and-play module integrated into point-wise feature extraction. In single-stage detectors like PointPillars [29], with a detection head SSD [30], GeoSPA enriches point-wise feature extraction without the need for proposal refinement. In two-stage detectors like PV-RCNN [17], where the proposal generation head is RFN [17], GeoSPA can be utilized in two aspects. It is applied not only in the point-wise feature extraction but also within the Region of Interest (RoI) to refine spatial features, aiding in the proposal refinement. The implementation of GeoSPA in different locations demonstrates its adaptability across different detection architectures as a plug-and-play module.

3.2 Geometric Spatial Pattern Analysis

In road object detection, cars often exhibit distinct rectangular shapes, particularly for stationary vehicles, where Doppler velocity provides less information. Meanwhile, cyclists differ from pedestrians in both width and height. To enhance the features obtained from deep learning alone, MUFASA integrates the GeoSPA based on the Lalonde descriptor, which is able to capture spatial features.

Definition of Lalonde Feature: The spatial descriptors are derived through two processes: Signature and Histogram. Following the methodology outlined in [18], we analyze the distribution of points within a local spatial domain by conducting Principal Component Analysis (PCA) on the covariance matrix of the 3D points' locations. The covariance matrix M is expressed as Eq. 1

$$M = \frac{1}{N}\sum_{i=1}^{N}(X_i - \bar{X})(X_i - \bar{X})^T, \quad (1)$$

where $\{X_i\} = \{(x_i, y_i, z_i)^T\}$ is the ith point in the point clouds and $\bar{X} = \frac{1}{N}\sum_{i=1}^{N} X_i$ is the mean value of all the points. The eigenvectors obtained from PCA are e_1, e_2 and e_3 with eigenvalus x_1, x_2 and x_3 while $x_1 \geq x_2 \geq x_3$. For different geometric representations, the eigenvalues showcase different features:

$$x_1 \approx x_2 \approx x_3 \text{ for scattered points,}$$
$$x_1 \gg x_2 \approx x_3 \text{ for a linear structure,}$$
$$x_1 \approx x_2 \gg x_3 \text{ for a solid surface.}$$

Then, $l_{scatter}$, l_{linear}, and $l_{surface}$ are defined as the scatter-ness, linear-ness, and surface-ness. They can be calculated as Eq. 2

$$l_{scatter} = x_1, \quad l_{linear} = x_1 - x_2, \quad l_{surface} = x_2 - x_3. \tag{2}$$

By taking the histogram of $l_{scatter}$, l_{linear}, and $l_{surface}$ for all points within the point clouds, we obtain the three Lalonde features L_1, L_2, and L_3 of the object.

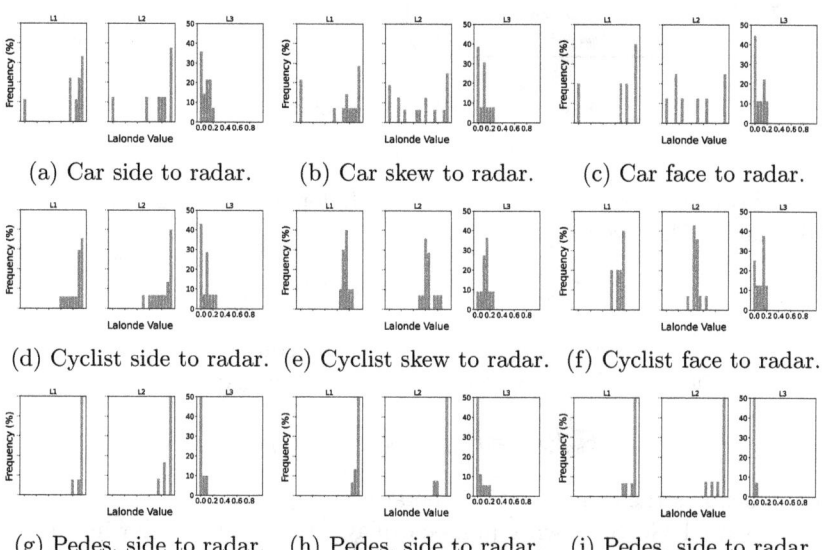

(a) Car side to radar. (b) Car skew to radar. (c) Car face to radar.

(d) Cyclist side to radar. (e) Cyclist skew to radar. (f) Cyclist face to radar.

(g) Pedes. side to radar. (h) Pedes. side to radar. (i) Pedes. side to radar.

Fig. 2. Lalonde features for car, cyclist, and pedestrian in different orientations.

The Lalonde features L_1, L_2, and L_3 for cars, cyclists, and pedestrians across different orientations in the VoD dataset are depicted in Fig. 2. Here, cars exhibit more pronounced planarity features in L_1 and L_2 compared to other objects, while cyclists can be more effectively detected from the side due to prominent point and planar features. Pedestrians consistently exhibit similar geometric characteristics across different orientations.

Implementation of GeoSPA: We introduced GeoSPA based on Lalonde features to capture the detailed spatial pattern. Its structure is shown in Fig. 3.

On one hand, a PointNet [16] architecture is used to extract point-wised feature as Eq. 3

$$F_{pw} = \text{PointNet}(S) = \max(\text{MLP}(S)), \tag{3}$$

where F_{pw} is the point-wised features within the subset S through the application of MLP layers and max pooling in PointNet. On the other hand, for each point $p_i \in S$, we compute the Lalonde descriptors $L(p_i)$ within its fixed neighborhood

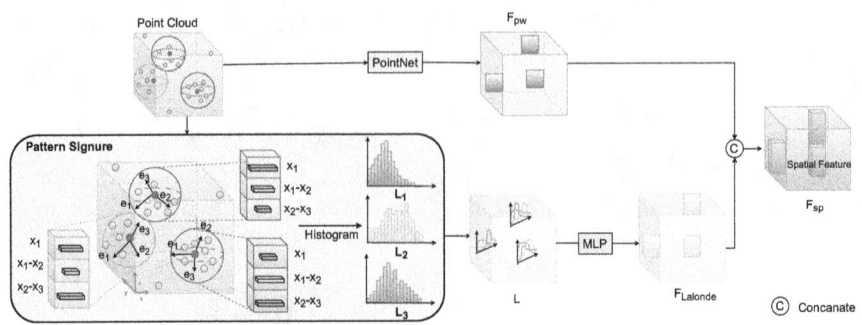

Fig. 3. GeoSPA implementation.

$N(p_i)$ and transform it into high-dimensional Lalonde features $F_{\text{Lalonde}}(p_i)$ using an MLP layer. This process is captured by Eq. 4

$$F_{\text{Lalonde}}(p_i) = \text{MLP}(L(N(p_i))). \tag{4}$$

The final spatial feature, $F_{\text{sp}}(p_i)$, is calculated by concatenating the point-wise features and the high-dimensional Lalonde features as Eq. 5

$$F_{\text{sp}}(p_i) = F_{\text{pw}}(p_i) \copyright F_{\text{Lalonde}}(p_i), \tag{5}$$

where $\copyright$ denotes the concatenation operation.

We designed GeoSPA with plug-and-play functionality, allowing it to be embedded into any point-wise feature extraction process. In single-stage networks, GeoSPA is incorporated into the initial feature extraction branch. For two-stage networks with proposal refinement, GeoSPA can also operate within the Region of Interest (ROI) to enhance local spatial features except in a point-wise feature extraction branch, thereby aiding in the refinement of proposals.

3.3 Distributed External Multi-view Attention

Our DEMVA module leverages dual-projection techniques: cylindrical and BEV views with external attention mechanisms. The multi-view extraction captures global features from multiple perspectives, while the distributed attention mechanism incrementally learns shared information across the entire dataset.

For BEV projection, each point $p_n(x_n, y_n, z_n)$ is systematically allocated to a defined pillar as defined in Eq. 6

$$\mathcal{M}_{BEV}(p_{BEV}^n) \to q_{BEV}^m, \tag{6}$$

where $\mathcal{M}_{BEV}$ symbolizes the mapping operation that assigns points to pillars in the BEV projection, p_{BEV}^n denotes the nth point in BEV coordinates, and q_{BEV}^m denotes the mth pillar. In the cylindrical projection, a transformation of points into cylindrical coordinates (ρ_n, θ_n, z'_n) is applied to maintain the fidelity of vertical dimensions as below:

$$\rho_n = \sqrt{x_n^2 + y_n^2}, \quad \theta_n = \arctan\left(\frac{y_n}{x_n}\right), \quad z'_n = z_n,$$

where ρ_n is the radial distance from the origin to the nth point, θ_n specifies the angular orientation around the z-axis, and z'_n upholds the original elevation data. Following this transformation, a similar pillar structuring is implemented in the cylindrical space as Eq. 7

$$\mathcal{M}_{cyl}(p_{cyl}^n) \rightarrow q_{cyl}^m, \tag{7}$$

where $\mathcal{M}_{cyl}$ means the function that maps the nth point to the mth pillar.

Later, q_{BEV}^m and q_{cyl}^m are mapped onto pseudo images. Utilizing two 2D CNNs, we further extract global features I_{BEV} and I_{cyl} with dimension $(B, C \times Z, H, W)$ from the BEV and cylindrical pseudo images. Here, B denotes the batch size, C indicates the number of channels, Z is the feature depth, H and W refer to the height and width of the feature maps.

Strong dataset-wide correlations, such as vehicles predominantly occupying central positions while pedestrians and cyclists are often at the edges, help to enhance the understanding of the road environment. Furthermore, objects within the same category always exhibit similar shapes and motion patterns. Therefore, we employ external attention mechanisms, effectively capturing and encoding shared information across the entire dataset.

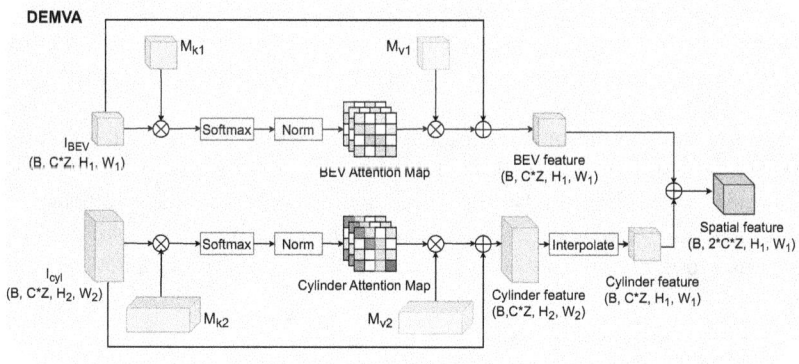

Fig. 4. Distributed Multi-View Spatial Attention

Figure 4 shows the process of extracting dataset-wide features by DEMVA. Initially, the inputs undergo a preliminary transformation by a matrix M_k, leading to an attention map via a Softmax and Normalization layer. This attention map is then multiplied with a second external matrix, M_v, leading to the feature graph. The resultant feature graph is subsequently fused with the original cylindrical and BEV features. The M_k and M_v are the key and value components in the attention mechanism. Both matrices, as the weight of one-dimensional convolution, are dynamically updated throughout the learning phase. Therefore, the matrices effectively function as memory units, continuously integrating information from the new frame into the matrices, thus enabling the extraction of dataset-wide features. As a result, the DEMVA applies this dataset-wide knowledge to each individual frame and facilitates the fusion of dataset-wide features with single-frame global features.

Given the inherent sparsity of radar point clouds, our DEMVA plays a crucial role in enhancing the model's performance by extracting global information through multiple perspectives and further enriching it with dataset-wide features via external attention mechanisms.

4 Experiment

4.1 Dataset and Metrics

The MUFASA network is evaluated on the VoD[1] and TJ4DRadSet[2] dataset to validate its efficacy. The VoD dataset comprises 8,693 frames of synchronized and calibrated data from LiDAR, cameras, and 4D radar. The data is mainly acquired in busy urban environments, including diverse traffic components. We evaluated our methods on the validation set, as the test server is unavailable. The TJ4DRadSet dataset includes 40,000 frames of synchronized LiDAR, camera, and radar data, with 7,757 frames annotated. This dataset spans various scenarios, including elevated roads, complex crossroads, single-direction lanes, and urban streets.

To assess our method, we employed Average Precision (AP) for each class and calculated the mean Average Precision (mAP) across all the classes. To calculate AP, we determined the Intersection over Union (IoU) between the ground truth and predicted 3D bounding boxes. A minimum IoU threshold of 50% was set for the car and truck categories, while a threshold of 25% was applied for pedestrian and cyclist categories. In the VoD dataset, the detection performance was analyzed in two distinct regions: the entire scene and the driving corridor, aligned with the original paper [10]. For the TJ4DRadSet dataset, evaluations are conducted in both BEV and 3D perspectives as in [11].

4.2 Implementation Details

The models are trained for 80 epochs with a batch size of 8, utilizing 4 NVIDIA Tesla P40 GPUs. For training, we used the Adam optimizer [31], with an initial learning rate of 0.03 and a weight decay rate of 0.01. Our implementation is based on OpenPCDet [32], a comprehensive library designed for point cloud tasks. Data augmentation is implemented, including rotation, flipping, and scaling, to improve the models' robustness and generalization capabilities.

---

[1] https://github.com/tudelft-iv/view-of-delft-dataset.
[2] https://github.com/TJRadarLab/TJ4DRadSet.

4.3 Quantitaive Results

We performed a comprehensive comparison of our proposed method with existing point cloud object detection techniques on the VoD and TJ4DRaDSet datasets. The results are detailed in Tables 1 and 2.

Table 1. Comparative AP results on VoD val. set. The values are in %. The best results are bold and the second best are marked with an underline.

Methods	Sensor	All area				Driving Corridor			
		Car	Ped.	Cyc.	mAP	Car	Ped.	Cyc.	mAP
SECOND[†] [33]	R	32.35	24.49	51.44	36.10	67.98	35.45	72.30	59.18
RPFA-Net[†] [34]	R	33.45	26.42	56.34	38.75	68.68	34.25	80.36	62.44
CenterPoint [35]	R	33.87	39.01	66.85	46.58	62.98	<u>49.22</u>	85.35	65.85
PointPillars [29]	R	37.92	31.24	65.66	44.94	71.41	42.27	87.68	67.12
MVFAN[†] [28]	R	34.05	27.27	57.14	39.42	69.81	38.65	84.87	64.38
MVFAN [28]	R	38.12	30.96	66.17	45.08	71.45	40.21	86.63	66.10
PV-RCNN [17]	R	41.65	38.82	58.36	46.28	<u>72.00</u>	43.53	78.32	64.62
BEVFusion [36]	R+C	37.85	**40.96**	**68.95**	49.25	70.21	45.86	**89.48**	68.52
RCFusion [37]	R+C	<u>41.70</u>	38.95	68.31	<u>49.65</u>	71.87	47.50	88.33	69.23
MUFASA(pp)	R	41.07	37.52	68.07	48.89	71.89	47.40	<u>89.02</u>	<u>69.44</u>
MUFASA(pv)	R	**43.10**	<u>38.97</u>	<u>68.65</u>	**50.24**	**72.50**	**50.28**	88.51	**70.43**

R denotes radar sensor, R+C denotes the fusion of radar and camera. The pp denotes MUFASA with Pointpillars head, and pv denotes MUFASA with PV-RCNN head. The results with [†] are inherited from [28]. The results of BEVFusion and RCFusion are reported from [38]

Table 1 demonstrates the remarkable performance of our method, surpassing state-of-the-art radar-based object detection methods on the VoD dataset. Leveraging the flexibility of key modules, the MUFASA can be embedded into different detection heads. The results also show a consistent enhancement in performance across different detection architectures. Notably, when incorporated with the PV-RCNN detection head, our approach achieves the highest mAP of 50.24% over the entire area and 70.43% within the driving corridor. This marks a significant improvement of 3.96% and 5.81%, respectively, over the PV-RCNN performance metrics.

Furthermore, compared to radar and camera fusion methodologies such as BEVFusion [36] and RCFusion [37], our approach maintains competitive performance with the highest mAP, underscoring its efficacy and robustness in capturing comprehensive features.

Table 2. Comparative AP results on TJ4DRaDSet test set. The values are in %. The best results are bold and the second best are marked with an underline.

Methods	Sensor	3D					BEV				
		Car	Ped.	Cyc.	Truck	mAP	Car	Ped.	Cyc.	Truck	mAP
PV-RCNN [17]	R	19.46	9.34	40.44	16.09	21.33	29.94	9.73	45.12	22.92	26.93
PartA^{2†} [13]	R	18.65	23.28	44.14	9.63	23.92	29.95	24.31	49.08	15.05	29.60
SECOND† [33]	R	18.18	24.43	32.36	14.76	22.43	36.02	28.58	39.75	19.35	30.93
PointPillars [29]	R	23.98	18.70	43.25	17.23	25.79	36.20	20.47	46.81	<u>30.60</u>	33.52
MVFAN [28]	R	23.37	23.58	45.35	17.62	27.48	33.79	25.92	47.96	30.15	34.46
RPFA-Net† [34]	R	26.89	**27.36**	<u>50.95</u>	14.46	29.91	**42.89**	<u>29.81</u>	<u>57.09</u>	25.98	38.94
MVX-Net† [14]	R+C	22.28	19.57	50.70	11.21	25.94	37.46	22.70	54.69	18.07	33.23
RCFusion† [37]	R+C	**29.72**	<u>27.17</u>	**54.93**	<u>23.56</u>	**33.85**	40.89	**30.95**	**58.30**	28.92	**39.76**
MUFASA(pp)	R	<u>27.86</u>	25.42	42.58	19.61	28.87	<u>41.72</u>	27.93	46.42	28.69	36.19
MUFASA(pv)	R	23.56	23.70	48.39	**25.25**	<u>30.23</u>	41.25	24.54	53.64	**36.97**	<u>39.10</u>

R denotes radar sensor, R+C denotes the fusion of radar and camera. The pp denotes MUFASA with Pointpillars head, and pv denotes MUFASA with PV-RCNN head. The results with $\dagger$ are inherited from [37]

From Table 2, MUFASA demonstrates robust performance in radar-based object detection, achieving the highest mAP among radar-only methods, with 30.23% for 3D detection and 39.10% for BEV detection. Notably, MUFASA excels in detecting trucks with PV-RCNN head, highlighting its effectiveness in large object detection. Furthermore, MUFASA with the PV-RCNN head (pv) significantly outperforms the PointPillars head (pp) in detecting cyclists and trucks on the TJ4DRaDSet dataset, showing improvements of 5.81% and 5.64% in 3D detection, respectively. This enhanced performance is due to the GeoSPA module in the ROI stage, which is particularly effective at refining bounding boxes with an obvious length-width ratio. However, in comparison to radar and camera fusion methods, such as MVX-Net [14] and RCFusion [37], MUFASA still exhibits a minor performance gap.

4.4 Qualitative Results

We visualize the bounding boxes generated by PointPillars [29], PV-RCNN [17], and MUFASA on the VoD dataset. Ground truth boxes are marked in green, while predictions are in red. From Fig. 5, it is evident that MUFASA performs better detection with fewer false negative bounding boxes.

4.5 Ablation Study

The effectiveness of the critical modules are illustrated through an ablation study. Additionally, the generalization of our methods is demonstrated by incorporating key models with different settings.

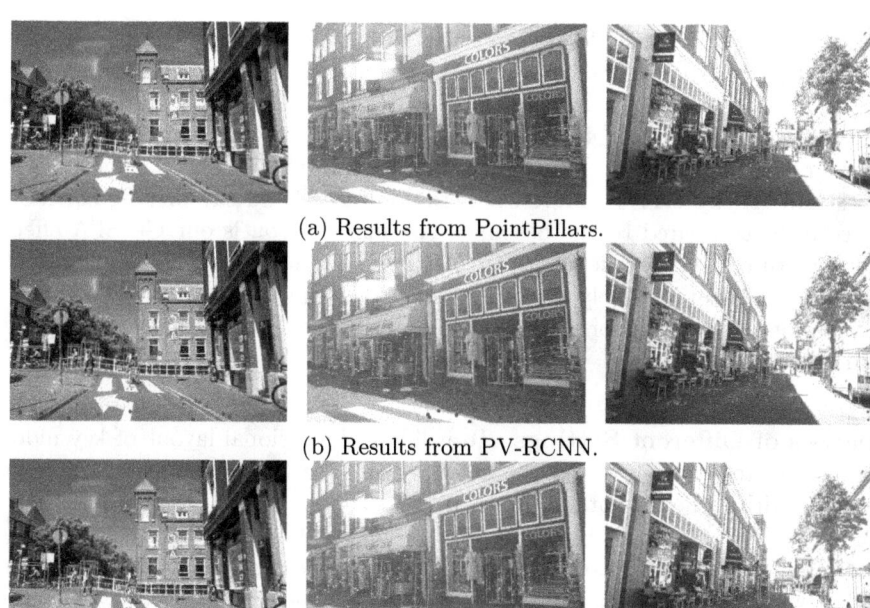

(a) Results from PointPillars.

(b) Results from PV-RCNN.

(c) Results from MUFASA (Ours).

Fig. 5. Visualization of detection.

Analysis of Key Modules. We first removed the DEMVA and GeoSPA from the MUFASA architecture. The remaining network was retrained with the same parameters as a baseline. Subsequently, we incrementally reintegrated each module into the baseline to observe their individual contributions.

Table 3. Module analysis on VoD val. set. The values are in %.

Module		All area				Driving Corridor			
D	G	Car	Ped.	Cyc.	mAP	Car	Ped.	Cyc.	mAP
		38.12	30.96	66.17	45.08	71.45	40.21	86.63	66.10
✓		40.86	32.11	67.96	46.98	72.04	42.94	86.74	67.24
	✓	41.25	37.10	66.95	48.43	71.86	47.84	87.08	68.93
✓	✓	**43.10**	**38.97**	**68.65**	**50.24**	**72.50**	**50.28**	**88.51**	**70.43**

D denotes the DEMVA module. G denotes the GeoSPA module. The detection heads are kept as PV-RCNN heads for better comparison

The analysis from Table 3 reveals that the DEMVA module enhances the detection performance for all the classes by integrating the dataset-wide features into each frame. Meanwhile, the GeoSPA module is particularly effective in improving the detection of pedestrians, which have fewer points. For instance, incorporating GeoSPA into our framework results in a substantial increase in pedestrian AP by 6.14% and 7.63% across all areas and the driving corridor, respectively, compared to the baseline. The main reason is our GeoSPA effectively captures the local features. Pedestrians, despite their varied movement patterns, maintain relatively consistent shapes. Learning the detailed geometric information in the neighborhood helps to identify the features that are uniquely from one category.

Analysis of Different Settings. To validate the rational layout of key modules, we strategically deployed the DEMVA and GeoSPA modules at different locations within the network architecture.

GeoSPA on Different Locations. Table 4 analyzes the impact of the GeoSPA module when applied at various locations within the network. Initially, we establish a baseline scenario where GeoSPA is not employed. Then, we apply GeoSPA in the early stage for the point-wise feature extraction and in the later stage to refine proposals with the PV-RCNN detection head.

Table 4. Layout of GeoSPA analysis on VoD val. set. The values are in %.

Layout		All area				Driving Corridor			
1st-Stage	2nd-Stage	Car	Ped.	Cyc.	mAP	Car	Ped.	Cyc.	mAP
		40.86	32.11	67.96	46.98	72.04	42.94	86.74	67.24
✓		42.52	36.95	**68.89**	49.45	72.19	48.84	86.89	69.31
	✓	41.67	33.94	67.49	47.70	72.36	46.20	87.79	68.78
✓	✓	**43.10**	**38.97**	68.65	**50.24**	**72.50**	**50.28**	**88.51**	**70.43**

1st Stage denotes point-wised feature extraction branch. 2nd Stage denotes proposal refinement in ROI. The detection heads are kept as PV-RCNN heads for analysis

The outcomes indicate that integrating GeoSPA at both stages yields improvements in mAP for the entire area as well as the driving corridor.

DEMVA on Different Branches. We implement external attention to different projection branches.

The results in Table 5 highlight the impact of external attention mechanisms within both the cylinder and BEV branches. Therefore, extracting hidden dataset-wide features with external attention mechanisms consistently enhances object detection accuracy.

Table 5. Layout of External Attention (EA) analysis on VoD val. set. The values are in %.

Layout Branch		All area				Driving Corridor			
BEV	Cylinder	Car	Ped.	Cyc.	mAP	Car	Ped.	Cyc.	mAP
		41.25	37.10	66.95	48.43	71.86	47.84	87.08	68.93
✓		41.98	37.58	68.13	49.23	71.89	48.82	87.56	69.42
	✓	42.55	38.19	68.18	49.64	72.11	49.43	88.14	69.89
✓	✓	**43.10**	**38.97**	**68.65**	**50.24**	**72.50**	**50.28**	**88.51**	**70.43**

The detection heads are kept as PV-RCNN heads for analysis

5 Conclusion and Discussion

Traditional radar object detection methods often struggle to fully exploit the detailed local and global features in a single frame, as well as the dataset-wide features across the entire dataset. In our method, MUFASA, the GeoSPA is designed as a flexible plug-and-play module, enhancing the model's capability to capture critical geometric details and recognize local spatial patterns across various detection networks. Additionally, the DEMVA module synthesizes shared information across different frames and integrates it into the global features of each individual frame. Empirical evaluations on the VoD and TJ4DRaDSet datasets demonstrate the superiority of our approaches over existing radar point cloud-based object detection techniques. Specifically, our method achieved an mAP of 50.24% and 70.43% on the entire area and driving corridor of the VoD dataset, representing a notable improvement of 3.96% and 5.81%.

However, when compared to sensor fusion-based detection methods, our approaches may still exhibit a lower mAP. This observation underscores the need for future research focusing on integrating camera, LiDAR, and radar data. Such integration aims to improve detection accuracy and robustness under various environments, thereby expanding the practical use of our methods in real-world scenarios.

Acknowledgement. This research has been conducted as part of the DELPHI project, which is funded by the European Union, under grant agreement No 101104263. However, views and opinions expressed are those of the author(s) only and do not necessarily reflect those of the European Union or the European Climate, Infrastructure and Environment Executive Agency (CINEA). Neither the European Union nor the granting authority can be held responsible for them.

References

1. Kaur, J., Singh, W.: Tools, techniques, datasets and application areas for object detection in an image: a review. Multimedia Tools Appl. **81**(27), 38297–38351 (2022)
2. Wu, Y., Wang, Y., Zhang, S., Ogai, H.: Deep 3D object detection networks using lidar data: a review. IEEE Sens. J. **21**(2), 1152–1171 (2020)
3. Tang, L., Shi, Y., He, Q., Sadek, A.W., Qiao, C.: Performance test of autonomous vehicle lidar sensors under different weather conditions. Transp. Res. Rec. **2674**(1), 319–329 (2020)
4. Raj, T., Hanim Hashim, F., Baseri Huddin, A., Ibrahim, M.F., Hussain, A.: A survey on lidar scanning mechanisms. Electronics **9**(5), 741 (2020)
5. Jiang, T., Zhuang, L., An, Q., Wang, J., Xiao, K., Wang, A.: T-rodnet: transformer for vehicular millimeter-wave radar object detection. IEEE Trans. Instrum. Meas. **72**, 1–12 (2022)
6. Ding, C., Zhang, L., Chen, H., Hong, H., Zhu, X., Fioranelli, F.: Sparsity-based human activity recognition with pointnet using a portable FMCW radar. IEEE Internet Things J. (2023)
7. Sun, S., Zhang, Y.D.: 4D automotive radar sensing for autonomous vehicles: a sparsity-oriented approach. IEEE J. Sel. Topics Signal Process. **15**(4), 879–891 (2021)
8. Meyer, M., Kuschk, G., Tomforde, S.: Graph convolutional networks for 3D object detection on radar data. In: Proceedings of the IEEE/CVF International Conference on Computer Vision, pp. 3060–3069 (2021)
9. Yang, B., Guo, R., Liang, M., Casas, S., Urtasun, R.: Radarnet: exploiting radar for robust perception of dynamic objects. In: Vedaldi, A., et al. (eds.) ECCV 2020, Part XVIII 16, pp. 496–512. Springer, Cham (2020). https://doi.org/10.1007/978-3-030-58580-8
10. Palffy, A., Pool, E., Baratam, S., Kooij, J.F., Gavrila, D.M.: Multi-class road user detection with 3+ 1d radar in the view-of-delft dataset. IEEE Robot. Autom. Lett. **7**(2), 4961–4968 (2022)
11. Zheng, L., et al.: Tj4dradset: a 4d radar dataset for autonomous driving. In: 2022 IEEE 25th International Conference on Intelligent Transportation Systems (ITSC), pp. 493–498. IEEE (2022)
12. Mao, J., Shi, S., Wang, X., Li, H.: 3D object detection for autonomous driving: a review and new outlooks. arXiv preprint arXiv:2206.09474 (2022)
13. Shi, S., Wang, Z., Wang, X., Li, H.:: Part-a$^\wedge$ 2 net: 3D part-aware and aggregation neural network for object detection from point cloud. **2**(3) arXiv preprint arXiv:1907.03670 (2019)
14. Sindagi, V.A., Zhou, Y., Tuzel, O.: MVX-net: multimodal voxelnet for 3D object detection. In: 2019 International Conference on Robotics and Automation (ICRA), pp. 7276–7282. IEEE (2019)
15. Zhou, S., et al.: Fastpillars: a deployment-friendly pillar-based 3d detector. arXiv preprint arXiv:2302.02367 (2023)
16. Qi, C.R., Su, H., Mo, K., Guibas, L.J.: Pointnet: deep learning on point sets for 3D classification and segmentation. In: Proceedings of the IEEE Conference on Computer Vision and Pattern Recognition, pp. 652–660 (2017)
17. Shi, S., et al.: PV-RCNN: point-voxel feature set abstraction for 3D object detection. In: Proceedings of the IEEE/CVF Conference on Computer Vision and Pattern Recognition, pp. 10529–10538 (2020)

18. Lalonde, J.-F., Vandapel, N., Huber, D.F., Hebert, M.: Natural terrain classification using three-dimensional Ladar data for ground robot mobility. J. Field Robot. **23**(10), 839–861 (2006)
19. Ghorbani, F., Ebadi, H., Sedaghat, A., Pfeifer, N.: A novel 3-d local daisy-style descriptor to reduce the effect of point displacement error in point cloud registration. IEEE J. Sel. Top. Appl. Earth Observat. Remote Sens. **15**, 2254–2273 (2022)
20. Khoury, M., Zhou, Q.-Y., Koltun, V.: Learning compact geometric features. In: Proceedings of the IEEE International Conference on Computer Vision, pp. 153–161 (2017)
21. Deng, H., Birdal, T., Ilic, S.: PPFNet: global context aware local features for robust 3D point matching. In: Proceedings of the IEEE Conference on Computer Vision and Pattern Recognition, pp. 195–205 (2018)
22. Deng, H., Birdal, T., Ilic, S.: PPF-foldnet: unsupervised learning of rotation invariant 3D local descriptors. In: Proceedings of the European Conference on Computer Vision (ECCV), pp. 602–618 (2018)
23. Qiu, S., Wu, Y., Anwar, S., Li, C.: Investigating attention mechanism in 3D point cloud object detection. In: 2021 International Conference on 3D Vision (3DV), pp. 403–412. IEEE (2021)
24. Nguyen, D.-K., Ju, J., Booij, O., Oswald, M.R., Snoek, C.G.: Boxer: box-attention for 2d and 3d transformers. In: Proceedings of the IEEE/CVF Conference on Computer Vision and Pattern Recognition, pp. 4773–4782 (2022)
25. Liu, Z., Zhao, X., Huang, T., Hu, R., Zhou, Y., Bai, X.: TANet: robust 3D object detection from point clouds with triple attention. In: Proceedings of the AAAI Conference on Artificial Intelligence, vol. 34, pp. 11677–11684 (2020)
26. Wang, G., Zhai, Q., Liu, H.: Cross self-attention network for 3D point cloud. Knowl.-Based Syst. **247**, 108769 (2022)
27. Yu, X., Tang, L., Rao, Y., Huang, T., Zhou, J., Lu, J.: Point-BERT: pre-training 3d point cloud transformers with masked point modeling. In: Proceedings of the IEEE/CVF Conference on Computer Vision and Pattern Recognition, pp. 19313–19322 (2022)
28. Yan, Q., Wang, Y.: MVFAN: multi-view feature assisted network for 4d radar object detection. In: Luo, B., Cheng, L., Wu, ZG., Li, H., Li, C. (eds.) ICONIP 2023. LNCS, vol. 14450, pp. 493–511, Springer, Cham (2023). https://doi.org/10.1007/978-981-99-8070-3_38
29. Lang, A.H., Vora, S., Caesar, H., Zhou, L., Yang, J., Beijbom, O.: PointPillars: fast encoders for object detection from point clouds. In: Proceedings of the IEEE/CVF Conference on Computer Vision and Pattern Recognition, pp. 12697–12705 (2019)
30. Liu, W., et al.: SSD: single shot MultiBox detector. In: Leibe, B., Matas, J., Sebe, N., Welling, M. (eds.) ECCV 2016. LNCS, vol. 9905, pp. 21–37. Springer, Cham (2016). https://doi.org/10.1007/978-3-319-46448-0_2
31. Kingma, D.P., Ba, J.: Adam: a method for stochastic optimization. arXiv preprint arXiv:1412.6980 (2014)
32. Team, O., et al.: OpenPCDet: an open-source toolbox for 3D object detection from point clouds. OD Team (2020)
33. Yan, Y., Mao, Y., Li, B.: Second: sparsely embedded convolutional detection. Sensors **18**(10), 3337 (2018)
34. Xu, B., et al.: RPFA-Net: a 4D radar pillar feature attention network for 3D object detection. In: 2021 IEEE International Intelligent Transportation Systems Conference (ITSC), pp. 3061–3066. IEEE (2021)

35. Yin, T., Zhou, X., Krahenbuhl, P.: Center-based 3D object detection and tracking. In: Proceedings of the IEEE/CVF Conference on Computer Vision and Pattern Recognition, pp. 11784–11793 (2021)
36. Liu, Z., et al.: BEVFusion: multi-task multi-sensor fusion with unified bird's-eye view representation. In: 2023 IEEE International Conference on Robotics and Automation (ICRA), pp. 2774–2781. IEEE (2023)
37. Zheng, L., et al.: RCFusion: fusing 4D radar and camera with bird's-eye view features for 3D object detection. IEEE Trans. Instrument. Measur. (2023)
38. Xiong, W., Liu, J., Huang, T., Han, Q.-L., Xia, Y., Zhu, B.: LXL: lidar excluded lean 3D object detection with 4D imaging radar and camera fusion. IEEE Trans. Intell. Veh. (2023)

One-Shot Object Detection with 4D-Correlation and 4D-Attention

Qiwei Lin[1], Xinzhi Lin[2], Junjie Zhou[3], and Qinghua Long[1(✉)]

[1] Beijing Institute of Radio Measurement, Beijing, China
cs.wishlab@gmail.com
[2] SKLSDE and BDBC Lab, Beihang University, Beijing, China
[3] Nanjing University of Aeronautics and Astronautics, Nanjing, China

Abstract. One-shot object detection (OSOD) is an emerging and important task to detect novel classes given only one query sample. This task is challenged by the significant variability in appearance and geometry within query-target image pairs, which blurs the lines between variations of the inter- and intra classes. To address such issue, we propose a novel framework called 4D-Correlation and 4D-Attention Networks (4DCA) to enhance the differentiation of these variations. Our 4DCA framework consists of two collaborative components: (1) During feature extraction, the 4D-Correlation-Pyramid (FCP) module dynamically fuses multi-layer features to construct high-dimensional representations that accentuate the correlations between query and target images. (2) For correlation learning, the 4D-Attention (FA) module employs multi-head cross-attention mechanisms learn the complex correlation between query-target image pairs. Our method focuses on extracting abundant visual correlations in limited samples, which strengthens intra-class robustness and inter-class separability. Extensive experiments on the MS COCO and FSOD datasets have proven the superiority of our method.

1 Introduction

Object detection is an important task in computer vision. Its success relies heavily on abundant labeled data, which often contains high labeling cost, and becomes a huge obstacle to practical applications. Therefore, it is important for novel class detection tasks with few labeled samples. In this work, we focus on the One-Shot Object Detection (OSOD) task, which aims at detecting all interesting objects in the target image with the same novel class of single query image patch.

We observe that, different from image retrieval [13] and object tracking [1,14,15], the query image and target image used for similarity measurement in the OSOD task tend to have more significant intra-class variation, which may be confused with the inter-class variation. In siamese network based object tracking [1,14,15], key and reference frames are typically aligned in terms of scale, viewpoint, and illumination, leading to minimal variation. In stark contrast, OSOD

Q. Lin, X. Lin and J. Zhou—These authors contributed equally to this work.

© The Author(s), under exclusive license to Springer Nature Switzerland AG 2024
M. Wand et al. (Eds.): ICANN 2024, LNCS 15017, pp. 185–199, 2024.
https://doi.org/10.1007/978-3-031-72335-3_13

confronts both inter-class and pronounced intra-class variations, exemplified by distinct instances within the same class, thereby complicating the process of feature extraction and similarity measurement. Furthermore, the number of query image samples is typically limited (one-shot), so one query image patch can not provide enough information for learning a discriminative representation, which further aggravates the problem of intra-class and inter-class variation confusion.

Our observation indicates the importance of integrating visual correlation extraction and learning to boost intra-class robustness and inter-class discrimination in one-shot object detection. Recent works [2,11,18,30,31] have explored correlation extraction but often overlook the depth of patterns accessible through the backbone's feature stages or fail to fully integrate these patterns. BHRL [30] incorporates FPN yet omits exhaustive correlation extraction, while HSNet [21] captures high-dimensional correlation patterns without subsequent multi-level learning. To address these gaps, we propose the innovative 4D-Correlation and 4D-Attention (4DCA) framework, which includes a Feature Correlation Pyramid (FCP) module for advanced multi-level extraction and a Feature Attention (FA) module for comprehensive learning of correlation patterns, as depicted in Fig. 1. Dense visual correlation matching in 4DCA architecture allows the model to comprehensively capture the diversity of inter-class variations of the target as much as possible, alleviating the generation of false positives due to a few intra-class variations.

Inspired by the human ability of capturing both low-level geometric and high-level semantic cues in coarse-to-fine manner for learning novel class, we propose a 4D-Correlation Pyramid (FCP) module to strengthen the intra-class robustness. The FCP module mines a broad array of geometric and semantic correlations from a multitude of intermediate layers, resulting in the formulation of a set of 4D correlation tensors that encapsulate a rich tapestry of visual correlations. By adopting a pyramidal structure, the module captures intricate geometric nuances and semantic insights. The fusion of correlation features between query image patches and target images is executed through a specialized transformation and fusion process, which refines the feature representation to emphasize discriminative attributes and suppresses attributes that often lead to misclassification, thereby mitigating the issue of intra-class ambiguity.

In addition, for the inter-class separability, a 4D-attention (FA) module is proposed to learn the rich visual correlation features extracted by the FCP module, which forms the basis for the subsequent head to detect the query-related instance. The FA module utilizes 4D convolution and channel attention to mine the potential correlation patterns. Firstly, we use region proposal network to extract instance-level correlation feature maps. Secondly, to obtain the similarity representations between query and target image, our module learns contrastive features, 2D correlation features and fusion features. Finally, we concatenate the above three features and the feature from the FCP to generate a learning feature. After the 4D-Attention module, the networks can better utilize the context information that is jointly embedded in the query and target images for subsequent classification and regression.

In summary, our contributions are:

- We propose an effective correlation extraction module named FCP, which simultaneously extracts effective correlations of query image patch and target image.
- We also propose the FA module to learn the rich visual correlation patterns extracted by the FCP module.
- Extensive experiments show that our 4D-Correlation and 4D-Attention Network (4DCA) improves 1.0% and 1.2% over the state-of-the-art method on FSOD and MS COCO data sets in unseen class detection, respectively, which validates its effectiveness.

2 Related Works

One-Shot Object Detection. The One-Shot Object Detection (OSOD) [2,5,11, 18,30–32] aims at detecting all interesting objects in the target image with the same novel class of single query image patch. [11] employs the non-local and squeeze-excitation modules to draw associations between query and target images. Research in [31] addresses the issue of false positives by minimizing interference between localization and classification heads. Work in [5] focuses on differentiating foreground from background via data augmentation and feature similarity techniques to reduce incorrect detections. BHRL [30] introduces the IHR module to underscore complex interdependencies in query-target pairs. Transformer architectures have been integrated into OSOD by studies [2,18,32], with SaFT [32] proposing a one-stage architecture that encourages semantic-aligned associations. While these recent works show promise, they often fail to sufficiently capture or learn from the complex correlation patterns. We introduce the correlation calculation into the OSOD task. Our 4D-Correlation and 4D-Attention (4DCA) framework, jointly extracts and learns visual correlation, is essential for strengthening intra-class robustness and inter-class separability.

Few-Shot Object Detection. The Few-Shot Object Detection (FSOD) [3,7,8,12, 24,25,28] task aims at learning to detect novel objects from only a few annotated examples. According to recent study [25], it has been highlighted that fine-tuning solely the final layer of pre-existing detectors for rare classes plays a pivotal role in Few-Shot Object Detection (FSOD) tasks. In a different approach [7], a novel model has been introduced that enables the detection of new objects without necessitating retraining or fine-tuning. Furthermore, a meta feature learner has been proposed by [24] to extract meta features alongside a reweighting module designed to specify the significance or correlation of these meta features. To address the challenge of detecting few-shot class objects while retaining prior knowledge, [8] has introduced a bias-balanced Region Proposal Network (RPN) and re-detector. Additionally, [3] has delved into the significance of loss functions and data augmentation during the fine-tuning process, advocating for the adjustment of their dynamics through the lens of meta-learning principles. Compared with the FSOD task, the OSOD task is more vulnerable to suffer from the overfitting due to its more limited number of samples (one-shot). Dense visual correlation matching in 4DCA architecture allows the model to comprehensively capture the diversity of inter-class variations of the target as much as possible, alleviating the generation of false positives due to a few intra-class variations.

4D Convolution for Visual Correspondence. Visual correspondence is fundamental to a variety of tasks, including image retrieval [13], optical flow estimation [29], and few-shot segmentation [10]. [23] introduces the Neighborhood Consensus Network, employing 4D convolution for visual correspondence. However, the utilization of multiple 4D kernels typically necessitates a high parameter count for learning. To mitigate this issue, [20] proposes a lightweight high-dimensional kernel for visual correspondence, aiming to reduce the number of involved parameters. [29] decomposes a 4D convolution kernel into two separate 2D kernels, thereby preserving a smaller memory footprint. In the context of few-shot segmentation, [21] puts forward efficient center-pivot 4D convolutions, further reducing computational demands. Additionally, [13] presents a Correlation Verification Network, comprising deeply stacked 4D convolutional layers that learn diverse geometric matching patterns from various image pairs. [10] introduces a 4D convolutional Swin Transformer for few-shot segmentation.

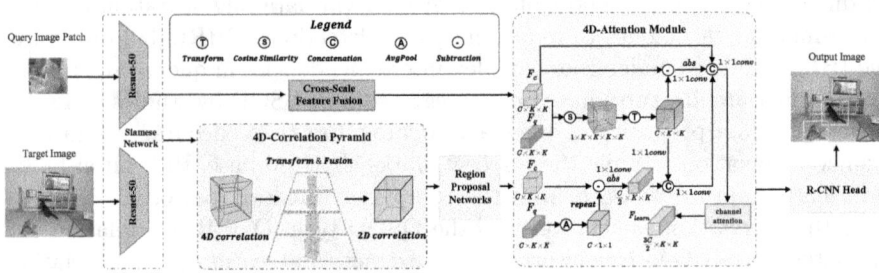

Fig. 1. The overall architecture of the proposed 4DCA network for one-shot object detection. Our 4DCA uses the siamese resnet-50 network as the backbone. The FCP module extracts high-dimensional correlation, then fine-grained correlation patterns are learned by the FA module, and finally the R-CNN head outputs the detection results.

3 Method

3.1 Problem Setup

We formulate the one-shot object detection as follows. Given an arbitrary query image patch I_q, the one-shot object detector aims at detecting all instances in the target image I_t that are consistent with this query patch class. The object classes are split into seen classes S and unseen classes U, which $S \cap U = \emptyset$. The one-shot object detector is trained with the data of seen classes S. The inference task is to detect unseen classes U with only one query image patch.

3.2 Overall Architecture

Figure 1 shows the overall architecture of our 4DCA (4D-Correlation and 4D-Attention). It mainly consists of three collaborative parts: the siamese networks, the 4D-Correlation Pyramid module, and the 4D-Attention module. Firstly, the shared-weight siamese ResNet-50 is adopted to extract the visual features of query image patch and target image. Secondly, our proposed 4D-Correlation Pyramid (FCP) module uses pyramidal design to capture both low-level geometric and high-level semantic cues, which includes transform units and fusion units to compute the correlation feature between the query image patch and target image. Subsequently, the correlation feature enables the standard Region Proposal Network (RPN) to generate a collection of potential region proposals that are more pertinent to the query patch. We extract the proposal features from the entire target feature using the RoI pooling operator. Thirdly, the 4D-Attention (FA) module learns the rich visual correlation patterns for query and target pairs. Finally, the R-CNN head is used to detect the query-related instances in target image, we follow the ratio preserving loss [30] to rebalance the involved samples.

3.3 4D-Correlation Pyramid Module

In this section, we propose a novel 4D-correlation pyramid module to extract multi-level feature correlations. Our FCP module expands the extracted feature map to a multi-scale feature pyramid, similar to FPN, which could capture both low-level geometric and high-level semantic cues between the query image patch and target image. Different from the previous methods [7,30], we designed the pyramidal architecture for the correlation extraction module, which could reduce intra-class variation interference.

Feature Correlation Construction. We compute the correlation of the multi-layer features, as shown in Fig. 2. The input is a pair of query image patch and target image $I_q, I_t \in R^{3 \times H \times W}$. The query-target feature maps (QF^l, TF^l) are extracted from the backbone network, where l represents the extracted layer. We compute the 4D correlation tensor $C^l \in R^{H_l \times W_l \times H_l \times W_l}$ using cosine similarity and ReLU function:

$$C^l(x_t, x_q) = ReLU(\frac{TF^l(x_t) \cdot QF^l(x_q)}{||TF^l(x_t)|| \, ||QF^l(x_q)||}), \quad (1)$$

where x_q and x_t are the 2D spatial positions of feature map QF^l and TF^l. The correlation of each layer forms the set $\{C^l\}_{l=1}^L$. We group 4D tensors of the same spatial size into a subset $\{C^l\}_{l \in L_s}$, where L_s is a subset of CNN layer indices at the pyramid layer s. The 4D tensors in $\{C^l\}_{l \in L_s}$ are concatenated along the channel dimension to form the visual correlations $C_s \in R^{|L_s| \times H_s \times W_s \times H_s \times W_s}$, where (H_s, W_s, H_s, W_s) represents the feature map scale of the visual correlation at the pyramid level s. We denote the S layers 4D-correlation pyramid as $\mathcal{C} = \{C_s\}_{s=1}^{S}$, which $\mathcal{C}$ represents feature correlations set.

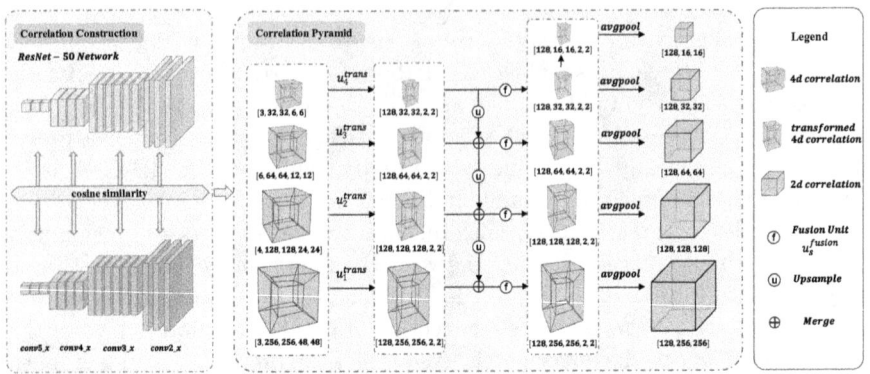

Fig. 2. Illustration of the proposed 4D-Correlation Pyramid (FCP) module. The annotations "[]" denote the "[$channel, H_1, W_1, H_2, W_2$]" format, where "$H_1, W_1$" corresponds to height and width of the target image and "H_2, W_2" corresponds to the query image.

4D-Correlation Pyramid. We design the transform unit u_s^{trans} and the fusion unit u_s^{fusion}, consisting of multi-channel 4D convolution, group normalization [27], and ReLU function, as shown in Fig. 3. Suitable convolution strides are designed according to the feature map scale to reduce the last two query space dimensions of C_s, while the first two target space dimensions are unchanged. After upsampling the target spatial dimension of the upper level outputs, we merge the outputs s and s+1 from adjacent pyramid levels. The fusion unit u_s^{fusion} propagates high-level semantics to lower layers. Using the previous studies, we follow the center-pivot 4D convolution [21] to alleviate the burden of using high-dimensional kernels and transform the 4D kernels into 2D kernels. After iterative propagation, the output tensor of the fusion unit is further compressed by average pooling in last two query spatial dimensions to obtain a multi-scale 2D representation of the 4D-correlation pyramid. Our 4D-correlation pyramid can effectively capture multi-scale semantic correlations, which forms the basis for subsequent correlation-learning.

3.4 4D-Attention Module

In this section, we propose the 4D-Attention (FA) module to learn the feature correlations extracted by the FCP module, which could strengthen the inter-class separability. We use high-dimensional convolution to mine the potential

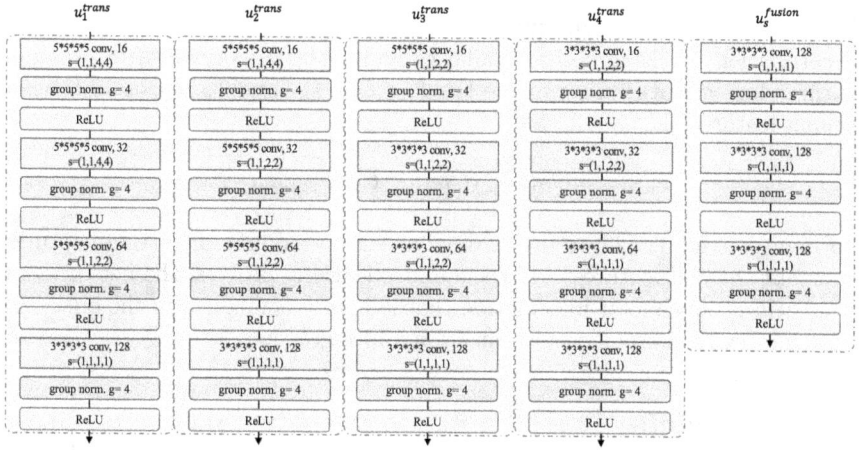

Fig. 3. Building blocks u_s^{trans} and u_s^{fusion} in FCP module. *stride* and g denotes strides of 4D convolution and the number of groups in group normalization. Note $s \in \{1,2,3\}$ for u_s^{fusion}.

correlation patterns. Figure 1 sketches the architecture of our FA module. Our FA module uses 2D correlation feature F_c as the input feature instead of the previous target feature. The advantage is that F_c merges more query image patch characteristics, which reduces the interference of intra-class variations and makes the module focus on the mining of inter-class variations.

Correlation Learning Stage. We introduce a simple cross-scale feature fusion module for the query feature extracted by the siamese Resnet-50, which is used to generate query feature input F_q. We extract four-scale query feature maps obtained by Resnet-50 and then use 1×1 convolution layer and linear interpolation to obtain feature maps of the same scale. Finally, we merge the feature maps of the same scale to obtain F_q. In the FA module, we aim at learning the correlation patterns between the query feature input F_q and the 2D correlation feature input F_c. The F_c is from the FCP module, as shown in Fig. 1. Firstly, similar to existing study [19], we compute the contrastive correlation feature between the F_c and the F_q, the contrastive feature F_{cc} is as follows:

$$F_{cc} = Conv_{\frac{C}{2}}(|R(AvgPool(F_q)) - F_c|), \qquad (2)$$

where $|\cdot|$ denotes the absolute value operator. $R(\cdot)$ is a repeat operator, which makes $F_{cc}^{C \times 1 \times 1} \longrightarrow F_{cc}^{C \times K \times K}$. $AvgPool(\cdot)$ is the average pooling operation. The $Conv_{\frac{C}{2}}(\cdot)$ is a 1×1 convolution layer with an output channel of $\frac{C}{2}$. Secondly, similar to our FCP module in Sect. 3.3, we compute the 2D correlation feature F_{2d} between the F_c and the F_q, and then we compute the fusion feature F_{dc} between the F_{2d} and the F_c. The F_{dc} is given by following:

$$F_{dc} = Conv_{\frac{C}{2}}(|F_c - F_{2d}|), F_{2d} = T(S(F_q, F_c)), \qquad (3)$$

where $T(\cdot)$ is the transform unit in Sect. 3.3, and the $S(\cdot)$ represents computing 4D correlation by using cosine similarity and $ReLU$ function. After obtaining the three fusion features, we merge the F_{cc}, F_{2d}, F_{dc} and F_c to obtain the final learning feature F_{learn}:

$$F_{learn} = Conv_{\frac{3C}{2}}(Conv_{\frac{C}{2}}[F_{cc}, F_{2d}], F_{dc}, F_c) \quad (4)$$

Finally, we follow [26] to use channel attention module for further capturing important channel features. After the above learning process, the networks can better utilize the context information that is jointly embedded in the query and target images to subsequent classification and regression.

4 Experiments

4.1 Datasets and Settings

Datasets and Evaluation Metrics. Following the previous works [2,11,25], we train and evaluate our model on PASCAL VOC and MS COCO benchmark datasets. For the PASCAL VOC dataset [6], we divide 20 classes into 16 seen classes and 4 unseen classes. For the MS COCO dataset [17], we use the same 4 splits over the 80 classes. We take 3 splits (60 classes) as seen classes and 1 split (20 classes) as unseen classes. For evaluation metrics, we follow [2,11,25] to report AP_{50} for both the PASCAL VOC and MS COCO datasets. We also test the performance of our model on the FSOD dataset [7], which uses AP, AP_{50}, AP_{75} as our evaluation metrics.

Table 1. Performance comparisons with state-of-the-art methods on the MS COCO dataset in terms of AP_{50}.

Method	Seen					Unseen				
	split-1	split-2	split-3	split-4	Average	split-1	split-2	split-3	split-4	Average
SiamMask [19]	38.9	37.1	37.8	36.6	37.6	15.3	17.6	17.4	17.0	16.8
CoAE [11]	42.2	40.2	39.9	41.3	40.9	23.4	23.6	20.5	20.4	22.0
AIT [2]	50.1	47.2	45.8	46.9	47.5	26.0	26.4	22.3	22.6	24.3
SaFT [32]	49.2	47.2	47.9	49.0	48.3	27.8	27.6	21.0	23.0	24.9
BHRL [30]	**56.0**	52.1	52.6	**53.4**	53.5	26.1	29.0	22.7	24.5	25.6
Ours	**56.0**	**52.2**	**52.6**	53.3	**53.5**	**26.3**	**29.6**	**25.7**	**25.7**	**26.8(+1.2)**

Table 2. Performance comparisons with state-of-the-art methods on the PASCAL VOC dataset in terms of AP_{50}.

Method	seen																	unseen				
	plant	sofa	tv	car	bottle	boat	chair	person	bus	train	horse	bike	dog	bird	mbike	table	Average	cow	sheep	cat	aero	Average
SiamFC [1]	3.2	22.8	5.0	16.7	0.5	8.1	1.2	4.2	22.2	22.6	35.4	14.2	25.8	11.7	19.7	27.8	15.1	6.8	2.28	31.6	12.4	13.3
SiamRPN [14]	1.9	15.7	4.5	12.8	1.0	1.1	6.1	8.7	7.9	6.9	17.4	17.8	20.5	7.2	18.5	5.1	9.6	15.9	15.7	21.7	3.5	14.2
OSCD [31]	28.4	41.5	65.0	66.4	37.1	49.8	16.2	31.7	69.7	73.1	75.6	71.6	61.4	52.3	63.4	39.8	52.7	75.3	60.0	47.9	25.3	52.1
CoAE [11]	24.9	50.1	58.8	64.3	32.9	48.9	14.2	53.2	71.5	74.7	74.0	66.3	75.7	61.5	68.5	42.7	55.1	78.0	61.9	72.0	43.5	63.8
AIT [2]	46.4	60.5	68.0	73.6	49.0	**65.1**	26.6	68.2	**82.6**	85.4	82.9	77.1	82.7	71.8	75.1	**60.0**	67.2	85.5	**72.8**	80.4	50.2	72.2
BHRL [30]	**57.5**	49.4	76.8	**80.4**	**61.2**	58.4	**48.1**	**83.3**	74.3	87.3	80.1	**81.0**	87.2	**73.0**	**78.8**	38.8	69.7	81.0	67.9	**86.9**	**59.3**	**73.8**
Ours	52.3	**68.6**	**78.0**	80.0	52.5	55.2	47.4	79.4	78.6	**88.0**	**84.4**	79.7	**87.5**	69.1	76.8	59.1	**71.0**	81.0	67.1	86.3	59.1	73.4

Table 3. Performance comparisons with the state-of-the-art method BHRL on the FSOD dataset.

Method	test-1			test-2			test-3			test-4			test-5			Average		
	AP	AP50	AP75	AP	AP50	AP75	AP	AP50	AP75	AP	AP50	AP75	AP	AP50	AP75	AP	AP50	AP75
BHRL(CVPR2022)	27.8	48.8	27.7	27.9	49.3	27.7	27.7	48.8	27.6	28.0	49.2	27.9	27.9	48.9	27.8	27.9	49.0	27.7
Ours	**28.3**	**49.8**	27.8	**28.5**	**50.3**	**28.2**	**28.3**	**49.9**	**28.0**	**28.6**	**50.0**	**28.5**	**28.4**	**49.7**	**28.2**	**28.4**(+0.5)	**50.0**(+1.0)	**28.1**(+0.4)

Target-Query Pairs. We adopt the approach outlined in [2,11,25] to generate target-query image pairs. Initially, target images are selected from the datasets. During training, a query seen-class image patch is randomly chosen for a given target image containing the same seen-class object. During the testing phase, query image patches of the same class within a target image are shuffled using a random seed derived from the target image ID. Subsequently, the average AP scores are calculated based on the selection of the first five query image patches.

Implementation Details. Our model is trained with a batch size of 16 across 4 GPUs using the SGD optimizer. Training on the PASCAL VOC dataset spans 12 epochs, while training on the MS COCO dataset lasts for 9 epochs. The initial learning rate is set at 0.02 and is subsequently reduced by a factor of 0.1 starting from the 7th epoch. Employing ResNet-50 as our backbone network, it is pre-trained on a modified ImageNet [4], excluding all COCO-related ImageNet classes [11] to prevent exposure to unseen classes. Following the methodology in [30], RoIAlign [9] is utilized to generate target proposals on the COCO dataset, while deformable RoI pooling is employed for generating target proposals on the PASCAL VOC dataset.

Table 4. Effects of each component in our design on the MS COCO dataset for unseen classes.

FCP	FA	split-1		split-2		split-3		split-4		Average	
		seen	unseen	seen	unseen	seen	unseen	seen	unseen	seen	unseen
		55.6	25.1	50.4	26.7	51.4	21.9	52.0	23.6	52.4	24.3
✓		55.9	25.8	51.2	28.6	51.8	22.1	52.9	23.9	53.0	25.1
	✓	55.8	26.1	51.4	28.5	52.0	21.9	52.2	24.2	52.9	25.2
✓	✓	**56.0**	**26.3**	**52.2**	**29.6**	**52.6**	**25.7**	**53.3**	**25.7**	**53.5**	**26.8**

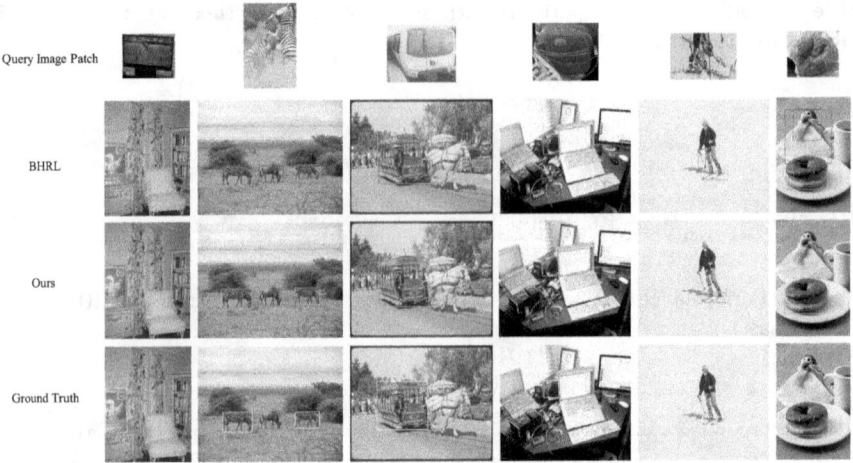

Fig. 4. Visualization comparison between BHRL and our 4DCA for unseen classes. Yellow boxes indicate the ground truth boxes, green boxes indicate the correct detection, and red boxes indicate the false detection. (Color figure online)

4.2 Results and Analysis

Evaluation on the MS COCO Dataset and the PASCAL VOC Dataset. Table 1 presents a comparative analysis of our 4DCA network with state-of-the-art methods [2,11,19,30] on the MS COCO dataset, considering both seen and unseen classes. The results demonstrate that our 4DCA network, labeled as 'Ours', achieves a seen-class AP_{50} of 53.3% and an unseen-class AP_{50} of 26.8%. Notably, our method exhibits a performance improvement of 1.2% in terms of AP_{50} for the unseen-class in comparison to the state-of-the-art BHRL method. Regarding seen classes, our approach performs on par with the leading BHRL method. However, for unseen classes, our method outperforms the widely-used CoAE by a considerable margin, with a AP_{50} gain of 4.8%. This significant enhancement can be attributed to the ability of our 4DCA network to enhance intra-class robustness and inter-class separability. In Table 2, we present a comparison between our model, BHRL, and several other methods [1,2,11,14,30,31] on the PASCAL VOC dataset. It can be observed that our model surpasses BHRL by 1.3% in AP_{50} on seen classes and performs slightly worse (0.4% AP_{50}) on unseen classes.

Evaluation on the FSOD Dataset. The essence of the OSOD task lies in the model's capacity for generalization when confronted with unfamiliar classes. However, the MS COCO dataset and PASCAL VOC dataset offer a limited range of categories and are not tailored for one-shot evaluation scenarios. To address this problem, we leverage the FSOD dataset [7] for detecting unseen objects and conducting a robust evaluation within a consistent one-shot setting. The FSOD dataset is purposefully crafted for few-shot object detection, comprising 1000 categories, with 800 designated for training and 200 for testing. Our

Fig. 5. Visualization results of the intermediate feature maps. With the deepening of visual correlation extraction and learning, the 4DCA outputs gradually focus on the objects of the query-related class.

model's performance, alongside the recent state-of-the-art method BHRL [30], is evaluated on this dataset. As depicted in Table 3, our model surpasses the current state-of-the-art BHRL by 0.5% in terms of AP, 1.0% in AP_{50}, and 0.4% in AP_{75} on unseen classes, showcasing enhanced generalization capabilities from seen to unseen classes.

Table 5. Comparison for seen classes on PASCAL VOC dataset.

method	AP_{50}
Faster R-CNN [22]	67.8
CoAE [11]	55.1
BHRL [30]	69.7
Ours	**71.0**

4.3 Ablation Studies

Effectiveness of FCP and FA. The 4D-Correlation Pyramid module and the 4D-Attention module are fundamental components of our model. The FCP is designed to capture both geometric and semantic cues in a query-target pair for better intra-class robustness. The FA module focus on the mining of inter-class variations. We conduct the experiments to verify the effectiveness of the proposed FCP module and FA module, and summarize the results for unseen classes on the COCO dataset in Table 4. The baseline in the 1st row adopts the widely-used FPN [16] to extract geometric and semantic cues, and feature matching [19] to learn the correlation patterns. The loss function is the same for both. As shown in the 1st and 2nd rows, the FCP module contributes to a 0.6% AP_{50} improvement and 0.8% AP_{50} improvement on seen classes and unseen classes, respectively. This benefits from the fact that the FCP module can extract effective correlations of query image patch and target image. As shown in the 1st and 3rd rows, the FA module contributes to a 0.5% AP_{50} improvement and 0.9% AP_{50} improvement on seen classes and unseen classes, respectively. This demonstrates that the FA can learn rich visual correlation patterns.

Performance Comparison for Seen Classes. We take Faster R-CNN [22] as baseline to verify the effectiveness of our model for seen classes. We use the same setting as our method to evaluate the Faster R-CNN model. As shown in Table 5, it can be seen that our model outperforms the Faster R-CNN by 3.3% in AP_{50} on seen classes.

Table 6. (a) Ablation studies for the FA module on the COCO split-3 dataset for unseen classes. (b) Performance comparison with the IHR module on the COCO split-3 dataset for unseen classes. "S.R." and "A.R." represent the salient-level relation and attention-level relation in the IHR module.

(a)

F_{cc}	F_{dc}	AP_{50}
		21.9
✓		23.5
	✓	23.6
✓	✓	**25.7**

(b)

S.R. + A.R. (IHR)	F_{dc}(Ours)	AP_{50}
		21.9
✓		22.4
	✓	**25.4**

Impact of Feature Branches in the FA Module. In Table 6, we analyse the importance of each feature branch in the FA module. As shown in Fig. 1, there are two main branches in the FA module that generate contrastive feature F_{cc} and fusion feature F_{dc} in parallel. F_{cc} and F_{dc} become an important part of the learning feature F_{learn} through concatenation. In Table 6a, we conduct ablation experiments on COCO split-3 dataset, and find that both branches can improve the performance of the model. The best performance is achieved by merging two features, as shown in the last row. This indicates that F_{learn} captures more comprehensive correlation information. We also compare the FA module with the similar method IHR [30] module. We keep the salient-level relation and attention-level relation of the IHR module and compare them with our F_{dc} branch, both of which are used to extract correlation information. As shown in Table 6b, our 4D relevance branch achieves better performance than the two branches of IHR.

4.4 Visualization

Visualizing the Comparison Between BHRL and Our 4DCA. In Fig. 4, we visualize the detection result of BHRL and our 4DCA for unseen classes. It can be observed that our 4DCA can effectively detect unseen class objects. Compared to BHRL, our method generates fewer false detections.

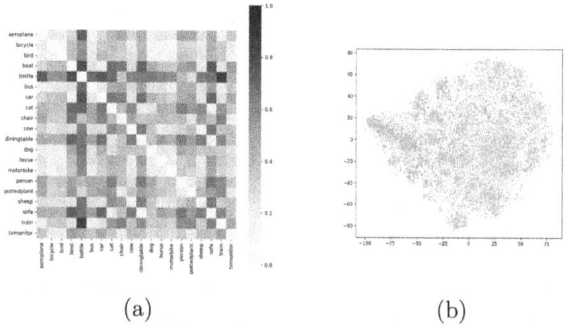

(a) (b)

Fig. 6. (a) Visualization of class-to-class pairwise distances based on 4D-Attention weights. Samples of the different classes have larger weights, that is, longer Euclidean distance. (b) t-SNE visualization of objects learned in the feature space with our designed 4DCA framework. Results are obtained on Pascal VOC split 3. The blue ones are positive samples. (Color figure online)

Visualizing the Results of the Intermediate Feature Maps. To enhance comprehension of our model, we visualize intermediate feature maps based on response intensity. In Fig. 5, query and target images are shown in the first two columns, with subsequent columns displaying 4DCA stage visualizations. The 4DCA outputs focus increasingly on objects of the query class as visual correlations are learned.

Visualizing the Inter-class Separability and Intra-class Robustness of Our 4DCA. During testing, we analyze the weight distributions of our 4DCA module for each class by aggregating FA module weights for query images. As depicted in Fig. 6a, visualizing pairwise euclidean distances of FA weight vectors for class pairs demonstrates distinct weight distributions for individual classes, enhancing inter-class separability. As illustrated in Fig. 6b, by using t-SNE, we visualize the separation of positive and negative samples in the feature space, showing clear clustering of samples from the same class while maintaining robust intra-class separability.

5 Conclusion

In this paper, we focus on the problem of intra-class variation confusion. We propose the 4DCA framework, which exploits high-dimensional convolutions to extract rich visual correlations and enhance intra-class robustness and inter-class separability. Extensive experiments on benchmark datasets demonstrate the effectiveness and efficiency of our method. We hope that our work can inspire more research regarding the OSOD task.

References

1. Bertinetto, L., Valmadre, J., Henriques, J.F., Vedaldi, A., Torr, P.H.S.: Fully-convolutional Siamese networks for object tracking. In: Hua, G., Jégou, H. (eds.) ECCV 2016. LNCS, vol. 9914, pp. 850–865. Springer, Cham (2016). https://doi.org/10.1007/978-3-319-48881-3_56
2. Chen, D.J., Hsieh, H.Y., Liu, T.L.: Adaptive image transformer for one-shot object detection. In: Proceedings of the IEEE/CVF Conference on Computer Vision and Pattern Recognition, pp. 12247–12256 (2021)
3. Demirel, B., Baran, O.B., Cinbis, R.G.: Meta-tuning loss functions and data augmentation for few-shot object detection. arXiv preprint arXiv:2304.12161 (2023)
4. Deng, J., Dong, W., Socher, R., Li, L.J., Li, K., Fei-Fei, L.: Imagenet: a large-scale hierarchical image database. In: 2009 IEEE Conference on Computer Vision and Pattern Recognition, pp. 248–255. IEEE (2009)
5. Du, Y., et al.: Augmentative contrastive learning for one-shot object detection. Neurocomputing **513**, 13–24 (2022)
6. Everingham, M., Van Gool, L., Williams, C.K., Winn, J., Zisserman, A.: The pascal visual object classes (VOC) challenge. Int. J. Comput. Vision **88**, 303–338 (2010)
7. Fan, Q., Zhuo, W., Tang, C.K., Tai, Y.W.: Few-shot object detection with attention-RPN and multi-relation detector. In: Proceedings of the IEEE/CVF Conference on Computer Vision and Pattern Recognition, pp. 4013–4022 (2020)
8. Fan, Z., Ma, Y., Li, Z., Sun, J.: Generalized few-shot object detection without forgetting. In: Proceedings of the IEEE/CVF Conference on Computer Vision and Pattern Recognition, pp. 4527–4536 (2021)
9. He, K., Gkioxari, G., Dollár, P., Girshick, R.: Mask R-CNN. In: Proceedings of the IEEE International Conference on Computer Vision, pp. 2961–2969 (2017)
10. Hong, S., Cho, S., Nam, J., Lin, S., Kim, S.: Cost aggregation with 4D convolutional SWIN transformer for few-shot segmentation. In: Avidan, S., Brostow, G., Cissé, M., Farinella, G.M., Hassner, T. (eds.) ECCV 2022, Part XXIX, pp. 108–126. Springer, Cham (2022). https://doi.org/10.1007/978-3-031-19818-2_7
11. Hsieh, T.I., Lo, Y.C., Chen, H.T., Liu, T.L.: One-shot object detection with co-attention and co-excitation. In: Advances in Neural Information Processing Systems, vol. 32 (2019)
12. Hu, H., Bai, S., Li, A., Cui, J., Wang, L.: Dense relation distillation with context-aware aggregation for few-shot object detection. In: Proceedings of the IEEE/CVF Conference on Computer Vision and Pattern Recognition, pp. 10185–10194 (2021)
13. Lee, S., Seong, H., Lee, S., Kim, E.: Correlation verification for image retrieval. In: Proceedings of the IEEE/CVF Conference on Computer Vision and Pattern Recognition, pp. 5374–5384 (2022)
14. Li, B., Wu, W., Wang, Q., Zhang, F., Xing, J., Yan, J.: SIAMRPN++: evolution of SIAMESE visual tracking with very deep networks. In: Proceedings of the IEEE/CVF Conference on Computer Vision and Pattern Recognition, pp. 4282–4291 (2019)
15. Li, B., Yan, J., Wu, W., Zhu, Z., Hu, X.: High performance visual tracking with SIAMESE region proposal network. In: Proceedings of the IEEE Conference on Computer Vision and Pattern Recognition, pp. 8971–8980 (2018)
16. Lin, T.Y., Dollár, P., Girshick, R., He, K., Hariharan, B., Belongie, S.: Feature pyramid networks for object detection. In: Proceedings of the IEEE Conference on Computer Vision and Pattern Recognition, pp. 2117–2125 (2017)

17. Lin, T.-Y., et al.: Microsoft COCO: common objects in context. In: Fleet, D., Pajdla, T., Schiele, B., Tuytelaars, T. (eds.) ECCV 2014. LNCS, vol. 8693, pp. 740–755. Springer, Cham (2014). https://doi.org/10.1007/978-3-319-10602-1_48
18. Lin, W., et al.: Cat: cross-attention transformer for one-shot object detection. arXiv preprint arXiv:2104.14984 (2021)
19. Michaelis, C., Ustyuzhaninov, I., Bethge, M., Ecker, A.S.: One-shot instance segmentation. arXiv preprint arXiv:1811.11507 (2018)
20. Min, J., Cho, M.: Convolutional hough matching networks. In: Proceedings of the IEEE/CVF Conference on Computer Vision and Pattern Recognition, pp. 2940–2950 (2021)
21. Min, J., Kang, D., Cho, M.: Hypercorrelation squeeze for few-shot segmentation. In: Proceedings of the IEEE/CVF International Conference on Computer Vision, pp. 6941–6952 (2021)
22. Ren, S., He, K., Girshick, R., Sun, J.: Faster R-CNN: towards real-time object detection with region proposal networks. In: Advances in Neural Information Processing Systems, vol. 28 (2015)
23. Rocco, I., Cimpoi, M., Arandjelović, R., Torii, A., Pajdla, T., Sivic, J.: Neighbourhood consensus networks. In: Advances in Neural Information Processing Systems, vol. 31 (2018)
24. Sun, B., Li, B., Cai, S., Yuan, Y., Zhang, C.: FSCE: few-shot object detection via contrastive proposal encoding. In: Proceedings of the IEEE/CVF Conference on Computer Vision and Pattern Recognition, pp. 7352–7362 (2021)
25. Wang, X., Huang, T.E., Darrell, T., Gonzalez, J.E., Yu, F.: Frustratingly simple few-shot object detection. arXiv preprint arXiv:2003.06957 (2020)
26. Woo, S., Park, J., Lee, J.Y., Kweon, I.S.: CBAM: convolutional block attention module. In: Proceedings of the European Conference on Computer Vision (ECCV), pp. 3–19 (2018)
27. Wu, Y., He, K.: Group normalization. In: Proceedings of the European Conference on Computer Vision (ECCV), pp. 3–19 (2018)
28. Xiao, Y., Lepetit, V., Marlet, R.: Few-shot object detection and viewpoint estimation for objects in the wild. IEEE Trans. Pattern Anal. Mach. Intell. **45**(3), 3090–3106 (2022)
29. Yang, G., Ramanan, D.: Volumetric correspondence networks for optical flow. In: Advances in Neural Information Processing Systems, vol. 32 (2019)
30. Yang, H., et al.: Balanced and hierarchical relation learning for one-shot object detection. In: Proceedings of the IEEE/CVF Conference on Computer Vision and Pattern Recognition, pp. 7591–7600 (2022)
31. Yang, H., Lin, Y., Zhang, H., Zhang, Y., Xu, B.: Towards improving classification power for one-shot object detection. Neurocomputing **455**, 390–400 (2021)
32. Zhao, Y., Guo, X., Lu, Y.: Semantic-aligned fusion transformer for one-shot object detection. In: Proceedings of the IEEE/CVF Conference on Computer Vision and Pattern Recognition, pp. 7601–7611 (2022)

Small Object Detection Based on Bidirectional Feature Fusion and Multi-scale Distillation

Lingyu Wang[1]([✉]), Zijie Zhou[2], Guanqun Shi[1], Junkang Guo[1], and Zhigang Liu[1]

[1] Xi'an Jiaotong University, Xi'an 710049, China
wly0226@stu.xjtu.edu.cn
[2] College of Artificial Intelligence, China University of Petroleum (Beijing), Beijing 102249, China

Abstract. In this paper, we present a novel approach to address the challenges of small object detection. The proposed method combines multi-scale distillation and bidirectional feature fusion to enhance the performance of small object detection models. By leveraging the knowledge of a teacher model, the student model captures both high-level and low-level features, leading to improved detection results. Then, bidirectional feature fusion aggregates multi-layer features within the student more effectively via a convolutional attention mechanism and pyramid pooling loss function. Extensive experiments demonstrate that the approach significantly improves small object detection performance over baselines, validating the use of multi-scale knowledge distillation and feature fusion techniques for this task.

Keywords: Small object detection · Knowledge distillation · Bidirectional feature fusion

1 Introduction

Object detection is a fundamental task that has been developed over the past few years in the computer vision community. Small object detection has gained significant attention due to its wide range of applications in fields such as surveillance, autonomous driving, and medical imaging. However, accurately detecting small objects remains a challenging task, mainly due to their limited spatial information and low signal-to-noise ratio. In order to detect small objects, the detection model needs to integrate both high-level and low-level feature information while considering the contextual information of the image. Current works strive to refine feature fusion modules [10,23], devise novel training schemes [36] to explicitly train on small objects, design new neural architectures [22,41] to better extract small objects' features, and leverage increased input resolution to enhance representation quality [1,47]. However, these approaches struggle to balance detection performance on small objects with computational costs at the inference stage.

Knowledge distillation [14] is to train a student network under the supervision of a larger network. In [14], knowledge information is distilled through the teacher's logit, which means the student is supervised by both ground truth labels and the teacher's logits. In recent years, some feature-based distillation methods have been proposed. Since only the head or predictor after the feature is different among various networks, theoretically, the feature-based distillation method can be used in various tasks. Because feature-based distillation enables the student model to improve detection performance while maintaining reasonable computational costs during the inference stage, we consider it a proper method for improving small object detection methods without increasing computational costs.

In this paper, we tackle the challenges associated with small object detection by presenting a novel approach that combines multi-scale distillation and bidirectional feature fusion. Our goal is to enhance the performance of small object detection models by enabling them to capture both high-level and low-level features from the teacher model and learn the vital information necessary for producing higher-quality detection results for small objects. Firstly, we introduce multi-scale knowledge distillation to the small object detection task. By leveraging the multi-level feature of the teacher model, we guide the student model to learn from these diverse levels of information and improve its performance in detecting small objects. This approach allows the student model to better benefit from the comprehensive knowledge provided by the teacher, enabling it to better understand the intricate details of small objects. Secondly, we introduce bidirectional feature fusion to the multi-scale distillation structure. This feature fusion mechanism facilitates the effective aggregation of multi-layer features within the student model, enhancing the distillation process. By fusing features bidirectionally, the student model can benefit from the complementary information from different layers, leading to a more comprehensive understanding of small objects and improved detection performance. To further improve the distillation process, we introduce the Convolutional Attention Feature Fusion (CAFF) module. This module enhances the fusion of features by incorporating attention mechanisms, allowing the student model to focus on the most relevant and informative regions for small object detection. Additionally, we propose the Pyramid Pooling Loss (PP Loss) function, which optimizes the distillation process by segregating the transfer of knowledge into different scales.

We validate the effectiveness of our proposed method through extensive experiments. The student model trained using our approach achieves significant improvements in small object detection compared to traditional methods. These results demonstrate the efficacy of our multi-scale distillation and bidirectional feature fusion approach in addressing the challenges of small object detection.

To sum up, our contributions are the following:

* We introduce multi-scale knowledge distillation to small object detection tasks, utilizing multi-level information of the teacher model to guide the student model and enhance its performance of small object detection.

* We propose a multi-scale distillation structure with bidirectional feature fusion to better aggregate multi-layer features of student model and improve the distillation efficiency.
* We propose a Convolutional Attention Feature Fusion (CAFF) module and the Pyramid Pooling Loss (PP Loss) function to improve the distillation process.
* We verify the effectiveness of our method via various experiments. The student model achieves significant improvements in small object detection.

2 Related Work

2.1 Object Detection

Object detection is one of the most challenging tasks in computer vision, which involves locating and classifying objects on the images. The current mainstream object detection algorithms are roughly divided into two-stage and one-stage detectors. Two-stage methods [2,12,23] represented by Faster R-CNN [32] maintain the highest accuracy in the detection field. These methods utilize region proposal network (RPN) and refinement procedure of classification and location to obtain better performance. However, high demands for lower latency bring one-stage detectors [27,30] under the spotlight, which directly achieve classification and location of targets through the feature map. In recent years, another criterion divides detection algorithms into anchor-based and anchor-free methods. Anchor-based detectors such as [24,27,31] solve object detection tasks with the help of anchor boxes, which can be viewed as pre-defined sliding windows or proposals. Nevertheless, all anchor-based methods need to be meticulously designed, and a large number of anchor boxes must be calculated, which takes much computation. To avoid tunning hyper-parameters and calculations related to anchor boxes, anchor-free methods [7,17,30,38] predict several key points of target, such as center and distance to boundaries, and reach a better performance with less cost. For object detection tasks, the imbalance of foreground and background is a crucial problem. R-CNN-like detectors use a two-stage cascade and sampling heuristics to narrow down the number of background samples, or online hard example mining(OHEM) [35] to ensure the balance between foreground and background. One-stage approaches, such as RetinaNet [24] proposed focal loss to solve this problem. Anchor-free detectors [16,38,48] attempt to discard the design of anchor boxes to avoid time-consuming box operations and cumbersome hyper-parameter tuning. Dynamic label assignment methods [9,29,44] are proposed to better define the positive and negative samples for model learning. Recently, attributing to the strong ability of the transformer block to encode expressive features, DETR family [4,18,26,28,43,49] has become a new trend in the object detection community.

2.2 Knowledge Distillation for Object Detection

Recently, some works have applied knowledge distillation to object detection tasks. Previous works mainly focus on designing proper distillation areas to cope with the extreme unbalance between positive and negative instances in object detection. [5] first deals with this problem by underweighting the background distillation loss in the classification head. [20] applies the L2 distillation loss to the negative and positive ROI features sampled by RPN in a certain proportion. [39] proposes a fine-grained feature imitation, distilling the near objects regions. [11] proposes to decouple the foreground and background features for distillation, adjusting each loss weight and temperature separately. [6] further proposes to distill the discriminative patches between students and teachers. However, all of those previous works take one fixed teacher for experiments, and none of them explore the relationship between teacher performance and student performance for object detection tasks. FGD [42] aligns the attention place for the teacher-student pair, while PKD [3] maximizes the Pearson Correlation Coefficient between the feature representations. As the earliest distillation strategy proposed in [14], prediction mimicking plays a vital role in classification distillation. Recently, some improved prediction-mimicking methods have been proposed to adapt to object detection. For example, Rank Mimicking [19] regards the score rank of the teacher as a kind of knowledge and aims to force the student to rank instances as the teacher. LD [46] proposes to distill the localization distribution of bounding box [21] to transfer localization knowledge.

3 Methodology

In this section, we present our proposed approach for small object detection based on multi-scale knowledge distillation and bidirectional feature fusion. We first describe the concept of multi-scale distillation between a student model and a teacher model to facilitate knowledge transfer from the teacher model's multi-scale representations. Then, we propose a distillation architecture with bidirectional feature fusion to enhance the student model's performance for small object detection by enabling the student model to capture both high-level and low-level features from the teacher model.

3.1 Multi-scale Distillation

The architectures of models vary significantly for different detection tasks. Since only the head or predictor after the feature is different among various networks, the feature-based distillation method can be theoretically used for different models. The primary method for distillation on single-layer features can be formulated as follows:

$$L_{skd} = D(F^T - f_{align}(F^S)) \tag{1}$$

where F^T and F^S are the feature maps from the teacher model and student model, and f_{align} is the adaptation layer to align the student's feature with teacher's feature. D is the L2 distance that measures the difference between student and teacher.

Multi-scale distillation is the concept of transferring multi-scale information from the teacher network to the student network, which allows the knowledge

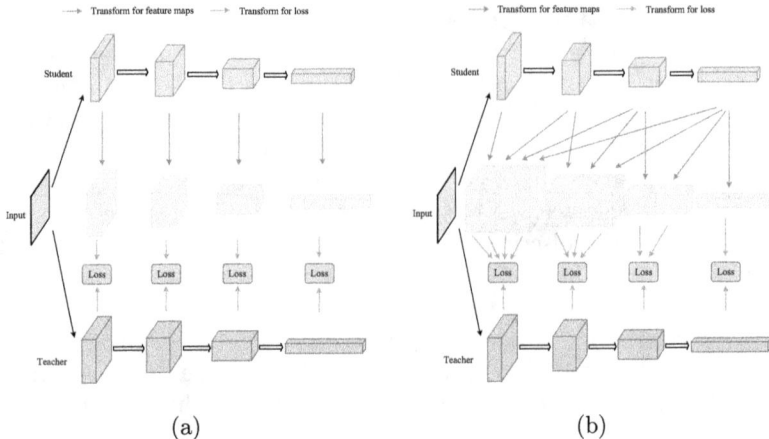

Fig. 1. (a) A simple architecture of multi-scale distillation. (b) An improved architecture of multi-scale distillation.

distillation process to take both high-level and low-level features into account to improve the student model's performance on small object detection. A simple way of multi-scale distillation is to conduct distillation for multiple feature layers between student and teacher, as shown in Fig. 1a. Similar to single-layer knowledge distillation, multiple-layer knowledge distillation of this structure can be written as:

$$L_{mkd} = \sum_{i \in I} D(F_i^T - f_{align}(F_i^S)) \qquad (2)$$

where I includes all the feature layers used to transfer knowledge.

A better way of conducting multi-scale distillation is to use all lower-level features of the teacher model to guide the current feature of the student model. The single-layer knowledge distillation with this mechanism is formulated as follows:

$$L_{skd} = \sum_{j=1}^{i} D(F_j^T - f_{align}(F_i^S)) \qquad (3)$$

where the feature of the student is fixed to F_i^S, and we use the teacher's first i levels of features to guide F_i^S. When we utilize this structure of distillation for multiple layers of the student model as illustrated in Fig. 1b, the distillation function can be formulated as:

$$L_{mkd} = \sum_{i \in I}(\sum_{j=1}^{i} D(F_j^T - f_{align}(F_i^S))) \qquad (4)$$

In our method, the L_{mkd} loss is added along with the original losses during the training process, and the inference is exactly the same as the original model. So, our method is totally cost-free at test time. We use factor λ to balance the distillation loss and original losses. The whole loss function is defined as:

$$L_{total} = L_{original} + \lambda L_{mkd} \qquad (5)$$

3.2 Bidirectional Feature Fusion Framework

Following the concept of multi-scale distillation in the previous section, we design the framework of distillation as shown in Fig. 2. In order to simplify the calculation and better aggregate different levels' features in the distilling process, we introduce the CAFF(convolutional attention feature fusion) module to progressively merge the features of the student model from the high-level layer to the low-level layer. Inspired by BiFPN structure from [37], we further improve the fusion process of distillation by a bidirectional feature fusion structure, which allows feature information to propagate bidirectionally across different resolution scales. This bidirectional fusion mechanism facilitates a better fusion of low-level and high-level features, promoting contextual propagation of features and thereby enhancing the efficiency of distillation and the detection performance of the student model. Additionally, we use PP Loss(Pyramid Pooling Loss) to better measure the difference between the feature maps of the student model and the teacher model. The details of CAFF and PP Loss are discussed in Sect. 3.3.

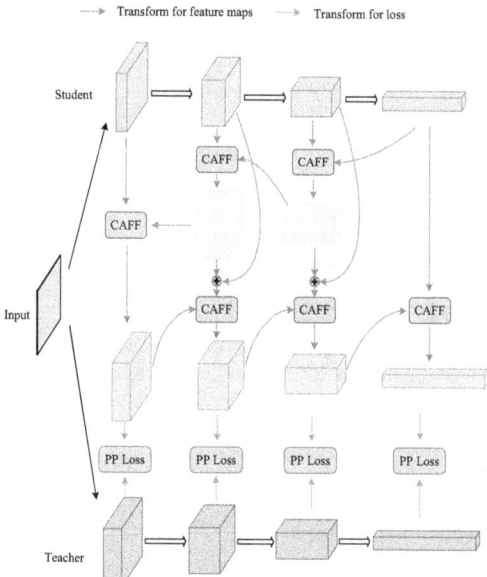

Fig. 2. The architecture of our proposed multi-scale distillation method with bidirectional feature fusion.

3.3 CAFF and PP Loss

There are two key modules in Fig. 2. They are convolutional attention feature fusion (CAFF) and pyramid pooling loss (PP Loss). We explain both of them in this section.

The CAFF module is inspired by [15], as shown in Fig. 3a. Firstly, higher-level feature maps are resized to match the lower-level feature maps' shape. Then, two feature maps from different levels are concatenated to produce two H × W attention maps. These two attention maps are element-wise multiplied with the corresponding features and are then added to yield the final output.

The CAFF module dynamically generates different attention maps based on input features, allowing the flexible aggregation of the two feature maps. This adaptive fusion proves superior to direct sum because the two feature maps originate from different network stages, which contain diverse information. The low- and high-level features may focus on different partitions. The attention maps can aggregate them more reasonably.

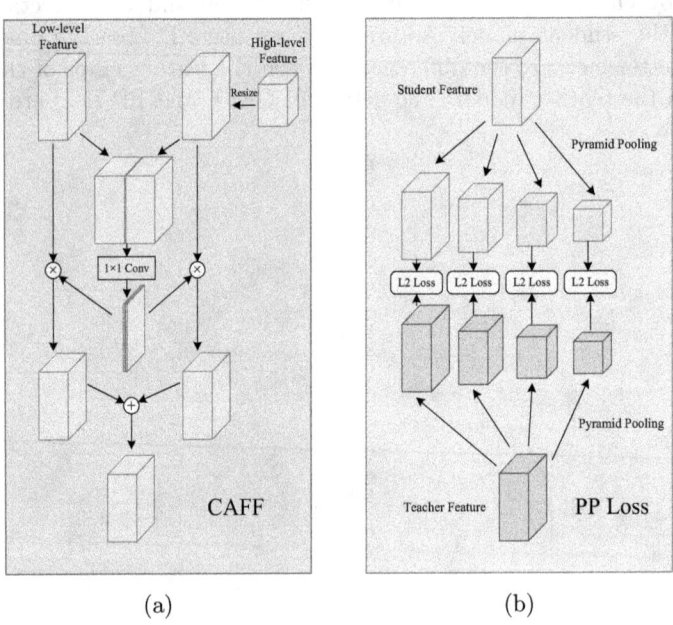

(a) (b)

Fig. 3. (a) Architecture of CAFF. Different levels' feature maps of the student model are adaptively aggregated together according to attention maps. (b) Architecture of PP Loss. The student model and teacher model's feature maps are pyramid pooled to extract different context information.

Details of the PP Loss are illustrated in Fig. 3b. Typically, the L2 distance serves as the loss function between two feature maps, which effectively transfer information within the same level. However, in our distillation framework, different levels' information is aggregated for learning from the teacher, and the conventional global L2 distance proves insufficient for transferring multi-scale information.

Motivated by [45], we introduce PP Loss, utilizing spatial pyramid pooling to segregate the transfer of knowledge into different levels' contextual information. This approach enhances information distillation across various resolution scales. The structure is straightforward: we initially extract knowledge from different levels using spatial pyramid pooling and then employ L2 distance to distill information between them individually.

4 Experiments

Our method is a feature-based distillation method that can be applied to different object detection models with a feature pyramid structure. In order to verify the performance of our proposed approach, we apply our method to several different models and conduct experiments on benchmark datasets commonly used for small object detection. By comparing the performance of our approach with previous state-of-the-art methods in terms of accuracy and efficiency, experimental results demonstrate that our approach significantly improves the small object detection efficiency of the student model while maintaining low computational costs.

4.1 Object Detection

Datasets. We conduct experiments of object detection on COCO2017 [25] datasets, which contain 1.5 million object instances of 80 categories, and 41.43% of the object instances in COCO2017 are small objects. We use the 120k training images for training and 5k validation images for testing. The performances of models are evaluated with Average Precision in different settings.

Implementation Details. For object detection experiments, we calculate the distillation loss between the student and teacher's output feature maps from the neck. The experiments are conducted with Detectron2 [40] as our baseline. We use the pre-trained model provided by Detectron2 as the teacher model. Student models are trained using the standard training policy following tradition [39], which initializes the student with the teacher's neck and head parameters to train the student when they have the same head structure. All performance is evaluated on the COCO2017 validation set.

Object Detection Results. For object detection, we conduct experiments on a classic two-stage detection method (Faster R-CNN [8]) with different backbones. We compare our method with three previous state-of-the-art distillation methods. As shown in Table 1, by comparison, we note that our method outperforms these methods. We observe that classic distillation methods like FitNet

Table 1. Object detection results

Method	mAP	AP50	AP75	APl	APm	APs
Teacher Faster R-CNN(ResNet101)	42.04	62.48	45.88	54.60	45.55	25.22
Student Faster R-CNN(ResNet18)	33.26	53.61	35.26	43.16	35.68	18.96
+FitNet [33]	34.13 (+0.87)	54.16	36.71	44.69	36.50	18.88
+FGFI [39]	35.44 (+2.18)	55.51	38.17	47.34	38.29	19.04
+GID [6]	36.27 (+3.01)	56.23	38.97	49.12	39.50	18.98
+Our Method	**36.52 (+3.26)**	**56.59**	**39.16**	**49.31**	**39.58**	**19.36**
Teacher Faster R-CNN(ResNet101)	42.04	62.48	45.88	54.60	45.55	25.22
Student Faster R-CNN(ResNet50)	37.93	58.84	41.05	49.10	41.14	22.44
+FitNet [33]	38.76 (+0.83)	59.62	41.80	50.70	42.20	22.32
+FGFI [39]	39.44 (+1.51)	60.27	43.04	51.97	42.51	22.89
+GID [6]	40.18 (+2.25)	60.68	43.81	53.19	43.97	22.69
+FGD [42]	**40.40 (+2.47)**	60.70	**44.30**	**53.50**	**44.50**	22.80
+Our Method	**40.40 (+2.47)**	**61.01**	44.24	53.30	43.96	**23.67**
Teacher Faster R-CNN(ResNet50)	40.22	61.02	43.81	51.98	43.53	24.16
Student FasterR-CNN(MobileNetV2)	29.47	48.87	30.90	38.86	30.77	16.33
+FitNet [33]	30.20 (+0.73)	49.80	31.69	39.69	31.64	16.39
+FGFI [39]	31.16 (+1.69)	50.68	32.92	42.12	32.63	16.73
+GID [6]	33.05 (+3.58)	52.71	35.23	44.67	36.07	16.59
+Our Method	**33.67 (+4.2)**	**53.42**	**35.75**	**45.13**	**36.34**	**17.42**

[33] contribute to enhancing the detection performance, but the enhancement is limited. FGFI [39] proposes a fine-grained feature imitation, distilling the near objects regions. GID [6] further brings a huge improvement to the object detection performance by proposing to distill the discriminative patches between students and teachers. Still, our proposed method exhibits a substantial performance advantage over these previous SOTA methods, further emphasizing its superiority in the context of detection tasks. FGD [42] is one of the most powerful distillation methods, which improves the distillation process by combining focal and global distillation. Even in comparison with FGD [42], our method achieves the same mAP in detection tasks and shows a considerable advantage in APs metric, which evaluates the small object detection performance of the student model.

We also change the experimental setting to test the generality. On the two-stage detection method Faster R-CNN, we change backbone architectures to test the effectiveness of our distillation method for the same-style backbones and different-style backbones. The knowledge distillation with ResNet101 [13] as a teacher model to train the identical style backbones brings a significant boost of mAP to ResNet18 and ResNet50 by 3.26 and 2.47, respectively. The distillation between ResNet50 and MobileNetV2 [34] still promotes the baseline from 29.47 to 33.71 despite the fact that they are different style backbones. For the metric APs, which evaluates the detection performance for challenging small objects, our method shows even more obvious advantages than previous methods, which demonstrates that our distillation method is particularly suitable to improve the performance of the student model in challenging small object detection tasks.

4.2 Instance Segmentation

We also apply our method to the more challenging instance segmentation task. We use Mask R-CNN [12] as our baseline models and distill between different backbone architectures. The models are trained on the COCO2017 training set and are evaluated on the validation set. The results are shown in Table 2.

Our method also improves the performance of instance segmentation tasks notably. For distillation between architectures of the same style, we boost the performance of ResNet18 and ResNet50 by 2.06 and 1.69 and reduce the gap between the teacher and student by 28% and 49% relatively. Even for the distillation on architectures of different styles, we better MobileNetV2 by 2.82. The fact that our method performs well on object detection and instance segmentation tasks illustrates the remarkable efficacy and applicability of our method.

Table 2. Instance segmentation results

Method	mAP	AP50	AP75	APl	APm	APs
Teacher Mask R-CNN(ResNet101)	38.63	60.45	41.28	55.29	41.33	19.48
Student Mask R-CNN(ResNet18)	31.25	51.07	33.10	45.53	32.80	**14.18**
+Our Method	**33.31 (+2.06)**	**53.43**	**35.44**	**50.25**	**34.95**	14.18
Teacher Mask R-CNN(ResNet101)	38.63	60.45	41.28	55.29	41.33	19.48
Student Mask R-CNN(ResNet50)	35.24	56.32	37.49	50.34	37.71	17.16
+Our Method	**36.93 (+1.69)**	**58.20**	**39.45**	**53.46**	**39.46**	**17.62**
Teacher Mask R-CNN(ResNet50)	37.17	58.60	39.88	53.30	39.49	18.63
Student Mask R-CNN(MobileNetV2)	28.37	47.19	29.95	41.70	29.01	12.09
+Our Method	**31.19 (+2.82)**	**50.78**	**33.01**	**47.00**	**32.43**	**13.18**

4.3 Ablation Study

To validate the effectiveness of different components of our proposed method, we use Faster R-CNN as the baseline to conduct several experiments on the COCO2017 dataset to evaluate the performance. In this section, all experiments utilize ResNet101 as the teacher network and ResNet 18 as the student network.

Overall Ablation Study. To analyze the importance of each proposed method, we use ResNet101 as the teacher to conduct knowledge distillation for ResNet18 on the object detection task of COCO2017 dataset. We gradually add CAFF (Convolutional Attention Feature Fusion), PP Loss(Pyramid Pooling Loss), and

Table 3. Overall ablation study results

Multi-scale KD	CAFF	PP Loss	Bidirectional Feature Fusion	mAP	APl	APm	APs
✓				36.00	49.24	38.84	18.73
✓	✓			36.25	48.78	38.97	18.86
✓	✓	✓		36.34	48.70	39.15	19.09
✓	✓	✓	✓	**36.52**	**49.31**	**39.58**	**19.36**

Table 4. Results of ablation study for pyramid pooling Loss

Loss function	mAP	AP50	AP75	APl	APm	APs
L2 loss of original feature	36.28	56.20	39.03	48.89	39.10	19.15
L2 loss of pooled feature (scale ratio = 0.5)	35.99	55.80	38.86	48.72	38.99	19.06
L2 loss of pooled features(scale ratio = 0.25)	35.08	55.08	37.64	47.76	37.99	17.90
L2 loss of pooled features(scale ratio = 1&0.5&0.25)	**36.52**	56.59	39.16	**49.31**	**39.58**	**19.36**
L2 loss of pooled features(scale ratio = 1&0.5&0.25&0.125)	36.33	56.59	39.52	48.47	39.40	19.60

Bidirectional Feature Fusion to the basic multi-scale distillation method. The result of the overall ablation study is reported in Table 3.

CAFF improves the mAP from 36.00 to 36.25. This result validates that the object detection accuracy of the student model is improved by the attention-based feature fusion structure in distillation. Moreover, PP Loss further improves the mAP to 36.34, and the result in APs is enhanced from 18.86 to 19.09, which indicates pyramid pooling loss can boost the performance of small object detection performance of student model by distilling knowledge through features of different resolution scales. Bidirectional Feature Fusion further improves mAP of the student model to 36.52, which validates that this feature fusion structure can better aggregate the features of the teacher model and improve the efficiency of knowledge distillation.

From the result, we can observe that each part of our proposed method separately brings consistent improvement to the result of mAP and APs, and when we aggregate them together, the best results are obtained. The overall ablation experiment demonstrates that each component of our proposed method improves the performance of object detection and especially small object detection of the student model.

Ablation Study for Pyramid Pooling Loss. We have also conducted the ablation study for Pyramid Pooling Loss to analyze the effect of PP Loss when different scales of pooled feature channels are included in the loss function. The result is reported in Table 4.

When each channel is separately utilized for loss calculation, the original feature without pooling works the best. Better results can be obtained when the losses of pooled channels of the pyramid pooling structure are combined. The combination loss of the original feature channel, the pooled channel with a scale ratio of 0.5 and the pooled channel with a scale ratio of 0.25 can bring the best mAP results. Although adding the loss of a smaller pooled feature channel can still enhance the APs result, the total mAP result becomes worse.

Analysis for Loss Weight of Knowledge Distillation. We also experimentally analyze the impact of loss weight for knowledge distillation on detection results. By verifying the loss weight for KD from 0.8 to 2.0, the results in Table 5 are obtained. We conclude that the best mAP results are obtained when we adopt 1.2 as the knowledge distillation loss weight.

Table 5. Results of different KD loss weight

Loss function	mAP	AP50	AP75	APl	APm	APs
KD Loss Weight = 0.8	36.34	56.45	39.19	48.68	39.25	19.53
KD Loss Weight = 1.0	36.35	56.59	39.05	48.55	39.08	19.35
KD Loss Weight = 1.2	**36.52**	**56.59**	**39.16**	**49.31**	**39.58**	**19.36**
KD Loss Weight = 2.0	36.34	56.32	39.20	49.08	39.15	19.23

5 Conclusion

In this paper, we have proposed a novel approach for small object detection based on bidirectional feature fusion and multiscale distillation. By leveraging knowledge from a teacher model, our approach enhances the performance of the student model, improving small object detection accuracy. Experimental results demonstrate the effectiveness and efficiency of our method. We believe that our work contributes to the advancement of small object detection techniques and opens up opportunities for further research in this area.

References

1. Bai, Y., Zhang, Y., Ding, M., Ghanem, B.: SOD-MTGAN: small object detection via multi-task generative adversarial network. In: Proceedings of the European Conference on Computer Vision (ECCV), pp. 206–221 (2018)
2. Cai, Z., Vasconcelos, N.: Cascade R-CNN: delving into high quality object detection. In: Proceedings of the IEEE Conference on Computer Vision and Pattern Recognition, pp. 6154–6162 (2018)
3. Cao, W., Zhang, Y., Gao, J., Cheng, A., Cheng, K., Cheng, J.: PKD: general distillation framework for object detectors via Pearson correlation coefficient. Adv. Neural. Inf. Process. Syst. **35**, 15394–15406 (2022)
4. Carion, N., Massa, F., Synnaeve, G., Usunier, N., Kirillov, A., Zagoruyko, S.: End-to-end object detection with transformers. In: Vedaldi, A., Bischof, H., Brox, T., Frahm, J.-M. (eds.) ECCV 2020. LNCS, vol. 12346, pp. 213–229. Springer, Cham (2020). https://doi.org/10.1007/978-3-030-58452-8_13

5. Chen, G., Choi, W., Yu, X., Han, T., Chandraker, M.: Learning efficient object detection models with knowledge distillation. In: Guyon, I., et al. (eds.) Advances in Neural Information Processing Systems 30, pp. 742–751. Curran Associates, Inc. (2017)
6. Dai, X., et al.: General instance distillation for object detection. In: Proceedings of the IEEE/CVF Conference on Computer Vision and Pattern Recognition (CVPR), pp. 7842–7851 (2021)
7. Duan, K., Bai, S., Xie, L., Qi, H., Huang, Q., Tian, Q.: CenterNet: keypoint triplets for object detection. In: Proceedings of the IEEE International Conference on Computer Vision, pp. 6569–6578 (2019)
8. Faster, R.: Towards real-time object detection with region proposal networks. In: Advances in Neural Information Processing Systems, vol. 9199, no. 10.5555, pp. 2969239–2969250 (2015)
9. Feng, C., Zhong, Y., Gao, Y., Scott, M.R., Huang, W.: TOOD: task-aligned one-stage object detection. In: Proceedings of the IEEE/CVF International Conference on Computer Vision (ICCV), pp. 3510–3519 (2021)
10. Ghiasi, G., Lin, T.Y., Le, Q.V.: NAS-FPN: learning scalable feature pyramid architecture for object detection. In: Proceedings of the IEEE/CVF Conference on Computer Vision and Pattern Recognition, pp. 7036–7045 (2019)
11. Guo, J., et al.: Distilling object detectors via decoupled features. In: Proceedings of the IEEE/CVF Conference on Computer Vision and Pattern Recognition (CVPR), pp. 2154–2164 (2021)
12. He, K., Gkioxari, G., Dollár, P., Girshick, R.: Mask R-CNN. In: Proceedings of the IEEE International Conference on Computer Vision, pp. 2961–2969 (2017)
13. He, K., Zhang, X., Ren, S., Sun, J.: Deep residual learning for image recognition. In: Proceedings of the IEEE Conference on Computer Vision and Pattern Recognition, pp. 770–778 (2016)
14. Hinton, G., Vinyals, O., Dean, J.: Distilling the knowledge in a neural network. arXiv preprint arXiv:1503.02531 (2015)
15. Hu, J., Shen, L., Sun, G.: Squeeze-and-excitation networks. In: Proceedings of the IEEE Conference on Computer Vision and Pattern Recognition, pp. 7132–7141 (2018)
16. Kong, T., Sun, F., Liu, H., Jiang, Y., Li, L., Shi, J.: Foveabox: beyound anchor-based object detection. IEEE Trans. Image Process. **29**, 7389–7398 (2020)
17. Law, H., Deng, J.: CornerNet: detecting objects as paired keypoints. In: Proceedings of the European Conference on Computer Vision (ECCV), pp. 734–750 (2018)
18. Li, F., Zhang, H., Liu, S., Guo, J., Ni, L.M., Zhang, L.: DN-DETR: accelerate DETR training by introducing query denoising. In: Proceedings of the IEEE/CVF Conference on Computer Vision and Pattern Recognition (CVPR), pp. 13619–13627 (2022)
19. Li, G., Li, X., Wang, Y., Zhang, S., Wu, Y., Liang, D.: Knowledge distillation for object detection via rank mimicking and prediction-guided feature imitation. In: Proceedings of the AAAI Conference on Artificial Intelligence, pp. 1306–1313 (2022)
20. Li, Q., Jin, S., Yan, J.: Mimicking very efficient network for object detection. In: Proceedings of the IEEE Conference on Computer Vision and Pattern Recognition, pp. 6356–6364 (2017)
21. Li, X., et al.: Generalized focal loss: learning qualified and distributed bounding boxes for dense object detection. In: Larochelle, H., Ranzato, M., Hadsell, R., Balcan, M., Lin, H. (eds.) Advances in Neural Information Processing Systems, vol. 33, pp. 21002–21012. Curran Associates, Inc. (2020)

22. Li, Y., Chen, Y., Wang, N., Zhang, Z.: Scale-aware trident networks for object detection. In: Proceedings of the IEEE/CVF International Conference on Computer Vision, pp. 6054–6063 (2019)
23. Lin, T.Y., Dollár, P., Girshick, R., He, K., Hariharan, B., Belongie, S.: Feature pyramid networks for object detection. In: Proceedings of the IEEE Conference on Computer Vision and Pattern Recognition, pp. 2117–2125 (2017)
24. Lin, T.Y., Goyal, P., Girshick, R., He, K., Dollár, P.: Focal loss for dense object detection. In: Proceedings of the IEEE International Conference on Computer Vision, pp. 2980–2988 (2017)
25. Lin, T.-Y., et al.: Microsoft COCO: common objects in context. In: Fleet, D., Pajdla, T., Schiele, B., Tuytelaars, T. (eds.) ECCV 2014. LNCS, vol. 8693, pp. 740–755. Springer, Cham (2014). https://doi.org/10.1007/978-3-319-10602-1_48
26. Liu, S., et al.: DAB-DETR: dynamic anchor boxes are better queries for DETR. arXiv preprint arXiv:2201.12329 (2022)
27. Liu, W., et al.: SSD: single shot MultiBox detector. In: Leibe, B., Matas, J., Sebe, N., Welling, M. (eds.) ECCV 2016. LNCS, vol. 9905, pp. 21–37. Springer, Cham (2016). https://doi.org/10.1007/978-3-319-46448-0_2
28. Meng, D., et al.: Conditional DETR for fast training convergence. In: Proceedings of the IEEE/CVF International Conference on Computer Vision (ICCV), pp. 3651–3660 (2021)
29. Nguyen, C.H., Nguyen, T.C., Tang, T.N., Phan, N.L.: Improving object detection by label assignment distillation. In: Proceedings of the IEEE/CVF Winter Conference on Applications of Computer Vision (WACV), pp. 1005–1014 (2022)
30. Redmon, J., Divvala, S., Girshick, R., Farhadi, A.: You only look once: Unified, real-time object detection. In: Proceedings of the IEEE Conference on Computer Vision and Pattern Recognition, pp. 779–788 (2016)
31. Redmon, J., Farhadi, A.: Yolo9000: better, faster, stronger. In: Proceedings of the IEEE Conference on Computer Vision and Pattern Recognition, pp. 7263–7271 (2017)
32. Ren, S., He, K., Girshick, R., Sun, J.: Faster r-cnn: Towards real-time object detection with region proposal networks. In: Cortes, C., Lawrence, N.D., Lee, D.D., Sugiyama, M., Garnett, R. (eds.) Advances in Neural Information Processing Systems 28, pp. 91–99. Curran Associates, Inc. (2015)
33. Romero, A., Ballas, N., Kahou, S.E., Chassang, A., Gatta, C., Bengio, Y.: Fitnets: hints for thin deep nets. arXiv preprint arXiv:1412.6550 (2014)
34. Sandler, M., Howard, A., Zhu, M., Zhmoginov, A., Chen, L.C.: Mobilenetv2: inverted residuals and linear bottlenecks. In: Proceedings of the IEEE Conference on Computer Vision and Pattern Recognition, pp. 4510–4520 (2018)
35. Shrivastava, A., Gupta, A., Girshick, R.: Training region-based object detectors with online hard example mining. In: Proceedings of the IEEE Conference on Computer Vision and Pattern Recognition, pp. 761–769 (2016)
36. Singh, B., Davis, L.S.: An analysis of scale invariance in object detection snip. In: Proceedings of the IEEE Conference on Computer Vision and Pattern Recognition, pp. 3578–3587 (2018)
37. Tan, M., Pang, R., Le, Q.V.: Efficientdet: scalable and efficient object detection. In: Proceedings of the IEEE/CVF Conference on Computer Vision and Pattern Recognition, pp. 10781–10790 (2020)
38. Tian, Z., Shen, C., Chen, H., He, T.: FCOS: fully convolutional one-stage object detection. In: Proceedings of the IEEE/CVF International Conference on Computer Vision, pp. 9627–9636 (2019)

39. Wang, T., Yuan, L., Zhang, X., Feng, J.: Distilling object detectors with fine-grained feature imitation. In: Proceedings of the IEEE/CVF Conference on Computer Vision and Pattern Recognition, pp. 4933–4942 (2019)
40. Wu, Y., Kirillov, A., Massa, F., Lo, W.Y., Girshick, R.: Detectron2 (2019). https://github.com/facebookresearch/detectron2
41. Yang, C., Huang, Z., Wang, N.: QueryDet: cascaded sparse query for accelerating high-resolution small object detection. In: Proceedings of the IEEE/CVF Conference on Computer Vision and Pattern Recognition, pp. 13668–13677 (2022)
42. Yang, Z., et al.: Focal and global knowledge distillation for detectors. In: Proceedings of the IEEE/CVF Conference on Computer Vision and Pattern Recognition (CVPR), pp. 4643–4652 (2022)
43. Zhang, H., et al.: Dino: Detr with improved denoising anchor boxes for end-to-end object detection. arXiv preprint arXiv:2203.03605 (2022)
44. Zhang, S., Chi, C., Yao, Y., Lei, Z., Li, S.Z.: Bridging the gap between anchor-based and anchor-free detection via adaptive training sample selection. In: Proceedings of the IEEE/CVF Conference on Computer Vision and Pattern Recognition, pp. 9759–9768 (2020)
45. Zhao, H., Shi, J., Qi, X., Wang, X., Jia, J.: Pyramid scene parsing network. In: Proceedings of the IEEE Conference on Computer Vision and Pattern Recognition, pp. 2881–2890 (2017)
46. Zheng, Z., et al.: Localization distillation for dense object detection. In: Proceedings of the IEEE/CVF Conference on Computer Vision and Pattern Recognition (CVPR), pp. 9407–9416 (2022)
47. Zhou, P., Ni, B., Geng, C., Hu, J., Xu, Y.: Scale-transferrable object detection. In: proceedings of the IEEE Conference on Computer Vision and Pattern Recognition, pp. 528–537 (2018)
48. Zhu, C., He, Y., Savvides, M.: Feature selective anchor-free module for single-shot object detection. In: Proceedings of the IEEE/CVF Conference on Computer Vision and Pattern Recognition, pp. 840–849 (2019)
49. Zhu, X., Su, W., Lu, L., Li, B., Wang, X., Dai, J.: Deformable detr: deformable transformers for end-to-end object detection. arXiv preprint arXiv:2010.04159 (2020)

SRA-YOLO: Spatial Resolution Adaptive YOLO for Semi-supervised Cross-Domain Aerial Object Detection

Junhao Huang, Jian Xue, Yuqiu Li, Hao Wu, and Ke Lu(✉)

School of Engineering Science, University of Chinese Academy of Science, Beijing, China
{huangjunhao22,liyuqiu20,wuhao22}@mails.ucas.ac.cn,
{xuejian,luk}@ucas.ac.cn

Abstract. This study introduces SRA-YOLO, a novel framework tailored for Semi-Supervised Cross-Domain Aerial Object Detection, leveraging the robust YOLOv5 architecture. Aimed at addressing the challenges of spatial resolution variances and data scarcity in aerial imagery, SRA-YOLO employs an innovative Teacher-Student strategy integrating strategic knowledge distillation to utilize both labeled and unlabeled data effectively. Our approach stands out by introducing adaptive training data generation techniques, specifically Adaptive Zoom-In and Zoom-Out methods, to counteract domain discrepancies and align Ground Sample Distance (GSD) across diverse aerial conditions. Through extensive experiments on benchmark datasets, notably DOTA-v1.5, DOTA-v2.0 and xView, our method demonstrates superior adaptability and performance, setting a new baseline for aerial object detection in semi-supervised and cross-domain scenarios.

Keywords: Semi-Supervised Learning · Cross-Domain Aerial Object Detection · Spatial Resolution · Domain Adaptation · Ground Sample Distance

1 Introduction

Recent advancements in object detection have been significantly propelled by deep learning, notably through supervised learning paradigms [6,14,20,25]. Yet, these methods are markedly data-dependent, necessitating large, well-annotated datasets, a demand particularly burdensome in aerial imagery and remote sensing due to logistical and resource constraints [5,7,15]. The emerging field of Cross-Domain Aerial Object Detection (CDAOD) seeks to mitigate these challenges by applying models trained on richly annotated datasets to less-documented, diverse domain scenes, confronting inevitable issues such as environmental and geographical disparities, alongside pronounced spatial resolution discrepancies, as highlighted in Fig. 1 [2,3,13,29].

This work is supported by the National Natural Science Foundation of China (U21B2049, 61929104, 61731022).

Addressing these challenges, this study unveils a novel Teacher-Student strategy, the Spatial Resolution Adaptive YOLO (SRA-YOLO), crafted for CDAOD tasks. This method integrates the robust YOLOv5 architecture [10] with strategic knowledge distillation, enabling effective utilization of both labeled and unlabeled data. Notably, the SRA-YOLO framework is adept at reconciling spatial resolution variances prevalent in aerial data, a critical factor for accurate detection.

Within our methodological exploration, we delve into innovative training data generation techniques to counteract domain discrepancy, crucially through Adaptive Zoom-In and Zoom-Out methods, which refine ground sample distance (GSD)[1] to mirror domain-specific spatial resolutions. This adaptive strategy, aimed at creating source-like and target-like pseudo images, significantly enhances the learning process under varying aerial conditions.

Our work is substantiated through rigorous experiments set against the backdrop of distinct datasets, notably DOTA-v1.5 and DOTA-v2.0, demonstrating the superior adaptability and performance of SRA-YOLO. This method not only champions aerial imagery scenarios but also sets new benchmarks in real-world application readiness.

Primary contributions of this study are manifold:

1. The formulation of the SRA-YOLO framework, an novel model tailored for CDAOD, specifically addressing the nuances of spatial resolution variances in aerial images.
2. The introduction of advanced data generation methodologies within the semi-supervised learning domain, aiming to ameliorate domain discrepancies through adaptive image transformation and cropping.
3. Comprehensive empirical validations that emphasize our approach's substantial enhancements in cross-domain detection accuracy.

(1) Example from the xView (2) Example from the DOTA-v1.5 (3) Example from the DOTA-v2.0

Fig. 1. The spatial resolutions of the DOTA-v2.0 [4] are tend to be much larger than the DOTA-v1.5 [22] and the xView [11].

---

[1] The GSD in remote sensing imagery, represents the size of a single pixel in real-world ground distance, usually measured in meters or centimeters per pixel.

2 Related Work

2.1 Semi-supervised Aerial Object Detection

Recent research in aerial object detection has evolved beyond the conventional fully supervised paradigm. Notably, H2RBox [24] introduces a weakly-supervised method that utilizes horizontal annotations to predict object angles. In the realm of ship detection in Synthetic Aperture Radar (SAR) images, SAR-Teacher [27] adopts a semi-supervised approach, enhancing pseudo-labels through consistency constraints and contextual adjustments. The KCR [28] method offers a co-training approach specifically designed for detecting rotated objects with axis-aligned annotations, demonstrating robust performance across domain gaps. RINet [5] proposes a weakly-supervised framework incorporating rotation-invariant modules to achieve consistent labeling and feature enhancement. This is facilitated through a complementary mining strategy. WSODet [18] takes a unique approach by using layerwise relevance propagation to clarify feature maps and introducing an end-to-end testing method, thereby bypassing the need for pre-generated proposals. In the context of aerial images, SOOD [9] presents a semi-supervised framework with novel loss functions that focus on object orientations. Additionally, it introduces dynamic weighting of pseudo-labels based on orientation differences. However, none of the mentioned methods have considered the impact of spatial resolution variations on the performance of the semi-supervised learning.

2.2 Cross-Domain Object Detection

Cross-domain object detection (CDOD) aims to adapt detectors trained on a labeled source domain to perform accurately on an unlabeled target domain. Previous methodologies primarily focus on domain alignment and self-training strategies, with a significant emphasis on the two-stage detector, Faster R-CNN [16]. SWDA [17] introduces a method emphasizing the alignment of features with overarching similarities rather than those with pronounced dissimilarities. This approach facilitates the alignment of local receptive fields within feature maps, enhancing detection performance by leveraging strong local and weak global feature alignments. HTCN [1] proposes a Hierarchical Transferability Calibration Network, which calibrates feature representations across different hierarchies (local-region/image/instance) to harmonize transferability and discriminability. It strategically aligns features between the source and target domains while ensuring the detector maintains discriminative capabilities for both domains' features. PA-ATF [8] develops an Asymmetric Tri-way Faster-RCNN tailored for DAOD tasks. It introduces an ancillary network to filter out irrelevant source-specific knowledge while preserving beneficial domain-invariant insights. A novel adversarial shuffling based strategy is employed for domain disentanglement, minimizing mutual information through domain-adaptive feature alignment. UMT [3] leverages an unbiased mean teacher framework to refine cross-domain object detection. It incorporates an out-of-distribution estimation to optimize sample selection, enhancing the distillation process across domains. The approach uniquely utilizes the teacher model's expertise and mitigates bias in the student model through pixel-level adaptation. TIA [26] embarks on a novel route by aligning features within task-specific spaces, thereby improving the detector's performance in both classification and localization tasks. Through the integration of auxiliary predictors for each subtask, TIA captures domain-specific nuances with a finer granularity, enabling a more precise feature alignment. However, the aforementioned efforts are all designed for the object detection on general domains, which may diminish their applicability in specific domains such as remote sensing imagery.

3 Method

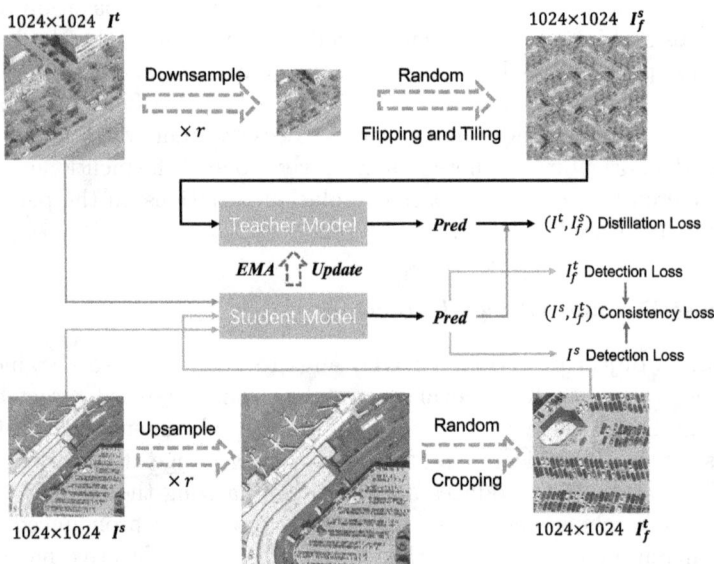

Fig. 2. Overview of the SRA-YOLO framework designed for cross-domain aerial object detection.

We introduce the SRA-YOLO framework, an abbreviation for Spatial Resolution Adaptive YOLO, designed for cross-domain aerial object detection. This framework utilizes the YOLOv5 detection system as its primary architecture and is optimized for semi-supervised learning in the domain of aerial image object detection. As shown in Fig. 2, this innovative approach integrates several key components. **Top:** The framework takes as input both real and pseudo-generated images. Specifically, real images from the target domain $\mathbf{I}^t$ are utilized alongside pseudo-generated source-like images $\mathbf{I}^s_f$, which are created to bridge domain-specific discrepancies. **Bottom:** The framework also uses real images from the source domain $\mathbf{I}^s$, combined with pseudo-generated target-like images $\mathbf{I}_f^t$, in the same manner to address domain discrepancies. **Middle:** At the core of the framework, the YOLOv5 detection system serves as the backbone, supporting both the teacher and student models within the semi-supervised learning setting. **Right:** The model incorporates a comprehensive loss design, integrating a distillation loss and a novel consistency loss, alongside standard detection loss, to refine and optimize cross-domain detection capabilities. Furthermore, the framework features four distinctive modules: a knowledge distillation framework incorporating a Humble Teacher [19] model to ensure progressive refinement of the student network; a strategy for generating pseudo cross-domain training images to bridge the gap between source and target domain image attributes; a refined distillation loss function tailored to address domain-specific variance; and a novel loss function for consistency that specifically targets the minimization of objectness discrepancy across domains. An exposition of these modules is presented herein.

3.1 Preliminary Definitions

In addressing the challenge of detecting objects across varying domains, we utilize a collection of labeled source domain images $\mathbf{I}^s$ that include N oriented bounding boxes $\mathcal{B} = \{B_j \mid_{j=1}^{N}, B_j = (x_j, y_j, w_j, h_j, \alpha_j)\}$, alongside a corresponding set of class identifiers $\mathcal{C} = \{C_j \mid_{j=1}^{N}, C_j \in (0, 1, ..., c)\}$ covering c distinct object categories. In parallel, the target domain is constituted of a series of unlabeled images $\mathbf{I}^t$. The source domain is characterized by N_s source images $\mathbf{I}^s$, bounding box coordinates $\mathcal{B}^s$, and class labels $\mathcal{C}^s$, hence defined as $\mathcal{D}_s = \{(\mathbf{I}_i^s, \mathcal{B}_i^s, \mathcal{C}_i^s) \mid_{i=1}^{N_s}\}$. The target domain, absent of annotations, consists of N_t images and is denoted as $\mathcal{D}_t = \{\mathbf{I}_i^t \mid_{i=1}^{N_t}\}$.

The aspiration of this research is to engineer a model with the capability to discern objects in the target domain to the utmost degree of precision, utilizing the dataset compositions $\mathcal{D}_s$ and $\mathcal{D}_t$. To this end, the YOLOv5 [10] framework is adopted. The associated supervised learning loss function, when training with the source dataset $\mathcal{D}_s$, is structured as follows:

$$\mathcal{L}_{\text{det}}(\mathbf{I}^s, \mathcal{B}^s, \mathcal{C}^s) = \mathcal{L}_{\text{box}}(\mathcal{B}^s; \mathbf{I}^s) + \mathcal{L}_{\text{cls, obj}}(\mathcal{C}^s; \mathbf{I}^s) \tag{1}$$

In this formulation, $\mathcal{L}_{\text{box}}$ denotes the Smooth L1 loss employed for the bounding box predictions, while $\mathcal{L}_{\text{cls, obj}}$ embodies the Seesaw Loss [21], which adeptly balances the classification task between frequent and infrequent categories and reinforces the learning of hard examples by dynamically adjusting the loss values. This loss function is particularly beneficial for dealing with class imbalance during object presence classification. Further elucidation of the domain adaptation mechanism for the unlabeled target domain images $\mathcal{D}_t$ is provided in the sections that follow.

3.2 Teacher-Student Training Scheme

We adopt the commonly used teacher-student training scheme for the semi-supervised training. The Humble Teacher (HT) approach [19] is innovatively designed for semi-supervised learning in image classification and adapted for modern object detection frameworks. This model, comprising two identical architectures (a student model and a teacher model), leverages the strength of knowledge distillation within a domain adaptation task. In this setup, the student model is trained on labeled data from the source domain using gradient descent, while the teacher model is dynamically updated via Exponential Moving Average (EMA) using the student's weights. Specifically, the teacher model's weight parameters $\mathcal{W}_t$ and student model's weight parameters $\mathcal{W}_s$ are iteratively updated as follows:

$$\mathcal{W}_t = \alpha \mathcal{W}_t + (1-\alpha)\mathcal{W}_s \tag{2}$$

Here, α is the EMA decay rate, optimally set to 0.999 to ensure that only small adjustments are made per iteration to foster stability and improved generalization.

The HT model's deployment for cross-domain object detection entails leveraging unlabeled target domain imagery, $\mathcal{D}_t$, as the input for the teacher model. This strategic approach allows the student model to be trained on these unlabeled samples ($\mathbf{I}^t$), thereby enriching the learning process through distillation. Diverging from traditional reliance on hard pseudo-labels, the HT framework advocates for the utilization of soft pseudo-labels. These labels, spanning a well-balanced assortment of region proposals, not only ensure comprehensive coverage of the image space but also prioritize the identification and learning of prominent foreground elements. Such a methodology inherently mitigates the risk of overfitting to any potential inaccuracies present in the teacher model's predictions.

In enhancing the robustness of the student model within the target domain, a notable phase involves the selection of bounding boxes, inferred from the teacher model's outputs, to serve as pseudo labels. This selection is predicated on their probability scores. Given the augmented inputs for the target domain, where $\tilde{\mathbf{I}}^t$ represents the input for the teacher model and $\hat{\mathbf{I}}^t$ denotes the input for the student model, both derived from the same set of images $\mathbf{I}^t$, a distillation loss function is implemented. This function aims to rectify the discrepancies in predictions observed between the teacher and student models. The formulation of this distillation loss is as follows:

$$\mathcal{L}_{\text{dis}}(\tilde{\mathbf{I}}^t, \hat{\mathbf{I}}^t) = \mathcal{L}_{\text{det}}(\hat{\mathbf{I}}^t, \mathcal{H}_\mathcal{R}[\mathcal{E}_\mathcal{R}(\tilde{\mathbf{I}}^t)], \mathcal{H}_\mathcal{C}[\mathcal{E}_\mathcal{C}(\tilde{\mathbf{I}}^t)]) \tag{3}$$

Here, $\mathcal{E}_\mathcal{R}(\cdot)$ and $\mathcal{E}_\mathcal{C}(\cdot)$ represent the predictive branches of the teacher model for oriented bounding box coordinates and class labels with the highest confidence scores, respectively. $\mathcal{H}_\mathcal{R}[\cdot]$ and $\mathcal{H}_\mathcal{C}[\cdot]$ function as filters for these predictions, ensuring that only the most reliable information is used to update the student model's understanding of instance-level features within the target domain.

3.3 Training Data Generation

In the realm of semi-supervised aerial object detection, generating training data that effectively reduces the domain discrepancy is crucial. To this end, the SRA-YOLO framework employs a method that adjusts the ground sample distance (GSD) of aerial images to emulate the variability in spatial resolution characteristic of different domains. This is achieved by two primary processes: the Adaptive Zoom-In technique for upscaling images from the target domain $\mathbf{I}^t$ to create source-like pseudo images $\mathbf{I}^s_f$, and the Adaptive Zoom-Out method for downscaling source domain images $\mathbf{I}^s$ to produce target-like pseudo images $\mathbf{I}^t_f$.

For $\mathbf{I}^t$, we apply a scaling rate r selected from a adaptively determined interval, dictated by the GSD of source images and average GSD of all previously processed images in target dataset. This interval is designed for spatial resolution alignment, with r chosen randomly within this range to enhance the robustness of the algorithm (see Eq. 4). Post upscaling, if the resizing rate exceeds a certain threshold, adaptive cropping is employed to prevent computational overload, resulting in the generation of $\mathbf{I}^s_f$. Conversely, $\mathbf{I}^s$ is downscaled at a rate chosen adaptively from an inverse range to mimic the target domain's GSD, followed by either direct output or a strategic tiling on a blank canvas, with potential flipping applied to enhance diversity, forming $\mathbf{I}^t_f$. These adaptive transformations, as visualized in Fig. 2, are integral to the training of our model, allowing it to learn from a dataset that encapsulates the spatial resolutions of both domains, thereby honing its detection capabilities.

$$r \in \begin{cases} (1, R] & \text{for upscaling} \\ [R, 0.5) & \text{for downscaling if } R \leq 0.5 \\ 0.5 & \text{for downscaling if } R > 0.5 \end{cases}, \quad (4)$$

$$R = \frac{G_{\text{avg}}}{G_{\text{org}}}$$

where r is the resizing rate, G_{avg} is the average ground sample distance of processed target images, and G_{org} is the original ground sample distance of the image from the source dataset.

This innovative approach to training data generation not only augments the dataset with diversified spatial resolutions but also aligns with the subsequent training stages where soft pseudo-labels, a core component of the HT model, facilitate the learning of the intricate details from both domains, effectively bridging the domain gap and enhancing the model's generalizability.

3.4 The Loss Function Design

To address cross-domain discrepancies, the SRA-YOLO framework incorporates both target-like and source-like pseudo images, $\mathbf{I}^s_f$ and $\mathbf{I}^t_f$, generated through spatial resolution transformations as discussed in the Sect. 3.3. A new supervised loss for the student model, which processes $\mathbf{I}^s_f$ similarly to the original source images $\mathbf{I}^t$, is defined by:

$$\mathcal{L}_{\text{det}}^{\dagger}(\mathbf{I}_f^t, \mathcal{B}^s, \mathcal{C}^s) = \mathcal{L}_{\text{box}}(\mathcal{B}^s; \mathbf{I}_f^t) + \mathcal{L}_{\text{cls, obj}}(\mathcal{C}^s; \mathbf{I}_f^t) \tag{5}$$

Concurrently, the teacher model, updated through EMA, now ingests source-like pseudo images $\mathbf{I}_f^s$ to learn source domain's global features. This necessitates a reformulation of the distillation loss previously defined in the Eq. 3, updating it to:

$$\mathcal{L}_{\text{dis}}^{\dagger}(\mathbf{I}_f^s, \hat{\mathbf{I}}^t) = \mathcal{L}_{\text{det}}(\hat{\mathbf{I}}^t, \mathcal{H}_{\mathcal{R}}[\mathcal{E}_{\mathcal{R}}(\mathbf{I}_f^s)], \mathcal{H}_{\mathcal{C}}[\mathcal{E}_{\mathcal{C}}(\mathbf{I}_f^s)]) \tag{6}$$

To foster consistency in predictions for the student model when exposed to both source and target domain images, we introduce a consistency loss. This is computed as the L2 norm between the supervised losses of the source and the source-like pseudo images:

$$\mathcal{L}_{\text{con}} = \|\mathcal{L}_{\text{det}}(\mathbf{I}^s, \mathcal{B}^s, \mathcal{C}^s) - \mathcal{L}_{\text{det}}^{\dagger}(\mathbf{I}_f^t, \mathcal{B}^s, \mathcal{C}^s)\|_2 \tag{7}$$

The overarching optimization of the model in an end-to-end training regime is achieved through a composite loss function that synergistically incorporates detection, distillation, and consistency losses:

$$\mathcal{L}_t = \mathcal{L}_{\text{det}}(\mathbf{I}^s, \mathcal{B}^s, \mathcal{C}^s) + \mathcal{L}_{\text{det}}^{\dagger}(\mathbf{I}_f^t, \mathcal{B}^s, \mathcal{C}^s) + \lambda \cdot \mathcal{L}_{\text{dis}}^{\dagger}(\mathbf{I}_f^s, \hat{\mathbf{I}}^t) + \eta \cdot \mathcal{L}_{\text{con}} \tag{8}$$

where λ and η are tunable hyper-parameters that balance the significance of each loss component during the training process.

4 Experiments

4.1 Dataset and Evaluation Protocol

To assess the efficacy of our semi-supervised learning framework within the context of cross-domain aerial object detection, we utilized two benchmark datasets: DOTA-v1.5 [4] and xView [11]. DOTA-v1.5 consists of 2,806 high-resolution aerial images with detailed annotations of small objects, across 16 categories. The xView dataset, containing over one million labeled objects across 60 classes, offers diverse scenes captured at a 0.3 m ground sample distance, providing high-resolution imagery for robust model training.

The adapted target domain, DOTA-v2.0-extra, is a subset of the comprehensive DOTA-v2.0. It is constructed by excluding the original images present in DOTA-v1.5, and instead, it incorporates only the additional images that were introduced in DOTA-v2.0. This selective composition results in a dataset that poses more complex challenges and offers a diverse array of scenes. This version, devoid of labels, is utilized as the unlabeled dataset in our semi-supervised training regimen.

In aligning with our cross-domain scenario, we define two distinct evaluation protocols:

DOTA-v1.5 → DOTA-v2.0-extra: Employing the labeled data from DOTA-v1.5 for training, the performance evaluation is conducted on the unlabeled

DOTA-v2.0-extra, showcasing the model's capability to adapt from the source domain to a more complex target domain.

xView → DOTA-v2.0-extra: Leveraging the comprehensive xView dataset as the source domain, this protocol evaluates the transferability of our model to the unlabeled DOTA-v2.0-extra, thus testing the model's generalization from civilian-grade imagery to intricate aerial views.

The aforementioned protocols are crucial in demonstrating our method's adaptability and robustness across varying domains and resolutions, pertinent for real-world aerial object detection applications. The two evaluation protocols mentioned above can concurrently assess the performance of the proposed method when the remote sensing data originates from the same dataset as well as from different datasets. During all the experiments, we use COCO [15] style metrics.

4.2 Implementation Details

For our semi-supervised cross-domain aerial object detection framework, YOLOv5 with Large parameters (YOLOv5-L) is the chosen detector due to its balance of real-time performance and accuracy. All images are cropped into 1024 × 1024 patches with an overlap of 200 pixels for both training and evaluation. During training, we utilize asymmetric data augmentation strategies in line with [23] and [12], while also adopting a batch size of 2 across two 24GB RTX3090 GPUs for 180k iterations. The initial learning rate is set to 0.0015, with momentum at 0.9 and weight decay at 0.0001. Training batches include two image pairs: labeled source images $(\mathbf{I}^s, \mathbf{I}^t_f)$ and unlabeled target images $(\mathbf{I}^t, \mathbf{I}^s_f)$, aligning with the semi-supervised paradigm.

We employ the EMA strategy for the teacher model updates, with γ set at 0.999, ensuring gradual model refinement. The IoU threshold for the filters $\mathcal{H}_\mathcal{R}[\cdot]$ is at 0.3, and the category score threshold $\mathcal{H}_\mathcal{C}[\cdot]$ is set to 0.8. The overall loss function $\mathcal{L}$ incorporates an emphasis on the consistency loss $\mathcal{L}_{\text{con}}$ using the L2 distance, with the hyper-parameters λ and η set to 0.05 and 2.0, respectively. These configurations will be further examined in our ablation studies.

4.3 Ablation Studies

We systematically examine the contribution of each loss component in the SRA-YOLO framework to understand their individual and combined impacts on the model's performance, specifically under the DOTA-v1.5 → DOTA-v2.0-extra adaptation scenario.

Distillation Loss Weight λ. We evaluate the role of the distillation loss by varying the weight parameter λ while keeping η fixed at zero. Table 1 presents the outcomes, pinpointing the optimal λ value for maximizing the detection performance.

Consistency Loss Weight η. This study investigates the impact of the consistency loss by adjusting η while setting λ to zero. Results detailed in Table 2

Table 1. Ablation studies on the weight λ of the distillation loss in the SRA-YOLO framework.

λ	AP_{50}	AP_{75}
0.01	49.5	31.7
0.05	**53.7**	**35.4**
0.1	52.6	34.1
0.5	51.4	32.8
1.	50.7	32.1

highlight the influence of varying η on model accuracy, indicating the importance of this parameter in enhancing cross-domain adaptability.

Table 2. Ablation studies on the weight η of the consistency loss for the SRA-YOLO framework.

η	AP_{50}	AP_{75}
0.5	50.8	33.0
1.0	52.4	34.7
2.0	**54.2**	**36.5**
5.0	52.3	34.9
10.0	51.1	33.6

Influence of Loss Components. The impact of individual components within the SRA-YOLO framework is assessed through a systematic ablation study, as delineated in Table 3. Initially, excluding both the distillation and consistency components results in a baseline AP_{50} of 48.7 and AP_{75} of 30.2. The introduction of distillation loss alone leads to significant performance improvements, increasing AP_{50} by 5.0 and AP_{75} by 5.2, illustrating the vital role of distillation in bridging the domain gap. Similarly, applying only the consistency loss results in a comparable enhancement, underlining its effectiveness in maintaining prediction consistency across domains. The combined application of both losses yields the most pronounced improvements, culminating in a AP_{50} of 56.0 and AP_{75} of 37.2, thereby validating the complementary nature of these components in the context of cross-domain aerial object detection.

4.4 Comparison with State-of-the-Art Methods

This section delineates a comprehensive quantitative evaluation between our proposed SRA-YOLO framework and state-of-the-art methods under two distinct domain adaptation scenarios: **DOTA-v1.5 → DOTA-v2.0-extra** and

Table 3. Incremental evaluation of different components in SRA-YOLO under the Extended Labeled Data setting for DOTA-v1.5 → DOTA-v2.0-extra.

Distillation	Consistency	AP_{50}	AP_{75}
-	-	48.7	30.2
✓	-	53.7 (+5.0)	35.4
-	✓	54.2 (+5.5)	36.5
✓	✓	**56.0 (+7.3)**	**37.2**

Table 4. Comparison with state-of-the-art methods on the DOTA-v1.5 → DOTA-v2.0-extra evaluation protocol.

Method	AP_{50}	AP_{75}
Source-Only	46.3	30.0
SWDA [17]	48.4	30.7
HTCN [1]	50.2	32.5
PF-ATF [8]	51.3	33.6
UMT [3]	52.1	34.8
TIA [26]	54.0	35.7
Direct-Label	60.4	40.8
SRA-YOLO (Ours)	**56.0**	**37.2**

xView → DOTA-v2.0-extra. Notably, we incorporate the Source-Only[2] and the Direct-Label[3] as baseline and ceiling protocols respectively, to frame the domain adaptation performance within realistic boundaries.

We first assess the performance of our SRA-YOLO framework against existing methods under the protocol from DOTA-v1.5 to DOTA-v2.0-extra. In Table 4, our SRA-YOLO architecture outstrips the leading method, TIA, enhancing the AP_{50} by 2.0 and AP_{75} by 1.5, respectively. This amplification from 54.0 to 56.0 in AP_{50} and from 35.7 to 37.2 in AP_{75} underscores the efficacy of SRA-YOLO in reconciling the spatial resolution variations and domain divergences inherent in transitioning from DOTA-v1.5 to DOTA-v2.0-extra datasets.

We further validate the robustness and adaptability of SRA-YOLO under the xView to DOTA-v2.0-extra evaluation protocol, challenging the framework with a distinct source domain. Contrasting the performance outcomes from Table 5, SRA-YOLO surpasses the current SOTA method, TIA, by augmenting the AP_{50} from 42.2 to 43.5 and AP_{75} from 24.0 to 25.8. And our method can achieve a

---
[2] The Source-Only denotes training with labeled source images and testing on target data without domain adaptation.
[3] The Direct-Label indicates training and testing with labeled target images.

Table 5. Comparison with state-of-the-art methods on the xView → DOTA-v2.0-extra evaluation protocol.

Method	AP_{50}	AP_{75}
Source-Only	32.3	17.1
SWDA [17]	36.7	19.4
HTCN [1]	38.5	21.2
PF-ATF [8]	39.6	22.1
UMT [3]	40.9	23.3
TIA [26]	42.2	24.0
Direct-Label	60.4	40.8
SRA-YOLO (Ours)	**43.5**	**25.8**

gain of +11.2 AP_{50} and +8.7 AP_{75} compared to the baseline without leveraging the source dataset images. This evidences a significant leap, establishing the superior domain adaptation efficacy of SRA-YOLO, especially when contending with the intrinsic challenges posed by differing aerial imagery characteristics between xView and DOTA-v2.0-extra datasets.

5 Conclusion

The SRA-YOLO framework marks a significant leap in Cross-Domain Aerial Object Detection, merging YOLOv5's robust architecture with sophisticated knowledge distillation and innovative data generation methods to tackle spatial resolution and domain variability challenges. Our method integrates adaptive spatial resolution techniques, enhancing detection across diverse aerial scenes by dynamically adjusting to resolution changes. Notably, our pseudo data generation process, crucial for model robustness, synthesizes varied aerial imagery through geometric transformations and domain adaptation techniques, enriching training data without additional real-world samples. This process, along with our unique Adaptive Zoom methods and tailored loss function, has been validated through comprehensive tests and ablation studies, demonstrating superior performance over existing approaches. Future efforts will aim at minimizing computational load and extending our framework with semi-supervised learning strategies to support a wider array of aerial images, thus advancing applications in urban planning and environmental monitoring with improved efficiency and adaptability.

References

1. Chen, C., Zheng, Z., Ding, X., Huang, Y., Dou, Q.: Harmonizing transferability and discriminability for adapting object detectors. In: Proceedings of the IEEE/CVF Conference on Computer Vision and Pattern Recognition, pp. 8869–8878 (2020)
2. Chen, Y., Liu, Q., Wang, T., Wang, B., Meng, X.: Rotation-invariant and relation-aware cross-domain adaptation object detection network for optical remote sensing images. Remote Sens. **13**(21), 4386 (2021)
3. Deng, J., Li, W., Chen, Y., Duan, L.: Unbiased mean teacher for cross-domain object detection. In: Proceedings of the IEEE/CVF Conference on Computer Vision and Pattern Recognition, pp. 4091–4101 (2021)
4. Ding, J., et al.: Object detection in aerial images: a large-scale benchmark and challenges. IEEE Trans. Pattern Anal. Mach. Intell. **44**, 7778–7796 (2021). https://doi.org/10.1109/TPAMI.2021.3117983
5. Everingham, M., Eslami, S.M.A., Van Gool, L., Williams, C.K.I., Winn, J., Zisserman, A.: The pascal visual object classes challenge: a retrospective. Int. J. Comput. Vision **111**(1), 98–136 (2015)
6. Ge, Z., Liu, S., Wang, F., Li, Z., Sun, J.: YOLOX: exceeding yolo series in 2021. arXiv preprint arXiv:2107.08430 (2021)
7. Gupta, A., Dollar, P., Girshick, R.: LVIS: a dataset for large vocabulary instance segmentation. In: Proceedings of the IEEE International Conference on Computer Vision and Pattern Recognition, pp. 5356–5364 (2019)
8. He, Z., Zhang, L., Yang, Y., Gao, X.: Partial alignment for object detection in the wild. IEEE Trans. Circuits Syst. Video Technol. **32**(8), 5238–5251 (2021)
9. Hua, W., et al.: Sood: Towards semi-supervised oriented object detection. In: Proceedings of IEEE International Conference on Computer Vision and Pattern Recognition, pp. 15558–15567 (2023)
10. Jocher, G., et al.: ultralytics/yolov5: v7.0 - YOLOv5 SOTA realtime instance segmentation (2022). https://doi.org/10.5281/zenodo.7347926
11. Lam, D., et al.: xView: objects in context in overhead imagery. arXiv preprint arXiv:1802.07856 (2018)
12. Li, G., Li, X., Wang, Y., Wu, Y., Liang, D., Zhang, S.: PseCo: Pseudo labeling and consistency training for semi-supervised object detection. In: Avidan, S., Brostow, G., Cissé, M., Farinella, G.M., Hassner, T. (eds.) Proceedings of European Conference on Computer Vision, vol. 13669, pp. 457–472. Springer, Cham (2022). https://doi.org/10.1007/978-3-031-20077-9_27
13. Li, G., Ji, Z., Qu, X., Zhou, R., Cao, D.: Cross-domain object detection for autonomous driving: a stepwise domain adaptive yolo approach. IEEE Trans. Intell. Vehi. **7**(3), 603–615 (2022)
14. Lin, T.Y., Goyal, P., Girshick, R., He, K., Dollár, P.: Focal loss for dense object detection. In: Proceedings of the IEEE International Conference on Computer Vision, pp. 2980–2988 (2017)
15. Lin, T.-Y., et al.: Microsoft COCO: common objects in context. In: Fleet, D., Pajdla, T., Schiele, B., Tuytelaars, T. (eds.) ECCV 2014. LNCS, vol. 8693, pp. 740–755. Springer, Cham (2014). https://doi.org/10.1007/978-3-319-10602-1_48
16. Ren, S., He, K., Girshick, R., Sun, J.: Faster R-CNN: towards real-time object detection with region proposal networks. In: Proceedings of the Advances in Neural Information Processing Systems, vol. 28 (2015)
17. Saito, K., Ushiku, Y., Harada, T., Saenko, K.: Strong-weak distribution alignment for adaptive object detection. In: Proceedings of the IEEE/CVF Conference on Computer Vision and Pattern Recognition, pp. 6956–6965 (2019)

18. Tan, Z., Jiang, Z., Guo, C., Zhang, H.: WSODet: a weakly supervised oriented detector for aerial object detection. IEEE Trans. Geosci. Remote Sens. **61**, 1–12 (2023)
19. Tang, Y., Chen, W., Luo, Y., Zhang, Y.: Humble teachers teach better students for semi-supervised object detection. In: Proceedings of the IEEE/CVF Conference on Computer Vision and Pattern Recognition, pp. 3132–3141 (2021)
20. Tian, Z., Shen, C., Chen, H., He, T.: FCOS: a simple and strong anchor-free object detector. IEEE Trans. Pattern Anal. Mach. Intell. **44**(4), 1922–1933 (2020)
21. Wang, J., et al.: Seesaw loss for long-tailed instance segmentation. In: Proceedings of the IEEE/CVF Conference on Computer Vision and Pattern Recognition, pp. 9695–9704 (2021)
22. Xia, G.S., et al.: DOTA: a large-scale dataset for object detection in aerial images. In: The IEEE Conference on Computer Vision and Pattern Recognition (CVPR) (2018)
23. Xu, M., Zhang, Z., Hu, H., Wang, J., Wang, L., Wei, F., Bai, X., Liu, Z.: End-to-end semi-supervised object detection with soft teacher. In: Porceedings of the IEEE International Conference on Computer Vision, pp. 3060–3069 (2021)
24. Yang, X., Zhang, G., Li, W., Wang, X., Zhou, Y., Yan, J.: H2RBox: horizontal box annotation is all you need for oriented object detection. arXiv preprint arXiv:2210.06742 (2022)
25. Yang, Z., Liu, S., Hu, H., Wang, L., Lin, S.: RepPoints: point set representation for object detection. In: Proceedings of the IEEE/CVF International Conference on Computer Vision, pp. 9657–9666 (2019)
26. Zhao, L., Wang, L.: Task-specific inconsistency alignment for domain adaptive object detection. In: Proceedings of the IEEE/CVF Conference on Computer Vision and Pattern Recognition, pp. 14217–14226 (2022)
27. Zhou, Y., Jiang, X., Chen, Z., Chen, L., Liu, X.: A semi-supervised arbitrary-oriented SAR ship detection network based on interference consistency learning and pseudolabel calibration. IEEE J. Sel. Topics Appl. Earth Observations Remote Sens. **16**, 5893–5904 (2023). https://doi.org/10.1109/JSTARS.2023.3284667
28. Zhu, T., Ferenczi, B., Purkait, P., Drummond, T., Rezatofighi, H., van den Hengel, A.: Knowledge combination to learn rotated detection without rotated annotation. In: Proceeding of the IEEE International Conference on Computer Vision and Pattern Recognition, pp. 15518–15527 (2023)
29. Zhu, Y., Sun, X., Diao, W., Wei, H., Fu, K.: DualDA-Net: Dual-head rectification for cross domain object detection of remote sensing. IEEE Trans. Geosci. Remote Sens. **61**, 1–16 (2023)

Computer Vision: Security and Adversarial Attacks

BiFAT: Bilateral Filtering and Attention Mechanisms in a Two-Stream Model for Deepfake Detection

Lei Zhang, Ceyuan Yi, and Liang Liu[✉]

School of Cyber Science and Engineering, Sichuan University, Chengdu 610065, China
{zhanglei2018,liangzhai118}@scu.edu.cn

Abstract. Addressing the significant societal concerns triggered by the widespread dissemination of Deepfake facial forgeries on the internet, and the shortcomings of existing Deepfake video detection methods in terms of generalizability and resistance to compression artifacts, we introduce a model named BiFAT. BiFAT synergizes bilateral filtering and attention mechanisms within a two-stream model to transcend the limitations of traditional binary classification approaches in Deepfake detection. Firstly, we employ an attention mechanism combined with the Steganalysis Rich Filters and Attention (SRMA) for spatial feature extraction, capturing intricate local textures and structures. Secondly, discrete Fourier transform and a complex adaptive filter are applied for frequency domain feature extraction, ensuring a comprehensive analysis of the image. This dual-domain approach, augmented by attention layers, refines the feature extraction and amalgamation process, significantly enhancing detection performance on benchmark datasets such as DF-1.0, DFDC, Celeb-DF, and FaceForensics++. Finally, our method demonstrates a notable improvement in model convergence speed, addressing the challenge of managing an excessive number of features, a common issue in contemporary DeepFake detection models, thereby boosting the model's generalizability and compression artifact resistance.

Keywords: DeepFake Detection · Face Forensics · Deep Learning

1 Introduction

While digital technology has undoubtedly brought convenience into our lives, it has concurrently introduced a slew of societal challenges. Among these challenges, Deepfake technology has emerged as a topic of increasing interest in recent years, drawing substantial attention from both academia and the public at large. Deepfake technology, as evidenced by a growing body of research [2,32,39], leverages artificial intelligence techniques to craft highly convincing counterfeit images and videos. These deceptively realistic creations have the potential to sow confusion by blurring the lines between fact and fiction, giving rise to a range of issues, including but not limited to, the manipulation of public opinion, identity theft, and the invasion of personal privacy. The burgeoning concerns surrounding Deepfake technology have spurred action from governments and the academic community alike. Researchers and policymakers have initiated comprehensive investigations into the nature, progression, and potential countermeasures against this technology, recognizing it as an essential area of study in the contemporary digital era. Some examples are shown in Fig. 1.

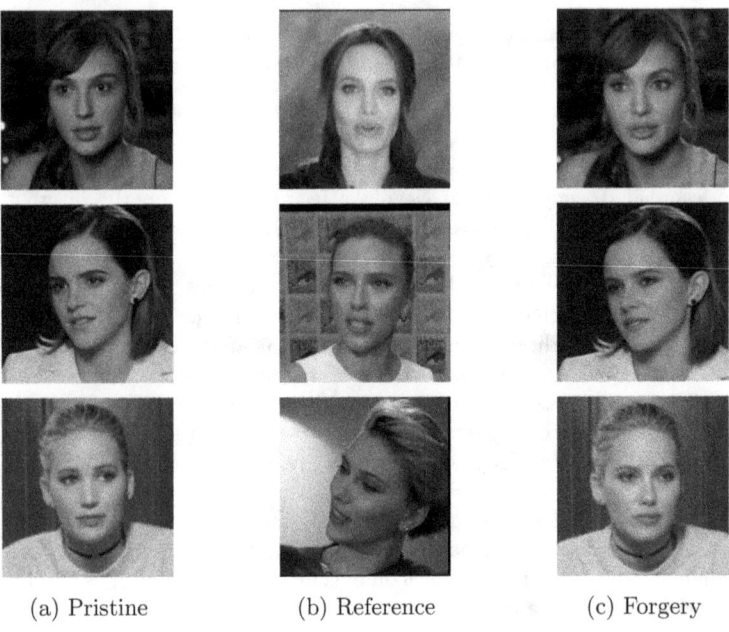

(a) Pristine   (b) Reference   (c) Forgery

Fig. 1. Examples of the input pristine, reference images, and their corresponding forgeries

Given the ominous and far-reaching implications of Deepfake technology, various organizations and researchers have intensified their efforts to address this pressing concern. A multitude of studies and initiatives have been put forth, focusing on the detection, prevention, and overall management of Deepfake technology [32]. Furthermore, there has been a concerted drive towards technical enhancements and innovations within the field of Deepfake technology, aimed at bolstering its security and controllability [20,39].

However, for most of the neural networks associated with DeepFake detection, the lack of detection generalization performance is particularly problematic when confronted with different deep forged datasets. This situation is largely attributed to the differences between the datasets involved in the training and testing phases of the neural networks. Specifically, the detection accuracy of the same model on different deep forgery datasets may vary significantly, and in some cases, the accuracy may even vary by as much as 30% [40].

In order to solve this problem, this paper utilizes bilateral filter neural networks as image extraction features while combining the attention mechanism for deep forgery detection. The spatial domain filter is constructed and the spatial domain features are extracted using the rich hidden write analysis algorithm, which can realize the extraction of detail information from the input image by the deep learning network. Meanwhile, this paper introduces a frequency filter designed to transform the image's frequency domain features into a spatial representation retaining these features. This transformed image is then utilized as the model's input to extract its frequency domain characteristics. Finally, an adaptive transfer learning approach is integrated to enhance the model's detection accuracy across various datasets.

The results demonstrate that our methodology not only exceeds the benchmarks set by standard binary classifiers but also achieves state-of-the-art performance. In summary, the key contributions of this paper are outlined as follows:

- We propose a effective framework to address deepfake forgeries, conceptualizing the deep-forged technique as a form of steganography applied to spatial images. This perspective leads us to develop an innovative methodology that significantly deviates from conventional deepfake detection strategies.
- The proposed framework enables two unique filters that extract feature information from both the spatial and frequency domains of images. These filters are integrated using an attention mechanism, a key innovation in our method. This integration is pivotal in enhancing the detection accuracy, enabling our method to effectively identify deepfake content with improved precision and reliability.
- We have conducted comprehensive tests, comparing our approach with the current state-of-the-art in deepfake detection. The results reveal that our method achieves superior performance, especially in scenarios that closely mimic real-world conditions,

2 Related Work

2.1 Deepfake Generation

For generating realistic faces, two principal generative approaches are employed: Generative Adversarial Networks (GANs) [13] and Variational AutoEncoders (VAEs) [18]. GANs utilize a dual network system consisting of a discriminator, tasked with identifying the authenticity of a video, and a generator, which modifies the video in a credibly deceptive manner. GANs have yielded highly credible and realistic results, with significant advancements including methods like StarGAN [4], DiscoGAN [17], and StyleGAN-V2 [16], which have achieved the best results in this field. On the other hand, VAE-based solutions employ a system comprising two pairs of encoders and decoders, each trained to deconstruct and reconstruct one of the two faces being exchanged. Subsequently, the decoding parts are swapped, enabling the reconstruction of the target persons face. The most renowned applications of this technique include DeepFaceLab [27], DFaker1, and DeepFaketf2.

In the realm of DeepFake technology, research predominantly focuses on two major categories: identity manipulation and attribute manipulation. Identity manipulation technologies, such as RSGAN [25] and FSGAN [19], emphasize extracting embedding information of facial and hair features for generating results, employing multi-scale architecture and occlusion-aware algorithms to handle various pixel situations and preserve the occlusion regions of the target face. Attribute manipulation, conversely, aims to alter facial attributes (like hair and skin color) or expressions (such as smiling or blinking). A notable work in this domain is StarGAN [4], which encodes facial attributes into a latent space. Additionally, researchers have extended image expression manipulation to the video level, creating facial animation techniques. These methods generate new videos wherein the source image displays the same expressions and actions as the face in the driving video.

2.2 Deepfake Detection

To tackle the issue of detecting deepfakes in videos, a variety of datasets have been developed over time. These are categorized into three evolutionary stages. The initial stage includes datasets like FaceForensics++ [29]. The second stage is marked by more advanced datasets such as the Google Deepfake Detection Dataset [10] and Celeb-DF [23]. The most recent stage, the third generation, features even more comprehensive datasets like the DFDC dataset [9] and DF-1.0 [15]. With each successive generation, these datasets have grown in size and in the number of frames they encompass.

Within the extensive and swiftly expanding body of research on deepfake detection, the predominant methods depend on supervised learning, utilizing extensive collections of authentic and fabricated videos. Early works [22,38] identified DeepFake by observing visual biological inconsistencies, such as atypical eye blinking or irregular head movements. In most instances, these techniques focus exclusively on video analysis, capitalizing on basic features or flaws originating from imperfections in the creation process. Generally, these strategies prove highly successful when the video under scrutiny has been produced using a manipulation technique that was included in the training data, but tend to be largely ineffective in other situations [34,36]. Considering the continuous emergence of new techniques for creating synthetic data, the frequency of these less effective scenarios is likely to increase.

In terms of DeepFake detection, most methods rely on supervised training, leveraging large datasets of real and fake videos. With learning-based approaches gaining popularity, certain studies [29,41] have introduced systems that derive attributes from the spatial domain, demonstrating remarkable results on particular datasets. Recently, new methodologies have started to explore a broader range of data domains. [40] formulated Deepfake detection as a fine-grained classification problem for research and proposed Multi-attentional Deepfake Detection

Network, which extracts texture information at the superficial level while localizing the forgery information at the deeper level. [31] proposed a new method for detecting deepfake videos is presented. This approach combines the strengths of Convolutional Neural Networks (CNNs) and Gated Recurrent Units (GRUs) to detect spatial and temporal inconsistencies in videos. The method uses a hybrid feature extraction process, incorporating a Histogram of Oriented Gradient (HOG)-based CNN and an enhanced XceptionNet method. These features are then merged and processed by GRUs to identify the authenticity of videos. These methods exploited frequency information but did not explicitly consider the relationship between different domains.

In addition to emphasizing the spatial domain, certain techniques also concentrate on the frequency domain to detect anomalies associated with forgery. Most of them use either Discrete Fourier Transform (DFT) or Wavelet Transform (WT), or Discrete Cosine Transform (DCT) to convert the spatial image to the frequency domain. Durall et al. [11] first proposed that averaging the amplitude of each frequency band with DFT can mine abnormal information of forgery in face manipulation detection. Masi et al. [30] employ a Laplacian of Gaussian (LoG) filter for frequency enhancement, aimed at diminishing the image content in the low-level feature maps. However, most of these studies largely depend on fundamental frequency statistical features, neglecting the correlation between frequency domain and spatial domain characteristics, resulting in suboptimal utilization of frequency information. In our work, considering the powerful feature extraction capabilities of CNNs, we utilize the Discrete Cosine Transform (DCT) to convert the frequency domain information of images into spatial domain images embedded with frequency information, which can then be extracted by CNNs. We have also theoretically analyzed and demonstrated its effectiveness, integrating it into the entire learning process of CNNs.

3 Method

In this paper, a bilateral filter is used to extract the features of the image in both the spatial and frequency domains to capture the general and local features of the image. This method contributes to the generalization and robustness of the model. The sensitivity of the steganalysis filters to the spatial information of the image is utilized to ensure the accuracy of the extracted features, and the self-attention structure is introduced to capture the correlation between the features in the spatial domain. The self-attention structure is also responsible for capturing the correlation between spatial and frequency domain features, which reduces the convergence time of the model and enhances the accuracy of the model.

The model structure is illustrated in Fig. 2, comprising a branch for extracting spatial domain features (the SRMA branch), and another for extracting frequency domain features (the Freq branch). The self-attention mechanism within the network is responsible for learning the correlations among feature maps from different domains of an image, selecting channel-wise attention to enhance model

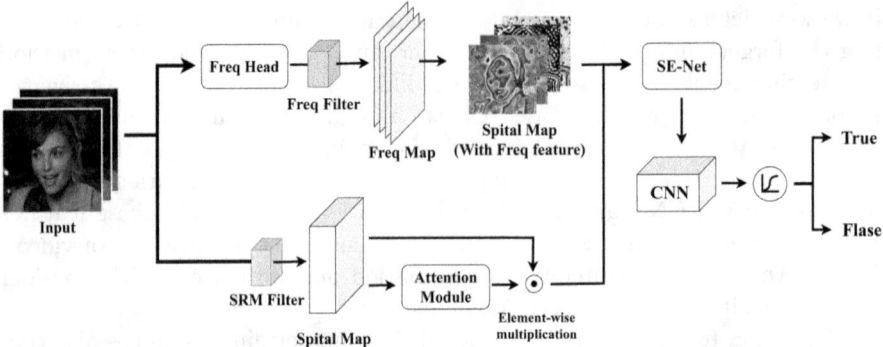

Fig. 2. The model utilizes a bilateral filter to extract features of the image in both the spatial and frequency domains to capture the overall and local features of the image, and consists of a branch for extracting spatial domain features (SRMA branch) as well as a branch for extracting frequency domain features (Freq branch)

performance. The input images for this model are sourced from the Celeb-DF dataset.

3.1 Spatial Filters Based on Rich Models

When detecting and analyzing steganographic techniques, the steganalysis method based on high-dimensional spatial features [12] can obtain excellent results. The method can effectively deal with high-dimensional spatial features. In this paper, the deep-forgery part of the image is regarded as the hidden information of the spatial image, and this perspective provides a completely new processing way to deal with depth forgery. In order to effectively extract the information in the spatial domain of the image, this paper proposes a new branch of information extraction called SRMA (Steganalysis Rich Filters and Attention, SRMA). This mechanism can solve the problem that the original module cannot effectively learn the correlation of multi-filter processing results. In this way, not only the feature learning ability of the model can be enhanced, but also the performance of the model in processing complex tasks can be improved. The specific structure of the SRMA branch is shown in Fig. 3. The input images for this model are sourced from the FF++ dataset.

Spatial Feature Extraction. To accurately extract pixel-level features in an image's spatial domain, precise computation of the residual image is crucial. 'Residuals' refer to the prediction errors that occur between local pixels after specific filtering, which arises due to the adjacent domain correlation within the image. Since a DeepFake-modified image exhibits subtle pixel-to-pixel variations, it increases the likelihood of detecting such prediction errors.

Different methods of residual calculation are designed to produce different types of filters. The residuals are calculated as a parameter for this pixel position

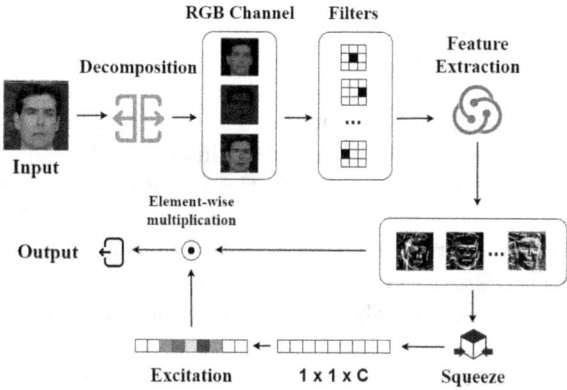

Fig. 3. Steganalysis Rich Filters and Attention

by gray value, and so on a residual map can be extracted from the original image. The equation can be expressed as

$$R_{i,j} = \hat{X}_{i,j}(N_{i,j}) - cX_{i,j} \tag{1}$$

where $R_{i,j}$ represents the residual of the image at pixel coordinates (i,j). $N_{i,j}$ is a number of neighboring elements of $X_{i,j}$, the number of neighboring elements is cc, and $\hat{X}_{i,j}(N_{i,j})$ is the predicted value of $cX_{i,j}$, that is, the data predicted by the filter.

The larger the magnitude of a pixel point in the residual image, the weaker the correlation of that pixel point corresponding to the domain pixel. Since the magnitude of each pixel point in the residual image varies, the image should be quantized and truncated first when acquiring the null domain feature map.

$$R_{i,j} \leftarrow \text{trunc}_T \left(\text{round} \left(\frac{R_{i,j}}{q} \right) \right) \tag{2}$$

$$\text{trunc}_T(x) = \begin{cases} x, & x \in [-T,T] \\ T\,\text{sign}(x), & x \notin [-T,T] \end{cases} \tag{3}$$

We define q as the quantization step and *roundround* as the rounding of the residuals, truncation nicely compresses the range of values of the residuals $R_{i,j}$ and also helps to reduce the dimensions of the subsequently extracted features.

And the final calculated matrix is the feature data needed by the neural network for deepfake detection in this paper, which can largely represent the spatial domain texture features of the input image, and its texture features are used as the parameter inputs of the spatial domain branch in the neural network, which makes the neural network to fuse the spatial features in order to improve the perception of the artifacts within the image.

Attention Module Addition. While the SRM structure is adept at extracting features from the image's null domain, there is a notable challenge: the weak correlation between features extracted by different filters, making it hard to discern direct connections, which in turn complicates model training. Incorporating an attention mechanism can effectively address this issue. By assigning weights to the feature maps produced by each filter, the attention mechanism enables the model to assess the relative importance of each feature map. This approach not only significantly reduces the time for model convergence and enhances training efficiency, but it may also improve model accuracy. Furthermore, employing this method can also reduce the number of training iterations needed when integrating spatial and frequency domain features.

This paper mainly carries out compression operation and excitation operation when injecting the attention mechanism. For the squeeze operation, We define z_c to represent the statistics of the cth channel in the feature map, u_c to represent the 2D data of the image of the cth channel, and H, W to be the length and width of the feature map matrix, respectively. $u_c(i,j)$ represents the (i,j) data in the feature map matrix. The global spatial information needs to be squeezed into a channel descriptor and its channel information is counted by global average pooling, at this time, the structure obtained is $1*1*C$, and C is the number of channels of the feature map at this time, which is given by the formula:

$$z_c = F_{sq}(u_c) = \frac{1}{H \times W} \sum_{i=1}^{H} \sum_{j=1}^{W} u_c(i,j) \qquad (4)$$

Then the excitation operation is performed, which learns the nonlinear relationship between the channels; the learned relationship is also not mutually exclusive, because multi-channel features are allowed here, instead of the one-hot form. In order to reduce the model complexity and improve the generalization ability in the excitation operation, this paper adopts a Bottleneck structure that contains two fully connected layers: a downscaling layer and an upscaling layer. The first fully connected layer is responsible for the dimensionality reduction operation, and its reduction coefficient r is used as a hyperparameter. The ReLU activation function is applied next. The last fully connected layer is used to recover the original dimension. The equation is provided in equation below, where σ refers to the Sigmoid function, δ represents the ReLU function, and W_1, W_2 are the descending and ascending layer parameters, respectively.

$$\begin{aligned} s = F_{ex}(z, W) &= \sigma(g(z, W)) \\ &= \sigma(W_2 \delta(W_1 z)) \end{aligned} \qquad (5)$$

After activation by Sigmoid function, s_c in the range of (0,1) is obtained, which can be interpreted as the weight of each feature channel, and the calibrated features can be obtained by multiplying this weight with the corresponding feature channel.

3.2 Frequency Filter Based on Image Reconstruction

Most current frequency domain filters, being manually designed, fail to encompass all image modes and struggle to adaptively discern forged modes within images. Frequency domain branching emerges as a viable solution to this challenge. This approach enables the adaptive capture of an image's frequency domain feature information before its integration into the neural network. Employing frequency filters for extracting features from an image's frequency domain not only leverages the neural network model's ability to adaptively process this information, but it also allows for the acquisition of a spatial image enriched with comprehensive frequency domain data. This dual benefit significantly enhances the saliency of feature parameters.

Inspired by F3-Net [28], the image is transformed using the Discrete Cosine Transform (DCT) [3,24] to constitute the frequency domain information for extraction, and the two-dimensional DCT transform equation is as follows.

$$F'(i,v) = \frac{1}{\sqrt{M}} C(v) \sum_{j=0}^{M-1} f(i,j) \cos\left[\frac{(2j+1)v\pi}{2M}\right] \quad (6)$$

$$F(u,v) = \frac{1}{\sqrt{N}} C(u) \sum_{i=0}^{N-1} F'(i,v) \cos\left[\frac{(2i+1)u\pi}{2N}\right] \quad (7)$$

where N is the number of rows, M is the number of columns, $f(i,j)$ is the pixel value of the input image at position (i,j), $F(u,v)$ is the frequency component of the transformed image at position (u,v), and $C(u)$ and $C(v)$ are the scale factors, which take the value of $\frac{1}{\sqrt{N}}$ or $\frac{1}{\sqrt{M}}$ if either u or v is 0, or $\frac{2}{\sqrt{N}}$ or $\frac{2}{\sqrt{M}}$ otherwise.

Also, three filters are designed for frequency decomposition of the DCT transformed image. The filters divide the frequency domain into three frequency bands: low, middle and high, but there is an uneven energy in the frequency domain information separated by the base filter, so the use of adaptive filters is added to implement it. The filter is divided into frequency domain base filter and adaptive filter which can be denoted by f_{base} and f_w respectively.

The frequency domain filter is used to filter the frequency distribution of the image after transforming the image by DCT operation. After grouping the images in the frequency domain, an inverse DCT transform operation is performed to transform them to the spatial domain, which allows their frequency domain features to be represented on the spatial domain. It ensures that it has some similarity with the features from the SRM branch and guarantees smooth model training. The spital maps with freq features are shown in Fig. 4.

Since the adaptive filter is a tuning of the underlying segmented filter, the value should not be too large, this paper uses normalization by normalizing the adaptive filter using σ, where $\sigma = \frac{1-e^{-x}}{1+e^{-x}}$, with the aim of restricting the value of the adaptive filter to be between (-1,1) and facilitating the superposition of subsequent filters on top of each other.

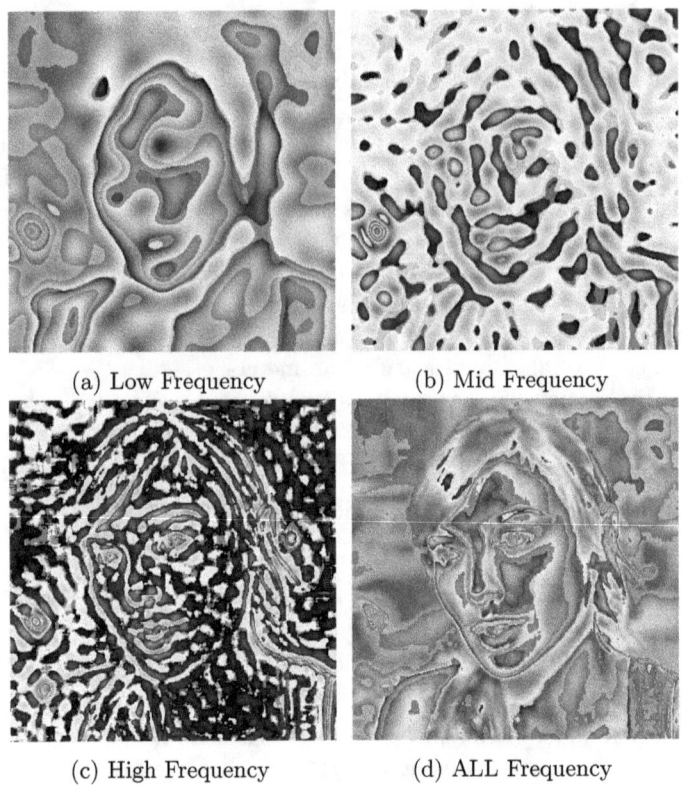

(a) Low Frequency (b) Mid Frequency

(c) High Frequency (d) ALL Frequency

Fig. 4. The Frequency level after frequency filter process

4 Experimental Results

DataSets. We use four commonly used datasets for evaluation: the FaceForensics++ [29], DFDC [9],DF-1.0 [15] and Celeb-DF [23]. Each dataset has its own characteristics. FaceForensics++ [29] is a large-scale face forgery dataset for deep learning, including four common face forgery techniques, i.e., Deepfakes, Face2Face, FaceSwap, and NeuralTextures, which cover a variety of different face forgery scenarios and situations. All of its videos are categorized into 3 versions according to different levels of compression: original version, C23 version and C40 version. Celeb-DF [23] is a dataset for Deepfake detection that contains facial videos from celebrities, both real and Deepfake videos. Celeb-DF includes 590 raw videos collected from YouTube with different age, race, and gender themes, and 5639 corresponding DeepFake videos that cover a wide range of different poses, expressions, and lighting conditions. The DFDC [9] dataset is an artificially synthesized video dataset collected by the DeepFake Detection Challenge, a joint initiative of the Facebook AI team and Microsoft and other organizations. It is divided into two parts: training set and validation set. Each video is 10 s long, with resolutions ranging from 320×240 to 3840×2160. Fake faces are generated using several mainstream fake face generation algorithms such as DeepFakes, Face2Face, etc. so that the dataset contains as many fake face videos as possible. The DF-1.0 dataset [15], also known as DeeperForensics-1.0, is a large-scale benchmark for real-world face forgery detection that features 60,000 videos, including both pristine and manipulated content, aimed at aiding the development and evaluation of deepfake detection methods.

Table 1. Experimental software environment

Typology	Software environment configuration Dependencies
Development platform	PyCharm 2023.2.1 (Professional Edition) Visual Studio Code 1.66.2
Compiler and interpreter environments	Python 3.9.0 GCC 11.3 MSVC++ 14.2
Software Packages and Frameworks	PyTorch 1.10.0 CUDA 11.4 Opencv-python 4.5.5.64 Numpy 1.22.3 Pillow 8.4.0

Experiments Settings. In order to validate the effectiveness of the model detection in this paper and to analyze its generalization for detection on different datasets, validation test experiments of this paper's method are conducted in this chapter. In the experiments, EfficientNet-B7 [33] included in the model uses a pre-trained version to perform convolutional operations on the input images, and its parameters are fine-tuned during the training process. For face image extraction, the Dlib module [8] was used to capture the faces in the dataset and the face size was set to 380-380 pixels and the learning rate was set to 0.004.

Our framework is implemented on PyTorch with a desktop PC equipped with an Intel Core E5-2696 v2 CPU and a GeForce RTX3080Ti GPU(12 GB memory, CUDA10.0). The experimental software environment and parameters are shown in Table 1.

Comparisons. In the comparative analysis, we included only the most advanced Deepfake detection methods with available and reproducible source code to ensure an equitable comparison. We adhered to experimental conditions identical to our own and preserved their best parameter configurations where relevant during the training and testing phases.

Table 2. Experimental results of comparative evaluation

Methods	Test Datasets							
	FF++		Celeb-DF		DFDC		DF-1.0	
	ACC	AUC	ACC	AUC	ACC	AUC	ACC	AUC
MesoNet [1]	61.12	59.32	50.02	50.46	35.63	50.04	50.05	50.21
Capsule [26]	76.54	83.24	52.33	54.36	60.96	59.13	56.29	60.46
FFD [7]	81.89	84.08	58.65	59.07	48.39	55.86	53.69	53.81
CViT [6]	84.36	94.07	53.76	59.21	46.41	54.33	50.75	51.76
TAR [21]	53.48	50.00	49.74	50.00	63.21	50.00	49.95	50.00
MADD [40]	76.07	86.42	56.99	60.84	62.94	64.99	**69.34**	69.47
NoiseDF [37]	81.36	**93.23**	59.17	63.19	70.10	**75.89**	67.49	70.88
BiFAT	**85.74**	89.21	**70.08**	**73.69**	**72.43**	74.27	68.70	**71.48**

[1] Comparative evaluation of frame-wise test accuracy (%) and AUC percentages (%) across various testing datasets following training on FF++

As shown in Table 2, the model in this paper is trained on the FaceForensics++ dataset and tested on other datasets, and its model design structure has good performance on cross-dataset testing and demonstrates excellent performance on cross-dataset testing, which indicates that the model has good generalization ability and robust robustness. The improvement of the model's generalization performance is achieved by combining the image bi-domain with the attention mechanism. The model is able to better understand and reveal the complex patterns hidden in the image, which improves its accuracy in detecting deep forged images. Its accuracy is more improved compared to the effect of MADD [40], which uses the spatial domain information as input, and improved with CViT [6], which also uses the attention mechanisms. This is due to the mutual complementation of spatial and frequency domain features and the weight allocation of global information by the attention structure.

Ablation Study. The model in this paper mainly consists of spatial filter branching, frequency filter branching and an attention layer. Among them, the features of the dual branch are the main structure to collect the Bi-Domain features of the image. The attention layer serves as an auxiliary module to add weights to the collection of features.

In order to verify the advantages of each module of this paper's model, this paper compares the cross-dataset generalizability comparison of each branch combination in the DFDC dataset to test its detection performance in cross-dataset scenarios. The main experiments are conducted on the following structures, 1) Efficient-B7 2) Efficient-B7+Freq branching 3) Efficient-B7+SRMA branching 4) Efficient-B7+ Freq branch + SRMA branch 5) Efficient-B7 + Freq branch + SRMA branch + SE-Net. The training sets are all DFDC datasets, and the evaluation metrics are AUC metrics.

Table 3. Ablation results

ID	Effi	Freq	SRMA	SE	FF++(c23)	Celeb-DF	DFDC	Average
1	✓	-	-	-	69.86	80.45	88.53	79.61
2	✓	✓	-	-	77.22	81.28	**91.58**	83.36
3	✓	-	✓	-	72.46	81.44	87.37	80.42
4	✓	✓	✓	-	77.50	82.51	89.62	83.21
5	✓	✓	✓	✓	**80.58**	**86.45**	90.43	**85.82**

[1] The results (AUC (%)) on FF++, Celeb-DF and DFDC. All models were trained on the DFDC dataset and tested on other datasets.

The experimental results are shown in Table 3. Among them, Freq represents the frequency-domain branch based on the frequency filter in the model of this paper, while SRMA represents the spatial filter branch based on the rich model, and the CNN network is selected as Efficient-B7. It can be seen that the combination of the CNN convolutional network alone and the Freq branch performs well on the DFDC, which indicates that the addition of the frequency domain of the image is on top of the CNN network alone to improves the accuracy of model detection. In terms of generalizability performance, SRMA combined with Freq branching slightly improves generalizability and slightly improves accuracy on cross-dataset detection.

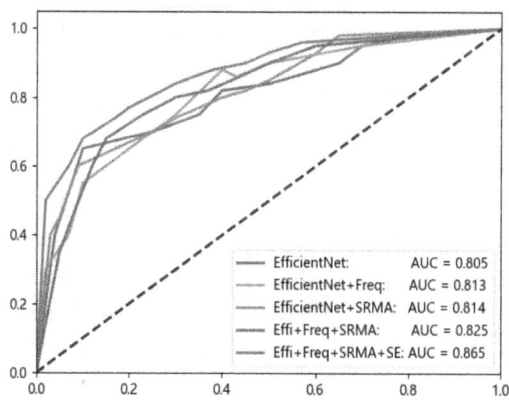

Fig. 5. AUC comparison on the Celeb-DF dataset

We show the area under the curve (AUC) results in our experiments in Fig. 5. One of the widely used datasets by researchers when confronted with deep forgery detection tasks is Celeb-DF, while another commonly used dataset is FaceForensics++. It is worth noting that the Celeb-DF dataset has higher quality forgery samples with more complex and hard-to-detect forgery features compared to the FaceForensics++ dataset. Therefore, in most of the studies, researchers usually use the Celeb-DF dataset as a benchmark for the evaluation of adversarial or cross-domain deep forgery detection tasks. This design is based on the consideration that the high-quality forgery samples of the Celeb-DF dataset can provide a more demanding and challenging testing environment, and better test the effectiveness and robustness of deep forgery detection algorithms.

Compression Resistance Test. In this paper, we investigate an experimental setup performed by training the model on the high-quality FaceForensics++ dataset (C23) and testing it on the low-quality FaceForensics++ dataset (C40). Considering that C40 video loses a lot of texture details during the encoding and compression process, which usually leads to a significant degradation of the model's accuracy when dealing with this type of low-quality data, the experiments designed in this paper aim to test the model's performance in this cross-compression scenario. It is worth noting that due to the poor quality of the C40 dataset, the model may exhibit large fluctuations and uncertainties on it, making our study challenging. In this experiment, this paper compares the detection performance of the model with the state-of-the-art deep forgery detection technique across compression rate scenarios on a dataset of four forgery methods (Deepfake, FaceSwap, Face2Face and NeuralTextures) from FaceForensics++. Specifically, we selected the corresponding HD and LD videos from the C23 and C40 datasets of FaceForensics++ for training and testing, respectively.

Table 4. Experimental results of cross compression on Faceforensics + + dataset

Methods	Accuracy (c23-c40)				Average
	Deepfake	FaceSwap	Face2Face	NeuralTextures	
Capsule [26]	67.75	54.50	54.50	53.75	57.63
MesoNet [1]	78.75	59.75	69.75	53.25	65.38
CNN-RNN [14]	71.93	52.01	50.95	51.76	56.67
3D-CNN [35]	79.55	54.52	69.10	59.80	65.74
Xception [5]	63.96	55.63	50.83	55.84	56.57
MADD [40]	**88.07**	**83.57**	62.14	52.85	71.66
CrossVitEfficientNet [6]	63.81	67.14	50.35	66.40	62.00
BiFAT	83.74	80.21	**74.08**	**70.69**	**77.18**

[1] C40 indicates low quality (heavy compression), C23 indicates high quality (light compression). The table data indicates that after training in the C23 environment, detection is performed in the C40 environment.

The experimental results are shown in Table 4, where it can be seen that the model in this study demonstrates excellent accuracy in detecting low-intensity forged videos generated by Face2Face and NeuralTextures, which can match the current best performance.

In particular, our model shows a significant improvement in accuracy when detecting forged videos generated by NeuralTextures. The fact that our model in this paper performs quite close to each other in the detection performance of the four types of forged videos proves that our chosen forged features are more broad and universal compared to other models, and thus it is more adaptive when facing detection across compression rates and cross-library scenarios.

5 Conclusion

In this study, we address DeepFake video detection challenges, such as limited generalizability and compression resistance, by introducing a method that leverages bilateral filtering and attention mechanisms for domain feature extraction. This method demonstrates superior generalization capabilities on datasets such as DF-1.0, DFDC, Celeb-DF, and FaceForensics++, with exceptional performance in resisting compression, particularly evident in the FaceForensics++ low-precision dataset. Our approach involves dual-domain feature extraction: spatial features are obtained using SRMA and attention for texture and structure, while frequency features are extracted via discrete Fourier transform and a complex adaptive filter. This multidimensional feature extraction boosts the model's generalization by overcoming the limitations of relying on a single feature source. Additionally, the incorporation of an attention mechanism enhances feature weighting and fusion, adapting feature responses globally and employing an SE-Net-like structure to weight spatial and frequency domain features adaptively. This results in a comprehensive feature set, addressing the challenge of feature overload and speeding up model convergence.

References

1. Afchar, D., Nozick, V., Yamagishi, J., Echizen, I.: MesoNet: a compact facial video forgery detection network. In: 2018 IEEE International Workshop on Information Forensics and Security (WIFS), pp. 1–7. IEEE (2018)
2. Ahmed, S.R., Sonuç, E., Ahmed, M.R., Duru, A.D.: Analysis survey on DeepFake detection and recognition with convolutional neural networks. In: 2022 International Congress on Human-Computer Interaction, Optimization and Robotic Applications (HORA), pp. 1–7. IEEE (2022)
3. Arai, Y., Agui, T., Nakajima, M.: A fast DCT-SQ scheme for images. IEICE TRANSACTIONS (1976–1990) **71**(11), 1095–1097 (1988)
4. Choi, Y., Choi, M., Kim, M., Ha, J.W., Kim, S., Choo, J.: StarGAN: unified generative adversarial networks for multi-domain image-to-image translation. In: Proceedings of the IEEE Conference on Computer Vision and Pattern Recognition, pp. 8789–8797 (2018)
5. Chollet, F.: Xception: deep learning with depthwise separable convolutions. In: Proceedings of the IEEE Conference on Computer Vision and Pattern Recognition, pp. 1251–1258 (2017)

6. Coccomini, D.A., Messina, N., Gennaro, C., Falchi, F.: Combining EfficientNet and vision transformers for video DeepFake detection. In: Sclaroff, S., Distante, C., Leo, M., Farinella, G.M., Tombari, F. (eds.) International conference on image analysis and processing, vol. 13233, pp. 219–229. Springer, Cham (2022). https://doi.org/10.1007/978-3-031-06433-3_19
7. Dang, H., Liu, F., Stehouwer, J., Liu, X., Jain, A.K.: On the detection of digital face manipulation. In: Proceedings of the IEEE/CVF Conference on Computer Vision and Pattern recognition, pp. 5781–5790 (2020)
8. davisking: Dlib c++ library. http://dlib.net/
9. Dolhansky, B., et al.: The DeepFake Detection Challenge (DFDC) dataset. arXiv preprint arXiv:2006.07397 (2020)
10. Dufour, N., Gully, A.: Contributing data to DeepFake detection research. Google AI Blog **1**(2), 3 (2019)
11. Durall, R., Keuper, M., Pfreundt, F.J., Keuper, J.: Unmasking DeepFakes with simple features. arXiv preprint arXiv:1911.00686 (2019)
12. Fridrich, J., Kodovsky, J.: Rich models for steganalysis of digital images. IEEE Trans. Inf. Forensics Secur. **7**(3), 868–882 (2012)
13. Goodfellow, I., et al.: Generative adversarial networks. Commun. ACM **63**(11), 139–144 (2020)
14. Güera, D., Delp, E.J.: DeepFake video detection using recurrent neural networks. In: 2018 15th IEEE International Conference on Advanced Video and Signal Based Surveillance (AVSS), pp. 1–6. IEEE (2018)
15. Jiang, L., Li, R., Wu, W., Qian, C., Loy, C.C.: DeeperForensics-1.0: A large-scale dataset for real-world face forgery detection. In: Proceedings of the IEEE/CVF Conference on Computer Vision and Pattern Recognition, pp. 2889–2898 (2020)
16. Karras, T., Laine, S., Aittala, M., Hellsten, J., Lehtinen, J., Aila, T.: Analyzing and improving the image quality of StyleGAN. In: Proceedings of the IEEE/CVF Conference on Computer Vision and Pattern Recognition, pp. 8110–8119 (2020)
17. Kim, T., Cha, M., Kim, H., Lee, J.K., Kim, J.: Learning to discover cross-domain relations with generative adversarial networks. In: International Conference on Machine Learning, pp. 1857–1865. PMLR (2017)
18. Kingma, D.P., Welling, M.: Auto-encoding variational Bayes. arXiv preprint arXiv:1312.6114 (2013)
19. Korshunova, I., Shi, W., Dambre, J., Theis, L.: Fast face-swap using convolutional neural networks. In: Proceedings of the IEEE International Conference on Computer Vision, pp. 3677–3685 (2017)
20. Kwok, A.O., Koh, S.G.: DeepFake: a social construction of technology perspective. Curr. Issue Tour. **24**(13), 1798–1802 (2021)
21. Lee, S., Tariq, S., Kim, J., Woo, S.S.: TAR: generalized forensic framework to detect DeepFakes using weakly supervised learning. In: Jøsang, A., Futcher, L., Hagen, J. (eds.) SEC 2021. IAICT, vol. 625, pp. 351–366. Springer, Cham (2021). https://doi.org/10.1007/978-3-030-78120-0_23
22. Li, Y., Chang, M.C., Lyu, S.: In Ictu Oculi: Exposing AI created fake videos by detecting eye blinking. In: 2018 IEEE International Workshop on Information Forensics and Security (WIFS), pp. 1–7. IEEE (2018)
23. Li, Y., Yang, X., Sun, P., Qi, H., Lyu, S.: Celeb-DF: a large-scale challenging dataset for DeepFake forensics. In: Proceedings of the IEEE/CVF Conference on Computer Vision and Pattern Recognition, pp. 3207–3216 (2020)
24. Loeffler, C., Ligtenberg, A., Moschytz, G.S.: Practical fast 1-D DCT algorithms with 11 multiplications. In: International Conference on Acoustics, Speech, and Signal Processing, pp. 988–991. IEEE (1989)

25. Natsume, R., Yatagawa, T., Morishima, S.: RSGAN: face swapping and editing using face and hair representation in latent spaces. arXiv preprint arXiv:1804.03447 (2018)
26. Nguyen, H.H., Yamagishi, J., Echizen, I.: Capsule-forensics: using capsule networks to detect forged images and videos. In: ICASSP 2019-2019 IEEE International Conference on Acoustics, Speech and Signal Processing (ICASSP), pp. 2307–2311. IEEE (2019)
27. Perov, I., et al.: DeepFaceLab: integrated, flexible and extensible face-swapping framework. arXiv preprint arXiv:2005.05535 (2020)
28. Qian, Y., Yin, G., Sheng, L., Chen, Z., Shao, J.: Thinking in frequency: face forgery detection by mining frequency-aware clues. In: Vedaldi, A., Bischof, H., Brox, T., Frahm, J.-M. (eds.) ECCV 2020. LNCS, vol. 12357, pp. 86–103. Springer, Cham (2020). https://doi.org/10.1007/978-3-030-58610-2_6
29. Rossler, A., Cozzolino, D., Verdoliva, L., Riess, C., Thies, J., Nießner, M.: Faceforensics++: learning to detect manipulated facial images. In: Proceedings of the IEEE/CVF International Conference on Computer Vision, pp. 1–11 (2019)
30. Sabir, E., Cheng, J., Jaiswal, A., AbdAlmageed, W., Masi, I., Natarajan, P.: Recurrent convolutional strategies for face manipulation detection in videos. Interfaces (GUI) **3**(1), 80–87 (2019)
31. Saikia, P., Dholaria, D., Yadav, P., Patel, V., Roy, M.: A hybrid CNN-LSTM model for video DeepFake detection by leveraging optical flow features. In: 2022 International Joint Conference on Neural Networks (IJCNN), pp. 1–7. IEEE (2022)
32. Seow, J.W., Lim, M.K., Phan, R.C., Liu, J.K.: A comprehensive overview of DeepFake: generation, detection, datasets, and opportunities. Neurocomputing **513**, 351–371 (2022)
33. Tan, M., Le, Q.: EfficientNet: rethinking model scaling for convolutional neural networks. In: International Conference on Machine Learning, pp. 6105–6114. PMLR (2019)
34. Tolosana, R., Vera-Rodriguez, R., Fierrez, J., Morales, A., Ortega-Garcia, J.: DeepFakes and beyond: a survey of face manipulation and fake detection. Inform. Fusion **64**, 131–148 (2020)
35. Tran, D., Bourdev, L., Fergus, R., Torresani, L., Paluri, M.: Learning spatiotemporal features with 3D convolutional networks. In: Proceedings of the IEEE International Conference on Computer Vision, pp. 4489–4497 (2015)
36. Verdoliva, L.: Media forensics and DeepFakes: an overview. IEEE J. Sel. Topics Sig. Process. **14**(5), 910–932 (2020)
37. Wang, T., Chow, K.P.: Noise based DeepFake detection via multi-head relative-interaction. In: Proceedings of the AAAI Conference on Artificial Intelligence, vol. 37, pp. 14548–14556 (2023)
38. Yang, X., Li, Y., Lyu, S.: Exposing deep fakes using inconsistent head poses. In: ICASSP 2019–2019 IEEE International Conference on Acoustics, Speech and Signal Processing (ICASSP), pp. 8261–8265. IEEE (2019)
39. Yu, P., Xia, Z., Fei, J., Lu, Y.: A survey on DeepFake video detection. IET Biometrics **10**(6), 607–624 (2021)
40. Zhao, H., Zhou, W., Chen, D., Wei, T., Zhang, W., Yu, N.: Multi-attentional DeepFake detection. In: Proceedings of the IEEE/CVF Conference on Computer Vision and Pattern Recognition, pp. 2185–2194 (2021)
41. Zhou, P., Han, X., Morariu, V.I., Davis, L.S.: Two-stream neural networks for tampered face detection. In: 2017 IEEE Conference on Computer Vision and Pattern Recognition Workshops (CVPRW), pp. 1831–1839. IEEE (2017)

EL-FDL: Improving Image Forgery Detection and Localization via Ensemble Learning

Bin Wang[1,2], Feifan Wang[1,2], Jingge Wang[3], Haonan Yan[1], Shaopeng Zhou[2,4], and Chaohao Li[2,4(✉)]

[1] Hangzhou Research Institute, Xidian University, Xian, China
wangbin02@xidian.edu.cn, 22151214404@stu.xidian.edu.cn
[2] Zhejiang Key Laboratory of Artificial Intelligence of Things (AIoT) Network and Data Security, Hangzhou, China
{abnerzhou,lchao}@zju.edu.cn
[3] The University of Sydney Camperdown, Hangzhou, NSW, Australia
jwan0689@uni.sydney.edu.au
[4] Zhejiang University, Hangzhou, China

Abstract. The widespread dissemination of diverse forgery images has profoundly impacted social life. Thus, image forgery detection techniques are becoming increasingly urgent. Existing models are usually trained to detect certain types of forgery images, leading to an insufficient generalization in detecting various forgery images (e.g., copy-move, splicing, inpainting). In this paper, we conducted extensive testing on SOTA models and revealed the limitations of individual models, including 1) insufficient generalization capability and 2) high false positive rates for pristine images. To address the above issues, we propose EL-FDL, a method based on stacking ensemble learning, which enhances the detection and localization abilities by integrating the output of heterogeneous SOTA models. Extensive experimental results demonstrate that our proposed EL-FDL significantly improved: +16.4% in detection, +11.1% in localization, and overall false positive rate decreased by at least -21.0% across the test dataset.

Keywords: forgery detection · ensemble learning · image forensics · decision fusion

1 Introduction

With the proliferation of image editing tools and image generation technologies, producing forgery images has become increasingly simple yet difficult to detect. This threatens personal privacy and risks public safety and social stability. For instance, spreading misinformation on social media, engaging in identity deception, and fabricating news have become prevalent tactics in online criminal

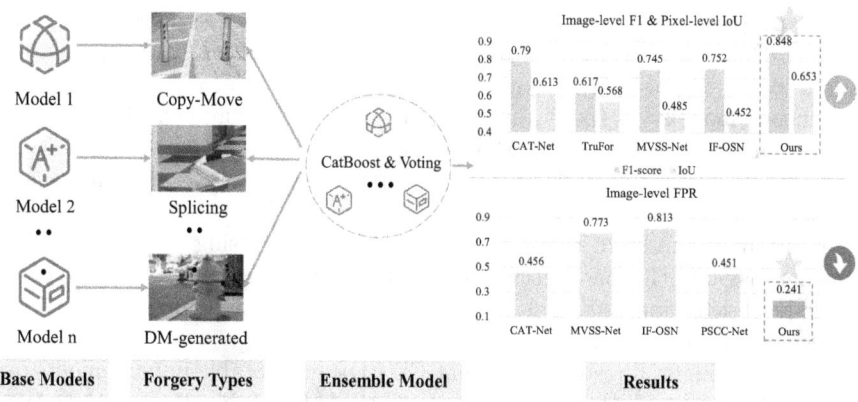

Fig. 1. An overview of EL-FDL. It uses stacking and voting ensemble learning methods to combine heterogeneous models for detecting different types of forgery images, thereby improving the detection performance while reducing the false positive rate.

activities. Moreover, the unethical utilization of manipulated images to deceive the public and undermine competitors' interests has become widespread, particularly in political elections and business competitions. Therefore, the threat of image forgery technology is fatal to various aspects of human life.

The main types of image forgery include manual tampering and artificial intelligence generation. The former includes copy-move, splicing, object-removal. The latter involves generative forgery images generated by artificial intelligence models, e.g., generative adversarial networks (hereafter referred to as GAN) and diffusion models [11,20].

Previous work has devoted much effort to addressing various forgery image detection. For instance, prior studies utilize fully convolutional networks for pixel-level semantic segmentation to detect splicing images [2]. Meanwhile, others employ SRM high-pass filters to emphasize edge features or region similarity matching for detecting copy-move forgeries [32]. For the GAN-generated images, extracting the features of the image block by deep CNN or replacing the discriminator of the GAN framework was applied in the detection [18]. Others detect DM-generated images by exploring forensic traces left by the diffusion model [4]. These methods and models show unsatisfactory performance when detecting forgery image types without pre-training.

To this end, we conducted a series of experiments on existing SOTA models and gained three insights. Firstly, the detection performance of the models varies notably depending on the type of forgery dataset. Then, the performance of the model varies even for the same type of forgery yet different datasets. In addition, we also find that the models exhibit high false positive rates on pristine images, which is not practical in real scenarios and increases maintenance costs. In summary, it can be described as 1) insufficient generalization, 2) limited robustness, and 3) high false positive rates.

We propose a practical framework for applying Ensemble Learning to image Forgery Detection and Localization (EL-FDL) to tackle the above issues, as shown in Fig. 1. EL-FDL is based on a stacking ensemble, which fuses the heterogeneous models via CatBoost [22] and Voting. For example, Model 1 excels in detecting copy-move, while Model 2 specializes in splicing, ..., and Model N is expert at detecting DM-generated. First, we process the original datasets using these base models and obtain their outputs. Then, we use Catboost to train the meta-model of the detection module, while using voting to perform decision fusion of the localization module. Finally, as shown in Fig. 1, we obtain image-level detection and pixel-level localization results with higher performance and lower false positive rates.

Our experimental results show that EL-FDL has notable improvements over the SOTA models. On these test datasets, CASIA, Columbia, Coverage, Defacto-inpainting, and CocoGlide, EL-FDL gained average improvements: 1) +18.1% and +14.8% in image-level ACC and F1-score, while reducing the FPR at least -21.0%, and 2) +9.3% and +12.9% in pixel-level F1-score and IoU. Our contributions are as follows:

1. We proposed an ensemble learning-based framework, integrating various heterogeneous detection models via Catboost and Voting.
2. We conducted extensive experiments that reveal the limitations of existing models, including insufficient generalization and high false positive rates.
3. The proposed EL-FDL presents better performances than the existing SOTA method over the test datasets with average gains being +16.4% in detection, +11.1% in localization, and -21.0% reduction in overall FPR.

2 Related Work

2.1 Forensic Detection and Localization

Traditional forgery detection techniques show poor performance with the development of manually tampered images towards deep forgery images. Therefore, to better address the challenges posed by forgery images, more effective deep-learning methods have been continuously proposed and widely applied.

Detection. Deep learning methods are usually analyzed by extracting various high-dimensional features (e.g., noise, frequency domain, pixels) in the forgery images. Chengbo Dong et al.(2022) develop multi-scale supervised and noisy views and explicitly extract boundary artifacts to learn the operational detection function [5]. In addition, to improve the robustness of image forgery detectors, Haiwei Wu et al.(2022) decompose noise on social networks into two parts [31], predictable noise and invisible noise, and model them separately then increase the accuracy of forgery detection. To further improve the forgery detection confidence, Guillaro et al. (2023) extracted traces in the image using learned noise-sensitive fingerprints, and introduced confidence map and integrity score mechanisms for image forgery detection [12].

Localization. Most SOTA model deep-learnings of forgery localization are inspired by semantic segmentation [12], but there are also unsupervised classification methods using contrastive learning. Xiuli Bi et al.(2019) make the features of image tampering regions more visible through residual propagation and feedback processes in CNN [1]. Kwon et al.(2022) deal with forgery localization by considering spliced objects of different shapes and sizes [14]. It uses dual JPEG detection of pre-trained DCT streams and JPEG artifacts to locate tampered regions. On the other hand, Haiwei Wu et al.(2023) use pixel-level contrastive learning to extract high-level features of an image [30]. The ReLoc framework [33] uses an image recovery module to identify and locate corrupted regions and further restore distorted tampered images.

Despite the good performance of these models, the challenges and limitations of detecting various forgeries remain. Therefore, this paper introduces ensemble learning to cope with the challenge.

2.2 Ensemble Learning

Ensemble learning is an effective method to improve model performance by combining various individual models [10]. Currently, ensemble learning has been employed in a wide range of applications (e.g., healthcare, speech systems, intrusion detection, image recognition) [23, 25–27]. Ensemble learning algorithms are at the heart of ensemble models and have been continuously developed. It can be broadly categorized into bagging, boosting, and stacking.

Boosting is an approach to convert weak models into a model with better generalization [10]. Its optimized algorithms are now widely used in various ensemble applications. AdaBoost [8] and GBDT [9] stand out as two mainly recognized boosting algorithms. Improved algorithms have been proposed by scholars in recent years, such as XGBoost [3], LightGBM [19], CatBoost [22], and NgBoost [7]. Stacking employs meta-learning techniques to improve model performance by fusing the outputs of heterogeneous models. Rajani et al.(2016) [24] introduced auxiliary features, confidence scores, and provenance, enhancing model accuracy.

Therefore, to address the challenge that a single model cannot detect various forgery images, we adopt a stacking-based ensemble approach combined with boosting to integrate multiple heterogeneous models for forgery image detection and localization.

3 Motivation

3.1 Design Goal

The design goal of EL-FDL is to **promote forgery detection performance while reducing the false positive rates**. Selecting the appropriate models and algorithms for the ensemble is the core of our work. Therefore, we have taken the following two paths to achieve our goals:

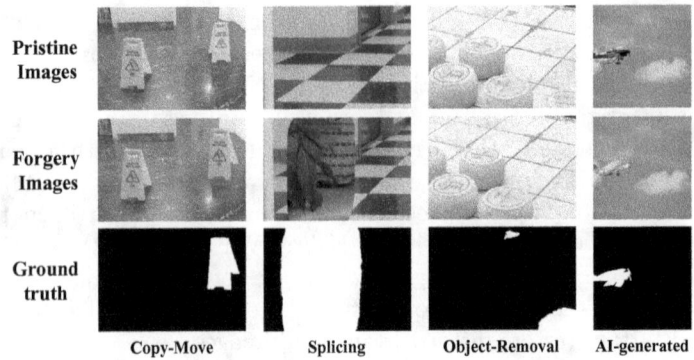

Fig. 2. Examples of different types of forgery images.

1. Select models: We experimented with existing models on various forgery datasets and chose the appropriate models for fusion by analyzing and comparing the performance of the models.
2. Select algorithms: We tried to apply various algorithms to the stacking ensemble and find apt algorithms to enable the ensemble model to have better detection performance in the face of multiple types of forgery images.

3.2 Threat Model

The attacker aims to generate forgery images(e.g., generate fake faces by GAN) for profit. Figure 2 shows examples of forgery types, and the definitions are also given below.

1. Copy-move forgery is a type of manipulation where a portion of an image is copied and pasted into the same image to form a new segment, which blends in with the surrounding area to create the illusion of a more complex scene.
2. Splicing forgery involves taking two or more images and merging them, to produce a realistic composite image.
3. Object-removal involves removing an object or region from an image and then replacing it with new content that is generally consistent with the surrounding area, intending to remove any information that could reveal the existence of the removed object or region.
4. AI-generated employs generative models such as GAN and diffusion models to create realistic but synthetic images for deceptive purposes.

Attackers often use one or more forgery image techniques for benefit fraud, and traditional detection models make it difficult to detect multiple forgeries simultaneously. Therefore, to address this challenge, we proposed EL-FDL, which aimed to detect various forgery types by an ensemble model.

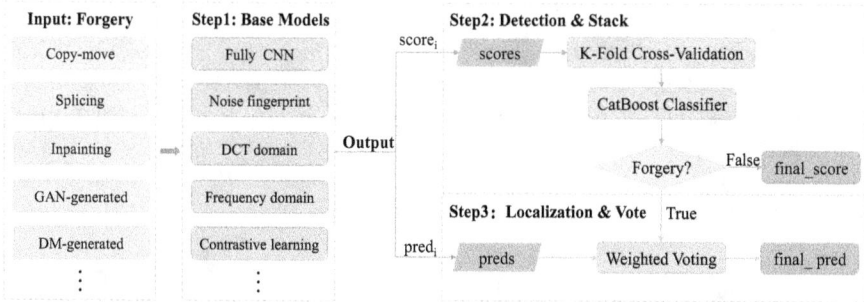

Fig. 3. The framework of EL-FDL. A variety of forgery images were first input into the base models. Base models will output the detection and localization results, namely $score_i$ and $pred_i$. The $scores$ will be first input into the detection module and given the final detection result $final\_score$ by the CatBoost classifier. Then, depending on the detection result, $preds$ will be input into the localization module and given the final localization result $final\_pred$ by voting.

4 Method

To tackle the challenge of detecting various types of forgery, we proposed an ensemble learning-based image forgery detection framework, EL-FDL.

This Section presents an overview of EL-FDL, illustrated in Fig. 3. Subsequent subsections will provide the details of each component. Initially, forgery images, are inputted. N base models, denoted as $\{L_1, L_2, \ldots, L_N\}$, are employed to detect forgery images. Each base model produces corresponding detection results, represented as $score_i$ or $pred_i$, where $score_i$ represents the forgery detection score output by base model L_i in the range $[0, 1]$. A score closer to 1 indicates a higher likelihood of forgery, while a score closer to 0 suggests a more pristine image. The $pred_i$ represents the predicted mask for locating forged regions, where 0 denotes real pixels and 1 denotes forged pixels. Next, the scores from all base models are concatenated into a matrix, denoted as $scores[N, 1]$, and fed into the image forgery detection module. This module outputs the final image forgery detection result in the range $[0, 1]$. If the result indicates pristine, the final detection score, denoted as $final\_score$, is outputted. If the result suggests forgery, the $pred_i$ values are concatenated into a matrix $preds[N, H, W]$, where each $pred_i$ has been pre-normalized to a size of 1024×1024. Finally, $preds[N, H, W]$ is inputted into the image forgery localization module, generating the final result, $final\_score$ for detection and $final\_pred$ for localization.

4.1 Base Models Layer

While single classifiers often exhibit excellent performance, they frequently suffer from drawbacks such as overfitting and insufficient generalization. In this module, we have aggregated various methods for simple and deep fake image detection and localization, aiming to empower ensemble learning models to cover an adequate range of image tampering types. We have standardized the input and output interfaces of all models, allowing for the detection of an image by simply inputting the detection image. Depending on the output type of each model, some models output only the confidence score, some only the localization mask, and some output both. These models are then concatenated in the order of their inputs, ultimately outputting $scores[N, 1]$ and $preds[N, H, W]$ for subsequent forgery detection and localization modules.

4.2 Forgery Detection Module

After the detection of the base model layer, we get the input $scores[N, 1]$ of the image forgery detection module, which represents the image-level forgery detection results of image x by N base models. It is only necessary to input the $scores[N, 1]$ into the meta-model, which the ensemble learning algorithm trains, to get the final forgery detection results.

Ensemble Method. The weak classifiers generated by bagging and boosting are isomorphic since the model structure varies across detection base models. Therefore, we cannot train the meta-model directly with the original dataset by bagging or boosting. Instead, we need to use the classification results of the base models as the training set to train the meta-model, which is called stacking. The integration by stacking does not affect the detection performance of the base models and produces a more powerful image detection meta-model.

Classification Algorithm. The choice of machine learning algorithms greatly impacts the generalization performance of Stacking. We are concerned that the number of features in the feature matrix of the stacking constructed meta-model is equal to the number of base models. However, there are usually only a few base models, so the feature matrix of the meta-model is often insufficient. When the meta-model is trained directly using traditional machine learning algorithms, the problem of overfitting often occurs.

To solve this problem, we introduce K-Fold Cross-Validation [29] to expand the feature matrix of the meta-model when training the model to improve its generalization performance. At the same time, we utilize the CatBoost [22] algorithm based on the GBDT [9] framework with ordered boosting and prediction shift mechanism and thus solve the problem of overfitting. Algorithm 1 presents workflow details in our ensemble framework.

4.3 Forgery Localization Module

Since the generalization of a single model is limited, we introduce a voting mechanism for localization ensemble. Traditional voting follows the majority rule to reduce variance but ignores the differences in model performance, so we introduce weight parameters to improve the voting method.

Algorithm 1. CatBoost application in EL-FDL

Input: Detection results and the labels $\{(\mathbf{x}_i, y_i)\}_{i=1}^n, I, \alpha, L, m, Mode$;
1: $\theta_t \leftarrow$ random permutation of $[1, n]$ for $t = 0..m$;
2: $M_0(i) \leftarrow 0$ for $i = 1..n$;
3: **if** $Mode = Plain$ **then**
4:     $M_t(i) \leftarrow 0$ for $t = 1..m, i : \theta_t(i) \leq 2^{j+1}$;
5: **end if**
6: **if** $Mode = Ordered$ **then**
7:     **for each** $j \in [1, \lceil \log_2 n \rceil]$ **do**
8:         $M_{t,j}(i) \leftarrow 0$ for $t = 1..m, i = 1..2^{j+1}$;
9:     **end for**
10: **end if**
11: **for each** $k \in [1, I]$ **do**
12:     $T_k, \{M_t\}_{t=1}^m \leftarrow BuildTree(\{M_t\}_{t=1}^m, \{(x_i, y_i)\}_{i=1}^n, \alpha, L, \{\theta_i\}_{i=1}^m, Mode)$;
13:     $leaf_0(i) \leftarrow GetLeaf(\mathbf{x}_i, T_k, \theta_0)$ for $i = 1..n$;
14:     $grad_0 \leftarrow CalcGradient(L, M_0, y)$;
15:     **for each** $leaf\ j$ in T_k **do**
16:         $b_j^k \leftarrow -avg(grad_0(i)$ for $i : leaf_0(i) = j)$;
17:     **end for**
18:     $M_0(i) \leftarrow M_0(i) + \alpha b_{leaf_0(i)}^k$ for $i = 1..n$;
19: **end for**
20: **return** $F(x) = \sum_{k=1}^I \sum_j \alpha b_j^k \mathbb{1}_{\{GetLeaf(\mathbf{x}, T_k, ApplyMode) = j\}}$;

The input of the localization module is denoted as $pred[N, H, W]$. For an image x, each pixel point is characterized by N channels, where the number of base models determines the value of N. Meanwhile, each base model is assigned a weight θ based on its performance in weighted voting. Usually, better-performing models receive a higher weight. Finally, we obtain the final prediction $final\_pred$ by calculating the weighted average of θ and $pred_i$.

$$final\_pred = \frac{1}{\sum_{i=1}^N \theta_i} \sum_{i=1}^N \theta_i \times pred_i \qquad (1)$$

5 Experiment

5.1 Experiment Setting

Unless otherwise noted, we used the same experimental setup and equipment to test the performance of the EL-FDL.

Training Datasets. We train the forgery detection model of EL-FDL using the 10000 forgery images of datasets tampCOCO [15], and the 2000 pristine images of IMD2020 [21]. We expanded IMD2020 to 10,000 images to ensure a balanced distribution of positive and negative samples.

Testing Datasets. We selected three commonly used public forgery image datasets, namely CASIA [6], Columbia [13], and Coverage [28]. These datasets contain copy-move and splicing, totaling 1203 forgery and 283 pristine images. Additionally, we included Defacto-inpainting including 20000 Object-Removals images from the DEFACTO [17], and CocoGlide [12] generated by diffusion models with 512 forgery and 512 pristine images.

Evaluation Metrics. We adopt the following metrics throughout the evaluation. **Accuracy(ACC)**: It characterizes the rate at which the classifier correctly classifies all samples, including positive and negative examples. **F1-score**: It is a metric that considers both precision and recall and provides a weighted harmonic mean of both measures to evaluate the accuracy of imbalanced datasets. **False Positive Rate (FPR)**: It characterizes the rate at which the classifier incorrectly classifies negative samples as positive. **Intersection over Union (IoU)**: It is a metric used in object detection that measures the overlap between the predicted and the ground-truth bounding boxes. It is calculated by dividing the intersection area between the two boxes by the union of both areas.

We utilize ACC, F1-score, and FPR to evaluate the image-level forgery detection ability. Meanwhile, employing F1-score and IoU to evaluate the pixel-level localization ability, with a preference for lower FPR indicating better performance and higher scores in other metrics being favorable. All metrics default to a threshold of 0.5 for consistency.

Implementation Details. We primarily utilized PyTorch deep learning framework to ensemble all methods, and the scikit-learn machine learning framework for training EL-FDL. 2 Xeon Gold 6226R(16C/2.90Ghz) and 2 NVIDIA RTX 3090 24GB were used for all experiments.

5.2 Experiment Results

We conducted extensive ensemble learning experiments for image-level forgery detection and pixel-level localization. After preliminary models and algorithms testing, we finally selected the following model for ensemble [5,12,14,16,30,31], and used CatBoost as the main ensemble algorithm. Detailed analysis of the experimental results will be provided in the subsequent sections.

Detection. Table 1 lists the ACC and F1-score for image-level forgery detection on the test dataset. We can observe that a single model might excel on one dataset, as seen in Trufor on Columbia, and PSCC-Net on CocoGide. However, their performance may need improvement on other datasets. For example, TruFor achieves only 11.8% and 20.8% and PSCC-Net only 1.6% and 2.7% on Defacto. In addition, CAT-Net is good at detecting splicing tampering types, so it performs well in CASIA, and Columbia datasets containing splicing. All the above results indicate the limitations of the generalization of a single model. In

Table 1. Image-level Accuracy and F1-score performance of image forgery detection. The best results are in **bold** and the second best results are in underlined.

Method	CASIA		Coverage		Columbia		Defacto		CocoGlide		Avg	
	ACC	F1	ACC	F1	ACC	F1	ACC	F1	ACC	F1	ACC	F1
CAT-Net [14]	0.908	0.951	0.635	0.640	0.802	0.831	**0.964**	**0.981**	0.520	0.548	0.766	0.790
TruFor [12]	0.680	0.810	0.690	0.581	**0.986**	**0.986**	0.118	0.208	0.644	0.498	0.624	0.617
MVSS-Net [5]	0.615	0.762	0.550	0.681	0.664	0.747	0.790	0.883	0.539	**0.654**	0.632	0.745
IF-OSN [31]	0.758	0.862	0.510	0.657	0.526	0.677	0.888	0.941	0.567	0.622	0.650	0.752
PSCC-Net [16]	0.372	0.541	0.550	0.297	0.504	0.667	0.016	0.027	**0.660**	0.528	0.420	0.412
EL-FDL(ours)	**0.961**	**0.980**	**0.975**	**0.975**	0.690	0.699	0.930	0.964	0.621	0.620	**0.835**	**0.848**

Table 2. Image-level forgery detection on some representative test images. ✓ represents a correct judgment, and ✗ represents an incorrect judgment.

Forgery Type	Image	Ground-truth	CAT-Net	TruFor	MVSS-Net	IF-OSN	PSCC-Net	EL-FDL(ours)
Splicing	Fig b	Fig b	✗	✓	✓	✓	✗	✓
Copy-Move	Fig b	Fig b	✓	✗	✗	✓	✓	✓
Inpainting	Fig b	Fig b	✗	✗	✓	✓	✗	✓
DM-generated	Fig b	Fig b	✓	✗	✓	✗	✗	✓

contrast, EL-FDL performs better on various datasets in different and same-type datasets. It outperforms the best-performing CAT-Net on average, improving ACC and F1 scores by +6.9% and +5.8%, respectively. Table 2 gives typical cases that cannot be fully detected by a single model but can be done by EL-FDL, which shows a better generalization of EL-FDL.

FPR (False Positives Rate). False positive rate is often focused on in statistics but is easily overlooked in machine learning due to the focus on accuracy. The false positive rate is significant in practical applications of forgery image detection, and an increase in the labor cost accompanies an increase in the false positive rate. From table reftab:image fpr, we observe that CAT-Net, MVSS-Net, and IF-OSN, which show high performance in the table (reftab:image ACC and F1), but have high FPR of 45.6%, 77.3% and 81.3%, respectively. Meanwhile, as can be seen from the data with * in the table, TruFor has a lower FPR of 11.7%, which is because its confidence map and integrity score mechanism reduce misclassification of the pristine image. However, the mechanisms also result in many forgery images not being successfully detected, so its accuracy remains low despite the low FPR. In contrast, the average FPR of EL-FDL is only 24.1%, which is much lower than all models except TruFor. Furthermore, we notice that the FPR of different models on different datasets varies(e.g., CAT-Net and MVSS-Net have relatively low FPR on the Columbia dataset, while PSCC-Net has relatively low FPR on Coverage and CocoGlide). Therefore, EL-FDL fuses the decision results of multiple models, tends to balance the performance of each model, and reduces the problem of a high positivity rate caused by a single model (Table 3).

Table 3. Image-level False Positives Rate performance in forgery detection.

Method	Columbia	Coverage	CocoGlide	Avg
CAT-Net [14]	0.377	0.380	0.611	0.456
TruFor [12]	0.036 *	0.150 *	0.166 *	0.117 *
MVSS-Net [5]	0.667	0.860	0.793	0.773
IF-OSN [31]	0.940	0.920	0.578	0.813
PSCC-Net [16]	0.984	**0.190**	**0.180**	0.451
EL-FDL	**0.005**	0.340	0.377	**0.241**

Table 4. Pixel-level F1-score and IoU performance of image forgery localization.

Method	CASIA		Coverage		Columbia		Defacto		CocoGlide		Avg	
	F1	IoU	F1	IoU	F1	IoU	F1	IoU	F1	IoU	F1	IoU
CAT-Net[14]	0.844	0.636	0.607	0.459	**0.852**	0.824	**0.702**	**0.585**	0.581	0.562	0.717	0.613
TruFor[12]	0.833	0.623	0.640	0.712	0.641	0.799	0.533	0.073	0.655	0.635	0.660	0.568
MVSS-Net[5]	0.707	0.397	0.628	0.667	0.695	0.744	0.495	0.010	0.597	0.609	0.624	0.485
IF-OSN[31]	0.741	0.465	0.526	0.504	0.606	0.708	0.484	0.010	0.624	0.575	0.596	0.452
PSCC-Net[16]	0.715	0.408	0.616	0.610	0.311	0.283	0.495	0.024	0.656	0.640	0.559	0.393
FOCAL[30]	**0.859**	**0.706**	0.670	**0.799**	0.690	0.842	0.622	0.210	0.533	0.595	0.675	0.630
EL-FDL (Hard)	0.802	0.578	**0.750**	0.713	0.754	0.872	0.548	0.088	**0.711**	0.619	0.713	0.574
EL-FDL (Weighted)	0.855	0.673	0.718	0.747	0.729	**0.879**	0.686	0.322	0.672	**0.643**	**0.732**	**0.653**

Localization. We conducted ensemble experiments for forgery localization using hard and weighted voting methods. Table 4 illustrates the pixel-level F1-score and IoU. In terms of average scores, Hard Voting has significantly outperformed all models except CAT-Net with an F1-score of 71.3%, and the IoU of 57.4% also shows improvement compared to other models such as TruFor, MVSS-Net, and IF-OSN. However, it is noteworthy that weaker models can still influence the hard voting method on specific datasets, such as Defacto, where most models underperform. In contrast, weighted voting allows us to make nuanced adjustments to models' weights, appropriately increasing the voting weight of outstanding models. Ultimately, the model outperformed all single models with 73.2% of F1 and 65.3% of IoU.

5.3 Ablation Study

Classification Algorithmic Comparison. To validate the machine learning classification algorithm chosen for the stacked ensemble model, we compared the commonly used classification algorithms KNN, DT, LogiR, and RF; all models were trained using default parameters. Table 5 indicates the results. On average scores, GBDT outperforms most other models with an ACC of 81.1% and an F1-score of 82.9%, while having the lowest FPR of 14.6%. Its ACC and F1-score

Table 5. Classification algorithmic comparison ablation results: Image-level ACC, F1-score, and FPR. The max ACC and F1 are in **bold** and the min FPR are underlined.

Alg.	CASIA		Columbia			Coverage			Defacto		CocoGlide			Avg		
	ACC	F1	ACC	FPR	F1	ACC	FPR	F1	ACC	F1	ACC	FPR	F1	ACC	FPR	F1
RF	0.878	0.935	**0.981**	0.025	**0.980**	0.680	0.190	0.584	0.688	0.815	**0.636**	0.339	0.533	0.773	0.185	0.769
DT	0.904	0.950	0.939	0.039	0.938	0.608	0.290	0.567	0.758	0.862	0.556	0.438	0.553	0.753	0.256	0.774
KNN	0.833	0.909	0.939	0.016	0.936	0.615	0.165	0.503	**0.864**	**0.927**	0.562	0.299	0.492	0.763	0.158	0.753
LogiR	**0.940**	**0.970**	0.970	0.016	0.959	**0.685**	0.370	**0.671**	0.830	0.907	0.589	0.439	0.584	**0.803**	0.275	**0.818**
GBDT	0.911	0.953	0.961	0.011	0.960	0.660	0.160	0.585	0.778	0.875	0.620	0.195	**0.643**	0.787	0.122	0.803

are 4.8% and 7.6% higher than the commonly used KNN algorithm, respectively. Although the ACC and F1-score of GBDT are not as good as those of LogiR, its FPR is much lower than that of LogiR. Therefore, given its performance metrics, it proves that our chosen GBDT algorithm has advantages for the training of the EL-FDL.

GBDT Optimisation. Optimization of the GBDT algorithm was attempted as the model is prone to overfitting due to the high learning capacity of GBDT. We finally used the GBDT-optimised Catboost [22] and compared it with several other GBDT-optimised algorithms, ngboost [7], lightgbm [19] and xgboost [3]. Table 6 shows the performance of each optimization algorithm on the test dataset. Compared to GBDT, XgBoost, LightGBM, and CatBoost, all have improved detection performance, but the false positive rates have also increased. Among these algorithms, CatBoost has the largest improvement in ACC and F1-score of 5.2% and 4.5% respectively, and the smallest increase in FPR of 11.9%. On the contrary, NgBoost shows a decrease of about 10% in detection and FPR compared to GBDT. It is demonstrated through experimental results that CatBoost has the greatest performance improvement in detection enhancement and false positive suppression. Meanwhile, NgBoost can significantly reduce the FPR, but a severe decline in detection capability accompanies it.

Table 6. GBDT optimization ablation results: Image-level ACC, F1-score and FPR.

Alg.	CASIA		Columbia			Coverage			Defacto		CocoGlide			Avg		
	ACC	F1	ACC	FPR	F1	ACC	FPR	F1	ACC	F1	ACC	FPR	F1	ACC	FPR	F1
GBDT	0.911	0.953	0.961	0.011	0.960	0.660	0.160	0.585	0.778	0.875	0.620	0.195	**0.643**	0.787	0.122	0.803
XgBoost	0.965	0.982	0.972	0.010	0.972	0.680	0.340	0.686	0.840	0.913	0.613	0.406	0.621	0.814	0.252	0.835
LightGBM	**0.973**	**0.986**	0.959	0.038	0.958	**0.695**	0.350	**0.708**	0.842	0.914	0.608	0.443	0.628	0.815	0.277	0.839
NgBoost	0.826	0.905	0.915	0.005	0.906	0.650	0.030	0.485	0.348	0.515	**0.625**	0.062	0.455	0.673	0.032	0.653
CatBoost	0.961	0.980	**0.975**	0.005	**0.975**	0.690	0.340	0.699	**0.930**	**0.964**	0.621	0.377	0.620	**0.835**	0.241	**0.848**

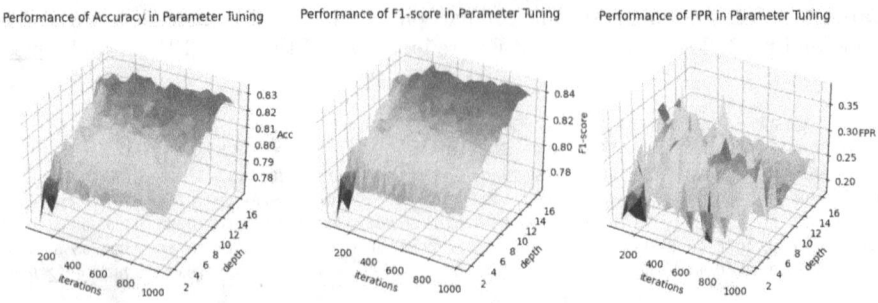

Fig. 4. Ablation results for fine-tuned *iteration* and *depth*: ACC, F1-score and FPR.

Parameter Finetune. The model parameters have a decisive impact on the model's performance. Therefore, we employed the Grid Search algorithm for optimal model parameters. CatBoost has many default parameters, such as *iterations*, $grow_{policy}$, *depth*, $min\_data\_in\_leaf$, max_leaves, etc. Through a series of experiments, we found that *iterations* and *depth* parameter values of the CatBoost model directly impacted the model's performance compared to other parameters. Specifically, we tried $iterationss = [50, 1001, 50]$ and $depth = [2, 17, 1]$. For each parameter set, we used 5-fold Cross-Validation to finetune the model. Figure 4 shows the tuning results. From the formula, $W = ACC + F1 - \frac{1}{2} \times FPR$, we determine that the model's performance was relatively optimal when $itrations = 300$ and $depth = 14$. In this case, the model's mean ACC and F1-score reached 83.5% and 84.8%, respectively, while the mean false positive rate was 24.1%.

6 Conclusion

In this paper, we propose EL-FDL, an efficient ensemble framework for image forgery detection and localization. We conducted extensive experiments that reveal the limitations of the existing SOTA methods, including insufficient generalization and high false positive rates. To tackle these limitations, we introduced stacking and Catboost for forgery detection and weighted voting for region localization. Our experimental results show that our ensemble model can better handle various types of forgery images compared to existing SOTA models, mainly in terms of +21.6 and +18.4%+ in average image-level ACC and F1-score, +9.3% and 12.9% in average pixel-level F1-score and IoU, and −21% decrease in FPR.

References

1. Bi, X., Wei, Y., Xiao, B., Li, W.: RRU-Net: the ringed residual u-net for image splicing forgery detection. In: 2019 IEEE/CVF Conference on Computer Vision and Pattern Recognition Workshops (CVPRW) (2019)
2. Chen, B., Qi, X., Wang, Y., Zheng, Y., Shim, H.J., Shi, Y.Q.: An improved splicing localization method by fully convolutional networks. IEEE Access **6**, 69472–69480 (2018)
3. Chen, T., Guestrin, C.: XGBoost: a scalable tree boosting system. In: Proceedings of the 22nd ACM SIGKDD International Conference on Knowledge Discovery and Data Mining (2016). https://api.semanticscholar.org/CorpusID:4650265
4. Corvi, R., Cozzolino, D., Zingarini, G., Poggi, G., Nagano, K., Verdoliva, L.: On the detection of synthetic images generated by diffusion models. In: IEEE International Conference on Acoustics, Speech and Signal Processing (ICASSP), pp. 1–5 (2023). https://doi.org/10.1109/ICASSP49357.2023.10095167
5. Dong, C., Chen, X., Hu, R., Cao, J., Li, X.: MVSS-Net: multi-view multi-scale supervised networks for image manipulation detection. IEEE Transactions on Pattern Analysis and Machine Intelligence, pp. 1–14 (2022). https://doi.org/10.1109/TPAMI.2022.3180556
6. Dong, J., Wang, W., Tan, T.: CASIA image tampering detection evaluation database. In: IEEE China Summit International Conference on Signal and Information Processing, pp. 422–426. IEEE (2013)
7. Duan, T., Anand, A., Ding, D.Y., Thai, K.K., Basu, S., Ng, A., Schuler, A.: NGBoost: natural gradient boosting for probabilistic prediction. In: International Conference on Machine Learning, pp. 2690–2700. PMLR (2020)
8. Freund, Y., Schapire, R.E.: A decision-theoretic generalization of on-line learning and an application to boosting. J. Comput. Syst. Sci. **55**(1), 119–139 (1997)
9. Friedman, J.H.: Greedy function approximation: a gradient boosting machine. Ann. Stat. **29**, 1189–1232 (2001)
10. Ganaie, M.A., Hu, M., Malik, A.K., Tanveer, M., Suganthan, P.N.: Ensemble deep learning: a review. Eng. Appl. Artif. Intell. **115**, 105151 (2022)
11. Goodfellow, I., et al.: Generative adversarial nets. In: Neural Information Processing Systems (2014)
12. Guillaro, F., Cozzolino, D., Sud, A., Dufour, N., Verdoliva, L.: TruFor: leveraging all-round clues for trustworthy image forgery detection and localization. In: Proceedings of the IEEE/CVF Conference on Computer Vision and Pattern Recognition (CVPR), pp. 20606–20615 (2023)
13. Hsu, Y., Chang, S.: Detecting image splicing using geometry invariants and camera characteristics consistency. In: IEEE International Conference on Multimedia and Expo, pp. 549–552. IEEE (2006)
14. Kwon, M.J., Nam, S.H., Yu, I.J., Lee, H.K., Kim, C.: Learning JPEG compression artifacts for image manipulation detection and localization. Int. J. Comput. Vision **130**(8), 1875–1895 (2022). https://doi.org/10.1007/s11263-022-01617-5
15. Lin, T.-Y., et al.: Microsoft COCO: common objects in context. In: Fleet, D., Pajdla, T., Schiele, B., Tuytelaars, T. (eds.) ECCV 2014. LNCS, vol. 8693, pp. 740–755. Springer, Cham (2014). https://doi.org/10.1007/978-3-319-10602-1_48
16. Liu, X., Liu, Y., Chen, J., Liu, X.: PSCC-Net: progressive spatio-channel correlation network for image manipulation detection and localization. IEEE Trans. Circ. Syst. Video Technol. **32**, 7505–7517 (2022)

17. Mahfoudi, G., Tajini, B., Retraint, F., Morain-nicolier, F., Dugelay, J.L., Pic, M.: DEFACTO: image and face manipulation dataset. In: 2019 27th European Signal Processing Conference (EUSIPCO), pp. 1–5 (2019). https://doi.org/10.23919/EUSIPCO.2019.8903181
18. Marra, F., Gragnaniello, D., Cozzolino, D., Verdoliva, L.: Detection of GAN-generated fake images over social networks. In: 2018 IEEE Conference on Multimedia Information Processing and Retrieval (MIPR) (2018)
19. Meng, Q.: LightGBM: a highly efficient gradient boosting decision tree. In: Neural Information Processing Systems (2017)
20. Nichol, A., et al.: GLIDE: towards photorealistic image generation and editing with text-guided diffusion models. arXiv preprint arXiv:2112.10741 (2021)
21. Novozámský, A., Mahdian, B., Saic, S.: Imd2020: A large-scale annotated dataset tailored for detecting manipulated images. In: 2020 IEEE Winter Applications of Computer Vision Workshops (WACVW), pp. 71–80 (2020). https://doi.org/10.1109/WACVW50321.2020.9096940
22. Prokhorenkova, L., Gusev, G., Vorobev, A., Dorogush, A.V., Gulin, A.: CatBoost: unbiased boosting with categorical features. In: Advances in Neural Information Processing Systems, vol. 31 (2018)
23. Rai, H.M., Chatterjee, K.: Hybrid CNN-LSTM deep learning model and ensemble technique for automatic detection of myocardial infarction using big ECG data. Appl. Intell. **52**(5), 5366–5384 (2022)
24. Rajani, N.F., Mooney, R.J.: Stacking with auxiliary features. arXiv preprint arXiv:1605.08764 (2016)
25. Tama, B.A., Lim, S.: Ensemble learning for intrusion detection systems: a systematic mapping study and cross-benchmark evaluation. Comput. Sci. Rev. **39**, 100357 (2021)
26. Tanveer, M., Rashid, A.H., Ganaie, M., Reza, M., Razzak, I., Hua, K.L.: Classification of Alzheimer's disease using ensemble of deep neural networks trained through transfer learning. IEEE J. Biomed. Health Inform. **26**(4), 1453–1463 (2021)
27. Wang, B., Xue, B., Zhang, M.: Particle swarm optimisation for evolving deep neural networks for image classification by evolving and stacking transferable blocks. In: 2020 IEEE Congress on Evolutionary Computation (CEC), pp. 1–8. IEEE (2020)
28. Wen, B., Zhu, Y., Subramanian, R., Ng, T.T., Winkler, S.: Coverage – a novel database for copy-move forgery detection. In: IEEE International Conference on Image Processing (2016)
29. Wong, T.-T.: Performance evaluation of classification algorithms by k-fold and leave-one-out cross validation. Pattern Recogn. **48**(9), 2839–2846 (2015)
30. Wu, H., Chen, Y., Zhou, J.: Rethinking image forgery detection via contrastive learning and unsupervised clustering. arXiv preprint arXiv:2308.09307 (2023)
31. Wu, H., Zhou, J., Tian, J., Liu, J.: Robust image forgery detection over online social network shared images. In: Proceedings of the IEEE/CVF Conference on Computer Vision and Pattern Recognition (CVPR), pp. 13440–13449 (2022)
32. Wu, Y., Abd-Almageed, W., Natarajan, P.: BusterNet: detecting copy-move image forgery with source/target localization. In: European Conference on Computer Vision (2018)
33. Zhuang, P., Li, H., Yang, R., Huang, J.: ReLoc: a restoration-assisted framework for robust image tampering localization. IEEE Transactions on Information Forensics and Security (2023)

Enhanced Image Manipulation Detection with TPB-Net: Integrating Triple-Path Backbone and Dual-Path Compressed Sensing Attention

Huaqing Song(✉)

Institute of Forensic Science, Ministry of Public Security,
Beijing, People's Republic of China
15298398611@163.com

Abstract. Tri-Path Backbone Network (TPB-Net) is introduced, trained end-to-end for effective detection of various image manipulations. Addressing the challenge of localizing image manipulations, which stems from the difficulty in extracting diverse forgery features, a Triple-path Interconnected Backbone (TIB) is employed for robust feature detection. The development of the Dual-path Compressed Sensing Attention (DCSA) module, featuring a dual-path attention mechanism, marks a significant advancement. This module efficiently compresses channels and spatial information, thereby enhancing learning efficiency, representation effectiveness, and model robustness. TPB-Net, an end-to-end framework with trainable modules, promotes joint optimization for optimal performance. Extensive experiments on four standard image manipulation datasets affirm TPB-Net's superior performance over existing state-of-the-art methods.

Keywords: Image forensics · Tampering localization · Triple-path Backbone · Dual-path Sensing Attention

1 Introduction

Digital images, vital in domains like media, social networks, and criminal investigations, are now facing a credibility crisis due to the easy access to tampering tools. This has led to serious social issues, such as the spread of seditious rumors, telecom fraud, academic misconduct, and the creation of false forensic evidence [1]. Common image manipulation techniques include copy-move, splicing, and inpainting, each altering the image's semantic content [2]. Copy-move replicates and moves a segment within the same image, while splicing transfers a segment from one image to another. Inpainting, or removal, replaces a part of the image with background pixels, erasing specific content. These techniques, often used maliciously, underscore the need for effective countermeasures in image manipulation detection.

Image manipulation typically leaves identifiable traces, leading to the development of algorithms targeting specific artifacts like resampling [6], median filtering [8], contrast adjustment [10], and double JPEG compression [12]. Although helpful, these methods are time-intensive and not always accurate [14]. Since each targets a specific artifact, multiple tests are required, making the process inefficient and error-prone, especially with the rise of new editing techniques.

Deep learning, thriving in pattern recognition and computer vision, has been applied to image forensics, yielding models that effectively localize manipulated image regions [15]. Image manipulation localization tasks (IMLTs) differ from standard image segmentation by focusing on regions not originally part of the image, emphasizing features like edge inconsistencies [15], noise patterns [20], color [21], and EXIF consistency [22]. These features, complex and varied, make IMLTs challenging compared to traditional segmentation tasks that rely on semantic information and edges.

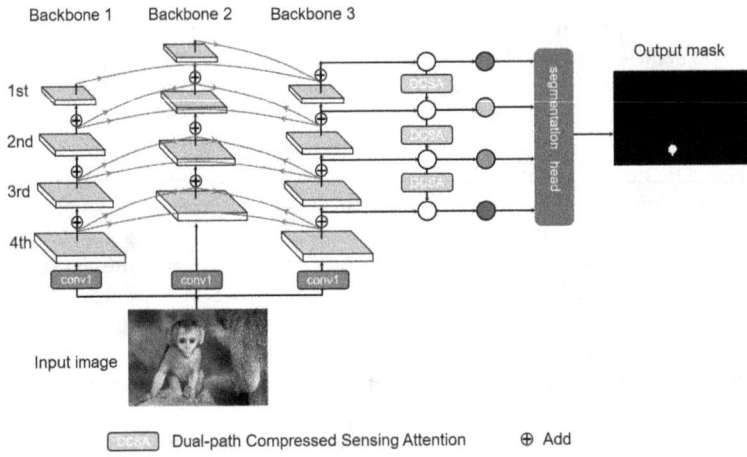

Fig. 1. Schematic of the Tri-Path Backbone Network (TPB-Net). This diagram illustrates the integration of a tri-path interconnected backbone designed to extract features from a raw image. Key components include the feature pyramid structure and the dual-path compressed sensing attention mechanism. The pyramid structure consolidates features at various scales, while the attention mechanism refines these features to enhance decision-making accuracy in image manipulation detection tasks. The output, a binary segmentation mask, clearly labels tampered areas, aiding in the accurate detection of manipulations

Building upon these insights, the Tri-Path Backbone Network (TPB-Net) is proposed for image manipulation localization. This approach utilizes a Triple-path Interconnected Backbone (TIB) to deliver potent feature detection capabilities. The resulting feature pyramid from TIB undergoes fusion and selection in subsequent networks, crucially focusing on minimizing semantic information while retaining non-semantic elements. Given that high-level, low-resolution features in the pyramid typically contain more semantic information [24], the fusion step incorporates a Dual-path Compressed Sensing Attention (DCSA) module. DCSA, distinct from the Dual Attention Network [25], employs a dual-path attention mechanism, compressing channels in the spatial path and spatial information in the channel path. These operations not only boost learning and representation efficiency but also enhance the model's robustness. TPB-Net, an integrated end-to-end framework with trainable modules, supports joint optimization for peak performance. Key contributions include:

- We introduce an innovative TPB-Net designed specifically for image manipulation localization, showing a robust capability for extracting and selecting prominent features. The structure of TPB-Net is illustrated in Fig. 1
- We developed a robust backbone network that excels in feature mining, complemented by an attention mechanism designed for effective feature filtering.
- Extensive experiment results conducted on public datasets unequivocally demonstrate the remarkable superiority of TPB-Net over the existing state-of-the-art methods.

2 The Proposed Methodology

The core concept of our methodology can be encapsulated in three key steps: Initially, a robust feature extractor is developed to capture a comprehensive array of features. This is followed by the integration of a module specifically designed to refine these features, primarily through the suppression of semantic information. The final decision-making process is then based on these refined features.

2.1 Overview

The schematic of our approach is depicted in Fig. 1. Our method distinctively relies on the raw image alone as the input, consciously excluding additional elements like noise patterns [23] and DCT [30]. This choice is underpinned by the idea that a sophisticated feature extractor is adept at discerning the necessary features directly from the raw image. Accordingly, the raw image is inputted into our custom-developed Triple-path Interconnected Backbone (TIB), comprising three DenseNet169 networks. The TPB (Tri-Path Backbone) enhances feature extraction by amalgamating feature maps from DenseNet169 after each block, resulting in a rich, diverse features. A feature pyramid structure is then employed, integrating features across various levels. An important aspect of this integration is the preservation of minimal semantic information at all scales. Recognizing that higher-level feature maps typically harbor more semantic content, our DCSA attention mechanism is incorporated within the top-down pathway to ensure efficient feature selection. The final decision is based on these meticulously fused features.

In contrast to using separate backbone networks, we employ three to obtain more diverse and comprehensive features. The output features from the previous (L_{th}) block of the three backbones (B_1, B_2, B_3) are summed and passed to L_{th}

block of each backbone. This process can be formulated as follows:

$$x^L = \sum_{k=1}^{3} F_k^L(x_1^L + x_2^{L-1} + x_2^{L-1}) \quad (1)$$

As a result, each individual backbone shares and collectively contributes to the feature maps between blocks. The obtained feature maps from different levels are fed into the following network. Given that this composition style utilizes three individual backbones and facilitates internal interconnections among them, we refer to it as the Triple-path interconnected backbone.

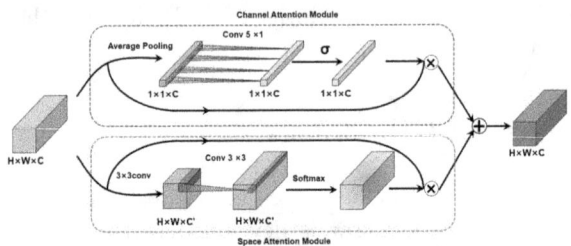

Fig. 2. The diagram of the Dual-Path Compressed Sensing Attention (DCSA). DCSA adopts a parallel structure, with the upper branch is channel attention and the lower branch is spatial attention. The innovation of DA lies in the adoption of compression cross interaction in both branches

2.2 DCSA for Feature Selection

Our method utilizes a feature pyramid, illustrated in Fig. 1, for multi-stage feature extraction. This pyramid enhances the model's capacity to capture and represent multi-scale information, thereby improving performance. However, it also introduces the challenge of managing excessive semantic information, particularly from the high-level, semantically-rich feature maps of the original Feature Pyramid Networks [31]. To mitigate this, our Dual-path Compressed Sensing Attention (DCSA) is integrated, specifically designed to filter out such unnecessary semantics.

DCSA, shown in Fig. 2, adopts a dual-branch structure similar to DAnet [25], focusing on both channel and spatial information. For channel attention, the model employs the Efficient Channel Attention (ECA) method [32], starting with feature aggregation via average pooling and leading to channel weight generation through a 1D convolution (kernel size 5) and sigmoid activation. The specifics of this process are outlined in the following equation:

$$X_C = o(Conv_{5 \times 1}(MaxPool(X_{input}))) \times X_{input} \quad (2)$$

The process involves X_{input} as the input and X_C as the output of the channel module. This module applies dimensionality reduction and facilitates interaction across channels. The space module, illustrated in the lower part of Fig. 2, begins by compressing features through a 3 × 3 2D convolution. Spatial weights are then generated using another 3 × 3 2D convolution, this time coupled with a softmax activation function. The spatial branch also reduces channel dimensionality while enabling interaction across spatial elements. The computational steps of the space module are outlined as follows:

$$X_s = \text{SoftMax}(\text{Conv}_{3\times3}(\text{Conv}_{3\times3}(X_{input}))) \times X_{input} \quad (3)$$

where X_S is the output of the space module. Hence the output X_{output} of the DCSA equals:

$$X_{out} = X_c + X_s \quad (4)$$

Both modules utilize dimensionality reduction and cross-interaction techniques, effectively simplifying the model's complexity without compromising its performance.

3 Experiments

This section details experiments carried out on four unique image manipulation datasets, designed to assess the efficacy of our TPB-Net. The results obtained from these experiments are then benchmarked against other leading state-of-the-art (SOTA) methods.

3.1 Experimental Setup

Table 1. Training and testing splits, along with the corresponding number of images, for the four standard datasets

Datasets	CASIA	COVERAGE	NIST16	Columbia
Training	5123	75	404	0
Testing	920	25	160	180

Datasets. Building upon the methodology presented in [41], we utilize the synthetic dataset suggested in [41] for pretraining. And we employ four well-known benchmarks, namely CASIA [33], COVERAGE [34], Nist Nimble 2016 (NIST16)[1], and Columbia [35] datasets, to evaluate our approach against state-of-the-art (SOTA) methods in manipulation detection. The division of the datasets is shown in Table 1.

---
[1] https://www.nist.gov/itl/iad/mig/nimble-challenge-2017-evaluation/.

Evaluation Metric. In this study, the focus is on binary segmentation, assigning each pixel in the input image a label as either tampered (white) or authentic (black). This process creates 2-dimensional binary arrays matching the input image's dimensions. To assess performance and facilitate comparisons, two evaluation metrics are employed: the pixel-level F1 score and the Area Under the receiver operating Characteristic Curve (AUC). Notably, while many previous studies fine-tune the decision threshold for the F1 score using the test set, this research takes a different approach. Recognizing the difficulty of identifying the optimal threshold for tampered images in real-world situations, a fixed threshold of 0.5 is used. This approach ensures a more objective comparison of performance across various methods, eliminating potential biases that might arise from threshold adjustments.

3.2 Results

Table 2. Comparison of our method with four SOTA methods on CASIA, NIST16, Columbia, and Coverage. We evaluated the AUC and F1 (%) metrics to assess the effectiveness of our approach

Datasets	CASIA		Coverage		NIST16		Columbia	
	AUC	F1	AUC	F1	AUC	F1	AUC	F1
ManTra-Net	75.2	40.6	77.5	40.9	91.2	60.7	73.5	52.1
SPAN	77.2	42.4	76.6	41.2	91.1	58.8	81.1	48.8
CAT-Net	72.4	31.2	70.2	32.6	87.5	42.8	73.3	49.7
MVSS-Net	76.8	42.8	78.9	42.1	89.1	61.2	76.4	53.4
Ours	**83.5**	**65.0**	**89.6**	**65.1**	**95.1**	**91.1**	**89.4**	**70.2**

Comparison with the State-of-Arts. To assess our approach's effectiveness, we compared its performance with baseline models, including ManTra-Net [16], SPAN [19], CAT-Net [30], and MVSS-Net [24]. The evaluation involved a two-step training process, carefully chosen based on prior successful applications in image manipulation detection. Initially, the model underwent pre-training on a synthetic dataset, designed to familiarize it with a broad spectrum of manipulations that might not be well-represented in real-world datasets. This approach is inspired by similar strategies in prior works which demonstrated that such pre-training can significantly enhance model robustness and adaptability [41]. Subsequent fine-tuning was carried out on CASIA, COVERAGE, and NIST16 datasets to tailor the model's response to specific characteristics of real-world data. Notably, the COLUMBIA dataset served exclusively for validation purposes, to assess the generalization capabilities of the model outside its training context. This structured training methodology ensures a comprehensive learning

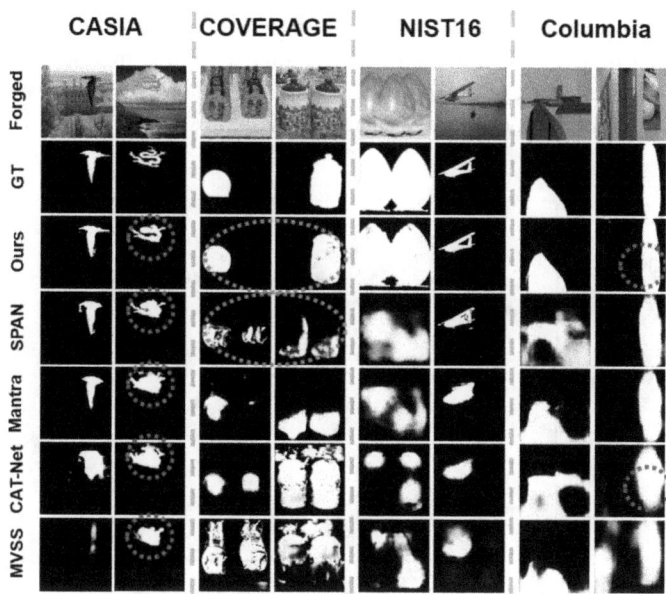

Fig. 3. Comparison of prediction results on CASIA, Coverage, NIST16, and Columbia datasets. From top to bottom: Manipulated Image, Ground-truth mask, SFEN prediction, SPAN prediction, Mantra-Net prediction, CAT-Net prediction, MVSS prediction

process, addressing both broad and specific manipulation scenarios. Pixel-level localization results, detailed in Table 2, reveal our method's clear edge over others, with significant score improvements.

Our method's AUC scores on all datasets show a substantial increase of 4–10%, exceeding 83%. Particularly noteworthy are the results on Coverage, NIST16, and Columbia, with AUC scores above 89%. TPB-Net, utilizing the Triple-path Interconnected Backbone (TIB), excels in extracting a broader and more diverse range of features compared to single-backbone architectures, leading to better localization accuracy. However, the AUC score for CASIA is slightly lower at 83.5%, possibly due to the cross-dataset training between CASIAv1 and CASIAv2.

The F1 score improvement is even more remarkable, nearly 20% higher than the AUC gain. This improvement is attributed to our method's ability to generate prediction masks with clear distinction, as shown in Fig. 3. Unlike other models [24], TPB-Net's high F1 score does not depend on an optimal threshold. The inclusion of the Dual-path Compressed Sensing Attention (DCSA) module in our model plays a crucial role in this success, filtering out irrelevant information and providing precise features for more accurate decision-making.

Number of Backbones in Interconnected Backbones. Experiments were carried out to investigate how the number of backbones in the TIB structure impacts performance. The dataset and training methodology employed remained consistent with prior experiments, with the outcomes depicted in Fig. 4.

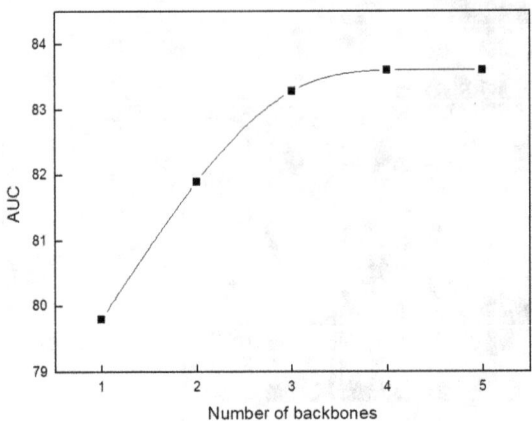

Fig. 4. Comparison results by using different number of backbones in TPB-Net

It was noted that the AUC score consistently rises with an increasing number of backbones, eventually stabilizing upon incorporating three backbones. This observation led to the selection of the Triple Backbone architecture, which offers the best performance in terms of AUC score.

The Influence of DCSA. To assess the extent of improvement DCSA brings to the final performance, ablation studies were performed comparing scenarios with and without DCSA in our framework. For comparison, element-wise addition was employed. It was observed that when using addition, the AUC score decreased by 2.4 points compared to the implementation with DCSA.

To gain a deeper insight, we visually examined and compared the feature maps extracted by the backbone using both the DCSA and the add operation. Figure 5 showcases examples with input images featuring a single tampered region. The visual comparison reveals that the feature maps display more pronounced activation values in the tampered areas when DCSA is implemented, as opposed to the add operation. This illustrative comparison underscores the effectiveness of DCSA in delivering more representative features for the task at hand.

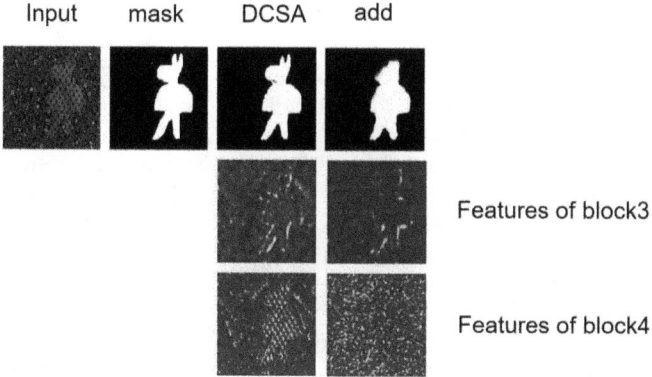

Fig. 5. Visualization comparison of the features extracted by backbone when DSCA or add operation is employed. We visualize the feature maps of 3rd and 4th block of the backbone as marked in Fig. 1. Notably, the feature maps exhibit more representational qualities when DSCA is employed, as evidenced by their stronger activation values and clearer boundaries

4 Conclusion

In conclusion, the Tri-Path Backbone Network (TPB-Net) is introduced as a novel and effective approach for localizing image manipulations. TPB-Net incorporates the Triple-path Interconnected Backbone (TIB) to bolster feature detection. A feature pyramid derived from TIB is further exploited for fusion and selection in subsequent network stages. A pivotal component of TPB-Net is the deliberate reduction of semantic content while retaining non-semantic elements, achieved via the Dual-path Compressed Sensing Attention (DCSA) module. This module employs a dual-path attention mechanism to compress both channel and spatial information, thereby increasing learning efficiency, enhancing representation quality, and boosting model robustness. Decisions are based on this refined structure. TPB-Net presents a comprehensive end-to-end framework with trainable modules, facilitating joint optimization for peak performance. This method has proven its accuracy and robustness in various general image manipulation localization tasks.

Acknowledgement. This work was supported in part by the Ministry of Science and Technology of the People's' Republic of China (Grant No. 2023YFC3303702), the Institute of Forensic Science of the Ministry of Public Security (Grant No. 2022JB024), the Ministry of Public Security of the People's Republic of China (Grant No. 2022JC16).

Disclosure of Interests. The author declares that he has no conflict of interest.

References

1. Zampoglou, M., Papadopoulos, S., Kompatsiaris, Y.: Large-scale evaluation of splicing localization algorithms for web images. Multimedia Tools Appl. **76**(4), 4801–4834 (2017)
2. Bappy, J.H., Roy-Chowdhury, A.K., Bunk, J., Nataraj, L., Manjunath, B.S.: Exploiting spatial structure for localizing manipulated image regions. In: Proceedings of the IEEE International Conference on Computer Vision, pp. 4980–4989. IEEE Computer Society, Venice, Italy (2017)
3. Bappy, J.H., Simons, C., Nataraj, L., Manjunath, B.S., Roy-Chowdhury, A.K.: Hybrid LSTM and encoder-decoder architecture for detection of image forgeries. IEEE Trans. Image Process. **28**(7), 3286–3300 (2019)
4. Mahfoudi, G., Tajini, B., Retraint, F., Morain-Nicolier, F., Dugelay, J.-L., Pic, M.: DEFACTO: image and face manipulation dataset. In: Proceedings of the 27th European Signal Processing Conference, pp. 1–5. IEEE, Spain (2019)
5. Verdoliva, L.: Media forensics and DeepFakes: an overview. IEEE J. Sel. Topics Signal Process. **14**(5), 910–932 (2020)
6. Popescu, A.C., Farid, H.: Exposing digital forgeries by detecting traces of resampling. IEEE Trans. Signal Process. **53**(2), 758–767 (2005)
7. Kirchner, M.: Fast and reliable resampling detection by spectral analysis of fixed linear predictor residue. In: Proceedings of the 10th Workshop on Multimedia & Security, pp. 11–20. ACM, Oxford, UK (2008)
8. Kirchner, M., Fridrich, J.J.: On detection of median filtering in digital images. In: Proceedings of the Media Forensics and Security II, vol. 7541, p. 754110. SPIE, San Jose, CA, USA (2010)
9. Kang, X., Stamm, M.C., Peng, A., Liu, K.J.R.: Robust median filtering forensics using an autoregressive model. IEEE Trans. Inf. Forensics Secur. **8**(9), 1456–1468 (2013)
10. Stamm, M.C., Liu, K.J.R.: Forensic detection of image manipulation using statistical intrinsic fingerprints. IEEE Trans. Inf. Forensics Secur. **5**(3), 492–506 (2010)
11. Yao, H., Wang, S., Zhang, X.: Detect piecewise linear contrast enhancement and estimate parameters using spectral analysis of image histogram. In: Proceedings of the IET International Communication Conference on Wireless Mobile and Computing, pp. 94–97. IET, Shanghai, China (2009)
12. Bianchi, T., Piva, A.: Detection of non-aligned double JPEG compression with estimation of primary compression parameters. In: Proceedings of the 18th IEEE International Conference on Image Processing, pp. 1929–1932. IEEE, Brussels, Belgium (2011)
13. Bianchi, T., Piva, A.: Image forgery localization via block-grained analysis of JPEG artifacts. IEEE Trans. Inf. Forensics Secur. **7**(3), 1003–1017 (2012)
14. Bayar, B., Stamm, M.C.: Constrained convolutional neural networks: a new approach towards general purpose image manipulation detection. IEEE Trans. Inf. Forensics Secur. **13**(11), 2691–2706 (2018)
15. Salloum, R., Ren, Y., Kuo, C.-C.J.: Image splicing localization using a multi-task fully convolutional network (MFCN). J. Vis. Commun. Image Represent. **51**, 201–209 (2018)
16. Wu, Y., AbdAlmageed, W., Natarajan, P.: ManTra-Net: manipulation tracing network for detection and localization of image forgeries with anomalous features. In: Proceedings of the IEEE Conference on Computer Vision and Pattern Recognition, pp. 9543–9552. Computer Vision Foundation/IEEE, Long Beach, CA, USA (2019)

17. Zhou, P., et al.: Generate, segment, and refine: towards generic manipulation segmentation. In: Proceedings of the AAAI Conference on Artificial Intelligence, vol. 34, no. 07, pp. 13058–13065. AAAI (2020)
18. Yang, C., Li, H., Lin, F., Jiang, B., Zhao, H.: Constrained R-CNN: a general image manipulation detection model. In: Proceedings of the IEEE International Conference on Multimedia and Expo, pp. 1–6. IEEE, London, UK (2020)
19. Hu, X., Zhang, Z., Jiang, Z., Chaudhuri, S., Yang, Z., Nevatia, R.: SPAN: spatial pyramid attention network for image manipulation localization. In: Proceedings of the 16th European Conference on Computer Vision, vol. 12366, pp. 312–328. Springer, Cham (2020). https://doi.org/10.1007/978-3-030-58589-1_19
20. Lyu, S., Pan, X., Zhang, X.: Exposing region splicing forgeries with blind local noise estimation. Int. J. Comput. Vision **110**(2), 202–221 (2014)
21. Fan, Y., Carré, P., Fernandez-Maloigne, C.: Image splicing detection with local illumination estimation. In: Proceedings of the IEEE International Conference on Image Processing, pp. 2940–2944. IEEE, Quebec City, QC, Canada (2015)
22. Huh, M., Liu, A., Owens, A., Efros, A.A.: Fighting fake news: image splice detection via learned self-consistency. In: Ferrari, V., Hebert, M., Sminchisescu, C., Weiss, Y. (eds.) ECCV 2018. LNCS, vol. 11215, pp. 106–124. Springer, Cham (2018). https://doi.org/10.1007/978-3-030-01252-6_7
23. Zhou, P., Han, X., Morariu, V.I., Davis, L.S.: Learning rich features for image manipulation detection. In: Proceedings of the IEEE Conference on Computer Vision and Pattern Recognition, pp. 1053–1061. Computer Vision Foundation/IEEE Computer Society, Salt Lake City, UT, USA (2018)
24. Dong, C., Chen, X., Hu, R., Cao, J., Li, X.: MVSS-Net: multi-view multi-scale supervised networks for image manipulation detection. IEEE Trans. Pattern Anal. Mach. Intell. (2022)
25. Fu, J., et al.: Dual attention network for scene segmentation. In: Proceedings of the IEEE/CVF Conference on Computer Vision and Pattern Recognition, pp. 3146–3154 (2019)
26. Zhuang, P., Li, H., Tan, S., Li, B., Huang, J.: Image tampering localization using a dense fully convolutional network. IEEE Trans. Inf. Forensics Secur. **16**, 2986–2999 (2021)
27. Zhu, H., Cao, G., Zhao, M.: Effective image tampering localization via semantic segmentation network. arXiv preprint arXiv:2208.13739 (2022)
28. Liu, Y., et al.: CBNet: a novel composite backbone network architecture for object detection. In: Proceedings of the AAAI Conference on Artificial Intelligence, vol. 34, no. 07, pp. 11653–11660 (2020)
29. Woo, S., Park, J., Lee, J.-Y., Kweon, I.S.: CBAM: convolutional block attention module. In: Ferrari, V., Hebert, M., Sminchisescu, C., Weiss, Y. (eds.) ECCV 2018. LNCS, vol. 11211, pp. 3–19. Springer, Cham (2018). https://doi.org/10.1007/978-3-030-01234-2_1
30. Kwon, M.-J., Yu, I.-J., Nam, S.-H., Lee, H.-K.: CAT-Net: compression artifact tracing network for detection and localization of image splicing. In: Proceedings of the IEEE/CVF Winter Conference on Applications of Computer Vision, pp. 375–384 (2021)
31. Lin, T.-Y., Dollár, P., Girshick, R., He, K., Hariharan, B., Belongie, S.: Feature pyramid networks for object detection. In: Proceedings of the IEEE Conference on Computer Vision and Pattern Recognition, pp. 2117–2125 (2017)
32. Wang, Q., Wu, B., Zhu, P., Li, P., Zuo, W., Hu, Q.: ECA-Net: efficient channel attention for deep convolutional neural networks. In: Proceedings of the IEEE/CVF Conference on Computer Vision and Pattern Recognition, pp. 11534–11542 (2020)

33. Dong, J., Wang, W., Tan, T.: CASIA image tampering detection evaluation database. In: 2013 IEEE China Summit and International Conference on Signal and Information Processing, pp. 422–426. IEEE (2013)
34. Wen, B., Zhu, Y., Subramanian, R., Ng, T.-T., Shen, X., Winkler, S.: COVERAGE-a novel database for copy-move forgery detection. In: 2016 IEEE International Conference on Image Processing (ICIP), pp. 161–165. IEEE (2016)
35. Ng, T.-T., Hsu, J., Chang, S.-F.: Columbia image splicing detection evaluation dataset. DVMM lab. Columbia Univ CalPhotos Digit Libr (2009)
36. He, K., Zhang, X., Ren, S., Sun, J.: Delving deep into rectifiers: surpassing human-level performance on ImageNet classification. In: Proceedings of the IEEE International Conference on Computer Vision, pp. 1026–1034 (2015)
37. Kingma, D.P., Ba, J.: Adam: a method for stochastic optimization. arXiv preprint arXiv:1412.6980 (2014)
38. El Biach, F.Z., Iala, I., Laanaya, H., Minaoui, K.: Encoder-decoder based convolutional neural networks for image forgery detection. Multimedia Tools Appl. **81**, 1–18 (2021)
39. Jadon, S.: A survey of loss functions for semantic segmentation. In: 2020 IEEE Conference on Computational Intelligence in Bioinformatics and Computational Biology (CIBCB), pp. 1–7. IEEE (2020)
40. Liu, X., Liu, Y., Chen, J., Liu, X.: PSCC-Net: progressive spatio-channel correlation network for image manipulation detection and localization. IEEE Trans. Circuits Syst. Video Technol. **32**(11), 7505–7517 (2022)
41. Bappy, J.H., Roy-Chowdhury, A.K., Bunk, J., Nataraj, L., Manjunath, B.S.: Exploiting spatial structure for localizing manipulated image regions. In: Proceedings of the IEEE International Conference on Computer Vision, pp. 4970–4979 (2017)

Generalizable Deepfake Detection with Unbiased Feature Extraction and Low-Level Forgery Enhancement

Zhihan Yu, JiaXin Li, Guangshuo Wang, Yuesheng Zhu(✉), and Guibo Luo(✉)

Institute of Electronic and Computer Engineering, Peking University, Beijing, China
{zhuys,luogb}@pku.edu.cn

Abstract. Deepfake detection has recently become an urgent issue since the deepfake technology has raised security concerns in society. However, current deepfake detection methods exist susceptibility when encountering unseen data, limiting their generalization ability. In this paper, we propose a straightforward yet effective framework of deepfake detection based on unbiased feature extraction and low-level forgery enhancement (UFELE). Obtaining unbiased features utilizing frozen Visual Foundation Models, we devise a Low-level Forgery Feature Enhancement (LFFE) module to extract and enhance the low-level features from the frozen intermediate block. Also, an Adaptive Feature Fusion (AFF) module is designed to amalgamate the enhanced low-level forgery features with the high-level semantic features flexibly. Extensive experiments on several datasets illustrate that our proposed method has better detection performance than the state-of-the-art methods in terms of generalizability and robustness.

Keywords: Face forgery detection · DeepFake detection · Visual foundation models

1 Introduction

Over the past few years, face manipulation (or deepfake) technology has developed rapidly. Concurrently, an increasing number of manipulated images are becoming widespread across the internet. These manipulated images are challenging to discern, even for human observers. They may lead to severe social issues and political threats if exploited maliciously. Even worse, they can originate from diverse sources or be generated by various manipulation methods, and there will undoubtedly be more forged forms in the future. Hence, developing deepfake detection methods with strong generalization abilities is increasingly crucial.

Most existing deepfake detection methods train deep neural networks on a particular set of real and fake images to perform binary classification [4,19,24,25]. These methods often achieve satisfactory results in detecting seen data learned in the training datasets (in-dataset evaluations). However, their performance usually dramatically declines when facing unseen data from different manipulation techniques. Research [16] attributes these methods' poor generalization ability to the learning-based framework, which biases the classifier's decision boundary towards specific fake domains during training. In real-world scenarios, the classifier tends to categorize all images generated through other manipulation methods different from the biased fake domains as real, which significantly hinders the models' generalizability. We aim to alleviate this issue by extracting features devoid of bias towards any specific domain. Visual Foundation Models (VFMs), such as Contrastive Language-Image Pre-training (CLIP), are capable of this purpose [16]. They ensure the obtained image features are unbiased since they have not been trained on any particular deepfake dataset. Moreover, they can capture more generalizable image features, benefiting from their training on a vast number of images. Another key to improving the generalizability of deepfake detection lies in discerning subtle artifacts between authentic and forgery images. Previous studies have shown that the artifacts are often more prominent in lower-level features [28]. Therefore, relying solely on high-level semantic features from the final layer for detection is limited.

Building upon these insights, we propose a framework called UFELE, leveraging unbiased features and low-level forgery feature enhancement for frame-level detection. We extract image representations using the VFMs, preventing the features from biasing toward any specific domain. Typically, the final output of the encoder consists of high-level semantic features. We design two modules to utilize low-level information simultaneously. Firstly, we introduce a Low-level Forgery Feature Enhancement (LFFE) module to extract and enhance the low-level forgery features. Subsequently, based on the attention mechanism, we devise an Adaptive Feature Fusion (AFF) module to integrate the low-level forgery features with the high-level semantic features. The AFF module adaptively selects and fuses the low-level and high-level features by generating attention maps for them, ensuring the maximal preservation of their respective informative characteristics.

The main contributions are summarized as follows:

- We propose a framework named UFELE for deepfake detection, which extracts unbiased features utilizing frozen VFMs, promoting generalizable deepfake detection.
- Based upon unbiased features, we design two novel modules, LFFE and AFF, to enhance the low-level forgery features and adaptively amalgamate them with the high-level semantic features, which is conducive to highlighting subtle artifacts.
- Experiment results demonstrate that our method not only exhibits excellent generalizability and robustness but also showcases applicability across diverse VFMs.

2 Related Work

2.1 Deepfake Detection Methods

Early deepfake detection methods mainly utilize handcrafted features for detection. For example, Li et al. [11] detect differences between real and fake images in the residual domain of chrominance components of HSV and YCbCr color spaces. Some works employ photo response non-uniformity [10] and PixelHop++ units [1] for detection. However, these methods are vulnerable to combating emerging manipulation techniques.

Deep learning has become the primary paradigm for current deepfake detection, and the model's generalization ability on unseen data is an urgent issue that needs to be addressed. Various methods adopt the attention mechanism to focus on more suspect areas. Zhao et al. [28] introduce multiple spatial attention heads and the regional independence loss for paying attention to different local parts. Wang et al. [25] use the attention mechanism for data augmentation, obscuring facial areas that the detector pays more attention to, guiding the detector to explore more representative forgery clues. Furthermore, to concentrate on local regions, which are more likely to contain subtle artifacts, some studies model the relationships between different patches [2,29], detecting fake images by measuring the self-consistency of features in different local regions. Dong et al. [4] harness multi-scale anchors to focus on local regions and learn generalizable artifact features. Some methods introduce frequency information [2,9,19,26] or noise residuals [23] to enhance the model's generalization ability and robustness. Nevertheless, these methods still need to improve in generalizability.

2.2 Visual Foundation Models

Visual Foundation Models (VFMs) have taken the computer vision field by storm. Among these models, CLIP [20] stands as one of the most influential in Vision-Language Pre-training. CLIP employs contrastive learning and trains on extensive 400 million image-text pairs, enabling exceptional performance even in zero-shot scenarios. In addition, DINOv2 [17], which is based on the Vision Transformer, learns visual representations via self-supervised training on unlabeled images, further closing the performance gap with supervised methods. The CNN-based InternImage [27] adaptively adjusts the sampling offsets and modulation scalars using dynamic sparse convolution operators, providing robust representations for visual perception.

There are works utilizing VFMs for forgery detection. Ojha et al. [16] explore the application of CLIP in fake image detection, achieving outstanding results in generalization ability. In this paper, we mainly leverage the frozen CLIP Visual Encoder to extract unbiased image representations and enhance the low-level forgery features.

3 Method

In this section, we describe our proposed UFELE framework in detail. As depicted in Fig. 1, we obtain unbiased features using the frozen CLIP Visual Transformer, which is assumed to comprise N blocks. Initially, we design a Low-level Forgery Feature Enhancement (LFFE) module to extract and enhance the low-level forgery features from the intermediate block. Subsequently, our Adaptive Feature Fusion (AFF) module facilitates the adaptive fusion of the enhanced low-level forgery features with the high-level semantic features.

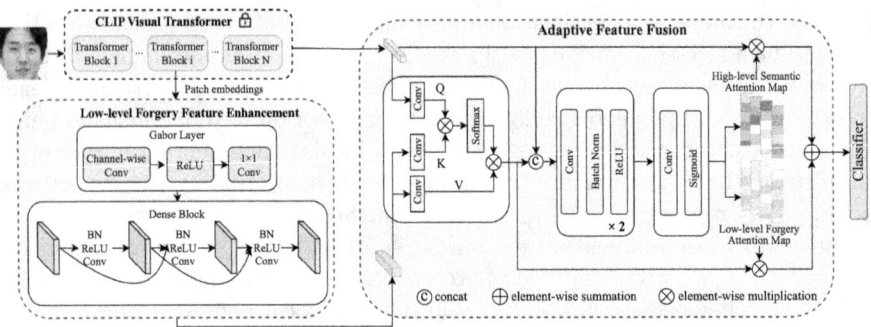

Fig. 1. Overview of our framework. We obtain unbiased features leveraging the frozen CLIP Visual Transformer and propose a Low-level Forgery Feature Enhancement (LFFE) module to extract and enhance low-level forgery features. Subsequently, our Adaptive Feature Fusion (AFF) module flexibly integrates the low-level forgery features with the high-level semantic features

3.1 Unbiased Feature Extraction

As previously stated, training deep networks directly for binary classification often biases learned features towards a specific fake domain, limiting the generalizability of models. To handle this issue, we extract unbiased features by employing frozen Visual Foundation Models. Different from previous methods, the VFMs are not trained on any specific deepfake dataset. Their feature space has yet to differentiate between real and fake images. Therefore, we can utilize it to extract unbiased features.

Specifically, we extract unbiased image representations using the frozen CLIP Visual Transformer. It can capture both high-level semantic information and low-level features [20] and is well-suited for our task. We obtain high-level semantic information from the class embedding of the final block, which represents the global semantic aggregation of tokens. Moreover, we extract the low-level forgery features from the intermediate block, taking advantage of patch embeddings containing local spatial information.

We also explore the performance of using DINOv2 [17] and InternImage [27] as image encoders in the experiment section. Experiment results demonstrate that our method exhibits excellent generalizability across various VFMs.

3.2 Low-Level Forgery Feature Enhancement

The distinctions between authentic and forgery images are often more prominent within the low-level features [28]. Our approach extracts and enhances the low-level forgery features from the intermediate block of CLIP Visual Transformer to effectively capture these subtle artifacts.

As shown in Fig. 1, the Gabor layer [18] is the initial step to obtain the low-level forgery features. It comprises convolutional layers with filters determined by learnable Gabor parameters. For a given input feature $F \in R^{c \times h \times w}$, where c, h, w denotes the number of channels, height, and width of F, respectively. The Gabor layer first conducts separate convolutions for each channel of F using different directional Gabor filters within the filter set K, and this process is based on depth-wise separable convolutions. After that, the results are passed through a ReLU activation function, generating corresponding responses R. The responses are then stacked and processed through a 1×1 convolution, culminating in the low-level forgery features F'. We can concisely formulate the above process as follows:

$$R = \{ReLU(F^i * f^j), F^i \in F, f^j \in K, \forall i, j\}$$
$$F' = Conv(R) \tag{1}$$

where F^i is the ith channel-wise slicing of F, f^j is the jth filter of K, $*$ signifies the convolution operation.

Then, we utilize a dense block [8] to enhance the obtained low-level forgery features. The dense block establishes connections between different layers. It directly concatenates channels from preceding layers to subsequent layers since the feature map sizes for each layer remain consistent. In other words, each subsequent layer in the dense block receives all inputs from the previous layers, enhancing the depth and interconnectedness of feature representations. The output x_k of the kth layer H_k within the dense block can be formulated as:

$$x_k = H_k([x_0, x_1, ..., x_{k-1}]) \tag{2}$$

With the densely connected approach, the dense block can facilitate gradient propagation, ensuring more effective utilization of the low-level forgery features. We limit the structure to 4 layers due to this block's rapidly increasing channel numbers.

3.3 Adaptive Feature Fusion

In deepfake detection tasks, low-level and high-level information both play essential roles [30]. Hence, we design an Adaptive Feature Fusion module to select and integrate the low-level forgery features with the high-level semantic features dynamically.

Firstly, We perform cross-attention to achieve initial fusion while maintaining dimensional consistency. The low-level forgery features and the high-level semantic features are denoted as F_l and F_h, respectively, $F_l \in R^{p \times c}$, $F_h \in R^{1 \times c}$, where p and c denote the number of total patches and the number of channels in the feature map. We project F_h into the query Q, F_l into key K and value V. The attention map Att is generated as:

$$Att = softmax(\frac{QK^T}{\sqrt{c}})$$
$$F_f = Att \cdot V \tag{3}$$

We concatenate the preliminary fused feature F_f with the high-level semantic feature F_h along channels. Subsequently, we apply two sets of Convolution - Batch Normalization - ReLU layers, followed by a convolution layer and a sigmoid layer, to generate a high-level semantic attention map and a low-level forgery attention map. Then, we multiply the feature map with corresponding features, adding the results together to obtain the ultimate features F_o.

$$F_o = F_f \cdot Att_{low} + F_h \cdot Att_{high} \tag{4}$$

where Att_{high} and Att_{low} represent the high-level semantic attention map and low-level forgery attention map, respectively. Finally, the fused features F_o are fed into the fully connected layer for classification.

Table 1. In-dataset evaluation results on FF++

Method	FF++	DF	F2F	FS	NT	Avg
Xception [21]	96.9	99.0	98.3	95.7	94.9	97.0
Face X-Ray [12]	98.5	99.1	99.3	99.2	99.3	99.2
DCL [24]	99.3	100	99.2	99.8	99.0	99.5
PCL+I2G [29]	99.1	100	99.0	99.8	97.6	99.1
SOLA [6]	99.2	100	99.5	**99.9**	99.8	99.8
SBIs [22]	99.2	100	99.8	99.8	98.8	99.6
Baseline [16]	97.0	97.6	97.3	98.1	95.9	97.5
Ours	**99.9**	100	**99.9**	99.8	**99.8**	**99.9**

4 Experiment

4.1 Datasets

We primarily evaluate our methods on the following four commonly used datasets:

FaceForensics++ (FF++) [21]. FF++ consists of 1000 original videos and 4000 manipulated videos generated by four forgery methods. In this paper, the performances are mainly based on FF++ with quantization parameters c23.

Celeb-DF (CD1)/Celeb-DFv2 (CD2) [13,14]. CD1 includes 408 original videos collected from YouTube and 795 manipulated videos generated from real videos. CD2 includes 590 original videos and 563 deepfake videos.

DFDC [3]. DFDC comprises 19,197 real videos filmed by actors and 100,000 fake videos created using various facial manipulation methods.

4.2 Implement Details

In the data preprocessing phase, we uniformly sample 100 frames from each video, crop and align the faces, and then resize each frame to 224×224. Common augmentations such as contrast and blur are employed. We choose ViT-L/14 as the encoder and extract low-level features from the twelfth block. The baseline consists of the ViT-L/14 with a fully connected layer, and we use cross entropy as the classification loss function. During the training phase, we used an Adam

Table 2. Cross-method evaluation on FF++

Training set	Method	DF	F2F	FS	NT	Avg
DF	Xception [21]	99.3	72.1	49.1	71.4	73.0
	DCL [24]	100	77.1	61.0	75.0	78.2
	LAV [23]	100	86.4	65.9	84.2	84.1
	Baseline [16]	99.0	82.1	94.7	72.0	87.0
	Ours	**100**	**94.0**	**95.3**	**90.3**	**94.9**
F2F	Xception [21]	80.3	99.4	76.2	69.6	81.4
	DCL [24]	91.9	99.2	59.6	66.7	79.4
	LAV [23]	82.6	99.9	90.1	90.5	79.4
	Baseline [16]	87.6	98.6	89.3	74.7	87.6
	Ours	**94.7**	**100**	**95.0**	**92.6**	**95.6**
FS	Xception [21]	66.4	88.8	99.4	71.3	81.5
	DCL [24]	74.8	69.8	99.9	52.6	74.3
	LAV [23]	70.6	93.3	100	90.5	88.6
	Baseline [16]	96.0	84.3	96.2	61.8	84.6
	Ours	**98.9**	**98.3**	**100**	**94.2**	**97.9**
NT	Xception [21]	79.9	81.3	73.1	99.1	83.4
	DCL [24]	91.2	52.1	78.3	99.0	80.2
	LAV [23]	86.9	96.9	**94.6**	99.4	94.5
	Baseline [16]	82.6	59.5	52.3	85.1	69.9
	Ours	**99.4**	**97.2**	93.1	**99.6**	**97.3**

optimizer, of which the initial learning rate is 2e−4 and gradually decreases to 1e−8. The evaluation metric utilizes the Area Under the Curve (AUC).

4.3 In-Dataset Evaluation

In-dataset evaluation mainly focuses on specialization, we compare our method with state-of-the-art methods on FF++. The results shown in Table 1 illustrate that our approach achieves remarkable performance on the in-dataset evaluation. Specifically, in contrast to the baseline, our method exhibits a 2.9% increase in AUC on the FF++ dataset. Furthermore, compared with the best-performing SOLA [6], we still improve the AUC of 0.7% on the FF++ dataset and 0.1% on its subsets. These results partially affirm the effectiveness of our method.

4.4 Cross-Dataset Evaluation

We conduct two experiments to evaluate the generalization ability of our method on unseen data. Initially, we evaluate our approach on four FF++ sub-datasets, and detectors are trained on one subset and tested on all four subsets. Table 2 presents the results, where the shaded area represents in-dataset results. Our method consistently outperforms competitors across various scenarios. Compared with the competitive LAV [23], our approach significantly improves the AUC of 16.2% on the F2F sub-dataset and approximately 10% on the DF and FS sub-datasets. One notable observation is that our baseline also demonstrates satisfactory generalizability. For instance, compared to Xception [21], the baseline shows a 14% improvement of AUC on the DF dataset, validating that utilizing frozen VFMs can yield more universal features.

Table 3. Cross-dataset evaluation results

Method	Celeb-DF	Celeb-DFv2	DFDC
Xception [21]	62.3	66.7	66.8
Face X-ray [12]	74.7	70.3	64.6
F3Net [19]	65.2	66.4	68.2
RFM [25]	79.1	71.7	75.8
Local-relation [2]	78.3	77.9	76.5
MAT [28]	67.4	68.3	66.3
PIL+I2G [29]	86.5	81.8	67.5
SBIs [22]	86.0	83.2	72.4
LAV [23]	84.7	86.0	76.3
IIL [4]	87.2	83.9	73.9
Baseline [16]	70.6	68.2	70.2
Ours	89.8(↑19.2)	87.7(↑19.5)	81.9(↑11.7)

Moreover, we train models on the FF++ dataset and evaluate them on the Celeb-DF, Celeb-DFv2 and DFDC datasets. As depicted in Table 3, our method exhibits considerable generalization performance, outperforming the baseline by 19.2%, 19.5% and 11.7% on the Celeb-DF, Celeb-DFv2 and DFDC datasets. Meanwhile, our approach raises Celeb-DF results from 87.2% to 89.8%, Celeb-DFv2 results from 86% to 87.7% and achieves a prominent 5.4% improvement on the challenging DFDC dataset. We attribute the significant progress to the effective extraction of unbiased features and the low-level feature enhancement, advancing the model's ability to capture inherent artifacts and significantly improve generalizability.

4.5 Robustness Evaluation

We also evaluate the robustness of our method against various types of image perturbations following the same setting as [7]. All the results are trained and tested on the FF++ dataset. As shown in Table 4, our approach achieves an outstanding AUC of 99.0%, with average performance exceeding 97% under various perturbations, which thoroughly validates our method's robustness.

Table 4. Robustness evaluation results on FF++

Method	Saturation	Contrast	Noise	Blur	Pixel	Avg
Xception [21]	99.3	98.6	53.8	60.2	74.2	77.2
FaceXray [12]	97.6	88.5	49.8	63.8	88.6	77.7
LF [7]	99.9	99.6	73.8	96.1	95.6	93.0
IIL [4]	99.6	99.8	87.4	**99.0**	98.8	96.9
Ours	**99.9**	**99.8**	**98.0**	97.7	**99.0**	**98.9**

4.6 Visualization Results

In this section, we visualize the learned feature distribution of the baseline and our method utilizing t-sne. Specifically, we train the models on the FF++ training dataset and extract features before the final fully connected layer.

The results are depicted in Fig. 2. (a), (b), and (c) illustrate the learned feature distribution of our model, (d), (e), and (f) represent the baseline. As depicted in Fig. 2, the baseline extracts features impartially for both real and fake faces, without learning to distinguish between them. This further confirms our motivation for utilizing a frozen visual foundation model to extract unbiased features. In addition, our approach shows significant separation between real and fake faces, whether considering results within the dataset (a) or across datasets (b)(c). This further demonstrates that our method learns distinctive features for differentiating between real and fake faces. These visual results validate the effectiveness and generalizability of our approach from another perspective.

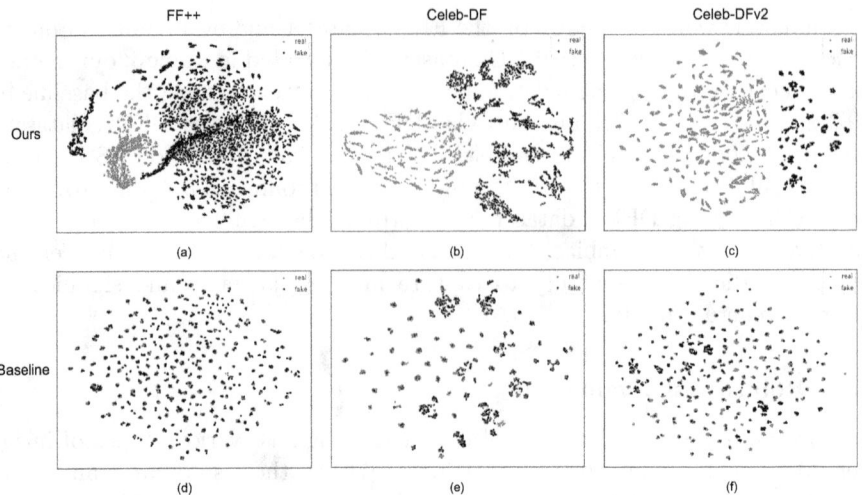

Fig. 2. The t-SNE feature visualization results

4.7 Ablation Study

Effectiveness of Components. We design the following variant models to validate the effectiveness of our proposed modules:

1) Variant 1, the baseline contains a frozen CLIP Visual Transformer and a fully connected layer, using only high-level semantic features for detection.

2) Variant 2, the baseline model equipped with our proposed LFFE, utilizing the extracted low-level forgery features for detection.

3) Variant 3, the baseline model with LFFE and concat strategy, trivially concatenating the extracted low-level forgery features with high-level semantic features for detection.

4) Variant 4, our UFELE with all components.

Table 5. Ablation study of different components

Variants	LFFE	Concat	AFF	Test Set (AUC)			
				FF++	CD1	CD2	DFDC
1	–	–	–	97.0	70.6	68.2	70.2
2	✓			98.6	82.1	80.3	75.5
3	✓	✓		99.4	83.2	85.9	75.7
4	✓		✓	**99.9**	**89.8**	**87.7**	**81.9**

The results are listed in Table 5. Comparison between variants 1 and 2 demonstrates the effectiveness of the LFFE module. Using only the low-level forgery features for detection also elevates the AUC by 11.5% and 12.1% on CD1 and CD2, respectively, emphasizing the significance of enhancing low-level features for deepfake detection. The results of variants 1, 2, and 3 reveal that integrating low-level forgery features with high-level semantic features can further improve detection performance, while the trivial concatenation strategy limits performance improvement. Contrasting between variants 2 and 4 illustrates that our proposed AFF module effectively combines high-level and low-level features, resulting in gains of 7.7%, 7.4%, and 6.4% on CD1, CD2, and DFDC datasets.

Performance on Different Encoders. We explore the effectiveness of utilizing DINOv2 [17] and InternImage [27] as Image Encoders. All the results are trained on the FF++ dataset and evaluated on CD1, CD2, and DFDC datasets. As shown in Table 6, our methods exhibit significant applicability across various Visual Foundation Models. For instance, upon integrating the DINOv2 encoder with our proposed LFFE and AFF, the AUC results on the CD1, CD2, and DFDC datasets increased by 20.1%, 24.2%, and 4.7% compared to the DINOv2 with a fully connected layer. Similar improvements can be observed with the InternImage encoder, with 18.5%, 15.3%, and 15% increases, respectively. These results demonstrate that our approach is applicable and effective across various Visual Foundation Models.

Table 6. Ablation study of different encoders

Method	CelebDF	CelebDFv2	DFDC
DINOv2 [17] + FC	66.1	64.9	75.5
DINO_v2 + LFFE + AFF	**86.2**	**89.1**	**80.2**
InternImage [27] + FC	64.4	65.1	63.7
InternImage + LFFE + AFF	**82.9**	**80.4**	**78.7**

Ablation Study on Different Intermediate Blocks. We conduct experiments to determine the optimal intermediate block for extracting the low-level forgery features. With the VIT-L/14 comprising 24 Transformer blocks, we obtain the low-level forgery features from patch embeddings every four blocks. The results are trained on the FF++ dataset and tested on other datasets.

As presented in Table 7, selecting the fourth or eighth block results in unsatisfactory performance. We attribute this to the inadequate learning of image representations, thereby hindering our LFFE module from effectively extracting low-level forgery information. Moreover, as the block depth increases, the Vision Transformer models high-level global semantic features [5,15] and potentially overlooks low-level local information that our LFFE module mainly relies on. Hence, selecting the 20th and 24th blocks also yields poor performance.

Our approach showcases optimal performance when selecting the 12th block. We attribute this to the fact that the twelfth block learns sufficient image representations and contains relatively adequate low-level information, facilitating the extraction of low-level forgery features. Consequently, the 12th block is the optimal choice for extracting low-level forgery features.

Table 7. Ablation Study on different intermediate blocks

Intermediate Block	FF++	Celeb-DF	Celeb-DFv2	DFDC
4th	94.9	77.7	76.0	76.5
8th	97.3	78.9	76.3	76.1
12th	**99.9**	**89.8**	**87.7**	**81.9**
16th	99.2	84.9	84.4	78.2
20th	98.4	79.7	75.2	76.0
24th	95.6	79.3	78.1	75.4

5 Conclusion

In this paper, we propose a generalizable deepfake detection method named UFELE. With unbiased feature extraction utilizing frozen VFMs, we incorporate LFFE and AFF to leverage high-level semantic information and low-level forgery information simultaneously. We design the LFFE module to extract and enhance low-level forgery features, while the AFF module amalgamates low-level forgery features with high-level semantic features. Extensive experiments on widely used benchmark datasets validate our method's remarkable detection performance in generalizability and robustness.

Acknowledgement. This work is supported by Shenzhen Science and Technology Program (No. JCYJ20230807120800001), and 2023 Shenzhen sustainable supporting funds for colleges and universities (No. 20231121165240001). The authors sincerely appreciate the computing environment supported by the China Unicom Shenzhen Intelligent Computing Center.

References

1. Chen, H.S., Rouhsedaghat, M., Ghani, H., Hu, S., You, S., Kuo, C.C.J.: DefakeHop: a light-weight high-performance DeepFake detector. In: 2021 IEEE International Conference on Multimedia and Expo (ICME), pp. 1–6. IEEE (2021)
2. Chen, S., Yao, T., Chen, Y., Ding, S., Li, J., Ji, R.: Local relation learning for face forgery detection. In: Proceedings of the AAAI Conference on Artificial Intelligence, vol. 35, pp. 1081–1088 (2021)

3. Dolhansky, B., et al.: The DeepFake detection challenge (DFDC) dataset. arXiv preprint arXiv:2006.07397 (2020)
4. Dong, S., Wang, J., Ji, R., Liang, J., Fan, H., Ge, Z.: Implicit identity leakage: the stumbling block to improving DeepFake detection generalization. In: Proceedings of the IEEE/CVF Conference on Computer Vision and Pattern Recognition, pp. 3994–4004 (2023)
5. Dosovitskiy, A., et al.: An image is worth 16 × 16 words: transformers for image recognition at scale. arXiv preprint arXiv:2010.11929 (2020)
6. Fei, J., Dai, Y., Yu, P., Shen, T., Xia, Z., Weng, J.: Learning second order local anomaly for general face forgery detection. In: Proceedings of the IEEE/CVF Conference on Computer Vision and Pattern Recognition, pp. 20270–20280 (2022)
7. Haliassos, A., Vougioukas, K., Petridis, S., Pantic, M.: Lips don't lie: a generalisable and robust approach to face forgery detection. In: Proceedings of the IEEE/CVF Conference on Computer Vision and Pattern Recognition, pp. 5039–5049 (2021)
8. Huang, G., Liu, Z., Van Der Maaten, L., Weinberger, K.Q.: Densely connected convolutional networks. In: Proceedings of the IEEE Conference on Computer Vision and Pattern Recognition, pp. 4700–4708 (2017)
9. Jeong, Y., Kim, D., Min, S., Joe, S., Gwon, Y., Choi, J.: BiHPF: bilateral high-pass filters for robust DeepFake detection. In: Proceedings of the IEEE/CVF Winter Conference on Applications of Computer Vision, pp. 48–57 (2022)
10. Koopman, M., Rodriguez, A.M., Geradts, Z.: Detection of DeepFake video manipulation. In: The 20th Irish Machine Vision and Image Processing Conference (IMVIP), pp. 133–136 (2018)
11. Li, H., Li, B., Tan, S., Huang, J.: Identification of deep network generated images using disparities in color components. Signal Process. **174**, 107616 (2020)
12. Li, L., et al.: Face X-ray for more general face forgery detection. In: Proceedings of the IEEE/CVF Conference on Computer Vision and Pattern Recognition, pp. 5001–5010 (2020)
13. Li, Y., Yang, X., Sun, P., Qi, H., Lyu, S.: Celeb-DF (v2): a new dataset for DeepFake forensics. arXiv preprint arXiv (2019)
14. Li, Y., Yang, X., Sun, P., Qi, H., Lyu, S.: Celeb-DF: a large-scale challenging dataset for DeepFake forensics. In: Proceedings of the IEEE/CVF Conference on Computer Vision and Pattern Recognition, pp. 3207–3216 (2020)
15. Naseer, M.M., Ranasinghe, K., Khan, S.H., Hayat, M., Shahbaz Khan, F., Yang, M.H.: Intriguing properties of vision transformers. Adv. Neural. Inf. Process. Syst. **34**, 23296–23308 (2021)
16. Ojha, U., Li, Y., Lee, Y.J.: Towards universal fake image detectors that generalize across generative models. In: Proceedings of the IEEE/CVF Conference on Computer Vision and Pattern Recognition, pp. 24480–24489 (2023)
17. Oquab, M., et al.: DINOv2: learning robust visual features without supervision. arXiv preprint arXiv:2304.07193 (2023)
18. Pérez, J.C., et al.: Gabor layers enhance network robustness. In: Vedaldi, A., Bischof, H., Brox, T., Frahm, J.M. (eds.) Computer Vision–ECCV 2020: 16th European Conference, Glasgow, UK, 23–28 August 2020, Proceedings, Part IX 16, pp. 450–466. Springer, Cham (2020). https://doi.org/10.1007/978-3-030-58545-7_26
19. Qian, Y., Yin, G., Sheng, L., Chen, Z., Shao, J.: Thinking in frequency: face forgery detection by mining frequency-aware clues. In: Vedaldi, A., Bischof, H., Brox, T., Frahm, J.-M. (eds.) ECCV 2020. LNCS, vol. 12357, pp. 86–103. Springer, Cham (2020). https://doi.org/10.1007/978-3-030-58610-2_6

20. Radford, A., et al.: Learning transferable visual models from natural language supervision. In: International Conference on Machine Learning, pp. 8748–8763. PMLR (2021)
21. Rossler, A., Cozzolino, D., Verdoliva, L., Riess, C., Thies, J., Nießner, M.: FaceForensics++: learning to detect manipulated facial images. In: Proceedings of the IEEE/CVF International Conference on Computer Vision, pp. 1–11 (2019)
22. Shiohara, K., Yamasaki, T.: Detecting DeepFakes with self-blended images. In: Proceedings of the IEEE/CVF Conference on Computer Vision and Pattern Recognition, pp. 18720–18729 (2022)
23. Shuai, C., et al.: Locate and verify: a two-stream network for improved DeepFake detection. In: Proceedings of the 31st ACM International Conference on Multimedia, pp. 7131–7142 (2023)
24. Sun, K., Yao, T., Chen, S., Ding, S., Li, J., Ji, R.: Dual contrastive learning for general face forgery detection. In: Proceedings of the AAAI Conference on Artificial Intelligence, vol. 36, pp. 2316–2324 (2022)
25. Wang, C., Deng, W.: Representative forgery mining for fake face detection. In: Proceedings of the IEEE/CVF Conference on Computer Vision and Pattern Recognition, pp. 14923–14932 (2021)
26. Wang, J., et al.: M2TR: multi-modal multi-scale transformers for DeepFake detection. In: Proceedings of the 2022 International Conference on Multimedia Retrieval, pp. 615–623 (2022)
27. Wang, W., et al.: InternImage: exploring large-scale vision foundation models with deformable convolutions. In: Proceedings of the IEEE/CVF Conference on Computer Vision and Pattern Recognition, pp. 14408–14419 (2023)
28. Zhao, H., Zhou, W., Chen, D., Wei, T., Zhang, W., Yu, N.: Multi-attentional DeepFake detection. In: Proceedings of the IEEE/CVF Conference on Computer Vision and Pattern Recognition, pp. 2185–2194 (2021)
29. Zhao, T., Xu, X., Xu, M., Ding, H., Xiong, Y., Xia, W.: Learning self-consistency for DeepFake detection. In: Proceedings of the IEEE/CVF International Conference on Computer Vision, pp. 15023–15033 (2021)
30. Zou, B., Yang, C., Guan, J., Quan, C., Zhao, Y.: DFCP: few-shot DeepFake detection via contrastive pretraining. In: 2023 IEEE International Conference on Multimedia and Expo (ICME), pp. 2303–2308. IEEE (2023)

Generative Universal Nullifying Perturbation for Countering Deepfakes Through Combined Unsupervised Feature Aggregation

Yuchen Guo[1,2], Xi Wang[1], Xiaomeng Fu[1,2], Jin Liu[1,2], Zhaoxing Li[1(✉)], and Jizhong Han[1]

[1] Institute of Information Engineering, Chinese Academy of Sciences, Beijing, China
[2] School of Cyber Security, University of Chinese Academy of Sciences, Beijing, China
{guoyuchen,wangxi1,fuxiaomeng,liujin,lizhaoxing,hanjizhong}@iie.ac.cn

Abstract. Incorporating adversarial perturbations into images to fool Deepfake models is a pivotal strategy in defending against manipulated content. However, most existing methods are image-specific, necessitating iterative optimization of perturbation for each image, which is time-consuming when applied to large-scale images and fails to achieve real-time inference. Meanwhile, even though the Deepfake models may be disrupt, the content of the original images is alerted, impeding the further delivery of information. To address these challenges, we proposed a method for universal nullifying perturbation generation. Our method integrates both pixel-wise and feature-wise information to generate the perturbation that influence the outputs of the Deepfake model, with the goal of preserving the holistic content of the image as much as possible. We present an unsupervised aggregation method to enhance the effectiveness of perturbation generation in leveraging feature information. Additionally, we advocate the use of neural networks for generating universal perturbations, particularly effective in addressing challenging tasks. Experimental results demonstrate that our proposed method achieves state-of-the-art performance, with our universal nullifying perturbation effectively maintaining the visual quality of original images. Moreover, cross-data experiments confirm that our perturbation remains efficient in protecting face images from forgery even in the presence of unknown data. Consequently, our proposed approach offers a robust and efficient solution to combat Deepfake, contributing to the safeguarding of personal privacy and prevention of reputational damage.

Keywords: Universal adversarial perturbation · Face manipulation · Nullification of deepfakes · Face protection

1 Introduction

The remarkable advancement in Artificial Intelligence Generated Content (AIGC) technologies such as GANs [26,34] has enabled models to achieve highly

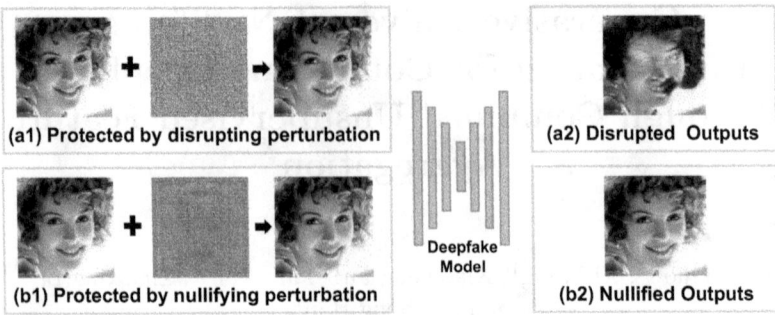

Fig. 1. Comparison of different protection effects. Distorted outputs can prevent the spread of inaccurate information to some extent. Nullified outputs, however, can defend against forgery while ensuring that information continues to be disseminated.

realistic manipulations, presenting substantial threats to both social and national security. Publicly available models further lower the threshold for the use of such models, and defenses against such forged models are imminent [2,4,11]. Current approaches against Deepfake can be broadly categorized into two strategies: passive defense and active defense. Passive defense methods [9,10,25,36] involve training Deepfake detectors to distinguish whether an image has been manipulated. However, this kind of method is limited to post hoc detection and cannot proactively prevent the occurrence of Deepfakes.

Recently, researchers have explored active Deepfake defense techniques, which entail injecting imperceptible adversarial perturbations into original images to disrupt Deepfake models [1,7,17,23,31,35] or nullify Deepfake models [12,40]. As illustrated in Fig. 1(a2), disrupting the outputs of Deepfake models can mitigate the risks posed by manipulated models, yet it simultaneously hinders the continued dissemination of information to a certain extent. In contrast, as demonstrated in Fig. 1(b2), nullified outputs maintain the integrity of the original information, thereby ensuring faithful information transmission. Yeh, et al. [40] obtain perturbation samples that invalidate the forged model through gradient estimation. He et al. [12] generate such nullified perturbed pictures using image reconstruction. Nonetheless, those image-specific methods need to generate individual perturbations for each original image. They face challenges in meeting the efficiency requirements for protecting extensive images and real-time scenarios.

Universal perturbation is one of the most efficient adversarial methods, especially when implemented in real-time systems. After acquiring a universal perturbation through training, it enables the direct addition of perturbation data into the vast majority of images, without the need for regeneration [27]. This approach emerges as one of the most efficient methods of perturbation. In contrast to image-specific perturbations, these methods [27] learn a singular universal pattern that aptly represents the entirety of the data distribution, thereby deceiving the model across a majority of samples. Recent researches [15,33] on universal perturbation for active defense predominantly adopts an untargeted approach.

However, this inclination towards an untargeted strategy results in the distortion of Deepfake models, potentially compromising the core objective of real-time systems: the prompt delivery of accurate information. In this paper, we endeavor to explore a targeted universal perturbation, named the Universal Nullifying Perturbation, to against deepfakes. Nevertheless, generating such a perturbation presents a considerable challenge. In the traditional targeted adversarial task, the perturbation expects to mislead models into predicting a specific label, while the universal nullifying perturbation aims to keep itself unaltered by the forgery models for each image. However, the configuration of this targeted perturbation poses increased complexity due to diverse targets across different examples while we aim to achieve this intricate task using only a single universal perturbation.

To tackle this challenge, our approach attempts to enhance the effectiveness of targeted perturbation by leveraging information extracted from the feature space. The deep feature space within a model typically consists of abstract, high-level semantic features. Attacks directed towards these high-level features prove advantageous in mitigating perturbation overfitting in specific images or models, as noted in previous works [8, 16, 37–39]. Importantly, the high-level feature space exhibits greater compactness than the pixel space, thereby facilitating the resolution of universal perturbation problems [33]. Tasks involving targeted attacks typically necessitate ground-truth information that aligns with the specified target for guidance in perturbation generation. However, in the case of conditional generative models, such as forgery models, obtaining the ground truth in the feature space is not trivial as it requires a complex reverse process.

To enhance the effective utilization of feature-wise information in guiding perturbation generation, in this paper, we analyze the generation process of the forgery model and propose an unsupervised feature aggregation method. Since unsupervised utilization of feature-wise information is insufficient, we further improve the constraints on pixel-wise and combine feature-wise and pixel-wise information to guide perturbation generation. Additionally, we advocate the adoption of a neural network for the generation of universal nullifying perturbations. In comparison to gradient-based methods, neural networks possess more robust fitting capabilities and offer increased flexibility in fitting universal perturbations through the sharing of model parameters.

We evaluate the effectiveness of our approach across different classes of deep forgery tasks to verify the general applicability of our proposed method. In particular, we focus on two prevalent and easily accessible yet highly detrimental deep forgery tasks: face attribute editing and face swapping. Furthermore, we conduct experiments on different datasets to verify the cross-dataset generalization of our perturbation. Our contributions can be summarized as follows:

- We extend the application of generalized perturbation for combating deep forgery models, which can efficiently protect face images from being edited by forgery models.
- We propose a new feature-wise perturbation method, where we effectively utilize feature information for perturbation generation through unsupervised feature aggregation.

- We improve the pixel-wise perturbation method, and we introduce reconstruction loss and identity loss to constrain the perturbation generation.
- We empirically verify the effectiveness of our proposed approach with different deep forgery tasks. Compared with state-of-the-art methods, experimental results show that our proposed method achieves a more effective defense against Deepfakes.

2 Related Work

2.1 Face Manipulation

Presently, GAN-based generative methods have demonstrated the capability to produce highly realistic facial images, capable of deceiving the human visual system. Noteworthy among these methods are PGGAN [18] and StyleGAN [19], which can generate high-resolution facial images that do not exist in reality. Another category of methods involves the manipulation of actual facial images for forgery. For instance, SimSwap [3] allows for face swapping across various identities, while AttentionGAN [32] permits the editing of multiple facial attributes. Given the heightened potential harm associated with forgery using real facial data, the defensive strategy in this paper centers on safeguarding against such methods.

2.2 Deepfake Active Defense

Active defense methods against deep forgery aim to deceive the forgery model by creating adversarial perturbations. Current active defense methodologies predominantly fall into two categories: disrupting methods and nullifying methods. The disrupting Deepfake approach introduced by Ruiz et al. [29], aimed at halting the dissemination of misleading content generated by Deepfakes. Wang et al. [35] achieve covert and resilient Deepfake disruption through the creation of adversarial perturbations in the Lab color space. Yeh et al. [40] initially introduced nullifying perturbation for Image-to-image Translation GANs. They implemented a query-based nullifying method, leveraging prior knowledge of the translation network and integrating a limit-aware RGF and gradient sliding mechanism. He et al. [12] implemented the nullifying perturbation method by exploring the feature space and reconstructing the image through an image reconstruction network. However, due to the necessity for a substantial number of queries or image reconstructions, it is difficult to extend existing methods to universal perturbation methods Fig. 2.

2.3 Universal Adversarial Perturbation

A Universal Adversarial Perturbation (UAP) is a unified perturbation capable of deceiving a specific model when applied to the majority of natural images. The concept was originally introduced by Moosavi et al. [27] for application in

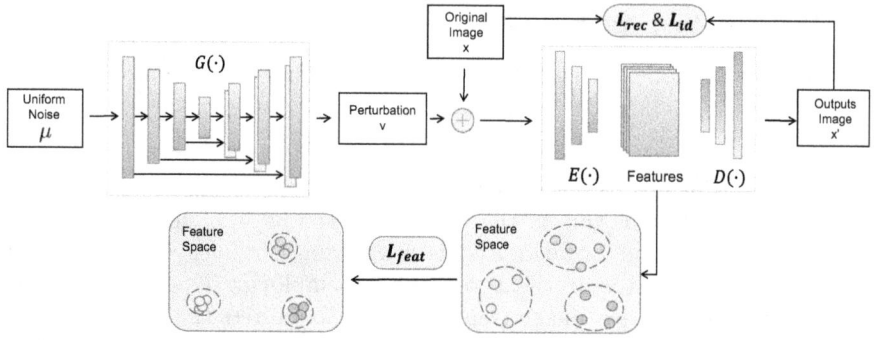

Fig. 2. Overview of our method. Different colored dots indicate the distribution of different image inputs x in the feature space. The L_{feat} encourages a greater concentration of features within the same image when edited under different conditions and pixel-wise losses ensure the ultimate objective of optimization.

classification tasks. Metzen et al. [13] extended the application of generalized adversarial perturbation to segmentation tasks, while Li et al. [20] applied it to image retrieval. Recently, Huang et al. [15] were the first to introduce a universal perturbation method capable of countering multiple forgery models. Tang et al. [33] proposed a method of fusing pixel-wise and feature-wise constraints to attain a more effective universal disrupting perturbation. Although these methods have advanced the generation of disrupting perturbations, they encounter challenges in achieving nullifying universal perturbations due to the complex targeted perturbation strategy and the difficulty of obtaining targeted-feature ground truth. This paper endeavors to address these challenges.

3 Method

This section provides a detailed description of our proposed universal nullifying perturbation generation method. Firstly, we state the problem for universal nullifying perturbation, and subsequently, we introduce the pixel-wise and feature-wise perturbation strategies respectively. The framework of our method is shown in Fig. 1.

3.1 Problem Formulation

Let $F : x \rightarrow x'$ represent a face editing model capable of attribute or face-swapping editing on the victim's face image. The main focus of this problem is to seek a targeted perturbation vector v that protects most face images from editing. That is, we seek a vector v such that:

$$v = \operatorname{argmin}(F(X+v), X) \qquad s.t. \|v\|_\infty \leq \varepsilon \qquad (1)$$

where ε denotes the maximum upper limit of the perturbation and X represents all images of the face dataset.

3.2 Feature-Wise Aggregation

The GAN-based model for conditional generation can be represented as:

$$x' = D(E(x,c)) \qquad (2)$$

where $E(\cdot)$ is the feature extractor, $D(\cdot)$ is the upsampling generator and c denotes the conditional. Due to the presence of condition c, acquiring the target feature information through $E(\cdot)$ is challenging. In such cases, obtaining ground truth features requires feature inversion employing $D(\cdot)$. However, performing inversion for each image is impractical. To address this issue, we introduce an unsupervised feature-wise cluster constraint. Although obtaining the ground truth of features is challenging, an ideal universal nullifying perturbation should ensure uniform features under different conditions, guaranteeing the preservation of the final image during the upsampling process. Consequently, we first calculate the clustering center for image x_i based on diverse conditions or distinct target faces. Subsequently, we enforce constraints on the features to converge towards this clustering center :

$$\mu C_i = \frac{1}{k}\sum_{j=1}^{k} E(x_i + v, c_j) \qquad (3)$$

$$L_{feat} = \sum_{j=1}^{k} MSE(E(x_i + v, c_j), \mu C_i) \qquad (4)$$

Table 1. Performance of our method in nullifying the two types of manipulation models with a comparison with three competitive baselines on CelebA. Best results are emphasized in **bold**.

Manipulation model	Method	MSE↓	SSIM↑	PSNR↑	CSIM↑	L_{per} ↓	SR↑
SimSwap	MIM [6]	0.003	0.943	29.436	0.396	2.492	54.00%
	Anti-forgery [35]	0.003	0.941	29.032	0.397	2.489	57.27%
	CMUA [15]	0.003	0.946	29.235	0.419	2.487	66.27%
	Ours	**0.002**	**0.953**	**32.808**	**0.824**	**2.379**	**93.87%**
AttentionGAN	MIM [6]	0.002	0.968	36.870	0.906	0.335	93.93%
	Anti-forgery [35]	0.002	0.971	37.032	0.919	0.315	95.12%
	CMUA [15]	0.002	0.977	38.587	0.927	0.262	97.97%
	Ours	**0.001**	**0.995**	**43.509**	**0.969**	**0.171**	**99.99%**

3.3 Pixel-Wise Perturbation

The universal nullifying perturbation can be efficiently applied to a diverse set of natural images, aiming to preserve the appearance of protected images after they have undergone processing by deepfakes. Intuitively, this perturbation compels the operation of the forgery model to shift from image editing to image reconstruction. Consequently, it is reasonable to contemplate introducing the common reconstruction loss as the primary constraint. The loss for the universal perturbation can be defined as follows:

$$L_{rec} = \|X - F(X+v)\|_1 + \sum_i \|\phi_i(X) - \phi_i(F(X+v))\|_1 \qquad (5)$$

where ϕ_i is the activation map of the i-th layer of the pre-trained VGG-19 [30] network.

On the other hand, the most profound repercussions associated with facial manipulation are the alteration and substitution of an individual's identity. Against manipulation, the nullification should also preserve accurate identity information. We introduce additional constraints on the facial identity information. We employ a pre-trained face recognition network [5] denoted as R for extracting identity features, and we minimize the cosine distance between the identity vectors of X and $F(X+v)$ as a constraint. The loss function is defined as:

$$L_{id} = Cosine(R(X), R(F(X+v))) \qquad (6)$$

Table 2. Performance of our method on cross-datasets.

Dataset	Manipulation model	MSE↓	SSIM↑	PSNR↑	CSIM↑	L_{per} ↓	SR↑
LFW	SimSwap	0.003	0.911	31.085	0.797	2.266	93.57%
	AttentionGAN	0.001	0.939	43.487	0.937	0.182	99.99%
Film100	SimSwap	0.003	0.913	31.570	0.802	2.235	94.28%
	AttentionGAN	0.001	0.941	43.532	0.989	0.172	100.00%

3.4 Generator

The generator G aims to transform a Gaussian noise into a nullifying perturbation signal. Initially, we randomly sample a Gaussian noise with the dimensions of the face image X, as the input to the generator G. In this context, the noise conforms to a normal distribution μ with a mean of (0, 1) and dimensions of $c*h*w$. We employ a Unet-based network as the core architecture of G, which keeps the dimension of output consistent with that of the input. We denoted the output nullifying perturbation as δ, and $\delta = G(\mu)$.

In order to render the presence of the perturbation imperceptible within images, we utilize the L-infinity norm to limit the perturbation strength. Ultimately, we superimpose the universal perturbation δ onto the original image with magnitude ε, resulting in the final perturbed image denoted as $\widehat{X}$:

$$v = Clamp(\delta, -\varepsilon, \varepsilon) \tag{7}$$

$$\widehat{X} = Clip(X + v), \ s.t. \ \|v\|_\infty \leq \varepsilon \tag{8}$$

The function Clip limits the perturbed image $\widehat{X}$ in the valid range. In this paper, the valid range is [-1, 1].

Finally, given the formidable generation and fitting capabilities inherent in deep neural networks, we advocate employing a DNN-based network for perturbation generation, the total loss can be defined as:

$$L_{total} = L_{feat} + \sum_{j=1}^{k}(L_{rec}(X, c_j) + L_{id}(X, c_j)) \tag{9}$$

The complete procedure is described in Algorithm 1.

Algorithm 1. Universal Nulifying Generation

1: **Input:** surrogate model F, uniform noise μ, $L_{\inf} - norm$ restriction ε, face image X, condition $C_{1...k}$, initialized generator G with parameters θ
2: **Output:** Universal nullifying perturbation vector v.
3: Initialize θ
4: **for** x_i **in** X **do**
5: $\quad \delta = G(\mu; \theta)$
6: $\quad v = Clamp(\delta, -\varepsilon, \varepsilon)$
7: $\quad \widehat{x}_i = x_i + v$
8: $\quad$ **for** c_i **in** C **do**
9: $\quad\quad$ Calculate losses L_{rec} and L_{id} using x_i and c_i
10: $\quad$ **end for**
11: $\quad$ Calculate losses L_{feat}
12: $\quad \theta \leftarrow$ Optimize $L_{total} = sum(L_{rec}, L_{id}, L_{feat})$
13: **end for**
14: Return v

---

4 Experiment

4.1 Experimental Setup

Implementation Details. The widely-used CelebFaces Attributes (CelebA) dataset [21] is utilized in our experiments. We randomly selected 10k images as the training set and evaluated our method on the CelebA test set. All facial images are uniformly cropped to a size of 256×256. In addition, to further validate the effectiveness of our perturbation across datasets, we evaluated the effect of our universal nullifying perturbation using LFW [14] and Films100 [15] as additional test sets.

To demonstrate our performance, we utilize two kinds of Deepfake models. They are the facial swapping model SimSwap [3] and the facial attribute editing model AttentionGAN [32].

We use a U-Net64 [28] encoder-decoder architecture as the generator G. We optimized the generator G for 5k iterations using an AdamW [22] optimizer with a learning rate of 0.0001. The upper magnitude of the disturbance intensity is $\varepsilon = 0.05$. All the framework is implemented by Pytorch and runs on Tesla-V100, and $batch\_size = 16$.

Evaluation Metrics. In evaluating the quality of the output images, We use the average MSE, PSNR, and SSIM based on previous studies [35]. Additionally, we gauge the similarity between the original images and the nullified outputs using the perceptual distance L_{per} calculated by the Vgg network features. We calculate the success rate SR to indicate the facial images that have been successfully protected. In reference to face recognition [5], we employ the CSIM metric to assess face identity similarity between images, with $CSIM > 0.5$ serving as a threshold to denote that two images correspond to the same identity. Consequently, the $SuccessRate$ is ascertained by evaluating $MSE < 0.05$ and $CSIM > 0.5$ between the original images and the nullified outputs.

Baselines. There is no UAP framework for combating Deepfakes using nullifying perturbation. To compare performance, we adapted three state-of-the-art methods: MIM [6], CMUA [15], and Anti-forgery [35] to the UAP scenario. MIM is a gradient-based method specifically designed to attack deep learning models. Anti-forgery is a deepfake defense method that employs adversarial disruption perturbation within the Lab color space and CMUA is a universal disrupt perturbation generation method. We adjust these methods to the universal setting refer to [27] and the nullification objective refers to [12].

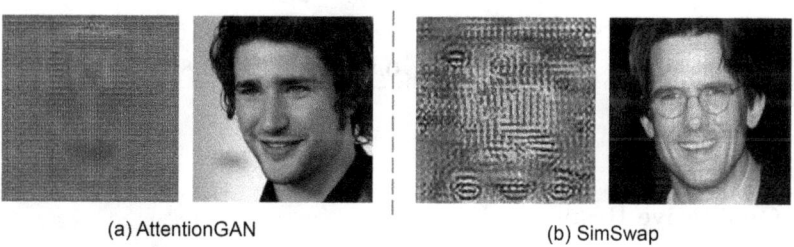

(a) AttentionGAN (b) SimSwap

Fig. 3. Universal perturbations and perturbed samples computed for different deepfake models. The pixel values are scaled for visibility.

4.2 Quantitative Results

In this section, we compare our approach with the 3 baselines against different Deepfake models. Table 1 demonstrates the quantitative results of the proposed method, and our proposed method achieves better results than the baseline method in all the metrics on SimSwap and AttentionGAN models. For the

Simwap and AttentionGAN models, our method achieves 93.87% and 99.99% defense success rates, respectively, which effectively protects the original facial images. Compared with the AttentionGAN model, our proposed method achieves a more obvious improvement in the defense effect for the SimSwap model. Sim-Swap is undoubtedly a forgery model with more complex conditions compared with AttentionGAN, yet the baseline method seems to be unable to effectively eliminate this more difficult SimSwap model. In addition to our improvements to feature-wise and pixel-wise perturbations, we also attribute this limitation to the fitting ability limitations of gradient-based methods. Gradient-based methods often require some perturbation superposition to achieve a generalized perturbation, whereas our proposed neural network generation-based method automatically fits a universal perturbation by sharing model parameters, which is still very effective even on difficult models.

We further assess the performance of the proposed method using the LFW [14] and Films100 [15] datasets, and the corresponding results are detailed in Table 2. Notably, despite the absence of LFW and Films100 data during the training phase, our method achieves defense success rates of 93.57%, 99.99%, 94.28%, and 100.00%, respectively. This underscores the robust protection offered by our method when confronted with unknown data in the real world.

Table 3. Ablation study for SimSwap model. Best results are emphasized in **bold**.

Method	MSE↓	CSIM↑	L_{per} ↓	SR↑
Baseline	0.003	0.661	2.485	84.76%
Ours w/o L_{rec}	0.004	0.819	3.39	89.45%
Ours w/o L_{id}	0.003	0.693	**2.232**	87.76%
Ours w/o L_{feat}	0.003	0.821	2.397	90.76%
Ours	**0.002**	**0.824**	2.379	**93.87%**

4.3 Qualitative Results

We present the qualitative results of our method in nullifying the SimSwap and AttentionGAN models in Fig. 4. For the attribute editing model, we show the comparison results for hair color editing and bangs editing in Fig. 4(a). The results demonstrate that the results of our method are closer in detail to the original images, as shown in Fig. 4(a) by reducing more of the bangs area as well as maintaining better details of the facial shadows. In the case of the face-swap model as shown in Fig. 4(b), previous methods face challenges, whereas our approach effectively preserves the original facial identity.

Our generated universal nullifying perturbations for SimSwap and AttentionGAN are shown in Fig. 3. It can be seen that the perturbation is almost imperceptible in perturbed images. The perturbation for AttentionGAN appears to

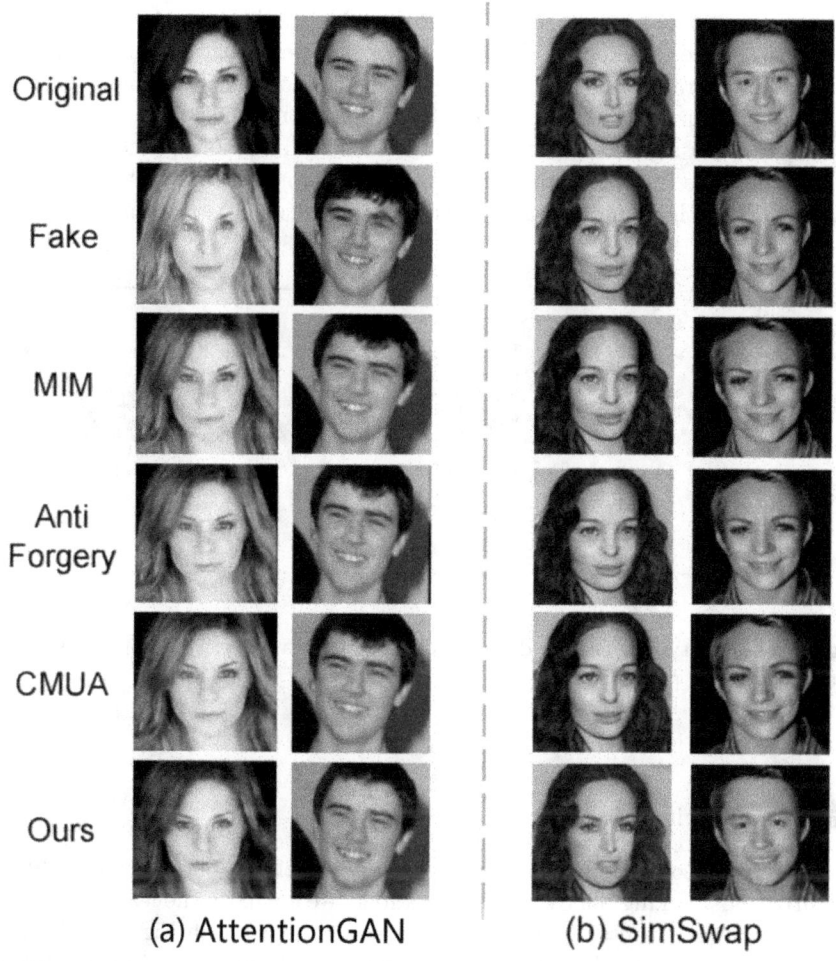

Fig. 4. Qualitative experiments on universal nullifying perturbation against for AttentionGAN and SimSwapmodel. The first row is the original face and the second row is the forged output of the original face. Rows three to six display the outcomes of various methods in nullifying.

have more overall regularity, which may be due to AttentionGAN's ability to do editing of multiple attribute regions of the image. In contrast, the perturbation for SimSwap is more distorted and complex, and the meshing is more severe.

4.4 Ablation Study

In this subsection, we perform ablation studies to unveil how each of the technical designs (i.e., the reconstruction loss, the identity loss, and the feature loss) affects the performance of the perturbation. Table 3 shows the ablation study to prove the effect of our method. The baseline method primarily utilizes L-norm distance loss at the pixel level to constrain perturbation generation. The results demonstrate that the introduced reconstruction loss function significantly enhances the quality of the nullified output. The constraint on displaying identity information significantly enhances the identity invariance, according to the obvious increase in CSIM score. Moreover, the proposed unsupervised feature aggregation method can effectively leverage the feature-wise information.

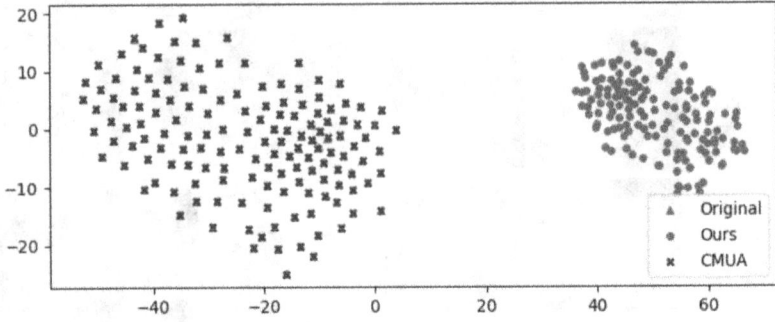

Fig. 5. Visualization of feature distribution. We illustrate the T-SNE [24] results for clean images and perturbed images.

4.5 Geometric Perspective

We provide a geometric perspective to explain the effects of universal nullifying perturbations. Taking SimSwap as an example, we compare the feature distribution of its layer outputs under different cases. As depicted in Fig. 5, the red triangle points represent the original images as input, the green points correspond to our perturbed images, and the blue fork points indicate CMUA's perturbed images as input. It can be seen that our perturbation effectively shifts the distribution of SimSwap model's layer output features and the feature distribution is more aggregated. However, the distribution of CMUA's perturbed images is almost consistent with that of the original images, which means CMUA failed to effectively change the SimSwap model's output.

5 Conclusion

In this paper, we present a methodology for generating universal nullifying perturbations, enabling the use of a single perturbation to safeguard the majority of facial images against Deepfake manipulations. Our approach employs a novel dual constraint method that combines feature-wise and pixel-wise constraints for generating universal perturbations. Furthermore, we propose an unsupervised feature space perturbation method designed to efficiently utilize feature-wise information to guide perturbation generation. Experimental results demonstrate that our proposed method can combat those popular and easy-to-use deep forgery models with a high success rate. Consequently, our universal perturbation can effectively eliminate manipulation models while maintaining the identity consistency of facial images.

References

1. Aneja, S., Markhasin, L., Nießner, M.: TAFIM: targeted adversarial attacks against facial image manipulations. In: Proceedings of the IEEE/CVF Conference on Computer Vision and Pattern Recognition, pp. 58–75. Springer (2022). https://doi.org/10.1007/978-3-031-19781-9_4
2. Bray, S.D., Johnson, S.D., Kleinberg, B.: Testing human ability to detect 'deepfake' images of human faces. J. Cybersecurity **9**(1), tyad011 (2023)
3. Chen, R., Chen, X., Ni, B., Ge, Y.: Simswap: an efficient framework for high fidelity face swapping. In: Proceedings of the 28th ACM International Conference on Multimedia, pp. 2003–2011 (2020)
4. Dash, B., Sharma, P.: Are chatgpt and deepfake algorithms endangering the cybersecurity industry? A review. Int. J. Eng. Appl. Sci.**10**(1) (2023)
5. Deng, J., Guo, J., Xue, N., Zafeiriou, S.: Arcface: additive angular margin loss for deep face recognition. In: Proceedings of the IEEE/CVF conference on computer vision and pattern recognition, pp. 4690–4699 (2019)
6. Dong, Y., et al.: Boosting adversarial attacks with momentum. In: Proceedings of the IEEE/CVF Conference on Computer Vision and Pattern Recognition, pp. 9185–9193 (2018)
7. Fang, Z., Yang, Y., Lin, J., Zhan, R.: Adversarial attacks for multi target image translation networks. In: 2020 IEEE International Conference on Progress in Informatics and Computing (PIC), pp. 179–184. IEEE (2020)
8. Feng, W., Xu, N., Zhang, T., Zhang, Y.: Dynamic generative targeted attacks with pattern injection. In: Proceedings of the IEEE/CVF Conference on Computer Vision and Pattern Recognition, pp. 16404–16414 (2023)
9. Frank, J., Eisenhofer, T., Schönherr, L., Fischer, A., Kolossa, D., Holz, T.: Leveraging frequency analysis for deep fake image recognition. In: International conference on machine learning, pp. 3247–3258. PMLR (2020)
10. Guarnera, L., Giudice, O., Battiato, S.: Deepfake detection by analyzing convolutional traces. In: Proceedings of the IEEE/CVF Conference on Computer Vision and Pattern Recognition Workshops, pp. 666–667 (2020)
11. Gunawan, I.J., Janisriwati, S.: Legal analysis on the use of deepfake technology: threats to Indonesian banking institutions. Law Justice **8**(2), 192–210 (2023)
12. He, Z., Wang, W., Guan, W., Dong, J., Tan, T.: Defeating deepfakes via adversarial visual reconstruction. In: Proceedings of the 30th ACM International Conference on Multimedia, pp. 1 (2022)
13. Hendrik Metzen, J., Chaithanya Kumar, M., Brox, T., Fischer, V.: Universal adversarial perturbations against semantic image segmentation. In: Proceedings of the IEEE/CVF International Conference on Computer Vision, pp. 2755–2764 (2017)

14. Huang, G.B., Mattar, M., Berg, T., Learned-Miller, E.: Labeled faces in the wild: a database forstudying face recognition in unconstrained environments. In: Workshop on Faces in 'Real-Life' Images: Detection, Alignment, and Recognition (2008)
15. Huang, H., et al.: CMUA-watermark: a cross-model universal adversarial watermark for combating deepfakes. In: AAAI. vol. 36, pp. 989–997 (2022)
16. Huang, Q., Katsman, I., He, H., Gu, Z., Belongie, S., Lim, S.N.: Enhancing adversarial example transferability with an intermediate level attack. In: Proceedings of the IEEE/CVF International Conference on Computer Vision, pp. 4733–4742 (2019)
17. Huang, Q., Zhang, J., Zhou, W., Zhang, W., Yu, N.: Initiative defense against facial manipulation. In: Proceedings of the AAAI Conference on Artificial Intelligence. vol. 35, pp. 1619–1627 (2021)
18. Karras, T., Aila, T., Laine, S., Lehtinen, J.: Progressive growing of GANS for improved quality, stability, and variation. In: International Conference on Learning Representations (2018)
19. Karras, T., Laine, S., Aila, T.: A style-based generator architecture for generative adversarial networks. In: Proceedings of the IEEE/CVF Conference on Computer Vision and Pattern Recognition, pp. 4401–4410 (2019)
20. Li, J., Ji, R., Liu, H., Hong, X., Gao, Y., Tian, Q.: Universal perturbation attack against image retrieval. In: Proceedings of the IEEE/CVF International Conference on Computer Vision, pp. 4899–4908 (2019)
21. Liu, Z., Luo, P., Wang, X., Tang, X.: Large-scale celebfaces attributes (celeba) dataset. Retrieved August **15**(2018), 11 (2018)
22. Loshchilov, I., Hutter, F.: Fixing weight decay regularization in ADAM (2018)
23. Lv, L.: Smart watermark to defend against deepfake image manipulation. In: 2021 IEEE 6th International Conference on Computer and Communication Systems (ICCCS), pp. 380–384. IEEE (2021)
24. Van der Maaten, L., Hinton, G.: Visualizing data using t-SNE. J. Mach. Learn. Res. **9**(11) (2008)
25. Masood, M., Nawaz, M., Malik, K.M., Javed, A., Irtaza, A., Malik, H.: Deepfakes generation and detection: state-of-the-art, open challenges, countermeasures, and way forward. Appl. Intell. **53**(4), 3974–4026 (2023)
26. Mirza, M., Osindero, S.: Conditional generative adversarial nets. arXiv preprint arXiv:1411.1784 (2014)
27. Moosavi-Dezfooli, S.M., Fawzi, A., Fawzi, O., Frossard, P.: Universal adversarial perturbations. In: Proceedings of the IEEE/CVF Conference on Computer Vision and Pattern Recognition, pp. 1765–1773 (2017)
28. Ronneberger, O., Fischer, P., Brox, T.: U-net: convolutional networks for biomedical image segmentation. In: Medical Image Computing and Computer-Assisted Intervention–MICCAI 2015: 18th International Conference, Munich, Germany, October 5-9, 2015, Proceedings, Part III 18, pp. 234–241. Springer (2015). https://doi.org/10.1007/978-3-319-24574-4_28
29. Ruiz, N., Bargal, S.A., Sclaroff, S.: Disrupting deepfakes: adversarial attacks against conditional image translation networks and facial manipulation systems. In: Proceedings of the IEEE/CVF Conference on Computer Vision and Pattern Recognition 2020 Workshops, pp. 236–251 (2020)
30. Simonyan, K., Zisserman, A.: Very deep convolutional networks for large-scale image recognition. arXiv preprint arXiv:1409.1556 (2014)
31. Sun, P., Li, Y., Qi, H., Lyu, S.: Landmark breaker: obstructing deepfake by disturbing landmark extraction. In: 2020 IEEE International Workshop on Information Forensics and Security (WIFS), pp. 1–6 (2020). 10.1109/WIFS49906.2020.9360910

32. Tang, H., Xu, D., Sebe, N., Yan, Y.: Attention-guided generative adversarial networks for unsupervised image-to-image translation. In: Proceedings: International Joint Conference on Neural Networks, IJCNN 2019. vol. 2019 (2019)
33. Tang, L., et al.: Feature extraction matters more: universal deepfake disruption through attacking ensemble feature extractors (2023)
34. Wang, K., Gou, C., Duan, Y., Lin, Y., Zheng, X., Wang, F.Y.: Generative adversarial networks: introduction and outlook. IEEE/CAA J. Automatica Sin. **4**(4), 588–598 (2017)
35. Wang, R., Huang, Z., Chen, Z., Liu, L., Chen, J., Wang, L.: Anti-forgery: towards a stealthy and robust deepfake disruption attack via adversarial perceptual-aware perturbations. Proceedings of the Thirty-First International Joint Conference on Artificial Intelligence (2022)
36. Wang, S.Y., Wang, O., Zhang, R., Owens, A., Efros, A.A.: CNN-generated images are surprisingly easy to spot... for now. In: Proceedings of the IEEE/CVF Conference on Computer Vision and Pattern Recognition, pp. 8695–8704 (2020)
37. Wang, Z., et al.: Towards transferable targeted adversarial examples. In: Proceedings of the IEEE/CVF Conference on Computer Vision and Pattern Recognition, pp. 20534–20543 (2023)
38. Wei, Z., Chen, J., Wu, Z., Jiang, Y.G.: Enhancing the self-universality for transferable targeted attacks. In: Proceedings of the IEEE/CVF Conference on Computer Vision and Pattern Recognition, pp. 12281–12290 (2023)
39. Xu, Q., Tao, G., Zhang, X.: Bounded adversarial attack on deep content features. In: Proceedings of the IEEE/CVF Conference on Computer Vision and Pattern Recognition, pp. 15203–15212 (2022)
40. Yeh, C.Y., Chen, H.W., Shuai, H.H., Yang, D.N., Chen, M.S.: Attack as the best defense: nullifying image-to-image translation GANS via limit-aware adversarial attack. In: Proceedings of the IEEE/CVF International Conference on Computer Vision, pp. 16188–16197 (2021)

HFDA-Net: Utilizing High-Frequency Feature and Dual-Attention to Enhance Image Manipulation Detection and Localization

Chengeng Liu, Xu Chen(✉), Tian Xu, and Xiangyang Jia

School of Computer Science, Wuhan University, Wuhan, China
xuchen@whu.edu.cn

Abstract. In this paper, we propose HFDA-Net, a novel approach for image manipulation detection and localization (IMDL) tasks. Unlike existing methods that only extract high-frequency features from the input image, HFDA-Net further extracts high-frequency features from RGB feature maps, capturing richer manipulation traces. In addition, HFDA-Net introduces a new module that efficiently calculates and combines position and channel attention, improving the accuracy and efficiency of manipulated region localization. Moreover, HFDA-Net supports feature extraction and aggregation at multiple scales and employs a coarse-to-fine pattern to predict manipulated regions, demonstrating remarkable generalizability. Thanks to its lightweight architecture, HFDA-Net achieves a processing speed of 65+ FPS when handling 1080P images. Extensive experiments on four image forensics benchmarks demonstrate that HFDA-Net generally outperforms existing advanced methods in manipulation detection by 1% to 15% and in manipulation localization by 1.5% to 5.4% under AUC. Furthermore, HFDA-Net exhibits good robustness compared to existing methods.

Keywords: Image manipulation detection and localization · Multi-scale learning · High-frequency feature · Attention mechanism

1 Introduction

With the development of image generation and manipulation techniques, the alteration of image content and the creation of high-fidelity images have gained popularity due to their increasing accessibility [26]. These manipulations encompass various techniques, such as object removal [3], face swapping [19], etc. These visually convincing manipulations often escape human perception, making them potentially harmful to individuals and society. Traditional image manipulation techniques primarily involve copying regions from the source image to the target image, as illustrated in Fig. 1. These techniques include copy-move (copying and pasting regions within an image), splicing (copying and pasting regions from a source image to a target image), and removal (removing and replacing parts of an image).

Pristine Image　　Manipulated Image　　Prediction

Fig. 1. Examples of image manipulation and its localization. The first two columns show examples of pristine and manipulated images, respectively, and the last column shows the output of manipulation localization.

Given the realistic and potentially harmful nature of these manipulated images, the development of advanced and reliable forensic algorithms is crucial. Over the past years, numerous methods have been proposed to address the tasks of image manipulation detection and localization (IMDL). Some early works identify specific types of forgeries by mining and analyzing artifacts in the images, including camera model information [6], local noise [18], and compression noise [4]. With the rise of deep learning, numerous approaches [13,16,29,31] have emerged that can detect a wide variety of image forgeries. However, existing methods still encounter several challenges:

Insufficient Feature Extraction. Realistic manipulated images can often deceive the human eye, necessitating that forensic models extract comprehensive forgery features to ensure effective manipulation detection and localization. While some prior methods [16,30] exclusively extract features from the RGB domain, others [13,29,31] additionally extract features from the frequency domain, employing filters like SRM [8] and Bayar [2]. High-frequency features within an image hold significance for detecting traces of manipulation, as they typically correspond to image details, such as edges and textures, which are pivotal for enhancing the accuracy and robustness of forensic methods. However, to the best of our knowledge, existing approaches utilize both features in a simple way. These methods directly extract high-frequency features from images and concatenate them with RGB features, without considering high-frequency features that may be hidden in the RGB features, which limits the performance of forensics.

Insufficient Learning of Image Feature Correlation. To localize manipulated regions in an image, some existing approaches [13,29] use *pooling* or *position attention* mechanism, which enables the model to focus on the features of the region most likely to be manipulated. However, these methods solely focus on local feature correlations and fail to fully capture global correlations, leading to limited generalization capability. In addition to position correlation, some approaches [16] also adopt *channel attention* to selectively amplify or suppress certain feature channels based on their importance. However, existing methods, such as PSCC-Net [16], typically use the same embeddings for calculating both attention mechanisms, without considering the difference between the two attentions. This may result in insufficient learning of image feature correlation and lower localization performance of the model.

To overcome these limitations, we present HFDA-Net, a novel image manipulation detection and localization framework. HFDA-Net enhances the feature extraction between the RGB domain and frequency domain with Dual-Domain Feature Extraction Module (DDFEM), utilizes a light-weight backbone proposed in [23] to extract multi-scale features, and enhances the attention mechanism by introducing a Position-Channel Fusion Module (PCFM) to effectively capture the global context of local features and improve the capability of manipulation localization. Thanks to the lightweight network design, HFDA-Net can process 1080P images at 65+ FPS.

In summary, the contributions of our work are as follows:

- We design a novel Dual-Domain Feature Extraction Module (DDFEM) that effectively extracts and fuses both RGB features and high-frequency features of manipulated images.
- We enhance the attention mechanism by introducing the Position-Channel Fusion Module (PCFM), which effectively extracts position and channel correlations, and aggregates the global context of local features to improve the capability of manipulation region localization.
- We extensively evaluate HFDA-Net on several standard image forensic benchmarks, and the results show that HFDA-Net generally outperforms existing advanced methods in manipulation detection by 1% to 15% and in manipulation localization by 1.5% to 5.4% under AUC.

2 Related Works

Image Manipulation Detection and Localization. Early approaches in the field of image manipulation detection and localization focused on specific types of manipulation, such as copy-move [28], splicing [14], and removal [27]. While these methods have achieved good results in detecting and localizing specific types of manipulation, they may not be able to cope with the diverse image manipulation techniques and unpredictable manipulating methods in the real world.

Recent research has aimed to address this limitation by developing algorithms capable of detecting multiple types of manipulations using a single model. For example, RGB-N [31] proposed a two-stream network that utilizes an object detection network for manipulation localization. However, it only provides bounding boxes for the manipulated regions without accurate masks. ManTra-Net [29] employed VGG [21] as a feature extractor and utilized a pooling and LSTM-based detection module for localization. Building upon this, SPAN [13] introduced local self-attention and pyramid propagation mechanisms to improve spatial correlation modeling. PSCC-Net [16] effectively modeled spatial and channel correlations while employing multi-scale feature representation to enhance manipulation detection.

High-Frequency Feature. Several works have emphasized the importance of high-frequency information in distinguishing between pristine and manipulated regions. RGB-N [31] incorporated SRM [8] noise in addition to images, while ManTra-Net [29] and SPAN [13] utilized BayarConv [2] and SRM filters to extract high-frequency features. However, these methods simply concatenate features from different domains, potentially leading to insufficient extraction of high-frequency information. In this paper, we not only extract RGB domain features and high-frequency features but also focus on further enriching high-frequency information from the RGB domain.

Attention Mechanism. Attention mechanism [1] has been extensively studied for its ability to capture the correlations between different features. Initially applied to machine translation tasks [22], the attention mechanism has demonstrated competence in various domains that require long-term feature modeling [5]. Within the computer vision field, channel attention [12] and position (spatial) attention [24] have been widely explored. Recent works have combined both attention mechanisms, and a dual attention mechanism [9] was proposed to capture rich contextual relationships. Some researchers have introduced attention mechanisms specifically for forgery detection [30]. In this paper, we propose a new dual attention mechanism, based on which a Position-Channel Fusion Module (PCFM) is designed to extract and aggregate position and channel correlations simultaneously.

3 Proposed Method

3.1 Overview

HFDA-Net, as illustrated in Fig. 2, comprises three key parts: the Dual-Domain Information Extraction and Fusion part, the Multi-scale Feature Extraction part, and the Detection and Localization part.

The input image is first passed through the Dual-Domain Feature Extraction Module (DDFEM) to acquire features containing both RGB domain and frequency domain information. Subsequently, in the Multi-scale Feature Extraction part, we adopt a lightweight backbone, HRNetV2p-W18, proposed in [23], utilizing its default settings. The backbone differs from previous methods [13, 29, 31]

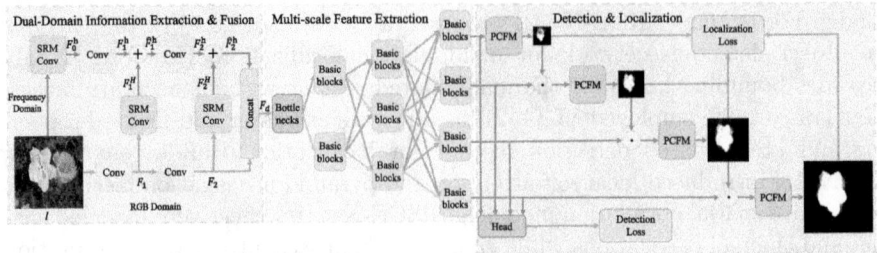

Fig. 2. The overall architecture of HFDA-Net. The image features containing high-frequency information are first extracted from the input image, after which the features are further extracted at multiple scales. The classification result is obtained through the detection head, after which the final mask prediction is obtained in a coarse-to-fine manner at multiple scales.

by extracting features at four scales that capture both local and global information in the input image. Multi-scale feature extraction makes the model robust to manipulated regions of different sizes, which is critical in the real world where the size and location of manipulated regions may vary greatly. Furthermore, this backbone incorporates dense connections among stages to facilitate the fusion of local and global features. This enables each scale to contain sufficient information for predicting the final manipulation mask.

After the features are extracted at multiple scales, HFDA-Net carries out detection and localization tasks. For manipulation detection, in contrast to most prior methods [13,29], which obtain detection results solely from the predicted mask, HFDA-Net inputs the features from multiple scales into a detection head for binary classification. This helps prevent false positives on pristine images.

Regarding manipulation localization, the proposed model feeds the features from each scale into the Position-Channel Fusion Module (PCFM) to predict the mask of the manipulated region. To utilize both local and global information, the model adopts the same strategy as in [16], which employs the predicted mask from each scale as a prior for the subsequent scale prediction . After the PCFM generates the predicted mask for each scale, the model outputs a predicted score and masks at the four scales as the final output.

3.2 Dual-Domain Feature Extraction Module

Conventional convolution operations are proficient at extracting features from images, yet their primary emphasis is on capturing predominant spatial characteristics rather than the subtler traces of manipulation. Recognizing that high-frequency features have the potential to reveal differences between pristine and manipulated regions [17], we introduce the Dual-Domain Feature Extraction Module (DDFEM) to extract both RGB and high-frequency features and further augment high-frequency features through RGB features.

In addition to the conventional convolution layers used in [16], which extract low-level RGB features, the proposed module applies SRM (Statistical Region

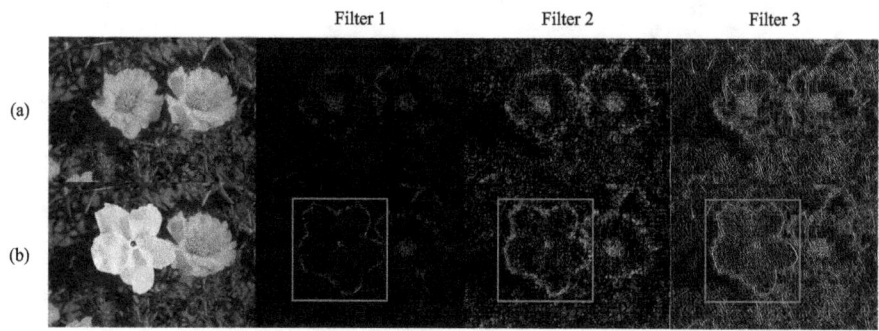

Fig. 3. Noises extracted by SRM filters from (a) the pristine image and (b) the manipulated image. Red rectangles highlight blended edge artifacts that are challenging to discern in the RGB domain but highly conspicuous in noises. In the pristine image, noise within the edge region displays a discontinuous pattern, while in the manipulated image, the edge noise exhibits a continuous and smoother or more pronounced profile. (Color figure online)

Merging) filters [8] to extract high-frequency features from both the original image and multiple low-level RGB feature maps. SRM filters are designed to capture fine-grained statistical information in the feature maps, which can help to reveal manipulation traces that are not easily detectable by conventional convolution operations. In Fig. 3, examples of the noise extracted by SRM filters are presented. It is evident that within the noise, discernible traces of edge manipulation in manipulated images can be identified.

As depicted in Fig. 2, given the RGB image I as input, we initially extract the high-frequency feature F_0^h using SRM filters. Subsequently, we feed the RGB image and F_0^h into conventional convolution layers to obtain output feature maps F_1 and F_1^h, respectively. To extract richer high-frequency information, we apply SRM filters to F_1 and add the resulting features F_1^H with F_1^h to obtain $\hat{F}_1^h$. This process is repeated for F_1 and $\hat{F}_1^h$ to obtain F_2 and $\hat{F}_2^h$, respectively. Finally, we concatenate F_2 and $\hat{F}_2^h$ to obtain the feature F_d, which contains information from both domains. Benefiting from multiple layers of high-frequency feature extraction, F_d exhibits an enhanced representation of high-frequency features.

3.3 Position-Channel Fusion Module

Attention mechanisms [9,22] excel at modeling long-term features and modulating them based on their relative importance. We aim to make features within the same region (manipulated or pristine) as similar as possible while ensuring distinctiveness between features from different regions. To accomplish this, we introduce attention mechanisms to enhance the ability to capture manipulated regions. Inspired by the Dual Attention Network proposed in [9], we present the Position-Channel Fusion Module (PCFM). This module employs both position and channel attention to aggregate correlations between different regions and channels, respectively.

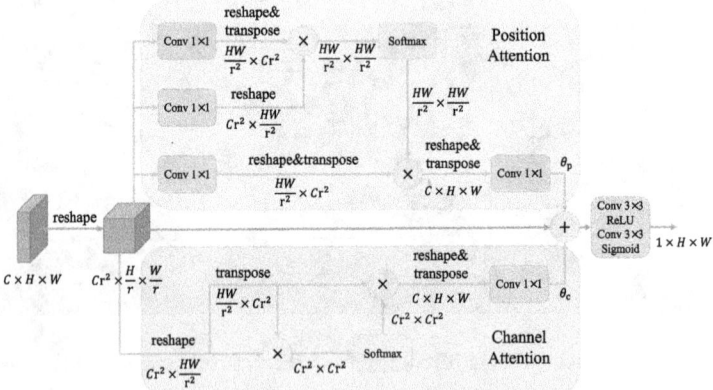

Fig. 4. The structure of PCFM. The green line denotes the feature flow of position attention and the orange line denotes the feature flow of channel attention. ⊗ denotes matrix multiplication and ⊕ denotes element-wise addition. (Color figure online)

As depicted in Fig. 4, the PCFM comprises two parallel attention mechanisms: position attention and channel attention. Position attention selectively updates features at each position based on the weights of all position features, while channel attention focuses on the relationships between channels and emphasizes interdependent channel feature mappings. Notably, to reduce computational position attention brought by position attention, the PCFM first performs feature reshaping. Finally, it outputs the prediction mask at the original size.

Specifically, for position attention, we employ three 1×1 convolutions to convert the feature X into three linear embeddings. Subsequently, we apply reshape or transpose operations on these embeddings to obtain three new embeddings: X_p^q, X_p^k, and X_p^v. The position correlation is calculated using X_p^q and X_p^k, and the position attention A_p is obtained by performing matrix multiplication with X_p^v after $softmax(\cdot)$ transformation. Regarding channel attention, it differs from position attention in that we compute the attention map directly from the original features. Specifically, we reshape the feature X to acquire X_c^q and then transpose X_c^q to obtain X_c^k and X_c^v. The channel correlation is computed using X_c^q and X_c^k, and the channel attention A_c is obtained by performing matrix multiplication with X_c^v after $softmax(\cdot)$ transformation. The two sets of attention can be expressed as:

$$A_p = softmax(X_p^q X_p^k) X_p^v. \tag{1}$$

$$A_c = X_c^v softmax(X_c^q X_c^k). \tag{2}$$

After obtaining the position and channel attention features, we restore them to their original sizes using transpose and reshape operations to obtain $\hat{A}_p$ and $\hat{A}_c$. Subsequently, we further process these two features separately using two 1×1 convolutions called μ_p and μ_c. To weigh the importance of the two attentions, we employ two learnable parameters, θ_p and θ_c, to multiply them with the corresponding features, respectively. Additionally, we introduce residual learning [11] to sum the two processed features with the original feature X, resulting in the final feature F for localization:

$$F = X + \theta_p \cdot \mu_p(\hat{A}_p) + \theta_c \cdot \mu_c(\hat{A}_c). \tag{3}$$

Finally, the PCFM module reduces the number of channels in the features through convolution operations and employs the $sigmoid(\cdot)$ function to generate the final prediction mask.

4 Experiments

4.1 Experimental Setup

Datasets. For localization performance evaluation, We conduct experiments on four standard datasets: Coverage [25], CASIA [7], NIST16 [10], and IMD2020 [20]. To ensure fairness, we use the same training/testing split as utilized in previous methods [13,16,31]. We use the same dataset as in [16] for detection performance evaluation.

For pre-training, Mantra-Net [29] and SPAN [13] are pre-trained on a non-public dataset consisting of 1.25 million images, while PSCC-Net [16] uses a synthetic dataset containing 81,910 pristine images and three types of manipulated images: splicing (116,583 images), copy-move (100,000 images), and removal (78,246 images). In comparison, we use the same dataset as PSCC-Net for pre-training and adopt the same pre-training strategy, where 0.1 million images are randomly sampled in each epoch for training. It's worth noting that the size of the pre-training dataset we use is much smaller than that of Mantra-Net and SPAN.

Metrics. To assess the localization performance, we employ the pixel-level Area Under Curve (AUC) and F1 score, following prior works [13,16,29]. For evaluating the detection performance, we utilize the image-level F1 score.

Loss Function. As both manipulation detection and localization tasks are binary classification problems, we employ binary cross-entropy loss as our loss function. For the manipulation detection task, we supervise the model's predictions using ground-truth labels, where a label of 0 indicates a pristine image and a label of 1 indicates a manipulated image. In the context of manipulation localization, we utilize ground-truth masks to supervise the output masks at four different scales. To ensure consistency, we scale the ground-truth mask to match the corresponding output mask. Within each mask, a value of 0 denotes a pristine pixel, while a value of 1 indicates a manipulated pixel. Additionally, we introduce a parameter, denoted as ω, to control the relative importance of the different scales. Consequently, our final loss function L_{total} can be defined as follows:

$$L_{total} = L_{BCE}(l_p, l_{gt}) + \frac{1}{4}\sum_{s=1}^{4} \omega_s L_{BCE}(m_p^s, m_{gt}^s), \quad (4)$$

where L_{BCE} represents the binary cross-entropy loss function. In the context of manipulation detection, l_p and l_{gt} correspond to the model's predicted label and the ground-truth label, respectively. As for manipulation localization on scale s, m_p^s and m_{gt}^s denote the predicted mask of the model and the corresponding ground-truth mask, ω_s signifies the importance weight assigned to scale s.

Implementation Details. HFDA-Net is implemented using PyTorch and consists of 3.75 Million (M) parameters. As a comparison, PSCC-Net [16], Mantra-Net [29] and SPAN [13] have 3.6 M, 3.8 M, and 3.7 M parameters respectively. All experiments are performed on a single NVIDIA Tesla A100 GPU. During training, the initial learning rate is set to 2e-4 and is reduced by half after every 5 epochs. The total training period is 25 epochs, with a batch size of 10. Training is conducted using the Adam [15] optimizer. For the loss function depicted in Eq. 4, we assign equal importance to each scale, so ω_s is set to 1 at each scale.

The training images are resized to a resolution of 256 × 256 pixels. During inference, our model can accept input images of arbitrary sizes. To alleviate the computational burden, we resample the features extracted by the backbone to 32 × 32, 64 × 64, 128 × 128, and 256 × 256 respectively, and subsequently input them into the corresponding PCFM module. After obtaining the final mask with a size fixed at 256 × 256, we resample it to the same size as the input image for evaluation.

4.2 Evaluation and Comparison

We evaluate HFDA-Net and compare it with 4 IMDL methods, namely RGB-N [31], Mantra-Net [29], SPAN [13], and PSCC-Net [16]. To evaluate the localization performance, we first assess the pre-trained model using the complete dataset. Subsequently, we fine-tune the pre-trained models on the training split of the dataset and evaluate their performance on the testing split.

The reported results of the compared methods are from their original papers. For the evaluation of the detection performance, considering that Mantra-Net does not have a corresponding fine-tuning model, we uniformly use the pre-training model for evaluation.

Localization Performance of Pre-trained Models. We first evaluate the pre-trained models on the complete datasets. We compare pre-trained HFDA-Net with Mantra-Net, SPAN, and PSCC-Net. The pre-trained models are selected based on their best validation scores on the validation set.

Table 1. Comparison of localization AUC (in %) using pre-trained models.

Method	Coverage 100 imgs	CASIA 6044 imgs	NIST16 564 imgs	IMD2020 2010 imgs	FPS
ManTra-Net [29]	81.9	81.7	79.5	74.8	7
SPAN [13]	**92.2**	79.7	84.0	75.0	9
PSCC-Net [16]	84.7	82.9	**85.5**	80.6	69
HFDA-Net	89.2	**84.5**	84.4	**81.4**	65

Table 1 presents the pixel-level AUC results of the pre-trained models on four public datasets. As shown in the table, HFDA-Net generally outperforms existing methods by 1.5% to 5.4% (by calculating the average of the AUC improvements across all datasets). HFDA-Net demonstrates the best localization performance on two large datasets CASIA (6044 images) and IMD2020 (2010 images). It achieves an AUC of 84.5% on CASIA and 81.4% on IMD2020, which is 1.6% and 0.8% higher than the second-best method, respectively. These results show that our proposed method has superior generalizability and localization ability. We attribute this success to our introduced DDFEM, which can capture the manipulation traces left behind by different manipulating methods, thus achieving better localization results.

HFDA-Net achieved the second-highest AUC on the other two small datasets Coverage (100 images) and IMD2020 (564 images). There may be two reasons why HFDA-Net did not achieve the best results. Firstly, the limited amount of data and randomized testing in these datasets could introduce variability in the results. Secondly, there might be differences in the distribution of the training data, which can impact the model's performance.

Running efficiency is critical for the practical application of IMDL models. HFDA-Net can achieve a processing speed of 65+ FPS when handling 1080P images, while PSCC-Net [16], Mantra-Net [29] and SPAN [13] achieve 69, 7 and 9 FPS, respectively. Despite its marginally slower processing rate when compared to PSCC-Net, HFDA-Net excels in achieving superior results. It effectively balances runtime efficiency and performance, making it an enticing choice for real-world applications.

Localization Performance of Fine-Tuned Models. We conducted fine-tuning using the training split of each dataset and evaluated the fine-tuned models on the corresponding testing split. Table 2 compares the results of fine-tuned HFDA-Net on three datasets with three methods RGB-N, SPAN, and PSCC-Net. As not provided in the original paper, the results of ManTra-Net are not listed in the table.

Table 2. Comparison of localization AUC / F1 score (in %) using fine-tuned models.

Method	Coverage	CASIA	NIST16
RGB-N [31]	81.7 / 43.7	79.5 / 40.8	93.7 / 72.2
SPAN [13]	93.7 / 55.8	83.8 / 38.2	96.1 / 58.2
PSCC-Net [16]	94.1 / 72.3	87.5 / **55.4**	99.1 / 74.2
HFDA-Net	**97.3 / 75.6**	**88.0** / 47.1	**99.6 / 75.3**

As shown in Table 2, HFDA-Net achieves the highest AUC on all datasets, with an average AUC improvement of 1.4% over the second-best method. Additionally, HFDA-Net gains the best F1 score on two datasets. The evaluation of the fine-tuned models demonstrates the excellent manipulation localization capabilities of HFDA-Net. We credit this achievement to the PCFM we have proposed, as it excels in extracting positional and channel correlations from the features obtained through DDFEM and backbone when dealing with particular manipulating techniques, which in turn yields better localization results.

HFDA-Net also demonstrates good localization performance on different scales. Figure 5 shows the manipulation localization results of some images. It can be observed that HFDA-Net accurately locates the manipulated regions regardless of their size and shape.

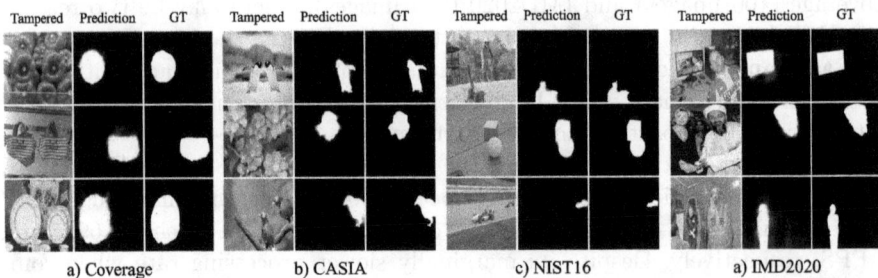

Fig. 5. Qualitative examples of manipulation localization on four standard datasets.

Detection Performance of Pre-trained Models. Table 3 presents the image manipulation detection performance of the pre-trained models. It is evident that HFDA-Net significantly outperforms the method presented in [13,29] by 8% to 15% under AUC. This improvement can be attributed to our utilization of a specialized classification head for detecting manipulated images, rather than relying on masks obtained through localization. Additionally, HFDA-Net demonstrates improvement over the method proposed in [16], which also employs a specialized classification head for manipulation detection. We attribute this performance enhancement to our proposed Dual-Domain Feature Extraction Module (DDFEM).

Table 3. Comparison of detection AUC / F1 score (in %) using pre-trained models.

Method	Image-Level AUC	Image-Level F1 score
ManTra-Net [29]	59.94	56.69
SPAN [13]	67.33	63.48
PSCC-Net [16]	74.40	66.88
HFDA-Net	**75.15**	**66.97**

4.3 Ablation Study

To assess the contribution of each proposed module, we conducted the ablation study by designing several network variants to validate the effectiveness of our network design. These variants were pre-trained on the same dataset and we report the AUC on four public datasets, as shown in Table 4.

Table 4. Ablation study of HFDA-Net. The AUC (in %) of variants is evaluated using pre-trained models.

Variants	Coverage	CASIA	NIST16	IMD2020
w/o DDFEM	85.6	82.2	80.6	78.9
w/o SRM Fusion	86.3	82.8	81.7	78.5
w/o DA	84.3	82.2	73.2	74.6
w/o PA	84.7	82.4	79.0	77.7
w/o CA	84.3	82.3	83.0	80.5
HFDA-Net	**89.2**	**84.5**	**84.4**	**81.4**

Firstly, we observe a significant performance degradation in the absence of the Dual-Domain Feature Extraction Module (DDFEM), as shown in row 1. This finding demonstrates the effectiveness of introducing high-frequency features for manipulation localization. We also explore the effectiveness of further extracting high-frequency information from low-level RGB features by retaining only the SRM filters that extract high-frequency information from the input image. The results in row 2 also show a large performance degradation, This suggests that only extracting the high-frequency information from the input image is insufficient and that further extraction and enrichment of the high-frequency information from the low-level RGB features can lead to performance gains.

Further analysis of the results in rows 3 to 5 reveals that all variants of the PCFM module exhibit degradation. Specifically, omitting both position and channel attention (w/o DA) results in a significant decrease in performance. Moreover, the model's performance shows varying degrees of decline when either position attention (w/o PA) or channel attention (w/o CA) is not employed. Notably, position attention demonstrates a greater contribution to the performance gain than channel attention. These ablation experiments on the PCFM module confirm that HFDA-Net can effectively extract and aggregate position and channel correlations, thereby enhancing the model's performance.

In summary, the results of the ablation study robustly affirm the effectiveness and significance of both the DDFEM and PCFM modules in augmenting the model's overall performance.

4.4 Robustness Analysis

To further validate the robustness and effectiveness of HFDA-Net, we conduct several experiments to assess its performance under various attack and post-processing operations. Following the distortion settings in [13], we apply corresponding standard functions available in OpenCV to degrade the images from the NIST16 dataset. These distortions include resizing the image to a different scale (Resize), applying Gaussian blur with a kernel size of k (GBlur), adding Gaussian noise with a standard deviation of σ to the image (GNoise), and performing JPEG compression with a quality factor of q (JPEGComp).

Table 5. Robustness analysis for various distortions over NIST16 dataset. The declines relative to the original dataset are reported in $-log$ form for easier comparison.

Distortion	Resize (0.78×)	Resize (0.25×)	GBlur ($k=3$)	GBlur ($k=15$)	GNoise ($\sigma=3$)	GNoise ($\sigma=15$)	JComp ($q=100$)	JComp ($q=50$)
ManTra-Net [29]	2.10	1.49	2.12	1.39	0.87	0.60	2.75	1.33
SPAN [13]	2.07	1.36	1.99	1.24	0.98	0.70	2.37	1.41
PSCC-Net [16]	2.68	2.27	2.98	1.19	1.08	0.99	**3.09**	**2.93**
HFDA-Net	**3.63**	**2.46**	**3.32**	**1.42**	**1.32**	**1.02**	2.85	2.67

Table 5 presents the results of the robustness analysis, where we report the metrics of the pre-trained models. Evaluating the performance degradation of the model solely based on the absolute declines in the metrics may not provide an intuitive assessment. Therefore, we utilize the $-log$ of the relative AUC decline for comparison, where higher values indicate better robustness of the model. As shown in Table 5, HFDA-Net demonstrates superior robustness under three distortions, namely Resize, GBlur, and GNoise. In addition, it exhibits slightly higher sensitivity to JPEG compression operations compared to PSCC-Net, but still better than other methods. While the overall performance may be affected to some extent, HFDA-Net maintains a favorable level of robustness across a range of attack and post-processing scenarios.

5 Conclusion

In this paper, we introduced HFDA-Net, a novel framework designed for the detection and localization of image manipulation. HFDA-Net capitalizes on the high-frequency information within images and incorporates a dual-attention mechanism to enhance the precision of detection and localization within manipulated regions. Notably, our contribution includes the Dual-Domain Feature Extraction Module (DDFEM), which effectively extracts features from both the RGB domain and the frequency domain while enhancing the high-frequency information derived from the RGB domain. Furthermore, our proposed Position-Channel Fusion Module (PCFM) adeptly captures positional and channel correlations at multiple scales, aggregating global context from local features. Extensive experiments on diverse benchmark datasets have demonstrated HFDA-Net's superiority when compared to existing advanced methods. In our future work, we aim to extend the applicability of HFDA-Net to detect deep learning-based image forgeries, further advancing our understanding and capabilities in the domain of image forensics.

References

1. Bahdanau, D., Cho, K., Bengio, Y.: Neural machine translation by jointly learning to align and translate. arXiv preprint (2014). arXiv:1409.0473
2. Bayar, B., Stamm, M.C.: Constrained convolutional neural networks: a new approach towards general purpose image manipulation detection. IEEE Trans. Inform. Forensics Secur. **13**(11), 2691–2706 (2018)
3. Bertalmio, M., Sapiro, G., Caselles, V., Ballester, C.: Image inpainting. In: Proceedings of the 27th Annual Conference on Computer Graphics and Interactive Techniques, pp. 417–424 (2000)
4. Bianchi, T., Piva, A.: Image forgery localization via block-grained analysis of jpeg artifacts. IEEE Trans. Inform. Forensics Secur. **7**(3), 1003–1017 (2012)
5. Chaudhari, S., Mithal, V., Polatkan, G., Ramanath, R.: An attentive survey of attention models. ACM Trans. Intell. Syst. Technol. **12**(5), 1–32 (2021)
6. Cozzolino, D., Gragnaniello, D., Verdoliva, L.: Image forgery localization through the fusion of camera-based, feature-based and pixel-based techniques. In: 2014 IEEE International Conference on Image Processing (ICIP), pp. 5302–5306. IEEE (2014)
7. Dong, J., Wang, W., Tan, T.: Casia image tampering detection evaluation database. In: 2013 IEEE China Summit and International Conference on Signal and Information Processing, pp. 422–426. IEEE (2013)
8. Fridrich, J., Kodovsky, J.: Rich models for steganalysis of digital images. IEEE Trans. Inform. Forensics Secur. **7**(3), 868–882 (2012)
9. Fu, J., et al.: Dual attention network for scene segmentation. In: Proceedings of the IEEE/CVF Conference on Computer Vision and Pattern Recognition, pp. 3146–3154 (2019)
10. Guan, H., et al.: MFC datasets: Large-scale benchmark datasets for media forensic challenge evaluation. In: 2019 IEEE Winter Applications of Computer Vision Workshops (WACVW), pp. 63–72. IEEE (2019)

11. He, K., Zhang, X., Ren, S., Sun, J.: Deep residual learning for image recognition. In: Proceedings of the IEEE Conference on Computer Vision and Pattern Recognition, pp. 770–778 (2016)
12. Hu, J., Shen, L., Sun, G.: Squeeze-and-excitation networks. In: Proceedings of the IEEE Conference on Computer Vision and Pattern Recognition, pp. 7132–7141 (2018)
13. Hu, X., Zhang, Z., Jiang, Z., Chaudhuri, S., Yang, Z., Nevatia, R.: Span: spatial pyramid attention network for image manipulation localization. In: Computer Vision–ECCV 2020: 16th European Conference, Glasgow, UK, August 23–28, 2020, Proceedings, Part XXI 16, pp. 312–328. Springer (2020). https://doi.org/10.1007/978-3-030-58589-1_19
14. Huh, M., Liu, A., Owens, A., Efros, A.A.: Fighting fake news: image splice detection via learned self-consistency. In: Proceedings of the European Conference on Computer Vision (ECCV), pp. 101–117 (2018)
15. Kingma, D.P., Ba, J.: Adam: A method for stochastic optimization. arXiv preprint (2014). arXiv:1412.6980
16. Liu, X., Liu, Y., Chen, J., Liu, X.: PSCC-net: Progressive spatio-channel correlation network for image manipulation detection and localization. IEEE Trans. Circ. Syst. Video Technol. **32**(11), 7505–7517 (2022)
17. Luo, Y., Zhang, Y., Yan, J., Liu, W.: Generalizing face forgery detection with high-frequency features. In: Proceedings of the IEEE/CVF Conference on Computer Vision and Pattern Recognition, pp. 16317–16326 (2021)
18. Lyu, S., Pan, X., Zhang, X.: Exposing region splicing forgeries with blind local noise estimation. Int. J. Comput. Vis. **110**, 202–221 (2014)
19. Nirkin, Y., Keller, Y., Hassner, T.: Fsgan: subject agnostic face swapping and reenactment. In: Proceedings of the IEEE/CVF International Conference on Computer Vision, pp. 7184–7193 (2019)
20. Novozamsky, A., Mahdian, B., Saic, S.: Imd2020: a large-scale annotated dataset tailored for detecting manipulated images. In: Proceedings of the IEEE/CVF Winter Conference on Applications of Computer Vision Workshops, pp. 71–80 (2020)
21. Simonyan, K., Zisserman, A.: Very deep convolutional networks for large-scale image recognition. arXiv preprint (2014). arXiv:1409.1556
22. Vaswani, A., et al.: Attention is all you need. Adv. Neural Inf. Process. Syst. **30** (2017)
23. Wang, J., et al.: Deep high-resolution representation learning for visual recognition. IEEE Trans. Pattern Anal. Mach. Intell. **43**(10), 3349–3364 (2020)
24. Wang, X., Girshick, R., Gupta, A., He, K.: Non-local neural networks. In: Proceedings of the IEEE Conference on Computer Vision and Pattern Recognition, pp. 7794–7803 (2018)
25. Wen, B., Zhu, Y., Subramanian, R., Ng, T.T., Shen, X., Winkler, S.: Coverage-a novel database for copy-move forgery detection. In: 2016 IEEE International Conference on Image Processing (ICIP), pp. 161–165. IEEE (2016)
26. Westerlund, M.: The emergence of deepfake technology: a review. Technol. Innov. Manage. Rev. **9**(11) (2019)
27. Wu, H., Zhou, J.: IID-net: image inpainting detection network via neural architecture search and attention. IEEE Trans. Circ. Syst. Video Technol. **32**(3), 1172–1185 (2021)
28. Wu, Y., Abd-Almageed, W., Natarajan, P.: Busternet: Detecting copy-move image forgery with source/target localization. In: Proceedings of the European Conference on Computer Vision (ECCV), pp. 168–184 (2018)

29. Wu, Y., AbdAlmageed, W., Natarajan, P.: Mantra-net: manipulation tracing network for detection and localization of image forgeries with anomalous features. In: Proceedings of the IEEE/CVF Conference on Computer Vision and Pattern Recognition, pp. 9543–9552 (2019)
30. Zhao, H.,et al.: Multi-attentional deepfake detection. In: Proceedings of the IEEE/CVF Conference on Computer Vision and Pattern Recognition, pp. 2185–2194 (2021)
31. Zhou, P., Han, X., Morariu, V.I., Davis, L.S.: Learning rich features for image manipulation detection. In: Proceedings of the IEEE Conference on Computer Vision and Pattern Recognition, pp. 1053–1061 (2018)

Noise-NeRF: Hide Information in Neural Radiance Field Using Trainable Noise

Qinglong Huang[1,2], Haoran Li[1,2], Yong Liao[1,2(✉)], Yanbin Hao[1], and Pengyuan Zhou[3(✉)]

[1] University of Science and Technology of China, Hefei, China
{qinglonghuang,lhr123}@mail.ustc.edu.cn, yliao@ustc.edu.cn,
haoyanbin@hotmail.com
[2] CCCD Key Lab of Ministry of Culture and Tourism, Hefei, China
[3] Aarhus University, Aarhus, Denmark
pengyuan.zhou@ece.au.dk

Abstract. Neural Radiance Field (NeRF) has been proposed as an innovative advancement in 3D reconstruction techniques. However, little research has been conducted on the issues of information confidentiality and security to NeRF, such as steganography. Existing NeRF steganography solutions have shortcomings in low steganography quality, model weight damage, and limited amount of steganographic information. This paper proposes Noise-NeRF, a novel NeRF steganography method employing Adaptive Pixel Selection strategy and Pixel Perturbation strategy to improve the quality and efficiency of steganography via trainable noise. Extensive experiments validate the state-of-the-art performances of Noise-NeRF on both steganography quality and rendering quality, as well as effectiveness in super-resolution image steganography.

Keywords: neural radiation fields · steganography · implicit neural representation

1 Introduction

The neural radiance field (NeRF) [31] can reconstruct three-dimensional photorealistic scenes from limited 2D images taken from different viewpoints with scene continuity [6]. NeRF holds great potential in digital media such as virtual reality, augmented reality, special effects games, etc. [17]. Meanwhile, the information confidentiality and data security issues of NeRF have garnered increasing attentions [12]. NeRF steganography is one of such challenges and has seen few studies only from recently [18,20]. Current approaches based on retraining the NeRF model have **three shortcomings**: 1) their embedded information into the model weights inevitably damage the model, resulting in unstable reconstruction qualities under different viewing angles [18]; 2) they can hide limited amount of steganographic information. Current methods mainly embed information in a single image or binary code for a single NeRF scene, which would face quality collapse when embedding too much information; 3) they mainly work with low-quality images while hiding information in super-resolution images is still overlooked.

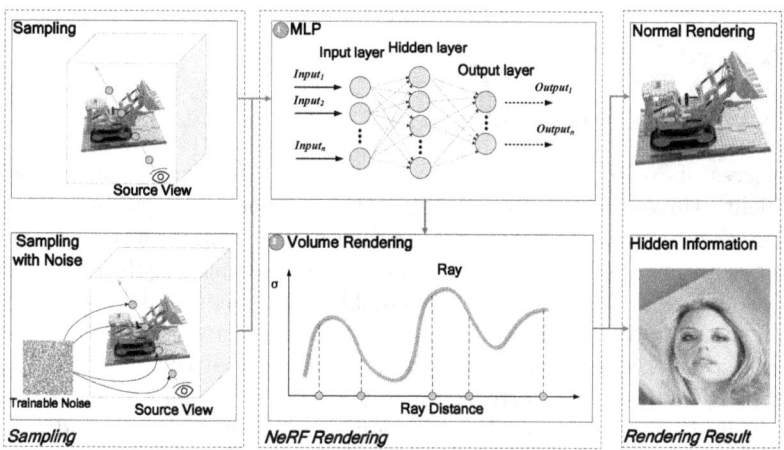

Fig. 1. Overview of Noise-NeRF.

To deal with the mentioned challenges, this paper proposes a novel NeRF steganography method namely Noise-NeRF based on trainable noise, as shown in Fig. 1. Noise-NeRF takes advantage of the neural networks in NeRF to query color and density information. We introduce trainable noise on specific views to achieve information steganography. Specifically, the NeRF model renders the secret information when we input the noise during sampling, otherwise renders the normal images. Noise-NeRF only requires to update the input noise without changing any weight, thus does not impact the rendering quality. To address the varying sensitivity of different pixels to embedded noise, we propose an Adaptive Pixel Selection strategy to ensure the steganography accuracy. Furthermore, we introduce a Pixel Perturbation strategy to accelerate the convergence with trainable noise. Our contributions can be summarized as follows:

- We propose the first lossless NeRF steganography method namely Noise-NeRF, by updating the input noise at a specific view instead of changing the model weights like other proposals. Our method ensures the NeRF model achieves information steganography without impacting its rendering quality.
- We propose an Adaptive Pixel Selection strategy and a Pixel Perturbation strategy to select pixels with greater differences according to the gradient to update the noise. We update the input noise in the early stage and finely process the pixel details of hidden content in the later stage. Our strategies significantly improve the recovery quality and steganography efficiency of NeRF.

– We conduct extensive experiments on ImageNet and several famous super-resolution image datasets using a series of pre-trained NeRF scenes. The results demonstrate the superior performance of Noise-NeRF in both steganography quality and rendering quality.

2 Related Work

2.1 Neural Radiance Field

The success of NeRF [25] has drawn widespread attention to the simple and high-fidelity three-dimensional reconstruction method of neural implicit representation. Implicit representation is a continuous representation that can be used for the generation of new perspectives and usually does not require 3D signals for supervision. NeRF realizes an effective combination of neural fields and graphics component volume rendering [25]. It uses a neural network to implicitly simulate the scene. By inputting the spatial coordinates of the three-dimensional object, NeRF outputs the corresponding geometric information. There are currently many improvements and application research on NeRF, including training acceleration [8,10,26], content edition [5,13,40], generalization [14,34,35,39], and large-scale scenes [23,30], etc. These studies have enabled efficient three-dimensional reconstruction and practical applications of NeRF in many use-cases. Meanwhile, with the launch of NeRF-related products such as Luma AI [1], issues such as information security and copyright protection for NeRF have become increasingly important.

2.2 Steganography for 2D Image

Steganography for 2D images is an important direction in the field of information security. Traditional image steganography methods generally use redundant information in the image to hide secret information [22]. For example, the most popular technique is "least significant bit" (LSB) steganography [19,29,42], which embeds secret information into the least significant bits of the pixel values of 2D images. LSB can hide a large amount of content via small changes to the image, and is difficult to detect. With the development of deep neural networks, there are also many studies using neural networks for information hiding [3,4,45]. DeepStega [3] can hide the steganographic image in a carrier of the same size. Nowdays, as the representation model of 3D scenes based on neural radiation fields has received widespread attention, steganography for NeRF is becoming an important research direction.

2.3 Steganography in NeRF

In the past, 3D scenes was mainly represented by explicit representation, such as mesh, point cloud, voxel, and volume [28]. These representations enable explicit modeling of scenes. They are also convenient for extending the steganography method of 2D images to 3D scenes, such as [27,38,44]. However, NeRF as an implicit representation functions in a completely different way. It maps the coordinate information of each point in the spatial scene to the color and density of the point. The internal weights make it difficult to accurately express the physical meaning with clear interpretability. Therefore, explicit translation, rotation, scaling, embedding, and other steganographic measures are difficult to apply to NeRF.

StegaNeRF [18] is the first study on hiding information in NeRF. They hide natural images in 3D scene representations by retraining NeRF parameters, and simultaneously train a decoder that can accurately extract hidden information from NeRF-rendered 2D images. In 2023, CopyRNeRF [20] studied copyright for NeRF, a research question that shares lots of similarities with steganography in NeRF. They proposed to protect the copyright of a NeRF model by replacing the original color representation with the color representation of watermarks. They use a decoder to recover the binary secret information from the rendered image while maintaining high rendering quality and allowing watermark extraction. Although effectively performing NeRF steganography, their method faces issues such as model retraining, limited amount of hidden data, and steganography quality. In this work, we propose Noise-NeRF to tackle these challenges.

3 Method

3.1 NeRF Preliminary

NeRF represents a continuous scene in space as a 5D neural radiation fields. It inputs the position information (x, y, z) and direction information (ψ, ϕ) of a specific point in the scene and outputs color information c and voxel density information *sigma*. The neural radiation fields F_θ with trainable parameters θ can be expressed as:

$$F_\theta : (x, y, z, \psi, \phi) \rightarrow (c, \sigma). \tag{1}$$

Next, NeRF uses the volume rendering formula to sample the rays along the observation direction and passes the sampled 3D points through the neural network to obtain the pixel value c and voxel density σ of each point for sampling and superposition to finally obtain the pixel value corresponding to this ray direction:

$$\hat{C}(\mathbf{r}) = \sum_{i=1}^{N} T_i \left(1 - \exp\left(-\sigma_i \delta_i\right)\right) \mathbf{c}_i, \text{ where } T_i = \exp\left(-\sum_{j=1}^{i-1} \sigma_j \delta_j\right), \tag{2}$$

where $\hat{C}$ denotes the color rendered by the camera ray $r(t) = o + td$, N represents the number of points sampled on the ray. σ_i represents the distance between adjacent sampling points i and $i+1$.

NeRF also adopts a hierarchical sampling strategy to train and optimize the network parameters θ through the mean square error (MSE loss) between the rendered and the true pixel colors. This enables NeRF to learn implicit representations and capture the features of 3D scenes:

$$L = \sum_{r \in R} \left[\left\| \hat{C}_c(r) - C_{GT}(r) \right\|_2^2 + \left\| \hat{C}_f(r) - C_{GT}(r) \right\|_2^2 \right], \qquad (3)$$

where R represents all the rays in the input viewpoint, $C_c(r)$ and $C_f(r)$ represent the color prediction of the ray by the coarse network and the fine network, respectively. $C_{GT}(r)$ denotes the ground truth.

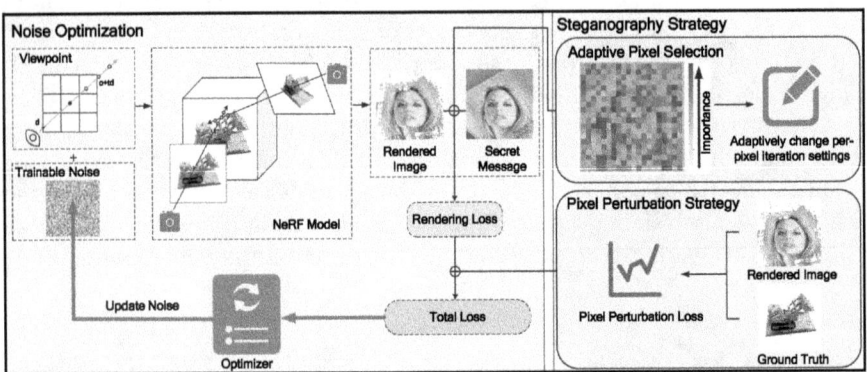

Fig. 2. Framework of Noise-NeRF. We first add random initial trainable noise to a specific view, and use pre-trained NeRF for prediction. Then, we perform supervised training on input noise using secret images. We employ Adaptive Pixel Selection strategy and Pixel Perturbation strategy during the training process to improve the quality and efficiency of steganography.

3.2 Noise Optimization

The goal of Noise-NeRF is to embed the steganographic information into the noise by calculating the gradient and updatting the noise. Let θ denote the weight of a pre-trained NeRF scene and M denote the hidden information. For a certain viewpoint P, a normal picture C can be obtained through NeRF rendering, that is, $f_\theta(P) = C$. We aim to generate noise δ through Noise-NeRF so that the model can render the steganographic content M, that is, $f_\theta(P + \delta) = M$.

The implementation framework of Noise-NeRF is shown in Fig. 2. Noise-NeRF is inspired by adversarial attack [43], which is a method that makes small perturbations to the original input samples to cause the neural network to produce misclassification or wrong output [21]. We add noise under a specific viewpoint to cause the NeRF's neural network to produce intentional error output, thus NeRF can render the hidden information. Since adversarial attack examples commonly show better results in high-dimensional space

[7], and NeRF maps low-dimensional coordinate points and directions to high-dimensional space through positional encoding [25] (Eq. (4)) to improve the network's ability to capture high-frequency information [32], we add noise after positional encoding in Noise-NeRF.

$$\gamma(p) = \left(\sin\left(2^0 \pi p\right), \cos\left(2^0 \pi p\right), \cdots, \cos\left(2^{L-1} \pi p\right)\right). \tag{4}$$

We add noise to the 5D coordinate points after positional encoding and then perform three-dimensional rendering through NeRF's MLP. The goal is to minimize the difference between the steganographic image and the image generated by the original NeRF by calculating the following loss.

$$L_{rgb} = \sum_{r \in R} \sum_{p \in r} \left[\left\| \hat{C}_f(\gamma(p) + \delta) - C_M(\gamma(p)) \right\|_2^2 \right], \tag{5}$$

where R represents all the rays in the input viewpoint, r represents one of the rays, δ is the added noise, C_M is the steganographic target information.

Noise-NeRF calculates the gradient of the model via backpropagation to find the best direction to perturb the input sample. We then update the input noise along the direction of the gradient so that the NeRF model can produce steganographic information, as follows.

$$\delta_p^i = \delta_p^{i-1} + \eta \cdot (\nabla_{\delta_p^t} \widetilde{L}_{rgb}), \tag{6}$$

where δ_p^t represents the noise added to the p sampling point in the i iteration process, and η is the learning rate.

3.3 Adaptive Pixel Selection

Though we calculate the gradient information of the input noise and update it through backpropagation, not all pixels are equally sensitive to the input noise. Different pixels between the steganographic target and NeRF's predicted image would cause different loss values and require different iteration settings to generate better noise. Therefore, we refer to the idea of batch size adaptation [33] and propose Adaptive Pixel Selection strategy, which adaptively selects pixels and sets different iterations.

Given a set of pixel batch sizes $S = s_1, ..., s_m$, we select each batch size s_i ($\forall s_i \in S$) in one iteration, compute the gradient, and update the input noise. To measure the impact of different batch sizes on steganography performance, we assume that the convergence speed remains stable within an iteration. If the batch size $s_i(s_i \in S)$ reduces the average loss the most in each query, it is considered the most appropriate batch size. Our method shares the gradients computed in the maximum batch size.

3.4 Pixel Perturbation Strategy

When updating noise, we aim to recover the steganographic information M from the camera pose P of the selected viewpoint. For the relatively NeRF network, using iterative loss calculation (Eq. (5)) and backpropagation is computationally heavy. Therefore, we target a fast deviation of the rendered image from the original image in the early stage of the noise update process. To achieve that, we need the noise to cause false positives in rendering $f_\theta(P+\delta)$ as much as possible. Therefore, we refer to the idea of batch size adaptation [33] and propose the Pixel Perturbation strategy as follows.

$$L_{perturb} = -\sum_{r \in R}\sum_{p \in r}\left[\left\|\hat{C}_f(\gamma(p)+\delta) - \hat{C}_f(\gamma(p))\right\|_2^2\right] \quad (7)$$

As such, we increase the efficiency of steganography by combining the fast deviation of the image in the early image thanks to the Pixel Perturbation strategy, and, optimize the rendered image thanks to the Adaptive Pixel Selection strategy. The overall training loss of Noise-NeRF can be expressed as:

$$\begin{cases} L = \lambda_1 \cdot L_{rgb} + \lambda_2 \cdot L_{perturb}, \; iteration \leq \mu \\ L = L_{rgb}, \; iteration > \mu \end{cases} \quad (8)$$

where λ_1 and λ_2 control the weights of the two loss functions, and μ is the boundary value of iteration.

In summary, the input noise is updated through backpropagation by calculating its loss gradient. This can generate the noise that causes the neural network to output incorrectly, and achieve lossless steganography in NeRF. Further, we propose Adaptive Pixel Selection and Pixel Perturbation strategies to significantly improve the quality and efficiency of NeRF steganography. The overall process of the Noise-NeRF is summarized in Algorithm 1.

Algorithm 1. Noise-NeRF on a single scene

Input: Pretrained NeRF model f and weights θ, Secret Message M, Viewpoint P
Output: Well-trained noise δ
for each iteration t **do**
    Conduct Adaptive Pixel Selection
    Add noise to NeRF rendering $f_\theta(P+\delta_p)$
    Compute rgb loss L_{rgb} in Eq. (5)
    Compute Perturbation loss $L_{perturb}$ in Eq. (7)
    Compute total loss L in Eq. (8)
    Update Noise $\delta^i = \delta^{i-1} + \eta \cdot Adam(\nabla_{\delta^t} L)$
end for

---

4 Experiments

4.1 Implementation Details

Datasets and Hyperparameters. We chose the standard NeRF as the experimental object. For forward and 360° scenes, we selected scenes in LLFF [24] and NeRF-Synthetic [25] as objects respectively. We randomly selected images from imagenet [9] as steganographic targets. We also selected several popular super-resolution datasets: DIV2K [2], OST [36], FFHQ [16], CeleA-HQ [15] to test the super-resolution steganography performance of Noise-NeRF. The hyperparameters in Eq.(8) are set as $\lambda_1 = 0.5$, $\lambda_2 = 0.5$, and $\mu = 50$. We use the Adam optimizer, the learning rate of each iteration is set to 1e-2, and the learning decay rate is set to 0.3. All the experiments were conducted on a server equipped with an NVIDIA RTX3090 GPU.

Metrics. We use PSNR, SSIM [37], and LPIPS [41], the classic indicators for measuring 3D reconstruction quality in NeRF, to evaluate the NeRF rendering effect. We use SSIM and SNR to evaluate the recovery quality of steganographic information.

Baselines. For the current SOTA method StegaNeRF [18], we use its original settings; for the traditional algorithm LSB [11] for two-dimensional pictures and the deep learning algorithm DeepStega [4], we hide the information in the two-dimensional images of the training dataset, and then use the traditional NeRF training method.

4.2 Multiple Scenes Steganography

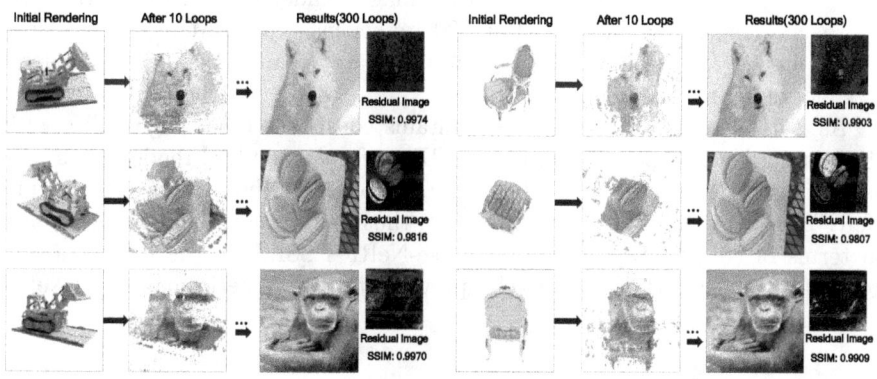

Fig. 3. Noise-NeRF performances on multiple scenes. Each column displays the initial rendering, rendering after 100 loops, rendering after 300 loops, and the residual image. We also show the SSIM between the steganography image rendered by Noise-NeRF and the real hidden image.

We first selected specified viewpoints on different scenes and used Noise-NeRF to generate noise. Then we input the noise into the NeRF model to render a steganographic image to verify steganography quality. In addition, we also test the performance of each baseline on NeRF rendering quality. The qualitative and quantitative results are shown in Fig. 3 and Table 1.

Table 1. Performance comparisons on multiple scenes. Standard NeRF is an initial NeRF scenario trained with standard settings. The upper part of the table is tested on the NeRF-Synthetic dataset; the lower part is tested on the LLFF dataset. The results are the average values across different scenes.

Method	NeRF Rendering			Embed Recovery	
	PSNR↑	SSIM↑	LPIPS↓	SSIM↑	ACC(%)↑
Standard NeRF [25]	27.74	0.8353	0.1408	N/A	N/A
LSB [29]	27.72	0.8346	0.1420	0.0132	N/A
DeepStega [3]	26.55	0.8213	0.1605	0.2098	N/A
StegaNeRF [18]	27.72	0.8340	0.1428	0.9730	**100.0**
Noise-NeRF	**27.74**	**0.8353**	**0.1408**	**0.9913**	**100.0**
Standard NeRF [25]	31.13	0.9606	0.0310	N/A	N/A
LSB [29]	31.12	0.9604	0.0310	0.0830	N/A
DeepStega [3]	31.13	0.9606	0.0313	0.2440	N/A
StegaNeRF [18]	30.96	0.9583	0.0290	0.9677	99.72
Noise-NeRF	**31.13**	**0.9606**	**0.0310**	**0.9847**	**100.0**

Figure 3 shows that Noise-NeRF continuously optimizes noise through iterations. After inputting the noise, the image rendered by NeRF gradually approaches the target image. After 300 iterations, the SSIM of the rendered hidden image and ground truth are both greater than 98%, meeting general steganography requirements.

As Table 1 shows, Noise-NeRF maintains consistent rendering quality with the standard NeRF. This is because NeRF performs standard rendering as long as no noise is input. On the other hand, all other methods require to modify NeRF's model weights to a certain extent, thus damaging the rendering quality. In terms of steganography quality, Noise-NeRF's SSIM on the two data sets got 0.9913 and 0.9847, respectively, proving its SOTA performance on NeRF steganography.

4.3 Super-Resolution Steganography

In this experiment, we tested the steganography ability of Noise-NeRF on super-resolution images. We randomly selected images from the super-resolution dataset as targets, each of which had a 2K resolution. Due to the huge number of bits required for steganography, baseline steganography algorithms will make a large update to the model weights, which would cause tremendous damage to NeRF-rendered images [18]. The visualization results of the experiment are shown in Fig. 4. We clip the super-resolution image into multiple sub-images and randomly select different viewpoints of the NeRF model. We align different sub-images to different viewpoints and stitch them together to obtain the final result. As shown in Table 2, in different NeRF scenes and different super-resolution datasets, Noise-NeRF achieves a 100% success rate in NeRF steganog-

Table 2. Noise-NeRF on super-resolution datasets. The amount of hidden information only depends on different trainable noises in our method. That is, by inputting different noises into the model, different hidden information can be rendered. Therefore, we use this to achieve the steganography of super-resolution images. The results are the average of NeRF-Synthetic and LLFF scenes.

Scene	Dataset	NeRF Rendering			Embed Recovery	
		PSNR	SSIM	LPIPS	PSNR	SSIM
NeRF-Synthetic [25]	DIV2K [2]	27.74	0.8353	0.1408	48.62	0.9889
	OST [36]				46.58	0.9748
	FFHQ [16]				48.75	0.9889
	CelebA-HQ [15]				46.80	0.9775
LLFF [24]	DIV2K [2]	31.13	0.9606	0.0310	47.90	0.9814
	OST [36]				44.91	0.9704
	FFHQ [16]				47.59	0.9807
	CelebA-HQ [15]				44.77	0.9799

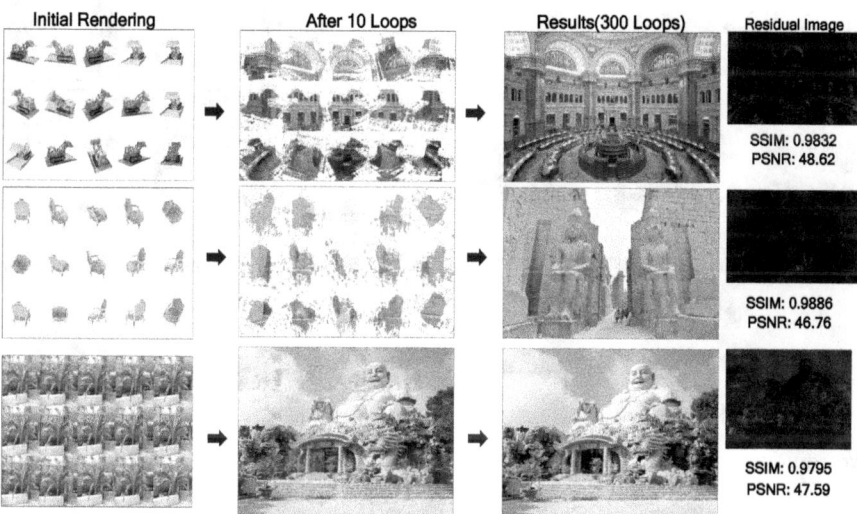

Fig. 4. Noise-NeRF performance on super-resolution images. Each column displays the initial rendering, rendering after 100 loops, rendering after 300 loops, and the residual image. We also show the SSIM between the steganography image rendered by Noise-NeRF and the real hidden image.

raphy, with the steganographic images achieving a similarity of more than 97%. Please refer to Fig. 5 for more details on the qualitative results. It proves the superiority of Noise-NeRF on super-resolution image steganography.

Fig. 5. More qualitative results of Noise-NeRF on multiple super-resolution results.

4.4 Ablation Study

We removed different components of Noise-NeRF as shown in Table 3 to verify the effectiveness of each part. We set the number of iterations to 300. As shown in Fig. 6, we take the standard NeRF rendering image and steganographic target as a reference. From Fig. 6 and Table 3, we observed that some pixels were completely blank in the output image without Adaptive Pixel Selection. This is because each pixel is different and has a different target pixel, thus requiring different iterations and batch size settings. Our Adaptive Pixel Selection strategy can handle this situation well by selecting pixels in a targeted manner. Removing the Pixel Perturbation strategy resulted in some pixel noise in the output image.

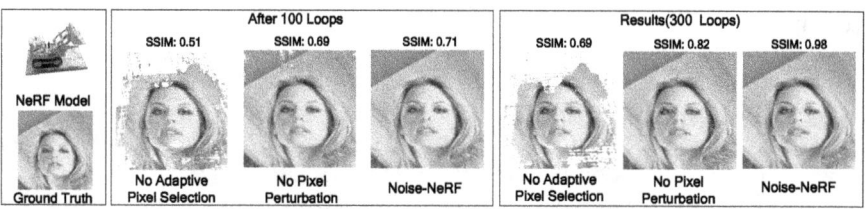

Fig. 6. Ablation study of Noise-NeRF.

This is because the huge neural network depth of NeRF requires many iterations of backpropagation to update the input noise and slowly gradually converge to the steganographic object. The Pixel Perturbation strategy increases the difference between the output image and the original image in the early stage, thus accelerating the noise's deviation from the original prediction of NeRF.

Table 3. Ablation study of Noise-NeRF.

Method	50 Loops		200 Loops		Results(300 Loops)	
	SSIM	Total Loss	SSIM	Total Loss	SSIM	Total Loss
No strategy	0.51	3143.79	0.62	2526.70	0.69	761.63
No Adaptive Pixel Selection	0.44	976.76	0.49	211.35	0.59	83.08
No Pixel Perturbation	0.69	83.67	0.76	66.15	0.82	26.40
Noise-NeRF (complete version)	**0.71**	**74.33**	**0.88**	**13.24**	**0.98**	**0.55**

5 Conclusion

In this paper, we propose a NeRF steganography method based on trainable noise, Noise-NeRF, to address challenges faced by NeRF steganography, namely low steganographic quality, model weight damage, and limited steganographic information. We propose Adaptive Pixel Selection strategy and Pixel Perturbation strategy to improve steganography quality and efficiency. Experimental results prove the superiority of Noise-NeRF over existing baselines in both steganography quality and rendering quality, as well as effectiveness in super-resolution image steganography.

Acknowledgement. This work is supported by the National Key Research and Development Program of China (2022YFB3105405, 2021YFC3300502).

References

1. https://lumalabs.ai/
2. Agustsson, E., Timofte, R.: Ntire 2017 challenge on single image super-resolution: dataset and study. In: Proceedings of the IEEE Conference on Computer Vision and Pattern Recognition Workshops, pp. 126–135 (2017)
3. Baluja, S.: hiding images within images. IEEE Trans. Pattern Anal. Mach. Intell. 1685–1697 (2019)
4. Baluja, S.: hiding images in plain sight: deep steganography. Adv. Neural Inf. Proc. Syst. **30** (2017)
5. Bao, C., et al.: Sine: semantic-driven image-based nerf editing with prior-guided editing field. In: Proceedings of the IEEE/CVF Conference on Computer Vision and Pattern Recognition, pp. 20919–20929 (2023)
6. Barron, J.T., Mildenhall, B., Verbin, D., Srinivasan, P.P., Hedman, P.: Mipnerf 360: unbounded anti-aliased neural radiance fields. In: Proceedings of the IEEE/CVF Conference on Computer Vision and Pattern Recognition, pp. 5470–5479 (2022)
7. Carlini, N., Wagner, D.: Towards evaluating the robustness of neural networks. In: 2017 IEEE Symposium on Security And Privacy (SP), pp. 39–57 (2017)
8. Chen, A., Xu, Z., Geiger, A., Yu, J., Su, H.: Tensorf: tensorial radiance fields. In: Proceedings of the European Conference on Computer Vision (ECCV) (2022)
9. Deng, J., Dong, W., Socher, R., Li, L.J., Li, K., Fei-Fei, L.: Imagenet: a large-scale hierarchical image database. In: 2009 IEEE Conference on Computer Vision and Pattern Recognition, pp. 248–255. IEEE (2009)
10. Fridovich-Keil, S., Yu, A., Tancik, M., Chen, Q., Recht, B., Kanazawa, A.: Plenoxels: radiance fields without neural networks. In: Proceedings of the IEEE/CVF Conference on Computer Vision and Pattern Recognition, pp. 5501–5510 (2022)
11. Fridrich, J., Goljan, M., Du, R.: Detecting LSB steganography in color, and grayscale images. IEEE Multimedia **8**, 22–28 (2001)
12. Horváth, A., Józsa, C.M.: Targeted adversarial attacks on generalizable neural radiance fields. In: Proceedings of the IEEE/CVF International Conference on Computer Vision, pp. 3718–3727 (2023)
13. Hyung, J., Hwang, S., Kim, D., Lee, H., Choo, J.: Local 3D editing via 3D distillation of clip knowledge. In: Proceedings of the IEEE/CVF Conference on Computer Vision and Pattern Recognition. pp. 12674–12684 (2023)
14. Irshad, M.Z., et al.: Neo 360: neural fields for sparse view synthesis of outdoor scenes. In: Proceedings of the IEEE/CVF International Conference on Computer Vision, pp. 9187–9198 (2023)
15. Karras, T., Aila, T., Laine, S., Lehtinen, J.: Progressive growing of gans for improved quality, stability, and variation. arXiv preprint arXiv:1710.10196 (2017)
16. Karras, T., Laine, S., Aila, T.: A style-based generator architecture for generative adversarial networks. In: Proceedings of the IEEE/CVF Conference on Computer Vision and Pattern Recognition, pp. 4401–4410 (2019)
17. Levy, D., et al.: Seathru-nerf: Neural radiance fields in scattering media. In: Proceedings of the IEEE/CVF Conference on Computer Vision and Pattern Recognition, pp. 56–65 (2023)
18. Li, C., Feng, B.Y., Fan, Z., Pan, P., Wang, Z.: Steganerf: embedding invisible information within neural radiance fields. In: Proceedings of the IEEE/CVF International Conference on Computer Vision, pp. 441–453 (2023)

19. Luo, W., Huang, F., Huang, J.: Edge adaptive image steganography based on LSB matching revisited. IEEE Trans. Inf. Forensics Secur. 201–214 (2010)
20. Luo, Z., Guo, Q., Cheung, K.C., See, S., Wan, R.: Copyrnerf: protecting the copyright of neural radiance fields. In: Proceedings of the IEEE/CVF International Conference on Computer Vision, pp. 22401–22411 (2023)
21. Madry, A., Makelov, A., Schmidt, L., Tsipras, D., Vladu, A.: Towards deep learning models resistant to adversarial attacks. arXiv preprint arXiv:1706.06083 (2017)
22. Marvel, L.M., Boncelet, C.G., Retter, C.T.: Spread spectrum image steganography. IEEE Trans. Image Proc. 1075–1083 (1999)
23. Mi, Z., Xu, D.: Switch-nerf: learning scene decomposition with mixture of experts for large-scale neural radiance fields. In: Proceedings of the International Conference on Learning Representations (ICLR) (2023)
24. Mildenhall, B., et al.: Local light field fusion: practical view synthesis with prescriptive sampling guidelines. ACM Trans. Graph. (TOG), 1–14 (2019)
25. Mildenhall, B., Srinivasan, P.P., Tancik, M., Barron, J.T., Ramamoorthi, R., Ng, R.: Nerf: representing scenes as neural radiance fields for view synthesis. Commun. ACM **65**, 99–106 (2021)
26. Müller, T., Evans, A., Schied, C., Keller, A.: Instant neural graphics primitives with a multiresolution hash encoding. ACM Trans. Graph. (ToG) **41**, 1–15 (2022)
27. Praun, E., Hoppe, H., Finkelstein, A.: Robust mesh watermarking. In: Proceedings of the 26th Annual Conference on Computer Graphics and Interactive Techniques, pp. 49–56 (1999)
28. Riegler, G., Osman Ulusoy, A., Geiger, A.: Octnet: learning deep 3D representations at high resolutions. In: Proceedings of the IEEE Conference on Computer Vision and Pattern Recognition, pp. 3577–3586 (2017)
29. Rustad, S., et al.: Inverted LSB image steganography using adaptive pattern to improve imperceptibility. J. King Saud Univ. Comput. Inf. Sci. 3559–3568 (2022)
30. Tancik, M., et al.: Block-nerf: scalable large scene neural view synthesis. In: Proceedings of the IEEE/CVF Conference on Computer Vision and Pattern Recognition, pp. 8248–8258 (2022)
31. Tancik, M., et al.: Nerfstudio: a modular framework for neural radiance field development. In: ACM SIGGRAPH 2023 Conference Proceedings, pp. 1–12 (2023)
32. Vaswani, A., et al.: Attention is all you need. Adv. Neural Inf. Proc. Syst. **30** (2017)
33. Wang, Q., Zheng, B., Li, Q., Shen, C., Ba, Z.: Towards query-efficient adversarial attacks against automatic speech recognition systems. IEEE Trans. Inf. Forensics Secur. 896–908 (2020)
34. Wang, Q., et al.: Ibrnet: learning multi-view image-based rendering. In: Proceedings of the IEEE/CVF Conference on Computer Vision and Pattern Recognition, pp. 4690–4699 (2021)
35. Wang, T., et al.: Rodin: a generative model for sculpting 3d digital avatars using diffusion. In: Proceedings of the IEEE/CVF Conference on Computer Vision and Pattern Recognition, pp. 4563–4573 (2023)
36. Wang, X., Yu, K., Dong, C., Loy, C.C.: Recovering realistic texture in image super-resolution by deep spatial feature transform. In: Proceedings of the IEEE conference on computer vision and pattern recognition, pp. 606–615 (2018)
37. Wang, Z., Bovik, A., Sheikh, H., Simoncelli, E.: Image quality assessment: from error visibility to structural similarity. IEEE Trans. Image Proc. 600–612 (2004). https://doi.org/10.1109/tip.2003.819861,

38. Wu, Y., Meng, G., Chen, Q.: Embedding novel views in a single jpeg image. In: Proceedings of the IEEE/CVF International Conference on Computer Vision, pp. 14519–14527 (2021)
39. Yu, A., Ye, V., Tancik, M., Kanazawa, A.: pixelnerf: neural radiance fields from one or few images. In: Proceedings of the IEEE/CVF Conference on Computer Vision and Pattern Recognition, pp. 4578–4587 (2021)
40. Zhan, F., Liu, L., Kortylewski, A., Theobalt, C.: General neural gauge fields. In: Proceedings of the International Conference on Learning Representations (ICLR) (2023)
41. Zhang, R., Isola, P., Efros, A.A., Shechtman, E., Wang, O.: The unreasonable effectiveness of deep features as a perceptual metric. In: 2018 IEEE/CVF Conference on Computer Vision and Pattern Recognition (2018). https://doi.org/10.1109/cvpr.2018.00068
42. Zhang, T., Ping, X.: Reliable detection of LSB steganography based on the difference image histogram. In: Proceedings of IEEE International Conference on Acoustics, Speech, and Signal Processing, 2003.(ICASSP'03), pp. III–545 (2003)
43. Zheng, T., Chen, C., Ren, K.: Distributionally adversarial attack. In: Proceedings of the AAAI Conference on Artificial Intelligence, pp. 2253–2260 (2019)
44. Zhu, J., Zhang, Y., Zhang, X., Cao, X.: Gaussian model for 3D mesh steganography. IEEE Signal Proc. Lett. **28**, 1729–1733 (2021)
45. Zhu, J., Kaplan, R., Johnson, J., Fei-Fei, L.: Hidden: hiding data with deep networks. In: Proceedings of the European Conference on computer vision (ECCV), pp. 657–672 (2018)

Unconventional Face Adversarial Attack

Ruoxi Wang[1], Baojin Huang[2(✉)], Zhen Han[2], and Dengshi Li[1(✉)]

[1] School of Artificial Intelligence, Jianghan University, Wuhan, China
reallds@jhun.edu.cn
[2] School of Computer Science, Wuhan University, Wuhan, China
huangbaojin@whu.edu.cn

Abstract. This paper advocates a kind of new and interesting adversarial attack concept, coined unconventional face adversarial attack (UFAA). In contrast to the traditional adversarial attack, UFAA can generate face images that can be identified by computers but cannot be recognized by human eyes. As for face recognition, we argue that humans and computers may follow different manners, focusing on latent identify features and visible appearance features, respectively. Accordingly, we propose a dual-branch face feature coupled network (FFCN) to disentangle the two components of appearance and identity of the face image. Particularly, we learn appearance and identity features separately and meanwhile use an identify-appearance coupled module to make the two branches exploit complementary information. Further, two reconstruction layers are employed to generate the corresponding appearance and identity images from the feature space. To ensure the completeness of information extraction, we propose a reunion module to fuse the appearance and identity image, reproducing the original input image as a self-supervision for FFCN learning. Experimental results on popular face datasets show that the attacked face images basically neither hinder the identification by face recognizers nor reveal discriminative appearance to human eyes, which quite agrees with the advocated UFAA paradigm. The new type of adversarial attack we advocate can be used to protect the privacy of facial identities, under scenarios where people can see but cannot understand.

Keywords: Unconventional adversarial attack · Face recognition · Privacy protection

1 Introduction

The adversarial attack is a typical artificial intelligence (AI) security problem. In the field of computer vision, adversarial attacks [13] aim to deceive machine learning models such as image classification and object recognition by adding noise that cannot be perceived by the human to the image. It causes machine learning models to produce incorrect classifications or predictions, but does not hinder human recognition. Under traditional adversarial attacks, adversarial samples subjectively look the same as normal samples, but the machine learning

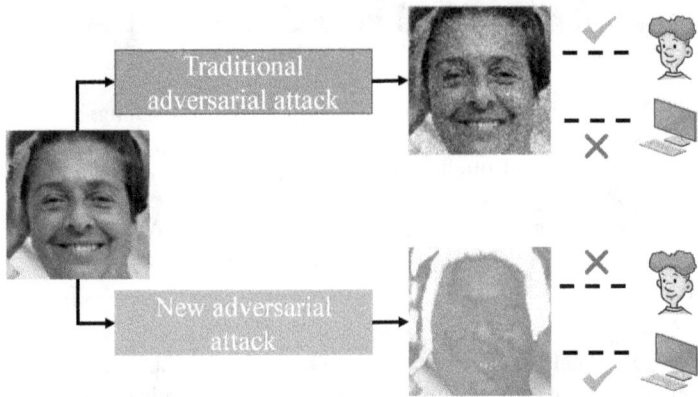

Fig. 1. The illustration of our coined unconventional adversarial attack. The top shows the traditional adversarial sample with adversarial noises added [5,17,19], which prevents from being recognized by computers but is still recognized by humans. In contrast, the unconventional adversarial sample is shown at the bottom, whose facial appearance is destroyed but its intrinsic identity information is retained, can be identified by computers but does not expose the visible identity to human eyes.

model will make prediction or classification errors. This paper proposes a completely new adversarial attack scheme, quite different from traditional adversarial attacks. On the contrary, the resulting adversarial samples cannot be recognized by human eyes, while without affecting the recognition of the machine, thereby coined an unconventional adversarial attack. In Fig. 1, a face image is taken as an example to illustrate our concept of unconventional adversarial attacks.

This unconventional adversarial attack also has its application value, such as face anonymization. Although the traditional anonymization by mosaicing can protect human facial identity, it also causes machine recognition to fail, which is not conducive to information interaction and sharing in the human-computer world. When the anonymized face is to be further used for subsequent computer processing, this mosaic anonymization is obviously not suitable. We take two specific application scenarios: 1) When the police solve the case, they must find the suspect from the surveillance video. However, the police do not want the given facial image of the suspect to be recognized by the computer operator, but it does not affect computer retrieval; 2) When data owners (such as banks or communication service providers) provide customer data to a third party or cloud for data analysis, they need to conceal or anonymize the key fields in advance, including facial images. In short, the proposed unconventional adversarial attack is an effective means of anonymizing image data in situations where the image data is prevented from being identified by the contact person but does not hinder the use of the computer.

In real life, face anonymization is usually realized by performing some irreversible processing, such as super pixel [1], blur [12], Gaussian noise [1] and low resolution [16], onto the original face image. However, these approaches are too crude to retain the semantic information of the image. Recently, some methods [2,9,11] based on generative adversarial network (GAN) have been proposed to anonymize the face image while maintaining the semantic attributes unchanged. Specifically, Maximov et al. [9] developed CIAGAN to remove the appearance characteristics of faces and bodies while producing high-quality images that can be used for detection or tracking. Chen et al. [2] proposed an image representation that is clearly separated from identity information, but has discriminative power for facial expression recognition. Ren et al. [11] proposed a video face anonymizer to remove appearance-sensitive information while maximizing facial action detection performance. These methods can retain such information as facial expressions or poses that is irrelevant to identity in destroying the facial appearance. However, they cannot retain identity information, so that the resulting faces cannot be used by computers for face identification. In other words, the generated anonymized faces can neither be identified by humans nor by computers.

The essence of the unconventional adversarial attack we proposed is to destroy the facial appearance but to retain the facial identity. Different from humans, deep learning based face recognizers are designed to know who it is, rather than who it looks like. Alternatively, as for face recognition, deep learning based face recognizers mainly rely on the discrimination of latent-space features (intrinsic identity information) while humans mainly rely on visible facial appearance. In view of this, we argue that the face image can be decomposed into two components, appearance and identity, with the appearance mainly perceived by humans and the identity mainly perceived by computers. Following this idea, we intend to accomplish the unconventional face adversarial attack by disentangling the blended appearance and identity. Particularly, we propose a novel face feature coupled network (FFCN) that is tailored for unconventional face adversarial attack. We first employ a feature extraction module to transform the image to convolutional feature maps. Then we design a dual-branch network composed of identify-appearance coupled module (IACM) to respectively learn the appearance and identity features. IACM further consists of a residual channel attention block (RCAB), a residual spatial attention block (RSAB) and a coupled block. RSAB and RCAB are used to extract rough appearance and identity features respectively, which are then input into the coupled block to adaptively exploit complementary and redundant information from each other. In this way, the extracted facial identity features are purified by eliminating irrelevant appearance information and supplemented with missing identity information. Meanwhile, facial appearance features are refined due to coupling learning. Next, the appearance and identity images are predicted through the reconstruction layer, where the identity image is treated as the unconventional adversarial sample of the input face. To facilitate the training, we also assemble a reunion module (RM) to merge the appearance and identity image to reproduce the original face.

The main contributions of this paper are highlighted as follows.

- In contrast to the traditional adversarial attack, we pioneer the concept of unconventional face adversarial attack (UFAA), which aims to convert the face image into its counterpart so that it cannot be recognized by human eyes but can be identified by computers. UFAA can be widely used to protect the privacy of facial appearance.
- Regarding face recognition, we argue that deep learning based face recognizers mainly rely on the discrimination of latent-space features (intrinsic identity information) while humans mainly rely on visible facial appearance. In view of this, we hold that a face image can be decoupled into two complementary components of appearance and identity, where the appearance image is served for the perception by humans while the identity image is served for the perception by computers. Conversely, given the appearance and identity image of the same subject, the original face image can be inversely reconstructed.
- We propose a dual-branch face feature coupled network (FFCN) to disentangle the blended correlations between the appearance and the identity for the face image, where IACM learns the coupled representations between RCAB and RSAB from different branches and adaptively explores complementary and redundant information from each other. In order to ensure the completeness of information extraction, RM is used to fuse appearance and identity images, reproducing the original input image as a self-supervision guide for FFCN learning.

2 Proposed Method

2.1 Problem Formulation

Given a deep learning model $f : R^m \longrightarrow \{1 \ldots k\}$, it can map an image to a concrete label set. We assume that f is trained by a continuous loss function $loss_f : R^m \times \{1 \ldots k\} \longrightarrow R^+$. For a given image $x \in R^m$ and target label $l \in \{1 \ldots k\}$, the unconventional adversarial attack can be formulated as

$$\text{Minimize } loss_f(x+r, l) - c \|r\|_\infty. \tag{1}$$

$r \in R^m$ denotes a noisy image, which may not be unique. c is a positive hyperparameter to trade off the noie and the loss of the attacked model. Obviously, we solve for a maximum r such that $f(x+r) = l$ by finding an optimal $c > 0$. Alternatively, $x+r$ is the farthest image to x labeled as l by f. This optimization objective would produce an optimal solution in the case of convexity. However, the deep learning model f is usually non-convex, thus the solution to this problem ends up with an approximation.

We take the face recognition model as f to achieve the optimization. Particularly, our designed face feature coupled network (FFCN) aims to decouple the appearance and identity of the face. In other words, we are committed to exploring the identity-invariant representation of the face for the deep face recognition. Based on this, we can learn special noise image r while ensuring $f(x+r) = l$ so that FFCN outputs a maximum appearance disturbance image while maintaining facial identity.

2.2 Architecture

We propose an end-to-end face feature coupled network that explicitly decouples the appearance and identity information of the face. In other words, we adopt a two-branch network to learn appearance and identity features separately and meanwhile use a coupling mechanism to make the two branches output complementary information. As shown in Fig. 2, given an original face image M_{ori}, we first employ a feature extraction module (FEM) to convert the raw pixels into the shallow convolutional feature map f_{ori}. Specifically, FEM consists of three convolutions with batch normalization and ReLU layers. Following that, f_{ori} is organized as the initial input pair ($A_0 = f_{ori}$, $I_0 = f_{ori}$), which is then fed into several cascaded IACMs. Thus we obtain the decoupled representation of appearance and identity (A_{final}, I_{final}). The above procedure can be described as

$$A_i, I_i = F^i_{iacm}(A_{i-1}, I_{i-1}), \qquad (2)$$

where $F^i_{iacm}(\cdot)$ refers to the i-th IACM, including a residual channel attention block, a residual spatial attention block and the coupled process of appearance and identity. A_{i-1} and I_{i-1} denote the outputs of the $(i-1)$-th IACM. The cascade modules independently and complementarily advance the feature extraction of each level.

Furthermore, the outputs of the last IACM generate the corresponding predicted images through two reconstruction layers. Specifically, we use two convolutions with the kernel of 3 to respectively project the A_{final} and I_{final} from the feature space to the image space, producing the appearance image M_{ap} and identity image M_{id}. Finally, to ensure that the decoupled representations ultimately hold the facial appearance and identity information, we fuse M_{ap} and M_{id} to obtain an approximate raw image M^*_{ori} using the reunion module $F_{reu}(\cdot)$. This procedure can be expressed as

$$M^*_{ori} = F_{reu}(F_{rec1}(A_{final}), F_{rec2}(I_{final})), \qquad (3)$$

where $F_{rec1}(\cdot)$ and $F_{rec2}(\cdot)$ indicate two reconstruction layers without shared parameters. Below we will elaborate the individual underlying modules.

2.3 Identity-Appearance Coupled Module

To decouple the appearance and identity feature of the face image, we propose the identity-appearance coupled module (IACM) that is shaped like a dual-branch network. As shown in Fig. 2, IACM is composed of a residual channel attention block (RCAB), a residual spatial attention block (RSAB) and a coupled block. Specifically, RSAB and RCAB are designed to extract rough appearance and identity features respectively, which are further input into the coupled block to refine the correlation. As such, we obtain the encoding representation with complementary and redundant information for RSAB and RCAB.

Especially, we construct RSAB using a residual block with spatial attention, which focuses on the relevancy between pixels and is more suitable for learning

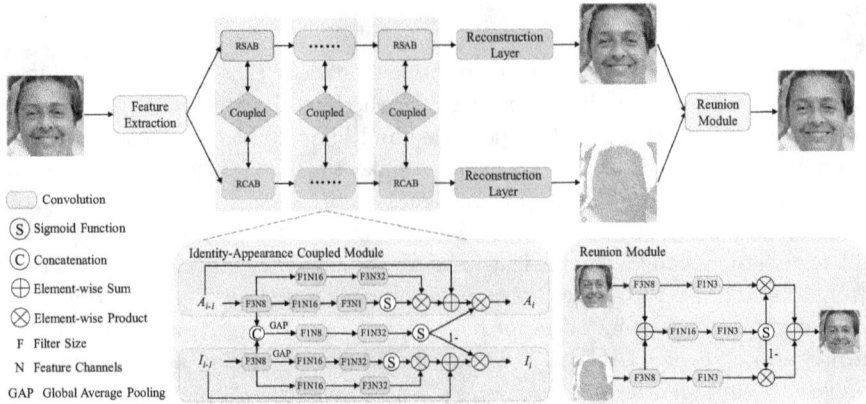

Fig. 2. The pipeline of our proposed framework. It consists of a feature extraction module, several identity-appearance coupled modules, two reconstruction layers and a reunion module. We first employ a feature extraction module to transform raw pixels to a convolutional feature map, which serves as the initial input of the first IACM. Furthermore, The output of the previous IACM is used as the input of the next IACM, constantly exploring the coupled relations among the identity and appearance features. Finally, the appearance and identity features produce corresponding predicted images through the reconstruction layer. Especially, the appearance and identity images are fused to generate the original input image by one RM, which serves as self-supervision to guide the learning of FFCN.

appearance representation. Likewise, RCAB is built upon a residual block with channel attention, which unevenly handles the importance between channels and is more suitable for the identity representation. The coarse appearance and identity representation process is formulated as

$$RS_{i-1} = A_{i-1} + F_{sa}(I_{i-1}) * F_{rb1}(A_{i-1}),$$
$$RC_{i-1} = I_{i-1} + F_{ca}(I_{i-1}) * F_{rb2}(I_{i-1}). \quad (4)$$

where RS_{i-1} and RC_{i-1} denote the outputs of $(i-1)$-th RSAB and RCAB, respectively. $F_{sa}(\cdot)$ and $F_{ca}(\cdot)$ refer to the spatial attention block and channel attention block, respectively. $F_{rb1}(\cdot)$ and $F_{rb2}(\cdot)$ are two residual blocks without shared parameters. Then the coupled block takes A_{i-1} and I_{i-1} as input to refine the correlation between RS_{i-1} and RC_{i-1}. Specifically, we first employ a convolution layer to map the A_{i-1} and I_{i-1} into the new features, which are concatenated in the channel dimension for further confidence prediction. Then the concatenated feature map generates the confidence map W_{re} via two convolutions and is normalized with the Sigmoid function. Finally, we can supplement insufficient information and eliminate redundant information for coarse appearance and identity representation as follows:

$$A_i = RS_{i-1} * W_{re}, \quad I_i = RC_{i-1} * (1 - W_{re}). \quad (5)$$

This way, we explore the coupled representations of appearance and identity by cascaded IACMs, which are further used to produce the corresponding subjective images through the reconstruction layer.

2.4 Reunion Module

To ensure the information integrity of appearance and identity images, we propose a reunion module to restore the input image based on the decoupled images. Specifically, we encode the appearance and identity images to the feature space, which are summed for further selective weight generation. Moreover, we employ an additional convolution to fine-tune the decoupled images, attaining generalized representation. Consequently, we fuse the images to reproduce the approximate input face image, expressed as

$$M^*_{ori} = M_{ap\_f} * SW + M_{id\_f} * (1 - SW), \quad (6)$$

where M_{ap_f} and M_{id_f} denote the fine-tune appearance and identity images, respectively. SW is the selective weight generated by two convolutions and a Sigmoid function. Especially, the M^*_{ori} serves as the self-supervision with the original input image to guide the whole network.

2.5 Optimization

To guide the optimization of FFCN, we introduce two loss functions to constrain the image pixels and identity respectively, including the Charbonnier penalty function [8] and recognition similarity function. Specifically, the former calculates the pixel difference of two images, which converges faster and has a certain error tolerance during training, avoiding to produce blurry and excessively smooth images like MSE-based loss ($L2$). The function is formulated as

$$F_{cp}(I^*, I) = \sqrt{(I^* - I)^2 + \varepsilon^2}, \quad (7)$$

where I^* and I denote the predicted and real images, respectively. And the penalty coefficient ε is set to 10^{-3}.

Recognition similarity function measures the Cosine similarity of two face embeddings extracted by existing face recognition models, which can reflect the identity information of the face as bellow:

$$F_{rs}(I^*, I) = \langle f_{reco}(I^*), f_{reco}(I) \rangle, \quad (8)$$

where $f_{reco}(\cdot)$ denotes the face embedding with feature normalization. We employ ArcFace [3] as the recognition model here. $\langle \cdot, \cdot \rangle$ represents the inner product operation.

To achieve the goal that the appearance image can be recognized but the identity image cannot be recognized by humans, we make the specific constraint on the image from the perspective of pixels as follows:

$$L_A = F_{cp}(M_{ap}, M_{ori}) - F_{cp}(M_{id}, M_{ori}). \quad (9)$$

Similarly, we maximize the recognition similarity between the identity image and the original image while minimizing the recognition similarity with the appearance image as bellow:

$$L_B = F_{rs}(M_{ap}, M_{id}) - F_{rs}(M_{id}, M_{ori}). \qquad (10)$$

To perform the consistency between the predicted input image and original image, we minimize their discrepancy, formulated as:

$$L_C = F_{cp}(M_{ori}^*, M_{ori}). \qquad (11)$$

By combining the above losses, our final total loss function for joint optimization is defined as

$$L = L_A + \alpha_1 \times L_B + \alpha_2 \times L_C, \qquad (12)$$

where α_1 and α_2 are trade-off hyperparameters to balance the pixel and recognition losses. We empirically set α_1 as 0.1 and α_2 as 0.2, respectively.

3 Experimental Results

Since the unconventional adversarial attack is pioneered by us, there is no existing comparison baselines. This section conducts experiments to verify whether our coined unconventional adversarial attack has achieved the primitive intention: the attacked faces can be identified by computers but cannot be recognized by humans. The former is testified using popular deep face recognition models and the latter demonstrates the subjective indiscernibility of generated faces. Finally, we discuss the practical applications of our model with a real example.

3.1 Experimental Settings

Datasets. Benefitting from our self-supervised optimization strategy, our proposed FFCN can be trained on any face datasets without labels such as identity ID. We adopt the widely used face recognition dataset LFW [6] as the training set, AgeDB-30 [10] and CFP-FP [14] as the testing sets. LFW comprises 13,233 face images with 5749 identities collected under unconstrained conditions, containing samples with different lighting conditions, angles, and occlusions. CFP-FP covers 7000 face images of 500 identities, with each identity containing 10 frontal and 4 non-frontal images. AgeDB-30 contains 16,488 images of various celebrities annotated with identity, age, and gender attributes.

Evaluation Metrics. We evaluate the performance of the images generated by our model from the face verification accuracy and the subjective recognition of human eyes since there are no real labels for our appearance and identity images. Specifically, the accuracy of face verification refers to the true positive rate (TPR) or false rejection rate (FRR) under a specific false acceptance rate (FAR). For face verification experiments, we report the TPR as accuracy when FAR is equal to 10^{-4}.

3.2 Implementation Details

The raw images in all datasets are detected by RetinaFace [4] detector and aligned to 112 × 112 pixels. In our FFCN, the number of cascaded IACM is empirically set to 20.

Our implementation is based on the Pytorch deep learning framework, with a batch size of 256 on two NVIDIA GTX 3090 GPUs. In training, we perform data argumentation (like flipping) on the training set, which improves the generalization ability of the trained model. The learning rate is initially 0.0001 and is divided by 10 at 10, 18, and 25 epochs. The training process is ended in 32 epochs with the above settings.

Table 1. Face verification performance (%) on attacked images by our unconventional adversarial attack model.

Dataset	CosFace [15]	ArcFace [3]	CurricularFace [7]
CFP-FP	95.67	96.56	96.64
CFP-FP-FFCN	88.26	92.14	90.94
AgeDB-30	94.31	94.10	93.75
AgeDB-30-FFCN	89.01	91.66	88.75

3.3 Results on Deep Face Recognition

We apply FFCN to AgeDB-30 and generate new face pairs (a normal face and a attacked face), called AgeDB-30-FFCN dataset. The CFP-FP is processed in the same way to obtain the CFP-FP-FFCN dataset. Furthermore, we employ three popular deep face recognition models to evaluate the AgeDB-30-FFCN and CFP-FP-FFCN, such as CosFace [15], ArcFace [3] and CurricularFace [7]. The results on face verification are tabulated in Table 1, where for the convenience of comparison, the results on the original datasets are also given. As shown, compared with the original faces, although the recognition accuracy of the attacked faces has decreased, it still maintains a sufficiently high accuracy overall. This proves that the unconventional adversarial attack we proposed is feasible provided that it basically does not affect the face recognition of computers. Admittedly, our FFCN results in a certain decrease in the face recognition accuracy, which is due to the fact that our model still causes some information loss during the decoupling process. In a further examination, we can find that the recognition accuracy by ArcFace on the attacked datasets is closest to the original datasets. This is mainly because ArcFace is used to guide FFCN training. It is worth noting out that CosFace, ArcFace and CurricularFace are extensively acknowledged deep face recognition models with the best performance in recent years. Therefore, this experimental verification is representative and convincing.

3.4 Results on Subjective Indiscernibility

The key of unconventional adversarial attack is to make face images discard appearance information and retain identity information so that the human eye cannot recognize the images. We hereby perform subjective analysis on identity images generated by our model. For more convincing evidences, we select some representative samples to report the final results, including face images of different skin tones, poses and expressions. As shown in Fig. 3, we can hardly recognize the original faces from the processed faces provide that the processed faces merely render facial sketch. We can see that our model can intuitively destroy the structure of facial features, such as the eyes, which are rich in identity information. Specifically, these identity images are more like the results of masking the facial landmarks, with the appearance information removed. Besides, this special mask can retain the distribution characteristics of the face identity, thus the processed image can still be recognized by computers.

We reckon the conventional face adversarial attack, preventing computers from identifying the face image with slight noises added. Contrarily, our coined unconventional face adversarial attack aims to interfere with human recognition instead of computers. Figure 3 indicates that our model adaptively concentrates the noise on the dominant facial components for human eyes, making it indiscernible by human eyes. That is due to the fact that humans are more inclined to identify identities through facial features, while computers can identify them based on latent-space features.

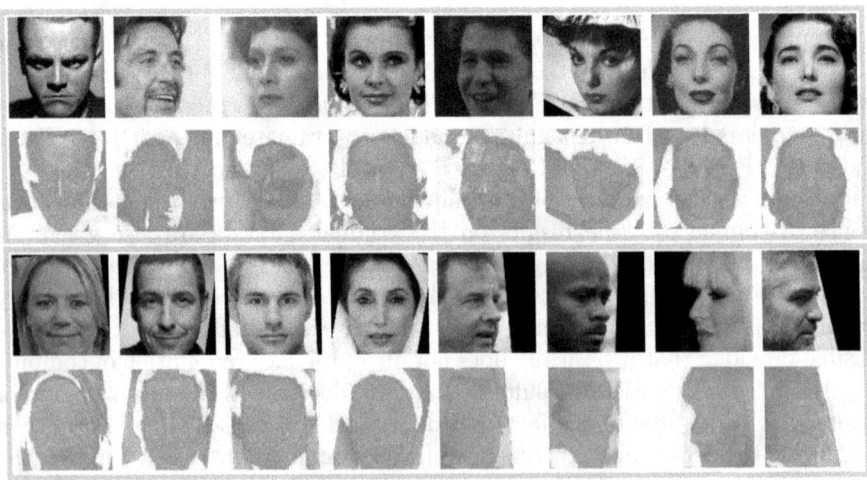

Fig. 3. Subjective results on AgeDB-30 and CFP-FP datasets. Each dataset is displayed in a pair of the original and corresponding attacked images. The orange and blue boxes denote AgeDB-30 and CFP-FP datasets samples, respectively. It can be seen that the attacked images lose the appearance information so that the human eyes fail to recognize them. (Color figure online)

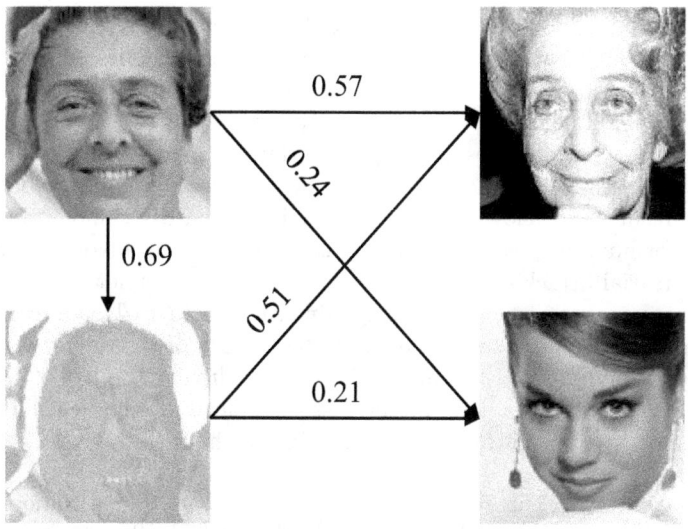

Fig. 4. Instance analysis for our model. The upper left corner represents the original input image, and the lower left corner represents its corresponding identity image. The upper right corner denotes the image with the same identity as the input image, marked as intra-class. The lower right corner denotes the image that is inconsistent with the input image identity, which is marked as the inter-class image. The value on the arrow indicates the Cosine similarity of the image embedding extracted by ArcFace trained on WebFace [18].

3.5 Instance Analysis

In this section, we choose a face recognition instance to analyze the application of unconventional adversarial attack. As shown in Fig. 4, given an original face image, the similarity (0.57) between it and the intra-class image is much greater than the similarity (0.24) with the inter-class image. In this way, it can be judged which identity the original image belongs to. Furthermore, we generate the identity image through our unconventional adversarial attack model. As expected, the similarity (0.51) between the identity image and the intra-class image also has a substantial degree of discrimination compared to the similarity (0.21) with the inter-class image. In other words, we can replace the original image with the identity image to complete the entire recognition process without revealing the appearance of the original image. Therefore, the unconventional adversarial attack model we proposed is practical for protecting facial appearance privacy.

4 Conclusion

In this paper, we have coined an completely new concept different from the traditional adversarial attack, unconventional face adversarial attack, where the converted face image cannot be recognized by human eyes but can be identified by computers. To achieve this purpose, we particularly design a dual-branch face feature coupled network (FFCN) to disentangle a face image into appearance and identity components, where the identity component is used as the attacked resulting image. Objective results on popular face recognizers show that the generated face images by our model basically do not hinder the face identification. Subjective results also show that the attacked faces hardly demonstrate the discernibility for human eyes. These results confirm that our advocated unconventional adversarial attack does fulfill the purpose that does not affect computers but humans, in contrast to the existing adversarial attack. This unconventional adversarial attack can be used to protect the privacy of face identify when face images are visibly exposed to humans but do not hinder the use of computers. This work has opened up a new and interesting topic, and other feasible solutions to implement this concept are worth exploring in the future.

Acknowledgements. This research was supposed in part by the National Natural Science Foundation of China (U22A2035, 62072347, 62371350), and in part by the Application Foundation Frontier Special Project of Wuhan Science and Technology Plan Project (No. 2020010601012288).

References

1. Butler, D.J., Huang, J., Roesner, F., Cakmak, M.: The privacy-utility tradeoff for remotely teleoperated robots. In: Proceedings of the Tenth Annual IEEE International Conference on Human-robot Interaction, pp. 27–34 (2015)
2. Chen, J., Konrad, J., Ishwar, P.: VGAN-based image representation learning for privacy-preserving facial expression recognition. In: Proceedings of the IEEE Conference on Computer Vision and Pattern Recognition Workshops, pp. 1570–1579 (2018)
3. Deng, J., Guo, J., Xue, N., Zafeiriou, S.: ArcFace: additive angular margin loss for deep face recognition. In: IEEE Conference on Computer Vision and Pattern Recognition, pp. 4690–4699 (2019)
4. Deng, J., Guo, J., Yuxiang, Z., Yu, J., Kotsia, I., Zafeiriou, S.: RetinaFace: single-stage dense face localisation in the wild. arXiv: Computer Vision and Pattern Recognition (2019)
5. Dong, Y., et al.: Boosting adversarial attacks with momentum. In: Proceedings of the IEEE Conference on Computer Vision and Pattern Recognition, pp. 9185–9193 (2018)
6. Huang, G.B., Mattar, M., Berg, T., Learned-Miller, E.: Labeled faces in the wild: a database for studying face recognition in unconstrained environments. In: Workshop on Faces in 'Real-Life' Images: Detection, Alignment, and Recognition (2008)
7. Huang, Y., et al.: CurricularFace: adaptive curriculum learning loss for deep face recognition. In: IEEE Conference on Computer Vision and Pattern Recognition, pp. 5901–5910 (2020)
8. Lai, W.S., Huang, J.B., Ahuja, N., Yang, M.H.: Deep Laplacian pyramid networks for fast and accurate super-resolution. In: IEEE Conference on Computer Vision and Pattern Recognition, pp. 5835–5843 (2017)

9. Maximov, M., Elezi, I., Leal-Taixé, L.: CIAGAN: conditional identity anonymization generative adversarial networks. In: Proceedings of the IEEE Conference on Computer Vision and Pattern Recognition, pp. 5447–5456 (2020)
10. Moschoglou, S., Papaioannou, A., Sagonas, C., Deng, J., Kotsia, I., Zafeiriou, S.: AgeDB: the first manually collected, in-the-wild age database. In: IEEE Conference on Computer Vision and Pattern Recognition, pp. 1997–2005 (2017)
11. Ren, Z., Lee, Y.J., Ryoo, M.S.: Learning to anonymize faces for privacy preserving action detection. In: Proceedings of the European Conference on Computer Vision, pp. 620–636 (2018)
12. Ryoo, M.S., Rothrock, B., Fleming, C., Yang, H.J.: Privacy-preserving human activity recognition from extreme low resolution. In: Thirty-First AAAI Conference on Artificial Intelligence (2017)
13. Sadeghi, K., Banerjee, A., Gupta, S.K.: A system-driven taxonomy of attacks and defenses in adversarial machine learning. IEEE Trans. Emerg. Top. Comput. Intell. **4**(4), 450–467 (2020)
14. Sengupta, S., Chen, J., Castillo, C.D., Patel, V.M., Chellappa, R., Jacobs, D.W.: Frontal to profile face verification in the wild. In: Workshop on Applications of Computer Vision, pp. 1–9 (2016)
15. Wang, H., et al.: CosFace: large margin cosine loss for deep face recognition. In: IEEE Conference on Computer Vision and Pattern Recognition, pp. 5265–5274 (2018)
16. Wang, Z., Chang, S., Yang, Y., Liu, D., Huang, T.S.: Studying very low resolution recognition using deep networks. In: Proceedings of the IEEE Conference on Computer Vision and Pattern Recognition, pp. 4792–4800 (2016)
17. Xie, C., et al.: Improving transferability of adversarial examples with input diversity. In: Proceedings of the IEEE Conference on Computer Vision and Pattern Recognition, pp. 2730–2739 (2019)
18. Yi, D., Lei, Z., Liao, S., Li, S.Z.: Learning face representation from scratch. arXiv: Computer Vision and Pattern Recognition (2014)
19. Zhong, Y., Deng, W.: Towards transferable adversarial attack against deep face recognition. IEEE Trans. Inf. Forensics Secur. **16**, 1452–1466 (2020)

Computer Vision: Image Enhancement

A Study in Dataset Pruning for Image Super-Resolution

Brian B. Moser[✉], Federico Raue, and Andreas Dengel

German Research Center for Artificial Intelligence (DFKI), Germany RPTU Kaiserslautern-Landau, Kaiserslautern, Germany
brian.moser@dfki.de

Abstract. In image Super-Resolution (SR), relying on large datasets for training is a double-edged sword. While offering rich training material, they also demand substantial computational and storage resources. In this work, we analyze dataset pruning to solve these challenges. We introduce a novel approach that reduces a dataset to a core-set of training samples, selected based on their loss values as determined by a simple pre-trained SR model. By focusing the training on just 50% of the original dataset, specifically on the samples characterized by the highest loss values, we achieve results comparable to or surpassing those obtained from training on the entire dataset. Interestingly, our analysis reveals that the top 5% of samples with the highest loss values negatively affect the training process. Excluding these samples and adjusting the selection to favor easier samples further enhances training outcomes. Our work opens new perspectives to the untapped potential of dataset pruning in image SR. It suggests that careful selection of training data based on loss-value metrics can lead to better SR models, challenging the conventional wisdom that more data inevitably leads to better performance.

Keywords: Super-Resolution · Dataset Pruning · Core-Set Selection

1 Introduction

Image Super-Resolution (SR) techniques are a cornerstone of image processing as they reconstruct High-Resolution (HR) images from their Low-Resolution (LR) counterparts [11,26,27,30]. It has wide-ranging applications, from enhancing consumer photography to improving satellite or medical imagery [3,24,28,37]. Despite its relevance, training SR models requires substantial computational resources due to large-scale datasets [13,24]. These datasets are pivotal for capturing the diversity of textures and patterns essential for effective upscaling, but they also pose significant storage challenges [19]. Recent advancements in deep learning have elevated SR techniques to new levels, with models like SwinIR and HAT setting new benchmarks for regression-based image enhancement quality [7,18].

However, the success of these models often hinges on their capacity to learn from extensive and diverse training data, exacerbating the resource-intensive nature of SR model training [24,28]. In response to these challenges, our work explores dataset pruning as a strategy to enhance the efficiency of SR model training without compromising the quality of the output images [1,8,33]. To the best of our knowledge, efforts to apply dataset pruning to image SR tasks have been scarce, except for the notable contribution made by *Ding et al.* [10], which we will discuss and improve on in this work. The concept of dataset pruning involves reducing the size of the training dataset by selectively identifying a subset of samples that are most informative for the optimization process. This approach is promising for mitigating the storage burden of large datasets while preserving or improving the training performance of SR models [13,25].

Our contribution is twofold. First, we propose a novel loss-value-based sampling method for dataset pruning in image SR, leveraging a simple pre-trained SR model, namely SRCNN [11]. Our method contrasts traditional approaches that indiscriminately use the entirety of available data, i.e., DIV2K [2]. Secondly, we empirically demonstrate that training SR models on a pruned dataset - comprising 50% of the original dataset selected based on their loss values - can achieve comparable or superior performance to training on the full dataset. Refining this selection by excluding the top 5% hardest samples, which we found were counterproductive, further enhances model training efficiency.

Through this work, we aim to spark a paradigm shift in how training datasets are curated for SR tasks. We advocate for a loss-value-driven approach to dataset pruning. Our strategy significantly reduces the storage requirements of SR model training and offers a scalable solution that can adapt to the evolving complexities and requirements of image SR.

2 Related Work

Dataset pruning is particularly interesting to deep learning [1,8,33]. It focuses on training set size reduction while attempting to maintain or even enhance the performance of models. This process is not just about economizing on computational storage; it also aims to improve model generalization by eliminating redundant or less informative samples [14,17]. Various methodologies have explored this concept, including importance sampling, core-set selection, and data distillation. In the following, we explore key contributions to dataset pruning and provide insights into its development.

Importance Sampling. One key approach in dataset pruning is importance sampling, where the idea is to prioritize training on samples deemed more important for the model. Works such as *Katharopoulos et al.* [17] have explored adaptive sampling methods that dynamically adjust the probability of selecting each sample based on the model's current state. These methods aim to focus computational effort where it is most needed. However, by weighting samples, importance sampling does not reduce the training set size as we do.

Data Distillation. Data distillation is a technique that generates a condensed and synthetic version of the training data, often through knowledge distillation [14], where a smaller dataset is created to capture the essence of the original data. The work by *Wang et al.* [38] on dataset distillation demonstrates how training on a distilled dataset can achieve comparable performance to training on the entire dataset, significantly reducing the computational burden regarding convergence and storage. Since then, various exciting developments have been made in dataset distillation [6,29]. Nevertheless, existing approaches to dataset distillation are predominantly aimed at capturing critical semantic details for image classification purposes [5,31,42,43]. Given the significant differences between image classification and image SR, applying dataset distillation techniques directly to SR tasks presents a considerable challenge [19].

Core-Set Selection. This approach involves identifying a subset of the training data that is a good representation of the entire dataset. Therefore, it reduces the dataset size in contrast to importance sampling. *Sener et al.* [34] introduced an optimization framework that selects samples constituting a core-set for training deep neural networks. This method minimizes the maximum loss over the dataset, ensuring the selected subset is as informative as the original dataset. Since then, core-set selection, also called proxy datasets, has been further developed in various fields, such as image classification or neural architecture search [8,10,25,35].

To the best of our knowledge, image SR tasks have primarily remained untouched by initiatives in dataset pruning, with a notable exception of the work conducted by *Ding et al.* [10]. The authors suggest using the Sobel filter to reduce the dataset, focusing specifically on selecting samples with rich textures. They further refine their selection by clustering these texture-rich samples to ensure a variety of textures is represented. In contrast, we opt for sampling based on SR reconstruction loss values. In the experiments section, we will demonstrate that our strategy, which prioritizes samples according to their SR reconstruction loss, performs better than a method based on Sobel filter selection.

3 Methodology

This section introduces our method for optimizing SR model training using dataset pruning. Our approach is found on the premise that not all samples in a dataset contribute equally to the learning process in the context of SR tasks [17,25,34]. By carefully selecting a core-set of samples that are most informative for SR model training, we aim to enhance the learning process.

After introducing the concept of core-sets and how they are sampled, we present our loss-based sampling method, which leverages a pre-trained SR model - a simple SRCNN [11] - to estimate the complexity in reconstructing HR samples from their LR counterparts. By focusing on challenging samples for the SR model, as indicated by higher loss values, we hypothesize that the model can learn more effectively, thereby improving its performance on unseen data.

3.1 Core-Sets

Consider a dataset $\mathcal{D} = \{(\mathbf{x}_i, \mathbf{y}_i)\}$ with a total number of elements denoted as $N_\mathcal{D}$. In this context, $\mathbf{x}_i$, where $0 \leq i < N_\mathcal{D}$, represents the i-th LR sample and $\mathbf{y}_i$

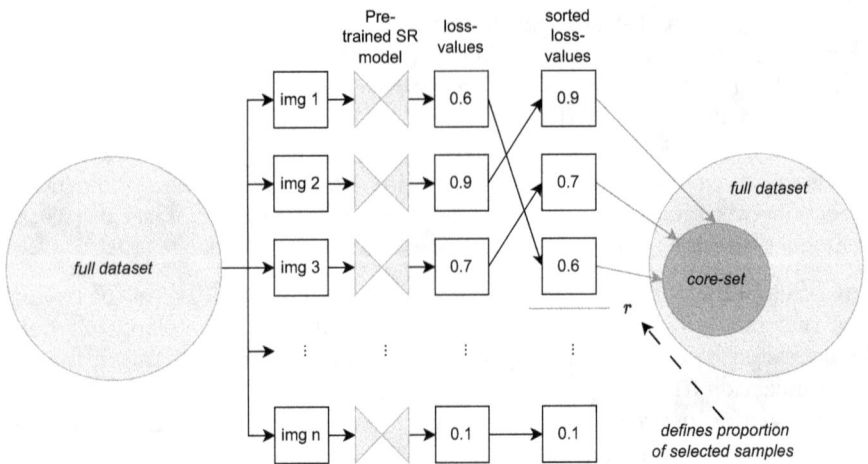

Fig. 1. Illustration of our loss-value-based core-set selection for image SR. Initially, the full dataset undergoes evaluation through a pre-trained SR model to calculate loss values for each image pair. These loss values are then sorted to identify samples with varying degrees of reconstruction difficulty. A pre-defined proportion r of these samples is selected to form a core-set.

its corresponding HR counterpart. We define a subset of $\mathcal{D}$, denoted by $\mathcal{D}_r \subset \mathcal{D}$, as a core-set with a size of $N_{\mathcal{D}_r}$. The proportion $r \in (0, 1)$ specifies the size of $\mathcal{D}_r$ relative to $\mathcal{D}$: $N_{\mathcal{D}_r} \approx r \cdot N_{\mathcal{D}}$. This approximation accounts for instances where the dataset size cannot be divided evenly. The core-set acts between the original dataset and the SR model to enhance the SR output quality by focusing on important samples during training. The objective is to construct a core-set $\mathcal{D}_r \subset \mathcal{D}$ such that its size $N_{\mathcal{D}_r} \approx r \cdot N_{\mathcal{D}}$, with $r \in (0, 1)$. To achieve this for any chosen r, the sampling strategy must satisfy the condition

$$N_{\mathcal{D}_r} = \sum_{(\mathbf{x}_i, \mathbf{y}_i) \in \mathcal{D}} \mathbb{1}_{\mathcal{D}_r}(\mathbf{x}_i) \approx r \cdot N_{\mathcal{D}}, \tag{1}$$

where $\mathbb{1}_{\mathcal{D}_r} : \mathcal{D} \to \{0, 1\}$ is the indicator that determines whether an element belongs to the core-set $\mathcal{D}_r$ within the larger dataset $\mathcal{D}$.

The concrete realization of the core-set selection depends on the sampling mechanism. *Ding et al.* [10] proposed to use the Sobel filter to identify texture-rich training samples. In contrast, we argue that a loss-value-based sampling is more efficient, which we will explain next and demonstrate empirically in the experiments section.

3.2 Loss-Value-Based Sampling

In image SR, one approximates $\mathbf{y}_i \approx \mathcal{M}(d(\mathbf{y}_i))$ with a SR model $\mathcal{M}$ and a degradation function d that represents the relationship between the HR and LR space (i.e., $d(\mathbf{y}_i) = \mathbf{x}_i$). As a result, a trained SR model can provide a distance metric based on a loss function. Let $\mathcal{L} : \mathbb{R}^{h \times w \times c} \times \mathbb{R}^{h \times w \times c} \to \mathbb{R}$ be a loss function, e.g., Mean Squared Error (MSE), with h, w, c as the height, width, and channel size, respectively. Given $r \in (0, 1)$, we can derive a core-set with

$$\mathcal{D}_r^{\text{ASC}} = \underset{\substack{\mathcal{D}' \subset \mathcal{D}, \\ \text{s.t. } |\mathcal{D}'| \approx r \cdot N_\mathcal{D}}}{\arg\min} \sum_{(\cdot, \mathbf{y}_i) \in \mathcal{D}'} \mathcal{L}(\mathcal{M}(d(\mathbf{y}_i)), \mathbf{y}_i), \quad (2)$$

where samples with high loss values are removed, denoted as ascending sampling (ASC). Likewise, we can define a sampling method based on removing the lowest loss values, thereby concentrating on hard samples by

$$\mathcal{D}_r^{\text{DES}} = \underset{\substack{\mathcal{D}' \subset \mathcal{D}, \\ \text{s.t. } |\mathcal{D}'| \approx r \cdot N_\mathcal{D}}}{\arg\max} \sum_{(\cdot, \mathbf{y}_i) \in \mathcal{D}'} \mathcal{L}(\mathcal{M}(d(\mathbf{y}_i)), \mathbf{y}_i), \quad (3)$$

denoted as descending sampling (DES). The concept is illustrated in Fig. 1. In the experiments section, we will determine whether ascending or descending sampling is preferable and which r value is beneficial. Intuitively, ascending sampling includes less complex, monochromatic training samples first, whereas descending sampling favors texture-rich, multi-colored training samples. In the following, we will use a simple pre-trained SRCNN [11] (composed of three layers of convolutions) and MSE for the loss calculation in Eq. 2 and 3.

4 Experiments

In this section, we empirically evaluate the performance of our loss-value-based sampling. We start by benchmarking whether ascending (ASC) or descending (DES) sampling is more beneficial. We also evaluate whether maintaining the same number of training steps is critical. Next, we compare our loss-value-based sampling with the sampling mechanism exchanged by using Sobel filters instead, as suggested by *Ding et al.* [10]. Finally, we analyze the pruned dataset and suggest a refined version. We will evaluate the original and refined core-set with state-of-the-art datasets and methods.

4.1 Datasets

Our method is assessed using well-established SR datasets. The DIV2K dataset [2] served as our primary source for training data, from which we extracted sub-images according to standard practice in literature [3,30]. As a result, we derive around 32K HR training samples from 800 2K HR images. LR samples are computed by following the standard procedure using bicubic interpolation and anti-aliasing [21,28]. These sub-images formed the basis for selecting the core-sets. For the evaluation phase, we utilized the test datasets Set5 [4], Set14 [39], BSDS100 [20], and Urban100 [15]. We assess our experiments based on two metrics: Peak Signal-to-Noise Ratio (PSNR) and Structural Similarity Index (SSIM), where higher values represent better image quality.

Table 1. Comparison of ascending and descending sampling on BSD100 with 2× scaling. Values with at least the same or better performance than their corresponding performance on the full dataset are highlighted in red.

Method	Train Steps	FSRCNN [12]		DRRN [36]		IDN [16]		RDN [41]		SwinIR [18]	
		PSNR	SSIM	PSNR	SSIM	PSNR	SSIM	PSNR	SSIM	PSNR	SSIM
full	15,608	31.09	0.8955	29.42	0.8781	31.98	0.9076	32.25	0.9103	32.23	0.9103
75% ASC	11,706	30.84	0.8928	28.11	0.8725	31.90	0.9065	32.21	0.9101	32.13	0.9091
50% ASC	7,804	30.25	0.8862	22.28	0.8370	31.67	0.9040	32.02	0.9080	31.90	0.9067
25% ASC	3,902	28.38	0.8303	14.66	0.7293	31.23	0.8976	31.66	0.9039	30.97	0.8957
75% DES	11,706	31.11	0.8960	29.32	0.8783	31.96	0.9071	32.26	0.9107	32.24	0.9104
50% DES	7,804	31.20	0.8968	29.40	0.8795	31.94	0.9070	32.25	0.9105	32.21	0.9101
25% DES	3,902	30.98	0.8937	29.32	0.8791	31.81	0.9052	32.22	0.9099	32.13	0.9088
25% DES	7,804	31.11	0.8969	29.39	0.8804	31.94	0.9068	32.24	0.9104	32.20	0.9096
25% DES	15,608	31.35	0.8986	29.46	0.8810	31.98	0.9076	32.26	0.9104	32.24	0.9101
50% DES	15,608	31.30	0.8983	29.39	0.8795	32.00	0.9076	32.28	0.9108	32.27	0.9104

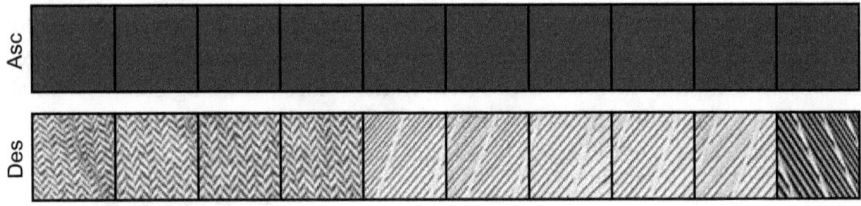

Fig. 2. Comparison of top-selected samples by ascending and descending sampling. We can observe that descending sampling selects primarily training patches with high textural details, whereas ascending sampling focuses on monochromatic samples.

4.2 Results

Ascending Versus Descending Sampling. We compare ascending (ASC) and descending (DES) sampling methods on the BSD100 dataset with 2× scaling in Table 1. Our primary focus is understanding their impact on various image SR models, namely FSRCNN [12], DRRN [36], IDN [16], RDN [41], and SwinIR [18]. The various models evaluate different categories of SR models, namely simple CNN, recursive CNN, residual CNNs, and Transformer-based [28].

We observe a general trend of declining performance, i.e., worse image enhancement quality, across all models when ascending sampling (ASC) is applied at reduced dataset sizes. Specifically, at 25% dataset size, the performance drop becomes more pronounced, with the PSNR dropping from 31.09 to 28.38 for FSRCNN and from 29.42 to 14.66 for DRRN. This indicates the ineffectiveness of ascending sampling in preserving model performance.

In contrast, descending sampling generally outperforms or matches the full dataset performance, especially notable in the 75% and 50% dataset sizes. For

Table 2. Quantitative comparison between sampling based on loss-value and Sobel filter (average PSNR/SSIM) with SwinIR for classical image SR on benchmark datasets (2× scaling, 50% pruning). The best performance is highlighted in red.

Sampling Method	Set5 [4]		Set14 [39]		BSD100 [20]		Urban100 [15]		Manga109 [22]	
	PSNR	SSIM	PSNR	SSIM	PSNR	SSIM	PSNR	SSIM	PSNR	SSIM
loss-based	38.32	0.9619	34.15	0.9232	32.45	0.9038	33.43	0.9396	39.55	0.9790
sobel-based	38.26	0.9612	34.09	0.9225	32.44	0.9037	33.38	0.9392	39.54	0.9789

instance, FSRCNN shows improved results at 75% DES and even higher scores at 50% DES, surpassing the full dataset baseline.

Note that decreased data size leads to fewer training steps if the number of epochs is fixed. Consequently, with fixed epochs, i.e., 200, SR models train effectively shorter because a single epoch has fewer training iterations due to the reduced data size. Remarkably, applying more epochs to match the number of training steps on the original dataset further enhances the results. Using 25% DES with 4x epochs, which is equal to the number of training steps employed in the full dataset, achieves the highest PSNR and SSIM for several models.

Our findings highlight that hard samples, defined by high loss, are crucial for maintaining or enhancing SR model performance. Therefore, texture-rich samples, contrary to monochromatic easy samples (see Fig. 2), are significant for training a SR model effectively. Additionally, maintaining the number of training iterations is essential, rather than merely focusing on reducing the dataset size for reduced training time. By keeping training iterations consistent, descending sampling effectively leverages a reduced but more potent subset of the original dataset, leading to improved or comparable performance across all evaluated SR models. Our findings about keeping the same training iterations present a distinct divergence from those reported by *Ding et al.* [10]. We speculate that this discrepancy may arise from using fewer training epochs, which likely prevented their models from achieving full convergence. Moving forward, we will further explore our loss-based sampling approach by maintaining a consistent number of iterations and employing the descending sampling technique.

Loss-Based Versus Sobel-Based As introduced by *Ding et al.* [10], utilizing the Sobel filter represents another strategy for curating a core-set for image SR. Therefore, we compare our loss-based sampling method with the Sobel filter approach. From Table 2, it is evident that the loss-based sampling method consistently outperforms the Sobel filter-based approach across all datasets. Specifically, for the Set5 dataset, loss-based sampling achieves a PSNR of 38.32 and an SSIM of 0.9619, compared to 38.26 (PSNR) and 0.9612 (SSIM) for the Sobel-based method. This trend continues across the Set14, BSD100, and Urban100 datasets, where loss-based sampling performs superiorly in both PSNR and SSIM metrics. By focusing on loss values, we prioritize samples the model finds challenging to reconstruct, potentially leading to a more robust learning process and

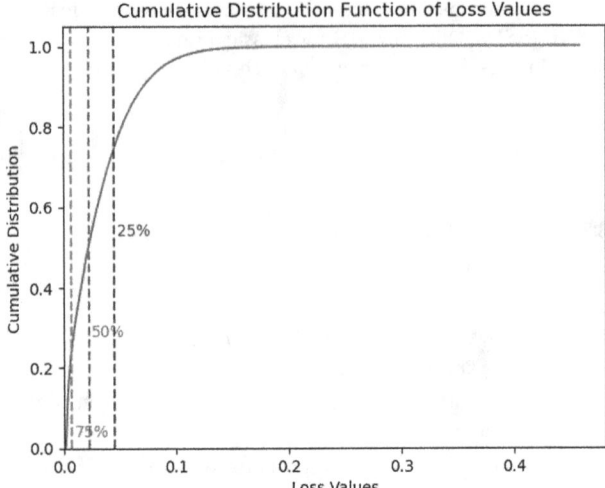

Fig. 3. Cumulative Loss-Value Distribution (sorted). Vertical lines represent different descending sampling endpoints for 25%, 50%, and 75% sampling. The right side of the respective vertical line shows the loss values included and found within the corresponding core-sets.

improved SR performance. In contrast, the Sobel filter-based approach, which selects samples based on texture richness, might overlook other crucial aspects contributing to the overall quality and effectiveness of SR reconstruction.

Analyzing Loss Values. This section examines the core-sets derived by descending sampling more closely. More specifically, we derive the loss values found by applying descending sampling at 25%, 50%, and 75%. Figure 3 shows the result. The distribution demonstrates that certain samples, characterized by notably higher loss values, are consistently included across all core-sets (see the long tail on the right side of the vertical lines). We theorize that these samples, possibly due to their high noise levels, could be detrimental to the training of SR models. To address this, we suggest refining the initially derived core-set by adjusting the selection threshold by 5% to favor samples with lower loss values and exclude those with the highest losses.

The modified core-set and associated loss values within this refined set are depicted in Fig. 4; see the area between the vertical lines denoted by start and end. This approach involves retaining 50% of the samples initially considered the most challenging but adjusting the selection to slightly favor easier samples (those with lower loss values) by shifting the inclusion criteria by 5%. In other words, the core-set still contains 50% of the original dataset's hardest samples, except the top 5% hardest. We will evaluate both core-sets, the original and the refined, in the following with state-of-the-art benchmarks.

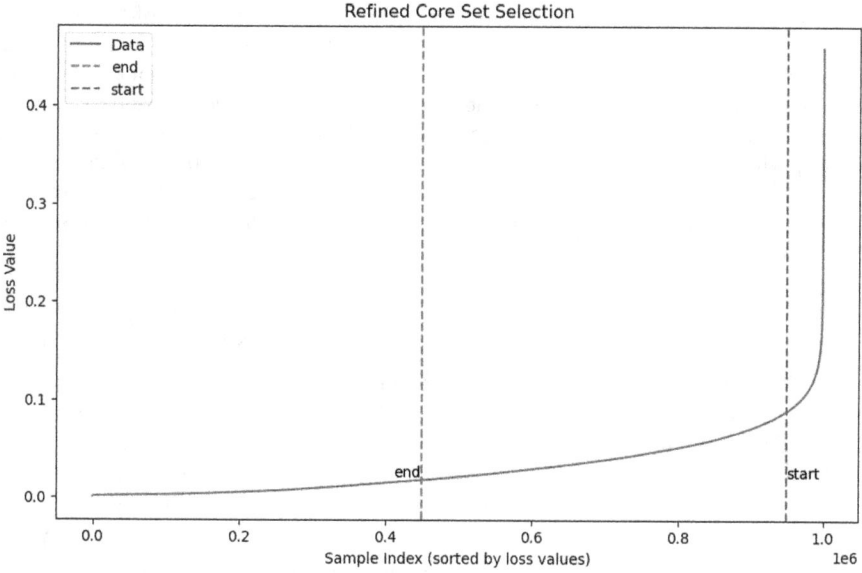

Fig. 4. Refined Core Set Proposal. This strategy selects the top 50% most challenging samples but modifies the selection by shifting the inclusion threshold by 5 % towards samples with lower loss values, aiming for a more balanced core-set. In other words, we keep 50 % of the hardest samples in our core-set after excluding the top 5 % from the dataset.

Benchmark with State-of-the-Art. We evaluate the quality of our core-sets by training the state-of-the-art SR model SwinIR [18] on them. The evaluation includes other state-of-the-art methods for classical image SR across benchmark datasets, including Set5 [4], Set14 [39], BSD100 [20], and Urban100 [15], with scaling factors of 2×, 3×, and 4×. Table 3 reports the results with notable performances being color-coded, with the best and second-best results marked in red and blue, respectively.

Interestingly, when SwinIR is trained on 50% of the dataset for 2× scaling, it maintains its superior performance on Set5 and improves upon the full dataset results on Set14, BSD100, and Urban100, suggesting efficient learning from a pruned dataset. The refined 50% core-set further improves performance, pushing the boundaries on Set14, BSD100, and Urban100 to achieve the highest metrics. Again, This indicates that a pruned dataset can match or even surpass full dataset training outcomes.

For a 3× scaling factor, the core-sets demonstrate competitive or superior performance compared to the full dataset, especially highlighted in the Set14 and BSD100 datasets. This reinforces the effectiveness of dataset pruning in enhancing model efficiency without significantly compromising output quality.

The core-sets yield closely competitive results at the most challenging scaling factor of 4. The refined core-set offers the best PSNR on BSD100 and closely

Table 3. Quantitative comparison (average PSNR/SSIM) with state-of-the-art methods for classical image SR on benchmark datasets (Set5, Set14, BSDS100, and Urban100). These experiments were evaluated under the lens of various scaling factors, specifically 2, 3, and 4. We trained SwinIR on our pruned datasets with 50 % of the size of the original datasets. Moreover, we included our refined version of our core-set, which excludes the top 5% hardest samples (see ref. 50 %). The best and second best performances are in red and blue colors, respectively. As a result, training SwinIR on half of the original datasets leads to comparable and, in most cases, superior performance.

Method	Scale	Train Set	Set5 [4]		Set14 [39]		BSD100 [20]		Urban100 [15]	
			PSNR	SSIM	PSNR	SSIM	PSNR	SSIM	PSNR	SSIM
RCAN [40]	×2	full	38.27	0.9614	34.12	0.9216	32.41	0.9027	33.34	0.9384
SAN [9]	×2	full	38.31	0.9620	34.07	0.9213	32.42	0.9028	33.10	0.9370
IGNN [44]	×2	full	38.24	0.9613	34.07	0.9217	32.41	0.9025	33.23	0.9383
HAN [32]	×2	full	38.27	0.9614	34.16	0.9217	32.41	0.9027	33.35	0.9385
NLSA [23]	×2	full	38.34	0.9618	34.08	0.9231	32.43	0.9027	33.42	0.9394
SwinIR [18]	×2	full	38.35	0.9620	34.14	0.9227	32.44	0.9030	33.40	0.9393
SwinIR [18]	×2	50%	38.35	0.9620	34.20	0.9230	32.46	0.9039	33.47	0.9399
SwinIR [18]	×2	ref. 50%	38.34	0.9619	34.23	0.9236	32.48	0.9041	33.52	0.9401
RCAN [40]	×3	full	34.74	0.9299	30.65	0.8482	29.32	0.8111	29.09	0.8702
SAN [9]	×3	full	34.75	0.9300	30.59	0.8476	29.33	0.8112	28.93	0.8671
IGNN [44]	×3	full	34.72	0.9298	30.66	0.8484	29.31	0.8105	29.03	0.8696
HAN [32]	×3	full	34.75	0.9299	30.67	0.8483	29.32	0.8110	29.10	0.8705
NLSA [23]	×3	full	34.85	0.9306	30.70	0.8485	29.34	0.8117	29.25	0.8726
SwinIR [18]	×3	full	34.89	0.9312	30.77	0.8503	29.37	0.8124	29.29	0.8744
SwinIR [18]	×3	50%	34.87	0.9307	30.70	0.8503	29.35	0.8134	29.19	0.8731
SwinIR [18]	×3	ref. 50%	34.84	0.9306	30.75	0.8506	29.37	0.8137	29.25	0.8740
RCAN [40]	×4	full	32.63	0.9002	28.87	0.7889	27.77	0.7436	26.82	0.8087
SAN [9]	×4	full	32.64	0.9003	28.92	0.7888	27.78	0.7436	26.79	0.8068
IGNN [44]	×4	full	32.57	0.8998	28.85	0.7891	27.77	0.7434	26.84	0.8090
HAN [32]	×4	full	32.64	0.9002	28.90	0.7890	27.80	0.7442	26.85	0.8094
NLSA [23]	×4	full	32.59	0.9000	28.87	0.7891	27.78	0.7444	26.96	0.8109
SwinIR [18]	×4	full	32.72	0.9021	28.94	0.7914	27.83	0.7459	27.07	0.8164
SwinIR [18]	×4	50%	32.71	0.9013	28.91	0.7908	27.80	0.7466	26.91	0.8113
SwinIR [18]	×4	ref. 50%	32.75	0.9012	28.87	0.7903	27.81	0.7469	26.92	0.8111

matches the full dataset's performance on Urban100. A general observation is that the refined core-set outperforms the original 50% core-set in most cases.

These findings underscore the potential of dataset pruning strategies, especially when applied to sophisticated models like SwinIR. The experiments suggest that thoughtful pruning can achieve comparable or superior performance using only a fraction of the training data.

5 Conclusion and Future Work

By introducing and comparing loss-value-based sampling strategies, our study highlights the potential of dataset pruning to maintain and, in most instances, enhance the performance of SR models while substantially reducing the computational storage. We use a simple pre-trained SR model, SRCNN, to determine which samples to remove based on a mean squared error loss. Our findings, particularly with the descending sampling method, underscore the value of selectively curating training datasets to include samples challenging for the model during training. In other words, as defined by loss values, training SR models on hard samples is more beneficial than training on easy samples. Furthermore, we concluded that loss-value-based sampling performed better than Sobel filter-based sampling. Moreover, we showed that our refined core-set, which excludes the top 5 % of hardest samples, further improves the performance. We have validated our approach against several benchmarks using current state-of-the-art models. Our experiments also verify our hypothesis on several SR models, including leading models like SwinIR, and on several datasets.

For future work, we see significant potential in advancing our dataset pruning strategies by integrating more nuanced measures of sample difficulty. This could involve leveraging insights from model uncertainty or incorporating adaptive feedback loops during training to adjust the core-set dynamically. Such refinements could pave the way for more efficient training methods, optimizing computational resources while achieving superior SR model performance.

Acknowledgements. This work was supported by the BMBF project SustainML (Grant 101070408).

References

1. Agarwal, S., Arora, H., Anand, S., Arora, C.: Contextual diversity for active learning. In: Vedaldi, A., Bischof, H., Brox, T., Frahm, J.-M. (eds.) ECCV 2020. LNCS, vol. 12361, pp. 137–153. Springer, Cham (2020). https://doi.org/10.1007/978-3-030-58517-4_9
2. Agustsson, E., Timofte, R.: Ntire 2017 challenge on single image super-resolution: dataset and study. In: CVPRW (2017)
3. Bashir, S.M.A., Wang, Y., Khan, M., Niu, Y.: A comprehensive review of deep learning-based single image super-resolution. PeerJ Comput. Sci. **7**, e621 (2021)
4. Bevilacqua, M., Roumy, A., Guillemot, C., Alberi-Morel, M.L.: Low-complexity single-image super-resolution based on nonnegative neighbor embedding (2012)
5. Cazenavette, G., Wang, T., Torralba, A., Efros, A.A., Zhu, J.Y.: Dataset distillation by matching training trajectories. In: CVPR, pp. 4750–4759 (2022)
6. Cazenavette, G., Wang, T., Torralba, A., Efros, A.A., Zhu, J.Y.: Generalizing dataset distillation via deep generative prior. In: CVPR, pp. 3739–3748 (2023)
7. Chen, X., Wang, X., Zhou, J., Qiao, Y., Dong, C.: Activating more pixels in image super-resolution transformer. In: CVPR, pp. 22367–22377 (2023)
8. Coleman, C., et al.: Selection via proxy: Efficient data selection for deep learning. arXiv preprint arXiv:1906.11829 (2019)

9. Dai, T., Cai, J., Zhang, Y., Xia, S.T., Zhang, L.: Second-order attention network for single image super-resolution. In: CVPR, pp. 11065–11074 (2019)
10. Ding, Q., Liang, Z., Wang, L., Wang, Y., Yang, J.: Not all patches are equal: hierarchical dataset condensation for single image super-resolution. IEEE Signal Process. Lett. (2023)
11. Dong, C., Loy, C.C., He, K., Tang, X.: Image super-resolution using deep convolutional networks. IEEE TPAMI **38**(2), 295–307 (2015)
12. Dong, C., Loy, C.C., Tang, X.: Accelerating the super-resolution convolutional neural network. In: Leibe, B., Matas, J., Sebe, N., Welling, M. (eds.) ECCV 2016. LNCS, vol. 9906, pp. 391–407. Springer, Cham (2016). https://doi.org/10.1007/978-3-319-46475-6_25
13. Ganguli, D., et al.: Predictability and surprise in large generative models. In: 2022 ACM Conference on Fairness, Accountability, and Transparency (2022)
14. Hinton, G., Vinyals, O., Dean, J.: Distilling the knowledge in a neural network. In: NeurIPS Workshop (2015)
15. Huang, J.B., Singh, A., Ahuja, N.: Single image super-resolution from transformed self-exemplars. In: CVPR, pp. 5197–5206 (2015)
16. Hui, Z., Wang, X., Gao, X.: Fast and accurate single image super-resolution via information distillation network. In: CVPR, pp. 723–731 (2018)
17. Katharopoulos, A., Fleuret, F.: Not all samples are created equal: Deep learning with importance sampling. In: ICML, pp. 2525–2534. PMLR (2018)
18. Liang, J., Cao, J., Sun, G., Zhang, K., Van Gool, L., Timofte, R.: Swinir: Image restoration using swin transformer. In: ICCV, pp. 1833–1844 (2021)
19. Liu, Y., Liu, A., Gu, J., Zhang, Z., Wu, W., Qiao, Y., Dong, C.: Discovering distinctive" semantics" in super-resolution networks. arXiv preprint arXiv:2108.00406 (2021)
20. Martin, D., Fowlkes, C., Tal, D., Malik, J.: A database of human segmented natural images and its application to evaluating segmentation algorithms and measuring ecological statistics. In: ICCV, vol. 2, pp. 416–423. IEEE (2001)
21. The Mathworks, Inc., Natick, Massachusetts: MATLAB version 9.3.0.713579 (R2017b) (2017)
22. Matsui, Y., et al.: Sketch-based manga retrieval using manga109 dataset. Multimedia Tools Appli. **76**, 21811–21838 (2017)
23. Mei, Y., Fan, Y., Zhou, Y.: Image super-resolution with non-local sparse attention. In: CVPR, pp. 3517–3526 (2021)
24. Moser, B., Frolov, S., Raue, F., Palacio, S., Dengel, A.: Waving goodbye to low-res: A diffusion-wavelet approach for image super-resolution. arXiv preprint arXiv:2304.01994 (2023)
25. Moser, B., Raue, F., Hees, J., Dengel, A.: Less is more: proxy datasets in nas approaches. In: CVPR, pp. 1953–1961 (2022)
26. Moser, B.B., Frolov, S., Raue, F., Palacio, S., Dengel, A.: Dwa: differential wavelet amplifier for image super-resolution. pp. 232–243. Springer (2023). https://doi.org/10.1007/978-3-031-44210-0_19
27. Moser, B.B., Frolov, S., Raue, F., Palacio, S., Dengel, A.: Yoda: you only diffuse areas. an area-masked diffusion approach for image super-resolution. arXiv preprint arXiv:2308.07977 (2023)
28. Moser, B.B., Raue, F., Frolov, S., Palacio, S., Hees, J., Dengel, A.: Hitchhiker's guide to super-resolution: introduction and recent advances. IEEE TPAMI (2023)
29. Moser, B.B., Raue, F., Palacio, S., Frolov, S., Dengel, A.: Latent dataset distillation with diffusion models. arXiv preprint arXiv:2403.03881 (2024)

30. Moser, B.B., Shanbhag, A.S., Raue, F., Frolov, S., Palacio, S., Dengel, A.: Diffusion models, image super-resolution and everything: survey. arXiv preprint arXiv:2401.00736 (2024)
31. Nguyen, T., Chen, Z., Lee, J.: Dataset meta-learning from kernel ridge-regression. arXiv preprint arXiv:2011.00050 (2020)
32. Niu, B., et al.: Single image super-resolution via a holistic attention network. In: Vedaldi, A., Bischof, H., Brox, T., Frahm, J.-M. (eds.) ECCV 2020. LNCS, vol. 12357, pp. 191–207. Springer, Cham (2020). https://doi.org/10.1007/978-3-030-58610-2_12
33. Paul, M., Ganguli, S., Dziugaite, G.K.: Deep learning on a data diet: finding important examples early in training. NeurIPS **34**, 20596–20607 (2021)
34. Sener, O., Savarese, S.: Active learning for convolutional neural networks: A coreset approach. arXiv preprint arXiv:1708.00489 (2017)
35. Shleifer, S., Prokop, E.: Using small proxy datasets to accelerate hyperparameter search. arXiv preprint arXiv:1906.04887 (2019)
36. Tai, Y., Yang, J., Liu, X.: Image super-resolution via deep recursive residual network. In: CVPR, pp. 3147–3155 (2017)
37. Valsesia, D., Magli, E.: Permutation invariance and uncertainty in multitemporal image super-resolution. arXiv preprint arXiv:2105.12409 (2021)
38. Wang, T., Zhu, J.Y., Torralba, A., Efros, A.A.: Dataset distillation. arXiv preprint arXiv:1811.10959 (2018)
39. Zeyde, R., Elad, M., Protter, M.: On single image scale-up using sparse-representations. In: Boissonnat, J.-D., et al. (eds.) Curves and Surfaces 2010. LNCS, vol. 6920, pp. 711–730. Springer, Heidelberg (2012). https://doi.org/10.1007/978-3-642-27413-8_47
40. Zhang, Y., Li, K., Li, K., Wang, L., Zhong, B., Fu, Y.: Image super-resolution using very deep residual channel attention networks. In: ECCV, pp. 286–301 (2018)
41. Zhang, Y., Tian, Y., Kong, Y., Zhong, B., Fu, Y.: Residual dense network for image super-resolution. In: CVPR, pp. 2472–2481 (2018)
42. Zhao, B., Bilen, H.: Synthesizing informative training samples with gan. arXiv preprint arXiv:2204.07513 (2022)
43. Zhao, B., Mopuri, K.R., Bilen, H.: Dataset condensation with gradient matching. arXiv preprint arXiv:2006.05929 (2020)
44. Zhou, S., Zhang, J., Zuo, W., Loy, C.C.: Cross-scale internal graph neural network for image super-resolution. NeurIPS **33**, 3499–3509 (2020)

EDAFormer: Enhancing Low-Light Images with a Dual-Attention Transformer

Jin Zhang, Haiyan Jin[✉], Haonan Su[✉], Yuanlin Zhang, Zhaolin Xiao, and Bin Wang

Faculty of Computer Science and Engineering, Xi'an University of Technology, Xi'an, China
{jinhaiyan,suhaonan}@xaut.edu.cn

Abstract. In low-light conditions, images often suffer from poor quality and unstable noise. Inspired by the global attention mechanism of transformers, most approaches for Low-Light Image Enhancement (LLIE) rely on fusing local and global features. However, this fusion, typically achieved through linear formulas, can lead to feature distortion and the wastage of useful information. Moreover, the contextual information contained in the extracted local and global features remains unchanged, making it challenging for this fusion method to adaptively restore details and remove noise in different regions of the image. Instead of local-global feature fusion, the EDAformer module utilizes a recursive framework and dual attention to fuse global and local attention, thereby realizing a scalable attention mechanism for image enhancement. Furthermore, we propose the Multi-scale Context-aware Convolutional Self-Attention (MCCSA) module, which aggregates local self-attention using a multi-scale approach. Evaluation on LOL-v1, LOL-v2, and SICE datasets demonstrates that our method outperforms existing techniques qualitatively and quantitatively in terms of denoising and detail preservation.

Keywords: Low-Light Image · Convolutional Self-Attention · Transformer · Self-attention

1 Introduction

Low-light image enhancement refers to the use of various image processing techniques to improve the quality of images captured under low-light conditions. Traditional methods, such as histogram equalization and gamma correction, aim to adjust the global brightness and contrast of an image to make its contents more visually discernible. However, they often overlook local details and structural features during the enhancement process. With the advent of the Retinex theory, images are divided into illumination and reflection components. Approaches like [1,2] focus on enhancing the estimated illumination and reflection elements,

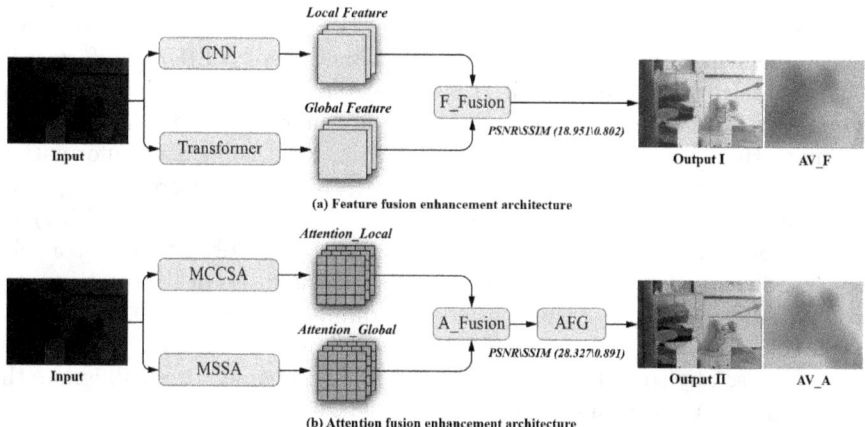

Fig. 1. Problem formulation. We utilize heatmap visualization [3] to illustrate the attention visualization (AV_F) after feature fusion and the attention visualization (AV_A) after attention fusion in the image. Darker colors indicate higher attention to specific areas. Input denotes the input image; output I and output II represent the final image enhancement results after feature fusion and attention fusion, respectively. (a) Feature fusion enhancement architecture; (b) Attention fusion enhancement architecture; MCCSA represents the Multi-scale Context-aware Convolutional Self-Attention module; MSSA represents the Multi-scale Self-Attention module; local feature and global feature are the final local and global features obtained through CNN and Transformer [4] networks; *Attention_Local* and *Attention_Global* are the local and global attention results obtained through our proposed MCCSA and MSSA modules, respectively; *F_Fusion* and *A_Fusion* represent Feature Fusion and Attention Fusion; AFG represents the module that processes attention into features.

combining the refined outcomes to produce an enhanced image. Nevertheless, due to the coexistence of noise and detailed information in the reflection component, recovering details in noisy scenarios becomes challenging.

With the evolution of deep learning, neural network-based methods have emerged. These approaches leverage convolutional neural networks to learn the non-linear enhancement function of the low-light image. For instance, Jin et al. [5] devised a multi-scale feature extraction module employing multiple convolutions and an illumination adjustment curve to enhance multi-scale features. Guo et al. [6] introduced zero reference curve estimation to fine-tune the brightness of input images by estimating high-order curves using neural networks. Jiang et al. [7] developed the EnlightenGAN network, utilizing a distinctive discriminator and generator architecture to achieve effective low-light image enhancement without pair supervision. However, these CNN-based methods are constrained by small receptive fields, making it challenging to recover the details among limited local features while denoising.

Different from CNN-based methods, with the introduction of the Transformer model, which enables long-range operations and global feature extraction, it facilitates establishing connections among all pixels in the image. Consequently, Transformers are applied to low-light image enhancement (LLIE). Retiformer [8] combines the Retinex theory with Transformers, adjusting the brightness of the illumination map through global attention and removing noise from the reflection map. However, due to the lack of focus on local contextual information, the detail recovery of the enhanced images is typically mediocre. Zhang et al. [9] proposed an efficient low-light restoration Transformer method (LRT) for images captured in low-light conditions, which sequentially connects convolutional modules and Transformers. Due to the repeated use of convolutions, the receptive field of global features continuously diminishes. Even with the addition of skip connections, it remains challenging to fully compensate for the information loss caused by convolutions. Relying solely on global features will ignore the contextual structure within local receptive fields.

So, some methods enhance low-light images by combining Transformer and CNN architectures, selectively utilizing both global and local features for detail enhancement. For instance, SNR-Transformer [4] constructs a dual-branch network where the Signal-to-Noise ratio (SNR) guides the Transformer to extract global features, while convolution operations are employed to acquire local features. The final enhancement result is obtained by fusing these two sets of features. However, the fusion of these two types of features is not always optimal, as some local and global features may become distorted before fusion. In contrast to SNR-Transformer's final feature fusion, LLFormer [10] utilizes Transformer blocks to fill the architecture of a U-shaped network, simultaneously extracting both local and global features. However, its essence still involves the utilization of global attention operations. The fusion strategies of these methods essentially rely on linear formulas to merge these two types of features, which can lead to feature distortion and waste valuable information during the fusion process.

Different from previous methods, we propose a novel Transformer architecture called Enhancing Low-Light Images with a Dual-Attention Transformer (EDAformer). Existing methods require extensive feature processing operations to extract global features after obtaining attention. Additionally, feature fusion typically occurs after the final feature processing, resulting in fixed contextual information in the final local and global features. This prevents the dynamic adjustment of feature fusion based on different regions of the input image. Furthermore, during the fusion process, feature redundancy may occur, leading to a significant amount of duplicate information. In contrast, we propose a novel attention fusion approach, combining the Multi-scale Context-aware Convolutional Self-Attention (MCCSA) module and the Multi-scale Self-Attention (MSSA) module to achieve a dual-attention mechanism, with fusion occurring during the attention acquisition phase rather than using feature fusion as in existing methods. This approach facilitates a scalable attention mechanism, avoids information waste during attention fusion, and enables adaptive adjustments in attention range. Meanwhile, the MCCSA module breaks the fixed nature of convolutional kernels by dynamically perceiving contextual information at different hierarchical levels using attention mechanisms and convolutional kernels combined. The MSSA module computes attention results within the maximum range at different scales.

Figure 1 illustrates the problem formulation of our work. Figure 1(a) and (b) depict the existing feature fusion framework and our proposed framework for enhancing low-light images with dual attention fusion, respectively. Their attention maps are presented in Fig. 1's AV_F and AV_A. AV_F and AV_A in Fig. 1 demonstrate attention with better contextual structures achieved by our proposed method compared to feature fusion methods (refer to the red blocks in output I and output II in Fig. 1). Additionally, the results in output I and output II in Fig. 1 show that our proposed method produces outcomes with superior structures compared to conventional feature fusion methods (refer to the blue blocks in output I and output II in Fig. 1). Finally, attention fusion is realized using a recursive framework to precisely focus on both local and global ranges. The main contributions of this paper are as follows:

- We propose an EDAformer network architecture for enhancing low-light images using a dual-attention mechanism, consisting of the MCCSA module and MSSA module. This network dynamically fuses local and global attention, thus enabling dynamic adjustment of attention range, resulting in enhanced images with minimal noise and rich detail.
- We introduce the Multi-scale Context-aware Convolutional Self-Attention (MCCSA) Module and the Multi-scale Self-Attention (MSSA) module, which gradually emphasize crucial features in a multi-scale manner. This approach leads to more precise attention calculations and captures richer details, enhancing the network's dynamic perceptual capability for contextual information and adaptability to complex scenes.
- We generalize local and global self-attention using a recursive approach to capture a more accurate global structure and local contextual details. The recursive EDAformer is proposed to achieve enhanced detail recovery and noise removal.

2 Related Work

In this section, we will provide a concise overview of low-light enhancement methods leveraging both local and global feature representations through deep learning.

For local feature processing, Zero-DCE [11] employs a DCE-Net consisting of seven convolutional layers to construct per-pixel high-order curves for brightness enhancement. However, the lack of supplementation with global information leads to failure in adaptively enhancing different brightness regions solely relying on local contextual features. Li et al. [12] proposed the lightweight unsupervised curve estimation network (LEES-Net), which offers adaptive brightness enhancement through curve fitting and a single attention mechanism. Nonetheless, it struggles to effectively handle significant noise due to its limited receptive field size.

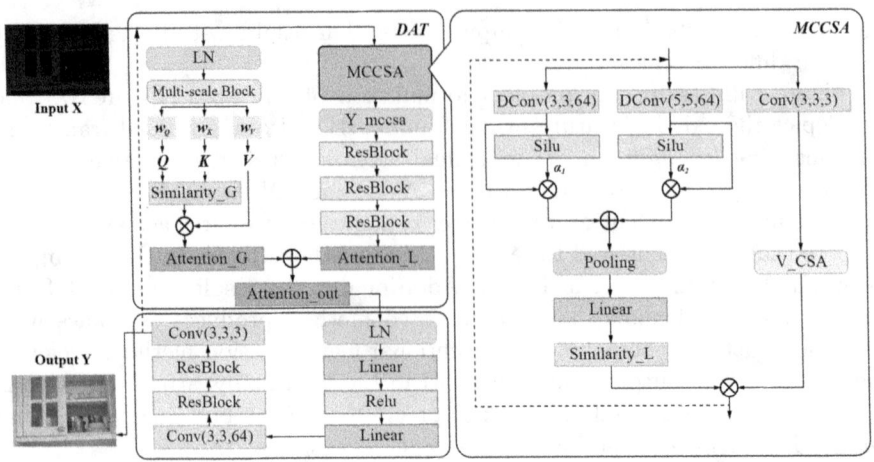

Fig. 2. Illustration of our proposed EDAformer. MCCSA represents the Multi-scale Context-aware Convolutional Self-Attention Module. DConv(3, 3, 64) and Conv(3, 3, 64) represent dilated convolution and regular convolution, respectively, with a kernel size of 3x3 and 64 channels. ⊕ represents element-wise addition. ⊗ represents element-wise multiplication. A dashed line indicates recursive operation. Similarity_G and Similarity_L represent the attention weights for global and local attention, respectively. The recursive iteration counts for the MCCSA and DAT modules are 2 and 6, respectively.

In global feature processing, the Transformer network model with global self-attention mechanism is introduced, utilizing the Vision Transformer (ViT) [13] for computer vision. This model extracts globally correlated features to enhance details through self-attention mechanism computation. The basic Transformer employs the multiplication of Queries (Q) with Keys (K) as self-attention weights and dynamically multiplies these weights with Values (V) to adaptively adjust global features for image enhancement. However, solely relying on global features disregards the contextual structure within local receptive fields. Jiang et al. [14] proposed a multi-stage Transformer network that processes a feature map into two differently sized feature maps, which are then fed into the Transformer network to extract global and local features, respectively. However, the fusion of these features still adopts a linear addition method, which can lead to information loss and redundancy.

Unlike previous methods, we propose the EDAformer with a dual attention mechanism. Through the Dual Attention Transformer (DAT) module composed of the Multi-scale Context-aware Convolutional Self-Attention (MCCSA) module and the Multi-scale Self-Attention (MSSA) module, and we aim is to achieve fusion at the attention level, avoiding information waste in feature fusion, particularly the distortion during the fusion process. We effectively merge local and global attention in the image, enabling dynamic adjustment within the attention range. This results in enhanced outcomes with higher visual quality, reduced noise, and improved details.

3 Methodology

The network architecture presented in this paper, as illustrated in Fig. 2, consists of two key components: the Multi-scale Context-aware Convolutional Self-Attention (MCCSA) Module and the Dual Attention Transformer (DAT) module. In the subsequent sections, we will provide a comprehensive explanation of both MCCSA module and DAT module, along with details on the Recursive Framework and the associated loss functions.

3.1 Multi-scale Context-Aware Convolutional Self-attention Module

The MCCSA demonstrates the enhanced feature extraction capabilities, characterizing by dynamic kernels and learnable filtering abilities. However, unlike previous methods that combine the convolutional output with attention weights, which combines local self-attention with convolutional kernels, our approach integrates multi-scale local convolutional self-attention within a 3×3 convolutional kernel. This enables the extraction of more nuanced features with greater hierarchical detail. The standard CSA module is represented as:

$$y_i = \sum_{j \in \phi(i)} \beta_{i \to j} W_{i \to j} \chi_j \tag{1}$$

where χ and $y \in R^d$ represent the input and output feature vectors, and d signifies the number of channels. Meanwhile, i and j represent spatial position indices, with j denoting pixel indices located in the window $\phi(i)$ centered at i. $|\phi(i)| \in k \times k$, where k represents the kernel size. The notation $i \to j$ indicates the relative spatial relationship from the center i to the neighboring pixels j. $W_{i \to j} \in R^{d \times d}$ is the projection matrix. When $\beta_{i \to j} = 1$, CSA is equivalent to performing a convolution operation on the input feature χ. $W_{i \to j}$ represents the weight values in the convolution kernel. β denotes the similarity attention within the local window of the convolution network.

In previous approaches, they predict β through simple linear operation in PyTorch, rather than the correlation computation of query and key in the basic self attention module. In this paper, we have employed a multi-scale approach to enhance the calculation of $\beta_{i \to j}$. This allows us to gather information at different levels and capture richer details, leading to a more accurate prediction of attention. The formula can be described as follows:

$$\beta_{i \to j} = Softmax(W_{qk} \sum_{m=1}^{2} \alpha_m \theta_m(\chi_i))$$
$$\alpha_m = Silu(\theta_m(\chi_i)) \quad m = 1,2 \tag{2}$$

where α_1 and α_2 represent the fusion weights for multi-scale feature maps obtained from two different dilated convolution operations, θ_1 and θ_2, with kernel sizes of 3×3 and 5×5, each having 64 channels. $\sum_{m=1}^{2} \alpha_m \theta_m(\chi_i)$ means the weighted summation of the multi-scale features from input χ_i. The $W_{qk} \in R^{d \times k^2}$ represents the projection matrices instead of the multiplication of the query and key features in basic self-attention module. The scalar $\beta_{i \to j} \in (0,1)$ controls the contribution of values at each spatial location within the kernel size. Dilated convolutions with multiple kernel sizes expand the receptive field, enhancing the network's perception of a multi-scale range of contextual features during attention computation.

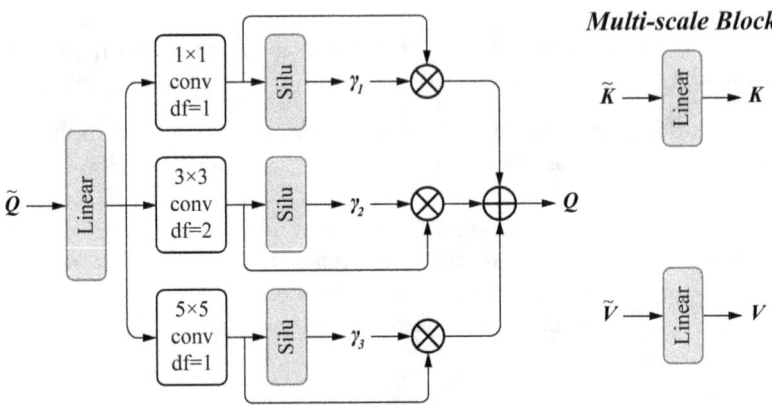

Fig. 3. In the illustration of the Multi-Scale Block, $\tilde{Q}$, $\tilde{K}$, and $\tilde{V}$ are derived from the input image after block processing, denoted as $\tilde{X}$. *conv* represents the convolution operation, with 1×1 indicating the kernel size and $df = 1$ representing a dilation rate of 1. *Sliu* represents the activation function in PyTorch. γ_1, γ_2, and γ_3 denote the fusion weights for multi-scale features. *Linear* refers to the linear transformation operation in PyTorch. $\oplus$ represents element-wise addition. $\otimes$ represents element-wise multiplication.

3.2 Dual Attention Transformer Module

As shown in Fig. 2, the proposed dual-attention mechanism consists of the MCCSA and the Multi-Scale Self-Attention (MSSA) modules, combining both local and global self attention. Firstly, we process the input image X in a block-wise manner and partition it into m patches of size $p \times p$. The processed image is denoted as $\tilde{X}$. Then, we calculate the local and global attention using the MCCSA and MSSA modules, respectively. Subsequently, multiple sets of convolution operations are applied to the local attention, effectively modifying both their size and channel dimensions. This iterative process continuously refines the attention results, ultimately yielding the refined attention representation, denoted as *Attention_L*. We employ the MSSA module to compute global attention. Unlike convolution, where feature responses are weighted sums of projected input vectors from all spatial positions, in self-attention, these weights depend on the similarity between queries and keys, representing the strength of relationships between any pair of feature vectors. Therefore, in generating these weights as shown in Fig. 3, we incorporate multi-scale information. Specifically, we transform the computation of queries from a linear operation to a multi-scale module. The specific formula is presented below:

$$Query = \sum_{n=1}^{3} \gamma_n(Dcov(W_q^k, d, \widetilde{X}))$$

$$\gamma_n = Silu(Dcov(W_q^k, d, \widetilde{X})) \quad n = 1, 2, 3$$

(3)

where $Dconv()$ represents dilated convolution operation, where W_q^k represents the projection matrix of kernel size k, where the value of k is 1, 3, 5. d represents different dilation rates, namely 1, 2, 1. $\widetilde{X}$ represents the feature map obtained by block-wise processing of the input image X. γ_1, γ_2 and γ_3 represent th feature fusion weights at different scales. $Silu()$ represents the activation function in PyTorch. Subsequently, we use the obtained Q, K, V to calculate the attention results according to the standard self-attention formula [4], denoted as $Attention\_G$.

Finally, the attentions are added for fusion, efficiently integrating local and global attention in the image, no longer performing final feature fusion, enhancing the network's feature capture and processing capabilities. We formulate the procedure as follows:

$$Attention\_out_z = \kappa_1 \times Attention\_G_z + \kappa_2 \times Attention\_L_z \quad (4)$$

where the $Attention\_G_z$ represents the global self-attention in the z_{th} head. On the other hand, the $Attention\_L_z$ are calculated from the local MCCSA module. κ_1 and κ_2 represent the weight coefficient, and here we set it to 1. The output of all heads are concatenated. The value of z is set to 8. The entire DAT module produces an attention fusion result, denoted as $attention\_out$. This result undergoes two linear layers, one layer normalization, and one ReLU activation function, followed by multiple convolutional modules, to obtain the first output result of the network, represented as Y_1. Six recursive iterations and corresponding feature processing operations are required to generate the final enhanced image output Y of the network.

3.3 Extension to an Efficient Recursive Framework

In this paper, we have devised a recursive framework that enhances the comprehension of images at multiple levels, assisting in the extraction of more representative and refined features. This, in turn, improves the effectiveness of detail recovery and noise removal in images. The computational formula for Recursive Framework can be described as follows:

$$X_{t+1} = F(\mu(X_t, h_{t-1})$$
$$h_{t-1} = X_{t-1}$$

(5)

where t represents the iteration state, and $h_t \in R^{d \times H \times W}$ represents the network input X from the t time step. F is defined as the MCCSA module or DAT module. To consider the balance between computational cost and performance, we set the recursive depth to 2 When F is the MCCSA module and we set the recursive depth to 6 When F is the DAT module. And X_2^{MCCSA} represents the attention map Y_{mccsa} of the MCCSA module and X_6^{DAT} represents the final attention fusion result, which undergoes corresponding attention processing operations to obtain the final enhanced result Y. We initialize the hidden state with $h_{-1} = 0$. The function $\mu(X, h) = Z_J \times X + D_J \times h$ combines input and hidden state through a linear function. Z_J and D_J are the projection weight parameters. However, based on our empirical observations, we have found that setting $Z_J = 1$ and $D_J = 1$ yields the best performance.

3.4 Loss Functions

In this paper, the total loss functions are formulated as follows:

$$L = \lambda_1 L_{loc-vgg} + \lambda_2 L_{dat-vgg} + \lambda_3 L_{rec} \qquad (6)$$

where λ_1, λ_2 and λ_3 are balancing parameters and are set to 0.50, 0.50 and 1.00.

(1) We design the Local-Vgg loss to constrain the output of MSCCSA module and ground truth:

$$L_{loc-vgg} = ||\Phi(Y_{mccsa}) - \Phi(\overline{Y})||_1 \qquad (7)$$

where $\Phi()$ is the extracted features from the VGG network [15]. Y_{mccsa} and $\overline{Y}$ denote the output feature of MCCSA module and the ground truth of input image, respectively.

(2) Then, we design the Dat-Vgg loss to constrain the output enhanced image and ground truth:

$$L_{dat-vgg} = ||\Phi(Y) - \Phi(\overline{Y})||_1 \qquad (8)$$

where $\Phi()$ is the extracted features from the VGG network [15]. Y and $\overline{Y}$ denote the output enhanced image and ground truth of input image, respectively.

(3) Then, we design the reconstruction loss to constrain the output enhanced image and ground truth:

$$L_{rec} = \sqrt{||Y - \overline{Y}||_2 + \epsilon^2} \qquad (9)$$

where Y and $\overline{Y}$ have the same definitions as $L_{dat-vgg}$. ϵ is set as 10^{-3} in all experiments.

4 Experiments

4.1 Experiment Setup

Implementation Detail. In the experiments, we used the LOL-v1 [16], SICE datasets [17] and LOL-v2-real [18]. Two NVIDIA GTX 4060Ti GPUs are employed to evaluate 11 compared methods, including LIME [19], RUAS [20],

Table 1. Quantitative performance comparisons on images from LOL-V1 and sice dataset.(red:best; blue:the second best;).

Method	LOL-V1				SICE			
	PSNR ↑	SSIM ↑	NIQE ↓	LPIPS ↓	PSNR ↑	SSIM ↑	NIQE ↓	LPIPS ↓
RUAS(2021)	16.405	0.503	6.349	0.213	14.891	0.707	6.149	0.376
ELGAN (2021)	17.556	0.666	4.581	0.270	20.707	0.801	4.581	0.254
LIME(2017)	17.182	0.562	4.992	0.316	19.221	0.795	4.992	0.273
DRBN(2020)	18.798	0.829	5.109	0.210	17.228	0.789	5.109	0.254
SGRDR(2021)	17.707	0.798	5.095	0.162	18.806	0.797	5.095	0.256
SCI(2022)	14.784	0.525	7.873	0.339	14.614	0.641	7.873	0.268
URetinex(2022)	21.328	0.833	4.259	0.121	21.242	0.783	4.259	0.228
LLMRECA(2023)	22.643	**0.838**	4.284	0.177	22.643	0.830	4.312	0.241
LLFormer(2023)	23.203	0.816	4.313	0.162	20.450	0.810	4.252	0.253
Ours	23.413	0.846	4.104	0.080	24.935	0.830	4.112	0.097

(a)input (b)RUAS (c)EnlightenGAN (d)LIME (e)SGRDR (f)DRBN

(g)SCI (h)URetinex (i)LLMRECA (j)LLFormer (k)Ours (l)GroundTruth

Fig. 4. Visual comparison of different methods on LOL-v1 dataset. (a) is the input image, (k) is the result of our method, (l) is the ground truth, (b)-(j) are the results for other methods. The blue region is for comparing the details between our method and others. (Color figure online)

(a)input (b)RUAS (c)EnlightenGAN (d)LIME (e)SGRDR (f)DRBN

(g)SCI (h)URetinex (i)LLMRECA (j)LLFormer (k)Ours (l)GroundTruth

Fig. 5. Visual comparison of different methods on SICE dataset. (a) is the input image, (k) is the result of our method, (l) is the ground truth, (b)-(j) are the results for other methods. The red region is for comparing the details between our method and others, while the blue region is for comparing the colors between our method and others. (Color figure online)

SGRDR [21], EnlightenGAN [7], DRBN [22], SCI [23], URetinex [24], LLM-RECA [5], LLFormer [10]. The LOL-v1 [16] contains 485 pairs of low-/normal-light images for training and 15 pairs for testing. Each pair includes a low-light input image and an associated well exposed reference image. The SICE [17] contains 360 pairs of low-/normal-light images for training and 133 pairs for testing. The LOL-v2-real [18] contains 689 low-/normal-light image pairs for training and 100 pairs for testing. The image size for all datasets is 600 × 400. We utilized the Adam optimizer, set the batch size to 6, and initialized the learning rate to 0.0001.

Evaluation Metrics. Four objective indices were adopted in our evaluation: PSNR, SSIM, NIQE [25], and LPIPS [26]. Peak Signal to Noise Ratio (PSNR) measures the fidelity between images, while Structural Similarity (SSIM) reflects the structural similarity between images. The Natural Image Quality Evaluator (NIQE) is a no-reference image quality assessment metric, and the Learned Perceptual Image Patch Similarity (LPIPS) is utilized to measure the perceptual difference between two images. A lower LPIPS value indicates a higher similarity between the two images. We verified the effectiveness and superiority of our method by comparing it with other state-of-the-art low-light image enhancement techniques.

Table 2. Quantitative results for cross-dataset test.(red:best; blue:the second best;).

Model	PSNR↑	SSIM↑	LPIPS↓
DRBN(2020)	18.421	0.760	0.261
RUAS(2021)	15.357	0.501	0.315
ELGAN(2021)	18.682	0.680	0.250
SCI(2022)	17.303	0.533	0.281
URetinex(2022)	21.093	0.817	0.161
LLMRECA(2023)	20.593	0.806	0.193
LLFormer(2023)	14.671	0.651	0.351
Ours	34.552	0.916	0.061

(a)input (b)SCI (c)URetinex (d)LLFormer (e)Ours (f)GroundTruth

Fig. 6. Visual comparison results for cross-dataset test. (a) is the input image, (e) is the result of our method, (f) is the ground truth, (b)-(d) are the results for other methods. The blue region is for comparing the details between our method and others, while the red region is for comparing the colors between our method and others. (Color figure online)

4.2 Comparison with State-of-the-Arts

1) Inter-test results: We compare our method with several state-of-the-art methods in LOL-v1 [16] and SICE datasets [17]. Figure 4 illustrates the results of compared methods on the images under extremely dark conditions. Enlighten-GAN [7], LIME [19], and SCI [23]'s enhanced images with color biases. RUAS [20], URetinex [24], LLMRECA [5], DRBN [22], and LLFormer [10] introduced considerable noise and blur details (see the blue regions in Fig. 4 (b), (h), (i), (f) and (j)). SGRDR [21] exhibited unclear details and excessively dark brightness. In contrast, our method achieved the best visual results with outstanding detail and brightness restoration compared to the ground truth (see the blue regions in the Fig. 4 (k) and (l)). Figure 5 illustrates the visualization results of the SICE dataset. Among all methods, only our approach achieves the closest resemblance to the GroundTruth in detail recovery (red regions for (k) and (I) in Fig. 5), while other methods exhibit noticeable blurring (red regions for (b), (c), (d), (e), (f), (g), (h), (i) and (j) in Fig. 5). Our method also closely resembles the GroundTruth in color restoration (blue regions for (k) and (I) in Fig. 5), whereas other methods differ from the GroundTruth (blue regions for (b), (c), (d), (e), (f), (g), (h), (i) and (j) in Fig. 5). The quantitative results on LOL-V1 and SICE datasets are presented in Table 1. It is evident that our method achieved the highest PSNR and SSIM values, indicating the superior performance in terms of noise removal and structural restoration. Our method also achieves the lowest NIQE and LPIPS scores, indicating that our enhanced images have the best natural quality and are closest to the GroundTruth.

2) Cross-test results: We conducted cross-dataset testing to further evaluate the generality of our method. The LOL-v1 [16] dataset was utilized for training, and LOL-V2-real [18] dataset was employed for testing. The subjective results are depicted in Fig. 6. The SCI [23] result displayed excessively low brightness (see the red regions in Fig. 6), URetinex's [24] outcome was notably blurred (see the blue regions in Fig. 6), and LLFormer's [10] result exhibited a significant amount of noise (see the blue regions in Fig. 6). Both URetinex [24] and LLFormer [10] showed color bias (see the red regions in Fig. 6). However, our method achieved results nearly identical to the ground truth. This demonstrates the superiority of our approach in generating high-quality images with enough enhancement, clear structure and similar colors to the ground truth. Quantitative comparison results are presented in Table 2, where our method achieves the best results in terms

Table 3. Quantitative results for component analysis.

Model	PSNR↑	SSIM↑	LPIPS↓
Z_0	18.663	0.777	0.256
Z_1	20.215	0.805	0.185
Z_2	21.291	0.811	0.131
Z_3	**23.413**	**0.846**	**0.080**

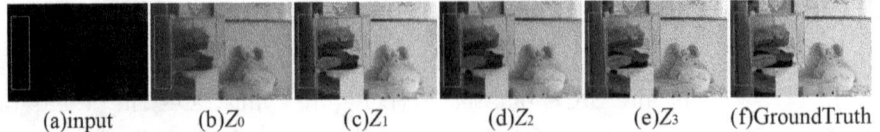

(a)input (b)Z_0 (c)Z_1 (d)Z_2 (e)Z_3 (f)GroundTruth

Fig. 7. Component analysis results. (a) is the input image, (f) is the ground truth, (b)-(e) are the results of other settings.

of PSNR and SSIM metrics. It is easy to conclude that our method exhibits stronger generalization capabilities.

4.3 Ablation Study

We conducted ablation experiments on 15 real images from the LOL-v1 dataset to evaluate our approach. For this purpose, we conducted four settings: Z_0 represents one scale feature for the estimation of $\beta_{i \to j}$ in Eq. 2, i.e. $\beta_{i \to j} = Softmax(W_{qk} \cdot \chi_i)$. Z_1 represents the fusion of two attention features outside the DAT module, i.e., after the last linear layer in Fig. 2, Z_2 represents the removal of the entire recursive framework, and Z_3 represents the proposed method with the combination of MCCSA and DAT modules. The results of different combinations are shown in Fig. 7 and Table 3.

Figure 7 demonstrates that the result of Z_0 exhibit dark brightness and considerable blur. The results of Z_1 exhibit blur in the wood texture on the left side of the image (see the red regions in Fig. 7) and display colors that differ from the ground truth. The resuts of Z_2 display both blur and noise problems (see the red regions in Fig. 7). However, the image generated by Z_3 closely resembles the ground truth image. Table 3 shows that when we remove the multi scale feature fusion(Z_0), the performance is the worst, indicating that the ability of α_m to fuse multi-scale feature maps is superior. If the dual attention framework is removed (Z_1), indicating a simple fusion of local and global features, it suggests that the feature fusion method still has deficiencies in capturing intricate details. When we remove the recursive framework (Z_2), its performance is unsatisfactory, indicating poor image structure restoration effects in extremely dark areas. However, our method achieves the highest performance metrics (Z_3). Ablation experiments indicate that the combination of MCCSA and DAT validate our approach as more effective for fusing local and global features.

5 Conclusion

In this paper, we propose an EDAformer based on a dual-attention mechanism for low light image enhancement. We have designed a novel fusion framework incorporating both local attention and global attention, effectively balancing the contributions of local and global receptive fields. Additionally, we have devised a new convolutional self-attention mechanism that more reasonably integrates attention in multi scale manner, yielding local attention enriched with more contextual information. Experimental results demonstrate that our approach effectively restores images. Particularly in extremely low-light scenarios, our method generates images with clear details and outstanding denoising effects. Cross-dataset testing results indicate that our method exhibits stronger generalization capabilities compared to other approaches.

References

1. Ren, X., Yang, W., Cheng, W.-H., Liu, J.: Lr3m: robust low-light enhancement via low-rank regularized retinex model. IEEE Trans. Image Process. **29**, 5862–5876 (2020)
2. Fu, X., Zeng, D., Huang, T.Y., Zhang, X.-P., Ding, X.: A weighted variational model for simultaneous reflectance and illumination estimation. In: Proceedings of the IEEE Conference on Computer Vision and Pattern Recognition, pp. 2782–2790 5862–5876 (2020)
3. Selvaraju, R.R., Cogswell, M., Das, A., Vedantam, R., Parikh, D., Batra, D.: Gradcam: visual explanations from deep networks via gradient-based localization. In: Proceedings of the IEEE International Conference on Computer Vision, pp. 618–626 (2017)
4. Xu, X., Wang, R., Fu, C.-W., Jia, J.: SNR-aware low-light image enhancement. In: Proceedings of the IEEE/CVF Conference on Computer Vision and Pattern Recognition, pp. 17714–17724 (2022)
5. Jin, H., Wei, D., Su, H.: Deep low light image enhancement via multi-scale recursive feature enhancement and curve adjustment. In: ICASSP 2023-2023 IEEE International Conference on Acoustics, Speech and Signal Processing (ICASSP), pp. 1–5. IEEE (2023)
6. Guo, C., et al.: Zero-reference deep curve estimation for low-light image enhancement. In: Proceedings of the IEEE/CVF Conference on Computer Vision and Pattern Recognition, pp. 1780–1789 (2020)
7. Jiang, Y., et al.: Enlightengan: deep light enhancement without paired supervision. IEEE Trans. Image Process. **30**, 2340–2349 (2021)
8. Ruan, J., Kong, X., Huang, W., Yang, W.: Retiformer: retinex-based enhancement in transformer for low-light image. In: ICASSP 2023-2023 IEEE International Conference on Acoustics, Speech and Signal Processing (ICASSP), pp. 1–5. IEEE (2023)
9. Zhang, S., Meng, N., Lam, E.Y.: LRT: an efficient low-light restoration transformer for dark light field images,. IEEE Trans. Image Process. (2023)
10. Wang, T., Zhang, K., Shen, T., Luo, W., Stenger, B., Tong, L.: Ultra-high-definition low-light image enhancement: a benchmark and transformer-based method. Proc. AAAI Conf. Artifi. Intell. **37**, 2654–2662 (2023)
11. Li, C., Guo, C., Loy, C.C.: Learning to enhance low-light image via zero-reference deep curve estimation. IEEE Trans. Pattern Anal. Mach. Intell. **44**(8), 4225–4238 (2021)
12. Li, X., He, R., Jian, W., Yan, H., Chen, X.: Lees-net: fast, lightweight unsupervised curve estimation network for low-light image enhancement and exposure suppression. Displays **80**, 102550 (2023)
13. Dosovitskiy, A., et al.: An image is worth 16x16 words: transformers for image recognition at scale, arXiv preprint arXiv:2010.11929 (2020)

14. Jiang, N., Lin, J., Zhang, T., Zheng, H., Zhao, T.: Low-light image enhancement via stage-transformer-guided network. IEEE Trans. Circ. Syst. Video Technol. (2023)
15. Simonyan, K., Zisserman, A.: Very deep convolutional networks for largescale image recognition, arXiv preprint arXiv:1409.1556 (2014)
16. Wei, C., Wang, W., Yang, W., Liu, J.: Deep retinex decomposition for low-light enhancement, vol. 2018, pp. 5862–5876. arXiv preprint arXiv:1808.04560 (2020)
17. Cai, J., Shuhang, G., Zhang, L.: Learning a deep single image contrast enhancer from multi-exposure images. IEEE Trans. Image Process. **27**(4), 2049–2062 (2018)
18. Yang, W., Wang, W., Huang, H., Wang, S., Liu, J.: Sparse gradient regularized deep retinex network for robust low-light image enhancement. IEEE Trans. Image Process. **30**, 2072–2086 (2021)
19. Guo, X., Li, Y., Ling, H.: Lime: low-light image enhancement via illumination map estimation. IEEE Trans. Image Process. **26**(2), 982–993 (2017), 5862–5876 (2020)
20. Liu, R., Ma, L., Zhang, J., Fan, X., Luo, Z.: Retinex-inspired unrolling with cooperative prior architecture search for low-light image enhancement. In: Proceedings of the IEEE/CVF Conference on Computer Vision and Pattern Recognition (CVPR), pp. 10561–10570 (2021)
21. Yang, W., Wang, W., Huang, H., Wang, S., Liu, J.: Sparse gradient regularized deep retinex network for robust low-light image enhancement. IEEE Trans. Image Process. **30**, 2072–2086 (2021)
22. Yang, W., Wang, S., Fang, Y., Wang, Y., Liu, J.: From fidelity to perceptual quality: A semi-supervised approach for low-light image enhancement. In: Proceedings of the IEEE/CVF Conference on Computer Vision and Pattern Recognition (CVPR) (2020)
23. Ma, L., Ma, T., Liu, R., Fan, X., Luo, Z.: Toward fast, flexible, and robust low-light image enhancement. In: Proceedings of the IEEE/CVF Conference on Computer Vision and Pattern Recognition, pp. 5637–5646 (2022)
24. Wu, W., Weng, J., Zhang, P., Wang, X., Yang, W., Jiang, J.: Uretinex-net: retinex-based deep unfolding network for low-light image enhancement. In: Proceedings of the IEEE/CVF Conference on Computer Vision and Pattern Recognition, pp. 5901–5910 (2022)
25. Mittal, A., Soundararajan, R., Bovik, A.C.: Making a "completely blind" image quality analyzer. IEEE Signal Process. Lett. **20**, 209–212 (2013)
26. Zhang, R., Isola, P., Efros, A.A., Shechtman, E., Wang, O.: The unreasonable effectiveness of deep features as a perceptual metric. In: Proceedings of the IEEE Conference on Computer Vision and Pattern Recognition, pp. 586–595 (2018)

Image Matting Based on Deep Equilibrium Models

Xinshuang Liu[1](✉) and Yue Zhao[2]

[1] UC San Diego, La Jolla 92093, USA
xinsliu01@gmail.com
[2] University of Pennsylvania, Philadelphia 19104, USA
yz2000@upenn.edu

Abstract. Recent works have shown that additional improvement stages can further enhance the performance of image matting models. Inspired by this, we propose deep equilibrium matting (DEQ-Matt), which improves the feature maps for infinite times to achieve optimal performance by using the deep equilibrium (DEQ) models. We further tailor a loss function to train the DEQ models on the image matting task. Besides, we propose to use saliency maps to guide the image matting models, because they can be automatically and reliably predicted. In experiments, our method outperforms state-of-the-art methods and is superior in both semantic estimation and detail processing. Furthermore, we observe an increasing trend in the model's performance as the number of feature improvement steps approaches infinity, which supports the motivation of this paper. The code is available at https://github.com/XinshuangL/DEQ-Matt.

Keywords: Image Matting · Deep Equilibrium Models

1 Introduction

Image matting is a fundamental task in computer vision that has board applications in film production, video conference, image edition, etc. Image matting extracts the foreground object from a given image by estimating its alpha matte, which can be formulated as:

$$I_i = \alpha_i F_i + (1 - \alpha_i) B_i, \quad \alpha_i \in [0, 1], \tag{1}$$

where I_i, F_i, B_i and α_i denote the image color, foreground color, background color, and the alpha matte at pixel i, respectively. Different from the object mask estimated in the image segmentation task [6,25,31], the alpha matte in image matting is precise and represents the transparency of the foreground object, which means image matting is more fine-grained than image segmentation. Also, Eq. 1 is an ill-posed problem to solve when only the image I is given. The ambiguity makes image matting methods [18,24,30,41] perform not well enough in

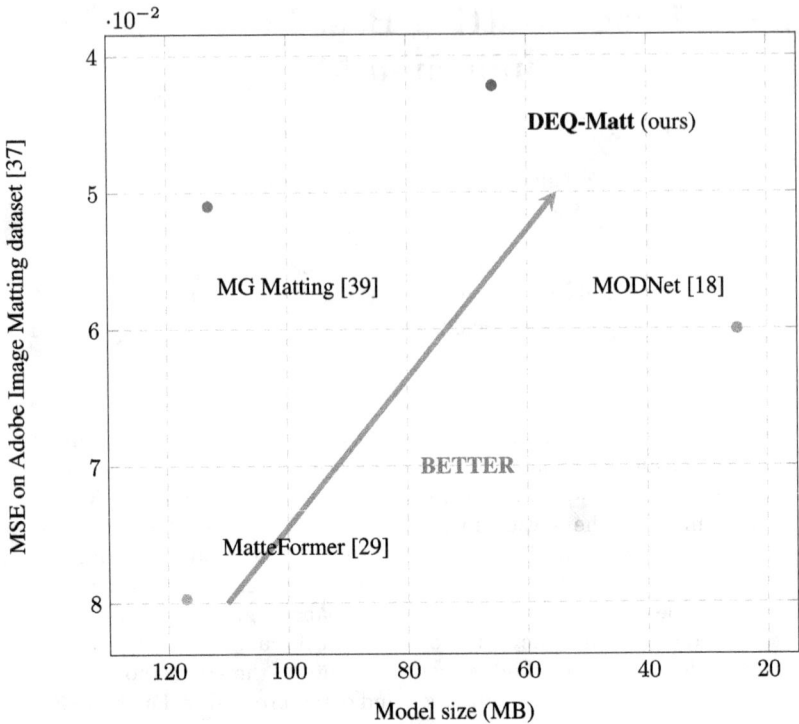

Fig. 1. Comparison between our proposed method and the state-of-the-art methods. Our method achieves the best performance with the second smallest model size

real-world applications when they only take RGB images as the input. To resolve the ambiguity in image matting, many previous works depend on an additional guidance like a trimap [17,21,29,37,38] or a background image [22,32]. However, those additional guidances are limited in real-world applications. Annotating a trimap requires additional user effort and may affect user experience. The additional background image should be precisely aligned with the original image that contains the foreground object, which is not always available.

In this paper, we propose to use object saliency maps to guide the image matting models. This is based on two facts. First, the object saliency maps can be automatically generated via salient object detection (SOD) methods [19], saving time for users. Second, the object saliency maps are relatively reliable because the SOD models can be trained on large-scale SOD datasets to obtain high performance, where annotating a SOD sample costs much less than annotating an image matting sample. For simplicity, we directly concatenate the saliency map with the RGB image to form a 4-channel input image, and use the neural network to fuse the information of these two sources and extract the alpha mattes. This modality fusion strategy has been well-studied by the previous trimap-based method [37].

Given the success of the improvement process in the previous image matting method [37], Cai et al. [3] proposed to recurrently improve the alpha mattes using the convolutional long short-term memory (LSTM) networks [33]. This pioneering work presented the idea that repeatedly improving alpha mattes yields better results than a single improvement. Ma et al. [28] further extended this idea to an infinite number of improvement steps. Moreover, they focused on improving intermediate feature maps rather than the prediction. This design enhances flexibility and efficiency. We follow this design, repeatedly improving the feature maps before decoding them to an alpha matte:

$$\mathbf{M}^{[i+1]} = f_\theta(\mathbf{M}^{[i]}; \mathbf{c}), \quad i = 0, \ldots, L-1, \tag{2}$$

where $\mathbf{M}$ denotes the feature maps, f_θ the function to improve the feature map, $\mathbf{c}$ the condition input, i the step index and L the entire step number. Similar to Ma et al. [28], we simulate infinite improvement steps using the deep equilibrium (DEQ) models [1], which find the root of the improvement function:

$$\mathbf{M}^\star = f_\theta(\mathbf{M}^\star; \mathbf{c}). \tag{3}$$

We name our model *deep equilibrium matting* (DEQ-Matt), which improves the feature maps infinite times to achieve optimal performance. Different from Ma et al. [28], we apply the improvement function on multi-scale feature maps. A comparison between our DEQ-Matt and the state-of-the-art methods [18,29,39] is shown in Fig. 1.

Due to the strong representability of the DEQ models, training a DEQ model for the image matting task involves two challenges: convergence to unsatisfied local optima, and overfitting on training data. To tackle these two issues, we tailor an effective loss function specifically for deep equilibrium models in the image matting task. First, we adopt the multiscale deep equilibrium (MDEQ) model [2] as our network backbone and match the feature maps at each resolution with the loss term in the progressive loss function [39] to aid the optimization process during training. Second, we use the Mean Square Error (MSE) between the output of the current model and its pre-trained model as a distillation loss to avoid overfitting the training data. The distillation loss can be used as an auxiliary loss function on the same training data with other loss functions, *i.e.*, no extra training data is required.

In experiments, our method significantly outperforms the state-of-the-art methods [18,21,29,39] on both the Adobe Image Matting dataset [37] and the Distinctions-646 dataset [30]. The qualitative experiments illustrate that our method is superior in both semantic estimation and detail processing. Also, we validate the effectiveness of each term in our loss function to train our DEQ-Matt through an ablation study. Finally, we observe that increasing the number of steps gradually improves the model performance, which supports our motivation of improving the feature maps for infinite times.

Our main contributions are summarized as follows:
- We propose to use the salient object detection (SOD) model to provide semantic guidance for the image matting model, because the SOD model can be trained on large-scale datasets to be more robust.

- We propose using deep equilibrium models in image matting models to enhance feature maps and achieve optimal performance.
- We tailor an effective loss function specifically for deep equilibrium models in the image matting task, resulting in higher performance.

2 Related Works

2.1 Conventional Image Matting Methods

There are two categories of the conventional image matting methods, the propagation-based [4,20,34] and the sampling-based [14–16]. These conventional image matting methods use a trimap to divide the image into known regions (including foreground regions and background regions) and unknown regions. Then, they solve the alpha values of the unknown regions based on the known regions. The propagation-based methods assume some statistical rules inspired by observing the training data to reduce the freedom of the image matting equations. Based on the constrained image matting equations, they can propagate alpha values from known regions to unknown regions. The sampling-based methods instead sample pixels from the known regions surrounding the unknown regions and use the image matting equations to estimate the alpha values of the unknown regions.

The conventional methods are designed with handcrafted rules to overcome the ambiguity of the image matting equations. However, since it's hard to convert the natural knowledge in the training dataset into handcrafted rules, these conventional methods have limited performance in complex cases.

2.2 Guidance-Based Image Matting Methods

The most common guidance for the image matting task is the trimap. Cho et al. [8] designed a deep convolutional neural network for image matting. Xu et al. [37] proposed a high-quality image matting dataset and trained an encoder-decoder-based image matting network on it to obtain a significantly better performance. The high-quality image matting dataset prompted the community to propose more methods [21,27,29,38]. Lu et al. [27] proposed to use a learnable indexing mechanism for downsampling and upsampling to accurate details in the alpha matte. Li et al. [21] integrated contextual information into the unknown regions based on the attention map calculated between image features. Yu et al. [38] proposed to achieve high-resolution image matting by processing the image matting on image patches guided by contextual information. Park et al. [29] designed an image matting model in the transformer architecture [12,36] to exploit the global information. In addition to using handcrafted trimaps, some works proposed to automatically generate trimaps [7,11]. Recently, image matting methods based on other guidances emerged [32]. Sengupta et al. [32] proposed to use an additional background image to replace the trimap. Lin et al. [22] further improved the efficiency of this method to make it perform at high-resolution images in real time. Yu et al. [39] instead proposed to use the object mask to guide the image matting process and designed a progressive improvement module to upsample the alpha matte.

Although the trimap-based methods have achieved impressive performance, annotating a trimap requires users' additional efforts and thus limits the applications of the methods. On the other hand, generating trimaps introduces an additional inference stage that may make mistakes and reduce the model's performance. The other guidances also require extra effort to obtain. In a word, there is still no perfect guidance for image matting by far.

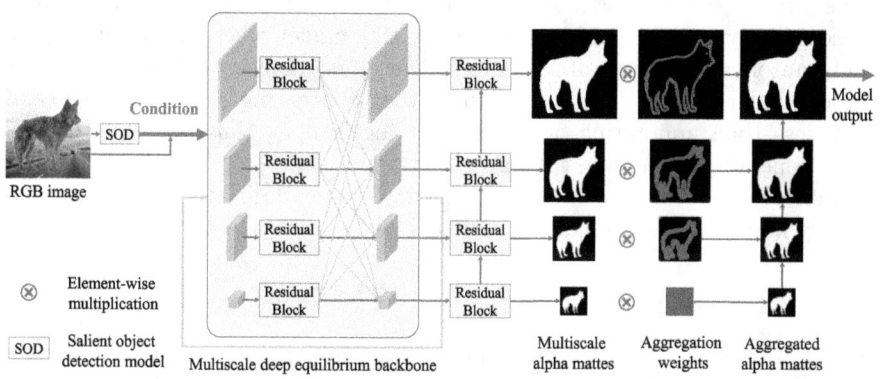

Fig. 2. Overview of our proposed method

2.3 Image Matting Methods Only Using RGB Images

Some recent works proposed to conduct image matting on only an RGB image [5,18,24,30,41]. Chen et al. [5] achieved automatic portrait matting by jointly estimating image semantics and processing image details. Liu et al. [24] improved this method by predicting masks, unify masks, and alpha mattes sequentially. Zhang et al. [41] proposed to first estimate the foreground and background probability maps and fuse them to obtain the alpha matte. Qiao et al. [30] proposed to aggregate the image features and appearance cues based on the attention mechanism. Ke et al. [18] designed a portrait matting model that decomposes the image matting task into three sub-tasks focusing on different regions of the image. However, these methods either are designed for portrait images [5,18,24] or cannot perform well on general objects [30,41].

3 Method

Figure 2 illustrates the overview of our proposed method. A salient object detection model first estimates the saliency map of the RGB image. Then, the RGB image and the saliency map are concatenated together and passed to the multi-scale deep equilibrium (MDEQ) backbone, serving as the condition for the feature improvement process. The MDEQ backbone finds the root of the improvement function and outputs them as multiscale results of the infinite feature improvement steps. Finally, we upsample and aggregate the multiscale feature maps to predict multiscale alpha mattes. The final alpha matte is aggregated from the multiscale alpha mattes.

3.1 Salient Object Detection

To help the image matting model robustly estimate image semantics, we propose to use saliency maps to guide the image matting model, where the saliency maps can be automatically generated from a salient object detection (SOD) model pre-trained on large-scale datasets. We note that annotating a SOD sample costs much less than annotating an image matting sample, thus the SOD dataset [40] is generally larger than the image matting dataset [37]. Specifically, we use the InSPyReNet [19] to estimate the saliency map and directly concatenate the saliency map with the RGB image as the input of our model.

3.2 Model Architecture

As shown in Sect. 4.6, we observe that repeatedly improving the feature maps gradually improves the performance. Thus, we propose deep equilibrium matting (DEQ-Matt), which improves the feature maps for infinite times to achieve optimal performance. This can be implemented by using a deep equilibrium (DEQ) model [1] to output the root of the improvement function. For the image matting task, where the images are generally in high resolution, we adopt the multiscale deep equilibrium (MDEQ) model [2] as our network backbone to efficiently process the input data.

Different from conventional image encoders, where the high-resolution feature maps lack semantics information, the MDEQ backbone has high-resolution feature maps that contain sufficient semantics information. This is because the semantics information is passed from low-resolution feature maps to high-resolution feature maps in the feature improvement step. Thus, we can simply employ a series of lightweight residual blocks to decode the multiscale feature maps and get the corresponding multiscale alpha mattes. We tailor the progressive improvement module for our model by extending it to have four resolution levels, and gradually aggregate the alpha mattes from low resolution to high resolution. This process is illustrated in Fig. 2, where we update the aggregated alpha matte with the alpha matte in the higher resolution within the blue regions in the aggregation weight.

In summary, the multiscale deep equilibrium (MDEQ) backbone improves the feature maps for infinite times to obtain optimal multiscale feature maps that contain both image semantics and image details. Then, the lightweight decoder predicts the corresponding multiscale alpha mattes. Finally, the multiscale alpha mattes are aggregated together to form the final alpha matte.

3.3 Loss Function

Although the MDEQ models have strong representability, training them for image matting tasks faces two challenges. First, the model parameters may converge to an unsatisfactory local optima. Second, the MDEQ model may overfit the training data since the size of the image matting dataset is small. To overcome the challenges, we tailor an effective loss function specifically for deep equilibrium models in the image matting task. First, we match the feature maps from the MDEQ model at each resolution with the loss terms in the progressive loss function [39]. This design introduces information flows from the loss function at each resolution to aid the optimization process during training, which leads to a well-optimized model parameter. Second, we use the Mean Square Error (MSE) between the output of the current model and its pre-trained model as a distillation loss to avoid overfitting the training data. The distillation loss can be used as an auxiliary loss function on the same training data with other loss functions, *i.e.*, no extra training data is required.

Table 1. Performance comparison on the Adobe Image Matting dataset [37]

Method	MSE ↓	MAD ↓
GCA Matting [21]	0.1102	0.1481
MatteFormer [29]	0.0797	0.1206
MODNet [18]	0.0600	0.1033
MG Matting [39]	0.0510	0.0871
Ours	**0.0422**	**0.0790**

Table 2. Performance comparison on the Distinctions-646 dataset [30]

Method	MSE ↓	MAD ↓
GCA Matting [21]	0.1125	0.1380
MODNet [18]	0.0514	0.0863
MatteFormer [29]	0.0437	0.0749
MG Matting [39]	0.0400	0.0712
Ours	**0.0347**	**0.0682**

4 Experiments

4.1 Dataset

We evaluate the methods on the Adobe Image Matting dataset [37] and the Distinctions-646 dataset [30]. During training, the background images are sampled from the MS COCO dataset [23]. For testing, we combine each foreground image with 20 background images in the Pascal VOC dataset [13]. To prevent interference with the evaluation, we eliminate background images that contain clearly visible humans.

4.2 Baselines and Evaluation Metrics

To evaluate the performance of our proposed DEQ-Matt method, the following state-of-the-art methods are selected for comparison:

- Guided Contextual Attention Matting (GCA Matting) [21]: integrates contextual information into feature maps guided by the image features.
- Matting Objective Decomposition Network (MODNet) [18]: decomposes the image matting task into three sub-tasks focusing on different regions of the image.
- Mask Guided Matting (MG Matting) [39]: progressively upsamples the alpha matte guided by the object mask.
- Transformer-based Image Matting (MatteFormer) [29]: adopts the transformer model to exploit global information for image matting.

We use Mean Square Error (MSE) and Mean Absolute Difference (MAD) as evaluation metrics.

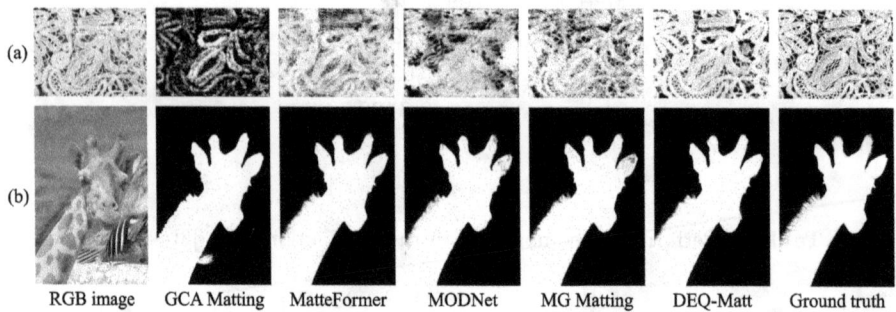

Fig. 3. Qualitative comparison with the state-of-the-art methods. (a) Our method obtains better fine details. (b) Our method estimates better image semantics

4.3 Implementation Details

For a fair comparison, all models are provided with the saliency maps generated by the InSPyReNet [19], and use the saliency maps in the additional input channel. Since our task is trimap-free image matting, we remove the parts that are designed for trimaps in the models. All models are trained in the same settings except for using their official loss functions. We train the models for 100 epochs with a learning rate initialized from 1×10^{-3} and scheduled by Warmup and cosine decay [26]. A weight decay of 1×10^{-4} is applied. The baseline models are initialized with their official network backbones weights pre-trained on the ImageNet [10] or Supervisely Person Segmentation (SPS) dataset

[35]. Our network backbone is pre-trained on the Cityscapes dataset [9]. During training, the size of the input image is 512 × 512. To avoid overfitting, we adopt the data augmentation methods: random combination of two foreground objects, random affine transformation, random cropping, and random color jitters.

4.4 Comparison with the State-of-the-Art Methods

We compare our method with the state-of-the-art image matting methods [18,21,29,39], where we use Mean Square Error (MSE) and Mean Absolute Difference (MAD) as evaluation metrics. The experimental results on the Adobe Image Matting dataset [37] and the Distinctions-646 dataset [30] are listed in Table 1 and Table 2, respectively. Our DEQ-Matt method outperforms all baseline methods in terms of both MSE and MAD on the two datasets. We further present the visual results in Fig. 3, which demonstrates that our method succeeds in estimating both image semantics and fine details.

4.5 Ablation Study

We validate the effectiveness of auxiliary loss functions for training our DEQ-Matt, by first removing these designs and gradually adding them back. The experimental results are listed in Table 3. We observe that the performance is improved gradually, which demonstrates that all the auxiliary loss functions improve the performance.

Table 3. The results of the ablation study. We evaluate the contribution of each auxiliary loss function to the MSE and MAD of the estimated alpha mattes. The presented values are the means of the values on the Adobe Image Matting dataset [37] and the Distinctions-646 dataset [30]. The best results are in **bold**

Progressive loss	Distillation loss	MSE ↓	MAD ↓
		0.0505	0.0886
✓		0.0418	0.0764
✓	✓	**0.0385**	**0.0736**

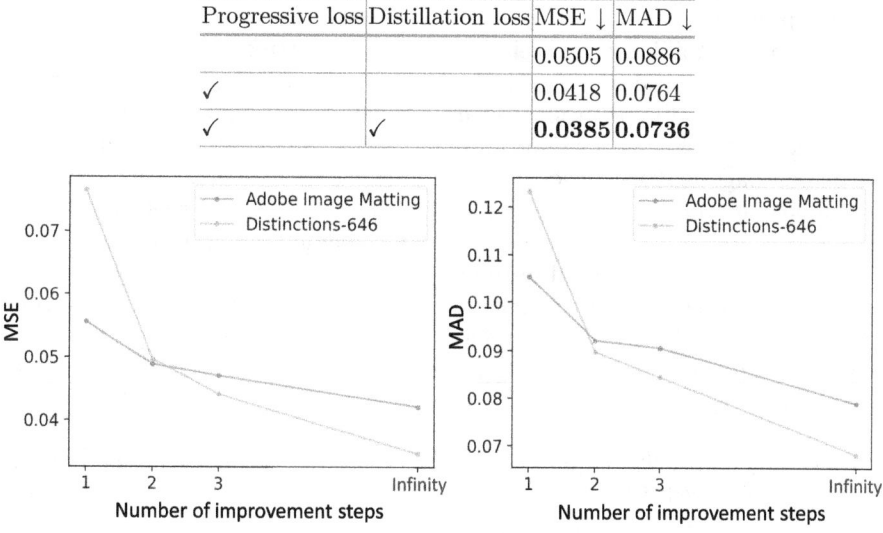

Fig. 4. Model performance with different numbers of improvement steps. For both MSE and MAD, the lower is better

4.6 Discussion on the Improvement Step

We study how the number of improvement steps affects the model's performance by conducting the improvement step multiple times and comparing their respective performances. The results are shown in Fig. 4. We observe that increasing the number of steps gradually improves the model performance in terms of MSE and MAD on both datasets. Also, the model reaches the optimal performance when using infinite steps. We further present the visual results in Fig. 5, where we observe that the improvement step gradually corrects the image semantics and sharps the fine details. These observations support our motivation of using infinite improvement steps to obtain optimal image matting performance.

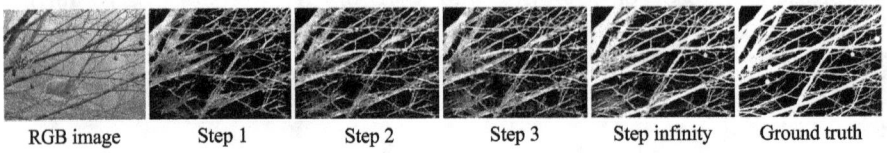

Fig. 5. Visual results of the improvement process

5 Conclusions

In this paper, we propose deep equilibrium matting (DEQ-Matt), which improves the feature maps for infinite times to obtain optimal performance. This is implemented by using the deep equilibrium (DEQ) models, which output the root of the improvement function. We further tailor an effective loss function specifically for deep equilibrium models in the image matting task to address two challenges: convergence to unsatisfactory local optima and overfitting on training data. Additionally, we propose using saliency maps to guide the image matting models. Saliency maps can be automatically and reliably predicted, making the entire image matting process both automatic and robust. In experiments, despite having relatively few parameters, our method outperforms state-of-the-art methods, excelling in both semantic estimation and detail processing. Also, we observe an increasing trend in the model's performance when increasing the number of feature improvement steps. This observation supports our motivation: improving the feature maps for infinite times to achieve optimal performance. Future work can explore extending our method to process videos and recover the color of foreground objects.

Acknowledgement. The authors gratefully acknowledge the ICANN 2024 reviewers for their valuable feedback.

References

1. Bai, S., Kolter, J.Z., Koltun, V.: Deep equilibrium models. In: Wallach, H.M., Larochelle, H., Beygelzimer, A., d'Alché-Buc, F., Fox, E.B., Garnett, R. (eds.) Advances in Neural Information Processing Systems, pp. 688–699 (2019)
2. Bai, S., Koltun, V., Kolter, J.Z.: Multiscale deep equilibrium models. In: Advances in Neural Information Processing Systems (2020)
3. Cai, S., et al.: Disentangled image matting. In: International Conference on Computer Vision, pp. 8818–8827. IEEE (2019)
4. Chen, Q., Li, D., Tang, C.: KNN matting. IEEE Trans. Pattern Anal. Mach. **35**(9), 2175–2188 (2013)
5. Chen, Q., Ge, T., Xu, Y., Zhang, Z., Yang, X., Gai, K.: Semantic human matting. In: ACM Multimedia, pp. 618–626. ACM (2018)
6. Cheng, B., Misra, I., Schwing, A.G., Kirillov, A., Girdhar, R.: Masked-attention mask transformer for universal image segmentation. In: Proceedings of the IEEE/CVF Conference on Computer Vision and Pattern Recognition, pp. 1280–1289. IEEE (2022)
7. Cho, D., Kim, S., Tai, Y., Kweon, I.S.: Automatic trimap generation and consistent matting for light-field images. IEEE Trans. Pattern Anal. Mach. Intell. **39**(8), 1504–1517 (2017)
8. Cho, D., Tai, Y.-W., Kweon, I.: Natural image matting using deep convolutional neural networks. In: Leibe, B., Matas, J., Sebe, N., Welling, M. (eds.) ECCV 2016. LNCS, vol. 9906, pp. 626–643. Springer, Cham (2016). https://doi.org/10.1007/978-3-319-46475-6_39
9. Cordts, M., et al.: The cityscapes dataset for semantic urban scene understanding. In: Proceedings of the IEEE/CVF Conference on Computer Vision and Pattern Recognition, pp. 3213–3223. IEEE Computer Society (2016)
10. Deng, J., Dong, W., Socher, R., Li, L., Li, K., Fei-Fei, L.: Imagenet: a large-scale hierarchical image database. In: Proceedings of the IEEE/CVF Conference on Computer Vision and Pattern Recognition, pp. 248–255. IEEE Computer Society (2009)
11. Deora, R., Sharma, R., Raj, D.S.S.: Salient image matting. arXiv preprint arXiv:2103.12337 (2021)
12. Dosovitskiy, A., et al.: An image is worth 16x16 words: Transformers for image recognition at scale. In: International Conference on Learning Representations. OpenReview.net (2021)
13. Everingham, M., Gool, L.V., Williams, C.K.I., Winn, J.M., Zisserman, A.: The pascal visual object classes (VOC) challenge. Int. J. Comput. Vision **88**(2), 303–338 (2010)
14. Feng, X., Liang, X., Zhang, Z.: A cluster sampling method for image matting via sparse coding. In: Leibe, B., Matas, J., Sebe, N., Welling, M. (eds.) ECCV 2016. LNCS, vol. 9906, pp. 204–219. Springer, Cham (2016). https://doi.org/10.1007/978-3-319-46475-6_13
15. Gastal, E.S.L., Oliveira, M.M.: Shared sampling for real-time alpha matting. Comput. Graph. Forum **29**(2), 575–584 (2010)
16. He, K., Rhemann, C., Rother, C., Tang, X., Sun, J.: A global sampling method for alpha matting. In: Proceedings of the IEEE/CVF Conference on Computer Vision and Pattern Recognition, pp. 2049–2056. IEEE Computer Society (2011)
17. Hou, Q., Liu, F.: Context-aware image matting for simultaneous foreground and alpha estimation. In: International Conference on Computer Vision, pp. 4129–4138. IEEE (2019)

18. Ke, Z., Sun, J., Li, K., Yan, Q., Lau, R.W.H.: Modnet: real-time trimap-free portrait matting via objective decomposition. In: Association for the Advancement of Artificial Intelligence, pp. 1140–1147. AAAI Press (2022)
19. Kim, T., Kim, K., Lee, J., Cha, D., Lee, J., Kim, D.: Revisiting image pyramid structure for high resolution salient object detection. In: Asian Conference on Computer Vision. LNCS, vol. 13847, pp. 257–273. Springer (2022). https://doi.org/10.1007/978-3-031-26293-7_16
20. Levin, A., Lischinski, D., Weiss, Y.: A closed-form solution to natural image matting. IEEE Trans. Pattern Anal. Mach. Intell. **30**(2), 228–242 (2007)
21. Li, Y., Lu, H.: Natural image matting via guided contextual attention. In: Association for the Advancement of Artificial Intelligence, pp. 11450–11457. AAAI Press (2020)
22. Lin, S., Ryabtsev, A., Sengupta, S., Curless, B.L., Seitz, S.M., Kemelmacher-Shlizerman, I.: Real-time high-resolution background matting. In: Proceedings of the IEEE/CVF Conference on Computer Vision and Pattern Recognition, pp. 8762–8771. Computer Vision Foundation / IEEE (2021)
23. Lin, T.-Y., et al.: Microsoft COCO: common objects in context. In: Fleet, D., Pajdla, T., Schiele, B., Tuytelaars, T. (eds.) ECCV 2014. LNCS, vol. 8693, pp. 740–755. Springer, Cham (2014). https://doi.org/10.1007/978-3-319-10602-1_48
24. Liu, J., et al.: Boosting semantic human matting with coarse annotations. In: Proceedings of the IEEE/CVF Conference on Computer Vision and Pattern Recognition, pp. 8560–8569. Computer Vision Foundation / IEEE (2020)
25. Long, J., Shelhamer, E., Darrell, T.: Fully convolutional networks for semantic segmentation. In: Proceedings of the IEEE/CVF Conference on Computer Vision and Pattern Recognition, pp. 3431–3440. IEEE Computer Society (2015)
26. Loshchilov, I., Hutter, F.: SGDR: stochastic gradient descent with warm restarts. In: International Conference on Learning Representations. OpenReview.net (2017)
27. Lu, H., Dai, Y., Shen, C., Xu, S.: Indices matter: learning to index for deep image matting. In: International Conference on Computer Vision, pp. 3265–3274. IEEE (2019)
28. Ma, L., Wang, T., Dong, B., Yan, J., Li, X., Zhang, X.: Implicit feature refinement for instance segmentation. In: MM 2021: ACM Multimedia Conference, Virtual Event, China, 20 - 24 October 2021, pp. 3088–3096. ACM (2021)
29. Park, G., Son, S., Yoo, J., Kim, S., Kwak, N.: Matteformer: transformer-based image matting via prior-tokens. In: Proceedings of the IEEE/CVF Conference on Computer Vision and Pattern Recognition, pp. 11686–11696. IEEE (2022)
30. Qiao, Y., et al.: Attention-guided hierarchical structure aggregation for image matting. In: Proceedings of the IEEE/CVF Conference on Computer Vision and Pattern Recognition, pp. 13673–13682. Computer Vision Foundation / IEEE (2020)
31. Qiu, Y., et al.: SATS: self-attention transfer for continual semantic segmentation. Pattern Recogn. **138**, 109383 (2023)
32. Sengupta, S., Jayaram, V., Curless, B., Seitz, S.M., Kemelmacher-Shlizerman, I.: Background matting: the world is your green screen. In: Proceedings of the IEEE/CVF Conference on Computer Vision and Pattern Recognition, pp. 2288–2297. Computer Vision Foundation / IEEE (2020)
33. Shi, X., Chen, Z., Wang, H., Yeung, D., Wong, W., Woo, W.: Convolutional LSTM network: a machine learning approach for precipitation nowcasting. In: Advances in Neural Information Processing Systems, pp. 802–810 (2015)
34. Sun, J., Jia, J., Tang, C., Shum, H.: Poisson matting. ACM Trans. Graph. **23**(3), 315–321 (2004)

35. supervise.ly: Supervisely person dataset. supervise.ly (2018)
36. Vaswani, A., et al.: Attention is all you need. In: Guyon, I., von Luxburg, U., Bengio, S., Wallach, H.M., Fergus, R., Vishwanathan, S.V.N., Garnett, R. (eds.) Advances in Neural Information Processing Systems, pp. 5998–6008 (2017)
37. Xu, N., Price, B.L., Cohen, S., Huang, T.S.: Deep image matting. In: Proceedings of the IEEE/CVF Conference on Computer Vision and Pattern Recognition, pp. 311–320. IEEE Computer Society (2017)
38. Yu, H., Xu, N., Huang, Z., Zhou, Y., Shi, H.: High-resolution deep image matting. In: Association for the Advancement of Artificial Intelligence, pp. 3217–3224. AAAI Press (2021)
39. Yu, Q., et al.: Mask guided matting via progressive refinement network. In: Proceedings of the IEEE/CVF Conference on Computer Vision and Pattern Recognition, pp. 1154–1163. Computer Vision Foundation/IEEE (2021)
40. Zhang, J., et al.: RGB-D saliency detection via cascaded mutual information minimization. In: International Conference on Computer Vision, pp. 4318–4327. IEEE (2021)
41. Zhang, Y., et al.: A late fusion CNN for digital matting. In: Proceedings of the IEEE/CVF Conference on Computer Vision and Pattern Recognition, pp. 7469–7478. Computer Vision Foundation / IEEE (2019)

Computer Vision: 3D Methods

ControlNeRF: Text-Driven 3D Scene Stylization via Diffusion Model

Jiahui Chen, Chuanfeng Yang, Kaiheng Li, Qingqiang Wu[✉],
and Qingqi Hong[✉]

Department of Digital Media Technology, Xiamen University, Xiamen, China
{wuqq,hongqq}@xmu.edu.cn

Abstract. 3D scene stylization aims to generate artistically rendered images from various viewpoints within a 3D space while ensuring style consistency regardless of the viewing angle. Traditional 2D methods usually used in this field struggle with maintaining this consistency when applied to 3D environments. To address this issue, we propose a novel approach named ControlNeRF, which employs a customized conditional diffusion model, ControlNet, and introduces latent variables, obtaining a stylized appearance throughout the scene solely driven by text. Specifically, this text-driven approach effectively overcomes the inconveniences associated with using images as style cues, and it not only achieves a high degree of stylistic consistency across various viewpoints but also produces high-quality images. We have conducted rigorous testing on ControlNeRF with diverse styles, which has confirmed these outcomes. Our approach not only advances the field of 3D scene stylization but also opens new possibilities for artistic expression and digital imaging.

Keywords: Stylization · Neural Radiance Fields · Diffusion Model · View Synthesis

1 Introduction

In recent years, there has been a growing focus on controlling the appearance of 3D real-world scenes across different fields, including gaming, film, virtual reality, and mixed reality applications. Traditional methods of stylizing 3D content typically involve modifying textures through either reference style images or semantic view synthesis. Explicit 3D representations, such as meshes and point clouds, have become the preferred choice due to their robust interactive editing capabilities. Nevertheless, these methods still face challenges in accurately rendering complex 3D scenes.

With the proposal of implicit 3D representation, especially neural radiation fields (NeRF) [14], various innovative methods [8,15] of stylizing novel views have emerged. Thanks to the high-fidelity rendering capabilities of NeRF, coupled with its implicit nature that offers significant expansibility, it has achieved significant success in stylizing 3D scenes. However, applying 2D stylization methods directly to 3D scenes might introduce cross-view artifacts due to individual stylization of each view without considering 3D consistency. Furthermore, relying solely on reference-style images may not adequately convey the desired outcomes of users. Existing 3D stylization methods [6,8] often necessitate multiple time-consuming training iterations. In this paper, we propose ControlNeRF, a method for stylizing 3D scenes using only text prompts, eliminating the need for reference style images. Our approach combines NeRF with a conditional diffusion model, enabling ordinary users to edit 3D scenes easily through text prompts with fewer iterations. For example, given a 3D scene, users can input a text prompt word that changes the style, such as *"As a bronze bust"* or *"Make him look like a Modigliani painting"*.

Although 3D generation models have been developed, such as [22], the availability of data sources for large-scale training of these models remains relatively limited. To overcome this limitation, we adopt the pre-trained 2D diffusion model, ControlNet [25], which has prior knowledge of the appearance and shape of scene images acquired from a large-scale dataset. To maintain the multi-view consistency of the scene, similar to DreamFusion [16] and Instruct-NeRF2NeRF (IN2N) [6], we adopt a two-stage alternating training methodology. In one stage, the diffusion model is used to edit NeRF input images, and in the other stage, the global 3D representation is updated to incorporate these edited images.

In summary, our paper makes the following contributions.

1. Firstly, we present a text-driven approach for 3D stylization, aiming to eliminate the requirement of reference style images.
2. Secondly, we introduce ControlNeRF, a novel method which integrates implicit 3D scene representation and a diffusion model conditioned on canny edge, effectively resolving the issue of inconsistent stylization commonly observed in 2D approach.
3. Finally, our extensive experiments demonstrate the exceptional stylized editing capabilities of our method for both 3D characters and 3D scenes, achieved with reduced iterations.

2 Related Work

2.1 Stylization in 2D

The stylization of artistic images has been a long-standing area of research. Image analogies [7] solve the problem by finding semantic correspondences between input images. Subsequently, a lot of approaches utilizing neural networks [5,10] for style transfer have emerged. However, image stylization is constrained by the given view. Simply combining neural style transfer with novel view synthesis methods, without incorporating 3D information, may lead to issues like blurriness or inconsistent views.

2.2 Stylization in 3D

As the 3D domain gains prominence, researchers are turning their attention to the stylization of 3D content. Explicit 3D stylization methods commonly leverage meshes [11] and point clouds [19] or employ textures [9] to edit individual objects. Despite their success, these methods are typically confined to stylizing a single object. In the realm of 3D scene-level style transfer, recent methods make use of point clouds [2]. However, constrained by the expressive capabilities of explicit 3D representations, these 3D stylization methods encounter challenges when extending to complex objects or scenes with specialized structures.

Implicit 3D representation, known for its ability to represent complex scenes effectively, has garnered more attention. NeRF [14] stands out as a popular method for generating realistic novel views of a scene, and recent research has explored artistic 3D stylization of NeRF [8,15,24]. While these methods achieve consistent 3D stylization of scenes, they primarily focus on global variations in scene appearance, frequently requiring reference images.

2.3 Text-Driven Stylization

In contrast to specifying style through reference images, natural language prompts provide a more intuitive and user-friendly approach. Supported by CLIP [17], which helps in establishing a latent space correspondence between text and images, some studies have delved into 3D stylization through text guidance instead of reference images. NeRF-Art [23], for instance, capitalizes on the similarity between the scene's CLIP embedding and concise textual prompts to tackle this task. Another example is IN2N [6], which employs an image editing model to iteratively edit multi-view images, subsequently reconstructing the edited 3D scene from them.

3 Methodology

Our approach can be simply divided into two processes: reconstruction and stylization. Firstly, we will provide a brief review of the representation of 3D scenes with NeRF [14]. Next, the reconstructed 3D scene and its associated source data will be taken as inputs for the stylization stage. In addition, we also need to use textual prompts as inputs, e.g., *"As a marble bust."* As output, our approach generate a stylized version of the NeRF representation based on the given prompts, along with a stylized version of the input images.

Inspired by IN2N [6], our approach tackles this task by iteratively updating images captured from observed viewpoints with the help of a diffusion model. Subsequently, these edited images are integrated into the 3D scene through NeRF training. Our approach builds on recent advances in image diffusion models, primarily ControlNet, which is a 2D text-and-image diffusion model designed for a variety of specific tasks.

3.1 Preliminaries

Neural Radiance Fields. We adopt NeRF as our representation for 3D scenes. NeRF utilizes neural network $\mathcal{F}$ to model a scene as a continuous function,

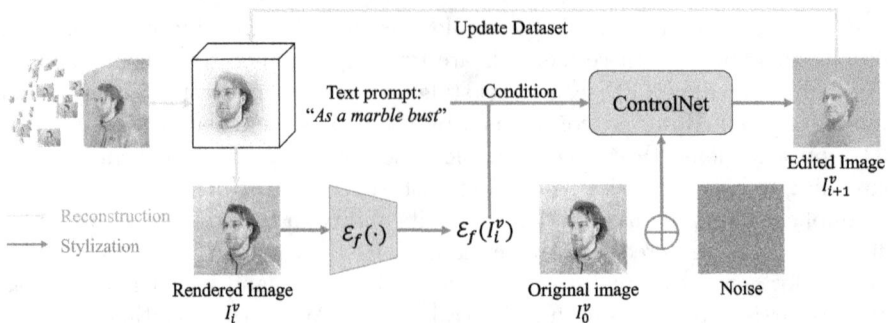

Fig. 1. Overview: Our approach involves iteratively updating the images in the dataset while training a NeRF. (1) Rendering an image I_i^v from a specific viewpoint v; (2) The image I_i^v is edited by ControlNet based on text prompts; (3) Updating the images I_{i+1}^v in the dataset; (4) Continuing the training of the NeRF

mapping 3D spatial coordinates to both color and density information. This capability enables the creation of highly detailed and realistic 3D reconstructions. Given 3D spatial coordinates (x, y, z) and their corresponding view directions $\mathbf{d} = (\theta, \phi)$, the network will predict the color $\mathbf{c} = (r, g, b)$ and density σ at each point in the scene.

To render images from a novel view, NeRF follows traditional ray marching techniques for volume rendering. For each pixel in the images, a ray $\mathbf{r}(t) = \mathbf{o} + t\mathbf{d}$ is cast from the camera's center $\mathbf{o}$ along the direction $\mathbf{d}$ passing through the pixel. The color $\hat{C}(\mathbf{r})$ of the pixel is determined by accumulating K sample points along the ray $\mathbf{r}$, as formulated in [14]:

$$\hat{C}(\mathbf{r}) = \sum_{i=1}^{N} T_i (1 - \exp(-\sigma_i(t_{i+1} - t_i))) \mathbf{c}_i, \tag{1}$$

$$\text{where } T_i = \exp(-\sum_{j}^{i-1} \sigma_j(t_{j+1} - t_j)). \tag{2}$$

During training, NeRF is optimized by minimizing the loss between predicted pixel color $\hat{C}(\mathbf{r})$ and the ground truth pixel color $C(\mathbf{r})$ for each ray, which is denoted by

$$\mathcal{L}_{rec} = \sum_{\mathbf{r}} \left\| \hat{C}(\mathbf{r}) - C(\mathbf{r}) \right\|_2^2. \tag{3}$$

ControlNet. Diffusion models were first introduced by Sohl-Dickstein et al. [20] and have been recently applied to image generation [3]. ControlNet [25] is a neural network architecture that can enhance large pre-trained text-to-image diffusion models with spatially localized, task-specific image conditions. In practice, ControlNet is based on a latent diffusion model [18], conditioned on various factors (e.g., edge, pose, depth, etc.). Text prompts are encoded using the CLIP text encoder [17], while diffusion timesteps are encoded with a time encoder using positional encoding. Unlike other latent diffusion models, ControlNet uses a tiny network $\mathcal{E}_f(\cdot)$ to encode an image-space condition $\mathbf{c}_i$ into a feature space conditioning vector $\mathbf{c}_f$ as

$$\mathbf{c}_f = \mathcal{E}_f(\mathbf{c}_i). \tag{4}$$

When given an input image z_0, image diffusion algorithms progressively add noise to the image, generating a noisy image z_t, where t denotes the number of times noise is added. The algorithms work within a set of conditions, including time step t, text prompts $\mathbf{c}_t$, and a task-specific condition $\mathbf{c}_f$. These conditions guide the learning process of a U-Net ϵ_θ, which is trained to predict the noise added to the noisy image z_t with

$$\mathcal{L}_d = \mathbb{E}_{z_0,t,\mathbf{c}_t,\mathbf{c}_f,\epsilon\sim\mathcal{N}(0,1)}[\|\epsilon - \epsilon_\theta(z_t,t,\mathbf{c}_t,\mathbf{c}_f)\|_2^2], \tag{5}$$

where $\mathcal{L}_d$ represents the overall learning object of the entire diffusion model.

3.2 ControlNeRF

We fine-tune the reconstructed NeRF model to align with the style of the given prompt word, thus resulting in a modified scene. An overview is provided in Fig. 1.

The core of our method revolves around the iterative updating of images within the NeRF dataset. We employ a diffusion model (ControlNet) for the gradual editing of images in the training dataset, facilitating the progressive integration of the diffusion prior knowledge into the 3D scene. Subsequently, NeRF is trained using these updated images, ensuring their seamless integration into a globally consistent 3D representation. Although our method involves significant edits to the scene, our use of the image-conditioned diffusion model effectively preserves the structure and identity of the original scene.

Editing a Dataset Image. Our innovation involves modifying the inputs of ControlNet to obtain more consistent images with fewer iterations. To edit the dataset image at a specific viewpoint v, as mentioned by SDEdit [12], we use the encoder $\mathcal{E}_l(\cdot)$ to map the unedited original image I_0^v to the latent space, obtaining z_0. Subsequently, we linearly combine it with Gaussian noise $\mathcal{N}(0,1)$ to generate z_t. For $\mathbf{c}_f$, we take the rendered image I_i^v after the i-th optimization as $\mathbf{c}_i$, and encode it according to Eq. 4. In summary, we define the process of replacing an image I_i^v with I_{i+1}^v as

$$I_{i+1}^v = \mathcal{D}_l(U_\theta(I_0^v, t; \mathbf{c}_t, \mathcal{E}_f(I_i^v))), \tag{6}$$

where $\mathcal{D}_l(\cdot)$ is the corresponding decoder. We define U_θ as the UniPC [26] sampling process with a fixed step s taken between initial timestep t and 0. During the image denoising process, we will obtain I_{i+1}^v that closely resembles I_0^v in terms of information content.

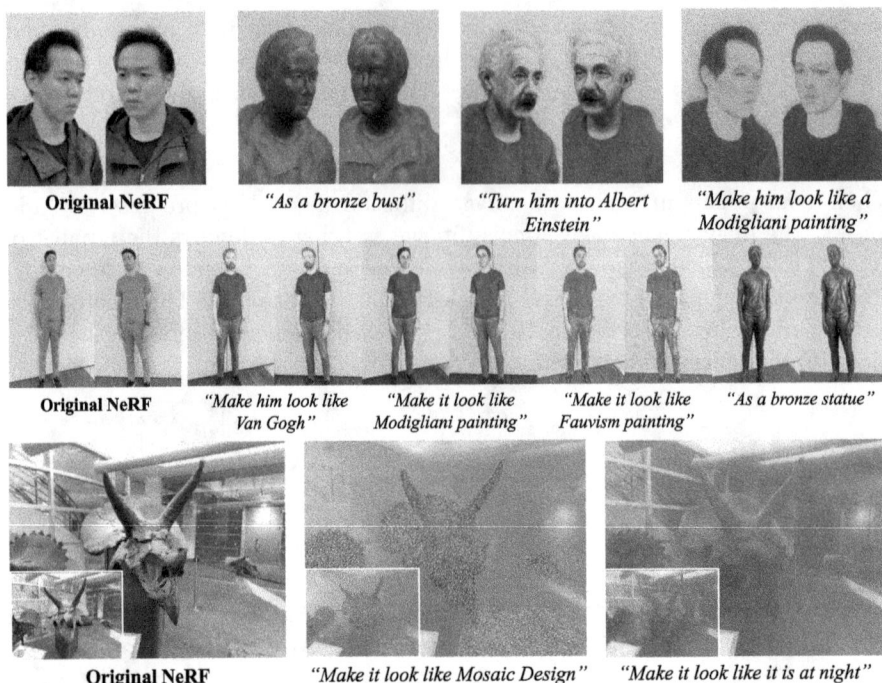

Fig. 2. Results. Our method is capable of handling various stylization tasks, including facial, full-body and interior style edits. Furthermore, we conducted experiments on a variety of datasets, including a proprietary dataset curated by our team, as well as the IN2N dataset and the LLFF dataset

Because the diffusion model edits the original image I_o^v based on textual prompts $\mathbf{c}_t$ and the noised image z_t passed to U-Net is partially noisy, this leads to the rendering of the current global 3D model affecting the diffusion model's final estimation of z_0. Considering that we use the features of rendered images I_i^v as conditional input, our method effectively suppresses the characteristic drift during iterative cycles.

Alternating Training Scheme. At first, we apply the aforementioned process to perform a stylized edit on the "realistic" images $\{I_0^v\}$ rendered from the reconstructed NeRF model. After this step, the stylized images may not necessarily maintain multi-view consistency. Secondly, we use these stylized images $\{I_{i=1}^v\}$ as target images for retraining the NeRF scene. During this phase, we can train the new NeRF scene with a batch of random rays across multiple views. Finally, we can render a new set of images through stylized NeRF.

As the diffusion model edits the original image I_0^v based on the textual prompt $\mathbf{c}_t$ and considering a certain spatial correlation among the original images, the current global NeRF scene plays a role in influencing the diffusion model's estimation of z_0. Through multiple alternating training sessions, we achieve a stylized and consistent NeRF. An essential point to note is that

Algorithm 1 Alternating training Pseudo Code

Require: The number of iterations, N; The images in dataset, $I^v \in I^V$; The prompt words, prompt.
Ensure: The stylized scene, $S_{stylized}$.
  Get rendered images I from any view $v \in V$ from the reconstructed scene
  for each i in N: **do**
    repeat
      $\mathbf{c}_t \sim$ token(prompt)
      $\mathbf{c}_f \sim$ encode(I_i^v)
      $z_t \sim q(I_0^v)$
      $t \sim$ Uniform$(1, \ldots, T)$
      $\epsilon \sim N(0, 1)$
      Take gradient descent step on
        $\nabla_\theta \|\epsilon - \epsilon_\theta(z_t, \mathbf{t}, \mathbf{c}_t, \mathbf{c}_f)\|^2$
    until Converged
    $I_{i+1}^v \sim$ decode(latentImage)
    Replace each image in dataset with edited image
  end for
  Alternate training and continue to reconstruct the scene with new dataset
---

during the rendering, editing, and updating processes of images, the diffusion model consistently incorporates the rendered image as a condition, ultimately leading to a stylized and consistent scene.

This process is similar to the approach proposed in IN2N [6], where the images are updated through style transfer in every alternate iteration. Unlike IN2N, our scheme retains both the edited and original images in the NeRF updates, effectively executing semi-permanent updates to the training dataset. In this process, each gradient update is derived from a random combination of rays from different viewpoints, and the computed gradients along these rays may originate from the most recent NeRF rendering. Due to the randomness and diversity of ray viewpoints in each alternating training session, this significantly enhances the stability and efficiency of the training.

4 Experiments

4.1 Implementation Details

We conduct our experiments using the 'nerfacto' model from NeRFStudio [21] and utilize the datasets from NeRF-Art [23], IN2N [6] and Local Light Field Fusion [13]. These datasets were chosen because they respectively include data on faces, human bodies, and indoor scenes. For NeRF training, we employ MSE and LPIPS losses. The first stage of NeRF training was limited to a maximum of 30,000 iterations, taking approximately 20 min on a single NVIDIA RTX 3090Ti. For stylization, the consistency of scene editing depends on several parameters of ControlNet [25]. We can use the default values of text guidance scalar ($s_t = 7.5$) and set the threshold for Canny edge detection [1] to [100, 200]. Regardless of

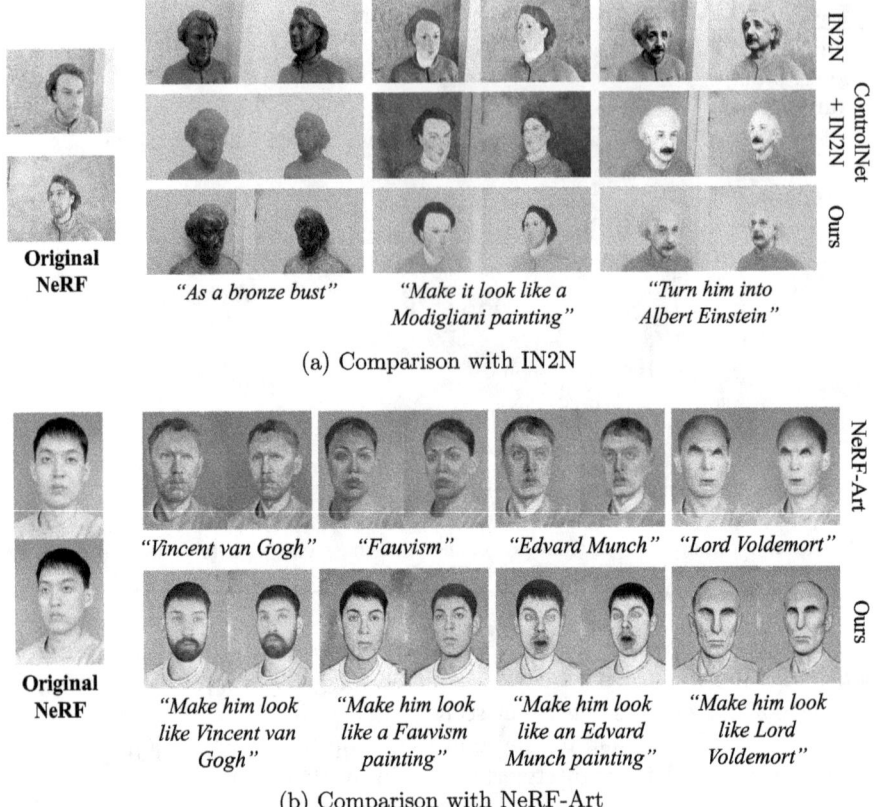

Fig. 3. Baseline Comparisons: We have conducted a comparative analysis of our model against other models described in Sect. 4.3

t, our denoising process for the image consistently underwent 20 iterations. The remaining parameters are fixed for all scenes.

4.2 Results and Analysis

As illustrated in Figs. 2 and 3, ControlNeRF maintains good stylization effects for faces, full-body images, and indoor scenes while preserving three-dimensional consistency. Firstly, we evaluate our method through various qualitative assessments. To validate the effectiveness of our approach, we compare it both qualitatively and quantitatively with IN2N [6] and NeRF-Art [23].

Our approach, by utilizing original images as latent variables in conjunction with the prior knowledge of pre-trained models, successfully generates consistent three-dimensional stylized scenes guided by textual prompts. This not only validates the efficacy of our method but also demonstrates its extensive applicability.

Table 1. Quantitative Evaluation. Our method outperforms in both user study and CLIP Directional Similarity [4] metrics

	User study ↑	CLIP Directional Similarity ↑
NeRF-Art [23]	9.48%	–
IN2N [6]	31.90%	0.1600
Ours	**58.62%**	**0.1913**

4.3 Comparisons

As illustrated in Fig. 3, qualitative comparisons were conducted between our method using ControlNet and the IN2N and NeRF-Art approaches. Notably, we integrated the original image as a conditional input in ControlNet, a technique inspired by IN2N, to facilitate a more comprehensive comparison. Selected results from the IN2N study were used for this analysis. Figure 3(a) demonstrates that ControlNet effectively captures finer details and minimizes distortions, unlike the IN2N method, which tends to overlook intricate features, such as the nuances in Einstein's wrinkles. This limitation in IN2N could be attributed to its treatment of rendered images as latent variables, potentially leading to a loss of critical positional information among images in the dataset. Conversely, ControlNet's consistent use of original images as latent variables helps preserve this crucial information during dataset updates. When comparing with NeRF-Art, it is observed that their approach relies on descriptive text inputs, which may introduce ambiguities in model editing. This is exemplified in their 'Van Gogh' scenario, where it remains unclear whether the objective is to emulate Van Gogh's artistic style or to replicate Van Gogh's facial features.

Since the effect of stylization is subjective, we leave it to users to decide their preferences. As shown in Table 1, we conducted quantitative comparisons based on user studies and CLIP direction similarity [4]. ControlNeRF outperforms IN2N in both aspects. Due to the absence of data pertaining to CLIP direction similarity in the NeRF-Art paper, Table 1 exhibits a data void. Besides, IN2N typically requires over 10k iterations to complete scene editing, while our method only necessitates 3k to 5k iterations.

4.4 Ablation Study

As demonstrated in Fig. 4, we conduct ablation experiments on ControlNeRF. When there is no original image to serve as the latent image variable for ControlNet, the generated scenes tend to be blurry. Concurrently, we conducted a quantitative comparison of our ablation experiments. The data in Table 2 indicates that in the absence of the original image serving as the latent variable, the performance temporarily surpasses that of methods utilizing the original image as latent with fewer iterations. However, as the number of iterations increases, the beneficial impact of employing the original image as latent becomes more pronounced, leading to a more consistent scene generation.

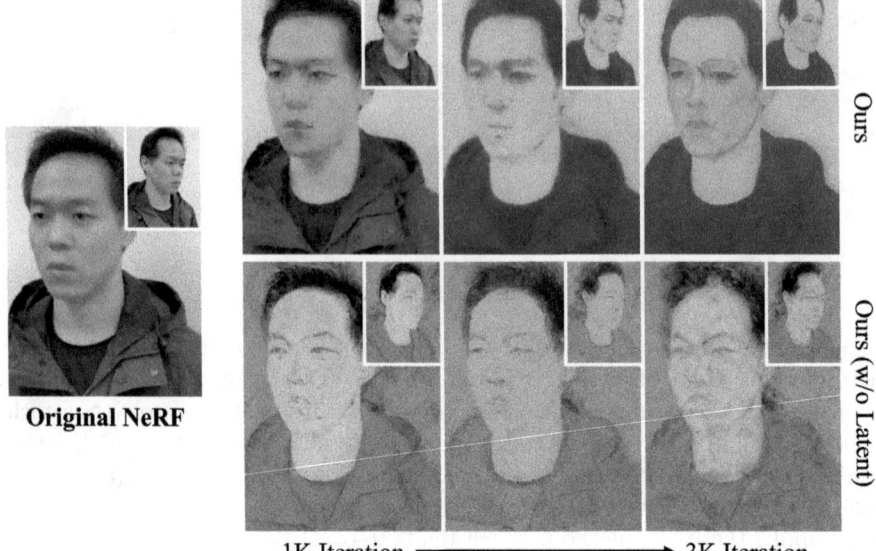

Fig. 4. Ablation study. Prompt: Make it look like a Modigliani painting. When the original images are not used as latent image variables, the entire scene tends to become blurry and exhibit artifacts. ControlNeRF effectively mitigates this issue

Table 2. Ablation Study on CLIP Direction Similarity. Quantitative comparison of our ablation studies in Fig. 4

	1K Iteration	2K Iteration	3K Iteration
Ours	**0.0663**	0.0470	0.0552
Ours (w/o Latent)	0.0050	**0.0656**	**0.1151**

In our ablation studies, we observed that ControlNeRF achieves a converged and consistent scene representation within approximately 3,000 iterations. This is notably faster and results in clearer stylized effects compared to methods that do not employ latent variables. This issue generally arises due to the lack of correlation in color information across various viewpoints in ControlNet, making it challenging to achieve 3D consistency in images from different perspectives. However, there exists a correlation in spatial color information among the images in the original dataset. Therefore, when using original images as latent image variables, ControlNet can more easily generate images with 3D consistency, leading to better stylization effects.

5 Conclusion

In this paper, we introduce ControlNeRF, a method that facilitates the intuitive and accessible stylization of NeRF scenes using textual prompts. Our approach manipulates already reconstructed NeRF scenes, ensuring that any generated edits maintain 3D consistency. We demonstrate the results of our method across various NeRF scenes, showcasing its capability to achieve stylization effects seamlessly within facial, full-body, and indoor settings. As NeRF garners increasing attention from the research community aiming to enhance generalization, quality, and speed during training and inference phases, we posit that leveraging implicit scene representations for 3D scene stylization will pioneer new applications in Virtual Reality and Augmented Reality.

Acknowledgements. This work was commissioned by MetaMaker and supported in part by the Open Project Program of State Key Laboratory of Virtual Reality Technology and Systems, Beihang University (NO. VRLAB2022AC04). Corresponding author: Qingqi Hong.

References

1. Canny, J.: A computational approach to edge detection. IEEE Trans. Pattern Anal. Mach. Intell. **6**, 679–698 (1986)
2. Cao, X., Wang, W., Nagao, K., Nakamura, R.: Psnet: a style transfer network for point cloud stylization on geometry and color. In: Proceedings of the IEEE/CVF Winter Conference on Applications of Computer Vision, pp. 3337–3345 (2020)
3. Dhariwal, P., Nichol, A.: Diffusion models beat gans on image synthesis. Adv. Neural. Inf. Process. Syst. **34**, 8780–8794 (2021)
4. Gal, R., Patashnik, O., Maron, H., Bermano, A.H., Chechik, G., Cohen-Or, D.: Stylegan-nada: Clip-guided domain adaptation of image generators. ACM Trans. Graphics (TOG) **41**(4) (2022)
5. Gatys, L.A., Ecker, A.S., Bethge, M.: Image style transfer using convolutional neural networks. In: 2016 IEEE Conference on Computer Vision and Pattern Recognition (CVPR) (2016)
6. Haque, A., Tancik, M., Efros, A.A., Holynski, A., Kanazawa, A.: Instruct-nerf2nerf: editing 3d scenes with instructions. In: Proceedings of the IEEE/CVF International Conference on Computer Vision, pp. 19740–19750 (October 2023)
7. Hertzmann, A., Jacobs, C.E., Oliver, N., Curless, B., Salesin, D.H.: Image analogies. In: Proceedings of the 28th Annual Conference on Computer Graphics and Interactive Techniques, pp. 327-340. Association for Computing Machinery (2001)
8. Huang, Y.H., He, Y., Yuan, Y.J., Lai, Y.K., Gao, L.: Stylizednerf: consistent 3d scene stylization as stylized nerf via 2d-3d mutual learning. In: Proceedings of the IEEE/CVF Conference on Computer Vision and Pattern Recognition, pp. 18342–18352 (2022)
9. Kato, H., Ushiku, Y., Harada, T.: Neural 3d mesh renderer. In: 2018 IEEE/CVF Conference on Computer Vision and Pattern Recognition (2018)
10. Li, Y., Chen, F., Yang, J., Wang, Z., Lu, X., Yang, M.H.: Universal style transfer via feature transforms. NeurIPS (2017)
11. Ma, C., Huang, H., Sheffer, A., Kalogerakis, E., Wang, R.: Analogy-driven 3d style transfer. Comput. Graph. Forum **33**(2), 175-184 (2014)
12. Meng, C., et al.: SDEdit: guided image synthesis and editing with stochastic differential equations. In: International Conference on Learning Representations (2022)
13. Mildenhall, B., et al.: Local light field fusion: practical view synthesis with prescriptive sampling guidelines. ACM Trans. Graph. (TOG) **38**(4), 1–14 (2019)

14. Mildenhall, B., Srinivasan, P.P., Tancik, M., Barron, J.T., Ramamoorthi, R., Ng, R.: Nerf: representing scenes as neural radiance fields for view synthesis. Commun. ACM **65**(1), 99–106 (2021)
15. Nguyen-Phuoc, T., Liu, F., Xiao, L.: Snerf: stylized neural implicit representations for 3d scenes. ACM Trans. Graph. (TOG) **41**(4), 1–11 (2022)
16. Poole, B., Jain, A., Barron, J.T., Mildenhall, B.: Dreamfusion: text-to-3d using 2d diffusion. In: The Eleventh International Conference on Learning Representations (2023)
17. Radford, A., et al.: Learning transferable visual models from natural language supervision. In: International Conference on Machine Learning, pp. 8748–8763. PMLR (2021)
18. Rombach, R., Blattmann, A., Lorenz, D., Esser, P., Ommer, B.: High-resolution image synthesis with latent diffusion models. In: Proceedings of the IEEE/CVF Conference on Computer Vision and Pattern Recognition, pp. 10684–10695 (2022)
19. Segu, M., Grinvald, M., Siegwart, R., Tombari, F.: 3dsnet: Unsupervised shape-to-shape 3d style transfer. arXiv preprint arXiv:2011.13388 (2020)
20. Sohl-Dickstein, J., Weiss, E., Maheswaranathan, N., Ganguli, S.: Deep unsupervised learning using nonequilibrium thermodynamics. In: International Conference on Machine Learning, pp. 2256–2265. PMLR (2015)
21. Tancik, M, et al.: Nerfstudio: a modular framework for neural radiance field development. In: ACM SIGGRAPH 2023 Conference Proceedings (2023)
22. Tang, J., et al.: Make-it-3d: high-fidelity 3d creation from a single image with diffusion prior. In: Proceedings of the IEEE/CVF International Conference on Computer Vision, pp. 22819–22829 (2023)
23. Wang, C., Jiang, R., Chai, M., He, M., Chen, D., Liao, J.: Nerf-art: text-driven neural radiance fields stylization. IEEE Trans. Visualizat. Comput. Graph. (2023)
24. Zhang, K., Kolkin, N., Bi, S., Luan, F., Xu, Z., Shechtman, E., Snavely, N.: Arf: Artistic radiance fields. In: European Conference on Computer Vision, pp. 717–733. Springer (2022). https://doi.org/10.1007/978-3-031-19821-2_41
25. Zhang, L., Rao, A., Agrawala, M.: Adding conditional control to text-to-image diffusion models. In: Proceedings of the IEEE/CVF International Conference on Computer Vision, pp. 3836–3847 (2023)
26. Zhao, W., Bai, L., Rao, Y., Zhou, J., Lu, J.: Unipc: a unified predictor-corrector framework for fast sampling of diffusion models. Adv. Neural Inform. Process. Syst. (2023)

Interactive Color Manipulation in NeRF: A Point Cloud and Palette-Driven Approach

Haolei Qiu[1](✉), Chenqu Ren[1](✉), and Yeheng Shao[2](✉)

[1] East China Normal University, Shanghai, China
{hlqiu98,renchenqu}@gmail.com
[2] Changchun University of Science and Technology, Changchun, Jilin Province, China
yehengshao@gmail.com

Abstract. Neural Radiance Fields (NeRF) technology has gained popularity for its ability to synthesize photorealistic new views of complex scenes. However, its editability is severely restricted due to its implicit representation. Existing color editing approaches often result in color contamination and distortion issues when editing NeRF-represented appearances. Additionally, these methods typically only support scene-level editing and cannot perform more fine-grained editing on objects within the scene. In this paper, we propose a fine-grained controllable color editing method that supports object-level operations while reducing the color contamination and distortion issues. Our method decomposes the color of each point in the scene into a linear combination of a set of palette bases. To ensure the sparsity of the decomposition, we propose Enhanced Sparse Regularizer (ESR) during the optimization process. We also propose a color correction function that reduces the error between the rendered color and the real color. Furthermore, we extend our model to support finer-grained local color editing through point cloud-level processing. Extensive experiments demonstrate that our color editing method outperforms baseline methods in terms of both qualitative and quantitative results.

Keywords: 3D reconstruction · Neural radiance field · 3D scene color editing

1 Introduction

NeRF [12] has proven highly effective in reconstructing 3D scenes from 2D images, with profound impacts on achieving complex multimedia tasks and connecting digital and real worlds. However, NeRF's implicit representation presents a challenging issue regarding its editability. Palette-based recoloring methods [13,20,22] allow users to adjust color artifacts by modifying a limited set of colors, which is a trade-off solution between user control and recoloring ability. In existing works, Gong et al. [6] and Tojo et al. [17] decompose the appearance of each 3D point into a linear combination based on the palette color bases, which is shared across the scene, to effectively edit the appearance of the 3D scene by modifying the palette color bases. PaletteNeRF [8] model the radiance of each point using a combination of specular and diffuse components, and further decompose the diffuse component into a linear combination of view-independent color bases that are shared across the scene. These works have decomposed images into multiple layers, where each pixel was represented as a weighted sum of these layers. However, when it comes to performing edits on a given image, these works were limited to global color editing or mixed editing, making it challenging to perform fine-grained editing for objects with similar colors. Although generative approaches such as CLIP-NeRF [19], Instruct-NeRF2NeRF [7], InstructPix2Pix [2] and others [10,14] can achieve color editing for specific objects to some extent, they often come with global scene color modifications and serious issues of three-dimensional consistency. Moreover, these methods require retraining for each editing operation. ICE-NeRF [9] and ProteusNeRF [18] introduces color editing by utilizing a pre-trained NeRF and a coarse user mask as input. However, it still requires retraining after each editing operation.

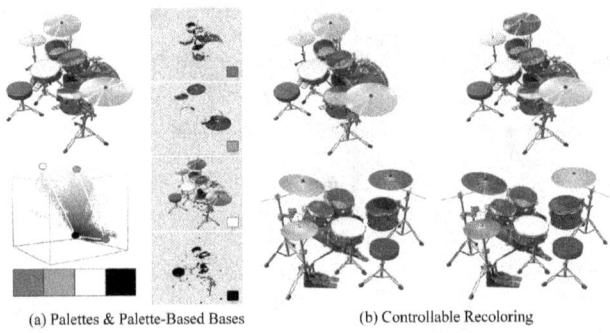

(a) Palettes & Palette-Based Bases   (b) Controllable Recoloring

Fig. 1. We propose a novel and controllable color editing method for recoloring 3D scenes that supports both scene-level and object-level color editing

In this paper, we propose Interactive Color Manipulation in NeRF (ICM-NeRF), a finer-grained color editing method that supports intuitive, artifact-free and view-consistent results. Specifically, we unify palette extraction, layer decomposition, and volume radiance field modeling into a single framework that treats the color of each point in the scene as a weighted mixture of colors in the palette. To minimize color contamination as much as possible, we propose Enhanced Sparse Regularizer (ESR) on the weights to ensure their sparsity, avoiding color contamination issues arising from the palette mixing. However, the sparsity of the palette may result in color distortion of the rendered images, so we propose a color correction function to mitigate errors between the render color and true color induced by sparse palette representation. To support independent color edits for different objects with identical colors, we propose an object-level color decomposition model. In summary, our main contributions include:

- We propose a novel palette-based editable NeRF framework that introduces Enhanced Sparse Regularizer (ESR) and color correction function to ensure the sparsity of color decomposition and maintain high fidelity.
- We develop a controllable color editing method that supports object-level adjustments. This allows for precise and interactive tuning of object colors within a scene, while ensuring consistent results across multiple views.

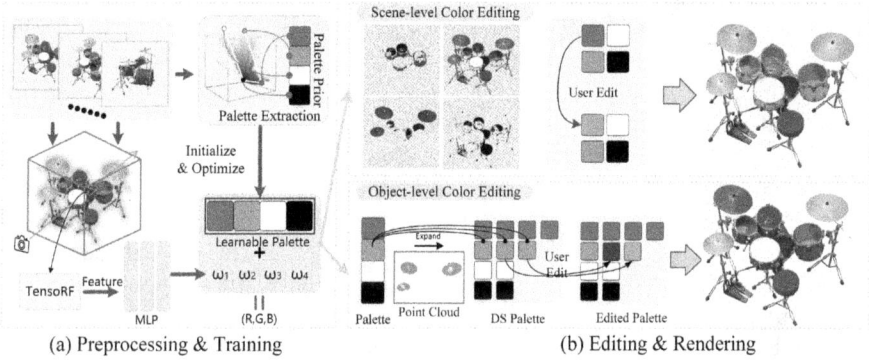

Fig. 2. The workflow of our methods

2 Method

2.1 Overview

Given that the geometric features of the scene are independent of color features, we can separate the training of geometric features and the editing of color features. To achieve fast geometric model training, we used the lightweight model TensoRF [3] as the backbone of our model. The workflow of our model is illustrated in Fig. 2. First, we obtain multi-view images of the scene with known poses and extract a palette from them. Then, we incorporate the extracted palette as a parameter into the model for training. Finally, we can modify the scene's colors by directly manipulating the palette. For object-level color editing, we use point cloud clustering to extract palette of DS (Different objects with the Same color) palette, enabling us to edit the colors of different objects with the same color.

2.2 Scene-Level Color Editing

Palette extraction is a crucial step in this type of palette-based color editing. Using a random palette can lead to serious color blurring issues [8]. Therefore, we adopt an advanced palette extraction method [16] to obtain initial palette parameters. To prevent color pollution resulting from the palette editing method, it is essential to ensure that the weights of the palette are as sparse as possible. However, excessively sparse weights may cause distortion in the final rendered image. Therefore, a color correction function is utilized to compensate for certain color distortions. As shown in Fig. 3, given a palette $\mathbf{P} = \{\mathbf{p}_1, \mathbf{p}_2, ..., \mathbf{p}_k\}$ of size K extracted, this paper aims to obtain color correction values C_{cor} and K optimized view-dependent palette parameters and weights by inputting the sample point coordinates $\mathbf{x}$ and viewing direction $\mathbf{d}$. The specific rendering formula is as follows:

$$C(\mathbf{x}, \mathbf{d}) = C_{cor}(\mathbf{x}, \mathbf{d}) + \sum_{i=1}^{K} w_i(\mathbf{x}) \mathbf{p}_i \quad (1)$$

The parameters w_i and C_{cor} are both dependent on the position of the point and the latter also depends on the viewing direction. As shown in the model 1 of Fig. 3, w_i is regularized using an activation function to ensure that the sum of its values equals 1, while C_{cor} is constrained to $[-1, 1]^3$. The color editing model consists of three multilayer perceptrons (MLPs): the Feature Extraction MLP extracts features from the input data, the Palette MLP obtains viewpoint-dependent palette weights, and the Color Correction MLP acquires viewpoint-dependent color correction values. The Learnable Palette is a set of parameters that can be learned, and finally we combine the network outputs with the Learnable Palette parameters using Eq. 1. to render the final color.

2.3 Object-Level Color Editing

In previous palette-based color-editable NeRF models [6,8,17,21], there existed a problem of not being able to edit the color of specific objects. To address this issue, we propose an object-level color editing model with the aim of enabling the editing of specific object colors within a scene.

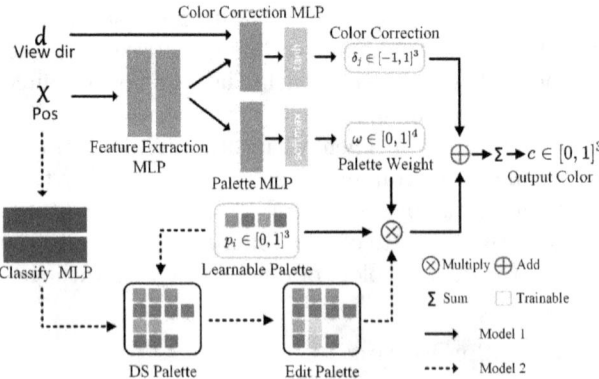

Fig. 3. The network architecture of our model

Point Cloud Construction. Directly constructing point clouds using NeRF results in significant deviations from the true coordinates and leads to many redundant points due to the lack of feature matching between images. To overcome these issues, we use an advanced MVS method called Transmvsnet [4] to construct the point clouds. By inputting multi-view images along with corresponding mask images that correspond to the target color, K clusters of point clouds are obtained, as shown in Fig. 4(a)(b).

Point Cloud Clustering. Since the algorithm for semantic segmentation of point clouds cannot effectively segment real-world objects that are relatively cluttered and not pre-trained, we use clustering algorithms to cluster the point clouds in the scene. We will record the number of objects with the same color as O_i based on their arrangement in the palette, and expand the corresponding color count in the palette to O_i. The final result is similar to the DS Palette shown in Fig. 3. In the real world, an object may be composed of multiple colors, and after color classification, the object will be divided into different components, where the point clouds with the same color will be segmented more clearly, as shown in Fig. 4(c)(d). We choose the DBSCAN [5] algorithm for clustering, which is more stable than other clustering algorithms in terms of segmenting object components.

Point Cloud Classification. After clustering the point clouds, it is necessary to classify the point clouds of different colors. As shown in model 2 of Fig. 3, we additionally use a Classify MLP to classify spatial points. Empirically, the color of a point in space tends to belong to a certain kind of base color in the palette, meaning that its weight for that color is higher. Therefore, when classifying it with a model that does not match its color, modifying the corresponding color in the classification model would hardly affect the color of this point, since the target color of the classification model has very little contribution to the color of this point. For example, if a point is green, then in a red classification model, modifying any color would hardly affect the color of this point.

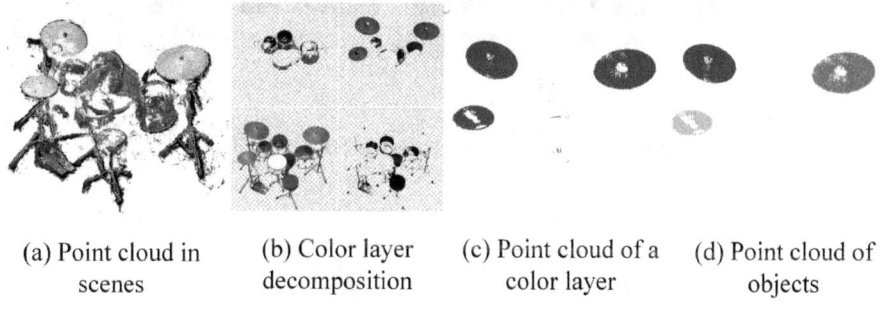

(a) Point cloud in scenes (b) Color layer decomposition (c) Point cloud of a color layer (d) Point cloud of objects

Fig. 4. The relevant processing of point clouds in object-level color editing

Object-Level Color Editing. When editing the color of a specific object in the scene, we first modify the color corresponding to that object in DS Palette, then freeze the trained Classify MLP, and combine the frozen Classify MLP with Edited Palette in the model, and finally re-render to generate a recolored 3D scene.

3 Optimization

Learning a set of palette bases and weights from the scene, while ensuring photo-realistic rendering of the resulting image, is a highly challenging task. Therefore, we must carefully design optimization schemes. To address this issue, we propose a series of loss optimization strategies for tuning the parameters and to avoid the problem of local optima as much as possible. Firstly, we introduce a scene reconstruction loss:

$$\mathcal{L}_{image} = \left\| C_{gt} - \sum_{i=1}^{K} \omega_i \mathbf{p}_i \right\|_2^2 + \left\| C_{gt} - (C_{cor} + \sum_{i=1}^{K} \omega_i \mathbf{p}_i) \right\|_2^2. \quad (2)$$

Here, C_{gt} represents the true color of image pixels, ω_i is the weight of the palette, $\mathbf{p}_i$ is the learnable palette, and C_{cor} is the corrected color obtained through a color correction function. All three variables can be constrained by Eq. 2. The first least squares constraint in Eq. 2. aims to obtain palette weights that better fits the scene, while the second constraint aims to correct the colors mixed through the palette to avoid color distortion issues.

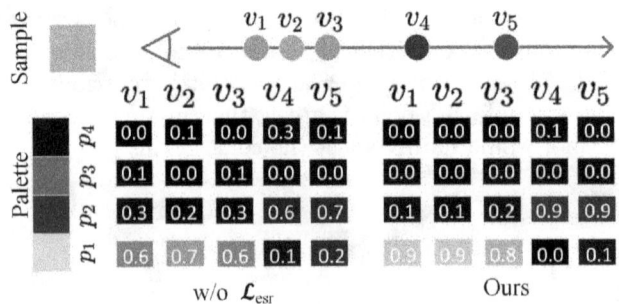

Fig. 5. The schematic diagram of the ESR

3.1 Enhanced Sparse Regularizer

To prevent color contamination caused by palette-based color editing methods, we need to make the palette as sparse as possible. To achieve this goal, we introduce a sparse regularization loss function used in PaletteNerf [8]. The definition of this loss function is as follows:

$$\mathcal{L}_{sp} = \frac{\sum_{i=1}^{K} \omega_i(\mathbf{x})}{\sum_{i=1}^{K} \omega_i^2(\mathbf{x})} - 1. \tag{3}$$

However, we found that although introducing $\mathcal{L}_{sp}$ can obtain sparse weights, the sparse weights obtained through $\mathcal{L}_{sp}$ constraints often have the problem of small differences between the maximum and the sub-maximum values. This leads to a prominent color contamination problem due to the influence of the sub-maximum values on the color. The schematic diagram is shown in Fig. 5. Therefore, we attempt to ensure that one weight value in the palette is as large as possible while the rest are as small as possible, and make these smaller values as evenly distributed as possible to avoid situations where the sub-maximum value is too large or even close to the maximum value. To this end, we propose an enhanced sparse regularization loss function $\mathcal{L}_{esr}$, defined as follows:

$$\mathcal{L}_{esr} = \sum_{i=1}^{K} (exp(\omega_i(\mathbf{x})(1-\omega_i(\mathbf{x})) - 1). \tag{4}$$

3.2 Appearance Constraint

In order to prevent the occurrence of extreme situations with respect to palette base and weights, certain constraints are imposed on the definitions of the palette base and color correction values. Specifically, they are defined as follows:

$$\mathcal{L}_p = \|\mathbf{P}_{train} - \mathbf{P}_{original}\|_2^2, \tag{5}$$

$$\mathcal{L}_{cor} = \|C_{cor}\|_2^2. \tag{6}$$

As a summary, we define the joint optimization loss of our model as shown in Eq. 7:

$$\mathcal{L} = \lambda_{image}\mathcal{L}_{image} + \lambda_{sp}\mathcal{L}_{sp} + \lambda_{esr}\mathcal{L}_{esr} + \lambda_p\mathcal{L}_p + \lambda_{cor}\mathcal{L}_{cor}. \tag{7}$$

where λ_{image}, λ_{sp}, λ_{esr}, λ_p and λ_{cor} represent the weights of the losses.

4 Experimental Configurations and Results

4.1 Configurations

In our experiments, the Classify MLP and Feature Extraction MLP are 2x32 networks, while the Color Correction MLP and Palette MLP are 1x32 networks. We set the hyperparameters λ_{image}, λ_{sp}, λ_{esr}, λ_p and λ_{cor} to 1.0, 0.005, 0.003, 0.0001 and 0.0001, respectively. For optimization, we utilize the Adam Optimizer and perform 25,000 iterations with a learning rate of 0.001.

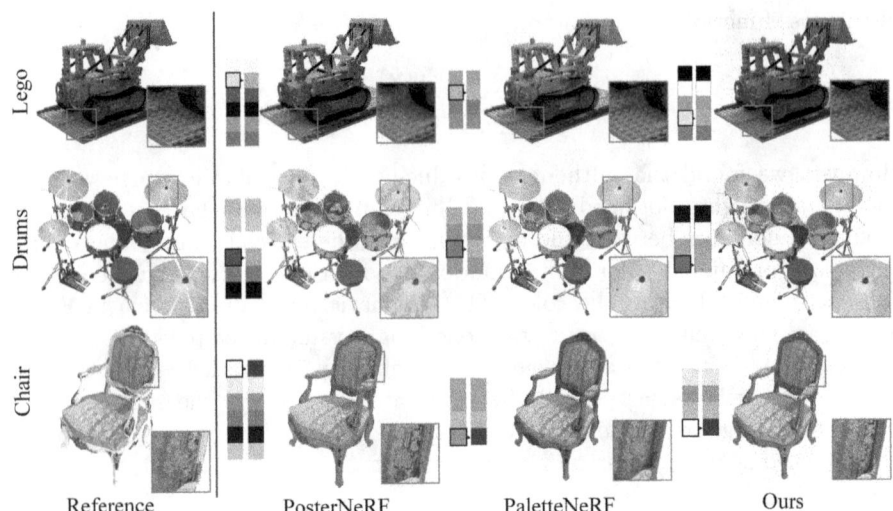

Fig. 6. Qualitative comparison with image palette-based recoloring methods on the Synthetic-NeRF [12]. We compare our method with PosterNeRF [17] and PaletteNeRF [8]. For each recolored image, we also show the corresponding palettes editing on its left side, and a zoom-in view on its right side

4.2 Comparisons

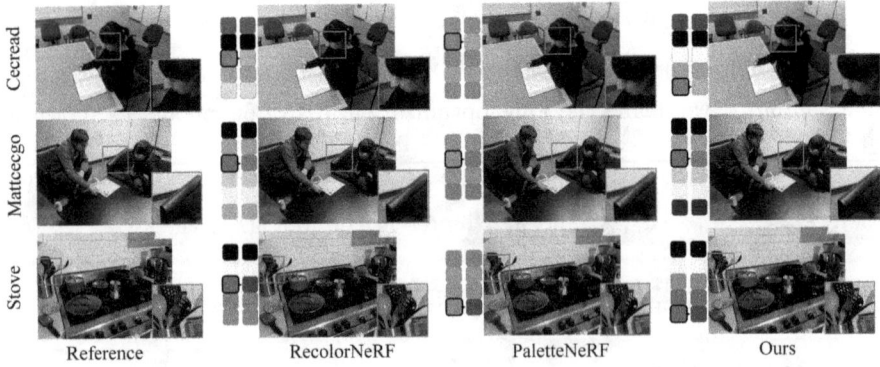

Fig. 7. Qualitative comparisons with RecolorNeRF [6] and PaletteNeRF [8] on the LLFF Datasets [11]

Qualitative Comparison. We compare our method with 4 recent state-of-the-art image-level or NeRF-level color editing baselines. As shown in Fig. 6, our method can accurately extract editable palette bases and recolor them without contaminating other regions. In contrast, PosterNeRF [17], RecolorNeRF [6], and PaletteNeRF [8] tend to mix the colors of the editing region with unwanted areas, resulting in color pollution. For instance, in Fig. 6, while changing the color of the drums from red to green, the results obtained by PosterNeRF and PaletteNeRF show that the color of the cymbals was also polluted with green. Figure 7 presents the comparison results of our approach with RecolorNeRF [6] and PaletteNeRF on the LLFF datasets [11]. Similarly, in Fig. 7, when attempting to change the red color of the chair to green, both RecolorNeRF and PaletteNeRF severely contaminated the facial colors of the person in scene. In Fig. 8, we also compared our model with the image-based recoloring method proposed by Tan et al. [15] on the real-world scenes LLFF datasets. Tan et al.'s method had to modify multiple palette bases simultaneously to achieve the goal of changing the green color of leaves to yellow, but it still severely contaminated the color of the flowers.

Fig. 8. Qualitative comparison with Tan et al. [15] on the LLFF Datasets

Quantitative Comparison. To evaluate the rendering quality of our method, we conducted a comparison between our approach and the original backbone model, RecolorNeRF, and PaletteNeRF in terms of photometric errors. As presented in Table 1, we reported PSNR, SSIM, and LPIPS metrics. The results obtained from our model, which initializes the palette using automatic RGB

Table 1. Quantitative comparisons with the original backbone, RecolorNeRF and PaletteNeRF on Synthetic-NeRF [12] and LLFF [11] Datasets. All scores are averages across all tested datasets

	PSNR ↑	SSIM ↑	LPIPS ↓
Original TensoRF	29.83	0.895	0.179
RecolorNeRF (User init.)	29.21	0.881	0.192
RecolorNeRF (Auto init.)	30.26	0.912	0.175
PaletteNeRF	29.74	0.886	0.181
Ours	30.61	0.913	0.173

Fig. 9. Qualitative ablation study on $\mathcal{L}_{esr}$ and $\mathcal{C}_{cor}$

4.3 Ablation Experiments

In order to verify the improvement of our proposed Loss on model performance, we conducted ablation experiments on the LLFF datasets [11]. As shown in Fig. 9, with the $\mathcal{L}_{esr}$ constraint, the rendered results have less contamination, while with $\mathcal{C}_{cor}$, the colors of the rendered results are closer to the real image. This is because the $\mathcal{L}_{esr}$ and $\mathcal{C}_{cor}$ integrated within our model produce more reasonable palette and blending weights, ensuring minimal color contamination when modifying the color of a specific palette due to mixing with other colors. Additionally, it avoids color distortion caused by overly simplified colors while ensuring sparsity in the weights. Meanwhile, we also compared their quantitative results, as shown in Table 2. Our method performs better on the PSNR, SSIM, and LPIPS metrics, further validating the effectiveness of our proposed $\mathcal{L}_{esr}$ and $\mathcal{C}_{cor}$.

Table 2. Quantitative ablation study results on $\mathcal{L}_{esr}$ and $\mathcal{C}_{cor}$

	PSNR ↑	SSIM ↑	LPIPS ↓
w/o $\mathcal{L}_{esr}$	30.24	0.906	0.175
w/o $\mathcal{C}_{cor}$	27.05	0.811	0.216
Ours	**30.61**	**0.913**	**0.173**

4.4 Object-Level Color Editing Experiment

As depicted in Fig. 10, our method enables individual color manipulation of objects with the same color. For instance, consider the image of "Drums" containing three yellow cymbals. With our solution, one can alter the color of either one, two, or all three cymbals without any impact on the color of other cymbals.

5 Conclusion

We present a novel framework called ICM-NeRF for achieving color editing functionality in NeRF based on palette methods. This framework can address the issue of color contamination and distortion by proposing ESR and color correction functions. Furthermore, this framework supports object-level recoloring capabilities.

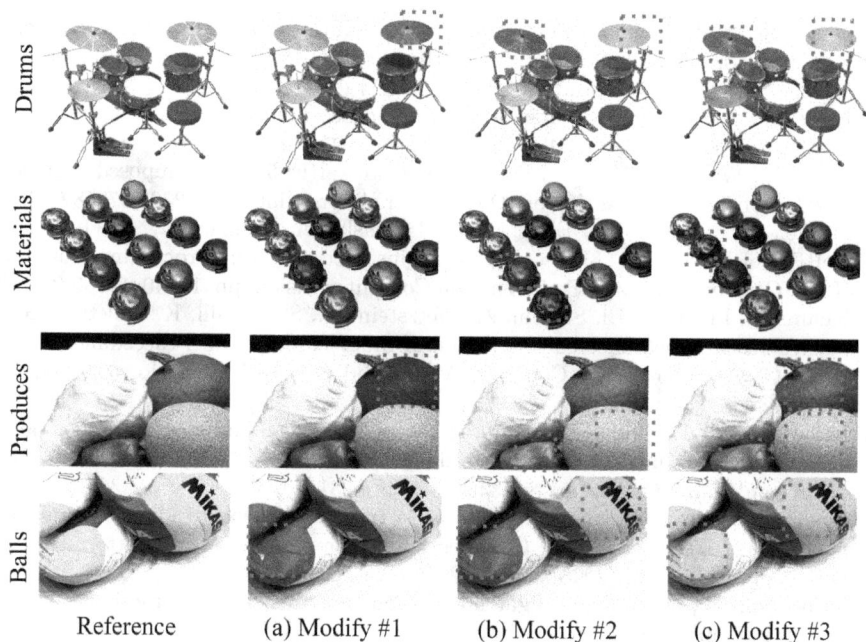

Fig. 10. Modify the color of multiple objects that share the same color individually on the Synthetic-NeRF [12] and DTU [1] datasets

Limitations. To achieve object-level recoloring, we utilize the information of point clouds. However, we also face some disadvantages of using point clouds. In certain scenarios, a limited number of images may result in an overly sparse point cloud. Additionally, objects with similar colors located too closely in the scene may lead to an overly dense point cloud, which can affect the final object clustering results. Therefore, ICM-NeRF's next steps will focus on optimizing the clustering effect of point clouds or incorporating object segmentation network models.

References

1. Aanæs, H., Jensen, R.R., Vogiatzis, G., Tola, E., Dahl, A.B.: Large-scale data for multiple-view stereopsis. Int. J. Comput. Vis. **120**(2), 153–168 (2016). https://doi.org/10.1007/s11263-016-0902-9
2. Brooks, T., Holynski, A., Efros, A.A.: InstructPix2Pix: learning to follow image editing instructions. In: Proceedings of the IEEE/CVF Conference on Computer Vision and Pattern Recognition, pp. 18392–18402 (2023)
3. Chen, A., Xu, Z., Geiger, A., Yu, J., Su, H.: TensoRF: tensorial radiance fields. In: Avidan, S., Brostow, G., Cissé, M., Farinella, G.M., Hassner, T. (eds.) Computer Vision – ECCV 2022: 17th European Conference, Tel Aviv, Israel, October 23–27, 2022, Proceedings, Part XXXII, pp. 333–350. Springer Nature Switzerland, Cham (2022). https://doi.org/10.1007/978-3-031-19824-3_20

4. Ding, Y., et al.: TransMVSnet: global context-aware multi-view stereo network with transformers. In: Proceedings of the IEEE/CVF Conference on Computer Vision and Pattern Recognition, pp. 8585–8594 (2022)
5. Ester, M., et al.: A density-based algorithm for discovering clusters in large spatial databases with noise. In: KDD. vol. 96, pp. 226–231 (1996)
6. Gong, B., Wang, Y., Han, X., Dou, Q.: RecolorNeRF: layer decomposed radiance field for efficient color editing of 3D scenes. arXiv preprint arXiv:2301.07958 (2023)
7. Haque, A., Tancik, M., Efros, A.A., Holynski, A., Kanazawa, A.: Instruct-NeRF2NeRF: editing 3D scenes with instructions. In: Proceedings of the IEEE/CVF International Conference on Computer Vision, pp. 19740–19750 (2023)
8. Kuang, Z., Luan, F., Bi, S., Shu, Z., Wetzstein, G., Sunkavalli, K.: PaletteNeRF: palette-based appearance editing of neural radiance fields. In: Proceedings of the IEEE/CVF Conference on Computer Vision and Pattern Recognition, pp. 20691–20700 (2023)
9. Lee, J.H., Kim, D.S.: Ice-NeRF: interactive color editing of nerfs via decomposition-aware weight optimization. In: Proceedings of the IEEE/CVF International Conference on Computer Vision, pp. 3491–3501 (2023)
10. Liu, K., et al.: StyleRF: zero-shot 3d style transfer of neural radiance fields. In: Proceedings of the IEEE/CVF Conference on Computer Vision and Pattern Recognition, pp. 8338–8348 (2023)
11. Mildenhall, B., et al.: Local light field fusion: practical view synthesis with prescriptive sampling guidelines. ACM Trans. Graph. (TOG) **38**(4), 1–14 (2019)
12. Mildenhall, B., Srinivasan, P.P., Tancik, M., Barron, J.T., Ramamoorthi, R., Ng, R.: NeRF: representing scenes as neural radiance fields for view synthesis. Commun. ACM **65**(1), 99–106 (2021)
13. Nguyen, R.M., Price, B., Cohen, S., Brown, M.S.: Group-theme recoloring for multi-image color consistency. In: Computer Graphics Forum. vol. 36, pp. 83–92. Wiley Online Library (2017)
14. Song, L., Cao, L., Gu, J., Jiang, Y., Yuan, J., Tang, H.: Efficient-NeRF2NeRF: streamlining text-driven 3D editing with multiview correspondence-enhanced diffusion models. arXiv preprint arXiv:2312.08563 (2023)
15. Tan, J., Echevarria, J., Gingold, Y.: Efficient palette-based decomposition and recoloring of images via RGBXY-space geometry. ACM Trans. Graph. (TOG) **37**(6), 1–10 (2018)
16. Tan, J., Lien, J.M., Gingold, Y.: Decomposing images into layers via RGB-space geometry. ACM Trans. Graph. (TOG) **36**(1), 1–14 (2016)
17. Tojo, K., Umetani, N.: Recolorable posterization of volumetric radiance fields using visibility-weighted palette extraction. In: Computer Graphics Forum. vol. 41, pp. 149–160. Wiley Online Library (2022)
18. Wang, B., Dutt, N.S., Mitra, N.J.: ProteusNeRF: fast lightweight NeRF editing using 3D-aware image context. arXiv preprint arXiv:2310.09965 (2023)
19. Wang, C., Chai, M., He, M., Chen, D., Liao, J.: Clip-NeRF: text-and-image driven manipulation of neural radiance fields. In: Proceedings of the IEEE/CVF Conference on Computer Vision and Pattern Recognition, pp. 3835–3844 (2022)
20. Wang, Y., Liu, Y., Xu, K.: An improved geometric approach for palette-based image decomposition and recoloring. In: Computer Graphics Forum. vol. 38, pp. 11–22. Wiley Online Library (2019)
21. Wu, Q., Tan, J., Xu, K.: PaletteNeRF: palette-based color editing for NeRFs. arXiv preprint arXiv:2212.12871 (2022)
22. Zhang, Q., Xiao, C., Sun, H., Tang, F.: Palette-based image recoloring using color decomposition optimization. IEEE Trans. Image Process. **26**(4), 1952–1964 (2017)

Multimodal Monocular Dense Depth Estimation with Event-Frame Fusion Using Transformer

Baihui Xiao[1], Jingzehua Xu[1], Zekai Zhang[1], Tianyu Xing[1], Jingjing Wang[2(✉)], and Yong Ren[3]

[1] Tsinghua Shenzhen International Graduate School, Tsinghua University, Shenzhen, China
[2] School of Cyber Science and Technology, Beihang University, Beijing, China
drwangjj@buaa.edu.cn
[3] Department of Electronic Engineering, Tsinghua University, Beijing, China

Abstract. Frame cameras struggle to estimate depth maps accurately under abnormal lighting conditions. In contrast, event cameras, with their high temporal resolution and high dynamic range, can capture sparse, asynchronous event streams that record pixel brightness changes, addressing the limitations of frame cameras. However, the potential of asynchronous events remains underexploited, which hinders the ability of event cameras to predict dense depth maps effectively. Integrating event streams with frame data can significantly enhance the monocular depth estimation accuracy, especially in complex scenarios. In this study, we introduce a novel depth estimation framework that combines event and frame data using a transformer-based model. Our proposed framework contains two primary components: a multimodal encoder and a joint decoder. The multimodal encoder employs self-attention mechanisms to analyze the interactions between frame patches and event tensors, mapping out dependencies across local and global spatiotemporal events. This multi-scale fusion approach maximizes the benefits of both event and frame inputs. The joint decoder incorporates a dual-phase, triple-scale feature fusion module, which extracts contextual information and delivers detailed depth prediction results. Our experimental results on the EventScape and MVSEC datasets affirm that our method sets a new benchmark in performance.

Keywords: Frame Camera · Event Camera · Multi-modal Fusion · Transformer self-attention · Monocular depth estimation

1 Introduction

Due to its simple structure, wide field of view, and low cost, monocular depth estimation has been widely used in many computer vision tasks such as simultaneous localization and mapping [30], autonomous driving [15,22], medical imaging [20]. This technology relies on a single viewpoint to predict pixel-level scene

---

B. Xiao and J. Xu—These authors contributed equally to this work.

© The Author(s), under exclusive license to Springer Nature Switzerland AG 2024
M. Wand et al. (Eds.): ICANN 2024, LNCS 15017, pp. 419–433, 2024.
https://doi.org/10.1007/978-3-031-72335-3_29

depth maps, enhancing the understanding of 3D scenes. Conventional monocular depth estimation primarily utilizes standard cameras, which are frame-based sensors. These include various learning frameworks [11,16,22,31,32]. However, frame-based depth estimation methods exhibit certain limitations, particularly when dealing with changes in illumination, which impair their ability to distinguish between different objects. In contrast, the emerging bio-inspired vision sensor, known as the event camera, can report changes in pixel brightness. This capability allows it to compensate for the shortcomings of frame-based cameras, earning it widespread attention in the field.

Compared to frame cameras, event cameras possess outstanding features such as high temporal resolution, low latency in the order of microseconds, and a high dynamic range of 140dB. They hold great potential in high dynamic range applications such as object tracking [5,10], optical flow estimation [1,7], depth estimation [12,14,24,34,35], and motion segmentation [21,34]. Due to the sparsity of event streams, early research on event-based monocular depth estimation focused mainly on sparse and semi-dense depth estimation [14,24,35]. With the development of deep learning and the introduction of large-scale event-based datasets like MVSEC [33], EventScape [8], and DENSE [12], significant progress has been made in dense depth estimation based on events. In [12], the authors utilized recursive networks to predict dense monocular depth maps purely based on events, demonstrating the event camera's ability to capture texture and edge detail changes with high spatiotemporal resolution. However, event-based estimation methods also have their limitations. On the one hand, triggering events only when the pixel intensity changes beyond a certain threshold can result in the loss of small details, while some textures may not trigger events, leading to edge blurring and detail loss in event-based predictions. On the other hand, it is inappropriate to solely use events as input and generate depth maps because it fails to provide intensity variations without initial intensity values.

The introduction of Dynamic and Active-pixel Vision Sensor (DAVIS) [2] has expanded the possibilities for research into algorithms based on events and frames [23]. Gehrig et al. [8] make the first attempt at monocular depth estimation using multimodal inputs, proposing a fully convolutional encoder-decoder architecture based on UNet. This architecture, employing Convolutional Neural Networks (CNNs) as feature extractors and integrating temporal contexts from different sensors through recurrency, outperforms pure frame-based or event-based methods in complex real-world scenarios. However, due to the inherent limitations of convolution operations, the modeling of dependencies between local patches is inadequate [32], leading to insufficient exploration of correlations between asynchronous events. To enhance feature learning and improve depth estimation accuracy, it is crucial for us to examine the relationships between events.

To address the challenges outlined above, we propose a Transformer-based multimodal monocular dense depth estimation framework fused with frames and events. This framework includes a multimodal encoder with a self-attention mechanism and a joint decoder. During the encoding phase, we aggregate frames and events into tensor-like voxels for input and feature extraction at different spatial resolutions. We then utilize a self-attention mechanism to examine the correlations between frame patches and event blocks, respectively. Through the self-attention layer, local events are associated with spatio-temporal global events, describing the dependencies between events. To better integrate information from events and frames, we fuse multimodal feature maps across multiple spatial resolutions. In the decoding phase, a two-stage triple-scale feature fusion module is employed to extract contextual information and generate detail-preserved predictions. To optimize the framework, we adopt a joint loss function, including scale-invariant loss and multi-scale scale-invariant gradient matching loss, to reduce the discrepancy between predicted depth maps and ground truth and smooth gradient changes. To evaluate the performance of our proposed method, we conducted experiments on the synthetic dataset EventScape and the real-world MVSEC dataset. Our method surpasses state-of-the-art methods [8,12,32] in both quantification and visualization.

The remainder of this paper is structured as follows: Sect. 2 reviews related work on monocular depth estimation and the progress of Transformers in computer vision. Section 3 introduces the proposed algorithmic framework, including the encoder, decoder, depth representation, and optimization objectives. Section 4 presents experiments and comparisons on the EventScape and MVSEC datasets. Finally, conclusions are drawn in Sect. 5.

2 Related Work

This section provides a brief review of several types of monocular depth estimation methods and the progress of Transformers in computer vision.

Frame-Based Methods: Frame-based monocular depth estimation often relies on CNNs and performs well on common datasets such as KITTI [9] and NYUv2 [25]. Lee et al. [16] used an encoder-decoder architecture and introduced a local plane-guided layer to enhance feature resolution. Song et al. [26] and Huynh et al. [13] improved depth estimation accuracy through continuous conditional random fields and attention mechanisms, respectively. Guizilini et al. [11] enhanced detail representation through 3D convolutional self-supervised learning. Facing the limitations of CNN's receptive field, Yang et al. [32] combined CNNs with Transformer layers, designing a unified attention gate decoder to enhance depth representation learning. The latest research [18] proposed an end-to-end unsupervised network that integrates a channel-space attention block to explore the correlation between features along the channel and spatial dimensions.

Event-Based Methods: Given that event streams are sparse and asynchronous, using event cameras for dense depth estimation poses challenges [12]. Zhu et al. [35] made significant progress in full 6-DoF camera estimation by combining asynchronous algorithms and inertial measurements. In [14], the 6-DoF motion of the camera, scene intensity gradients, and inverse depth were estimated by processing keyframes, enabling the construction of indoor scenes. For the first time, Zhu et al. [34] adopted a joint learning strategy to predict optical flow, ego-motion, and depth, proposing a discretized volume to represent a large number of asynchronous events. Differing from standard feedforward architectures, Hidalgo-Carri'o et al. [12] utilized the temporal consistency of event streams through a recursive architecture, being the first to use the event modality for monocular dense depth prediction and significantly outperforming model-based methods.

Event and Frame-Based Methods: To our knowledge, [8] is the first work that combines events and frames for monocular depth estimation. To leverage asynchronous events and synchronous absolute intensity frames, Gehrig et al. [8] proposed a recurrent asynchronous multimodal network to process asynchronous and irregular data from multiple sensors, achieving state-of-the-art performance in real-world scenes.

Transformer in Computer Vision: Recently, Transformer and self-attention technologies have achieved significant success in computer vision tasks [3,6,28,29]. For instance, axial attention [29] effectively expanded the receptive field without significantly increasing computational costs. DETR [3] leveraged Transformers in object detection, significantly improving detection performance through the self-attention mechanism. ViT [6] interpreted images as a sequence of patches and fed them into a standard Transformer encoder, achieving top-tier results in image classification. TransDepth [32] was the first to combine linear Transformers with ResNet for depth prediction and surface normal estimation tasks using the attention mechanism. To date, no studies have introduced Transformer models with self-attention mechanisms into event-enhanced depth estimation.

3 Method

Figure 1 presents our proposed algorithm framework, comprising a multimodal encoder and a joint decoder. Section 3.1 explains the use of self-attention mechanism within the encoder to explore correlations between frame patches and event tensors, integrating frame and event information through a multimodal feature fusion mechanism. Section 3.2 details a two-level triple-scale fusion module in the decoder for capturing context and generating detailed depth maps. Section 3.3 introduces converting metric depth to logarithmic depth to emphasize changes. Lastly, Sect. 3.4 discusses a joint loss function combining scale-invariant and multiscale gradient matching losses to minimize pixel differences and smooth gradients, enhancing the framework's overall performance.

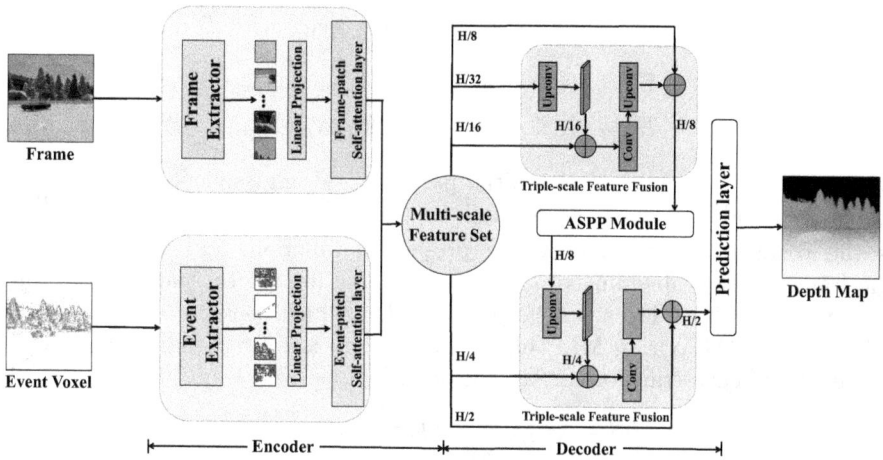

Fig. 1. The pipeline of the proposed method. Taking the frames obtained from standard cameras and events from event cameras as input, the proposed method generates the dense prediction depth map via the encoder-decoder framework. A self-attention mechanism is leveraged to investigate the correlation between patches of frames and event tensors, respectively, which can effectively improve the performance of predicting dense depth maps

3.1 Encoder

Event Representation: Since the input form of the convolutional neural network (CNNs) is synchronous, asynchronous events need to be transformed into synchronous representations. Based on [8,12,34], we transform a set of input events $I_k = \{e_k^i\}_{i=0}^{S-1}$ within the time window $\Delta t = t_{S-1} - t_0$ into a tensor-like voxel grid $G_k \in \mathbb{R}^{H \times W}$ with B temporal bins

$$G_k(\boldsymbol{u}, t) = \sum p_i \Delta(\boldsymbol{u}_i - \boldsymbol{u}) \max\{0, 1 - |t - t_i^*|\}, \forall e_i \in I_k, \quad (1)$$

where $\boldsymbol{u}_i$ and p_i denote the coordinates of the trigger time e_k^i, and the polarities, respectively. $t_i^* = \frac{B-1}{\Delta t}$ and t_i represents the timestamp. The parameters are set to $B = 5$ and $\Delta t = 50$ ms, [8,12].

Self-attention Mechanism: The ImageNet-based pre-trained ResNet is used to extract features for multiple modalities and spatial resolutions. Then, a sequence of flattened local 2D event patches $E_p \in \mathbb{R}^{N \times H}$ and frame patches $F_p \in \mathbb{R}^{N \times H}$ are obtained, where N and H denote the total number of patches and the dimension of the patch-based features, respectively. Since the potential vector size D keeps constant for all transformer layers, we must project the 2D patches individually into a potential embedding space with D dimensions

$$E^0 = \{\lambda_e^1 \Phi, \lambda_e^2 \Phi \ldots, \lambda_e^N \Phi\}, \lambda_e^i \in E_p, \quad (2a)$$
$$F^0 = \{\lambda_f^1 \Psi, \lambda_f^2 \Psi \ldots, \lambda_f^N \Psi\}, \lambda_f^i \in F_p, \quad (2b)$$

where E^0 and F^0 represent the initial patch embedding sequence of events and frames. λ_e^i and λ_f^i denote each patch of the events and frames. $\Phi \in \mathbb{R}^{H \times D}$ is the voxel grid patch embedding projection function, and $\Psi \in \mathbb{R}^{H \times D}$ is the frame patch embedding projection. Then, we import the patch embedding sequence into the L-layer transformer encoder, which consists of a multi-head self-attention (MSA), an MLP block (MLP), and a layer paradigm (LN). The processing of each transformer layer is described as

$$\begin{cases} \hat{E}^l = \mathbf{MSA}\left(\mathbf{LN}\left(E^{l-1}\right)\right) + E^{l-1}, \\ E^l = \mathbf{MSA}\left(\mathbf{LN}\left(\hat{E}^{l-1}\right)\right) + \hat{E}^{l-1}, \\ \hat{F}^l = \mathbf{MSA}\left(\mathbf{LN}\left(F^{l-1}\right)\right) + F^{l-1}, \\ F^l = \mathbf{MSA}\left(\mathbf{LN}\left(\hat{F}^{l-1}\right)\right) + \hat{F}^{l-1}. \end{cases} \quad (3)$$

The multi-head attention mechanism is used to evaluate the relationship between local patches. The attention function can be depicted as a projection operation from the input to the output vector [6,28]. In multi-head attention, the features are divided into N_d heads and corresponding N_d subspaces, where the sub-features are $D_d = D/N_d$ dimensions. A tuple containing a query (Q_d), a key (K_d), and a value (V_d) is the input of the MSA layer, and the d-th head of the l-th transformer layer is described based on the learnable parameters W_Q^d, W_K^d and $W_V^d \in \mathbb{R}^{D_d \times D}$

$$Q_E^d = W_Q^d \cdot E^{l-1}, K_E^d = W_K^d \cdot E^{l-1}, V_E^d = W_V^d \cdot E^{l-1}, \quad (4a)$$
$$Q_F^d = W_Q^d \cdot F^{l-1}, K_F^d = W_K^d \cdot F^{l-1}, V_F^d = W_V^d \cdot F^{l-1}. \quad (4b)$$

Consequently, the weights of the values are calculated as

$$\gamma_E^d = softmax\left(\frac{Q_E^d \times K_E^{d^T}}{\sqrt{D_d}}\right), \quad (5a)$$

$$\gamma_F^d = softmax\left(\frac{Q_F^d \times K_F^{d^T}}{\sqrt{D_d}}\right). \quad (5b)$$

The MSA operation is gained as

$$\mathbf{MSA}(E^l) = concat\left(\gamma_1 \cdot V_E^1, \gamma_2 \cdot V_E^2 \ldots, \gamma_{N_d} \cdot V_E^{N_d}\right) \cdot W^O, \quad (6a)$$
$$\mathbf{MSA}(F^l) = concat\left(\gamma_1 \cdot V_F^1, \gamma_2 \cdot V_F^2 \ldots, \gamma_{N_d} \cdot V_F^{N_d}\right) \cdot W^O. \quad (6b)$$

Finally, $E^L, E^L \in \mathbb{R}^{N \times D}$ are obtained, and the patches embedded in the D-dimensional space are projected into the feature space separately.

Multi-modal Feature Fusion Mechanism: The obtained event and frame feature maps with different spatial resolutions are noted as M_E and M_F, respectively. The feature map set in different modal spaces is projected into a common space based on the dominance of events and frames. Then, the multi-scale fusion feature is obtained by element-wise addition

$$M_E = \{m_E^i\}_{i=1}^K, M_F = \{m_F^i\}_{i=1}^K, \tag{7a}$$

$$m^i = m_E^i \oplus m_F^i, M = \{m^i\}_{i=1}^K, \tag{7b}$$

where $\oplus$ is the point-wise addition. In the feature map $m^i = \left[BC \times 2^i, \frac{H}{2^i}, \frac{W}{2^i}\right]$, BC denotes the base channel.

3.2 Decoder

The two-stage Triple-Scale Feature Fusion (TSFF) module is connected by using the Atrous Spatial Pyramid Pooling (ASPP) module [4,16]. The TSFF module is depicted as a projection from the input with size $\{[\frac{H}{N},\frac{H}{N}],[\frac{H}{2N},\frac{H}{2N}],[\frac{H}{4N},\frac{H}{4N}]\}$ to the output with size $\{[\frac{H}{N},\frac{H}{N}]\}$. The parameters in the two stages are set to $N=8$ and $N=2$. The ration parameters in the ASPP are set to $[3,6,12,18,24]$. The output map $o \in \mathbb{R}^{H \times W \times BC}$ of the last upconv layer is fed into the final convolutional layer to get the final depth estimate $\tilde{D}$.

3.3 Depth Representation

Based on [8,12], the metric depth maps are converted to log depth maps, which allows the proposed method to possess adaptive learning of significant depth variations and predict log depth maps. For the metric depth map $D_m(u)$, the log depth map $D_l(u)$ is pixel-wise computed as

$$D_l(u) = \frac{1}{\beta} \log \frac{D_m(u)}{D_{max}} + 1, \tag{8}$$

where D_{max} is the maximum metric depth, and β is used to align the 0 depth position with the nearest position of the original depth map. Followed by E2Depth and RAMNet [8,12] in the experiment, the EventScope dataset uses parameters $\beta = 5.7$ and $D_{max} = 1000$, while the MVSEC dataset uses parameters $\beta = 3.7$ and $D_{max} = 80.0$.

3.4 Problem Formulation

A supervised learning mechanism is used for the experiments, and the predicted log-depth map $\tilde{D}(u)$ and the ground true log-depth map $D(u)$ denote the corresponding log-depth values of the pixels with coordinates u. A joint loss function consisting of the scale-invariant loss function and the multi-scale scale-invariant gradient matching loss function is used to optimize the framework.

Algorithm 1 The generation and objective of our proposed method.

Require: The training dataset $\mathcal{S} = \{(P_k, I_k, D_k)\}_{k=1}^{N}$, the mini-batch size n_m, the learning rate ς, the maximal number of epochs $\mathcal{M}$.
1: Randomly initialize the parameters of the encoder θ_E and the parameters of the decoder θ_D.
2: **for** $i = 1$ to $\mathcal{M}$ **do**
3:    **for** $j = 1$ to $\left\lfloor \frac{n}{n_j} \right\rfloor$ **do**
4:      **Construct** training mini-batch by randomly selecting n_m samples from $\mathcal{S}$.
5:      **Aggregate** a group of input events I_k into the tensor-like voxel grid G_k.
6:      **Extract** the feature frames map set M_F and events map set M_E for each sample in the mini-batch by forwarding propagation.
7:      **Flatten** a sequence of local 2D event-patch maps $E_{k,p}$ and frame-patch maps $F_{k,p}$ in the specific dimension.
8:      **Projection** $E_k^0 = E_{k,p}\Phi, F_k^0 = F_{k,p}\Phi$.
9:      **for** $l = 1$ to L **do**
10:        $E_k^l = \mathbf{MSA}\left(\mathbf{LN}\left(E_k^{l-1}\right)\right) + E_k^{l-1}$.
11:        $F_k^l = \mathbf{MSA}\left(\mathbf{LN}\left(F_k^{l-1}\right)\right) + F_k^{l-1}$.
12:      **end for**
13:      **Feature Fusion:** $M_k = M_{k,E} \oplus M_{k,F}$.
14:      **Decoder:** $o_k = \mathbf{TSFF}(m_1, m_2, \mathbf{ASPP}(\mathbf{TSFF}(m_3, m_4, m_5)))$.
15:      **Prediction:** $\tilde{D}_k = \mathbf{Prediction\ Layer}(o_k)$.
16:      Calculate the loss function L_{pg} and L_g by Equations 9 and 10.
17:      Update the parameters of the encoder and the decoder by minimizing L with: $\theta_E = \theta_E - \varsigma \frac{\partial L}{\partial \theta_E}$, $\theta_D = \theta_D - \varsigma \frac{\partial L}{\partial \theta_D}$.
18:    **end for**
19: **end for**

The difference between the predicted pixel depth and the ground truth pixel depth [7] is decreased by using a scale-invariant loss function, which is described as

$$L_{pg} = \frac{1}{n}\sum_{u}\left(\tilde{D}(u) - D(u)\right)^2 - \frac{1}{n^2}\sum_{u}\left(\tilde{D}(u) - D(u)\right)^2, \qquad (9)$$

where n is the total number of valid pixels.

The multi-scale scale-invariant gradient matching loss function smooths the change in gradient [17], which is expressed as

$$L_g = \frac{1}{n}\sum_{k}\sum_{u}\left(\left|\frac{\partial\left(\tilde{D}(u) - D(u)\right)^k}{\partial x}\right| + \left|\frac{\partial\left(\tilde{D}(u) - D(u)\right)^k}{\partial y}\right|\right), \qquad (10)$$

where k stands for four different scales. Consequently, the total loss is calculated as

$$L = \omega_1 L_{pg} + \omega_2 L_g, \qquad (11)$$

where $\omega_1 = 1.0$ and $\omega_1 = 0.25$ are used to construct the loss function L [8].

Thus, Algorithm 1 shows the generation and objective of our proposed method.

4 Experiments

In this section, we conducted experiments on the EventScape and MVSEC datasets, and compared our algorithm with advanced methods [8,12,32] through both qualitative and quantitative analysis, presenting the results.

4.1 Dataset

We conduct experiments on the EventScape and MVSEC datasets. EventScape is a large-scale synthetic dataset based on the CARLA simulator, documenting about 2 h and 743 driving sequences, including scenes of pedestrians, cars, and buildings [8]. The dataset's event and frame data simulate DAVIS outputs, achieving alignment and synchronization. On the other hand, the MVSEC dataset is collected under various lighting and environmental conditions, covering driving sequences during both day and night. It uses two DAVIS sensors with a resolution of 346 × 260 pixels to record events and frames, and ground truth depth measurements are made with LiDAR [33].

4.2 Metrics

Following the previous work [11,12,22,32], we adopt the following metrics to quantify our algorithm.

- Abs relative difference (Abs Rel): $\frac{1}{n}\sum_{i=1}^{n} \frac{|d_i - \tilde{d}_i|}{\tilde{d}_i}$.
- Squared relative difference (Sq Rel): $\frac{1}{n}\sum_{i=1}^{n} \frac{|d_i - \tilde{d}_i|^2}{\tilde{d}_i}$.
- Average mean depth error: $\frac{1}{n}\sum_{i=1}^{n} |d_i - \tilde{d}_i|$.
- Mean log error (RMS-log): $\sqrt{\frac{1}{n}\sum_{i=1}^{n} |\ln(d_i) - \ln(\tilde{d}_i)|^2}$.
- Scale Invariant log error (SI-log): $\frac{1}{n}\sum_{i=1}^{n} |\ln(d_i) - \ln(\tilde{d}_i)|^2 - \frac{1}{n}\sum_{i=1}^{n} |\ln((d_i) - (\tilde{d}_i))|^2$.
- Accuracy with threshold t: percentage(%) of $\tilde{d}_i$, subject to $\max\left(\frac{\tilde{d}_i}{d_y}, \frac{d_i}{d_y}\right) = \Delta < t, t \in [1.25, 1.25^2, 1.25^3]$,

where $\tilde{d}_i$ and d_i are the predicted value and ground-truth value at i-th pixel respectively, while n is the total number of valid pixels.

4.3 Experimental Setup

Our proposed algorithm model is implemented in PyTorch on four NVIDIA 1080Ti GPUs with 11 GB memory each. We optimize the network using Adam with a minibatch size of 16 and an initial learning rate of 0.003, which is halved every 50 epochs. For compatibility and improved learning, the input data is

Table 1. The quantitative results on evenscape dataset. The predictions generated by our method outperforms those generated by TransDepth and RAM Net. Ours (event), ours (frame), our (baseline) denote the proposed method without frames inputs, events inputs and the self-attention layer respectively. ↓ indicates lower is better and ↑ indicates higher is better. The best scores are shown in bold

Method	Abs Rel↓	Sq Rel↓	RMSE log↓	SI log↓	$\Delta < 1.25$ ↑	$\Delta < 1.25^2$ ↑	$\Delta < 1.25^3$ ↑
Ours(event)	0.321	4.849	0.384	0.129	0.804	0.892	0.936
Ours(frame)	0.269	4.683	0.313	0.092	0.825	0.906	0.954
TransDepth	0.261	1.555	0.393	0.114	0.755	0.848	0.904
RAM Net	0.157	0.886	0.315	0.096	0.821	0.907	0.954
Ours(baseline)	0.262	0.909	0.406	0.120	0.747	0.845	0.910
Ours	**0.134**	**0.739**	**0.274**	**0.065**	**0.846**	**0.932**	**0.967**

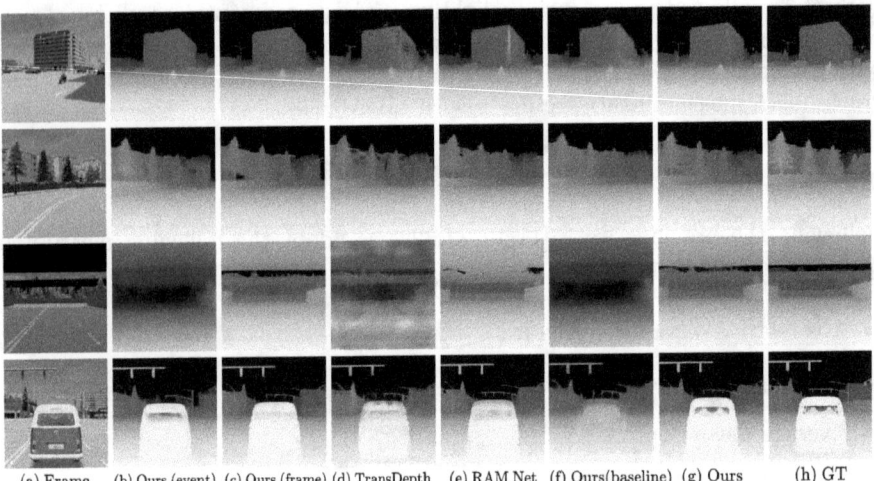

(a) Frame (b) Ours (event) (c) Ours (frame) (d) TransDepth (e) RAM Net (f) Ours(baseline) (g) Ours (h) GT

Fig. 2. Visualization results of monocular depth estimations on EventScape dataset. From left to right: the input frames, results generated by our method with only events, our method with only frames, TransDepth, RAMNet [8], our method without self-attention layer, and our method

normalized and randomly cropped to 224 × 224 for EventScape and 320 × 256 for MVSEC. First, we train and evaluate our algorithm model on EventScape, following the split in [8]. To assess robustness and generalization under abnormal lighting conditions, we pre-train the model on synthetic dataset, fine-tune it on outdoor day2 sequences in MVSEC, and evaluate on outdoor daytime and night sequences.

4.4 Experimental Results and Analysis

First, we compare our proposed method with two leading monocular depth estimation methods: TransDepth, a frame-based approach, and RAMNet, a multi-

Table 2. Average absolute depth error (in meters) at different cut-off depth distance (lower is better) on outdoor night sequences in mvsec dataset. The best scores are shown in bold

Dataset	Distance	Frame-based		Event-based		Event- and Frame-based		
		TransDepth	Ours (frame)	E2Depth	Ours (event)	RAMNet	Ours (baseline)	Ours
day1	10 m	1.38	1.41	1.85	1.22	1.39	1.40	**1.03**
	20 m	2.31	2.17	2.64	2.20	2.17	2.21	**1.73**
	30 m	2.88	2.59	3.13	2.65	2.76	2.89	**2.20**
night1	10 m	1.44	1.34	3.38	1.75	2.50	1.56	**1.34**
	20 m	2.46	2.25	3.82	2.74	3.19	2.28	**2.09**
	30 m	3.46	3.42	4.46	3.22	3.82	3.25	**3.04**
night2	10 m	1.60	1.21	1.67	1.77	1.21	1.59	**1.21**
	20 m	2.94	2.70	2.63	2.85	2.31	2.60	**2.24**
	30 m	4.12	4.16	3.58	3.40	**3.28**	3.66	3.35
night3	10 m	1.43	1.05	1.42	1.50	1.01	1.42	**1.01**
	20 m	2.83	2.64	2.33	2.64	2.34	2.50	**2.11**
	30 m	4.07	4.15	**3.18**	3.18	3.43	3.58	3.25

modal approach, on the EventScape dataset. The quantitative comparison results are shown in Table I, demonstrating that our proposed method achieves favorable results across various evaluation metrics. In terms of the key metric Abs Rel, our method improves by 15% compared to RAMNet and nearly 50% compared to TransDepth. Figure 2 provides qualitative comparisons, revealing that our method effectively preserves local information by utilizing self-attention mechanisms within modalities, outperforming RAMNet. Furthermore, our method combines frame and event data, enabling the capture of richer scenes and more details, surpassing pure frame-based and pure event-based methods. To demonstrate the superiority of our proposed method in real-world scenarios, we compare it with TransDepth, event-based method E2Depth [12], and RAMNet. All methods are pretrained on synthetic datasets, fine-tuned on outdoor day2 sequences in MVSEC, and evaluated on outdoor daytime and night sequences in MVSEC. The quantitative comparison results in Table 2 indicate improvements in terms of mean depth error in different cutoffs in different sequences for our method. Compared to TransDepth, our method achieves an average improvement of 20%, 22%, and 17% at 10 m, 20 m, and 30 m, respectively. Compared to E2Depth, the average improvements are 45%, 27%, and 14% at 10 m, 20 m, and 30 m, respectively. Compared to RAMNet, the average improvements are 25%, 18%, and 8% at 10 m, 20 m, and 30 m, respectively. Qualitative comparison results in Fig. 3 show that under low-light night conditions, frame-based methods miss a significant amount of information and fail to recognize scenes. Event-based methods can capture detailed brightness changes with high spatiotemporal resolution, compensating for the limitations of pure frame methods

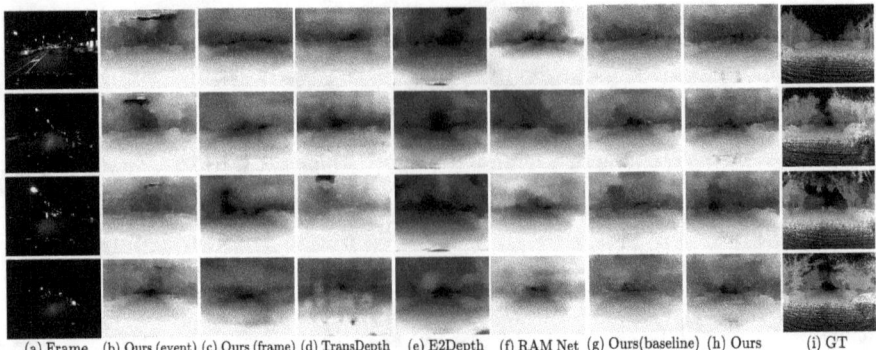

(a) Frame (b) Ours (event) (c) Ours (frame) (d) TransDepth (e) E2Depth (f) RAM Net (g) Ours(baseline) (h) Ours (i) GT

Fig. 3. Visualization results of monocular depth estimations on MVSEC dataset. From left to right: the input frames, results generated by our method with only events, our method with only frames, TransDepth [32], E2Depth [12], RAMNet [8], our method without self-attention layer and our method. From top to bottom, they correspond to the scene samples in outdoor night1 sequences, outdoor night2 sequences, and outdoor night3 sequences respectively

in low-light conditions. However, pure event-based methods may miss some subtle details and textures in-depth estimation due to events being triggered only when pixel brightness crosses a certain threshold. By exploring the correlations between frame patches and event tensors, our proposed method exhibits better local feature preservation than the frame and event-based RAMNet. Experimental analysis in challenging real environments confirms that the combination of frame and event modalities, along with the utilization of self-attention mechanisms through self-attention layers to study patch correlations, is crucial for predicting depth maps with more accurate details and contours, thus validating the rationality and effectiveness of our proposed method.

Effect of Different Modalities: We compare the depth estimation results of our proposed method using different modalities as input. From the quantitative comparison results on EventScape in Table I, it can be observed that using a combination of frame and event inputs (ours) improves the Abs Rel metric by 58% compared to using pure event inputs (ours(event)) and by 50% compared to using pure frame inputs (ours(frame)). Similarly, from the quantitative comparison results on MVSEC in Table 2, it can be seen that the combination of event and frame inputs significantly enhances performance across different sequences in the dataset. The qualitative results shown in Figs. 2 and 3 further support these findings. The pure frame input method misses crucial information, leading to the inability of our proposed method to recognize scenes. Although the pure event input method shows some improvement in detail, it fails to provide a hierarchical representation of objects at different distances. Additionally, the presence of black dots in the predicted depth maps degrades the overall evaluation metrics. The combination of frame and event inputs leverages the information from both modalities, resulting in a significant improvement in the performance of our proposed method.

Effect of Transformer Layers: We perform ablation experiments to demonstrate the effectiveness of the transformer layer, referred to as "Ours" (baseline). The quantitative results of our method without the transformer layer are shown in Tables 1 and 2. The experimental results indicate that removing the transformer layer leads to a significant decrease in most evaluation metrics. Compared to the baseline, our approach achieves a 15% improvement in Abs Rel in the EventScape dataset and an average improvement of 22% at 10 m, 12% at 20 m, and 8% at 30 m in terms of mean depth error in the MVSEC dataset. As depicted in Fig. 2 and Fig. 3, the predictions of our method without the transformer layer lack silhouette details and contain more noise.

5 Conclusion

In this paper, we propose a framework for multimodal monocular dense depth estimation based on the Transformer, which takes frames and events as input to leverage the advantages of both modalities on monocular depth estimation tasks. A self-attention mechanism is introduced to investigate the correlation between patches of frames and event tensors, respectively. Then, we fuse the feature maps of both modalities with different spatial resolutions and obtain depth predictions with distinct and layered details via the decoding stage. Experimental qualitative and quantitative results show that the proposed method significantly outperforms the state-of-the-art method on the synthetic dataset EventScape and the challenging real scenarios MVSEC dataset. The ablation study and visualization results further show the effectiveness of the self-attention mechanism and the necessity of the combination of events and frames.

Acknowledgement. This work of Jingjing Wang was partly supported by the National Natural Science Foundation of China under Grant No. 62071268 and No. 62222101, partly supported by the Young Elite Scientist Sponsorship Program by the China Association for Science and Technology under Grant No. 2020QNRC001, and partly supported by the Fundamental Research Funds for the Central Universities. This work of Yong Ren was partly supported by the National Natural Science Foundation of China under Grant 62127801, partly supported by the National Key Research and Development Program of China under Grant 2020YFD0901000.

References

1. Benosman, R., Clercq, C., Lagorce, X., Ieng, S.H., Bartolozzi, C.: Event-based visual flow. IEEE Trans. Neural Netw. Learn. Syst. **25**(2), 407–417 (2013)
2. Brandli, C., Berner, R., Yang, M., Liu, S.C., Delbruck, T.: A 240 × 180 130 db 3 μs latency global shutter spatiotemporal vision sensor. IEEE J. Solid-State Circuits **49**(10), 2333–2341 (2014)

3. Carion, N., Massa, F., Synnaeve, G., Usunier, N., Kirillov, A., Zagoruyko, S.: End-to-end object detection with transformers. In: European Conference on Computer Vision, pp. 213–229 (2020)
4. Chen, L.C., Papandreou, G., Kokkinos, I., Murphy, K., Yuille, A.L.: DeepLab: semantic image segmentation with deep convolutional nets, atrous convolution, and fully connected CRFs. IEEE Trans. Pattern Anal. Mach. Intell. **40**(4), 834–848 (2017)
5. Delbruck, T., Lang, M.: Robotic goalie with 3 ms reaction time at 4% CPU load using event-based dynamic vision sensor. Front. Neurosci. **7**, 223 (2013)
6. Dosovitskiy, A., et al.: An image is worth 16x16 words: transformers for image recognition at scale. arXiv preprint arXiv:2010.11929 (2020)
7. Eigen, D., Puhrsch, C., Fergus, R.: Depth map prediction from a single image using a multi-scale deep network. In: Proceedings of the 27th International Conference on Neural Information Processing Systems, pp. 2366–2374 (2014)
8. Gehrig, D., Rüegg, M., Gehrig, M., Hidalgo-Carrió, J., Scaramuzza, D.: Combining events and frames using recurrent asynchronous multimodal networks for monocular depth prediction. IEEE Robot. Autom. Lett. **6**(2), 2822–2829 (2021)
9. Geiger, A., Lenz, P., Stiller, C., Urtasun, R.: Vision meets robotics: the KITTI dataset. Int. J. Rob. Res. **32**(11), 1231–1237 (2013)
10. Glover, A., Bartolozzi, C.: Event-driven ball detection and gaze fixation in clutter. In: IEEE/RSJ International Conference on Intelligent Robots and Systems, pp. 2203–2208 (2016)
11. Guizilini, V., Ambrus, R., Pillai, S., Raventos, A., Gaidon, A.: 3D packing for self-supervised monocular depth estimation. In: Proceedings of the IEEE/CVF Conference on Computer Vision and Pattern Recognition, pp. 2485–2494 (2020)
12. Hidalgo-Carrió, J., Gehrig, D., Scaramuzza, D.: Learning monocular dense depth from events. In: International Conference on 3D Vision, pp. 534–542 (2020)
13. Huynh, L., Nguyen-Ha, P., Matas, J., Rahtu, E., Heikkilä, J.: Guiding monocular depth estimation using depth-attention volume. In: European Conference on Computer Vision, pp. 581–597 (2020)
14. Kim, H., Leutenegger, S., Davison, A.J.: Real-time 3D reconstruction and 6-DoF tracking with an event camera. In: European Conference on Computer Vision, pp. 349–364 (2016)
15. Laidlow, T., Czarnowski, J., Leutenegger, S.: DeepFusion: Real-time dense 3D reconstruction for monocular slam using single-view depth and gradient predictions. In: 2019 International Conference on Robotics and Automation (ICRA), pp. 4068–4074. IEEE (2019)
16. Lee, J.H., Han, M.K., Ko, D.W., Suh, I.H.: From big to small: multi-scale local planar guidance for monocular depth estimation. arXiv preprint arXiv:1907.10326 (2019)
17. Li, Z., Snavely, N.: MegaDepth: learning single-view depth prediction from internet photos. In: Proceedings of the IEEE Conference on Computer Vision and Pattern Recognition, pp. 2041–2050 (2018)
18. Ling, C., Zhang, X., Chen, H.: Unsupervised monocular depth estimation using attention and multi-warp reconstruction. IEEE Trans. Multimedia **24**, 2938–2949 (2021)
19. Litzenberger, M., et al.: Embedded vision system for real-time object tracking using an asynchronous transient vision sensor. In: IEEE 12th Digital Signal Processing Workshop and 4th IEEE Signal Processing Education Workshop, pp. 173–178 (2006)

20. Liu, X., et al.: Dense depth estimation in monocular endoscopy with self-supervised learning methods. IEEE Trans. Med. Imag. **39**(5), 1438–1447 (2019)
21. Ni, Z., Ieng, S.H., Posch, C., Régnier, S., Benosman, R.: Visual tracking using neuromorphic asynchronous event-based cameras. Neural Comput. **27**(4), 925–953 (2015)
22. Palafox, P.R., Betz, J., Nobis, F., Riedl, K., Lienkamp, M.: SemanticDepth: fusing semantic segmentation and monocular depth estimation for enabling autonomous driving in roads without lane lines. Sensors **19**(14), 3224 (2019)
23. Pini, S., Borghi, G., Vezzani, R., Cucchiara, R.: Video synthesis from intensity and event frames. In: International Conference on Image Analysis and Processing, pp. 313–323 (2019)
24. Rebecq, H., Horstschaefer, T., Scaramuzza, D.: Real-time visual-inertial odometry for event cameras using keyframe-based nonlinear optimization, pp. 1–12 (2017)
25. Silberman, N., Hoiem, D., Kohli, P., Fergus, R.: Indoor segmentation and support inference from RGBD images. In: Fitzgibbon, A., Lazebnik, S., Perona, P., Sato, Y., Schmid, C. (eds.) Computer Vision – ECCV 2012: 12th European Conference on Computer Vision, Florence, Italy, October 7-13, 2012, Proceedings, Part V, pp. 746–760. Springer, Berlin, Heidelberg (2012). https://doi.org/10.1007/978-3-642-33715-4_54
26. Song, W., Li, S., Liu, J., Hao, A., Zhao, Q., Qin, H.: Contextualized CNN for scene-aware depth estimation from single RGB image. IEEE Trans. Multimed. **22**(5), 1220–1233 (2019)
27. Stoffregen, T., Kleeman, L.: Simultaneous optical flow and segmentation (sofas) using dynamic vision sensor. arXiv preprint arXiv:1805.12326 (2018)
28. Vaswani, A., et al.: Attention is all you need. Adv. Neural Inf. Process. Syst. 6000–6010 (2017)
29. Wang, H., Zhu, Y., Green, B., Adam, H., Yuille, A., Chen, L.-C.: Axial-DeepLab: stand-alone axial-attention for panoptic segmentation. In: Vedaldi, A., Bischof, H., Brox, T., Frahm, J.-M. (eds.) Computer Vision – ECCV 2020: 16th European Conference, Glasgow, UK, August 23–28, 2020, Proceedings, Part IV, pp. 108–126. Springer International Publishing, Cham (2020). https://doi.org/10.1007/978-3-030-58548-8_7
30. Wang, Z., Liu, H., Wang, X., Qian, Y.: Segment and label indoor scene based on RGB-D for the visually impaired. In: Gurrin, C., Hopfgartner, F., Hurst, W., Johansen, H., Lee, H., O'Connor, N. (eds.) Multimedia Modeling, pp. 449–460. Springer, Cham (2014). https://doi.org/10.1007/978-3-319-04114-8_38
31. Xu, D., Alameda-Pineda, X., Ouyang, W., Ricci, E., Wang, X., Sebe, N.: Probabilistic graph attention network with conditional kernels for pixel-wise prediction. IEEE Trans. Pattern Anal. Mach. Intell. **44**(5), 2673–2688 (2020)
32. Yang, G., Tang, H., Ding, M., Sebe, N., Ricci, E.: Transformer-based attention networks for continuous pixel-wise prediction. In: Proceedings of the IEEE/CVF International Conference on Computer vision, pp. 16269–16279 (2021)
33. Zhu, A.Z., Thakur, D., Özaslan, T., Pfrommer, B., Kumar, V., Daniilidis, K.: The multivehicle stereo event camera dataset: an event camera dataset for 3D perception. IEEE Robot. Autom. Lett. **3**(3), 2032–2039 (2018)
34. Zhu, A.Z., Yuan, L., Chaney, K., Daniilidis, K.: Unsupervised event-based learning of optical flow, depth, and egomotion. In: Proceedings of the IEEE/CVF Conference on Computer Vision and Pattern Recognition, pp. 989–997 (2019)
35. Zihao Zhu, A., Atanasov, N., Daniilidis, K.: Event-based visual inertial odometry. In: Proceedings of the IEEE Conference on Computer Vision and Pattern Recognition, pp. 5391–5399 (2017)

SAM-NeRF: NeRF-Based 3D Instance Segmentation with Segment Anything Model

Xi Wang[1], Linglin Xie[2(✉)], Peng Qiao[1], Yong Dou[1], Sidun Liu[1], Wenyu Li[1], and Kaijun Yang[2]

[1] National University of Defense Technology, Changsha 410073, China
{xiwang,pengqiao,yongdou,liusidun,wenyu18}@nudt.edu.cn
[2] The Second Surveying and Mapping Institute of Hunan, Changsha 420001, China
{xll,ykj}@img.net

Abstract. Existing NeRF-based instance segmentation methods lift 2D annotated or predicted semantic and instance masks into 3D through radiance field, but still insufficient in segmenting on the unlabeled semantic classes. The Segment Anything Model (SAM) introduces a foundation model for image segmentation, and achieves impressive zero-shot performance. In this paper, we take advantage of SAM and propose SAM-NeRF for 3D instance segmentation agnostic to semantic labels. Unlike existing SAM-based 3D instance segmentation methods which rely on user provided prompts, SAM-NeRF only uses 2D posed images and SAM generated segmentation results to render novel view images with 3D consistent instance masks. To account for the inconsistencies on the instance identifiers across views, we represent the 3D instances with a neural instance field, and propose a mask matching method to lift SAM segmentation results to 3D scene consistently without any semantic supervision. As SAM segments the scene under various granularity, causing divergence cross views, we further propose a merging algorithm to improve the 3D segmentation performance with unified granularity between different views. Without any semantic guidance, our method outperforms the start-of-the-art 2D and 3D supervised panoptic segmentation methods on unlabeled classes in all evaluated datasets.

Keywords: 3D instance segmentation · NeRF · Segment Anything Model · Zero-shot segmentation

1 Introduction

3D scene segmentation, a task for decomposing 3D scene into individual objects, has many applications in areas such as VR, autonomous driving and so on. 3D instance segmentation is a subtask of 3D scene segmentation that segmenting the scene into individual instances. Over the past years, 3D instance segmentation has experienced an impressive progress.

Existing NeRF-based 3D instance segmentation methods [11,16,24,27] lift 2D instance masks of the training views into 3D scene consistently. However, in some specific areas such as autonomous driving, medical segmentation and indoor scenes with numerous targets, the annotations of pixel-accurate segmentation is highly expensive and time-consuming. Some methods use supervised 2D panoptic segmentation models to generate semantic and instance labels of the training views, with a semantic field to the lift the 2D semantic-consistent segmentations into the 3D scenes. But the 3D segmentation performance and consistency of their results are strongly restricted by the semantic knowledge of the 2D models. The limitations increase the difficulty of 3D instance segmentation across different views, especially the number of open-world semantic classes are much more than the labeled classes of 2D segmentation methods. Thus, there is a increasing demand for generating the 2D labels of a 3D scene beyond the annotations and the semantic limitations.

Recently, the Segment Anything Model (SAM) [14] is developed as a visual foundation model for image segmentation with a impressive zero-shot performance. Previous SAM-based NeRF segmentation [2,5] leverage the segmentation ability of SAM to take prompts from one single view and lift the prompted object segmentation of the first frame to the 3D scene. However, it can't handle the demand of panoptic segmentation where all objects of the scene need to be segmented. It is also ineffective to prompt appropriate multi-targets and train a NeRF only on the user selected objects at once. There are also some methods [2,10] integrate textual prompts with SAM for 3D semantic segmentation. But the textual prompts are not efficient enough to support instance segmentation task and the result is still strongly limited by the semantic prompts. To alleviate these problems, we adapt SAM to 3D instance segmentation to segment all instances in the scene without any user prompt.

However, the SAM generates results in an inconsistent segmentation granularity when applying on different views of the same scene without any prompt. This problem will influence the consistency of 3D segmentation granularity when lifting the SAM segmentation to the 3D scene. Besides, the semantic labels of panoptic segmentation methods can strongly supervise the 3D consistent object identifiers because the segmentation results of the training views have the same semantic classes. But SAM segmentations lack semantic guidance, causing instance identifiers mismatched across diverse views. It's non-trivial to lift the SAM segmentation results into 3D scene representation consistently.

To tackle the above issues, in this work, we introduce SAM-NeRF, a new method for NeRF-based instance segmentation with SAM (Fig. 1). Our method represents the 3D scene with neural radiance field and segment the 3D instances without any semantic guidance. We employ a merging algorithm to merge the SAM segmentation results of different views, which ensure the consistency of segmentation granularity across all views. The instance field, represented as a simple MLP, is adopted to lift the merged segmentations to the 3D instances. An instance loss with a matching method is designed to supervise the 3D consistency of instance identifiers. In general, our method takes advantage of SAM to segment instances in the 3D scenes by lifting SAM results to 3D instance field.

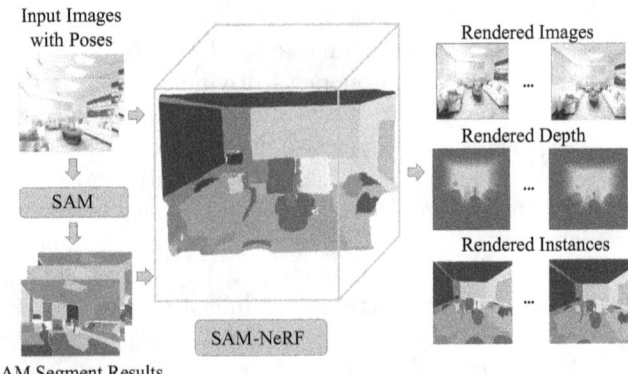

Fig. 1. Our method with only input posed images and SAM segmentation masks for training. We use SAM with no user input required to get the 2D segmentation mask. Our method can render images and segmentation masks of the novel views

Our model is trained from only 2D posed images and corresponding SAM-generated segmentation results. After training, each 3D instance is assigned with a unique instance identifier, thus achieving 3D consistency across all views. Besides, the color and depth are also rendered from SAM-NeRF. We use TensoRF architecture to encode density and color information with a separate MLP to represent the 3D instance field. We propose a merging algorithm to unify the 2D segmentation granularity and a mask matching method to match 2D segmentations with 3D instance identifiers.

Our main contributions are highlighted as follows:

- We take advantage of the zero-shot performance of SAM and propose a novel method for 3D instance segmentation. Our method is able to segment all instances in a scene without semantic guidance.
- We address the inherent inconsistency in the segmentation granularity of SAM results across different views. We use a merging algorithm to unify the segmentation granularity of the same instance.
- We use a simple instance MLP with a mask matching method to lift merged SAM segmentation results into a coherent 3D instance representation without any semantic-consistent supervision.

2 Related Work

Neural Radiance Fields (NeRF). NeRF address novel view synthesis with an implicit radiance field based on a multilayer perceptron (MLP) [1,3,17,18,28] and inspires subsequent works on different tasks [12,23]. NeRF is first proposed by Midenhall et al. [17] and achieves high quality in 3D scene representation. And TensoRF [3] models the radiance field as a 4D tensor to reduce the memory cost with better rendering quality. Our method uses TensoRF to reconstruct appearance and geometry, with a simple MLP to encode the instance field.

2D Instance Segmentation. Earlier approaches for 2D instance segmentation classified the objects in semantic classes or detection bounding boxes to segment the instances. The first and most important attempt called Mask R-CNN [13] is introduced for generating a high-quality segmentation mask, and inspires many subsequent works [4,6,8]. Based on Transformer [26], Mask2Former [7] develops a state-of-the-art method to address any image segmentation task. However, the segmentation results of these methods are strongly depended on the semantic classes of the training labels and it will limit the application of these methods in the open world. Recently, Segment Anything Model (SAM) [14] has been proposed to build a foundation model for interactive and automatic segmentation task, it delivers a impressive zero-shot segmentation performance. In our method, we use SAM as our pretrained 2D segmentation model to generate input masks of SAM-NeRF automatically without user interaction input.

3D Instance Segmentation. 3D instance segmentation has been explored for a long time. Unlike 3D semantic segmentation with consistent semantic guidance, 3D instance segmentation is a challenging task because the same object can be assigned different instance identifiers across views. Previous methods lift semantic segmentation to 3D and divide the scene into semantic classes with basic consistency and distinguish instances of the same class.

Segmentation on explicit 3D representation (e.g., voxel based, point based) [19,20] divide the 3D space into different classes and instances, but the explicit representation [22,29] lacks the ability to synthesize photo-realistic novel views. And NeRF-based segmentation methods are proposed for novel view synthesis with simultaneous 3D segmentation from 2D posed images. Bing Wang et al. [27] decomposes 3D scene by using the ground truth 2D labels that are expensive to collect. Panoptic NeRF [11] unifies coarse 3D annotations and 2D semantic for 3D panoptic segmentation. Panoptic Lifting [24] lifts 2D panoptic segmentation into a neural field representation. There are also several investigations [16] using object detection for 3D segmentation. However, the 3D instance segmentation performance of these methods relies on 3D object detection or semantic segmentation with limited 2D object or semantic annotations, thus hindering the extension to open-world scenarios.

3 Method

This section will introduce the pipeline of our method. As shown in Fig. 2, our method only uses images with poses and SAM segmentation results of the images as input. We use TensoRF supervised by the RGB loss to represent the appearance field and a simple MLP with the instance loss to represent the 3D instance field. For inconsistency problem of SAM results on segmentation granularity and instance identifiers across different views, we use a merging algorithm and

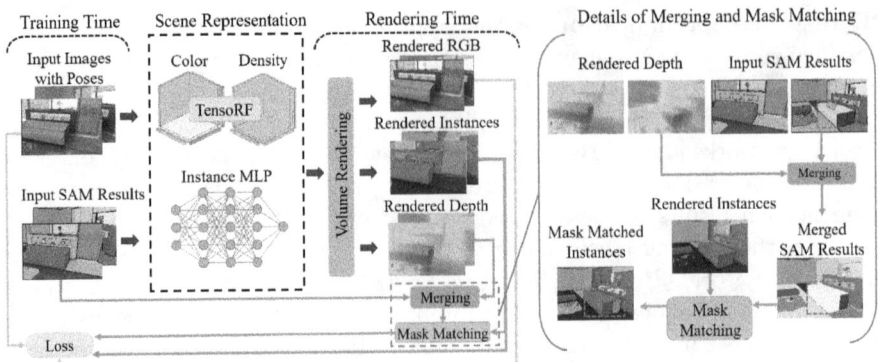

Fig. 2. Overview of SAM-NeRF. We use TensoRF architecture with a simple MLP for instance field. We use the merging algorithm and mask matching method to generate 3D consistent segmentation results

calculate the instance loss with the mask matching method. In Sect. 3.1, we introduce the details of the scene representation. In Sect. 3.2, we propose a bidirectional merging algorithm. In Sect. 3.3, we explain the loss function and the mask matching method.

3.1 Scene Representation

We use TensoRF architecture to represent the color and density field with a simple MLP for instance field.

Radiance Field Representation. Our method uses a neural radiance field to represent a 3D scene, it maps 3D location $\mathbf{x} = (x, y, z)$ and 2D viewing direction $d = (\theta, \phi)$ to a volume density σ, an emitted color c and an instance label distribution over $\mathcal{N}$ labels. The neural radiance field $\mathcal{F}_\theta$ can be formulated as

$$\mathcal{F}_\theta : (\mathbf{x}, d) \mapsto (\sigma, c) \tag{1}$$

and the instance field $\mathcal{G}_\theta$ can be formulated as

$$\mathcal{G}_\theta : (\mathbf{x}) \mapsto \mathcal{P} \tag{2}$$

where $\mathcal{P}$ is a $\mathcal{N}$-dimensional vector representing the instance label distribution.

Volume Rendering. To render images, for each pixel, we render a single ray $r = o + td$ with sampling N shading points along the ray, and then computing the result of output channel C including color c and instance distribution $\mathcal{P}$ we wish to render by the rendering equation:

$$C = \sum_{i=1}^{N} T_i(1 - exp(-\sigma_i \delta_i))c_i \qquad (3)$$

$$T_i = exp(-\sum_{j=1}^{i-1} \sigma_j \delta_j)$$

where σ_i and c_i represent the corresponding density and the output features computed at the point i. $\delta_i = t_{i+1} - t_i$ is the ray step size and T_i is the transmittance probability at point i.

3.2 Merging Algorithm

We use a bidirectional merging algorithm for unifying the segmentation granularity of SAM results.

Projection. Before merging between different views, first our method renders the depth maps of the training views. To project 2D pixels into 3D space, the camera to world projection takes the rendered depth value $s_{u,v}$ of pixel coordinates $p = (u, v)$ to project the pixel to the world coordinates $z = (X, Y, Z)$. The world to camera projection function is shown in Eq. 4:

$$s_{u,v} \begin{bmatrix} u \\ v \\ 1 \end{bmatrix} = K(R \begin{bmatrix} X \\ Y \\ Z \end{bmatrix} + T) \qquad (4)$$

the solution for camera to world projection is deduced as

$$\begin{bmatrix} X \\ Y \\ Z \end{bmatrix} = R^{-1}(K^{-1} s_{u,v} \begin{bmatrix} u \\ v \\ 1 \end{bmatrix} - T) \qquad (5)$$

where K is the camera calibration matrix, R is the rotation matrix and T is the translation matrix.

Merging Between Two Views. We represent the world coordinates of two images as $Z^1 = \{z_1^1, z_2^1, ..., z_m^1\}$ and $Z^2 = \{z_1^2, z_2^2, ..., z_n^2\}$, m and n are the number of points in Z^1, Z^2. For each instance id i in image I_1, the world points of instance id i is denoted as a point set Z_i^1, and the number of the points in the point set is β_i^1. The points in Z_i^1 that have same 3D position as Z^2 are denoted as Z_i^2. For the instance id j in Z_i^2, the number of the points is β_{ij}^2. And the number of points with instance id j in Z^2 is β_j^2. The points with id i in I_1 and j in I_2 are highly overlapping mask if they satisfy the inequality:

$$\beta_{ij}^2 > \delta \times min(\beta_i^1, \beta_j^2) \qquad (6)$$

δ is the threshold of overlapping. We merge the mask by assigning j as the new mask id of the points in Z^2 that have same id as points in Z_i^2.

Bidirectional Merging. Our bidirectional merging algorithm can merge the segmentation results in forward and reverse direction of input image sequence alternately. This enables the method adequately unify the SAM segmentation granularity between adjacent views.

3.3 Loss Functions

We use RGB loss for the optimization of neural radiance field and instance loss for instance field.

RGB Loss. The RGB loss is a squared error between the rendered and the ground truth color:

$$\mathcal{L}_{RGB}(R) = \frac{1}{|R|} \sum_{r \in R} \|c_r - \hat{c}_r\|^2 \qquad (7)$$

where R is a batch of sampled rays.

Instance Loss. Given a batch of rays R, each ray r in R is assigned the most compatible 3D instance id with mask matching function Q_R to match the 3D instance, and the instance loss is a cross entropy loss between matched 2D segmentation mask and the rendered 3D instance mask:

$$\mathcal{L}_{ins}(R) = -\frac{1}{|R|} \sum_{r \in R} p_r log(Q_R(\hat{h}_r)) \qquad (8)$$

where $\hat{h}_r \in \mathcal{H}_I$ is the 2D instance id and p_r is the instance distribution of ray r. The mask matching function Q_R is a linear assignment problem that can be formulated as

$$Q_R = \arg\max_{\mathcal{P}_R} \sum_{h \in \mathcal{H}_R} \sum_{r \in R_h} \frac{p_r(\mathcal{P}_I(h))}{|R_h|} \qquad (9)$$

$\mathcal{H}_R \subseteq \mathcal{H}_I$ is a subset of 2D instances in rays R, R_h is the subset of rays in R that belongs to instance id h.

Total Loss. The total loss $\mathcal{L}$ for training is:

$$\mathcal{L}(R) = \lambda_{RGB}\mathcal{L}_{RGB}(R) + \lambda_{ins}\mathcal{L}_{ins}(R) \qquad (10)$$

4 Experimental Results

4.1 Implementation Details

In our model, we use pretrained SAM for 2D segmentation masks generation of the training set. Our model is implemented with pytorch in Python environment on a NVIDIA TESLA V100 GPU with 32GB memory. For training, we use Adam optimizer with 1×10^{-2} as the learning rate of TensoRF and 5×10^{-4} of instance MLP. For merging algorithm, our method uses $\delta = 0.5$. For the total loss $\mathcal{L}$, we use $\lambda_{RGB} = 1$ and $\lambda_{ins} = 0.1$. Our instance field optimization starts training at intermediate training stage of NeRF and our merging algorithm is applied bidirectionally during instance field optimization at a fixed step of training epochs.

4.2 Dataset and Evaluation Metrics

Datasets. In our method three public datasets are used: Hypersim [21], Replica [25] and ScanNet [9]. For each of the datasets, we choose two scenes for evaluation and use the available ground truth poses and RGB images as input. The ground truth semantic and instance labels are only used in evaluation.

Evaluation Metrics. We evaluate the zero-shot 3D instance segmentation performance of SAM-NeRF by using the intersection over union (IoU) metric to calculate the accuracy of predicted instances on the unlabeled classes of the baselines. Also we use semantic mean intersection over union (mIoU) to evaluate the SAM-NeRF segmentation performance on labeled classes of the baselines.

4.3 Results

We compare our results with the start-of-the-art 2D panoptic segmentation method: Mask2Former [7] and 3D panoptic segmentation method: Panoptic Lifting [24]. Mask2Former uses the pretrained model and Panoptic Lifting uses the posed images with Mask2Former-generated segmentations for training. Since the Mask2Former pretrained model was trained on COCO [15], we map COCO panoptic classes to 21 ScanNet classes for evaluation. We calculate the mIoU on the labeled semantic classes and IoU on unlabeled classes of the baselines. For the comparison on unlabeled classes, we choose two classes in each scene to evaluate the segmentation performance. More details about classes and data splits are available in Appendix A.

For SAM-NeRF, we match each ground truth instance labels with 3D instance segmentation results of the views in the test set. For example, semantic class s_{gt}^1 has instances $\{i_{gt}^1, i_{gt}^2...i_{gt}^m\}$ in the ground truth label, and the instances predicted by SAM-NeRF are $\{i_{sam}^1, i_{sam}^2...i_{sam}^n\}$. For instance identifier i_{gt}^1, we calculate the IoU with the instances predicted by SAM-NeRF, if instance i_{sam}^1 has the best IoU result with i_{gt}^1, we choose i_{sam}^1 as the predicted instance of

Fig. 3. Visual performance of rendered color and instances on Hypersim [21], Replica [25] and ScanNet [9]. In each dataset, the first column is the rendered color images and the second column is the panoptic segmentation results of baselines and instance segmentation results of SAM-NeRF. Mask2Former does not render color images, thus the rgb images are from the label

Table 1. Quantitative comparison of instance segmentation on the unlabeled classes of test set. The metric is IoU(%)

Datasets			Mask2Former [7]	Panoptic Lifting [24]	**Ours**
Hypersim [21]	ai_001_008	picture	10.9	17.7	**67.9**
		blinds	0.0	0.0	**58.5**
	ai_010_005	picture	0.6	4.0	**72.4**
		pillow	0.0	0.0	**89.8**
Replica [25]	room_0	rug	0.0	0.0	**95.3**
		indoor plants	7.6	16.0	**60.2**
	office_3	cushion	3.9	0.6	**55.9**
		blinds	4.9	0.0	**38.8**
ScanNet [9]	scene0050_02	tissue box	7.9	6.7	**49.4**
		cooler	0.1	4.7	**56.4**
	scene0144_01	pillow	0.0	0.0	**61.8**
		printer	5.1	14.2	**63.3**

Table 2. Quantitative comparison of instance segmentation on the labeled classes of baseline. The metric is mIoU(%)

Datasets	Mask2Former [7]	Panoptic Lifting [24]	**Ours**
Hypersim [21]	57.4	60.0	49.3
Replica [25]	63.1	69.1	59.3
ScanNet [9]	50.0	55.9	46.4

i_{gt}^1. Finally we obtain the best match of s_{gt}^1 through our prediction and calculate the IoU of this semantic class. For the baselines, We use the prediction of "otherprop" class as the segmentation result of unlabeled classes.

Instance segmentation of views in different datasets can be obtained from SAM-NeRF. As shown in the bottommost row of Fig. 3, our method can segment instances of the 3D scene without semantic guidance. The result of the scene on ScanNet dataset shows that our method can segment the cushion that even not annotated in the ground truth labels. Our zero-shot method achieves the best IoU on the unlabeled classes and it significantly outperforms the supervised methods as shown in Table 1. Though it is unsurprisingly that the state-of-the-art supervised segmentation methods slightly perform better performance on the labeled classes as shown in Table 2. The Mask2Former and Panoptic Lifting can easily learn semantic specific classes that consistent in different views but difficult to learn classses beyond the annotations, since it was trained on semantic labeled datasets. Our method can segment instances without any semantic guidance or annotation and significantly shows an impressive zero-shot performance. More visualization results are provided in Appendix B.

4.4 Ablations

In Table 3 and Fig. 4, we perform ablations of the rendered segmentation results on the Hypersim dataset. We disable merging algorithm and its bidirectional design as described in Sect. 3.2, obtaining a drop in segmentation performance on the semantic labeled classes. The quantity result shows that merging algorithm will strongly influence the segmentation granularity of the result (see Fig. 4 (a) and (b)). And SAM-NeRF with bidirectional merging (see Fig. 4 (c)) shows the best segmentation performance.

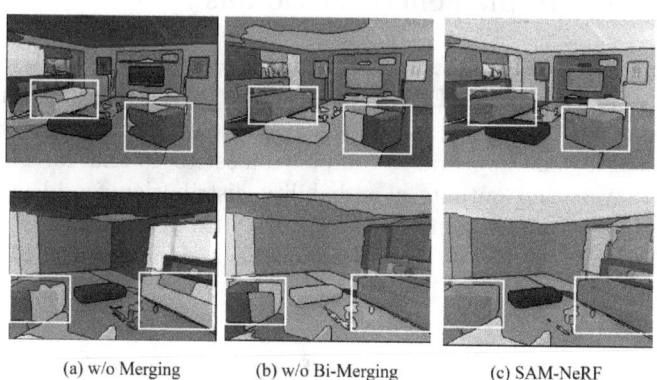

Fig. 4. Ablations of merging algorithm. (a) 3D scene segmentation without merging algorithm. (b) 3D scene segmentation with only once forward-direction merging. (c) 3D scene segmentation of our method with bidirectional merging

Table 3. Ablation Study over 2 test scenes on Hypersim. The Bidirectional-merging ablation uses only once forward-direction merging

Method	mIoU
w/o Merging	46.4
w/o Bidirectional-merging	45.9
Ours	**49.3**

5 Conclusion

In this paper, we propose a NeRF-based method with SAM for 3D instance segmentation. By a merging algorithm, we merge the SAM segmentation masks to unify segmentation granularity of different views. Without any semantic guidance, our method can lift merged SAM segmentation results to 3D instance field and generate color images together with 3D consistent instance segmentations of the novel views. We perform comparison to the start-of-the-art 2D panoptic segmentation and 3D panoptic segmentation methods with semantic consistent guidance, and results show better segmentation performance on unlabeled classes. We also discuss the importance of merging algorithm in the ablation study. We believe SAM-NeRF will contribute to the application of Segment Anything Model and the research on NeRF-based segmentation methods.

Acknowledgements. This work is supported by the Open Fund of Science and Technology on Parallel and Distributed Processing Laboratory (PDL). The grant number is WDZC20235250106.

Appendix A Implementation Details

SAM-NeRF. In SAM-NeRF, we use TensoRF for modeling the scene density and radiance with a simple MLP for instance field. The settings of TensoRF are same as Panoptic Lifting [24] which using Vector-Matrix decomposition with number of density and appearance components set to 16 and 48. The instance MLP has 5 layers and outputs a probability distribution for identifiers. Our model is trained with a learning rate of 1×10^{-2} for TensoRF and 5×10^{-4} for instance MLP. We use the publicly available Segment Anything [14] code and models without retraining or fine-tuning.

Baselines. The public implementation of pretrained Panoptic Lifting [24] and Mask2Former(swin_large_IN21K) [7] are used as baselines. For Panoptic Lifting, we use the publicly available Mask2Former code and models for machine-generated instance labels. Because the pretrained Mask2Former model was trained on COCO [15] dataset, so we map the Mask2Former predictions and the ground-truth labels across all datasets to 21 ScanNet classes.

Data and Labels. Table 4 shows 21 ScanNet classes used in our experiments. The evaluation scenes and their number of frames are shown in Table 5. We use the same data splitting as Panoptic Lifting [24].

Table 4. Classes and their types of training labels in the baseline

Class	Type
wall	Stuff
floor	Stuff
cabinet	Stuff
bed	Thing
chair	Thing
sofa	Thing
table	Stuff
door	Stuff
window	Stuff
counter	Stuff
shelves	Stuff
curtain	Stuff
ceiling	Stuff
refrigerator	Thing
television	Thing
person	Thing
toilet	Thing
sink	Thing
lamp	Stuff
bag	Thing
otherprop	Stuff

Table 5. Scenes used for evaluation in our experiments

Dataset	Scene	#Frames
HyperSim	ai_001_008	100
HyperSim	ai_010_005	100
Replica	room_0	900
Replica	office_3	900
ScanNet	scene0050_02	874
ScanNet	scene0144_01	678

Appendix B Additional Results

We provide more visualization results on different datasets and on various views of the same scene in Fig. 5 and Fig. 6.

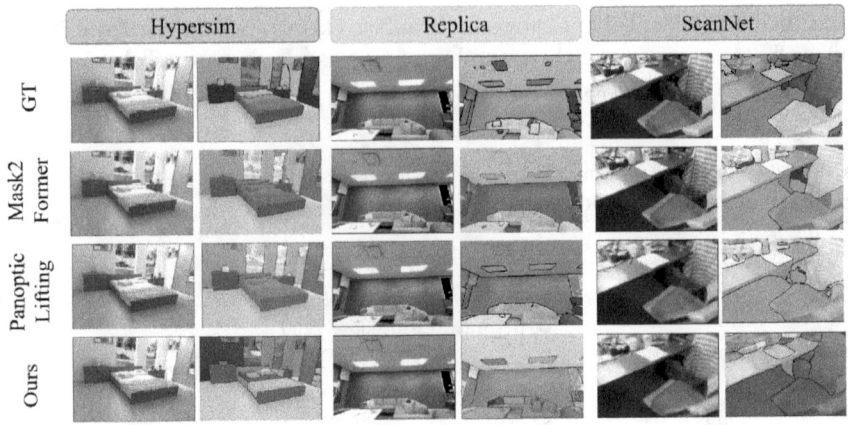

Fig. 5. More visual performance of novel views and rendered instances

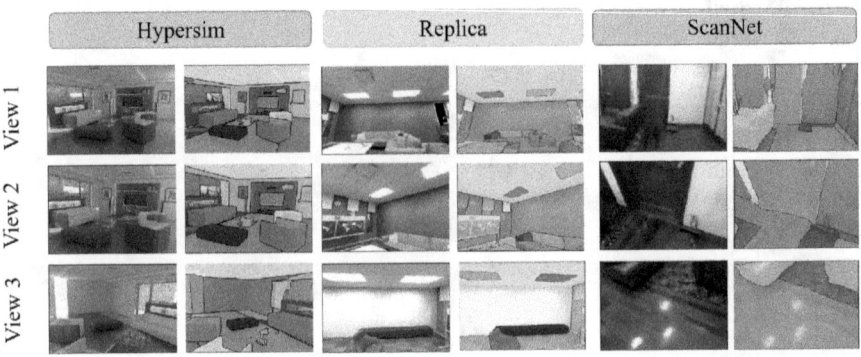

Fig. 6. Visualize results on different views in the same scene. In each dataset, the first column shows the rendered color images and the second column shows the rendered 3D consistent instance segmentations

We further report some visualization results of merging algorithm on training data in Fig. 7. The merging algorithm can unify the segmentation granularity of SAM results with the reference of the adjacent views. For example, the ceiling in Replica scene of the view (the second row of the Figure) is over-segmented by original SAM. The merging algorithm refers the segmentation granularity of the pre-view (the first row of the Figure) and unifies the segmentation granularity with the pre-view result.

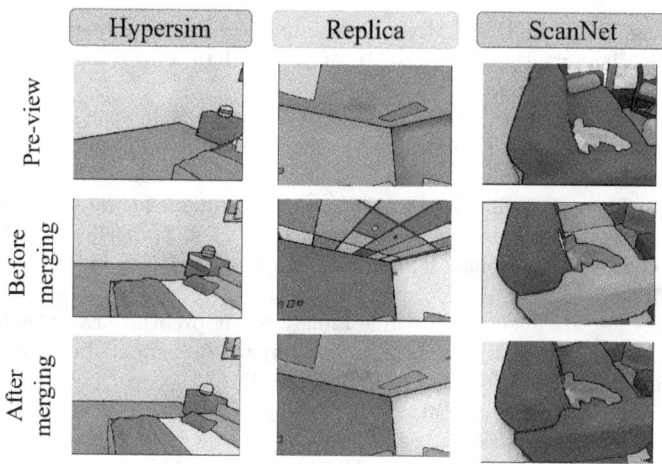

Fig. 7. Visual performance of merging algorithm. For each dataset, first row is the SAM segmentation result of the reference view, second row is the SAM segmentation result before merging and last row is the result after merging. Merging algorithm is able to unify the segmentation granularity of views

References

1. Barron, J.T., Mildenhall, B., Tancik, M., Hedman, P., Martin-Brualla, R., Srinivasan, P.P.: Mip-NeRF: a multiscale representation for anti-aliasing neural radiance fields. In: ICCV, pp. 5855–5864 (2021)
2. Cen, J., et al.: Segment anything in 3D with NeRFs. In: NeurIPS (2023)
3. Chen, A., Xu, Z., Geiger, A., Yu, J., Su, H.: TensoRF: tensorial radiance fields. In: Avidan, S., Brostow, G., Cissé, M., Farinella, G.M., Hassner, T. (eds.) Computer Vision - ECCV 2022. ECCV 2022. LNCS, vol. 13692, pp. 333–350. Springer, Cham (2022). https://doi.org/10.1007/978-3-031-19824-3_20
4. Chen, K., et al.: Hybrid task cascade for instance segmentation. In: CVPR, pp. 4974–4983 (2019)
5. Chen, X., Tang, J., Wan, D., Wang, J., Zeng, G.: Interactive segment anything NeRF with feature imitation. arXiv preprint arXiv:2305.16233
6. Chen, X., Girshick, R., He, K., Dollár, P.: TensorMask: a foundation for dense object segmentation. In: ICCV, pp. 2061–2069 (2019)
7. Cheng, B., Misra, I., Schwing, A.G., Kirillov, A., Girdhar, R.: Masked-attention mask transformer for universal image segmentation. In: CVPR, pp. 1290–1299 (2022)
8. Cheng, T., Wang, X., Huang, L., Liu, W.: Boundary-preserving mask R-CNN. In: Vedaldi, A., Bischof, H., Brox, T., Frahm, J.-M. (eds.) ECCV 2020. LNCS, vol. 12359, pp. 660–676. Springer, Cham (2020). https://doi.org/10.1007/978-3-030-58568-6_39
9. Dai, A., Chang, A.X., Savva, M., Halber, M., Funkhouser, T., Nießner, M.: ScanNet: richly-annotated 3D reconstructions of indoor scenes. In: CVPR, pp. 5828–5839 (2017)

10. Feng Wang, Z.C., Liu, H.: SAMNeRF: A simple baseline for segmenting anything in NeRF with language prompts (2023). https://github.com/WangFeng18/Explore-Sam-in-NeRF/tree/main
11. Fu, X., et al.: Panoptic NeRF: 3D-to-2D label transfer for panoptic urban scene segmentation. In: 2022 International Conference on 3D Vision (3DV), pp. 1–11. IEEE (2022)
12. Gafni, G., Thies, J., Zollhofer, M., Nießner, M.: Dynamic neural radiance fields for monocular 4D facial avatar reconstruction. In: CVPR, pp. 8649–8658 (2021)
13. He, K., Gkioxari, G., Dollár, P., Girshick, R.: Mask R-CNN. In: ICCV, pp. 2961–2969 (2017)
14. Kirillov, A., et al.: Segment anything (2023). arXiv preprint arXiv:2304.02643
15. Lin, T., et al.: Microsoft COCO: common objects in context. In: European Conference on Computer Vision, pp. 740–755 (2014)
16. Liu, Y., Hu, B., Huang, J., Tai, Y.W., Tang, C.K.: Instance neural radiance field. In: ICCV, pp. 787–796 (2023)
17. Mildenhall, B., Srinivasan, P.P., Tancik, M., Barron, J.T., Ramamoorthi, R., Ng, R.: NeRF: representing scenes as neural radiance fields for view synthesis. Commun. ACM **65**(1), 99–106 (2021)
18. Oechsle, M., Peng, S., Geiger, A.: UNISURF: unifying neural implicit surfaces and radiance fields for multi-view reconstruction. In: ICCV, pp. 5589–5599 (2021)
19. Qi, C.R., Su, H., Mo, K., Guibas, L.J.: PointNet: deep learning on point sets for 3D classification and segmentation. In: CVPR (2017)
20. Qi, C.R., Yi, L., Su, H., Guibas, L.J.: PointNet++: deep hierarchical feature learning on point sets in a metric space. In: Advances in Neural Information Processing Systems, vol. 30 (2017)
21. Roberts, M., et al.: Hypersim: a photorealistic synthetic dataset for holistic indoor scene understanding. In: ICCV, pp. 10912–10922 (2021)
22. Schönberger, J.L., Frahm, J.M.: Structure-from-motion revisited. In: CVPR, pp. 4104–4113 (2016)
23. Shi, Y., Xi, J., Hu, D., Cai, Z., Xu, K.: RayMVSNet++: learning ray-based 1D implicit fields for accurate multi-view stereo. TPAMI (2023)
24. Siddiqui, Y., et al.: Panoptic lifting for 3D scene understanding with neural fields. In: CVPR, pp. 9043–9052 (2023)
25. Straub, J., et al.: The replica dataset: a digital replica of indoor spaces (2019). arXiv preprint arXiv:1906.05797
26. Vaswani, A., et al.: Attention is all you need. In: Advances in Neural Information Processing Systems, vol. 30 (2017)
27. Wang, B., Chen, L., Yang, B.: DM-NeRF: 3D scene geometry decomposition and manipulation from 2D images (2022). arXiv preprint arXiv:2208.07227
28. Wang, P., Liu, L., Liu, Y., Theobalt, C., Komura, T., Wang, W.: NeuS: learning neural implicit surfaces by volume rendering for multi-view reconstruction. In: NeurIPS, pp. 27171–27183. Curran Assoicates, Inc. (2021)
29. Zhang, J., Zhu, C., Zheng, L., Xu, K.: ROSEFusion: random optimization for online dense reconstruction under fast camera motion. TOG **40**(4), 1–17 (2021)

Towards High-Accuracy Point Cloud Registration with Channel Self-attention and Angle Invariance

Jinhong Hong, Songwei Pei[✉], and Shuhuai Wang

School of Computer Science (National Pilot Software Engineering School), Beijing University of Posts and Telecommunications, Beijing 100876, China
peisongwei@bupt.edu.cn

Abstract. Point cloud registration, which plays a vital role in various applications, remains a very challenging task, especially in scenarios with low overlap between source and target 3D point clouds. This paper proposes a high-accuracy and robust point cloud registration method by designing a fused geometric feature extraction module and a two-stage outlier pruning strategy. In the fused geometric feature extraction module, we introduce a non-local feature aggregation block that adopts a channel self-attention mechanism, named the CHNonlocal block, to enhance geometric features extracted from point-to-point correspondences using the known SCNonlocal block. The two-stage outlier pruning strategy further refines outlier removal by leveraging angle invariance to obtain consensus sets targeting point-to-point correspondences, initially identified by pruning outliers based on feature similarity. Similar to PointDSC, candidate pose transformation parameters can be calculated from these consensus sets, and the best hypothesis can be selected as the final registration result. Experiments on various point cloud datasets demonstrate that our method achieves higher registration accuracy and better generalization ability compared to mainstream point cloud registration algorithms, especially in low-overlap scenarios.

Keywords: Point cloud registration · Angle invariance · Channel self-attention

1 Introduction

With the maturity and rapid development of 3D point cloud data acquisition equipment, such as laser radar and Kinect, 3D point cloud has become an important approach to represent the 3D world [1, 2], and has been applied in many fields such as autonomous driving and smart cities [3–5]. Point cloud registration is known as the technique of aligning two 3D point clouds of the same scene, which is almost indispensable in the applications fields relying on 3D point cloud data. Point cloud registration is a very challenging task, because the 3D point cloud data is unstructured and larger in volume, and typically contains a large amount of outliers [6, 7]. How to implement accurate point cloud registration has been a significant concern for researchers [8–10].

In the task of point cloud registration, preliminary registration of the point clouds is typically indispensable because the point clouds to be registered may have a large difference in the initial pose. The feature-based point cloud registration algorithm is commonly used to implement the preliminary registration of point clouds [10, 32]. This method first extracts local features of the point clouds, such as point features, line features, surface features, and texture features [11–14], and then conducts feature matching of the point clouds based on the extracted local features. However, under the scenario of low overlap between the source and target point clouds, point-to-point correspondences generated by feature matching are prone to large false matches. Therefore, it is necessary to prune the outliers in the matching pairs through the outlier removal method first, and then estimate the transformation between the source and the target point clouds. With the development of deep learning, learning-based point cloud registration methods have been extensively researched and developed. The application of deep learning technology to point cloud registration methods [15–19] improves the accuracy and robustness of point cloud registration. However, the initial point-to-point correspondences using only learned features still contain many outliers, resulting in unsatisfactory registration between the source and target point clouds. It is thus imperative to obtain robust point-to-point correspondences with reduced outliers to improve the accuracy of point cloud registration, especially under the scenario of low overlap between the source and the target point clouds.

Traditional outlier removal methods such as RANSAC [20] and its variants [21] are the mainstream methods for removing outliers from the set of point-to-point correspondences. However, the main disadvantage of this type of algorithm is that the convergence speed is very slow, and the performance of outlier removal is poor when a large number of outliers exist. In 3D point cloud registration, outliers are prominent due to the lack of useful texture features for 3D points with irregular density and the relatively weaker descriptive ability of 3D feature descriptors. Therefore, the spatial consistency under rigid transformation can be leveraged for pruning outliers. Spectral matching and voting mechanisms [22, 23] explicitly utilize spatial consistent features based on Euclidean distance to remove outliers. With the development of deep learning, the learning-based outlier pruning method has been gradually proposed, and it was first introduced into the 2D image matching task. In the learning-based 3D outlier removal algorithm, the outlier removal is typically defined as an outlier classification problem. 3D outlier removal methods, such as DGR [17] and 3DregNet [18], belong to this category, using architectures such as sparse convolution and Multilayer Perceptron (MLP) to implement outlier classification.

Learning-based point cloud registration algorithms can also take advantage of spatial consistency to obtain robust point-to-point correspondences. PointDSC [19] proposes a robust point cloud registration network that exploits spatial consistency explicitly in feature extraction and outlier removal. However, the spatial consistency feature used in this work only considers the spatial characteristic of the Euclidean distance between the point pairs. Consequently, the feature similarity matrix formed by SCNonlocal may still show high similarity between incorrect and correct matching pairs, resulting in poor performance in removing outliers. Moreover, during the feature extraction stage, the method focuses solely on the feature correlation among different matching point pairs, ignoring the correlation among different dimensions within matching point pairs.

Based on PointDSC [19], this paper leverages the channel self-attention mechanism and the angle invariance of rigid body transformation to improve the accuracy of 3D point registration. In view of the limitations of geometric feature extraction and outlier removal in PointDSC, this paper has made the following major contributions:

1) We propose a fused geometric feature extraction module, in which a non-local feature extraction block inspired by the channel self-attention mechanism, namely the CHNonlocal block, is designed to work with the SCNonlocal block [19] to obtain better geometric features for each input correspondence.
2) We propose a two-stage outlier pruning strategy that leverages spatial angle invariance to further remove outliers, resulting in a more accurate consensus set.
3) The proposed method is verified on the 3DMatch and 3DLoMatch datasets. Comparative experiments with state-of-the-art methods demonstrate the effectiveness and superiority of our method.

2 Related Work

Recently, deep learning-based point cloud registration methods have been widely studied, which include keypoint detection [16, 29, 30], feature description [15, 16, 30], end-to-end registration[31], outlier rejection [17, 18, 32, 33], etc. In this section, we will review the works that are closely related to deep learning-based point cloud registration methods briefly.

USIP [29] proposes to detect the keypoints in 3D point clouds in an unsupervised manner and achieve high repeatability and accuracy for keypoint detection. In USIP [29], a feature proposal network is implemented to learn the features of keypoints, and the probabilistic chamfer and point-to-point losses are proposed to obtain keypoints with high repeatability. 3DMatch [15] implements a data-driven model to create correspondences between 3D point clouds by adopting the local volumetric patch descriptor. In this work, a large number of correspondence labels from 3D reconstructions are leveraged for feature learning. D3Feat [30] adopts a KPConv-based fully convolutional network and a density-invariant keypoint selection method to detect and describe keypoints in 3D point clouds. A self-supervised detector loss is also proposed to guide the model training. FINet [16] proposes to promote feature interaction during the feature extraction stage to better solve the 3D point cloud registration. In FINet [16], a dual branch structure is implemented to improve feature interactions. PointNetLK [31] proposes an effective 3D point cloud registration method by leveraging PointNet and the modified LK algorithm. The generalization ability of PointNetLK [31] to unseen objects is remarkable due to the explicit encoding in the alignment. However, for the above works, the robustness against the outliers in complex scenes, especially under the scenario of low overlap between point cloud groups, is expected to improve the accuracy of point cloud registration.

RPM-Net [32] proposes an end-to-end differentiable deep network for robust point matching. In RPM-Net [32], the robustness against outliers is inherited from RPM, and hybrid features are learned to desensitize initialization for improving 3D point cloud registration. DGR [17] proposes to implement a differentiable framework for 3D point cloud registration with high robustness by incorporating three main modules, which are a 6D convolutional network, a weighted Procrustes algorithm, and a robust SE(3) optimizer. The weighted Procrustes algorithm is implemented to be differentiable and has linear computational complexity, allowing accurate registration with dense correspondence sets. 3DRegNet [18] is also a robust deep learning architecture for 3D point cloud registration. In 3DRegNet [18], the point correspondences can be classified into inliers/outliers by the Classification Block built upon ResNets. The Registration Block is also designed in 3DRegNet to cooperate with the Classification Block to calculate the 6D transformation parameters. In [33], a variational non-local network is implemented for outlier rejection by learning the discriminative feature representations with the Bayesian-driven contextual dependencies. A Wilson score-based voting method is also adopted in [33] to select inliers with high quality. However, how to better take advantage of the geometric feature of 3D point clouds for higher accuracy registration remains to be improved.

3 The Proposed Method

In this work, we propose to improve the accuracy of 3D point cloud registration by designing a fused geometric feature extraction module and a two-stage outlier pruning strategy, which will be presented in detail below.

3.1 Fused Geometric Feature Extraction

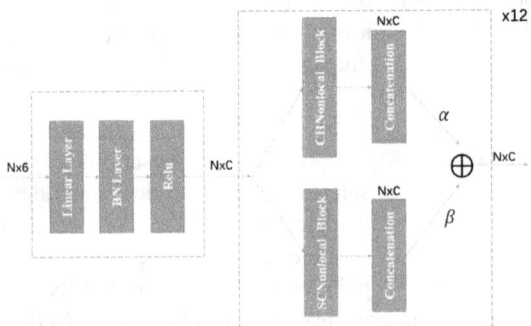

Fig. 1. Architecture of the proposed fused geometric feature extraction module. This module takes correspondences as input and generates geometric features for each correspondence.

The channel self-attention mechanism can capture the long-distance dependencies among the different dimensions of features. Inspired by this, we strengthen the features of point cloud matching pairs by learning the dependencies among the feature dimensions of input point-to-point correspondences, which is thus conducive for the subsequent pruning of wrong matching pairs, thereby improving the accuracy of point cloud registration. In this work, we propose to enhance the feature extraction for point-to-point correspondences by designing a fused geometric feature extraction module, in which a non-local feature aggregation block that adopts the channel self-attention mechanism, namely the CHNonlocal block, is designed to complement the geometric features extracted by SCNonlocal block [19] for each point-to-point correspondence. The architecture of the proposed fused geometric feature extraction module is shown in Fig. 1. In the figure, N represents the number of input correspondences, C represents the feature dimension of input correspondences, and α and β are learnable weight parameters.

The fused geometric feature extraction module mainly consists of two parts:

The first part, as shown in the left dashed box of Fig. 1, expands the feature dimension of the input correspondences from N × 6 to N × C with a Linear layer. A BN layer and Relu activation function are added later. After normalization with the BN layer, a more stable feature distribution can be obtained.

The second part, as shown in the right dashed box of Fig. 1, consists of 12 residual blocks, each composed of two different feature extraction blocks, the CHNonlocal block and the SCNonlocal block. The CHNonlocal block and the SCNonlocal block are shown in Fig. 2 (a) and Fig. 2 (b), respectively.

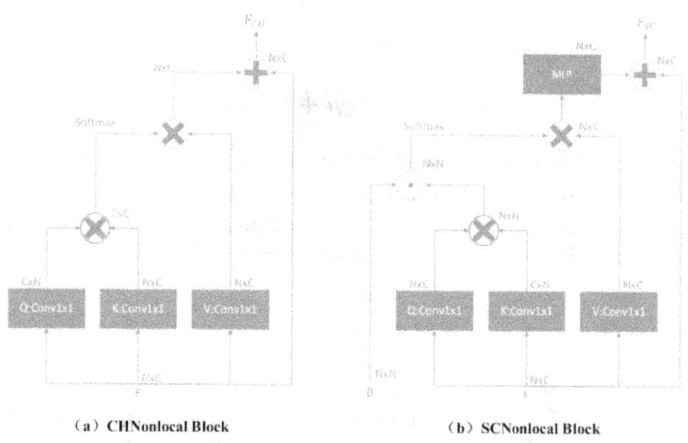

(a) CHNonlocal Block   (b) SCNonlocal Block

Fig. 2. (a) Channel Nonlocal (CHNonlocal) block fuses different dimensional feature information within the same point-to-point correspondence. (b) Spatial Consistency Nonlocal (SCNonlocal) block fuses feature information from different point-to-point correspondences.

CHNonlocal is a non-local feature extraction module guided by the channel self-attention mechanism. First, the input feature map of CHNonlocal is linearly mapped to three feature matrices of θ, ϕ, and g. Then we use a non-local neural network to obtain the correlation between different feature channels for each matching pair, and use the Softmax algorithm to obtain the self-attention coefficient matrix. The output feature of each channel is first calculated by weighted summing of the features of all input channels with the self-attention coefficient matrix, and then aggregated with the output feature of the previous block (the input feature of this block) as the output features of the CHNonlocal block. The output feature of this module is formulated as:

$$F_{CH} = F_{input} + \sum_i^{|C|} \text{softmax}_i\left(\theta^T \otimes \phi\right) g(f_i) \tag{1}$$

The SCNonlocal block is a non-local feature module guided by the spatial consistency matrix. By introducing the spatial feature similarity to strengthen the features extracted in the non-local network, this module can effectively extract and aggregate feature information of the same dimension between different matching point pairs, which is consistent with the PointDSC [19]. The output feature calculation method of the SCNonlocal block is formulated as:

$$F_{SC} = F_{input} + \text{MLP}\left(\sum_i^{|C|} \text{softmax}_i(\alpha\beta) g(f_i)\right) \tag{2}$$

In the equation, α is the non-locality coefficient, which is calculated by the Nonlocal network, and β is the spatial distance similarity coefficient.

Finally, the features extracted by the two modules are fused as the final output feature, as shown in Eq. (3), where F_{CH} is the feature matrix output by the CHNonlocal module, F_{SC} is the feature matrix output by the SCNonlocal module.

$$F_{out} = \alpha * F_{CH} + \beta * F_{SC} \tag{3}$$

Our fused geometric feature extraction module can better extract the geometric features by fusing features from different dimensions of matching point pairs, and the generated feature matrix can be used for seed selection and obtaining consensus sets in the subsequent procedure of point cloud registration.

3.2 Two-Stage Outlier Pruning Strategy

In the PointDSC algorithm [19], it first leverages the learned feature similarity matrix to obtain the consensus set corresponding to each seed by performing k-nearest neighbor searching. Then, it uses Neural Spectral Matching (NSM) on each consensus set to estimate the transformation as a hypothesis. The neural spectrum matching method constructs the compatibility matrix for each consensus set. The leading eigenvector of the compatibility matrix can be computed by the power iteration algorithm. The leading eigenvector represents the confidence level between the point-to-point correspondences. Finally, this method uses the leading eigenvector and the SVD algorithm to obtain the transformation of each consensus set. Therefore, a consensus set with a high inlier rate facilitates neural spectral matching in finding the correct clustering..

However, the spatial feature matrix composed of three-dimensional Euclidean distances may still exhibit significant similarity between outliers and inliers. Figure 3 (a) shows the feature similarity matrix formed by the geometric feature extraction module, where C1, C2, C3, and C4 represent correct correspondences, C5 and C6 represent wrong correspondences. Clearly, the feature similarity between C1 and C6 is still very high, up to 0.96, under the Euclidean distance spatial feature. Therefore, it is hard to effectively remove outliers in the process of building a consensus set with similar features. It is thus difficult for Neural Spectral Matching to find an obvious correct matching point pair cluster when the consensus set contains many wrong matching point pairs, which leads to the inability to accurately complete the point cloud registration. Therefore, this paper proposes to further remove the outliers based on the invariance of spatial angles to realize the coarse-to-fine pruning of the consensus set and improve its inlier rate. The proposed two-stage outlier pruning strategy is mainly divided into the following two steps:

In the first step, we find the K1 nearest neighbors of each seed point in the similarity matrix formed by the fused geometric feature extraction module. As mentioned above, even if the seed is a correct matching point pair, its corresponding consensus set still contains outliers because the feature similarity matrix may exhibit high similarity between outliers and inliers. Assume that the correspondence C1 is selected as the seed point, and the value of the nearest neighbor of Top-K1 is set to 4. Hence, {C2, C3, C4, C6} will be added to the consensus set of C1 according to the similarity, but it still contains a wrong matching point pair C6. Therefore, it is necessary to perform a second pruning on the consensus set to remove the wrong matching point pairs left over after the first round of pruning for outliers.

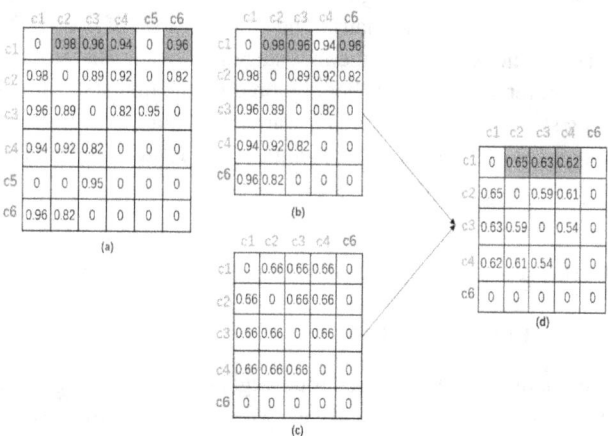

Fig. 3. (A) The feature space generated by the geometric feature extraction module. (b) The feature space after performing KNN nearest neighbor search (K1). (c) The feature space constructed based on Spatial Angle Invariance. (d) The feature spaces are fused with Hadamard products to reconstruct a new feature space.

In the second step, the feature space similarity matrix shown in Fig. 3 (b) is first constructed for each consensus set, which characterizes the feature similarity between all matching point pairs in that set. Then we perform a K-nearest search on the matrix, setting the value of the nearest neighbor of Top-K2 to 3, and further obtaining matching point pairs as {C2, C3, C6} according to the similarity. The outlier C6 is still not successfully pruned during the screening. The main reason is that the wrong matching point pair C6 and the correct matching point pair C1 have strong feature similarity in the Euclidean distance feature space and are still within the Top-K2 similarity range. Therefore, in the second stage, the feature of invariant spatial angle is incorporated in the process of reconstructing the feature space similarity matrix. First, we construct a feature similarity matrix according to the spatial angle invariance after rigid body transformation. The formula for constructing the matrix is formulated as:

$$M_{ij} = \frac{\sum_{k \notin i,j}^{K1}[|\angle kij - \angle k'i'j'| < \theta_{thr}]}{K1 - 2}, (1 < i,j,k < K1) \quad (4)$$

where K1 represents the size of the consensus set, i, j, and k represent points in the source point cloud for three correspondences Ci, Cj, and Ck in the consensus set, respectively. I', j', and k' are the corresponding points in the target point cloud.

Firstly, we respectively calculate the angle between the vector $\rightarrow_{ij}$ formed by the source matching points i and j and the other vectors $\rightarrow_{ik}$ starting from i except the vector $\rightarrow_{ij}$ in the consensus set. A similar angle calculation is conducted for i', j', and k'. Then we preset the angle threshold θ_{thr} and count the number of angle difference that is smaller than the threshold θ_{thr} to obtain the angular characteristic similarity M_{ij} between the correspondences Ci and Cj. Reconstructing the new feature space similarity matrix is to aggregate the space angle consistency feature matrix on the basis of the original space feature matrix. K2 nearest neighbor search is performed on this new similarity matrix. According to this similarity matrix, the consensus set of matching pairs of C1 is {C2, C3, C4}. The outlier C6 kept in the first stage is pruned. Therefore, the pruning in the second stage can remove some outliers ignored by the first stage. Consequently, the two-stage pruning strategy based on angle invariance is beneficial for pruning incorrect matching point pairs and effectively improving the inlier rate of the consensus set of the seed.

4 Experiments

4.1 Datasets and Evaluation Metrics

We evaluate our method on the point cloud registration dataset 3DMatch [15]. For each pair of point cloud data in the dataset, we first set a 5cm voxel grid to realize voxel filtering and downsampling. Then we use two different feature descriptors, FPFH [24] and FCGF [25], to generate the initial point-to-point correspondences of the point clouds as the initial input data. We select Registration Recall (RR), Rotation Error (RE), Translation Error (L2 Translation Error, TE), Inlier Precision (IP), Inlier Recall (IR), and comprehensive evaluation index (F1-measure, F1) to evaluate the proposed method. The performance of the proposed method is further verified on the 3DLoMatch dataset with a low overlap rate [26].

4.2 Implementation Details

As usual, we train the network on the training set of the 3DMatch dataset, and evaluate it on the test set. Since different point clouds in the dataset have different numbers of point-to-point correspondences, 1000 point-to-point correspondences are fixedly sampled from each pair of point clouds. In the seed selection stage, the seed selection ratio is set to 0.1. In the consensus set sampling stage, 40 nearest neighbor point pairs (K1 = 40) of the seed point are selected in the first stage, and 10 correspondences are selected from the K1 nearest neighbor point pairs in the second stage (K2 = 10) to form a consensus set. In the stage of predicting the matching point pair label, the inlier threshold is set to 10cm. In the stage of evaluating the registration performance, the rotation error threshold and translation error threshold are set to 15° and 30 cm, respectively. We use the Adam gradient descent optimizer [27] to optimize the network, the batch size is 16, and the initial learning rate is 0.0001. The weight decay rate is set to 1e−06, and the network is trained for 100 epochs. All experiments are trained on a GPU server equipped with an RTX 3090 graphics card.

4.3 Ablation Study

First, we conduct ablation studies for the proposed fused geometric feature extraction module and the two-stage outlier pruning strategy on the 3DMatch dataset. We leverage the PointDSC network as the baseline, and gradually apply the two proposed schemes to the baseline and test the results. The results are shown in Table 1.

Table 1. Ablation study.

Method	RR(%)	IP (%)	IR(%)	F1(%)
PointDSC	77.57	68.45	71.56	69.75
PointDSC+Fused model	79.11	69.27	71.91	70.37
PointDSC+TS	81.95	70.79	75.73	72.98
PointDSC+Fused model+TS	83.18	71.34	77.08	73.93

Table 1 shows the ablation results of the proposed method on the 3DMatch dataset, in which the fused module denotes the fused geometric feature extraction module and TS represents the two-stage outlier pruning strategy. It can be seen that after using the fused geometric feature extraction module, the four metrics, RR, IP, IR, and F1, have achieved significant improvement, which is 1.54%, 0.82%, 0.35%, and 0.62% higher than that of the baseline. These results verify that the fused geometric feature extraction module can better learn point cloud features for feature matching. When the proposed fused model is combined with the two-stage outlier pruning strategy, it yields +5.61% of RR, +2.89% of IP, +5.52% of IR, and +4.18% of F1 Recall improvements. It helps the network become more sensitive to outlier correspondences, which improves the pruning effect of outlier correspondences and hence elevates the accuracy of point cloud registration.

4.4 Comparison with State-of-the-Art

First, we compare our method with the baseline model as well as other state-of-the-art outlier-rejection based point cloud registration algorithms. In the comparison, four traditional point cloud registration algorithms SM [22], RANSAC [20], GC-RANSAC [21], TEASER [28] and two partial learning-based point cloud registration algorithms 3DRegNet [18] and DGR [17] are selected. The hand-extracted FPFH descriptor is used to generate initial matching point pairs, and the average inlier rate of the generated matching point pairs is 6.84%.

Table 2. Registration results on 3DMatch with FPFH.

Method	RR(%)	RE(°)	TE (cm)	IP (%)	IR(%)	F1(%)
3DRegNet	26.31	3.75	9.60	28.21	8.90	11.63
DGR w/o s.g.	27.04	2.61	7.76	28.80	12.42	17.35
DGR	69.13	3.78	10.80	28.80	12.42	17.35
SM	55.88	2.94	8.15	47.96	70.69	50.70
RANSAC(10k)	60.63	4.35	11.79	62.43	54.12	57.07
RANSAC(100k)	73.57	3.55	10.04	68.18	67.40	67.47
GC-RANSAC	67.65	2.33	6.87	48.55	69.38	56.78
TEASER	75.48	2.48	7.31	73.01	62.63	66.93
PointDSC	77.57	2.05	6.41	68.44	71.75	69.48
Ours	83.18	2.13	6.71	71.34	77.08	73.93

As shown in Table 2, compared with the baseline, the proposed point cloud registration network improves the "Reg Recall" from 77.57% to 83.18%, which effectively improves the performance of point cloud registration. Due to the large translation and rotation errors caused by the registration failure, only the successfully registered matching pairs are considered in the calculation of RE and TE. Therefore, this calculation method makes methods with high registration recall more likely to produce large rotation errors and translation errors. Nevertheless, our method is slightly weaker than PointDSC on TE and RE metrics, but still outperforms other works. For the outlier removal effect, our method has significantly improved the three metrics of classification precision (IP), classification recall rate (IR), and comprehensive evaluation index F1-measure (F1). Our method is 4.18% higher than the PointDSC network on the F1 metric, which verifies that our method can remove false matching pairs more effectively. Although the accuracy of the TEASER algorithm is higher than our method in Inlier Precision, it is significantly lower than our method in Inlier Recall (62.63% for TEASER and 77.08% for our method). Therefore, our method achieves a better balance between inlier prediction accuracy and recall.

In order to further verify the performance of the proposed method, we also use the latest learning-based FCGF descriptor to generate initial point-to-point correspondences and test the registration results. The average inlier rate of the generated matching point pairs is 25.61%. As shown in Table 3, since FCGF descriptor-based method generates significantly fewer false point-to-point correspondences than that of FPFH descriptors, the performance of all point cloud registration algorithms based on feature matching is improved when applying FCGF feature descriptors. However, the proposed method still obtains the highest Registration Recall among all comparison works, and the registration recall rate is 0.14% higher than that of the PointDSC network. When combined with FCGF feature descriptors, the traditional point cloud registration algorithm RANSAC also exhibits better registration results when the number of iterations is 100k, but our method can still achieve higher accuracy. At the same time, our method is also superior to other methods in terms of F1 score, which shows that our method can still effectively remove outliers after applying FCGF feature descriptors.

Table 3. Registration results on 3DMatch with FCGF.

Method	RR(%)	RE(°)	TE(cm)	IP(%)	IR(%)	F1(%)
3DRegNet	77.76	2.74	8.13	67.34	56.28	58.33
DGR w/o s.g.	86.50	2.33	7.36	67.47	78.94	72.76
DGR	91.30	2.40	7.48	67.47	78.94	72.76
SM	86.57	2.29	7.07	81.44	38.36	48.21
RANSAC(10k)	90.70	2.69	8.25	78.54	83.72	80.76
RANSAC(100k)	91.50	2.49	7.54	78.38	85.30	81.43
GC-RANSAC	92.05	2.33	7.11	64.46	93.39	75.69
TEASER	85.77	2.73	8.66	82.43	68.08	73.96
PointDSC	92.85	2.08	6.51	78.71	86.19	82.12
Ours	92.98	2.04	6.54	78.91	86.22	82.55

As shown above, since the inlier rate of the initial point-to-point correspondences generated by the FCGF descriptor is higher than that of the FPFH feature descriptor, the accuracy of the point cloud registration algorithm combined with FPFH is improved significantly as compared to the algorithm combined with FCGF in terms of registration recall. As compared with other works, it also verifies that the proposed point cloud registration algorithm is robust to the initial point-to-point correspondences generated by different feature descriptors.

4.5 Robustness to Lower Overlap

To evaluate the robustness of the improved method in the paper under low overlap rate scenarios and its generalization ability to new data sets and unseen scenes, we directly use the model trained on 3DMatch to evaluate it on the 3DLoMatch data set. In the experiment, the model trained on 3Dmatch is not tuned. We use different numbers of points on the 3DLoMatch dataset to construct input correspondence sets, and the numbers of selected points are 5000, 2500, 1000, 500, and 250, respectively. The point-to-point correspondence set is generated based on the FCGF feature descriptor.

As shown in Table 4, our method performs better than RANSAC and PointDSC on a different number of matching pairs, which proves the effectiveness and robustness of our method in low-overlap scenarios. In the case of 5000 matching pairs and 2500 matching pairs, our method improves the registration recall by 4.3% and 4.1% as compared to PointDSC, respectively. When only a small number of points (such as less than 250) are used to construct input matching pairs, the effect is not significant, mainly because some

Table 4. Registration results on 3DLoMatch Dataset with FCGF.

Method	5000	2500	1000	500	250
FCGF+RANSAC	35.7	34.9	33.4	31.3	24.4
FCGF+PointDSC	52.0	51.0	45.2	37.7	27.5
Ours	56.3	55.1	51.0	44.6	31.6

point cloud pairs have fewer matching relationships and cannot effectively calculate the pose parameters between point clouds. However, the proposed model trained on 3DMatch can still achieve significant results when applied to the 3DLoMatch dataset, verifying the strong generalization ability of the proposed method in new datasets and scenarios.

5 Conclusions

In this work, we propose a fused geometric feature extraction module and a two-stage outlier pruning strategy. The combination of CHNonlocal and SCNonlocal modules effectively aggregates the global feature information of matching point pairs. To alleviate the problem that the outlier cannot be effectively pruned by a single sampling of the consensus set, we further propose a two-stage pruning strategy by leveraging the angle invariant. Ablation research has demonstrated the effectiveness of our proposed method. Experiments on different point cloud datasets have shown that our method significantly improves point cloud registration performance as compared to current mainstream methods. It also verifies the robustness of our method to the initial point-to-point correspondence set generated by different feature descriptors.

Acknowledgement. This work was supported in part by National Natural Science Foundation of China (NSFC) under Grant No. 61772061.

References

1. Qian, K., He, Z., Zhang, X.: 3D point cloud generation with millimeter-wave radar. Proc. ACM Interact. Mobile Wearable Ubiquit. Technol. 4(4), 1–23 (2020)
2. Li, J., Li, R., Li, J., Wang, J., Wu, Q., Liu, X.: Dual-view 3d object recognition and detection via lidar point cloud and camera image. Robot. Auton. Syst. **150**, 103999 (2022)
3. Fernandes, D., et al.: Point-cloud based 3D object detection and classification methods for self-driving applications: a survey and taxonomy. Inf. Fusion **68**, 161–191 (2021)
4. Hu, Q., Yang, B., Khalid, S., Xiao, W., Trigoni, N., Markham, A.: Towards semantic segmentation of urban-scale 3D point clouds: a dataset, benchmarks and challenges. In: Proceedings of the IEEE/CVF Conference on Computer Vision and Pattern Recognition, pp. 4977–4987 (2021)
5. Cui, Y., et al.: Deep learning for image and point cloud fusion in autonomous driving: a review. IEEE Trans. Intell. Transp. Syst. **23**(2), 722–739 (2021)

6. Zhang, Z., Dai, Y., Sun, J.: Deep learning based point cloud registration: an overview. Virtual Reality Intelligent Hardware **2**(3), 222–246 (2020)
7. Sultani, Z.N., Ghani, R.F.: Kinect 3D point cloud live video streaming. Procedia Comput. Sci. **65**, 125–132 (2015)
8. Zhang, Y.X., Gui, J., Cong, X., Gong, X., Tao, W.: A Comprehensive survey and taxonomy on point cloud registration based on deep learning. arXiv preprint arXiv:2404.13830 (2024)
9. Xiao, A., Huang, J., Guan, D., Zhang, X., Lu, S., Shao, L.: Unsupervised point cloud representation learning with deep neural networks: a survey. IEEE Trans. Pattern Anal. Mach. Intell. **45**(9), 11321–11339 (2023)
10. Huang, X., Mei, G., Zhang, J., Abbas, R.: A comprehensive survey on point cloud registration. arXiv preprint arXiv:2103.02690 (2021)
11. Tian, B., Jiang, P., Zhang, X., Zhang, Y., Wang, F.: A novel feature point detection algorithm of unstructured 3D point cloud. In: Huang, D.S., Han, K., Hussain, A. (eds.) Intelligent Computing Methodologies: 12th International Conference, ICIC 2016, Lanzhou, China, 2–5 August 2016, Proceedings, Part III 12, pp. 736–744. Springer, Cham (2016). https://doi.org/10.1007/978-3-319-42297-8_68
12. Prokop, M., Shaikh, S.A., Kim, K.S.: Low overlapping point cloud registration using line features detection. Remote Sens. **12**(1), 61 (2019)
13. Chen, S., Nan, L., Xia, R., Zhao, J., Wonka, P.: PLADE: a plane-based descriptor for point cloud registration with small overlap. IEEE Trans. Geosci. Remote Sens. **58**(4), 2530–2540 (2019)
14. Zhang, X., Gao, R., Sun, Q., Cheng, J.: An automated rectification method for unmanned aerial vehicle lidar point cloud data based on laser intensity. Remote Sens. **11**(7), 811 (2019)
15. Zeng, A., Song, S., Nießner, M., Fisher, M., Xiao, J., Funkhouser, T.: 3DMatch: learning local geometric descriptors from RGB-D reconstructions. In: Proceedings of the IEEE Conference on Computer Vision and Pattern Recognition, 1802–1811 (2017)
16. Xu, H., Ye, N., Liu, G., Zeng, B., Liu, S.: FINet: dual branches feature interaction for partial-to-partial point cloud registration. Proc. AAAI Conf. Artif Intell. **36**(3), 2848–2856 (2022)
17. Choy, C., Dong, W., Koltun, V.: Deep global registration. In Proceedings of the IEEE/CVF Conference on Computer Vision and Pattern Recognition, pp. 2514–2523 (2020)
18. Pais, G.D., Ramalingam, S., Govindu, V.M., Nascimento, J.C., Chellappa, R., Miraldo, P.: 3DRegNet: a deep neural network for 3D point registration. In: Proceedings of the IEEE/CVF Conference on Computer Vision and Pattern Recognition, pp. 7193–7203 (2020)
19. Bai, X., et al.: PointDSC: robust point cloud registration using deep spatial consistency. In: Proceedings of the IEEE/CVF Conference on Computer Vision and Pattern Recognition, pp. 15859–15869 (2021)
20. Fischler, M.A., Bolles, R.C.: Random sample consensus: a paradigm for model fitting with applications to image analysis and automated cartography. Commun. ACM **24**(6), 381–395 (1981)
21. Barath, D., Matas, J.: Graph-cut RANSAC. In: Proceedings of the IEEE Conference on Computer Vision and Pattern Recognition, pp. 6733–6741 (2018)
22. Yang, J., Xiao, Y., Cao, Z., Yang, W.: Ranking 3D feature correspondences via consistency voting. Pattern Recogn. Lett. **117**, 1–8 (2019)
23. Sahloul, H., Shirafuji, S., Ota, J.: An accurate and efficient voting scheme for a maximally all-inlier 3D correspondence set. IEEE Trans. Pattern Anal. Mach. Intell. **43**(7), 2287–2298 (2020)
24. Rusu, R.B., Blodow, N., Beetz, M.: Fast point feature histograms (FPFH) for 3D registration. In: 2009 IEEE International Conference on Robotics and Automation, pp. 3212–3217 (2009)
25. Geiger, A., Lenz, P., Stiller, C., Urtasun, R.: Vision meets robotics: the KITTI dataset. Int. J. Robot. Res. **32**(11), 1231–1237 (2013)

26. Huang, S., Gojcic, Z., Usvyatsov, M., Wieser, A., Schindler, K.: Registration of 3D point clouds with low overlap. In: Proceedings Computer Vision and Pattern Recognition, pp. 1–60 (2021)
27. Kingma, D.P., Ba, J.: Adam: a method for stochastic optimization. arXiv preprint arXiv:1412.6980 (2014)
28. Yang, H., Shi, J., Carlone, L.: Teaser: fast and certifiable point cloud registration. IEEE Trans. Rob. **37**(2), 314–333 (2020)
29. Li, J., Lee, G.H.: USIP: unsupervised stable interest point detection from 3D point clouds. In: Proceedings of the IEEE/CVF International Conference on Computer Vision, pp. 361–370 (2019)
30. Bai, X., Luo, Z., Zhou, L., Fu, H., Quan, L., Tai, C.L.: D3Feat: joint learning of dense detection and description of 3D local features. In: Proceedings of the IEEE/CVF Conference on Computer Vision and Pattern Recognition, pp. 6359–6367 (2020)
31. Aoki, Y., Goforth, H., Srivatsan, R.A., Lucey, S.: PointNetLK: robust & efficient point cloud registration using pointnet. In: Proceedings of the IEEE/CVF Conference on Computer Vision and Pattern Recognition, pp. 7163–7172 (2019)
32. Yew, Z.J., Lee, G.H.: RPM-Net: robust point matching using learned features. In: Proceedings of the IEEE/CVF Conference on Computer Vision and Pattern Recognition, pp. 11824–11833 (2020)
33. Jiang, H., Dang, Z., Wei, Z., Xie, J., Yang, J., Salzmann, M.: Robust outlier rejection for 3D registration with variational bayes. In: Proceedings of the IEEE/CVF Conference on Computer Vision and Pattern Recognition, pp. 1148–1157 (2023)

Author Index

B
Bierzynski, Kay 168

C
Cao, Yifei 137
Chen, Jiahui 395
Chen, Xu 304
Chuah, Joon Huang 17

D
Dengel, Andreas 351
Dong, Aimei 46
Dong, Xiangjun 46
Dou, Yong 434

F
Fu, Xiaomeng 289

G
Guo, Junkang 200
Guo, Yuchen 289

H
Han, Jizhong 289
Han, Zhen 335
Hao, Yanbin 320
Hong, Jinhong 449
Hong, Qingqi 395
Hu, Xiaopei 46
Hu, Zhigang 31
Huang, Baojin 335
Huang, Junhao 215
Huang, Li 61
Huang, Qinglong 320

J
Jia, Xiangyang 304
Jiang, Le 3
Jin, Haiyan 364

K
Kang, Guxia 93
Kuang, Xiaomei 79

L
Li, Chaohao 248
Li, Dengshi 335
Li, Guoming 3
Li, Haoran 320
Li, Jiangquan 137
Li, JiaXin 275
Li, Kaiheng 395
Li, Pengyu 120
Li, Shufang 93
Li, Tengfei 120
Li, Wenyu 434
Li, Yuqiu 215
Li, Zhaoxing 289
Liao, Yong 320
Lin, Qiwei 185
Lin, Wei 31
Lin, Xinzhi 185
Liu, Chengeng 304
Liu, Chenhe 120
Liu, Jin 289
Liu, Liang 231
Liu, Ningzhong 108
Liu, Sidun 434
Liu, Xinshuang 379
Liu, Yang 3
Liu, Yu 137
Liu, Zhigang 200
Long, Qinghua 185
Loo, Chu Kiong 17
Lu, Ke 215
Luo, Guibo 275
Lv, Jing 61

M
Ma, Mengyuan 153
Moser, Brian B. 351

O
Ouyang, Ye 3

P
Pei, Songwei 449
Peng, Xiangyuan 168

Q
Qian, Lin 153
Qiao, Peng 434
Qiu, Haolei 407

R
Raue, Federico 351
Ren, Chenqu 407
Ren, Yong 419

S
Servadei, Lorenzo 168
Shao, Yeheng 407
Shen, Jiaquan 108
Shi, Guanqun 200
Song, Huaqing 263
Su, Haonan 364
Sun, Han 108
Sun, Huawei 168

T
Tang, Miao 168

W
Wang, Bin 248, 364
Wang, Feifan 248
Wang, Guangshuo 275
Wang, Jingge 248
Wang, Jingjing 419
Wang, Lingyu 200
Wang, Ruoxi 335
Wang, Shuhuai 449
Wang, Xi 289, 434
Wang, Xinyu 120
Wei, Hongkui 137
Wermter, Stefan 17
Wille, Robert 168
Wu, Hao 215
Wu, Jihao 93
Wu, Qingqiang 395

X
Xiao, Baihui 419
Xiao, Zhaolin 364
Xie, Linglin 434
Xing, Tianyu 419
Xu, Jingzehua 419
Xu, Kaiping 137
Xu, Qingzhen 79
Xu, Tian 304
Xue, Jian 215

Y
Yan, Haonan 248
Yang, Chuanfeng 395
Yang, Kaijun 434
Yang, Liu 31
Yang, Ming 61
Yang, Yuqing 93
Ye, Xiaozhou 3
Yi, Ceyuan 231
Yin, Hujun 153
Yin, Zixuan 108
Yu, Dongyang 120
Yu, Jizhe 137
Yu, Zhihan 275
Yuan, Junbin 79
Yuan, Lu 46

Z
Zhang, Jin 364
Zhang, Lei 231
Zhang, Shihui 120
Zhang, Xingzhong 17
Zhang, Xuerong 61
Zhang, Yuanlin 364
Zhang, Zekai 419
Zhao, Guixin 46
Zhao, Yue 379
Zheng, Hao 31
Zheng, Meiguang 31
Zhou, Huiyu 108
Zhou, Junjie 185
Zhou, Pengyuan 320
Zhou, Shaopeng 248
Zhou, Zijie 200
Zhu, Aiqing 79
Zhu, Yuesheng 275

Printed in the USA
CPSIA information can be obtained
at www.ICGtesting.com
CBHW051508161024
15929CB00004B/169